El inglés práctico superior

El inglés práctico superior
Tomo I

Josep Capdevila Batllés

www.librosenred.com

Dirección General: Marcelo Perazolo
Diseño de cubierta: Laura Gissi

Está prohibida la reproducción total o parcial de este libro, su tratamiento informático, la transmisión de cualquier forma o de cualquier medio, ya sea electrónico, mecánico, por fotocopia, registro u otros métodos, sin el permiso previo escrito de los titulares del Copyright.

Primera edición en español - Impresión bajo demanda

© LibrosEnRed, 2021
Una marca registrada de Amertown International S.A.

ISBN: 978-1-62915-454-1

Para encargar más copias de este libro o conocer otros libros de esta colección visite www.librosenred.com

Publicaciones anteriores

ILUSTRACIONES CAPDEVILA. Pintadas a mano para un método conceptológico de La Salle, 1972 (época estudiantil, pedagógicas sí, pero sin trascendencia filosófica).

ELABORACIÓN DE LOS APUNTES DE GENÉTICA Y DE BIOMETRÍA, para universitarios, 1973 (época estudiantil).

FRUTALES Y HORTALIZAS, Erradicación de elementos hostliles, Ed. Aedos, 1981. Destaca la utilización de productos fitosanitarios de química básica, descartando las marcas comerciales.

APLICACIÓN DE LA LEGISLACIÓN SANITARIA DE LA COMUNIDAD ECONÓMICA EUROPEA (CEE) EN ESPAÑA (repercusiones económicas), Universidad de Tolbiac, París 1983.

AGRICULTURA E INDUSTRIA ESPAÑOLAS FRENTE A LA CEE: aspectos jurídicos, económicos y políticos, Ed. Aedos 1985. Se insistió más sobre los peligros de la competencia europea.

BASE DE DATOS (versión española) elaborada por el CENTRO NACIONAL DE INVESTIGACIÓN CIENTÍFICA (CNRS), París, 1987. Personalmente me encargué de cuatro secciones: agroindustria, medicina, biología y química.

¿SE PUEDE GOBERNAR EL MUNDO? Más allá de la globalización, Bosch editor, 2004.

ÉTICA, DIGNIDAD Y TRAUMA, Rotundo fracaso de las Humanidades, Ed. Libros en Red, 2007.

DROGADICCIÓN, Acción y combate y límites, Ed. Bubok, 2011.

LA DIALECTIQUE DE LA DOMINATION, La Science et les religions on la parole, Ed. Bubok, 2012.

SURLENISMO, Integración de Surrealismo y Helenismo, segunda edición, Ed. Bubok, 2013.

VALL d'ASSUA, Himalaya del Pallars, exemple per Europa i Egipte d'Occident, Ed. Bubok, 2014.

PENSOLOGÍA, más allá de las Humanidades, Ed. CEP - i - La - Nansa, 2016.

Desde 1981 (cuando entré en La Sorbona) me esmero en archivar cuanto desconozco de esta lengua gracias a mis variadas lecturas, las cuales constituyen el lecho de mis personales críticas y consecuentes teorías temáticas. Un inglés más práctico es imposible.

También con respecto a mi pintura "El SURLENISMO: integración del Surrealismo con el Helenismo", usando del pragmatismo anglosajón, con frecuencia inscribo explicaciones en inglés a las telas. Así lo aprendido, aprendido está.

Lástima que en el orbe hispano hablante todavía no nos avocamos a informarnos de cuanto más nos concierne y en consecuencia muchos útiles libros se consideran demasiado técnicos y elitistas. ¿Ocurrirá más a partir de ahora, cuando el conocimiento del inglés es cada vez más de primerísima necesidad?

Conviene destacar la **complementariedad evolutiva** de estas investigaciones: desde la ciencia pura más allá de las Humanidades y la creación de la nueva escuela pictórica arriba mencionada, pasando por la economía, el derecho y la geopolítica. Mi pintura queda así integrada en este esquema global, pues aparte de los paisajes, suelo plasmar también en las telas los temas que trato en mis publicaciones. Recuerdo también cómo los mejores y más acertados reconocimientos se me han otorgado desde los Estados Unidos de América, aunque critique algunos abusos americanos en la arena internacional.

Introducción

Para ahorrar tiempo recomendaré esta obra con una frase: vayan al inglés cotidiano de grado avanzado que un servidor ha escogido en las revistas de prestigio: día tras día, año tras año y decenio tras decenio.

Me animé a este útil proyecto después de escuchar copiosas quejas tales como: "He estudiado con tal o tal método, pero llego a los Estados Unidos y me pierdo", "Llevo x años estudiando inglés y debo recurrir excesivamente al diccionario", "Aunque saqué un excelente en la escuela, si sabes de un buen método, me lo indicas, buena falta me hace", etc. ¡Es, pues, hora de buscar algo estratégico!

Comprendo perfectamente las quejas mencionadas arriba, pues yo mismo aún tengo problemas, a pesar de mis insistencias. Soy la persona indicada para sostener que los resultados académicos suelen ser insuficientes: con un sobresaliente en 5º de bachiller y el haberme acercado a notables en la lengua extranjera de La Sorbona, París, sin este último prolongado esfuerzo hubiese andado siempre muy cojo, por no decir impotente. Pues los periodistas y los escritores anglófonos también se lucen con expresiones y vocabulario complicados. Y mi caso puede extenderse a muchos colectivos.

¿Por qué he contado esto? Pues para subrayar mejor que se trata de un universo realmente complejo y difícil. Veamos los pilares de apoyo:

- Pretendo que se pueda aprender cómodamente este ya mencionado inglés práctico elegante de cada día.

- Se supone que los estudiosos a quienes me dirijo ya conocen la gramática, así como los verbos y el vocabulario elementales, tal como me ocurría a mí. Así queda más espacio para este proyecto que les ofrezco.

- El objetivo principal es que se pueda leer cualquier texto con mínimas consultas al diccionario. Entonces la escritura elegante y poética irá emergiendo automáticamente y sin esfuerzo. Aquí está la novedad práctica.

- En buena medida mi proposición también puede servir para que los angloparlantes perfeccionen el español.

- Sabiendo que esta lengua resulta cada vez más imprescindible para cualquier profesión, ahora que yo he masticado un poco el terreno, los invito a digerirlo.

- Será un placer más tarde complementar este tomo 1 con una temática más compleja. Pero por el momento, ahí está la novedad del método con un nivel satisfactorio.

- Además, matemos dos pájaros de un tiro. Me refiero a la metodología que presento abajo, cuya estructura obedece a nuestras ansias de facilitar la memorización y también estimular la creatividad. De la misma manera que hacer *footing* siempre por la misma ruta atrofia nuestros cerebros, también los métodos monótonos lo hacen. Por lo que recomendamos razonablemente un esquema muy **variado**, para mejor asociar ideas.

- Finalmente, desde el flanco formativo e informativo, con tanta pena como razón expresaré mi desconsuelo al comparar posiciones de fuerza y competitividad dentro de la Unión Europea (UE): España lidera algunos deportes, primerísimamente el fútbol, también sobresalen los playeros y los esquiadores, aún más el deambular por las calles..., pero nuestras bibliotecas están excesivamente vacías. Esto repercute en nuestros resultados: en patentes, en atracción de materia gris (en

España es más bien al revés), en exportación de tecnologías... Cuento todo esto porque el conocimiento de lenguas extranjeras, con el inglés en primerísima fila, es más común en el norte que en el sur de Europa. Aunque en España estamos avanzando agradablemente.

Metodología

Muchos son los trucos que nos hemos inventado para un objetivo común: aprender al máximo esta bonita lengua sintetizando estratégicamente los espacios con un **mínimo esfuerzo**. La siguiente lista parece complicada, pero su pura lógica la convierte en sencilla:

- Tanto en el vocabulario como en las pequeñas frases y en los giros, sobresaldrá la dirección inglés → español, aunque por razones prácticas y para mejor facilidad de aprendizaje, a veces será conveniente la dirección contraria: por ejemplo la expresión "A trancas y barrancas", por tener dos equivalentes en inglés: *with great difficulty/overcoming many obstacles*.

- A veces la dirección pedagógica inglés → español quedaba corta, por lo que un determinado vocablo así rubricado en español se complementará más con otros términos que también sean útiles, sirviéndonos del signo (+), simplificando de paso el aprendizaje. Así, por ejemplo, el término *crest* significa cresta, cima, etc. Entonces conviene reseñar que "cima" significa también y sobre todo *top* (para edificio), *summit* (para montaña) y *peak* y *height* (de su carrera). En nuestro texto leeremos: *crest*: cresta, cima + *top, summit, peak, height*. Tan decisivas son estas añadiduras que me atrevo a decir "Las traducciones unilaterales y tradicionales provocan impotencias y graves errores". Debemos pues reaccionar, no soslayando más los términos imprescindibles. Esta idea revolucionaria y de muy exigida labor de consulta constituye uno de los puntos fuertes del libro. En todos esos casos, de no consultar en dirección contraria, nos quedaríamos con conceptos <u>parcialmente equívocos</u> y limitados.

- Dada la fabulosa cantidad de verbos utilizados, optamos por prescindir del *"to"*. Así participaremos del ahorro de un texto excesivamente voluminoso. Pero cuidado: sólo prescindiremos de él en las traducciones de verbos infinitivos considerados aisladamente (ejemplo: llevar: *carry, wear, bring*); no en las frases (quedaría realmente confuso y feo). Así, por ejemplo, lo respetaremos en "The right *to* testify".

- Con vías a facilitar el aprendizaje de los diferentes términos, en muchos casos agruparemos estratégicamente los <u>diversos significados</u> de cada palabra. Insisto en ello porque de manera incomprensible incluso los más prestigiosos diccionarios lo han olvidado excesivamente. Cojamos las diferentes acepciones de la dicción *clash*: en los diccionarios se agrupan sin criterio alguno, repito, pero hay que facilitar enormemente la memorización. Así, para *clash* tendremos: conflicto; enfrentamiento, oposición; choque, estruendo, ruido metálico. Utilizamos en signo";" dos veces.

- El signo "/" se utilizará con frecuencia: ante todo para separar sinónimos, por ejemplo "*The lower/ bottom bunk*" (litera) y para dos adjetivos del mismo substantivo, por ejemplo "*Downriver/stream*" (aquí ahorramos un "down" y subrayamos los dos sustantivos a los cuales califica), etcétera.

- Dada la infinidad de veces que se utilizaría el término "and", lo reemplazaremos por el simple signo "&". Ahorraremos espacio.

- También, para mejor aprovechar el espacio, nos serviremos de dos estrategias esenciales: a) En los diccionarios, para tal o tal término se suelen presentar primero los significados sustantivos, adjetivos y adverbios, y luego los verbos. Aquí presentaremos el primer grupo y cuando corresponda añadiremos la V (que significa verbo de estos términos). Por ejemplo *plug* (tapón,V, enchufe,V,). O sea que significa también tapar y enchufar. Para los plurales es mejor utilizar el Vs, aquí será tapón, enchufe, Vs. b) ¿Para qué cargar el espacio con términos ya comprensibles? Nos referimos a los que se parecen mucho en las dos lenguas. Por ejemplo *nanometre* = nanómetro, *tumult* = tumulto... y todos los acabados en *um*, así *vacuum* = vacío. En todos estos casos pondremos un (=) en lugar de esos términos.

- No hemos eludido el ajuste de términos opuestos o diferentes: con el signo ↔ si tienen significado opuesto. Así: *It was favourably received* ↔ -- -- *badly/poorly received*; con el signo =/= si lo tienen simplemente diferente, pero que gráficamente se parezcan o al revés. Por ejemplo, el término *belie* (defraudar, desdecir, ocultar) =/= *belief* (creencia). Encontrarán infinidad de aplicaciones. La flecha→ se utilizará para enriquecer con pequeñas frases prácticas.

- A cada palabra traducida de un idioma al otro le suelen corresponder muchas en el segundo, sobre todo en los verbos. Al escoger cuál palabra es la adecuada, frecuentemente dejamos al lector (o estudiante) el placer de ejercitarse, según la lógica y el contexto de la frase. Así, por ejemplo, en *hinge on* (depender de, moverse sobre) *the weather,* es de lógica aplastante el escoger "depender de".

- Descubrirán Uds. muchas pequeñas frases sin traducir, por fáciles, ante todo en la primera parte. Aunque alojarán algo estratégico, o al menos interesante. Por ejemplo: *he was good at his job, I work on them, I'm scared of you...* Aquí se deben retener *at*, *on* y *of* en su lugar.

- Encontrarán hartas veces palabras divididas con un paréntesis, por ejemplo: *(black)smith.* Se interpretarán como de igual valor con o sin el contenido del paréntesis: aquí tanto *smith* como *blacksmith* significan herrero. También paréntesis para ahorrar espacio, por ejemplo en *pick up*: (re)coger se traduce por coger + recoger.

- En las primeras páginas he sido muy generoso, recapitulando muchas pequeñas frases y un rico vocabulario. Luego, poco a poco he ido hacia lo más difícil, aunque exquisito.

- Sobre todo, la **familiaridad** de los protagonistas y espacios conocidos que van apareciendo en el texto facilitarán más la memorización que la superabundancia de ejemplos fríos.

- Las abreviaciones son las corrientes: Agr.: agricultura; Atm.: atmósfera; Aut: autoridad; Biol. (Biología); Com.: comercio; Comp.: computer; Ec.: economía; Electr. (electricidad). Geog.: geografía; Hist.: historia; Jur.: jurídico; Líq. (líquido); m.: metros y mercancías (según contexto); Med.: medicina; o.s.: uno mismo; Mil.: militar; Náut.: náutica; pers.: personas, pb.: problema; Pol.: política; Rel.: religión; sb: alguien; Sp.: deporte; sth: algo; T.: temperatura; Téc.: técnico; Tf.: teléfono, recordamos que =/= significa distinto, etcétera.

Organizaremos el texto en dos partes:

a) Primera parte: Ante todo los giros y el vocabulario intermedios entre sus respectivos conocimientos básicos mencionados (más o menos al nivel de cuanto he expresado para mi experiencia) y la más técnica segunda parte. Asimilar este conjunto de ideas ya nos permitirá hablar y escribir con cierta ligereza, aunque necesitando aún excesivamente el uso del diccionario en las lecturas más elegantes.

b) Segunda parte: Me tacharán de excesivamente ambicioso, pero les aseguro que la lógica es práctica, la de adquirir el nivel exigible para pasearnos holgadamente por el mundanal universo anglosajón. Aquí me he esmerado en incluir el hueso duro de esta lengua, tanto en vocabulario como en expresiones, giros, etcétera.

Primera parte: el inglés más común

Aquí distinguiremos dos capítulos complementarios: (I) Vocabulario y algunas expresiones y vocabulario básicos son sacados de diccionarios de prestigio, algo por encima del aprendido en la enseñanza básica y (II) El vocabulario y las muy variadas y ricas expresiones elegidas de libros pedagógicos utilizados por profesores ingleses.

Capítulo I - Algunas expresiones y vocabulario básicos, son sacados de diccionarios de prestigio, algo por encima del aprendido en la enseñanza básica

Dividiremos el capítulo en dos secciones. Primera sección: vocablos variados y simples; segunda sección: palabras y pequeñas frases sencillas.

Primera sección: vocablos variados y simples

Esforcémonos en retener este conjunto de significados tan embarazosos (primera serie: español → inglés; segunda serie: inglés → español):

Abandonado: (pueblo) =, deserted, (terreno, jardín) neglected → They fled abandoning their weapons (armas).

Acelerar: brisk the pace (acelerar el paso), acceleration (la mec.) =/= speed-up (en un proceso), speed-in (customs procedure), gas pedal, step on the gas (daros prisa), (acontecimientos) hasten, quicken one's pace, don't accelerate at the bends, he put his foot to the floor (a fondo), come on, get a move on, hurry up, they're waiting for us, rapidly (rápidamente), accelerator.

Agotamiento: be worn out (estar agotado), the toyshop sold out (ha vendido todo), they have exhausted all legal avenues (avenidad, vías), exhausted/finished provisions, all my extensions (prórrogas) have run out, the government aims (pretende) to last out (agotar) its terms, running in the heat tires you out, I ran out of petrol, they ran out of arguments to defend their thesis, my patience is running out/wearing thin, time was running out, this job wears me out.

Agua: fish in troubled waters (pescar en río revuelto), don't be a dog in the manger (pesebre): -- que no has de beber, déjala correr; it's no use crying over spilt/spilled (de spill: verter, derramar) milk: -- pasada no mueve molino; running water, dish -- (de fregar), tap -- (de grifo), meltwater (de fusión de nieve), rain --, seltzer (con gas) --, distilled --, fresh --, salt --, hard --, sleet (aguanieve), hydrogen peroxide (-- oxigenada), drinking --, the cold -- of the Atlantic, down/upstream, down/up river; sit on the fence (valla): nadar entre dos --s; things are returning to normal (las -- vuelven a su cauce); sewage (-- fecales/ residuales), territorial (jurisdiccionales) waters, faces (-- mayores), urine (-- menores); aguardiente + eau de vie =/= cognac/ brandy: coñac.

Aguantar: put up with/endured/bore the pain/the insults as best as I could; capacidad de resistir: this plant withstands/can take heat (calor) well + he stands (tolera) the work in the mine pretty well (bastante), stand the pace (-- el ritmo), he can take a joke, I can't bear/stand to see an animal suffering, this cold is just unbearable (insoportable), hold the parcel a minute, these beams (vigas) can take any weight, she couldn't hold back her laughter, do you think this nail will hold? Why do we have to keep quiet (aguantarnos) & no one responds? Can you hold on (--te) until we get home? Capacity for patience (aguante), you have no staying power/stamina! (¡Qué poco aguante tienes!).

Agudo: (instrumento) sharp, pointed, (enfermedad, dolor, acento, pregunta) acute, (de mente) sharp, keen, (ingenio) ready, lively, (observación) smart, (gracioso) witty, (crítica) penetrating, (voz) piercing.

Ahogar: (en agua) drown, (al aire) suffocate, choked by the neck of the shirt, choked with emotion, her voice trembles, (ahogar, paralizar) cripple → Cuba with the economic blockade, (lucha y rebelión) crush, (llamas) smother, (voces) stifle, (derechos) curtail, (plan) hinder, block; make a mountain out of a molehill (topera): ahogarse en un vaso de agua; me ahogo: I'mt out of breath + I'm suffocating with this heat, a feeling of breathlessness (asfixia + asphyxia).

Ajeno: it laid its eggs in another (ajeno) bird's nest, with other people's money (con dinero ajeno), at sb' else's expenses (a cuenta ajena), things unconnected (ajenas) with work, he would remain outside (ajeno) of politics, reasons beyond our control (ajenas a nuestra voluntad), oblivious (ajeno) to what happens.

Ajustar: a pair of tight jeans (vaqueros ajustados), the election results were tight/close, I need some pliers (alicates) to tighten the valve (la válvula)/the screws, fix the motorbike's engine (motor), adjust product to demand, settle their differences, the top (tapón)/cork (corcho) doesn't fit in the bottle, fill the joints (empalmes, junturas) that don't fit together with putty (masilla), adjust my tie, rumo(u)rs do not reflect the real situation, financial/budget settlement, wage/structural adjustment.

Alegrar: cheer her up (alegrarla) + (reunión, fiesta) liven up → alegre: (Mús.) lively, (día, habitación, color) bright, we are pleased to hear that you passed (aprobaste), cheer up! (¡Alegra esa cara!), I'm pleased/happy (me alegro) for her, merry (alegre), I'm delighted (me alegro muchísimo), she is a cheerful/happy person. How marvellous! (¡Qué alegría!).

Coger: (tomar) take, (levantar) pick up, (con fuerza) grasp + seize: (pers.) detener, (poder) tomar, (psíquicamente) agarrar, (propiedad) incautar, (flor/fruta) pick, (enfermedad/pez) catch.

Damn: condenar, damned (maldito) → the effort was damned (condenado al fracaso) from the start, the critics damned (tiraron por los suelos) the book, -- it! (¡Maldito sea!), it's a -- (verdadera) shame, it's -- awkward (terriblemente difícil),

I don't give a -- (me importa un pito), it's not worth a -- (no vale nada).

Herencia: get anything under the will (herencia + inheritance), Biol.: heredity, cultural heritage, legacy/bequest: legado; he will inherit my money; genetic/property/assets inheritance; bequeath sth. to sb; heir/ heiress.

Mediano: (tamaño, porción) medium, (de mediana edad) middle-aged, the sister who got married is the middle one, medium-sized business (mediana empresa)/car.

Presagio y demás: it (fore)bodes/betokens (presagia) well/no good, foreshadow (presagiar), omen (augurio), premonition (presentimiento), foresee/predict (prever), have a sense/feeling/ sensation (sensación) of foreboding (tener un mal presagio), predictable (predecible), prediction/forecast (pronóstico), they have foretold... (predicho...), prognosis (pronóstico médico), prescient (proféticamente, con clarividencia) warned, foresight (previsión).

Resistente: =), (tela) hard-wearing, vegetales/animales resistentes: hardy; cold/heat-resistant, damp (humedad) proof, the shanty town (chabolas) didn't withstand the hurricane/a shock (golpe), I can't stand it any longer, (Med.: hacerse resistente) build up a resistance, (contain yourself) (contenerse).

Superior: at the top of the page, feel superior to sb, a superior quality carpet, any number higher than two, any higher casta, he has a higher-ranking post than you, my superiors; en educación: (curso) advanced, (enseñanza) higher.

Tejer: hand-woven rugs (alfombras), (telas) weave, (de araña) spin, (tejido a mano) hand-woven, knit (tricotar) → knitting/ knitted fabric, crochet (ganchillo,V), (bordar) embroider.

Tela: cloth, fabric; poner en tela de juicio: call into question; spider's web, (lienzo para arte) canvas, (hay tela para rato) there's lot to talk about; telar: (máq.) loom, (planta textil) textile mill + molino.

Tiempo: Full-time → part-time, if you tell me beforehand (con tiempo), we'll manage it eventually (al fin): con el -- lo conseguiremos; save (ganar) time, at the wrong time (fuera de --), pass time (pasar el --), waste time, without delay (demora,V): sin perder el tiempo; let matters take their course (darle -- al --), time is precious (el -- es oro), one must try to put a brave face (a mal -- buena cara), time is a great healer (el -- lo cura todo), everything in good time (cada cosa a su --), he was premature (nacido antes del --), you took a long time (has tardado mucho), in due time (a su debido --), in the good old times, these days (en estos -- que corren), formerly (en otros --), recently/lately/in recent times (en los últimos --), through the ages, these are troubled (revueltos) times, her clothes are really old fashioned (de -- de Mª Castaña), first/second half, time out (-- muerto), what's the time like there? (¿Qué -- hace allí?), I prefer fruit that's in time, time sharing (-- compartido), run -- (tiempo de ejecución), real-time conversation/playing, downtime (-- inactivo).

Tierra: tocar --: (pers.) disembark, (m.) unload, go overland (por --)/by land across the country; by land & by sea, grain-growing land (de cereales), arable land, agricultural land (de labor), dry land (de secano); wasteland(-- baldía), no man's land (-- de nadie), native land/soil (-- natal), building land (urbanizable), Holy Land, ground-to-air missile, the plane hit the ground (el avión cayó a --), solid ground (-- firme), fall to the ground (caer por --), throw o.s. to the ground (echarse al suelo), let me die! (¡-- trágame!), the desert is advancing inland (-- adentro), non-cultivated land (-- no cultivada), leap ashore (saltar a --), a dust cloud blew up (se levantó mucha --), the shoes covered with dust, soil (para plantas) land, soil erosion, a bag of soil (--), clay court (-- batida).

Tieso: stiff, rigid, (erguido) erect, (derecho) straight, ponte – (stand up straight, I found him chirply (--, animado) in spite of all his illness, proudy (--) with his girl on his arm, be frozen stiff (quedarse tieso), with his ears pricked (--).

Todo, global...: throughout/all over the world, be on the ball (estar en todo), all the rest (todo lo demás), all of you (todos vosotros), that's all torn (rota), first of all (ante todo), give sth one's all (ir a por todas), I've to take care of all of you, fourteen altogether, all together (todos a la una), in global terms, how much is it altogether?

Tratamiento: (Med., téc., tema, resíduos) treatment, (datos, textos, gráficos, información) processing, batch, (lotes, grupos, remesas, hornadas) processing: -- por lotes; problema: handling; be careful with it (trátalo bien), treat sb like dirt (suciedad): -- a patadas, how should we address him (tratarlo)?

Trucos, chollos...: It's been fixed! (¡Hay tongo!), vote-rigging (apaño), pre-electoral rigging, the elections were rigged! He has a snack (--), souped-up (trucados) voting rights, that's cheating! (¡Aquí hay trampa!), the referee (árbitro) accepted a bribe (se vendió), be at the mercy of sth/sb (estar vendido a), you always cheat, where is the trick? Jiggery-pokery (gato encerrado, trampas), I've been conned, rip sb off (timar a alguien), swindler (estafador, timador) → they swindled him out of € 40.

Venta: sale of arms, be on sale, clearance sale (de liquidación), peddling/hawking sales (ventas en la calle y puerta a puerta), door-to-door (puerta a puerta, a domicilio) selling, forward sales (a término), retail sales (al por menor), wholesale (al por mayor), cash sale, mail order (venta por correo). También para peddling: (drugs) pasar, (ideas) difundir → peddling of political favours (tráfico de influencias).

Verdad: the plain truth (la pura --), there is some truth (una parte de --), be untruthful (faltar a la --), in all honesty (en honor a la --), be honest (a decir --) I don't know, be completely open about things (ir con la -- por delante), it was you, wasn't it? (¿-- que has sido tu?), are those real (de --) bullets?, give sb a piece of one's mind (decir a alguien las cuatro --es), the real (verdadera) reason is..., it's really a shame (vergüenza) + it's really/truly sad, your true friend, your true opinion.

Vista: to the nacked eye (a simple --), look away (apartar la --), turn a blind eye (hacer la -- gorda), keep sb in sight → lose sight of sb, he was several seconds ahead (--) of his rival, frontal view of the castle, payable within thirty days (a 30 días --), not pleasant to look at (a la --), with a view to (con --s a), the approval/go-ahead (visto bueno) for the investigation.

Voluntad: he has no will (--) of his own (propia), the last wish, thy will be done! (¡Hágase su --!), willpower (fuerza de --), ¿Cuánto es)?, la -- (as much as you think, it's worth), volunteer (alistarse/ofrecerse como voluntario), voluntary (voluntario).

Volver: he turned his back (espalda) on me/the gun on himself, return (--) sth to the place, drive (--) sb mad, I've never gone back (vuelto) there, start again (-- a empezar), I restarted (volví a poner en marcha) the engine, they pulled/backed out (volvieron atrás) at the last moment, troubles come thick/back to him (todo se le vuelve dificultad).

Voto: floating (de los indecisos) vote, spoiled/blank ballot paper (-- en blanco), opinion polls (encuestas), a show of hands (-- a mano alzada), secret/postal vote, gain by two votes, put sth to a/the vote (someter algo a votación), she was --ed into the board (elegida para integrar la junta), vote of chastity/of obedience.

Voz: in a voice choked with emotion (entrecortada), my voice was trembling/shaking, whisper (a media --), cantar a dos voces (a duet), be the lead singer (llevar la -- cantante), raise the alarm (dar la -- de alarma), give me a shout (--) when you're finished, here is a rumour going down that (corre la...), spread the rumours/word that...; have no say (--) in the matter, there was shouting in the distance (se oían voces a lo lejos).

Average & medium. Average: a girl of -- intelligence, a rather -- piece of work (un trabajo de mediana calidad), an -- (promedio) of ten people a day, a rather -- piece of work. Medium: (objeto/tamaño) mediano) → available in three sizes: small, -- & large size, a man of -- build (de constitución mediana), of -- height (de altura --), air is a -- for sound, happy -- (término medio), a -- -sized company =/= look for a compromise or middle way, middle brother, the advertising media (medios).

→Damn: condenar, damned (maldito) → the effort was damned (condenado al fracaso) from the start, the critics damned (tiraron por los suelos) the book, -- it! (¡Maldito sea!), it's a -- (verdadera) shame, it's -- awkward (terriblemente difícil), I don't give a -- (me importa un pito), it's not worth a -- (no vale nada).

Early: an -- birthday, be -- (llegar pronto), he was half an hour --, summer is -- this year, -- in the morning, an -- riser (un madrugador), we arrived -- (antes de tiempo), her -- thirties (sus treinta y poco), from an -- age (desde pequeño), it's too -- (prematuro), an -- (precoz) diagnóstico, the train arrived 15 m. --, the project is at a very -- stage (el proyecto está muy verde), in -- childhood (en la más tierna infancia), at weekends I get up --, different from the --ier models.

Get with its simpler expresiones: -- back: regresar, recuperar, devolver; -- across: we'll have to swim, there's no other way to -- -- (de pasar al otro lado); -- ahead: tomar la delantera/adelantar, progresar; I don't -- on with sb: no me llevo bien con alguien; it is easy to get on with (volverse tratable) → be easy/ hard to "go" on with (llevarse bien/ mal); -- by (pasar, arreglárselas) → we'll -- by; get in: llegar, entrar; entregar, meter; get away with: salir impune; get down to: ponerse a trabajar, get onto: ponerse en contacto con, encargarse de, viajar: I -- -- a fair bit (bastante); correr el rumor, divulgarse, saberse → it soon -- -- that they were getting divorced.

Get along: I must be getting along now (me tengo que ir), -- -- with you! (¡Vete, váyanse!), the firm couldn't -- -- (funcionar) without her, we -- -- for years without a computer (nos las arreglaremos) ..., she is --ting -- just fine at the school (le va muy bien en el colegio), how are you --ting -- with the preparations? (¿Qué tal marchan los preparativos?).

Get around: she finds it hard to -- -- (andar), having a car enables her to -- -- (desplazarse) better, it's the best way to -- -- (desplazarse por) the town, -- -- (ir) to the hospital as quickly as possible, you certainly -- -- in your job (tú sí que viajas en tu trabajo), it soon got -- that he is having an affair (pronto corrió la voz de que estaba teniendo una aventura), don't let it -- -- that... (que no se sepa que...), we can't -- -- this table (no cabemos todos alrededor de esta mesa), I managed to get her -- to my point of view (pude convencerlo de que tenía razón), -- -- (ir) to the hospital as quickly as possible.

Get around to: I don't know whether the general practitioner (médico de medicina general) will -- -- -- you this afternoon; I meant to write to you, I just never -- -- -- it (tenía intención..., pero nunca llegó el momento); by the time they got -- -- telling us, everybody knew already (cuando al fin nos lo dijeron, todo el mundo lo sabía); we never got -- -- discussing the price (nunca llegamos a discutir el precio), I must -- -- -- writing those letters (debo ponerme a ...).

Get at: the screw/wire (cable) is very hard to -- -- (es difícil llegar al --/--), don't let John -- -- the truffles! (¡No dejes que John se acerque a las trufas!), he can't -- -- the money (disponer de dinero) until he's (cumpla) 18, I can't wait to -- -- (deseo utilizar) the computer; you are always --ting at him (siempre te estás metiendo con él), I'm not --ting -- you, I merely said (no te critico, simplemente dije...), she's always --ting at me (dándome la lata) to buy her a diamond (de brillantes) ring, what are you --ting at? (¿Qué quieres decir?).

Overall & whole. Overall: -- dimension (dimensión exterior), --/global impression, -- majority (mayoría absoluta), the zone's influence, an -- (total) view; over € 80 b -- for the whole period. Whole: four quarters make a -- (unidad), on the -- (en general), it rained for three -- days, -- (integrales) grains, the -- of Paris, the -- of our output, the -- of July, the -- morning/family/world, he swallowed it -- (entero), eat a -- cake, his -- body ashed, there are only five in the -- of Spain, the -- team came, the -- length of the building, he cleaned the -- house/population.

Take away: (restar): -- nine -- from twelve, seven -- -- four is three; take me away (llévame), take the children away from the school, -- -- a sailboat (velero) off the coast.

Segunda sección: palabras y pequeñas frases sencillas

Sin duda, para muchos se tratará de un recordatorio, pero no para otros. Veamos:

Accuse/charge (acusar), give notice of appeal (interponer un recurso), give a sentence, sentence to death (pena de muerte), convict (condenar). Calf (lechal), veal (ternera), beef, stew (estofado), steak (filete), dairy (lechera) cow. Aguijón: (de insecto) sting, (de planta) prickle, spine. Golden (real) eagle. Full of holes (agujereado). Black/ozone hole. My legs are stiff (tengo agujetas en la pierna). That woman over there. Down there (ahí abajo) → up there. Downriver (río abajo) → two miles -- from here. Outside (exterior) swimming pool: p. al descubierto. I live right there. That way (por ahí); look over there (por ahí). Hence (de ahí que, por lo tanto) the tenants (inquilinos)... There you are (ahí tiene). There goes the ball, catch it! The crux (meollo, quid) of the matter (cuestión). Adopt → godson/daughter: ahijado/a. Impute sth to sb. I fell into the (al) river. I got on the train (subí al tren). They climbed onto (subieron) the (al) roof. They stepped out of the train onto the (al) platform (andén). Sit next/beside me, next to the cinema. He was sitting at his desk (a su mesa de trabajo). In the morning, at noon (mediodía), in the afternoon, at midnight. Twice a day, once a week. He knocked him to the ground (lo derribó a puñetazos). They stabbed (acuchillaron) him to death. It smells of wine. Wake at the slightest (más ligero) sound. Washed by hand (a mano). A hand embroidered (bordada) piece. At a high price. Little by little (poco a poco). The criterion to be adopted (por adoptar). Items (artículos) to be discussed (tratados). The path to take (el camino por seguir). Did you give him (a él) the book? Convince/persuade: convencer. If this were not the case, I'd leave (me iría). You don't dare (te atreves) to dive in headfirst (a tirarte de cabeza). Down (abajo) at the river. Down here (aquí abajo). I sleep in the lower/bottom bunk (litera, cucheta). From below (desde abajo). There's a pharmacy further down the road (un poco más abajo). I study chemistry (química). I live three floors below. See note below. The bottom of the coat is all muddy (enfangado). It had cobwebs/spider's webs (telarañas) underneath; underneath the carpet/under the table. The kitchen and the lounge (salón) are downstairs. The downstairs neighbours. A party in the flat downstairs. Downstream (aguas abajo). We followed the street down to the square. Down the hill (cuesta abajo). Down the hillside (ladera abajo). They were sliding (deslizando) down/downstairs. With his head bent down/bowed (agachada). Don't look down (para abajo). This country has been ruined (venido abajo) by the war. In the photo below. The undersigned (el abajo firmante). Those of us at the bottom (los de abajo). Changes/revolution should begin/start at the bottom. Thirty years old and under (de 30 años para abajo). Under the shirt. Down with the government! Everyone rushed (avalanchados) towards the exit. It's worthless. Standard-bearers (cultura: poseedores; novedades/cheque: portadores). I was overcome by (me invadió) a feeling of desolation. He led (llevaba) a life of excess & indulgence. The chapter covers (abarca) three centuries. You can take in (abarcar; recoger, hacer entrar) the whole valley from here. Abatimiento: (derrumbamiento) demolition, knocking down, (depresión) depression, dejection. Your flies (bragueta + zip: cremallera) are undone, open. He left the top of the jar open (dejó el tarro abierto). He's very open-minded (de miras amplias). Ablandar: soften, (culinario) tenderize, (conmover) touch. Abobado (stupid-looking). Slap/hit (abofetear) in the face. Plead for/defend (abogar por). Abollado: (dented). Chemical fertilizer (abono). Tackle: Sp. --: equipo de deporte, fishing -- (aparejo), the book --s (aborda, se enfrenta a) controversial (controvertidos) subjects. Abortar: (accidentado) have a miscarriage, (deliberado) abortion. Best wishes/kind regards (un abrazo afectuoso o cordial). Bulky (abultado). There was plenty (abundancia) of drink. The olive trees are plentiful (abundantes) in the south. A gentrified (aburguesado) area (barrio). Unfairly (abusivamente, deslealmente). Become bourgeois. Take advantage (abusar): he's very generous but you mustn't take advantage; everyone takes advantage of the weak; the defendant took advantage of... It's a fine drink as long as you don't overdo (abuses de) it. It's outrageous (atroz, abusivo, escandaloso, vergonzoso, indignante...) what they've charged you for.... I think she's taking liberties (abuso de confianza). Indecent assault (agresión,V, asalto): abusos deshonestos. Walk up & down the street. Move over here (vente para acá), move over this way (más acá), move it this way (tráelo más acá) = bring it closer; move your chair closer (cerca) to the table; he brought his lips close to mine; common interest that brings us closer; come closer so that I can see you; don't get any closer, you could burn yourself. Let's do away (acabemos) with him! On top of everything, we left without even saying goodbye. Eventually I got fed up (hasta las narices) with all these parties. I've run out (my) patience. Hoard (tesoro, atesorar, acumular) food supplies (provisiones) for the winter; we have exhausted/used all our supplies. The left hold all the Council (ayuntamiento) posts. The accident took up the front pages in all the newspapers. I suggested (propuse) it & they agreed (accedieron). They have no access to the labour market because they have no qualifications (estudios). Assent (asentimiento), consent (consentimiento). This coincided with his assuming (acceso) to power. Entry to the estate (finca, propiedad; estado social) by road. A fish/mink (visón) farm. The main entrance to the museum. They didn't let him join the course (carrera) he wished. An uneventful (sin incidentes) life. Plane crash, road accident, industrial (laboral) accident. It's time to take action (pasar a la acción). A reprehensible (condenable) act (acción). He condemned the attack. Fair (justo) punishment for their evil (malas) deeds (acciones). A fast-acting slimming (adelgazante) cream. The majority (mayoritario) shareholding (accionariado). Crude oil (petróleo crudo) =/= fuel oil (aceite combustible), cottonseed (de algodón) oil, coconut (de coco) oil, castor (de ricino) oil, rapeseed (de colza) oil, lubricating oil, cod (de bacalao)-liver (hígado) oil, refined olive oil, virgin olive oil, table oil. The task he was assigned/he accepted. They refuse to face (aceptar) the facts. No refunds (no se admiten devoluciones) =/= you will be refunded for your expenses (se le reembolsarán los gastos). Irrigation ditch (cuneta, acequia)/channel. Toughen (endurecer, fortalecer), harden o.s. (aferrarse). We're approaching the target, aim. Unemployment is approaching 10%, he's approaching the retirement age. Our tastes tend more towards opera. The music is appropriate for a funeral. The best (más acertado) purchase of my life. Hit the target (acertar los disparos). You get it right (acertaste). You made just the right choice (acertaste) with that present. I didn't manage to express myself clearly. Champagne-flavoured (achampañado). Flattened (achatado, allanado). Count the correct & incorrect answers. I doubt the wisdom (acierto) of that decision. The so right (con tanto acierto) called... Successes & failures. Clarify (hacer una aclaración de) sth. Rinsed (aclarado) in cold water. Diluir: thin (down). Get lightened (amanecer) =/= lighten (hacer el pelo más claro) + clear (aclarar el bosque), clear up (despejar las nubes), make up your mind! (¡A ver si te aclaras!), clear (airear) the air (atm.). Our country took in the exiled, some families took in students. The hotel where they are staying. They received us with affection. Athens hosted the Olympics. The theatre will seat/hold 1,500 people. This building houses (alberga) the Science museum. The corridors (pasillos) will accommodate an exhibition. They have invoked the right not to testify. He afforded (dispensó, concedió) the show a cold reception (acogida) + it was favourably received ↔ bad/poorly received. Host (de acogida) family. Tremendous/brilliant (acojonante). You can go with me (acompañarme). Don't you want me to go with you? He was with him at the press conference (rueda de prensa). See sb home (acompañar a alguien a casa)/ to the door. We stayed a while to keep grandmother company. He stood by her side throughout the illness. They offered me to join in the search (búsqueda) of... He's got a complex about his nose. Push to safety (poner a salvo). Distress (angustia, aflicción, apuro, dolor) → don't distress yourself! (¡No te acongojes!). An engine that complies/in compliance/in conformity with regulations. Be used/accustomed to doing sth. He got into the habit of drinking chocolate, chocolate cookie/biscuit (galleta de). Aerial acrobatics (acrobacia aérea). The documentary proof is in the minutes (actas de reunión), let it be noted in the record (acta del organismo), write up the minutes (levantar acta de), certificate (acta) of baptism, death certificate, bill (acta) of indictment (acusación). In defiant posture (actitud). In state (actitud, estado) of total concentration.

Serving officer (oficial en activo). Opening ceremony (acto inaugural). Repairs (reparaciones) while you wait (en el acto) =/= he died instantly. Actualmente: presently, currently, nowadays. Tema de actualidad (topicality): a highly topical (de mucha actualidad) question. La actualidad: current affairs, current news. They settled (llegaron a un acuerdo) out of the court. Tiredness (el cansancio) showed in their faces. Acumular: pile up, gather, amass. The seismometer picks up/ registers (acusa) the least vibration. The work is advanced; people advanced in years. The alarm clock is 5 m. fast. He is ahead of/advanced for his age. For children of three & upwards (en adelante). An improvement in the current method. From now on/in the future. Carry on/go ahead with their plans. The advances of Science. The retirement age will be lowered. Come in (entre, siga)! =/= Go on (siga)! He released (liberó, cedió, hizo público) the results in advance. The article is just a taster (degustador, muestra) of his latest book. An advance of € 50 + cash deposit (adelanto en metálico). Besides somewhere to stay (alojamiento), we need food. Out at sea (mar adentro) → inland (tierra adentro). Put the finishing touch (sazon, el toque final, aderezo,Vs). Adicto: addicted to heroin/oysters, a devoted audience filled the hall, the press loyal to/supportive of the government. Train (adiestrar, entrenar, educar...). Guess who called? Foresee the future. Fortune teller (adivino/a). Knock down (adjudicar + award) to the highest bidder (postor). Assistant lecturer (professor adjunto). I enclose my CV (le envío adjunto mi CV). We accept/take credit cards. Honorary citizen (hijo adoptivo) of the city. Become sleepy/drowsy (adormecerse). Full of ornaments (adornos). Christmas decorations. Semi-detached house = duplex (casa adosada). He ignored my warnings (hizo caso omiso de mis advertencias). Crop dusting (aerofumigación). Airbrush (cepillo...) = aerógrafo (para pintar con aire comprimido). Affable: (=), sociable, cortés, afectuoso. An educational (educador, docente) work.

Strengthen/secure (afianzar). Avalar: (en Com.) guarantee, vouch for sth/sb. Keen/enthusiastic (aficionado). Not professional (amateur). They have become very fond of him (le han tomado mucho cariño), in a fond embrace (tiernamente abrazado). In tune: Mús. (afinado,V), (automóvil) puesto a punto. Afligir: afflict, distress, don't get upset (don't upset yourself). Influx (afluencia) of tourists, of foreign capital. Aphonia: loss of voice, voiceless (afónico). Out of the way! (¡Afuera! + Get out!). From outside: (de)sde afuera. Bend down (encorvarse, agacharse + stoop). He held him until the police arrived. Hold it by this end (extremo). He gripped her arm tightly (él se agarró con fuerza a su brazo), he grabbed (agarró) the child by the shoulder, he grabbed her hair & refused to let her go. Stiffening (agarrotamiento) of muscles. This tie is strangling me. Haulage company (agencia de transporte) =/= travel agency (agencia de turismo, de viajes). I shook the injured man to bring him round (volviera en sí). His assassination stirred up (agitó) the country. They use the fear of war to win votes. Be grateful (sentirse agradecido) for..., I'm much obliged to you (se lo agradezco), I would be grateful if you would send me..., she looked at me gratefully (con gratitud) & said "Many thanks! I appreciate it!" I've the pleasure of informing you that... Worsening/aggravating for the worst. Cultural, press, military... attaché (agregado). Organic (biológical) farming (agricultura); subsistence farming, food & agriculture (sector agroalimentario); agriculture, fishing & livestock (sector agropecuario). Get flu (engripsarse). Gather/assemble (pers., datos: agrupar). Crowd together (agrupar + form a group). Water-cooled (refrigerado) engine/motor. A very wet (con mucha agua + with a lot of rain) winter. Launch (botar) a boat. Take the plunge: aventurarse, arriesgarse. It makes my mouth water. Be in it up to one's neck. Eagerness: (afán, entusiasmo, ansia, ilusión, impaciencia) of profit (lucro) + thirst for knowledge, desire to better o.s. (superación). They are eagerly (con entusiasmo...) awaiting (esperan como agua de mayo...) the privatisations. He searched eagerly through the files =/= earnestly (seriamente, formalmente). Piss one's laughing (mearse de risa) =/= Wet o.s... Thermal springs. Shower (aguacero, ducha, chubasco). Deepen (ahondar). For the moment it turns out (parece, resulta) that... They've just (acaban de) told me... A little while ago (hace poco tiempo) ↔ a long way ago... An energy saving scheme (plan). Ahumar (smoke, cure). The controversy hung in the air. The concert was outdoors/in the open air (aire libre). Frighten off/away (ahuyentar). Blow up (volar por los aires). They learned in their own air (a su aire). An airconditioned vehicle. Compressed (comprimido) air. What brings you here? He replied wearily (con aire cansado). He looks a bit like a Carlist. Lentils give me a lot of air. Well/badly ventilated. Soundproofing (insonorización). Insulation (aislamiento térmico, acústico), insulating (aislante) =/= isolation (pers., estado: aislamiento), cut off (aislados) by the floods (inundaciones), an isolated case. Get some air (airearse). Sb's praises (alabanzas), praise (alabar) sth. Wire-netting (alambrada, tela metálica). He is showing off (alardeando de) his wealth. He boasts about his sexual prowess. Car/fire alarm, anti-theft alarm, burglar (ladrón) alarm, public alarm (inquietud pública), don't be alarmed! Bricklaying (albañilería). Shelter (albergue, refugio,Vs), provide accommodation for..., youth hostel (albergue, residencia), the stadium can hold many people, state-owned tourist hotel, road house. Cause a commotion (armar un alboroto). Lagoon (albufera: está cerca del mar y comunicada con él). Artichoke (alcachofa). Mayoress (alcaldesa). The scope (alcance) of the human mind (mente). She used all the means availables to her. Grasp (agarrar, captar una idea, aprovechar una oportunidad) → be within sb's reach/grasp (alcance). Keep out of reach of children/out of the gunfire (disparos). Short range (alcance)/long --/medium --. The extent of the problem. On the point (a punto) of catching the leader of the race. I caught her up (la alcancé) as she was going out of the door. They reached the summit (la cima). The agreement was reached. Bring about peace. The change will affect us. He couldn't reach the doorbell. Bull/rising (alcista) market, the upward (alcista) trend. Instructive/enlightening: aleccionador + (castigo) exemplary. Alegar: a plea (of not guilty, …), he claims/alleges/argues/puts forward that she… The two planets have shifted (movido) slightly apart/away from each other. A few months away from each other. A rift (alejamiento) between the government & the people. Move away (alejarse). Move the vase away a little. This smell keeps the mosquitoes away. Let's get/go/move a bit further away. I saw two youths running away. The road veers (vira) away from the coast. They gradually (poco a poco) drifted apart from their friends. Get off the subject (alejarse del tema). Encouraging (alentador) → encourage sb to do sth. Watch out! (¡Alerta!) → all the rescue services are on standby (alerta), raise the alarm (dar la voz de alerta). On 24-hour standby. Dorsal fin (aleta de pez) → move its fins (aletear) =/= en aves: flutter/flap their wings. Treachery (alevosía, maquinación, traición). Alforja: caballo (saddlebag), moto (pannier), a cuestas (knapsack). He is a musician or sth like (o algo así). I'm in a hurry (prisa). There is a certain likeness between them. These shoes are rather/a little uncomfortable. The inflation has gone up by a little over two points. We've done it at one time or another/at some point (todos lo hemos hecho alguna vez). Out of all these shirts (de entre tantas camisas) there's bound to be (tiene que haber) one that you like. One or two (alguno que otro). He has bad breath (aliento). The exercise left me breathless/out of breath. Get one's breath back (recobra…). Feed pump (bomba de alimentación). Some animal fodder (piensos) is not at all (nada) nutritious/nourishing. Her stories strengthened/fuelled my desire to… They feed on carrion (carroña). While shipwrecked (en naufragio), they survived on fruit. Whole food (alimentos integrales).

Health (natural) foods. Aliño: flavouring, (de ensalada) dressing, (de guiso) seasoning. Alistar: put on a list, matricular (enrol). Aliviar: ease/relieve the effects/problems. What a relief (alivio)! It's a great relief to have passed at last, console/comfort (consolar). The (great) beyond: el más allá. Fall down/tumble down (derrumbarse, allanarse). In there (allí dentro). Near there. Wherever he goes (allí donde va)... He makes a favourable impression (despierta admiración). Shortly afterwards (de allí a poco). That is why (de allí que)... Kind (amable, caritativa + charitable) soul. I'm eternally/deeply grateful (te lo agradezco en el alma). From the bottom of my heart. Good God! (¡Dios mío de mi alma!). I shudder (me estremezco, vibro) to think (tiemblo de pensar en) =/= stammer/mumble (balbucear, hablar entre dientes) =/= stutter/stammer (tartamudear) =/= shatter (hacer añicos, destrozar: --ed by the news) + I'm completely shattered (hecho polvo, no puedo con mi alma) =/= shutter (obturador) → the reactor should be shuttered (con postigos cerrados). I want it desperately (con toda mi alma). He's the life and soul of the party. Air cushion (almohada neumática). Piles (=, montones, almorranas). I've had lunch (vengo almorzado), luncheon (comida, almuerzo). Wedding breakfast (banquete nupcial). Official (de gala) luncheon. Small/boarding house: pensión. Lark (alondra). Ropesoled sandal (alpargata). Renter/hirer ←→ tenant (inquilino). Dar en alquiler: (casa, local) rent, let; (coche, bicicleta, TV) rent, let + hire → apartment for rent, flat to let, to let (se alquila) → tomar en alquiler: (casa, local, TV) rent, (coche, bicicleta) rent, hire. Pay the rent. Substitute/surrogate (sustituta) mother. Raise sb's rent. Alchemy (alquimia). Coal tar (alquitrán de hulla). Alquitranado: (acción) tarred, (carretera/ superficie) tarmac,V. All around the church. Look around/about me. The sick note (baja médica) ←→ discharge sb (dar el alta médica). I applied for a phone line. Disturb (alterar) the peace (orden), the humidity spoiled the food + sour (agriar) the milk. She was visibly shaken/upset (volcado, afectado, disgustado, turbado). Keep calm! Don't be upset! (¡No te alteres!). Alternately (alternativamente). Take turns in office (alternarse en el poder). Have alternatives/options/choices; alternative energy sources. Crop (cultivo) rotation. High plateau (altiplano, meseta). Arrogance, haughtiness (altivez, altanería). At this stage of the year. Alucinado: stunned, gobsmacked, mind blowing. Allude to/ mention (aludir). Boarder (alumno interno, huésped). Alzar: (copa/ brazo) raise, (objeto) lift, (objeto pesado) hoist. The meteoric raise to fame. Suckle/nurse (amamantar). Suck (chupar), sucker (ventosa). Entertaining/pleasant (ameno). Tonsil (amígdala). Pile up (amontonar). Shock absorber (amortiguador). Distress/make anxious (angustiar). Entertainment/amusement/fun (entretenimiento, diversión). Ajusticiar: put to death, execute (+ un plan, una obra de arte). Encouraging (alentador). Alineación: (Pol.) alignment, (Sp.) line-up. Clam (almeja), almond (almendra), starch (almidón). Alejar: move the vase (jarro) away, keep sb away =/= alojar (put up, accommodate), alojamiento (accommodation, lodging). Climbing (alpinismo). Quarrel (alboroto, pelea) → pick a -- (buscar camorra). Meet people (alternar). Ansia (yearning/longing) for freedom + anxiety, worry, anguish. Con antelación: beforehand, in advance. Show antipathy for sth, dislike sth. Apaciguar: (tranquilizar) calm down, (manifestaciones) pacify, (político) appease. Appeal (apelar) for people's common sense. Grieve (afligir, apenar). Scarcely (apenas, con dificultad). Take pity on sb (apiadarse). Adjournment (aplazamiento). Hard working (aplicado). Support (apoyo, sostén). Trainee (aprendiz + apprentice). Squeeze together (apretarse). Aprisionar (imprison). Trap (trampa, atrapar). Arancel: customs duty, tariff. Embarrass (poner en aprietos, avergonzar). Filing cabinet (archivador). Deeply rooted (arraigado). Pull along (arrastrar + drag) → drag oneself (arrastrarse). Seize (arrebatar, tomar el poder...). Outburst (arrebato). Tidy/neat: arreglado. Fixed (fijado, establecido). Sort it out (ordénalo) as best as you can. Regretful (arrepentido + repentant). Fling o.s. (arrojarse). Run over (derramarse, desbordarse; atropellar; pasarse del tiempo, echar un vistazo). Lend a hand (arrimar el hombro). Wage earner (asalariado). Ascender: promote, climb/go up. Besiege (asediar). Consent (asentimiento). Allocate (asignar). As well (así mismo). Asistenta: charwoman, charlady, cleaning woman =/= asistente: assistant, (Mil.) orderly (ordenanza), social worker (asistente/a social). As the saying goes (como dice el dicho). Applicant (aspirante), contender for the title, aspirant to power. Asombrar: astonish, stun, amaze, frighten + asustar. Shrewdness (astucia). Traffic jam (atasco). Landing (aterrizaje). Atizar: (fuego) poke, stir, (horno) stoke, discordias/pasiones (stir up). Atrasar: (salida) delay, (reloj) put back, (progreso) slow down. Stay behind (atrasarse). Atrevido: daring, audaz (bold) =/= bald (calvo) =/= bolt/latch (pestillo,Vs) → quemar el último cartucho (shoot one's bolt). Daring neckline (escote). Cheeky (descarado, indiscreto). Stunt: proeza, truco, ardid, maniobra; acróbata; detener, atrofiar → stun (dejar pasmado, aturdido, sin sentido, V); stunning: (success) sensacional, (defeat) aplastante, (punch) contundente, (beauty) despampanante =/= stint (escatimar) → -- sb of sth; hacer su parte → I've done my --; período → a five year --. Bewilderment (aturdimiento, perplejidad, desconcierto). Appealing (atractivo + =). Audiencia (hearing). Owl (búho) =/= howl (aullido,V) → he teaches his dog to howl =/= haul (transportar, trayecto, arrastrar, pesca: redada) → he was hauled off by the police. Self-taught (autodidacta). Perpetrator (autor de un crimen). Hitchhiking (auto-stop) + he gave me a lift/ride. Fast (rápido, firme, firmemente, ayuno, V). At random (al azar, imprevisto). Mishap (contratiempo). Bullet (bala) → -- train (tren a gran velocidad). Bajar: go/come down, descend, (la voz): lower. Hairdresser (peluquero/a). Vulgar: (=, ordinary). Dustman (basurero). Quarrel (riña, pelearse). Becar: award a grant/scholarship. Aubergine (berenjena). Rudely (a lo bestia). Bug (bicho, chinche). Communal property (bienes gananciales: lo que aporta cada uno). That is quite enough (ya está bien). Well meaning (bien intencionado). Fork (bifurcación, tenedor, horca) → -- out (desembolsar, aflojar). Birria (mess, horrible, garbage, rubbish + basura, tonterías; be rubbish: ser un manta). Crosseyed (bizco). Sponge cake (bizcocho). Launder (blanquear dinero). Ingenuo (innocent, naive). Borde (edge, brim). Borrador: (proyecto, contrato) draft, (carta) rough draft, (dibujo) sketch. Drop out: derramarse, (de competición) retirarse, (universidad) abandonar, (de un equipo) salirse. Abandonar: (trabajo) give up, (asociación) leave. Retract (retractarse). Muzzle (bozal). Bravo: (=, fierce). Booing (abucheo) → he was --ed + give sb the bird (abuchear a alguien). Suntanned (bronceado por el sol). Sprout (brotar). Sharp: (temperatura) repentino cambio, (persona) avispada, (curva) abrupta, (instrumento) afilado, (grito) agudo, (viento) cortante; sharpen (afilar una herramienta) =/= put a point on (sacar punta)... Bulto: (abultamiento) bulge, (silueta) shape, (ropa, papel) bundle → a bulto (at a rough guess). Bochornoso: (tiempo) sultry, muggy, (calor) sticky. Cansancio: tiredness, exhaustion, weariness → be worn out. Boredom: aburrimiento, hastío. Canturrear (hum, croon, sing softly). Pipes (cañerías). Foreman (capataz). Surrender (capitular). Fanciful/whimsical: caprichoso (=). Pick up: levantar, comprar, (ir a) recoger, coger ideas, ganar dinero, "Ligar". Cheeky/so & so (caradura). Loud laugh/guffaw (carcajada) → roar (rugir, bramar) with laughter (a carcajadas). Delicacy: (=, fragilidad + frailty; exquisitez, manjar exquisito) =/= charcutería (cooked) pork, delicatessen). Load (cargamento) → maximum load. Abrazar: embrace, hug. Toast (tostado, V, brindis) =/= dedicatoria (dedication) =/= devote a lot of time to reading. Bust (busto, romper) → go -- (quebrar). Corpse (cadáver). Caduco (out of date). Caer: (temperatura) drop, (agua) waterfall, have a fall on the floor, (hair) loss, (Gobierno) fall, collapse, (oil prices, $) fall. Calcular: figure, reckon. Randy (caliente sexualmente, cachondo). If you are hot... (si tienes calor...). Stray dog (perro callejero). Pain killer (calmante). Calmar: (el dolor) relieve, (los ánimos) calm. Underpants (calzoncillos) ↔ knickers, panties. Campana (bell) extractora: extractor hood, fan + ventilador. Belfry/bell tower (campanario). Swine/rotten/mean/bastard (canalla). Cancelar: cancel, (cuenta) close off, (deuda) settle. Cuddle (abrazo,V). Hoarding: acumulación, valla (publicitaria), cartelera + billboard.Cartón: cardboard. Rattlesnake (serpiente cascabel). Kennel (caseta de perro). At best (en el mejor de los casos). Nut: tuerca, cojones, chiflado → be nuts about sth. (chiflado por algo), go -- (volverse loco), be nuts (estar como un cencerro) =/= nuez → walnut (de nogal), chestnut (castaña), peanut (cacahute), hazelnut (avellana). Dandruff (caspa). Breed (criar, engendrar; raza, variedad + strain). By a chance (por una casualidad). Catalogar (catalogue, label, classify). A fair cause (una causa justa). Ponder/consider. Celebrar: (boda...: celebrate), be delighted. Celo: professional commitment, (diligencia) zeal, (hembra) oestrus, (adhesivo) sellotape, scotch tape, (celos) jealousy → be jealous of sb, make sb. jealous. Take a census (censo). Scrapyard (cementerio de coches). Centrifugar: (=, spin dry). Frente (forehead, brow) → a furrowed brow: una frente surcada de arrugas; ceño (entrecejo) fruncido: frown, scowl → fruncir el -- (frown/knit one's brow). Cerca (fence, wall). Nearby (cercano). Cherry (cereza). Locksmith (cerrajero), plumber (fontanero), blacksmith (herrero), joiner/carpenter. Cerrar el grifo (turn off/switch off the tap/faucet). Foodstuffs: (comestibles → (en tienda) groceries, (tienda de comestibles) grocer's (shop), grocery (tendero de comestibles), shopkeeper (tendero), greengrocer (frutero) =/= drugstore (farmacia + otros productos), tender/fresh food. Contest (contienda, lucha; impugnar, rebatir). Resign: cesar en un cargo. Make up: compensar, inventar, (cama/lista) preparar, (resolver) -- -- one's differences, (decidirse) -- -- one's mind; maquillar, constituir (10% of...). Contundente: (arma) offensive, (instrumento) blunt, (argumento, tono) forceful, (victoria, derrota) crushing, overwhelming, (efecto) severe, (arbitraje) severe, strict, (prueba) conclusive. Con creces (amply, fully) → she far exceeded/surpassed all expectations, he beat the record by a long way, she smashed (rompió, dio al traste, aplastó) the record, he is very big/tall for his age, sb's old enough to know... Talkative (charlatán). Gossip (cotilleo, chismorreo) → it's just idle -- (sólo son habladurías). Chiflado: crazy, barmy → he is crazy about that girl. Color chillón (gaudy, garish, lurid). Custard apple (chirimoya). Chiripa (fluke, stroke of luck). Give a tip-off (dar el chivatazo). Blind/sightless (ciego). Stork (cigüeña). Plum (ciruela). Quotation (cita de un autor) → quote, cite, the sources quoted =/= citar: we arranged to meet at 4. Sow discord (sembrar cizaña). Cry out (clamar). Clara de huevo (white), yema de huevo (yolk), del dedo (fingertip), (Bot.) leaf bud. Variety (variedad). Clase/tipo (kind), kind of... (especie de...) =/= class of teachers =/= lesson (lección) of music, classroom (aula). Clavel (carnation). Collarbone (clavícula). Coastal (áreas costeras) → coastal navigation. Coerce (coaccionar). Squalid (cochombroso, miserable, asqueroso, vil). Filthy (sucia, obscena) person. Stew (guisado, estofado), boiled (hervido), cooked (cocinado), grilled (a la parrilla/brasas). Talk nonstop (hablar por los codos). Coherencia: (=), consistence. Colmena: (bee)hive → colmenar (apiary). Appear (comparecer, aparecer, salir). Inhibited (cohibido). Cojera: limp, (cojo) lame people, (cojear) hobble. Collar: alaja (necklace), de animales (collar). Remark (comentario, observación). Trade (comercio, V). Assignment/task/mission (cometido, misión). Feel sorry for (compadecer). Appearance (comparecencia). The height (colmo) of stupidity. Laundry (colada) → do the laundry. Hanging (colgando). Colonia (summer camp). Fuera de combate (out of action/the running).

Compartir: (casa, comida, ganancias, opinión) share. Full (completo). Consist of (consistir en). Common (usual). A brilliantly conceived (concebido) plan. Conciencia: =, awareness concienciar: make aware → be aware that, politically/sexually aware. Specify (concretar). Conducir: this way leads to, (coche) drive, (Electr.) conduct. Confiture/preserve/jam. Entrust/trust/confide (confiar). Intake (consumo, entrada, toma). Achieve (conseguir). Concertar (arrange, set up), acordar (agree). Concurso: competition, (TV) quiz show, (administración) open competition. Condescending/complacent. Admission (en un club) → free -- (entrada libre), the closing date for application has been extended. Converge (confluir). Confuse/mix up (confundir). Conmoción: (cerebral) concussion, (Geol.) shock, tremor; conmocionar (shake). Expert (entendido/conocedor). Devote oneself (consagrarse) to... Conservar: keep his letters, keep food fresh, (calor) retain. Thoughtful: considerado, pensativo. Left luggage (equipaje en depósito). Constancy (constancia). Constar: appear on the planes, consist of 50 tasks, figure in, be included in. Enquiry (consulta, investigación). Query (duda, pregunta,V; la metodología, ...: cuestionar). Fait accompli (hecho consumido). Consumar: (delito) carry out, (matrimonio) commonmate. Adjoining (contigua) room. Anti-establishment (contestatario). Escaso: short (of money, ...), little help, barely 5 kg., slim chance, scare/scant(escaso)/slender (+ delgado) food =/= spare part (recambio). Hold back/restrain (contener) the passion... Back page (contraportada). Convalidar: (title) accreditation, (subject: asignatura) recognition. Corazonada/presentimiento: hunch, feeling. Cordial = warm, (--mente): warmly, cordially, (en carta) sincerely. Common sense (cordura). Coro: (Mús.) chorus, (coral) choir. Correcto: polite, courteous (=) → courtesy (cortesía). Proper (apropiado). Corrupt (=, corrompido,V). Cortar: (césped) mow, (luz) cut off. Coser: (vestido) sew, (Med.) stitch up, (a balas) riddle sb with bullets. Big head (creído). Roaring (rugiente, estruendoso) =/= rear (parte trasera), crianza: rearing + para reproducción: breeding =/= upbringing (educación), descendencia (offspring) → die without issue/offspring =/= local offshoots (ramas, vástagos, retoños, filiales) of Guggenheim... Crítica: criticism of the government, the play got excellent reviews (ídem en los diarios), the exhibition was well received. Cronista: feature writer, reporter, columnist, sports writer, (Hist.) chronicler. Cuantioso: considerable, substantial. Cubierto: (cielo) overcast, covered (in stains, by the insurance), bed: with a sheet (sábana). Countdown (cuenta regresiva). The moon is waxing (creciendo). They involved (implicados)? Carefully (con cuidado). Cockroach (cucaracha). Spoonful (cucharada). Cuartel (barracks, quarters). Uphill (cuesta arriba). Worship (culto). Culture (cultivar) =/= educated, cultured. At any moment (de un momento a otro), in due course (en su momento), en un momento dado (at a certain point) =/= up (hasta) to a certain point. Harm (molestia, daño), tobacco is harmful (dañino) for the health + the chemical is -- to the plants + harmless (inofensivo). Give a shout (dar una voz). Provide with lunch (dar de comer). Come across: -- -- well/badly (dar buena/mala sensación), tropezar con; dar con → I'd never -- -- the word before. Get people talking (dar que hablar). Keep quiet (no decir nada). Desgracia (bemoan, misfortune, bad luck). Behead (decapitar). Molesto: (tos/ruido) annoying, (enfadado) annoyed, (ropa...) uncomfortable. Infer/deduce (deducir) + deduct (descontar). Defensa: body's defence, -- of a team, he defended freedom. Stop that nonsense (déjate de tonterías). He flopped down on the bed (se dejó caer en la cama). Delincuente (offender, infractor). Draughtman (delineante). Delito: crime (+ infracción), offense. Emaciated (demacrado). Plaintiff (demandante). Insane (=, demente + mad, mental patient). Delay (demora,V). He renounced (renegó) his faith. Refuse (rehusar). Set of teeth (dentadura). Denunciar: report, condemn, denounce → he reported the theft/a formal complaint to the police. Shop assistant (dependiente). Depositar: put on, place one's trust on sb, store, deposit. Derrotar (defeat, beat). Derrumbar: pull down, shoot down, (casa) demolish/knock down. Undo (desabrochar; damage: reparar; Comput.: cancelar). Displease (desagradar). Desajustar: upset/loosen. Discouraging (desalentador). Derivar (derive, stem from). Depurar: (agua) treat/purify, (Pol.) purge, (información, problemas) debug. Derogar/abrogar: abolish, (contrato) revoke, (ley) repeal =/= repel (repeler, rechazar). Pay out (desembolsar, pagar). Lack of respect (desacato). Unwise (desacertado, imprudente). Defiant (desafiante). Desafinar (play out of tune). Desahogo: (alivio) relief, (comodidad) comfort. Desalentador (discouraging, dishearting). Un<u>tidy (ordenado, arreglado)</u>: desordenado, descuidado → --ness: desaliño, lo descuidado, desorden; his hair is always untidy. Heartless (desalmado). Eviction (desalojo, deshaucio). Desamparar: desert, abandon, forsake. Unnoticed (desapercibido). Unscrupulous (desaprensivo). Rootless (desarraigado) =/= uproot (desarraigar). Develop (desarrollar). Dismantle (desarticular). Take place (suceder). Come undone (desatarse). Unblock (desatascar/desatrancar). Desautorizar: deprive of authority, deny permission, discredit + desprestigiar, refutar. Disorder/mess (desbarajuste).Overflow (desagüe, rebosar, desbordarse). Alimentary canal: tubo digestivo. Be in the wrong track (desencaminado). Waste ground (descampado). Descargar: (mercancías) unload, (Electr.) discharge. Tranquilizarse (calm down). ¡Qué descaro! (What a cheek!). Derailment (descarrilamiento). Descifrar/entender/resolver un problema (figure out). Descomposición: (=, diarrea). Rot (podrir). Descomponer: (sustancia/frase...) break down, (cadáver) decompose, (mat. orgánica.) rot/decay. Thoughtless (desconsiderado). Desconsolado: disconsolate, grief stricken (con pena, dolor). Distressing (descorazonador, angustioso, acuciante). Neglected (descuidado). Descuido: oversight, carelessness. Poor devil/ unlucky (desdichado). Nonreturnable containers (envases). Desempeñar: (deber/función) carry out, hold the post of dean, fulfill... Contorted/out of join (desencajado). Pull out/draw (desenfundar). Disappointment (decepción, desilusión). Move with ease (desenvoltura). Unbalanced (desequilibrado). In despair (desesperado). Reject: (offer, candidate) rechazar, no aceptar, (Med.) rechazar. Lack of appetite (desgana). Tear (desgarrar) =/= wear out (desgastarse). Misfortune (desgracia). Desechos: waste, leftovers, scraps. Desigual: (terreno) uneven, (Ec./Pol.) unequal, (letra, pulso) erratic. Desmaquillarse (remove one's make up). Deny (desmentir). Desmenuzar: (pan) crumble, (pescado, pollo) flake. Disrupt (interrumpir, alterar). Serve: servir, despachar + sack/fire sb. Stunning (asombroso, despampanante). Self-confident (con desparpajo, que confía en sí mismo). Scorn (despreciar) → despectivo: disparaging, scornful. Take off (avión: despegar) =/= detach (separar/despegar algo). Despeinado: ruffled, messed up. Skin (despellejar). Waste/squander (despilfarrar). Scatterbrained/ absent-minded (despistado). Desplazar: displace, (cargo) remove from office, (objeto) move, (tropas) transfer, (suplantar) take the place of, (desbancar) supersede =/= dismiss/sack (despedir). Despicable (despreciable). Despojar: (bienes) strip, (honores, derechos...) divest + deshacerse de); despojarse, (ropas) undress, (cubierta) take off. A deshora (at odd time). Stretch: extensión, estirarse; elasticidad; alcanzar, trecho → stretch oneself (desperezarse). Desplomarse: collapse, slump (bolsa 1929...), fall sharply. Despise/look down on (despreciar). Despreocuparse (don't bother or worry about). Outstanding (destacado, sobresaliente; pendiente). Ramshackle: (casa, coche) destartalados, (ejército) maltrecho. Desteñirse: fade, run, discolour. Destinado: (carta) addressed, (dinero...) set aside for sth., (obra) the play is destined to fall. Drawback: inconveniente, desventaja. A tasteful touch (un detalle de buen gusto). Damage: deterioro, desperfectos, (suerte, reputación) perjuicio. Debtor → creditor. Desviar: (flecha/balón) deflect, (golpe) parry, (pregunta) evade, (tren) switch, (avión/circulación) divert, (desviar a alguien del buen camino) lead sb astray. Dibujar: sketch, draw, (técnico) design. Dictamen: report, (jurídico) legal opinion → issue a report. Slip: resbalón,V, (nudo) correrse, (moral) decaer, (oportunidad) escape, (en el cajón) meter, salir desapercibido =/= slid (slide, d, d): deslizar + tobogán, resbalón, corrimiento de tierras) → a smile as he -- a set of photos/a book across the table + América showed them a -- (filimina) with two charts (carta, mapa, lista de éxitos). Differentiate (diferenciar). Spread: desplegar, difundir, propagar, untar, (-- out): dispersarse, extenderse. Deceased (difunto). Digno: worthy (of attention, ...) → praise -- (-- de elogio), trust -- (-- de confianza). Willing God (si Dios quiere). Discurrir el tiempo: time goes by/off, pass. Argument/discussion. Displeased (disgustado), disgustarse (be annoyed, get upset, be displeased). Disminución (drop, fall, decrease) =/= drip (gota, goteo) from the tap (grifo, llave del gas). Distinguirse: (objeto) stand out, (pers.) distinguish o.s. Amuse oneself (distraerse). Distributor (distribuidor). Divagar: digress, ramble. Wander (pasear, vagar). Have a good time (divertirse). Doblegarse (give in, bend) → give in to anyone/anything. Dominar: rule the World, they dominated the second half. Weekend tripper (dominguero). Sleepyheaded (dormilón). Elaborar: prepare/ produce, (plan...) draw up. Ejecución: (a muerte) execution, (orden) carry out, (deseos) fulfilment. Ejemplar (issue, specimen). Ejercer (practise, exert). Ejercicio económico (financial year). Estorbar: be in the way, bother, (progreso) hinder, (camino) obstruct. Pocket (embolsarse). Eminencia: (=, leading figure). Emitir: (señal) send out, (veredicto) bring in, (dinero) issue, (TV) broadcast, (sonido/ olor) emit. Emocionante: moving, touching, exciting, thrilling. Junction: empalme, confluencia de ríos... Emparejar:

(calcetines) match socks, (pers.) pair. Become enraged (enfurecerse). Treacherous (engañoso). Wreck: destrozar, naufragio,Vs. Express his satisfaction. Strangeness/oddness (extrañeza). Exuberante: exuberant, lush (+ lozano, suntuoso), luxuriant. Fábrica (factory) → fabricar: manufacture, produce. The appearance (la facha + look). He is quite likely to come (probable que venga). He has a gift (facilidad) for expression. Feasible (factible). Provide (faciltar, suministrar). Facturar las maletas (check in + registrarse en el hotel). Household chores (faenas de casa). There are not enough + be missing (faltan). Fame/renown (fama). Starving/famished (famélico). Fanfarronear: as soon as there are women around, he shows off/you are always boasting. Famoso: (en positivo) famous ←→ (en negativo) notorious → he is a -- liar). Annoyed/bothered (fastidiado, molestado). Fastidiarse: I've hurt my knee again, our holiday is ruined, the car's broken down. Fate/misfortune (fatalidad). Fatigar: walking tires me out, get breathless + exhausting (fatigante). Favorecer: red suits you, these measures favour us. Fenomenal: terrible, marvellous. Penoso: it is distressing (lamentable) to see poverty, a difficult job, painful. Perishable (perecedero). Fierce (feroz, violento, encarnizado) =/= fiercy (ardiente, exaltado) speech... =/= farcical (obscuro, ridículo) =/= forceful: (pers.) con carácter, (discurso) contundente, (argumento) convincente → forcefulness: fortaleza, contundencia. Stinking/fetid (fétido). Reliability (formalidad, fiabilidad) =/= trustworthiness (credibilidad); trust (confianza) → a position of -- (de confianza o de responsabilidad). Sell on credit (fiar). Card index (fichero). Faithfulness (fidelidad). Fiel: loyal, faithful. I'mangry (enfadado) with you/ about what happened. We'll hold a party (daremos una fiesta). Stare: mirar fijamente. Filigrana: filigree, intricacy → intricate work. Filtrar (leak) un dato. Purpose/aim (finalidad). In order to/so as to (a fin de que). Terminus (fin de trayecto). Feign (fingir) → fingido (feigned, false) → Trump is a master feigning; I tried to feign indiferente/appear indifferent. Finura: delicacy (=, fragilidad), refinement, politeness + cortesía). Flute (flauta). Lock: mechón de pelo, cerradura,V. He did it very reluctantly (actuó con desgana). You don't seem very hungry. Flojo: loose, slack + slackening of American resolve (resolución, determinación) to depose Mr Assad; slackness: dejadez, negligencia/falta de movimiento/de tensión. Florecer: flourish, thrive (+ prosperar). Rubber ring (flotador). Flabby (fofo, soso). Spirited (fogoso). Foliage (follaje). Struggle (forcejeo, lucha,Vs). Express (formular) a desire. Fray (lucha, crispar los nervios, deshilvanarse) =/= fail (fracasar, fallar, no aprobar, reprobar) =/= frail/weak (débil, frágil). Monk (fraile). Overcome (franquear) an obstacle + vencer, apoderarse (a strange feeling --ed her). Perfumed soap (jabón perfumado). Glasses/spectacles (gafas) → reading --, sun--, prescripted (graduadas) --, diving goggles (para bucear). Prizewinner (galardonado) → he was awarded a prize. Full dress (traje de gala). Rooster (gallo) → hen. Prawn (gamba). He is always up to (en condiciones de hacer) some mischief (travesura). I don't want to argue (discutir, reñir, exponer) + discuss (un plan). Reach the peak (ganar la cumbre). Charm ("Gancho"). Imponerse: we have set ourselves a heavy schedule, assert one's authority. Wisdom prevailed in the end. Garbanzo (chickpea) =/= guisante (pea). Tener garra: be compelling + fascinante, convincente). Expenditure (gasto). Seagull (gaviota). Genio (genius, temper) → what a -- you have! Solicitor: procurador, abogado, (para testamentos) notario. Gilipollas (prat, wanker, dickhead, asshole) → the only woman this man looks up (consulta) is his mother, who turned him into the asshole that he is. Enjoyment (goce) → gozoso (joyful). You rascal! (¡Golfo!). Golpe (blow, hit, knock, bump). Fatty (gordo) =/= le cae gordo (she can't bear him). Gracioso: graceful, funny, amusing. I need to have my eyes tested (graduar la vista). A granel (en grandes cantidades): in bulk → sell by the loose/by the liter. Grumpy (gruñón). Guapo: cute, pretty, handsome. Bodyguard (guardaespaldas). Armario: (cocina) cupboard, closet, (guardarropa) wardrobe, (teatro, discoteca) cloak (capa) room, (cuarto de baño) cabinet. Watchman (guardián). Filthy/disgusting (guarro). Humorous (guasón). Warrior (guerrero). Steer: (automóvil) conducir, (ship) gobernar, (pers.) dirigir → your columnist (articulista) tries to steer him off the topic. Wink (guiñar) at sb =/= wince (mueca). ¿Gustas? (Would like some?). A tasteless (insípedo, soso, de mal gusto) remark → a joke (broma) in very poor taste (gusto). Smart (hábil, listo, elegante, rápido). Habilitar: (local) convert, (poder) provide, authorize. Get used to (habituarse a). A grotty (asquerosa) image. Piece of gossip (habladuría). Hacer la maleta (pack up) ←→ unpack. Go old (hacerse mayor). Promising/encouraging (halagüeño). What a find! (¡Qué hallazgo!). Hartarse (get tired of/fed up/ sick of). Wizard/sorcerer (hechicero). Stench/stink (hedor). Propeller (hélice). Grass eating (herbívoro + =). Horseshoe (herradura). Moisturizing (hidratante). Weed (hierbajo). Bonfire (hoguera). The house was ablaze (en llamas). Deciduous (de hoja caduca). Comfortable: ropa/zapatos (=), (hotel) cómodo; holgado de dinero. Be idle (estar ocioso). Werewolf (hombre lobo). Uprightness (honestidad, =). Footprint/footstep (huella), track (rastro de animal y coche). Vegetable garden (huerta). Humility/humbleness (humildad). Humos: conceit (+ vanidad (=), engreimiento), airs → with a triumphant air. Sunken (hundido). Shy (vergonzoso, huraño, asustadizo) → on the shy (con sigilo, a hurtadillas). Hurto (robbery, pilfering). Idear (devise, think up, conceive). Unreadable (ilegible). Ilusionar: (excite, thri<u>ll</u> + emocionar); thriller (obra de suspenso y emoción) =/= thri<u>ft</u> (frugalidad) =/= thrive: (plan) prosperar, (niño) desarrollarse. Distinguished/famous/illustrious (ilustre). Magnet (imán). Indelible (imborrable) memory/pen. Impactar: crash, hit, shock (conmoción), stun (asombrar, atontar). Disabled (minusválido). Prevailing (imperante). Safety pin (imperdible). Fallible/imperfect/flawed (imperfecto). Imperturbable (=) ↔ disturbing, upsetting. Ungodly/irreligious atheistic (impío) ↔ believer =/= agnostic. Faultless (impecable). Implement (implanter, poner en marcha) a model/reform... Involvement (implicación). Matter (importarle) + and what business is it of yours? (¿Y a tí qué te importa?). Make impossible (imposibilitar). Powerlessness (impotencia, =). Unworkable (impracticable). Impressive/striking (impresionante). Unforeseeable/unpredictable (imprevisible). Unexpected (imprevisto). Instill (inculcar). Imprudencia: (=), indiscretion, rashness, it was a driver's carelessness. Challenge: desafío, reto, cuestionamiento,Vs Prohibitive/unapproachable (inaccessible, =). Maladjusted/misfit (inapropiado). Unnoticed/unobserved/unseen (inadvertido). Inagotable: (recursos) inexhaustible, (paciencia) tireless. Unbearable (inaguantable). Unattainable (inalcanzable). Incapacidad (inability), unfit for military service. Disabled/unfit (incapacitado). Incauto: (=, unsuspecting), gullible (crédulo, =). Neverending/incessant (incesante). Instar/incitar (urge). The general incited the army to... Incomodar(se) (embarrass, makesb feel uncomfortable): put oneself out. Isolate/cut off (incomunicar). Inconceivable. Changeable (inconstante (=). Countless (incontable). Annoy/pester (incordiar, molestar). Built in: incorporado, =). Discourteous: =, incorrecto (=). Lack of culture. Concern (incumbencia). Fail to fulfill (incumplir). Terrible (=, dreadful, awful). Defenceless (indefenso). Unharmed/unhurt (indemne). Irresolution (indeterminación). Point out (indicar). Índice: (Mat.) index, (biblioteca) catalogue. Indicio: sign; Jur.: circumstancia evidence. Poverty stricken (indigente, muy pobre). Unlucky/unfortunate/unhappy (infeliz). Poor wretch (desgraciado + unhappy). Indisponer (se): (upset/make sb unwell): fall/become ill. Untameable (indomable). Lenient (indulgente, benevolente, poco severo). Induce/lead/infer (inducir). Exempt/pardon/reprieve (indultar). Unpublished/unknown (inédito). Unavoidable (ineludible). Incompetent (inepto). Motionless (inerte). Mediator/middleman (intermediario). Abarrotar: overrun, a hall packed with pers. Unfaithful (infiel). Blow up: inflar, explotar. Informal: (charla) informal, (pers.) unreliable. Infringement (infracción). Infringe (infringir).Clever/witty (ingenioso). Disqualify (=, inhabilitar). Impending (inminente). Inmobilizar (=, tie up). Innato (innate). Undeniable (innegable). Harmless (inofensivo, =). Inappropriate (inapropiado). Register/enroll (inscribir). Foolishness (insensatez). Useless (inservible). Trifle (baratija, insignificancia, =). Sunstroke (insolación). Soundproof (insonorizado,V). Unsuspected (insospechado). Instancia: (solicitud) application, request, (Jur.) petition, (formulario) application form. Instauración: setting-up/establishment =/= fundación (founding) → founding fathers. Examining magistrate (juez de instrucción). Unsurpassable/unbeatable/insurmountable (insuperable) =/= invencible: (enemigo) invincible, unbeatable, (obstacle) insuperable. Intensify (intensificar). Set up: levantar, erigir, (casa) montar, (reunión) organizar. Attempt (intento, intentar + try). In spite of my best endeavours (intentos) =/= make/use all endeavours (intentar por todos los medios) to do sth. Unsociable/difficult (intratable, huraño). Intriguing (intrigante, enigmático). Intruder/trespasser (intruso). Render useless (inutilizar). Vote of confidence: investidura + investiture speech. Irradiate (=) =/= expel: arrojar, (pers.) expulsar. Burst into (irrumpir). Flood (inundación, diluvio) → the areas affected by (flood)ing =/= floating (flotante). Jarra: (leche) jug, (cerveza) mug/tankard. Police headquarters (jefatura de policía). Rank/hierarchy (jerarquía). Syringe (jeringa). Working day (jornada laborable). Good-humoured (jovial). Retirement (jubilación), jubilar (pension sb off, retire). Juego de palabras (pun, play on words). Juntarse: gather, move/get together. The country's reputation is at stake (en juego) =/= sake: for safety's -- (para más seguridad), for your own -- (bien), die for their country's--; safety regulations (normas). A compulsive gambler (un jugador empedernido). Junta: (reunión) meeting, (junta directiva) board of directors. Task (labor) → teamwork (labor de equipo). Labrado: (metal) wrought (del verbo work), (madera) carved. Bark (corteza, ladrar). Lay/secular (laico). Lanzado: he's so forward!, he rushed out (salió precipitado) of the house. Lápida (headstone, memorial tablet). Having one is useless (inútil) if you don't use it =/= it was unusable/useless after the accident. Lastre: be a burden for his family, (Náut.) ballast. Injure: (pers.) herir, (pride) lastimar, (reputation) dañar. Nuisance (lata, fastidio) → what a bore! Feel his heart beating (latiendo). Laudable (loable). Toilet/washbasin (lavabo). I gave the girl a ribbon (regalé una cinta a la niña). Suckling pig (lechón). Lettuce (lechuga). Eyes full of sleep (ojos llenos de lagañas). Legitimidad: legitimacy, authenticity, lawfulness. Slogan (lema). Firewood (leña), woodcutter (leñador). Seriously (fatalmente) injured. Lesionado: hurt, injured, (por arma) wound. Letrero: (luminoso) neon sign, (carretera) sign. Lifting/r_a_ising (levantamiento de objetos). Word list (léxico). Liar/envolver: wrap up =/= involved in drug trafficking. Liberar (release). Permission/ licence (licencia) =/= licenciar (confer a degree, graduate), licenciado (graduate). A general feeling of discomfort (malestar). He sensed (presintió, percibió) her unease (inquietud + concern) + uneasiness (desasosiego). File (carpeta, archivo,V, hilera, fila). Shoeshiner (limpiabotas). Cleanliness (limpieza). Lindar: (a) frontera: bordear → bordering (limítrofe), + out of bounds (límites): zona prohibida; (b) colindante: boundary, adjoining. Listing (cotización bursátil). Lawsuit (litigio). Sore/ ulcer (llaga). Appeal (llamamiento, súplica, (Jur.) recurso) =/= call a strike (huelga). Blaze (llamarada) → -- of anger (arranque de cólera) =/= flare up (llamear, ponerse furioso). Catching (contagioso, =). Llanta (de rueda): rim → the -- (borde) of the sun. Keyring (llavero). Insult (insultar). We haven't been here long (llevamos poco tiempo aquí). Praiseworthy (loable). Lose one's mind/get mad (volverse loco). He'll achieve this purpose (logrará su propósito). Achievement/accomplishment/attainment (logro). Lomo: back, (cocina) loin → sirloin steaks. Long lived (longevo). Healthy looking (lozano). Struggle (lucha,V, refriega, forcejear). Remote spot (lugar apartado). Lúgubre: gloomy, speak with a lugubrious voice. Flowerpot (maceta). This job wears me out (este trabajo me agota). Piece of junk (trastos), piece of lumber (madero). Think out (madurar una decisión). Hide (out), hiding place (escondite). Skill/mastery (maestría). I don't know the scale (magnitud) of... Mago: magician, wizard (+ genio). Beyond (más allá del) good (bien) & evil (mal). Bad-mannered (mal criado). Spoil (estropear, mimar, malcriar). Grow stiff (ponerse rígido/duro). Foulmouthed (malhablado). Malice/mischievousness (picardía), mischievous (pícaro). Cunning (malicioso, astuto, ingenioso). Spiteful (rencoroso + resentful, malicioso, malintencionado). Dirty minded (mal pensado). Maltreated/abused (maltratado). Flimsiness (ligereza, poca solidez, inconsistencia). Bossy (mandón). Easy to use (manejable). Handle: please do not -- (tocar) the fruit, -- (tratar) gently, -- (manejar) a gun. Demonstration (manifestación). Manifestar: state (declarar, expresar + declare, show, demonstrate). Handyman (manitas). Hands up! (¡Manos arriba!). Manso: (animal) tame, (pers.) meek + sumisa. Maintenance (manutención). Blanket (manta, global) =/= sheet (sábana, hoja, chapa, lámina). In small scale. Marvel/wonder (maravilla). Departure (marcha). Marchoso (lively, fun-loving, partygoer). Dropout (marginado) =/= drop out (salirse, abandonar, marginarse). Masseur (masajista). Overcrowding: (masificación) in the University, (abarrotamiento) in the train. Pet (mascota, =). Slaughterhouse (matadero). I racked (sacudí) my brains (me maté pensando). Motherly (maternal). Matiz: (color) shade, nuances of meaning, subtlety of performance. Some clarifications (matizaciones) are required. Matizar: (arte) blend + mezclar, armonizar), (intervención) qualify; deal with certain points. Jawbone (maxilar). Mallet (mazo). Birch (abedul). I promised myself... Pee (pipí), urine (orina), urinate (orinar) → piss blood, (hacer pipí): do a wee-wee, go for a pee. By means of (mediante). Jellyfish (medusa). Mussel (mejillón). Improvement (mejora). Honeyed (meloso). He doesn't have the slightest (la menor) idea. Undermined (salud menoscabada) by work. Menospreciar (despise/underestimate). Courier/messenger (mensajero). Strange as it may seem (aunque parezca mentira). Menudo (thin, slight, tiny). What a bump I had! (menudo golpe me di). Bonded goods/marchandises (mercancías en depósito). Worth the trouble (merecer la pena). Merienda: tea, (al aire libre) picnic. Spoil/pamper (mimar). Lavish (suntuoso, espléndido, generoso...) with the champagne, with her praise (elogios). Prowl/loiter (merodear: vagar robando por los campos). It was just a blunder (metedura de pata). Get mixed with (mezclarse). We mingled (nos mezclamos) with the spectators. Miedo: lose fear (miedo) of flying, I'm worried that he will fail (suspender), frighten (dar miedo). Detailed/meticulous (minucioso). You can take it (abarcar) with a glance (mirada). A reproachable (de reproche) look. Poverty (miseria) =/= pittance (poca cantidad). Misericordia (compassion/mercy → have -- on sb). Around midweek (entre semana, a mediados de semana). Backpackers (turistas de mochila). Have a runny nose → blow your nose. Manners (modales). Moderate (moderado) =/= mild: (pers.) afable, (clima) templado, (ataque) ligero, (tabaco, cerveza) suave. Moderador: (debate, política) moderator, (TV) presenter. Presidente: (comité) chairperson, chairman, (país, asociación) president, (de la cámara) speaker. Dressmaker (modisto). Moldear: (barro/carácter) mold, (bronce, yeso) cast. Molestar (bother, interrupt, disturb) → molesto: annoying, unpleasant, uncomfortable, awkward (+ malo, peligroso, incómodo, embarazoso). Cute (monada, precioso, listo). Instructor

(=, monitor) → swimming --, ski. Huge (enorme, inmenso) → it was a -- success (exitazo). Morbid (morboso). Blood sausage/ black pudding (morcilla). Morro: (Zool.) snout, nose; you've got a nerve! (¡Qué morros tienes!), (cara dura) cheeky, (auto) nose, (hozico) muzzle. Mortandad: road deaths, infant mortality. At the most (como mucho) you need... by far (con mucho). No way: de ningún modo + no way! (¡Ni hablar!). Murmurar: (viento) whisper, (agua) murmur, (quejarse) grumble, (hojas) rustle. Disabled person (mutilado). Nacionalizarse (become naturalized). Don't make remarks (comentarios) of that kind (naturaleza). Molestar → (importunar) sorry to bother/trouble you, but...; (interrumpir) don't disturb her, she's studying; (offender) I'm sorry if I've upset you. Mist/thin fog (niebla). Vanidad: vanity. I felt the need to hug her (abrazarla). Affirmation ←→ denial/negation. You are useless (eres un negado/inútil/inservible). She dances with a lot of spirit (nervio). Niñera (nanny, nursemaid). Nivelar: (terreno) level, (desigualdad) even, (finanzas) balance =/= aplanar/allanar (flatten). Harmful (nocivo). Normalizar: (relaciones, situación) normalize, tech.) standardize. Bronca: (follón) row, (regañina) ticking off + kick up a fuss (armar una --). Well-known (notorio, famoso). Novato: raw, green, beginner. Novelty (novedad). Persist in (obstinarse). Impede (dificultar, obstaculizar) =/= block (=, tarugo, obstruir, bloquear). Not obvious symptoms of crisis. They opted for the war. Ocio(leisure, free time)so: idle. Squatter (ocupante illegal). Ocupar: it takes up a page, have an adjoining (contigua) room, (cargo) hold, (vacante) fill. Ocurrencia (witty/funny remark). Odio (loathing, hat<u>r</u>ed) → hate (odiar). Off-colour (salud) indispuesto, (broma y observación) subida de tono. Buttonhole (ojal). Quick look (ojeada). Ojeras (bags under the eyes). Ondulado: (carretera) uneven, rough, (terreno) undulating, rolling, (superficie) undulating, uneven, (cartón, hierro) corrugated, (pelo) wavy haired. Timely/appropriate (oportuno, =). Opresión: (sensación) oppression, (Med.) breathing difficult, tightness of the chest. Osadía: (audacia) daring (+ atrevido), insolence. Get dark (oscurecer). Ostentar: flaunt, show off... Otorgar: (premio) award a prize, (subvención/beca/permiso) grant; be rewarded (recompensar) for his effort; premiado (prize-winning); otorgar poderes (bestow). Overseas (en el extranjero). Suffer from (padecer de). Stepfather (padrastro). Turn pale (palidecer). Beating (paliza). Palpitar: =, throb (with emotion, (corazón) beat. (Bread) roll: panecillo. Paraglider (parapente), parachute (paracaídas), paratrooper/parachutist (paracaidista). Papelera: (en inmueble) wastepaper basket/bin; (en la calle) litter bin =/= stationer's (papelería), furrier's (peletería). Parcel (paquete). Steady: continuo, constante, firme, fijo, formal, estable. Eyes fixed on me, table -- to the wall, -- (fija) crane (grúa), stationary (vehículo/objeto estacionado). Paralizarse: Med. (=), obras: come to halt/a standstill. Lightning conductor (pararrayos). Talkative (parlanchín). Partir: cut in half, (con manos) break, split + rajar, (grieta) fissure, crack. Pasar la vida: spend one's life + -- the whole time. Take a walk (pasear). Patear: (en el suelo) stamp down, (pelota) kick. Gradual (=, paulatino). Take sth to heart (a pecho). Objection/drawback (pega). Fishbowl (pecera). Stony (pedregoso). Oblivious/insensible to my entreaties (súplicas). Catchy (pegadizo, fácil de recordar) =/= sticky (pegajoso, adhesivo) → come to a -- end (acabar mal). Crawler (pelota, adulador + flatterer, sycophant, fawning). Wig (peluca). Pending/unresolved (pendiente). Penetrar: hardly any light enters the room, the smoke is filtering through the cracks (grietas), (eyes, cry, pain) pierce. Do penance (hacer penitencia). Think over (examinar una idea). Pensión: =, guest house. Humble (humilde) → humiliate/humble (humillar). Cucumber (pepino). Mishap (percance, contratiempo). Hanger (percha, gancho para la ropa). Forgiveness (perdón). Everlasting (perdurable) ↔ perishable (perecedero). Idler/lazy (perezoso). Improvement (mejora) → there's still plenty of room for -- =/= perfeccionamiento → an advanced course (un curso de --). Profile (perfil) → shape (forma, silueta, estructura, molde, estado físico; perfilar una idea). Perforar: perforate, (mina) drill, bore, (tarjeta, ficha) punch; drilling (perforación) =/= punzar: prick, pierce, (billete) punch. Parchment (pergamino). Percatarse (notice). Expert's report (peritaje). Perjudicar: harm, (salud) damage, (derechos, intereses) prejudice. Continuance (permanencia) in her post, in the association. Allow oneself (permitirse). Petición: by popular request or demand, petition for divorce. Persona: person, character + = → she is an odd --. Embody (personificar). Shrewdness (perspicacia). Persuade (=), convince (=). Unbalanced (desequilibrado, perturbado). Crib (pesebre, cuna, chuleta, plagio + plagiarism/piracy). Banger/cracker (petardo). He blinked (parpadeó). Picarse: (fruta) rot, (mar) become choppy =/= picante: (comida) hot, peppery, spicy, (chiste/libro) risqué. Pico: (ave, insecto) beak, (monte) peak, (herramienta) pick, (picotazo,V, besito) peck. Picado: (cebolla) chopped, (carne) minced. Fodder/feed (pienso). Looting/plunder (pillaje, saqueo) + looter (saqueador). Atropellar: run over, (ser --do): be knocked down (by a car). Paint brush (pincel) + brushstroke (pincelada). Pisotear: tread on sth, trample. Pito: (tren) whistle + silbato), (coche) horn → pitar: (policía, árbitro) blow, (claxon) horn, hoot, (abuchear) boo. Quit (dejar de hacer algo, abandonar; irse, dimitir). Plazo: term → a short term loan, application period (período de solicitud), a fixed term. Folding (plegable). Fullness (plenitud). More than a job (pluriempleo). Cope (arreglárselas) → he's coping very well; can you --? Cope with (poder con, enfrentarse a). Ponerse nervioso: lose one's cool. Put off/postpone (posponer). Preciado (prized). Precipitar: rush (towards the exit), hasten. Accuracy (precisión), accurate (preciso). Preacher (predicador). Prevail: prevalecer, predominar → predominio (predominance). Worry/concern (preocupación). Prey: (animal, víctima) presa → hacer presa (seize). Prescindir:

(do without) many things; we are obliged to dispense with your services. Presenciar: (attend, witness + testigo). Presentarse: they turned up unexpectedly, the robber gave himself up to the police, let me introduce myself, stand/run in the elections. Pressure cooker (olla a presión), pressure gauge (indicador de presión). Imprisoned (preso). Préstamo (lending) ↔ pedirlo (borrowing), dinero prestado: loan → we need a loan of... =/= let (permitir, alquilar). Bank loan, grant (conceder) a loan, mortgage loan. Presumir: he presumes he is innocent =/= he loves showing off. Supposed/alleged (presunto). Pretendiente: (de una mujer) suiter, (cargo) applicant. Far-sighted/well-prepared (previsor). First born (primogénito). Privación (deprivation, lack, hardship) → hardship clause: cl. de salvaguardia. Probabilidad: chance, (Mat.) probability. Procedure/proceedings (procedimiento). Secure: seguro, firme, sujetar bien; proteger; garantizar. Take place (producirse). Desecrate/defile/profane (profanar). Prolongar: =, extend + continuar (carry on, go on) → the road goes on beyond the wood. "Get engaged" (prometerse). A prompt reply (pronta respuesta). Provide/supply (proporcionar). Proposal (propuesta). Overtime, extra time (prórroga en Sp.). Objection, =, protesta. Good sense, prudence (prudencia) =/= wealthy (pudiente). Pudrirse: rot, putrefy, decay → decay: (dientes) caerse, (casa) desmoronarse, (alimentos) pudrirse; decadencia humana. Booming/thriving: pujante. Neat/tidy (pulcro). Rabo (tail) → oxtail (cola de buey) soup. Ramo: (flores) the bride's bouquet, bunch of roses, (laurel/árbol) branch. Raquítico: paltry, (pers.) skinny. Irk (molestar, irritar), irksome (irritante). Itch (picor) =/= sting (aguijón, picadura, picar, ardor). Raspar: (pintura,...) scrape off, (toalla) be rough, (barba) scratch. Rastrear (trail/track). Rastreador: tracker. Petty-thief/light-fingered (ratero). Reluctant/unwilling (reacio). Feasible (realizable). Enhance: realzar una idea, incrementar de valor, mejorar una posición. Come round (reanimarse). Abase oneself (humillarse, rebajarse). Exceed/go beyond (rebasar). Distrust/suspicion (recelo). Receta: (culinaria) recipe, (Med.) prescription. Rejection (rechazo). Lean back (reclinarse). Recruit (recluta). Recover/regain one's health. Pick up/gather (recoger) → -- la mesa: clear the table =/= gather (recolectar). Horas de recreo: leisure times, (escuela) break. Reproach (recriminar). Rectitude/honesty (rectitud). Draw up/write (redactar). Reimburse/refund/repay (reembolsar). Reinforce/strengthen (reforzar). Effortlessly (fácilmente), effortlessness (facilidad). Refrescar: cool (down), (conocimiento) brush up, (memoria) refresch. Be crazy (como una regadera). Statutory (reglamentario). Reinstate (reincorporar). Recidivist/reoffender (reincidente). Sender (remitente). Rebosar: (embalse) overflow, (de algo) brim/bubble (with health, ...), abound =/= Resaltar: (highlight, stand out) → green -- the colour; emphasize, stress the importance of, the speaker highlighted... Claim/demand (reivindicación). Reja: (ventana) grille/bars, (escalera) banister, (balcón/cercado) railing → be behind bars. Relate/link (relacionar). Get in with the right people (relacionarse bien) + hobnob with (alternar con) the top people (gente bien). Consign to oblivion (relegar al olvido). Relinquish (renunciar, ceder). Landing: aterrizaje, rellano (de escalera). Reluciente (glittering, sparkling, gleaming,Vs). Roll up (remangarse) one's sleeves/one's trousers. Rematar: (matar) finish off, (actuación) round off, conclude, (tenis) smash. Put right: remediar =/= mend (remendar). As a last resort (como último remedio). Beetroot (remolacha) → sugar beet. Remolino: (agua) whirlpool, (aire) whirlwind, (pelo) cowlick. Remorse (remordimiento). Remover: (objetos) move round, (tierra) turn on, dig up. Feel renewed (sentirse renacer). Rencor (rancour, resentment). Disown: (repudiar, =; creencia: renegar de). Renewal (renovación). Share out (repartir los beneficios). Unbearable/intolerable (insoportable). Sudden/unexpected (repentino). Replantear: raise again/reopen; reconsider/

rethink. Restock (repoblar animales). Repostar → provisiones: supply, stock up with, replenish, (gasolina) refill, full up. Get one's strength back (reponer las fuerzas). Leave to stand (dejar algo en reposo) =/= (Med.) be at rest. Scold (reprender). Represalia (reprisal) → retaliate (tomar represalias) =/= reprimir: (deseos) repress, (rebelión) suppress. Requirement (requisito). Repeler: (agresión) repel, repulse + I find snakes repellent/repulsive→ repulsivo: revolting, disgusting; repugnancia: revulsion, aversion, loathing =/= asco: how revolting/disgusting! (¡Qué asco!). It made me feel sick, I really loathe/detest him, it's deathly/deadly boring in this village. Burst out laughing (echarse a reir). Rescue/save: rescatar. Reservar: (habitación, mesa) reserve, book, (en exceso) overbook, (guardar) keep in reserve. Gaming/fishing preserve (=). Receipt/slip/ticket (resguardo). Respondón: cheeky, lippy =/= rebelde: rebellious, (Jur.) defaulting. Responsibility: = + (Jur.) liability → hold liable (responsabilizar). Restore (restablecer, restaurar). Resurrect/revive (resucitar). Resolute (resuelto). In short (en resumen). Delayed (retardado). Hold up: sujetar/sostener, levantar la mano, atracar (un banco...), mostrar (como modelo), (tráfico) retrasar (+ delay, jam) → the train was held --; (trabajo) interrumpir, demand for energy is likely to -- up (levantarse, sostenerse erguida, mantenerse), (progreso) entorpecer =/= hold out: (manos, armas) tender, alargar; durar, resistir, (posibilidad) ofrecer, (pers.) aguantar, (zapatos) durar, -- -- for sth: insistir hasta conseguir algo =/= hold my bag while ..., -- sb down (a la fuerza), -- sway (ejercer dominio) over sb, hold (retener) sb in thrall (esclavitud) =/= keep hold of the child's hand (no lo sueltes) =/= hold back (contener, ocultar). Retirar: (subvención, permiso, apoyo) withdraw, (alejar, apartar) move away, retired (jubilado), in a remote (retirada) place. Retract/withdraw (retractarse). Retrasado mental (retarded, backward, mentally handicapped). Retrasar: fall behind, be late/delayed. Be the spitting (viva) image of sb. Disclosure (revelación) of a secret. Resell (revender). Reventón: blowout, flat-tyre. Revisar: check the data, check-up (revisión médica), revise a decision/text/lesson, take the car for a service, the annual salary review + examinar, (tropas) pasar revista. Revoltoso: rebellious, troublemaker. Revolucionar: stir up + remover, provocar. Turn upside down (revolver los cajones/la cama...). Toss (lanzar, agitarse) & turn: revolverse en la cama. Sacudir: shake, (ala) flop, (alfombra) beat. Drop behind (rezagarse). She put on a gorgeous (rico) dress. Irrigación: irrigation, watering. Stiffness/rigidity (rigidez). Rivalry (rivalidad). Rizado: (pelo) curly, (mar) slightly choppy, (superficie) crimped, ridged, crinkled. Oak (roble). Robusto: =, sturdy, tough, strong. Request/beg (rogar, pedir). Rompecabezas: puzzle, jigsaw. He tore (rompió) the contract. The truce (tregua) has been broken. Roto: (camisa) torn, ripped, (vaso, brazo, TV) broken, (papel) torn, (pers.) broken, (zapatos) worn out. Rotundo → (éxito) resounding; (respuesta) categorical, emphatic. Coarseness/roughness: rudeza. Rígido: (moral, educación) strict, (actitud) rigid, inflexive, (material) rigid, stiff. Beg/implore sb not to do sth: I beg you to stay (te quedes). Ruido/rugido/estruendo (roar). Noisy (ruidoso). Nightingale (ruiseñor). Sacar: take sth out of sth, (diamantes) extract. Savour (savorear) his coffee. Saciar: (hambre, deseo, curiosidad) satisfy, (thirst) quench. Assembly hall (sala de actos). Splash/spatter/sprinkle (salpicar) =/= you have scattered (esparcido) papers all around the office. Saltar: he jumped out of the car/into the water, the cork shot out of the bottle, (botón) come off, a spark (chispa) flew out of the fire, (plomos) blow. Bulging eyes (ojos saltones). Saludar (say hello to, greet, send regards). Sergeant. Savagery (salvajismo). Bran (salvado). Cure/recover (sanar). Sanear: clean up the premise (local)/administration, restructure the economy, (terreno) drain + drenar. Holy See (Santa Sede), Holy Land (Tierra Santa), Holy Scriptures (Sagrada). Kick off (saque, iniciar). Frying pan (sartén). Blot (borrón) → blotting paper (papel secante). Everything goes smoothly (como una seda). Seductive/tempting (seductor). Simplicity (sencillez), simple: (estilo, ropa, asunto) sencillo... =/= sensible (sensato) =/= sensitive: susceptible, (sensible) skin... + a noticeable (sensible) improvement. Good sense (sensatez). Consciente: conscious/aware of sth, politically aware (entendido). Secret sign (contraseña). Move apart/separate (separar). The couple have split up. Move away from the wall. He is despicable (despreciable). Sedative: a -- (calmante) to calm him down (serenarlo). Lose one's temper, be in a bad -- (de al humor), be in a – (estar furioso). Serious look, you are looking serious. Reliable (serio, cumplidor). Sawdust (serrín). Handsaw (serrucho). Napkin (servilleta); tablecloth (tapete); nappies (pañales de bebé). Stealth (sigilo, furtivo, insensible) =/= sleuth (detective). Meaningful (significativo, coherente). Silenciar: → the papers silenced/hushed up (acallaban) the incident (suceso). Folding chair (silla plegable). Resemblance (similitud) between... + similar names. Pleasant/nice/likeable (simpático). Supporter (simpatizante, seguidor). Peculiar/odd (singular). Mermaid/siren. Besieged (sitiar): sitiado =/= located (situado). Soborno: (acción) bribery, (dinero, regalo) bribe. Leftover (sobrante/restantes): sobras. Parental pressure, pressure cooker/group. He endured (soportó) his illness. Overestimate/overrate/overvalue (sobrevalorar). Fly over (sobrevolar), fly away/in/out: irse/entrar/salir volando. Socio (partner). Stifle (sofocarse, ahogo,V, contener) =/= stiff/rigid (tieso). Blush (sonrojo, rubor). Downright (patente, magnífico, categórico) piece of nonsense: solemne tontería. Solidario: caring, sympathetic to our cause, declare one's support for. Soundness (solidez de estructura, de ideas, solvencia) =/= strength (solidez de un material). Snivelling (lloriqueo) =/= sob (sollozar) =/= sot (borrachín) =/= sip (sorbo, traguito) =/= gulp (sorbo grande). A screw come loose (soltarse un tornillo), don't let it go of my hand, the dog breaks loose from the chain. Subject (someter) prisoners to torture. Submit the project to a council. Sunshade (sombrilla). Drill: taladro, perforación,V; drill into (sondear) → drill-ships: these ships are designed for work in the deepest of waters; rig (aparejo: velas y cuerdas) → Oil rig (torre de perforación + drilling rig, derrick); the centrepiece of the vessel is the derrick. Blow/puff (of steam): soplo. Surprise (sorpresa). Sorprender: I'm surprised he hasn't arrived, she caught them stealing. Suspicious (sospechoso). Uprising/revolt/revelion (sublevación). Subsanar: (defecto) put right, (error) correct, (dificultad) overcome. Persist (subsistir). Subsoil (subsuelo), underground (metro, subterráneo) → -- passage, -- store/park. Suburbio: =, outlying área. Slum area (barrio bajo). Subsidized (subvencionado). Underlying (subyacente). Suceder: that had happened to him =/= succeed sb in a post. Event (suceso). A detergent that banishes (elimina) dirt (suciedad). Succinctly/concisely (sucintamente). Talk dirty (decir chorradas). Tastiness/richness (suculencia). Sweat buckets (sudar a chorros, sudar la gota gorda), sweat it out (sudarlo con esfuerzo), by the sweat of one's brow (frente). Sueldo atrasado (back pay). Fall to the ground, hurl o.s. (echarse) to the ground. Demolish: (edificio, estructura) demoler, derribar, (teoría) demoler, (oposición) hacer polvo. Those goods are dirt cheap. A marble floor. Suelto: (criminal) free, (animal) loose, (cordones) untied, undone → those shoelaces are undone, the book has two pages loose, loose change, they are not sold singly/separately. A separated (suelto) extract from the nobel. Be a light sleeper (tener el sueño ligero) ←→ I haven't caught up on sleep (no he recuperado el sueño atrasado). Coffee keeps me awake. This is my lucky number, be in luck, luckily/fortunately (por suerte) ←→ unfortunately. The fate (suerte) which awaits (espera) him. All sorts/kinds of remarks (comentarios). The votes (sufragios) cast (emitidos) for the candidate. He can't bear/stand (sufrir) his boss. She gets terribly worried if I'm late home. Nail sth down (sujetar con clavos). My duties as a politician bind me.

He is rebellious, his parents can't control him. He came out holding his trousers up. Is the rope secure (sujeta)? The wheels are held on/secured with nuts (tuercas). Children should be properly strapped/secured when travelling by car. What are the total expenses? Add up/addition, subtraction, division, multiplication. A whole host (anfitrión, huesped, gran cantidad; radio/TV: presentador) of great contributions to the motoring (automóvil) world. Amount (cantidad) → it --s to...: asciende a... Sink beneath the surface. Superar: (contrincante/dificultad) overcome, (límite) go beyond, (récord/marca) break, get past the first round, you have excelled yourself, remontar (un problema): overcome, surmount. Surplus (superavit). Useful área/usable space (superficie útil). He lives on the top (último) floor. Overcrowded/overpopulated. Supervise. Single room/Sunday supplement. Súplica: (ruego) request, (petición) plea, (instancia Jur.) petition, pleading. I suppose so. Surco: (Agr.) furrow, (metal) groove. Overwork (surmenage). The game was rained off (suprimido a causa de la lluvia). Aplazar: (pago) defer; (viaje) postpone, put off, (juicio, reunión): (antes de iniciarse) postpone, (ya iniciados) adjourn. Go one's own way (ir a lo suyo) → get - - - (salirse con la suya). Ignition switch. Chop: cortar, hachazo, chuleta. Tabla: (cocina) chopping board =/= (dibujo) drawing board. Borrar: cross/take sb off a list, tippex, rub out, erase, remove, clean off, (fichero, mensaje) delete. Brand (tildar) sb as incompetent. Get into a mess (hacerse un taco). Tap with one's heels (taconear). Be rough (áspero) to the touch (tacto). He identified coins by touch. A sticky (viscoso) feel. They were categorical (tajantes) =/= a sharp (tajante) criticism of the Government; I categorically (tajantemente) refuse (niego, rehuso)... Do anything (lo que sea) to (con tal de) attract attention. Provided/as long as (con tal de que) you get back at 11 o.k. A liberal-minded (de talante) man. Be in a good mood, do sth willingly. Be talented/gifted for music. Be tall enough (dar la talla).

Shirts of all sizes. Cheque payable to bearer. Bad cheque (talón sin fondos). Tantear: (con la mano) feel, (probar) test, try out, probe, (terreno) see how things stand, (tela...) make a rough estimate of, (situación) weigh up. He has so much (tanto) money he doesn't know what to do with it. There were so many cars that there was nowhere to park. There's no need to exaggerate. He scored twice, a goal for (a favour), consolation goal (del honor). Be fully abreast (al día) of events. Blow one's brains out (levantarse la tapa de los sesos). Tapar/abrigar: (con ropa) wrap up, (olla) put the lid on, (botella) put the top on, (tubo/túnel/ agujero) obstruct, block. Fill: rellenar, (espacio) ocupar, (necesidad) satisfacer. Go and fetch it (ve a buscarlo), but don't be long. I expect you at 8, don't be late. It takes a while to take effect (surtir efecto). It's late to complain now. Tariff (=, precios fijados) + tasa: exchange/interest/growth/unemployment/birth/ (de suministros: supplies) rate + (de transportes) fare + tarifa plana (de internet): flat rate. Tarjeta de felicitaciones: greeting card, (de fidelidad) loyalty card, (de presentación) business card, (perforada) punched card. European health insurance. Tarta: cheese cake, apple tart, wedding/birthday cake. Legal (judiciales) fees, garbage collection charge. Valuation (tasación) of a building. A homeless (sin techo) person. It has reached its upper limit. Arrow key (tecla con flecha). Tecla de iniciación (booting-up switch). Tecleo (keying/typing). Intrigue: =, tejemaneje. Politicians and shady (dudosos, sombríos) deals. Devise: concebir, idear... High season (temporada) → low --. Tempting (tentador). Deputy mayor (teniente de alcalde). We've run out of coffee. Bring sth to a successful conclusion (llevar algo a feliz término). In the final/last analysis (en último análisis). Ultimately (en última instancia) =/= if the worst comes to the worst (en último término), you can... A revolutionary in the good sense (sentido) of the word. Millions in terms of productivity. A list of medical terms, conciliatory terms, the terms of the contract, in good terms (relaciones) with sb. Reverse (invertir) the roles. Municipal area/district. Water heater (calentador). Heat-insulating (aislamiento). Unevenness (accidentes) of the ground. All-terrain vehicles. In the field of chemistry, economic sphere or field. Give (ceder) ground (terreno). Be on (pisar) safe/firm/solid ground. Be familiar (conocedor) of the ground. Solve the pbs. as we go along (sobre el terreno). It is a breeding (abonado) ground for vice/the opposition, etcétera. These trends (tendencias) have found a fertile breeding ground (caldo de cultivo) for... Pickings: ganancias, restos, sobras de alimentos → the country provides rich -- (está abonado) for foreign investors. Testing ground (terreno de pruebas). They lost in their home ground, drew (empate) at home, a fresh (nueva) defeat away. Attachment to one's native soil. Tertulia: (social/regular/informal) gathering → -- televisiva (talk show). Literary circle/gathering. His theory (tesis) is untenable. We cannot refuse the defence's arguments. Be worth a fortune (valer un tesoro), a mine of information (un tesoro de datos). Comprehensive (global, completo, de conjunto, integral) test. Testificar: attest, bear witness, (Jur.) testify, give evidence → a person who had witnessed the accident gave evidence (declaró). The streets bear witness of its Arab past. Baby at the breast (niño de teta). This doesn't refer to you. It all depends on you now. Cool/unenthusiastic welcome (recepción). Quite: (1) completamente → Are you sure? -- sure, I can -- believe it, I -- agree with you, (2) bastante → it's -- warm today, we see them -- often. Staying power (aguante, resistencia). I haven't seen you for ages (desde hace mucho tiempo)! He can't stay any longer. We got there in time, water chilled or at room T.? <u>Grope</u> one's way <u>along</u>/feel one's way (andar a tientas), grope around <u>for</u> sth (buscar algo a tientas), lose one's touch (perder el contacto). Lime tree (tilo) → lime flower tea. Ring the bell (timbre) → alarm bell. Know sth on good authority (de buena tinta). Indian ink (tinta china). Without the slightest hint (indicio...) of politics. Tintinear: (campanillas) tinkle, (llaves) jingle. Who is that guy/bloke (tipo, tío), blockhead (bruto, zopenco, tarugo). He won't leave me alone (en paz)! It's typical of him =/= traditional costume. It's the most charming/picturesque (=) pub (taberna) of the county (condado). That was ages ago (de eso hace la tira). Sling/catapult/slingshot: honda, cabestrillo, tirachinas. He scored ten points in the first throw. Read the novel in one go (tirada). A print run (tirada) of 200 copies. A weekly circulation magazine. Be dirt (muy) -cheap + a dead (muy) easy subject (asignatura). Tiralíneas (drawing/ruling pen). Tyrannical/possessive/domineering. Tirantes (braces/ suspenders). Tirantez (tension, strain, tightness). This dress is a bit tight (tira un poco) here. Throw the leftovers to the bin (papelera). These trousers are about ready for the dustbin (cubo de la basura): están para tirarlos. Stop kicking (de tirar patadas) + the mule kicked him. Pull a bit harder (un poco más fuerte). A donkey (burro) was pulling the cart (carro) along. One's native land always exerts a powerful pull. We can get by (arreglarnos) on less money. How's your health? → we are getting by. The engine (motor) isn't pulling. Go on with it! (¡Tira de una vez!). Reddish blond hair (pelo rubio tirando a rojo). It's middling (mediocre) to (tirando a) bad. He takes after (tira a) his father. Petrol for 10 km at the most. Plunge (tirarse) into the water. Rush after (correr tras) sb/ spring on sb. He spent (se tiró) two hours fixing it (arreglando, reparando + repairing, mending). They shot him dead (lo mataron de un tiro). He shot his lover (amante). He shot himself. I wouldn't do it for love or money. It backfired on him (le salió el tiro por la culata). Me sienta como un tiro: (obligación) it's a real pain, (ropa/peinado) it looks really terrible/awful on me, (comida) it really doesn't agree with me, I was really miffed (disgustado) that nobody turned up (apareció). Target practice (tiro al blanco) =/= butts, shooting range (campo de tiro) =/= trap (trampa, atrapar...) → trap shooting (tiro al plato), clay pigeon shooting (tiro al pichón), archery (tiro con arco). Coup de grace. She's always asking the first person who comes along (se presenta) for money. Come along! (¡Vamos!, ¡de prisa!). How is the book coming along? (¿Cómo va el libro?). Be within one's reach. Draught animal (animal de tiro). Tiroteo: shooting, exchange of shots, have a gunfight with sb. Tísico (consumptive, tubercular). Turn sth upside down: poner algo boca abajo, darle la vuelta a algo. Burglars --ed the house -- (la revolvieron). He hung the picture -- --. Not to hesitate (titubear)/vacillate to do sth. Act resolutely (=, con determinación). Universitary degree (titulación) required → with a degree in engineering; graduate student (estudiante de posgrado). Regular first team player (titular) + juez titular (a judge assigned to a particular court) + titular de puesto (holder incumbent) + press headlines + (news) headlines (TV, radio). Title of nobility, the qualifications (títulos) for a job, posthumously (a título póstumo), worthy (merecidos, dignos) attributes, be worthy (digno, meritorio) of sth/sb. Chalk (tiza). Dressing table: tocador (mueble con espejo). Toilet kit, vanity kit Neceser (estuche...). Don't let anyone touch my papers. Feel his forehead (tócale la frente) =/= in/at the forefront of sth (al frente/a la vanguardia de algo). The forward (delantero) handled (tocó con la mano) the ball. Stand up against the wall over there (ponte ahí, tocando la pared). The pictures (imágenes) moved/touched me deeply (me tocaron en lo más profundo). They are ringing the bell (campana, timbre) for mass. It's not due to be done until next month. Whose turn is it? (¿A quién le toca?). It is up to you to reprimand him (reprenderle) if you see fit (adecuado + físico: en forma, Med: sano. This borders/verges on the ridiculous. Summer was drawing (tocaba) to a close (su fin). Don't pick your spots (lunares, manchas, granos; apuros, lugar, TV espacio. ¡No te toques los granos! Cables (wires + alambres, telegramas). Tocino: (alimento) fat, salted fresh lard (manteca de cerdo), (con vetas de carne) salt pork, (tocino veteado) streaky bacon; graso: (pelo, guiso) greasy, (carne) fatty; grasa: fish oil, (de ballena, foca) blubber, (de panceta) bacon, cream (de nata) cake. He hit (golpeó) him with all his might/force. Me dieron ganas de reír tontamente (I got the giggles, I started giggling), dimwit (lerdo, torpe). In the first place. In spite of being new (con todo y ser nuevo)... Toma de aire (air inlet/intake). The taking/capture of Granada. Toma de conciencia (realization) =/= toma de contacto (initial contact). He'll take office (tomará posesión) tomorrow. They took (down) our statement (declaración) at the police (comisaría). We will take steps (medidas) to... The project is taking shape (va tomando forma). I took a dislike (asco) to snails. The boss has (got) it in for me (la tiene tomada conmigo). They haven't taken it seriously/taken it as a joke (en broma). Wow! (¡Toma!). What an amazing (asombroso, extra, alucinante) guy!: ¡Qué tío más bueno! Don't take it that way (así) + so badly (tan mal). Turn as red as a beetroot (ponerse como un tomate). Sin ton ni son: (motivo) for no particular reason, (lógica) without rhythm or reason. A shade (tonalidad) of green. Invigorating/stimulating (tonificador). In a low tone of voice. Turn down/up the TV a little + soften one's tone to talk,... Grow/become heated (climatizado, acalorado). They began to raise their voices. Very much in keeping with... (muy a tono con el resto de la película...). An ideology more in tune with the times. A whisky to perk myself up (para ponerme a tono). That's nonsense/rubbish/garbage (tonterías) → don't talk --/--/--! What a silly thing to say! (¡Qué tonterías acabas de decir!). Come with us, don't be silly! How silly/stupid of me! Don't be silly (no seas tonto)! He's a total/complete idiot! Tontear: fool about, act/play the fool, act dumb. Topar con: (pers.) run, bump into, come across, (objeto) find, come across, (obstáculo) run into/hit an obstacle. Fecha tope (closing date, deadline). The theatre was poked out (a tope), the container was overloaded, up to my ears/neck in work. Trabajar a tope (work flat out). Wage ceiling (tope salarial). A tap (toque) on the shoulder. There are some taps (toquecitos) at/on the door (llaman...). Pull him up (dale un toque de atención, regáñalo) for being late. I'll give you a telling-off (bronca) if you keep behaving badly. On the stroke (toque) of twelve. Give sb a bell (toque Tf.). Reveille: (toque de) diana. A personal touch → a few touches to finish it. Toquetear: handle, finger, (acariciar) fondle, caress, (magrear) feel up. He turned (his head) to look at her, the car turned left. He twisted his neck/ankle. Turn the steering wheel, you aren't driving straight. Go astray/off the rails (ir por mal camino). Neglect one's duty: saltarse su deber a la torera; flout (desobedecer, desacatar) a law. Sandstorm (tormenta), snow--, dust--, he unleashed (desencadenó) a -- of passions. He was jealously watching the skaters (patinadores). They gathered round him. Remain uncommitted (no comprometido). Roughly/crudely: a grandes rasgos, aproximadamente; bruscamente, toscamente. Tostar: (pan) toast, (café) roast, (carne, pez...) brown. A complete revision of this theory. A total disaster. The insurer (aseguradora) will cover all expenses. Stubbornness/obstinacy (tozudez). He sells/handles that line (género). I've an hour's work left. She's a very willing worker (tiene una enorme capacidad de trabajo). The ironing is the job I like least, the housework (los quehaceres de la casa), this is really work! (¡Esto es un trabajo de chinos!), temporary job (trabajo eventual). I have to hand (entregar) two essays (ensayos, trabajos) tomorrow. Translator → simultaneous translation. Can you bring/fetch/bear me a glass of water? The lad (muchacho, chaval) who delivers/brings the newspaper. Give it to me (tráemelo). The recession brought/about an increase in employment, the recession makes me very anxious (inquieto, angustioso). This case is a headache (trae de cabeza) for the police. The shopping hours (horarios comerciales) for the consumers. It's a real nightmare (pesadilla) of a pb.: es un problema que se las trae.

Dress shabbily (vestirse mal). Interrupt (cortar) traffic. I bit my tongue (tragué saliva) out of respect for his father, the ground (tierra) soaks (traga) the water up, he had to put up with (tragar) his boss's threats. A drop of wine could not come amiss (no vendría mal), say sth amiss (inoportuno, =). Traje: (de etiqueta) dress suit, dinner dress, (de novia) wedding dress, (del espacio) spacesuit. Vestir de paisano: (soldado) be in/wear civilian clothes, (policía) be in/wear plain clothes, (sacerdote) be in/wear secular dress, (sin uniforme) be in mufti, vestir sport (dress casually). Fall into the trap + set/lay a trap for sb. Catch sb lying. We're going through a difficult period/patch (estamos pasando un mal trago). The countryside is so peaceful! (¡Qué tranquilidad se respira en el campo!). Take it home & read it at your leisure (cuando te convenga). What a relief (tranquilidad)! The exams are over in the end/lastly/finally! Give sb a telling-off/rocket (echar un rapapolvo a alguien). Jet (avión a chorro), cohete espacial (r̲ocket) → --ed to fame, --ed upwards (subido como un rayo), prices have --ed =/= r̲acket (raqueta, alboroto, jaleo, asunto: drugs --, debt --); transbordador: (Náut.) f̲erry, (Aér.) s̲huttle → car f̲., space s̲. Transcribe (copiar, transcribir) =/= transliterate (transcribir un alfabeto) =/= translate (traducir). We have bowed/given in or away/tolerated (transigido) with popular demand. I cannot tolerate this sort of outrage (atrocidad, escándalo, ultraje). No thoroughfare (prohibido el tráfico). Rush (punta) hour = peak hours. Calle transversal (cross street). Trapicheo (negocios poco limpios): fiddle/shady deals. Pasar un trapo (cloth, rag) por: (suelo) give a wipe over/down, (muebles) dust. Estropajo (scourer; de acero: steel wool) + seca platos: tea towel, dish towel. We do not want her remarks (comentarios) to leak out/get out (transciendan) + transcend beyond the boundaries (confines) of reason. The back/rear (parte trasera) of the building + back/rear engine/wheel. He has been transferred/moved to... + the filing cabinets are moved into the other office. Stay up late = go to bet late; stay up all night. Business for sale (se traspasa el negocio), devolve (traspasar poderes) to Catalonia... Trastada: (travesura) prank, mischief, (mala pasada) play a dirty trick (truco, travesura, broma) on sb. Trasudar: (pers.) sweat lightly, (cosa: seep + filtrarse). Unpleasant appearance (aspecto, aparición). There's still quite a bit to do. Walk a good way (un buen trecho). Tregua: (military) truce, (descanso) lull/respite. Train: mail train (tren correo), goods (carga) train, suburban (de cercanías) train, passenger train. Live in style (a todo tren). The lifestyle (tren de vida). Trillar: (Agr.) t̲h̲resh, (tema...) overuse. Losses (pérdidas) are three times bigger than (triplican) the profits (ganancias). Tristeza (sadness, sorrow). Triturador: grinder, crushing machine + (Culin.) mincer. Triumph over one's enemies + be successful in his profession. Trompa: (elefante) trunk, (insecto) proboscis; fallopian tube. Tropezar: (pies) trip, stumble, (contra algo) bump into sth, run into a difficulty. Knuckle (nudillo) under: someterse, pasar por el tubo =/= knuckle down (ponerse a trabajar en serio). Tumbar: (pers.) knock down/over, (puerta a golpes) batter down, (viento) blow down. Turbio: (agua) cloudy, muddy, turbid, (vista) dim, blurred, (mente) disturbed, (tema) confused, (período) turbulent, unsettled, (negocio) shady. Tutela: guardianship → bajo tutela (in ward). Duty: do one's – (cumplir con su deber), go on – (empezar el turno), be on – (estar de turno) ←→ be off duty; -- chemist (farmacia de turno), all-night chemist's =/= pharmacy (la ciencia de la farmacia). His bad humor (mal humor). Back row (última fila). As a last resort (instancia). Deep-freeze (ultracongelar). Descongelar: (congelador) defrost, (salarios, créditos) unfreeze. Ultrajar: offend, insult, abuse. A ra̲b̲i̲d̲ (a ultranza/fanático) nationalist + he looks for peace at any price, he fights to the death. Poverty line (umbral de pobreza + break-even point (punto de equilibrio, umbral de rentabilidad). Intensive care (cuidado) unit. Unir: unite the parts, join forces, join wires with insulating tape (cinta), united by the desire of..., the road unites the two towns, (Mec.) jointion, stick (unir) the edges together with adhesive tape, the taxi drivers joined the lorry drivers' strike. Cross-country skiing (esquí de fondo + mountaineering. Unventilated (sin ventilación). Be inseparable (ser carne y uña). Urban area ↔ rural area. Building (urbanizable) land ↔ green belt. In case of emergency (urgencia). You don't need t use the "Ud." form with me. Usable (utilizable), usefulness (utilidad). Grape harvest (vendimia) → raisin (uva pasa). The lean years (vacas flacas) ↔ fat years. He jumped into the space/the wind. A feeling of emptiness (vacío). Vacuum power + a gap in the legislation. A rather vague answer. Vagar (wander, roam, prowl about). Be a lazy devil (ser muy vago). Voucher (vale de compra), (bank note) billete. Holiday maker (veraneante). Undoubted (indudable) musical value. Vary (variar) the menu. Vaso sagrado (liturgical vessel/blood), lugar sagrado (holy/sacred place). You would see it coming (eso ya se veía venir). So it seems (se ve que sí). The two properties are adjoining (las dos fincas son vecinas). Look after sth (velar por algo). We hardly see each other nowadays (ahora apenas nos vemos). Slit: abertura, corte,V → -- one's wrists (cortarse las venas). Beating/overcoming (venciendo) the virus, sleep (el sueño) overcame him, he didn't manage (no consiguió) to complete all the tests (vencer todas las pruebas). Give in (ceder, consentir; entregar, presentar). Keep going (sigue adelante) & don't give in/up. I give in/up! (¡Me rindo/me entrego!) + don't give up (te entregues, abandones) in the face of difficulties, -- up smoking... His contract runs out/expires tomorrow + the deadline for paying the rent (alquiler) is (vence) tomorrow = the rent is due tomorrow. Al vencimiento (expiry) del título (title). After overcoming (luego de superar) the first obstacles. In a spirit of revenge/vengeance. The news (noticias) were (venían) in the paper (periódico). The best bit (lo mejor) in the film is coming (viene) now. How tough (forzudo, severo) they've become! I could do with a cup(me vendría bien una copa). That's what I've been saying all along (desde hace tiempo). Come what may come (venga lo que venga). Come along, don't be such a bore! (¡Venga ya, no seas pesado!). Be on sale (estar a la venta), available (de venta) only in chemists (farmacias). Summer resort (lugar de veraneo), holiday resort. Dirty old man (viejo verde). Executioner (verdugo). How embarrassing! (¡Qué vergonzoso!) → I almost died of embarrassment. Verificar: (inspeccionar) inspect, check, (Mec.) test, (hechos) verify. Verruga: (cara/espalda) wart, (manos/pies) verruca. Original version of a film. Half-dressed (a medio vestir), naked (desnudo). The best dressed (vestida) woman at the party. Start wearing my summer clothes. Vestirse de fiesta/gala (get dressed up). The smart way (elegancia) he dresses. Veteado: (mármol) veined, (carne) streaked. Mostly/in most cases (la mayoría de las veces). Seldom/rarely (raras veces). Knock down (derribar) in one go (de una vez). Let's get it over with! (¡Acabemos de una vez!). Once & for all (de una vez para siempre). A su vez (in turn)...) =/= when his turn comes + give up (ceder) one's turn. I saw her come downstairs (... bajando las escaleras). Please, make way! (¡dejen la vía libre!). Supply route (vía) + access route. One-way street/route. A single track/trail (pista + carril: lane). He was run over when he was crossing the track/lane =/= digestive/respiratory/urinary tracts (vías). Go away (salir de viaje). Viciar (corrupt, pervert). We can't get him out of the habit (vicio, costumbre) + complain for no reason at all (de vicio), he has the habit of not answering letters. Vicioso/depravado: dissolute, depraved, degenerated; a (sexual) pervert; addict; hooked on football. Claim (cantar) victory. A lifelong friend. For life (de por vida). He looks very old for his age. The skirt (falda) is too loose (viene ancha) for her ↔ it's too tight round your shoulders. Viento en popa (atrás: stern): following wind → ir viento en popa (go splendidly/go great guns/prosper). At all costs/come what may come (contra viento y marea). Regulation currently in force (legislación vigente). The custom that still prevails. They evaded (burlaron) the watchful (atento, vigilante) eye of.... Watch the children to see they don't get hurt. They kept a close watch (vigilancia de cerca) on the suspect + keep watching outside while (mientras) I hide. Vigorización: invigorating, (física) strengthening, (estímulo) encouraging. Vigoroso: (fuerte) strong, tough + duro), (esfuerzo) strenuous, (protesta) vigorous + energetic, forceful. Closely bound together (estrechamente vinculados entre sí). A lot of problems suddenly cropped up (vinieron). I felt like crying (me vinieron ganas de llorar), because I didn't feel like going. The job is <u>too much for/beyond</u> me (me viene grande). I'm famished (tengo un hambre que no veo). Many happy returns! (¡A celebrar con salud el año que viene!). Viscoso: viscous, (Líq.) thick, (secreción animal/vegetal) slimy. The child comes (viene) all on his own (sólo). I feel awkward/not don't feel at ease (violento) when I'm with you. The housing (vivienda) pbs. Box office (ventanilla). His memory (recuerdo) will always be with us (vivo). The age (época) in which we happen to live (nos ha tocado vivir). The papers blew out (salieron volando) the window + all my papers blew away (volaron). The document went all round the office (dio vueltas por toda la oficina). I'll be right there (llego volando + rush to do sth.). Go ballooning (montar en globo). The husband ran off with his lover. The lorry turned over twice and landed upside down + the plane circled round & round (dio muchas vueltas) before landing + turn down: poner boca abajo, dar media vuelta + somersault: voltereta, salto mortal, (coche) vuelco + (derrocar gobierno) overturn, overthrow, topple. Extinct volcano (volcán apagado) + dormant --. You will be rewarded (recompensados). Backward step (vuelta atrás). Turn on/spin round an axis. Go/revolve round (girar alrededor de) a plane. I was dizzy (mareado) & everything was going/spinning round (me daba vueltas). Turn round (date la vuelta) so I can do (peinar) your hair. Turn the glass the <u>right way up</u> → - - - <u>upside down</u>. Turn the socks the <u>right</u> way <u>out</u> → - - - <u>inside out</u>. The elections are almost upon us/around the corner (a la vuelta de la esquina). He gave us a ride (vuelta) in his car = he took us for a spin in his car. The road twists & turns up to the summit (el camino da muchas vueltas hasta llegar a la cima). We went for a stroll in the park. Return match. The ups & downs (vicisitudes) of life. Change things completely (dar la vuelta a la tortilla). A friend of yours. Whose is this? It's yours + theirs is in the garden. Vulgar y corriente: ordinary =/= a man above the --. Popular work (obra de vulgarización). Commonly/popularly known as... Vulnerar: (fama) damage, harm, (costumbre, derechos) interfere with, affect seriously, (jurídico, comercial) violate, break. I've just got the marks (notas). Wacky (chiflado, extravagante...) =/= wakeful (desvelado). Wade: caminar por el agua, barro, nieve + -- into (arremeter contra, meterse con). Apuesta: wager → -- € 1,000 on a horse, lay a -- on sth. + bet: the bet was..., place your bets, please! I bet you that... Waistcoat (chaleco). Waive (no aplicar, exonerar, renunciar a derechos). Be worthless. Wan (pálido, lánguido). Waning (menguante, decreciente). Weary (cansado) =/= wary (precavido, cauteloso), wariness (celo, cautela), warily (cautelosamente). Wastage (desperdicio, merma) =/= wasteful (derrochador). Watchdog (perro guardián). De primera calidad: a top quality product, work of high-quality, he had a first degree (la nota más alta). Water down (diluir). Watering (riego) can: regadera. Waxwork (figura de cera). Weaken (debilitar). Weather-beaten (curtido). Weathercast (boletín meteorológico). Weave (tejido) =/= wedge (cuña/calza, porción) → --ed in (encajado) between two lorries, -- a door open, this is the thin end of the wedge (eso puede ser el principio de muchos males). Weigh down (sujetar con un peso/piedra). Weird (raro, extraño) ness: rareza. Windblown (arrancado por el viento) → windborne (llevado por el v.). Winding (tortuoso, serpenteante). Windpipe (tráquea + trachea). Wiring (instalación eléctrica). Wittiness (agudeza, ingenio), wittingly (a sabiendas) =/= wistful (pensativo, triste, melancólico) =/= glum (triste, malhumorado + moody, bad - tempered) =/= sullen: (pers.) huraña, (cielo, día) triste. Wizardly (brujería). Womanliness (feminidad + femininity). Wonky (cojo, que tambalea). Woodcraft (conocimiento de la vida del bosque). Woodman (leñador). The wording is unclear (está mal redactado). Work like a slave (esclaco). Workroom (taller). Worthiness (valía, mérito), a worthy (digno) opponent. Wrongdoer (malhechor, delincuente). Wrongly (equivocadamente). Forsake: abandonar → God --en + renunciar (a un plan); --n spot (sitio). She wears her age/years well (se conserva muy bien). Have you finished already? It's all over (ya se acabó). Time's up (ya es la hora). I want to start right now/away (desde ya). He doesn't live here anymore (ya no...) /he no longer lives here/ comes to see us any more. This really is robbery (esto ya es un robo). (That's) quite enough! (¡Ya está bien!). They could have said they were coming (podían haber avisado de que venían). As/since she's not coming, we'll go. Yunta de bueyes (oxen): yoke, team. Zambullida (dive, plunge,V). Lace-up (con cordones) shoes. The cat scratched me (me dio un zarpazo). Shopping areas (zonas comerciales). Fox (zorro) ↔ vixen (zorra). He's a sly (astuto, travieso)/crafty old fox (viejo zorro). Zozobrar: (barco) founder, sink, capsize, overturn, (plan) fail, founder, (negocio) be ruined, (pers.) be anxious, worry. Portrayal: descripción, representación, (arte) retrato + portrait. Back: reforzar, respaldar, retroceder.

Capítulo II: El vocabulario y las muy variadas y ricas expresiones elegidas de libros pedagógicos utilizados por profesores ingleses

Dividiremos el capítulo en dos secciones. Primera sección: vocablos complementarios del capítulo anterior; segunda sección: palabras y pequeñas frases algo más complejas que las del capítulo anterior.

Primera sección: vocablos complementarios del capítulo anterior

Este hermoso repertorio de enseñanza fue elaborado por profesionales de la lengua inglesa, Recomendamos su imprescindible estudio, como también del capítulo anterior. Primero la dirección español → inglés y luego al revés.

Acosar: (fugitivo) pursue, the reporters (periodistas) were hounding the MP (Member of Parliament: diputado), the children pestered me with questions, ply sb with questions, harass.

Barco: ship, (-- grande) vessel, warship =/= boat → fishing boat; (barco cisterna) tanker, sailing boat, patrol boat =/= a leisurely (relajado, sin prisas) task for a slothful (perezosa) crew with a seaworthy (en condiciones de navegar) barge (barcaza) =/= he gets aboard (sube a bordo de) a dinghy (lancha, bote) launched from the ship; we got off the ship & put the boat into the sea; I jumped out (salí de un salto) & ran down the shore.

Cartera: (hombre) walle<u>t</u> + billetero =/= a walle<u>d</u> (amurallado) complex, (mujer) purse, (bolso) handbag, (de documentos, maletín) briefcase, (de valores, negocio, político) portfolio → Minister without --, (suit)case (maleta).

Crítica: la -- (the critics, -- literaria (literary criticism), reseñas (reviews → the movie has had a very good-- + well received by the critics worldwide; he strongly attacked the bishop; he has been object of a lot of criticism, criticable (reprehensible).

Interrumpir: don't interrupt me, (tráfico) block, (suministro) cut off, power cut, (obras en las calzadas) roadworks are disrupted, (planes) ruin the negotiations, the bus services have been suspended.

Llorar: cry (llorar), whimper: lloriqueo, quejido; llantos/gemidos: wailing → the -- of the wind/sirens; quejarse (grumble, whine, moan) → weep/cry with joy (llorar de alegría), mourn (llorar la muerte) + mourning (luto); lamentarse: moan, grumble, complain.

Miedo: he's afraid of the dark, -- of her, he's -- of his parents will find out..., don't be --,..., he fears for his family/business, I exposed my fears to the director; are you coming? I'm afraid so/no, they were -- of change, I was -- of that (me lo temía), there's nothing to be -- (temer), I'm -- of the police/of being alone/falling/missing the train, what are you -- of? =/= frighten: don't be --ed (no te asustes), you look scared/frightened ←→ don't be --/--, take fright at sth. (be scared), a --ning (espantosa, aterradora) place, what a fright! fearful (temible, horrible).

Pinchar: a loutish (grosero, gamberro + hooligan, troublemaker) slashed the tyre, (objeto punzante) prick → -- with a pin (alfiler...), (balon) punctuation/ burst, give an injection, (navaja) stab, (presionar) prod (into playing sport...).

Reserva: reserve, (prod. alim.) stock, (agua) supply at a minimum, currency/gold reserves, hidden reserves, reserve books by phone, (Biol.) wildlife sanctuary, game (caza) reserve, (deporte) be at reserve.

Retardar/retardado: he was late for the meeting, mental deficiency, cultural backwardness, backward university system + (ideas) outdated, the watch is three m. slow, he postponed/put off his appearance before the press, the draw (sorteo) has been postponed/put back, put back the date of the examen, raise the retirement age, delayed/held up the departure of the plane/the traffic, I'm sorry I'm late/sorry for the delay + the plane was three m. late, (estudios) get/fall behind, (andando) lag behind, they complained about the delay in payments.

Reventar: (precios) slash, the robbers blew the safe/strongbox (caja fuerte), (plan) wreck, (mitin) disrupt, we got a flat tyre (pinchazo: puncture), (neumático) blowout, (proyectil) blow up, (presa: dam) burst, tense relations that will blow up, I'm full to bursting.

Revés: (tela, documento, mano) back, (prenda) inside, you are holding the book upside down, you've got your socks (calcetines) on inside out, shoes in the wrong feet, turn the other way (volver al revés), do sth opposite of what you say, contrary to popular belief, suffer a setback.

Saltar: jump with joy, come out to the pitch (campo), jump/leap out of a window, leap ashore (a tierra), the oil is spitting, the ball flew out of the ground/over the bar (portería), the car was blown up (saltó por los aires), the alarm goes off, the fusses (plomos) have blown, skip from one thing to another/of several pages, a leap forward in technology, we jumped across the river, unpredictable leaps of the progress, he leapt/leaped to one's feet (se levantó de un salto), he leaped up onto the branch of a tree, his leap to the fame/into the theater, pole (palo, percha, Tf.: poste, cortina: barra) vault (salto,V; bóveda/sótano, panteón): salto de pértiga. High jump, ski jump (+ trampolin), long jump, springboard/diving board (trampolín), a gap of three years.

Saludar: wave at, he waved to us; he never says hello, say hello to; give my regards to your husband, send warmest regards; greet with a slight nod (con la cabeza), they greeted each other with a kiss, he didn't respond to my greetings; give my best wishes to him.

Servicio: yours faithfully (su seguro servidor), serve the people (pueblo), on guard today, serve one's country (patria), it might be useful. I's is no good any more/is no longer valid, what is it for?, what's this gadget for?, to stir up controversy (crear controversia), this strike is not achieving anything, I wouldn't be good as a doctor, the second showing (sesión, servicio), in case that's any use (por si sirve de algo) ↔ you are completely useless (inútil), it's no good complaining.

Simple: through sheer carelessness (por simple descuido); plain (decoro, comida) sencilla; franca, clara) decoration; single (de ida) ticket, -- combat, soltero, by a -- (sólo) point, -- room, -- (única) currency; single-minded (resuelto, firme) =/= simple-minded (simple, ingenuo) =/= gullible (crédulo, simplón) → gullibility/simpleness. I'll just/simply have to accept it. I was just (simplemente) calling to confirm.

Suave: (surface) smooth, even, (color, movim., brisa) gentle, (clima, sabor) mild, (trabajo) easy, (voz) soft + las drogas), (olor) slight, sweet → suavidad: (piel, superficie) smoothness, evenness.

Temblar: she was so nervous she began to stutter (tartamudear), (hand/voice, de miedo) tremble, (frío) shiver with cold, (fiebre) you are shivering, (edificio, muebles) shake: the earthquake made the village --, she is getting very shaky, the news shock Wall Street.

Due: where is the plane --? The book is -- out in December, I'm -- in Paris tomorrow, it's -- to happen, ..., it's -- on 30th (el plazo vence el 30), when is the rent (alquiler) --? Drive with

-- (debido) care, after -- consideration, -- to repairs (obras) the garage will be closed.

Either & neither. Either: he doesn't know her --; I didn't buy it --; my sister didn't go --; this wouldn't be a problem --; cualquiera: -- day (would suit me), -- of us; you can do it -- way (de una u otra manera), take -- route (cualquiera de las dos); in -- hand (en cada mano) + on -- side of the road; which bus do you take? I've never been either to Paris or Rome; I can't speak -- Spanish or Italian, you can have --, ice or cream. Neither: -- he nor I can go, he -- smokes nor drinks; if you aren't going, -- am I; you don't like it, -- do I; -- she did; -- of them were informed; -- too much nor too little; I didn't go, me --; I've -- been to Paris; lo sabes tu? Tampoco (-- do I); he doesn't like caviar, -- do I; -- company wanted this problem; -- good nor bad.

Excel & superar. Excel: → -- o.s.: pasarse → she is always generous, but this time she's excelled herself (se pasó); -- at/in: sobresalir en; -- as (destacar como). Superar: exceed the forecasts, (pb, adversary/opponent, fear, poverty, difficulties) overcome, (récord) beat, (exam.) pass → querer superar_se_: desire to better himself.

Fancy: (capricho) → we will leave when the -- take us =/= give himself a treat/caprice (darse un capricho), changeable weather, a decision taken on a whim (capricho); do you -- watching TV? Whatever takes your -- (lo que más te apetezca), -- goods (géneros de fantasía); imaginarse → I rather – he's gone out.

Faint: (sonido) débil, ligero, (cosa) casi imperceptible/invisible, imagen borrosa (+ blurred), (aroma) ligero, -- from/with hunger: agotado por el hambre; desmayo/desvanecimiento: I nearly --ed!, (-- - hearted) pusilánime/tímido.

Feel: -- (tantear) our way towards a deal, I felt (sentí) sth move, I do -- (noto, soy consciente de) the importance of this, I felt like crying (me vinieron ganas de llorar), I felt (me sentí) like a new man, he --s the cold, he --s (se siente afectado por) the death of his father, what do you -- about it? (¿Qué te parece eso?), how do you -- (te sientes) now? -- himself old, sick, I -- (tengo la sensación) as if there's nothing we can do, he liked the -- of the breeze (brisa) on her face, a general -- (sensación), sticky -- (tacto viscoso), it --s like silk, it --s like (parece que va) to rain, I felt like a fool (me sentí estúpido)/a new man, I don't longer -- like travelling. He --s emotion like any human being. He felt he was being watched (se sentía observado). -- at (como en) home. I felt ill/bad. The decision does not reflect the --ing of the majority.

Forward: leaning -- (echado para adelante + self assured: (seguro de sí mismo), the mirror was tilted (inclinado) --, row (fila) two is too far --, that law marks a great step -- (un adelanto), the elections will be brought --, put sth forward: adelantar, (proposición) presenter, put sb forward (proponer a alguien), we brought the wedding --, bring -- (adelantar) peace & spare Syrian lives.

Go: -- with (armonizar con), -- without/dispense (prescindir) with the detail, -- after (perseguir), -- along (ir, proceder), -- along with (estar de acuerdo con), -- around with (ser suficiente), -- by (pasar + atenerse a), -- in (entrar, caber), -- into (investigar), -- off (marcharse, estallar), -- over (reviser), -- under (hundirse), --/come up, get closer, --/come round (acercarse). Go through: (pasar por una capital...), atravesar, (dinero) gastar, (comida) comerse, aguantar → I know what you are going -- (como lo estás pasando).

Hardly: va con (+): hardly (casi) ever/anybody/anything. I could -- (apenas)..., it's -- (no hace ni) ten minutes since you came in. I could -- believe my ears (apenas podía creer lo que escuchaba).

Have: the United Kingdom would -- to try; if no one had pulled them apart/separated them, they would -- killed each other; we would -- failed (fracasado), had it not been...; he would -- won, had he...; if it hasn't been for him...; do I -- to obey Mr Smith? You shouldn't -- taken it like that; we shall -- to walk; he had to pretend love to her; he is black as he had been beaten; he had to make him take the pills; if this were the case, we'd -- to rid of them, the pipeline might -- to pass through...; if it hadn't been for him, I'd -- drowned; I'll just/ simply -- to accept it; a fifth of what he could -- had to pay to handover (traspasar, ceder, entregar) under the new scheme; I'd -- to reapply (nueva solicitud); power would -- to be handed to the next generation; we would -- nothing left; it will -- taken heart (cogido ánimo); Britain would -- Brexit.

Heave: tirón, jalón, empujón, arrastrar, esfuerzo → -- (cargar) bricks, -- (tirar) on a rope, -- a sigh (suspirar); I heaved (lancé) a sigh (suspiro) of relief (alivio), he --ed himself off the floor (se levantó haciendo un gran esfuerzo). An upbeat (optimista) view on more heave is needed.

Hurry: I'm in a -- (tengo prisa), they left (salieron) in a -- (a todo correr), -- up!/do --! he --ed in/out (entró, salió corriendo), stop --ing me! I was --ed into that decision (me hicieron tomar esta decisión precipitadamente).

Hurt: hacer daño → -- your finger, -- (heridas) in the accident, -- o.s. (hacerse daño), did you -- yourself? Mind you don't -- yourself! He's not badly (gravemente) --ed, he wouldn't -- a fly, did I -- you? -- by his attitude, I didn't mean to -- you, my arm --s (me duele), where does it --s? My shoes are --ing, kick him "where" it--s! It --s to admit it, but...

Indeed: (de hecho): -- I know...; that is praise -- (eso sí es un elogio); answer a question: isn't it a beautiful day? Yes --! Did you know him? Yes, --, I did the best I could, --! (¡Por supuesto!).

Isssue/item/subject: Issue (asunto) → avoid/confuse the --, the issue of slavery split the country, the bank will -- (proveer) you with a chekbook, -- notes & actions, death without --... Item: itemize (detallar), artículo: de diario, mercancía → household

--, -- of clothing; (asuntos) → several useful –s (puntos por tratar en la agenda). Subject: on the -- (sobre el tema, asunto, asignatura), change the --, -- to (propenso/expuesto a), -- sb to sth (someter a alguien a algo).

Junk (basura, trastos viejos, baratijas, chatarra; tirar a la basura, desechar una teoría) → -- (pulgas) market + the play (obra) is a -- (chapuza), he talks a lot of -- (tonterías), the outflow (desagüe, flujo de capital) signalling the end of the junk bonds (correo basura) depends on weather, Renano did not -- the peace deal.

Mind: a creative -- (mente), he has the -- of a three years old, it came to my -- that... (se me ocurrió...), my -- was elsewhere (en otro sitio), it never entered my --, have one's -- on sth., bear sth/sb in -- (cuenta), time out of -- (immemorial), change one's -- (intención), nothing was further from my --, change sb's --, to my -- (a mi juicio), with one -- (unánimemente), be of the same --, lose one's -- (perder el juicio), in his right -- (en su sano juicio), be out of one's --, one of the fines (privilegiados) --s (cerebros) of the period (época), don't -- me (por mí no se preocupe), -- you don't fall/don't get wet! -- your head/what you're doing, -- my bags, I don't -- (no me molesta) the cold, I don't -- waiting, do you -- telling me...? --! (¡Cuidado!), -- bender (alucinógeno: hallucinogenic + go on a bender: ir de juerga/borrachera), make up one's -- (decidirse), be mindful (tener en cuenta) of..., --less (sin sentido), minder (guardaespaldas + bodyguard, -- don't get drunk, do you mind the noise? Go out of one's mind (perder la razón).

Pack: =, mochila (back--, rucksack), pelotón, empaquetar, envasar, recoger las cosas; package (paquete,V, oferta...), packed/jam-packed (abarrotado), -- deal (viaje organizado), packaged (envasados) foods ↔ packet: (de cerillas, de cigarrillos...) cajita; sobre, bolsa, dineral; pack up: (coche) dejar de funcionar/estropearse, (pers.) parar la actividad → -- -- for a day, (cosas) recoger.

Plain (franco, claro, sencillo) → make sth -- (evidente), it's plain that (es evidente que)..., her guilt (culpa) was -- to see, I shall be -- with you, (plain/prairie) llanura; plain_ly_: he dresses -- (sobriamente), speak -- (sencillamente, claramente), it was -- explained/put forward (clarísimo).

R_u_sh: movimiento o avance impetuoso/avalancharse; prisa, ráfaga, apurar... → with a -- (de golpe), -- hour (hora punta), empuje, I'm in a dreadful (terrible) rush, so I can't stop, he --ed off to get a doctor =/= r_a_sh: temerario/precipitado; erupción, avalancha, arrebato, racha → a -- of strikes; in a -- I promised her... (en un arrebato le prometí...), set off (provocar, hacer estallar) a rash (erupción, racha, avalancha; imprudente) decision.

Service: he didn't charge (cobró) anything for the service, an off-duty policeman ↔ be in duty, he served as a lieutenant, a computing --s company, we deliver home, inflight (a bordo) service, fire --, emergency --, broadcasting --, do sb a disservice (perjudicar a alguien), be fit for military --, casualties/emergency department --, the toilets --, a six – piece-coffee set --, servants (servicio doméstico), after 3,000 km. It's due (le toca) a --, at your --! Go out of --, the public sector --es.

So: I'm -- (tan) worried, it's about -- (más o menos así de) high, I don't need -- many (tantos), we spent -- much (tanto), I love you -- (tanto), it is -- (es así), is that --? (¿De veras?), that's -- (eso es), -- far (hasta ahora), I expect -- (supongo que sí), -- he says (eso dice él), -- to speak (por decirlo así), -- do I (yo también), -- that (para que), ten or -- people.

Stand: posición, postura, actitud, puesto, estar de pie → make a -- (hacer parada), -- waiting (esperar de pie); resistencia,V → make/take -- against sth; parada de taxis, quiosco, (Sp., Jur.) tribuna, -- on sth (pisar algo), encontrarse/ubicarse. Take breaks to -- & stretch your legs, don't -- (quedarse) here arguing (discutiendo).

Still (sentido de tranquilo): he stood -- (se quedó quieto, apacible) → in the -- (silencio) of the night, a -- evening, get it -- (inmóvil), keep --! (¡No te muevas!), stand -- (quedarse quieto), all was -- (tranquilo), -- (acallar) the gossiping tongues (rumores + rumours).

Throw: echar, derribar, desmontar, lanzar → the blast (explosión) threw them (los lanzó) across the room) → -- one's hat/cap into the ring (lanzarse al ruedo), -- a party (dar una fiesta) → -- away (tirar a la basura, ...), (oportunidad) desperdiciar, -- back: (pelota, pez al agua) devolver.

Tighten, tense, strain...: tighten the strings of a racket =/= not to tense your muscles, the relations; feel one's tense =/= put sth under strain (tensión/presión + raza/variedad), high voltage tension (voltaje de alta tensión), blood pressure, the rope is taut (tirante), stiff (tiesos) collars, stiff with (plagados de) customers, (carne) tough, be frozen stiff.

Trial (juicio) & try: Trial: on -- for murder, go on --/stand -- (ser procesado), flight -- (de prueba), be on -- (de prueba), the Olympic -- (pruebas de selección para...) =/= try: intento, give sth a -- (intentar hacer algo), let me have a --, give sth a -- (probar algo), give sb a -- (poner alguien a prueba), -- to do sth (intentar hacer algo), I tried not to think..., -- not to cough, -- turning the key, -- one's look, you --! (¡Hazlo y verás!) =/= tray (bandeja).

Would: If you asked him he -- do it, I said I -- do it (te dije que lo haría); -- you close the door, please? Cain -- overcome (vencería) the sin, what -- you want me to? I --n't worry too much if I were you, he --n't do it, the car --n't start (no quería arrancar), I -- if I could; if I had known, I --n't have come, I wish you --n't worry, -- you like a cup of coffee?

Segunda sección: palabras y pequeñas frases algo más complejas que en el capítulo I

Adopt (ahijar). Godchildren (ahijados) → godson, goddaughter. Golddigger (cazafortunas). Pointless (inútil, inmotivado, sin sentido) → it's pointless trying to convince him. Good-tempered (apacible). Brillante: (bright, shiny, brilliant) people... Graceful (cortés + courteous). Decorate, adorn. Gown (bata de casa, togo). Grapple (forcejear). A solemn promise. Greediness (glotonería + gluttony). Gregarious (=, sociable). Mareado: air/sea/car sick, tipsy (achispado). Trick (truco) =/= figure sb out (cogerle el truco). Wiry (enjuto: delgado y flaco; fuerte, áspero, nervioso) =/= tough/robust (robusto) shelter (protección, refugio, alojamiento). Grief (pena, dolor) → grief-stricken (apesadumbrado). Dirt (suciedad) → the streets have got dirtier. Bewitch (seducir, cautivar + =) the public. We went to see them off (a despedirnos) at the station =/= dismiss (despachar un trabajador). The volcano spews out =/= he vomits/brings up (vomita). Bending Germany's energy market out of shape (deformando...). A foiled (frustrado + frustrate, thwart) attack. The appeal of Spain for the tourists/investors + charm to get work + one attraction of the city. To the audience's delight (regocijo, deleite). Frame: estructura, marco, cuerpo. I despair (pierdo la esperanza) of my son + don't despair (no abandones). Pull off: quitar, llevar a cabo, conseguir. Freshwater (agua dulce). Uproar (alboroto) in the parliament. Disturbance (disturbio). Excess luggage. Fussy (quisquilloso, exigente) → stop fussing (de ser quisquilloso) & eat it. Jump for joy (alegría). Talkative (habla mucho + gossipy). Gape: estar abierto, mirar boquiabierto: don't just stand there gaping.... Old people's home (asilo) + (-- de huérfanos) orphanage. Trust (confianza) is the basis of friendship. Groundless (infundado). Grouse: queja + grumble, complaint. Grub (larva) → grubby (sucio, manoseado) =/= grumpy (gruñón). Agotador (exhausting, gruelling). Bad-tempered (mal-humorado). Cautious/well prepared (precavido). Guía/consejo (guidance). An expected turn (vuelta) in politics. Guild (gremio). Gunrunner (traficante de armas). Racha → a run of victories, a series of misfortunes, a gust of wind, a run or spell of bad luck recently...

Tragar: swallow; stop stuffing! Guzzle (zamparse, engullirse. Hack (hacer trizas, cortar con hacha). Half-caste (mestizo + =) + animal: crossbred, planta: hybrid). Hamper (cesta, entorpecer). Handicapped/disabled (minusválido). Handshake (apretón de manos). Useful (útil) ↔ useless. Handicraft (artesanía + craftsmanship), arts and crafts (artes y oficios), skill/cleverness (habilidad), technical skill (destreza) → the experienced developers with teamwork (trabajo de equipo) skills become the best managers =/= handy: práctico, útil, hábil) → keep sth -- (a mano), (manitas), craft fair (feria artesanal), craft work (artesanía). Percance/contratiempo: the project suffered setbacks, we arrived without mishaps. We long/yearn for (anhelamos) a prosperous future. Haphazard (caótico, desordenado). Relaxed/unworried (despreocupado). Hard cash (dinero contante y sonante), hard drinker (empedernido). Insensitive (insensible) to cold. Numb: (nervio, miembro) entumecido. A sturdy (robusto) tree/young man. A qu̲ick phone call =/= a fa̲st runner. Hasty (precipitado, apresurado) + hasten: acelerar, apurarse. Handbook (manual) + brochure (folleto de viajes) + booklet (manual de instrucciones) + pass the leaflet (octavila) with the timetable to him to put it in the notebook (agenda) + (de escuela) cuaderno. Hairpin (horquilla de moño) → a -- bend/curve: curva en herradura o muy cerrada. Hairdo (peinado). Frantic (desesperado, frenético + frenzied). Harness: arnés/arreos → to -- a horse to a wagon, (río, energía) aprovechar, (potencial) explotar. Don't talk nonsense (disparates). Block/obstruct the way. Hustle (apresurar, empujar) → the police --ed the thief. Deadly boring (aburridísimo). Careless (descuidado). Laze around/about: holgazanear, no hacer nada =/= idle (perezoso, vano, estar sin trabajo) away: desperdiciar el tiempo. Join (juntar, confluir con, ingresar en...) in: tomar parte, participar en. Jolt: sacudir, conmover, golpear → give a -- (susto) =/= jo̲stle (empujar) → -- way through (abrirse camino por medio de) the crowd =/= jo̲tter (bloc de notas) =/= Jitter (ponerse nervioso). Don't push me (no me empujes). Junk (trasto, basura, baratija). That sort of behaviour is not justifiable. The children will knock the wheelie bin (contenedor) over (tirar, atropellar). The lorry was dumping (volcando, vertiendo) sand. Suspicious bags (bolsas). Stick out/stand out (sobresalir). Give up: ceder, entregar(se), abandonar, romper con. Keyboard (teclado). Kind-hearted (bondadoso). Equip/fit (equipar). Knight (caballero) in shining armour (armadura): príncipe azul. Knock down (derribar, atropellar + run over) =/= knotty: nudoso, (pb) espinoso. Involve (involucrar) → involved in his shady (sucios) deals. Knowingly (adrede). Lax (poco estricto, relajado). Outstanding/leading (destacado). A jump of 2 m → high --, ski --, long --, a great leap forward. Waterfall (catarata). Leap year (año bisiesto). Defraud/disappoint/let down. Estallar: (bomba, globo) explode, (neumático) burst, (vidrio) shatter, (epidemia, sublevación) break out. Live-off sth (alimentarse a costa de algo) =/= live through sth (sobrevivir algo). Aborrecer: (pers, actividad) detest, loathe, (crías) reject =/= hate: odiar, aborrecer, detestar. Lodger (huésped, inquilino en casa particular). Despise (despreciar + reject, spurn). They spurned (rechazaron) our offer of help. Disregard (no tener cuenta de) the danger. Look into (investigar), look out (tener cuidado), look round (mirar por ahí). Lousy: piojoso + fatal, pésimo, asqueroso. Politeness/courtesy (cortesía). Opening ceremony → stand on (andarse con) ceremonies. Formality (lo ceremonioso, formalidad), without ceremony. Correctness (corrección). Madden (enloquecer). Creep (trepar, arrastrarse poco a poco; asqueroso, adulador) → -- along (avanzar a paso de tortuga), the pain was creeping in her hands → creepy: (pers.) asquerosa, (film, Hist.) escalofriante, repulsivo, horripilante) =/= he crawled (se arrastraba) through the long grass =/= crippled (lisiado, inutilizado; Ind.: paralizada....) =/= crumple: (currency: abollarse; tela: arrugarse) =/= disabled (discapacitado, minusválido, mutilado; Mil: inutilizado). Exaggerate = magnify. Improvise a tune (melodía, =). Makeshift (provisional, =) =/= maverick (inconformista + nonconformist). Compulsory/mandatory (obligatorio). Manned (tripulado). Homicide/murder =/= manslaughter (homicidio involuntario). Estropear (spoil, break)se la ropa: get spoilt. Rebajar: reduce a sentence, 15% of reduction, lose 2 kg, lower the level (techo), (color/tono) soften, (Líq.) dilute, humiliate (humillar). Abandonar: (animal, idea, pers.) abandon, leave a political party, they left the room, my strength deserts me, (cargo, esperanza) give up, (derecho) renounce, (obligación) neglect. Dominant flavour/ideology. Prevailing opinion. Élite (=, diligent class, upper class) ↔ lower class, working class. Domineering (autoritario, dominante) =/= masterful: capaz, autoritario, dominante, (rendimiento) magistral. Mastery (dominio). At mealtimes (a la hora de comer). Meaningless (sin sentido). Mean: tacaño + stingy, malo, humilde...; promedio, significar/querer decir → means: recursos, medios, manera → by any means (del modo que sea), by all means → by no means. Mellow: (fruta) madura; añejo, (color) suave, (sonido) dulce, (actitud) plácida. Meantime (entretanto) → in the -- (por ahora, mientras tanto). Meddle (entrometerse) → -- with sth (jugar con algo) → don't -- with witchcraft (brujería) =/= intercede/intervene/mediate (mediar). Mess up (desordenar). Merely (simplemente, solamente). Pass the time/get talking (entretenerse), amuse oneself =/= keep busy. Mouthwatering (muy apetitoso). Murky: (oscura) night, (turbio) past. Unpleasant (antipático). Nasty (desagradable, repugnante + disgusting/revolting) → a nasty (mal) temper (genio), a nasty (grave) accident ↔ Neat: (habitación) ordenada, (jardín, ropa) bien cuidado, (pers.) ordenada, pulcra, (solución) ingeniosa), (figura) atractiva. Angustioso: (grito) anguish, (situación) distressing. News flash: noticias de última hora. The teacher nodded (hizo signo con la cabeza) in agreement, she nodded me a welcome, he nodded me to leave the room. Lazo: shoelace, (para asegurar) knot, (escurridizo) slipknot, (decorativo) bow, ties of friendship, family ties, ribbon (cinta), lasso. Noteworthy (digno de mención). Anular: (partido, viaje) cancel, (matrimonio) annul, declare sth invalid, (ley, multa) revoke, (sanción) lift, (sentencia) overturn, (gol) disallow, (invalidar) overrule. Mirage (espejismo). Miserly/mean (avaro). Misbehave (portarse mal). Misfire (tiro/máquina/plan: fallar). Misuse (abuso, uso incorrecto). Húmedo: the socks are /the ground is damp, (ojos, labios) moist, (Atm.) humid, (clima, región) wet + (lluvioso, mojado) rainy, wet. Sullen (huraño, atmósfera de resentimiento, sombrío, triste) =/= moody (malhumorado, deprimido, taciturno, temperamental). Riddle: enigma, acertijo; criba (+ sieve) → the moth (polilla) has riddled (carcomido) the jumper (jersey); the cancer has riddled his lungs, --ed with bullets. Mothball: (barco) mandado a la reserva; aparcar un proyecto. Afligir (distress, afflict, mourn + estar de luto) → afligido: mournful + lúgubre. Overconfident (excesivamente seguro de sí mismo). Over<u>haul (trayecto)</u>: poner a punto, revisar, alcanzar, adelantar a. Overhead (gastos generales). Override (hacer caso omiso, anular, ignorar) → of overriding (de fundamental) importance. Unconscious/oblivious (inconsciente). Encroach: invadir, (derechos) usurpar. Overrun by tourists. Surrounded (rodeado) by the police. Oversleep (quedarse dormido). Excedente (surplus) → the luggage must not exceed the limit. He is the wittiest (el de más genio) of all. Go too far (excederse). Overtake: adelantar, sobrepasar → --n (sobrecogido) by fear. Overwhelming: insoportable, irresistible, (abrumadora) majority → an -- 80% voted against + people voted overwhelmingly (rotundamente, abrumadoramente) in favour of the proposal. Pad: almohadilla, rellenar... Painstakingly (laboriosamente) =/= obliging (servicial). Nurture (cuidar, alimentar, crianza,) → -- of new talents. Obstructive (que pone obstáculos o dificultades). Off-duty (fuera de servicio), off-line (desconectado). Waterproof jacket (chubasquero). One-off: (único, extraordinario + =; excelente). Orchard: vegetable garden. Without apparent reason. Outbreak (brote, arrebato) of war. Outburst (arrebato de ira, estallido, explosión). Outcast/alienated (marginado). Outlast (durar más que). Overbearing = authoritarian. Derisory (irrisorio). Pardon/exemption/reprieve (indulto). Pauper (indigente + destitute) → he fainted (se desmayó) from hunger; paupers' grave (fosa común + common grave). Sketch (dibujo, bosquejo,V) → outline (contorno, esbozo,Vs) → drawing (dibujo) → design (diseño). Paw (pata, manaza, manosear). Ingresar: (servicio militar) join, (dinero) pay in. Payee (beneficiario). Repressed (reprimido). Perk (ventaja, beneficio adicional) → one of the --s of the job) → -- up (animarse, sentirse mejor) → our business/she is --ed up a bit. Dominar: (población, territorio, Sp.) dominate → the Spanish -- the whole set, (país) rule, (adversario) overpower, (epidemia, incendio) bring under control, (rebelión) put down, (técnica, tema) master. Apuro: awkward situation, (vergüenza) embarrassment, (dificultades) troubles. Agujerear: make holes; pierce + perforar. Estrellarse: (contra): crash, (fracasar): fall. Robar: (objeto, dinero) steal, (banco) rob → we have been robbed, (los ladroncillos) pilfer, take up your time, you have been cheated/robbed in that deal, kidnap (raptar). Beg/implore/plead (suplicar) → he pleaded her not to leave him. Steer: (dirigir, conducir) → your columnist (articulista) tries to steer him off the topic. Plunge: zambullirse, inmersión,V/baño, desplome; (puñal: dagger) clavar, arrojarse → -- into a war. The weather difficulties notwithstanding (a pesar de). Injustice/unfairness. Sincerity/openness. Aparente (=, oblivious). Go on an excursion/outing/trip. Overnight (de la noche a la mañana) → the plants came up --; durante la noche → we drove --, an -- accommodation, -- (repentino) success. Encantado (, pleased), "Enchanted castle". Pass over (pasar por encima de; pasar por alto, omitir).

Complacer: please. Not well/indisposed (indispuesto). Partridge (perdiz). Patronize: ser cliente de, frecuentar (hotel...), utilizar un servicio, tratar con condescendencia. Patrocinar: sponsor, back, support. Act as godfather (apadrinar). Pave (pavimentar). Annoying (molesto). Penance (castigo, penitencia, =). Pervasive: (generalizado) belief, (penetrante) smell, (dominante) mood (humor). Pitcher (cántaro, jarra). Patético/conmovedor: moving, poignant, touching. Rejection (rechazo) of an offer, he rejected me. Ecuánime: impartial, (sereno) calm. Pool (piscina, charco, estanque). Pop in (entrar un momento). Destination of funds, of tourists... → funds-raising for third world children. Poverty-stricken (sumido en la pobreza). Motor launch (lancha motora). Pounce on/upon (abalancharse sobre). Practitioners (profesionales, =). Pilgrimage (peregrinación). Joke/prank (broma) → prankster: bromista + be in a joking mood; practical joke (broma pesada). Preposterous (absurdo, ridículo). Presumption (suposición). Pre-eminent (=, predominante). Prevailing: (opinión, viento) predominance, (precio) imperante, (incerteza) reinante, the -- (actual) fashion + prevalecer. Prior (anterior, previo). Prize-giving (entrega de premios). Survey/poll (sondeo) + enquiry (indagación, investigación + probe (sond(e)ar). Profess: (religión) profesar, (sorpresa) manifestar. Political tendencies. Downward/upward trend. Let through (dejar pasar). Level off: nivelarse, (precios, inflación, crecimiento) estabilizarse. Tapa: (párpado, bomba, cacerola) lid, (libro) cover, (con rosca) screw top =/= tapón de corcho: cork, de lavabo: plug; de oídos: ear plug. He blew his brains out. Lie back (recostarse). Lifeless (sin vida). Life-sized (de tamaño natural). Exaltado: overexcited, hotheaded, impetuous, elated (eufórico, =), exalted, (político) extremist. Nice/likeable (simpático). Gusto (taste, pleasure, liking) → I trust (confío) the meal was to your liking. Liner (transatlántico). There's a curse (maldición) on us. Hassle (follón, jaleo, fastidiar) → we --ed them for an answer + it's not worth the -- (no vale la pena). Goldplated (chapado de oro). Leave (permiso, vacaciones), -- behind (dejar detrás), -- out (excluir + exclude, reject). Leek (puerro). Lending rate (tipo de interés). Lenient/indulgent (indulgente). He blew out the candles in one go. Puff: calada de tabaco, soplo de aire → that run (carrera) has puffed me out (dejado sin aliento). Desmantelar: (fábrica) dismantle, (estantería, tienda de campaña) take down, (teoría) demolish, (máquina) strip down, (organización) disband. Pull: (-- up) levantar, (-- off) quitar, (-- on) tirar de, (-- away) arrancar. Push aside (dejar de un lado). Fasten (abróchate) the seat belts. Aggressive attitude. Violent scenes. Pushy (agresivo, avasallador). Put by (ahorrar; guardar + put away, keep, save him a cake). Put out (sacar). Puzzling (disconcerting, =). Picturesque/colourful (pintoresco). Extraer: (petróleo, muela) extract, (cirujía) remove, take blood. Quarry (cantera, explotar una cantera) =/= quash: (sentencia) anular, (rebelión) sofocar, (rumor) poner fin. Muelle: (objeto) spring =/= the ship tied up (atracó) at the wharf. Apagar: (luz) switch off, (fuego) put off, (cerilla) blow out, (sentimiento) lessen + reducir, aliviar, (sed) quench. Interrumpir: interrupt, (vacaciones) cut short, (tráfico) block, hold up, (embarazo: pregnancy) terminate, (suministro) cut off. Distinctive features (peculiaridades) + each country has its own peculiarities/special characteristics. Silencioso: (callado) silent, (barrio... tranquilo) quiet. The years leading up (que precedieron) the war. Just this once (sin que sirva de precedente + preceding, previous). Set a precedent ↔ unprecedented. Heinous (atroz) =/= hideous: feísimo, monstruoso, horroroso, perverso, malo. He is always acting the fool (siempre está haciendo payasadas). Hoyo: hole, pit (en los Estados Unidos de America: piñón de fruta), (de tumba): grave. Lair: guarida, refugio + shelter. He vehemently/hotly denied it. Henceforth (de ahora en adelante). Political interest is at its height (auge, apogeo + heyday). Horrific accident.

Highbrow (intelectual).+ Tyrannical/high-handed (despótico). shrill/high-pitched (estridente, agudo + strident). Excursion (=, trip, outing si es larga, (a pie: hike) → --ista: (campo) hiker, (viaje) tripper. Hilly (montañoso, accidentado). Vagabundo: (pers.) wandering, (animal) stray. Pay (rendir) tribute/homage (homenaje). Chapuza: botched job/odd job, kludges =/= grudges (rencillas). Bungle (metedura de pata, echar a perder) → bungling (torpe) Government. Stubborn/headstrong (testarrudo). Heady (embriagador, excitante). Hearsay (rumor, =). Hearse (coche fúnebre). Heartbroken (desconsolado). Heartless (desalmado) ↔ heartfelt (sincere) → my -- sympathy/apologies/condolences. Hearty (campechano, cordial) → heartiest (las más cordiales) congratulations (enhorabuena). Heated: (piscina) climatizada, (casa) air-conditioned. Forthcoming (próximo, comunicativo). Well-off: (de dinero) acomodado → the -- (las clases acomodadas). A lifestyle suited to our means... Hellish (infernal). Patrimonio: =, wealth/cultural heritage, national wealth, asset (activos) management, World heritage. Devolver: return, give back, handback, (dinero) refund, (deuda) repay, restore, (vomitar) bring up. Hand in: (trabajo) entregar + -- -- one's resignation. Transmitir: (sonido) =, (bienes, saludos, enfermedad) pass on. Hand down (bajar algo, dejar en herencia, transmitir). Haphazard (al azar, irregular) → -- guess (cálculo aproximado). Disregard (no tener en cuenta). Decorate/embellish/garnish (adornar). Nice/kind/pleasant (amable). Gently/smoothly/mildly (dulcemente, suavemente...). An evenly distributed load. Distribuir: (tareas) allocate, (a domicilio) deliver. Give out (anunciar, emitir, distribuir, repartir algo). Delight/glee (regocijo). Categorically (rotundamente + flatly, roundly, emphatically). Flick (coletazo, capirotazo) through: hojear, leer superficialmente. Flippant (ligero, poco formal). Prosperous/thriving, flourishing. Confusing/blurred image. Failure/flop (fracaso). Follow up (poner en práctica) → follow through (llevar a cabo). Frustrate: (plan) thwart, (esperanzas) dash (una operación) foil + desbaratar planes. Discretion forbides (prohíbe, impide) me to repeat it. Forceful (vigoroso, enérgico). Foregoing (precedente, ya mencionado) =/= the result is a foregone (cantado, previsible, inevitable) conclusion (resultado). Forge (forjar, falsificar + fake, counterfeit). They are fake (falsos + false). Forcible (por la fuerza) reparation. He advanced me € 11. Pay in advance, a favourable result is anticipated, anticipate a solution, forestall (prevenir, impedir) criticism. Doubt/hesitate/ mistrust (desconfiar). Make up my mind between two cars. Fail as an actor, -- by five votes, (in one's duty): don't -- me! Without -- (sin falta) =/= the film was a flop (fracaso), the book fell flop (de golpe) on the table. A farce/absurd life. Farmyard (corral). Intrepid/daring/fearless. Decipher/decode a message. Fearsome/fearful (temible). Do your coat up (abróchate el abrigo) + fasten the belt (abrochar el cinturón) =/= tighten one's belt (ajustar_se_ el cinturón) =/= fast (ing): ayuno, V =/= fatten (engordar) pigs, ... =/= fake (falso, falsificar) =/= tempt the fate (suerte, destino), the fate which awaits him; resigned to one's fate; left (abandonado) to his fate =/= fad (manía, maña, moda pasajera)ish: maniático, mañoso =/= fade (apagarse, debilitarse, fundirse, desteñirse, marchitarse) → -- away: apagarse lentamente, irse consumiendo. Banquete (banquet, feast, dinner), (en bodas) wedding + reception. Fed up (harto). Why on earth didn't you ring me? A mouse caught in a trap. Fall into a trap → (en el juego): play fair, no cheating. Suplente: substitute teacher, covering doctor, substitute or reserve goalkeeper. Eliminar: (equipo/candidato) eliminate, (juego) get him out of game, (mancha, obstáculo) remove; eliminatoria: (torneo) qualifying round, (competición) qualifying competition. Realize (darse cuenta). The reunion is made up of four countries. The first volume covers (comprende...). Filling (empaste en odontología) + this dish is -- (llena). Finesse (sutileza, artimaña, diplomacia). Filthy (asqueroso) → -- hands, -- clothes, -- conditions, -- mind, -- temper (insoportable), -- weather, "-- rish". Firing (tiroteo), first-rate (excelente, de primera categoría). Fit in (adaptar) =/= fit out (acondicionar): -- -- premises (locales) for fashion shows (desfiles), -- -- the road network; a fit of laughter (ataque de risa). Flounder (debatirse, luchar; perder el hilo, quedarse sin saber qué hacer). Inflate the figures (cifras). Dotar: (proveer) provide, equip, (conceder derechos) grant, (finanzas) some money was allocated for prizes. Endowment: donación, don; dote, calidad → endowed with authority + the qualities for leadership, gift for painting, a school for gifted/endowed children. Entitle (autorizar) =/= enforceable (ejecutable) → enforce (hacer cumplir) the law, enforce sb on sth. Be lost/engrossed (absorto) in thought. Engaging: encantador, atractivo, =. Llano: (terreno) flat, (no inclinado) level, (lenguaje) simple. On the eve (víspera) of sth. Of medium height. How are things? So-so (regular + normal/usual). As a rule (por lo regular). Evenly: (movimiento, crecimiento, respiración) regularmente, (repartir) equitativamente. Evict (desahuciar). Aventajar: be ahead, (superar) excel, surpass. Excruciating (atroz, espantoso, terrible). Exposición: (arte) exhibition, (agriculture/flowers) show, (tema) presentation, (meteorología) exposure, (comercio) trade fair. Hazaña: my father's exploits, passing the exam was quite a feat. Prescindir: I can do without the computer, dispense with the details, my son disregards my advice. Anonymous (faceless). Let's face it (reconozcámoslo + recognize, admit). Joker/facetious/funny/cute (gracioso). Those savings mean a lot to us. It would mean investing more. He is about forty. As you may expect (esperar, suponer). Presumably (es de esperar) they have contacted them. Opposing (antónimos) groups. He has been sent (destinado) into the air force. Set aside your savings to pay... → destinatario (addressee). Be eaten up (consumido) with envy, eat up the miles (1609 m.), eat up electricity, jealousy is eating him up.

Don't tempt me! Capaz: who passed an aptitude test, suitable for this job, fit (físico) for military service. The doctor told me not to overdo (hacer esfuerzos). Enclosure: cercamiento, recinto. Things enclosed in the annex. Embellecer: beautify, embroider (bordar), make more beautiful. Embody (encarnar). Endure: perdurar, he endured (soportó) his illness with stoicism. Compromiso: commitment, engagement, awkward position (aprieto). Seducir: (sex) seduce, the idea appealed to me. Culto: enlighted, cultured; worship (adoración); personality cult. Enmity (enemistad). Heckle (interrumpir, molestar con cuestiones). A request for aid. Demands for the Prime Minister's resignation. Petition to reopen the swimming pool. Edgy = nervous. Inattentive/rude (desatento). Heighten: acrecentar, realzar, intensificar + intensify. Perspicacia (insight, shrewdness). Piercing: (olor, ojos, bala, frío...) penetrante, (dolor) punzante. Property (propiedades), the heir to the throne/fortune. Tone: the violin is not in -- (no armoniza) with the piano, the -- of the speech, the -- (tónica) of the market, a conciliatory tone =/= an outlook (vista, perspectiva, mentalidad) in tune (en sintonía con) with young people =/= tuneful (melodioso + melodious); -- in (afinar, (TV) sintonizar), be tuned in to sth (estar al corriente de algo); overstep the mark (subirse de tono). Subsoil (subsuelo) =/= underground (subterráneo). With subtitles (subtítulos) =/= subtly (sutilmente). Suburb (=, poor area). Subvención (=, grand, subsidy) =/= (de vejez) pension, (de matrimonio, inválido) allowance. Is the second in the line (sucesión) to the throne. The streets have got dirtier. The delicious (= + suculenta) grilled (a la parrilla) hake (merluza). Many men succumbed to her charms (encantos). We slogged our guts out (trabajamos mucho) to finish it in time. Sweaty (sudoriento), sweatshirt (sudadera). Half soles (medias suelas). Basic salary (meses)/wage (semanas). Knock sth down (echar algo al suelo). An odd (suelto) sock. Be at large (andar suelto). Toss: sacudida, tirada +Vs → we tossed (nos jugamos a cara y cruz) for it. Jammy/lucky (suertudo). Proof of their ability/aptitude → put on airs (darse aires de aptitud). Universal suffrage. Be under house (domiciliario) arrest. Go through hell (sufrir como un condenado). He suggested a plan to me. The seat belt holds you firmly. A strap (correa, tira)less (sin tirantes) dress → a strapless bra (sostén), watch strap, dog's leash. Paper clip (sujetapapeles). I clipped (=) the bills together (sujeté...) with staples (con grapas). Keep sth up (sostener). Abide (soportar, acatar) the laws of a country. The luggage was securely fastened to the roof rack. Suspicious looking character (sujeto). Do one's sums (hacer cuentas), do sums in one's head (hacer un cálculo mental), sums to do for homework, sum up (resumir), think a number, add ten & take away four. Debts amounting to several millions. Divide: (=), the road --s (se bifurca) into two lanes, (ganancias) split =/= dive: the submarine dived (se sumergió) → nosedive: (Ec...) bajar en picada, (popularidad, reputación) dar un bajón. I immersed myself in the subject. The supplying (suministradora) company. Submissive (sumiso). At most (a lo sumo) a project dependent (supeditado + subordinated) on... Four-star (super) petrol. Her post is a higher grade than mine. Barça was superior to his rival. Upper/middle class. Crop's overproduction. Supply teacher, I do supply teaching in primary school, a replacement for the director, replaceable (sustituible), interino (temporary, interim..., Med.: locum), a substitute goalkeeper. You stand in for me (me suples)? I don't want to have to beg him for forgiveness (perdón), I beg your pardon. The trip was a terrible ordeal (suplicio). As you may expect (como es de suponer). The suppression (=, abolición + =) of a demonstration of firearms control. Take sth for granted (sentado, descontado). Weep/ooze/suppurate (supurar). Southern regions. His brow/forehead (frente) was furrowed (surcada) with age =/= (tierra surcada: plowed through). The reservoir (pantano) supplies the surrounding (vecinos) villages. The firm is liable (susceptible) to be privatized. Annual/yearly subscription → fee/rate --, a monthly -- of 30 €, cancel a -- ↔ take out (abrir) a -- =/= (en una asociación) become member. The referee suspended the game, postponed the trial, the temporary postponement (aplazamiento) of the match, moratorium (suspensión) on payments, the project has been deferred (diferido, aplazado). Thinking about him makes her sigh (suspirar + he gave a -- of relief when he saw me). Grey matter (sustancia gris). Support (sustentar) a family/theory + the pillars -- the bridge. What do you base your suspicions on? He whispered (susurró) sth in my ear. Sutil (subtle) → sub<u>t</u>lety/fineness/delicacy (sutileza). Good willing (si Dios quiere), God almighty (Dios Todopoderoso). Inasmuch as (en tanto que, dado que, ya que) =/= insofar as (en la medida en que) =/= so long as (mientras) =/= so far as I know (que yo sepa). Nicotine poisoning (tabaquismo). Dar la tabarra (be a nuisance) → -- -- -- a alguien (pester sb.). Taberna: pub, bar, inn (+ posada). Plank (<u>t</u>abla de <u>m</u>adera) → a plank bridge =/= board (<u>t</u>. de <u>m</u>. pulida) =/= a slab: (de hormigón) bloque, (de piedra) losa, (de pan) pedazo, (de madera) tabla; (in a mortuary/morgue: depósito de cadáveres): plancha de mármol; chessboard (tablero de ajedrez), end in a stalemate (tablas). Wipe the slate (pizarra) clean. Tablado: (tarima) platform, (escenario) stage. The departure board (tablero de), notice board, drawing board, instrument panel (-- de mandos). The subject is taboo. A faultless (sin tacha) employee. Full of crossings outs (tachaduras) + cross out all the adjectives. She plugged (tapó con un taco) the hole. Swear word (palabrota). He gets muddled up (se hizo un taco, confundirse). (Sense of) touch (tacto) → recognise sb by touch =/= the feel of wool, the towels feel soft, lack of tact. He did very well out of (sacó tajada de). To such an extent that... As things stand (tal y como están las cosas). Pneumatic drill (taladradora mecánica). He is in a good mood (talante) reluctantly (de mala gana). Have talent for sth. What size (talla) shirt? He's small of stature. They bought an ebony (de ébano) carving (escultura + sculpture), carve a statue. Diamond cutting. Crystal (vidrio fino). Be tall enough/be tall up to (dar la talla), neither of the candidates was up to the job. A prominent (de talla) lawyer. A tight-waisted jacked. A girl with a slim (esbelta) figure. A joiner (carpintero de obra)/carpenter's workshop (taller), (de arte) studio, (reparaciones) garage, (talleres gráficos) printing works. Shoot (brote, coto de caza; tirar, disparar, firmar). Pay in cash/with a cheque (talón). Cheque book/receipt book (talonario) + I sold two books (talonarios) ofraffle (rifa, sorteo) tickets. Medium-sized/by size/a $ size, a Passport sized picture (fotos). The bottom/ top sheet (sábana). Shake (hacer tambalear) → the news shook Wall Street. The officials sifted (tamizaron) the data/the applications. Rubber (goma: de borrar, de bala...; caucho), -- stamp (tampón, sello,V) → I got/I was given the -- -- (visto bueno). I don't think she is so (tan) naïve. I wasn't expecting such an expensive present. Not even (ni tan siquiera). Spend as much as you can. I don't mind (tanto me da). So much the better/worse (tanto mejor/peor). Whether... or... (tanto si... como si...). His company is just a cover (tapadera) of shady (turbios, dudosos) deals. Cover a wound + wrap her up in a blanket. A lid on a saucepan (cazuela). Block sb's view (vista, opinión). Some tapas (=) for dinner. Build a wall round (tapiar). Tapices: (pared) tapestries, (maqueta) carpet, (sillas...) upholster. Openly (sin tapujos) ↔ be cagey (reservado, cauteloso). This film will be a box-office (taquilla) hit: golpe... éxito ↔ flop/failure (fracaso). A long time to reply. Get better (recuperarse). At the latest (a más tardar). Not to be long (no tardar). Se tarda... (it takes...). We are going to be late. Thankless task (tarea ingrata). Tarifas: (entrance, physician, membership ...) fee, (eléctricas, hotel) prices, reduced fares for the children, night rate, customs duties. A jar of honey/jam... Sand/hail/snow<u>storm</u>. Stormy weather/relationship. Templado: (clima) mild, (zona) temperate, (beber) of sober habits, drink in moderation, (alimento, bebida) lukewarm, (pers.) even tempered. Warm sth up ↔ cool sth down. His words have a calming effect. Seasonal (de temporada) vegetable. Caza (hunt), open season (temporada de caza). Temporada/un período determinado (season) =/= <u>in</u>determinado (period); temporal: (provisional) temporary, (tormenta) storm → weather the storm (campear el temporal). Keep sb from doing sth (impedir)... The new encroaching (usurpación) on our liberty. Rustle (susurro, crujido hacer susurrar, crujir; robar) up: preparar, improvisar. Keep sth. from sb (ocultar...). Lime (cal, lima) → limestone (piedra caliza). The nipples (pezones, tetinas) lightly (suavemente) puckered (arrugados, fruncidos). Trundle (empujar, tirar) up & down. Skittish (caprichoso, delicado). She was lying (tendido) on the settee (sofá) → settee bed (sofá cama). Hang up (cuelga) the washing (ropa), do the washing. Have a high opinion of sth/sb ↔ have no regards for... Tape (cinta) → --worm (tenía). In accordance with (a tenor del) art. 10... At the third attempt, the third age (edad). The oil stained (ensuciaba) the sea black. Ténue: (luz, sonrisa, sonido) faint, (color) pale, (brisa) light, (humo, niebla, tela) thin. A theoretical case =/= a theory exam. Activities for senior citizens/third age (pers. de la tercera edad). The festivities ended in tragedy. She went out as soon as she'd finished eating. We ended up laughing like sb. Get rid of the flies, the sugar has run out. The party's over, we closed the meeting. Our relationship is finished, have a happy ending. That's nonsense (tonterías)/rubbish/silly (bobas) things. Treat sb tenderly (with tenderness). Terraza: flat roof =/= balcony. His statement (testimonio) was decisive → the ruins are evidence of an ancient civilisation. Testify (dar testimonio) that... A reference book/number... A nervous tic. Have you been waiting long? How long have you studied? You'll understand in time (con el tiempo). In plenty (de sobras) time to do sth. For some time now (de algún tiempo para acá). Time is pressing (el tiempo apremia). In those (aquellos) days + in my times (época). It's been a long time since you... Spare (libre, disponible) time. Boutique (tienda de modas). Gift shop/store. I felt my way to the exit (encontré la salida a tientas). A tender (tierno) steak, at the tender age of five. Work the land. Return the computer to the upright position =/= stand up straight! (¡Ponte tieso!); sit with your back straight, so your hips (caderas) form right angles; try to keep your writing straight! → a crooked (torcido) tooth/nose. Leave sb speechless (mudo, estupefacto). Make a cut (dar un tijeretazo). He's been branded (tildado) a liar (de mentiroso). A time of darkness (tinieblas). An ink for drawing. I don't like vagueness (medias tintas). Inkpot + leave sth. out/unsaid (dejar algo en el tintero). Classify/typify (tipificar). What an ugly (feo, peligroso) guy (tipo)! This magazine has a big circulation. Lying (mentiroso). Dirt cheap pieces. This subject (asignatura) is dead easy. Throw away (desechar) an opportunity/rubbish. I dropped (dejé caer, lancé) all my shopping. Knock (golpe, choque,V) → -- into sth/sb (chocar con), -- over/down (tumbar una persona). Print (imprimir). Waste the money on clothes. The skirt is too tight round the waist. This car is not going at all well. Jump into the water =/= throw myself out of the window. A bullet wound in the head. The coach/carriage (carroza) was drawn by a pair of horses. There is a draught (cte. de aire, bocanada) from the window, draft/draught beer (cerveza de barril) =/= drought (sequía). Within range (a tiro) → come within range (ponerse a tiro). Know what's going on (por donde van los tiros). Tug (tirón,V; remolcar, arrastrar), give sb's hair a tug, I felt a -- in my sleeve, he yanked (arrancó de un tirón) the plug (tapón, enchufe...), move jerkily (coche: a tirones, ...). Pullet (pollita) muscle → muscly. He slept for ten hours solid (sin parar) + freeze -- (por completo). He died in the shoot-out (tiroteo)... We heard shooting (disparos). He wavered (titubeó, tambaleó, flaqueó) before shooting. Shaky (temblorosa) voice. Unhesitatingly (sin titubeo). Qualified staff required, academic qualification (título). The incumbent (titular) president. It was in the headlines (titulares) this morning. Get a degree in law. Baccalaureate: (inf.) lower examination, (sup.) higher certificate. Frame my degree certificate (título de licenciado). The necessary qualifications for the job. A letter sent in a private capacity (a título personal)/posthumously. I've strained (torcido) my ankle (tobillo). Still (afirmaciones e interrogaciones afirmativas): I'm still here; do you still live in London? Yet: (negaciones e interrogaciones negativas): they are not ripe yet, haven't they written the book yet? Oraciones comparativas: even → you are even more... I haven't had a rest today, we are trying to -- (descansar), have a -- (tomarse un respiro). A real (verdadero) genius, a real occasion. I'm really dirty/shattered (hecho polvo). He isn't totally (del todo) stupid. Todopoderoso: all-powerful. Wire: enrollar, dar cuerda. Wind up (recoger) the awning (toldo) if it rains. I can't bear (tolerar) people... I can't eat shellfish (mariscos). The taking (toma) of the city. The last feed is at ten. This story is a joke (tomadura de pelo). Took on (asumió, aceptó...) the form of a human being, take down sb's name/address. There you are: toma, aquí tienes (el cambio...). Take a few days off (d. libres). You shouldn't have taken it like that. He has got it in (entrado, recogido) for us. Take sth the wrong way. Haunt (aparecerse, lugar predilecto)ed: (lugar) embrujado =/= (pers.) bewitched. Hostage (reén). Implement: instrumento → a farm -- + llevar a cabo. Incarcerate. Innate/ inbred (innato). Conspicuous (llamativo, visible, destacado) ↔ inconspicuous (discreto, apenas visible). Exhaust: -- pipe (tubo de escape), be --ed (estar agotado), in depth/thorough (riguroso, a fondo). Aliciente/ incentivo (=, inducement). He indulges (permite, complace, satisface) his whim (caprichos) + she's taken a fancy (se ha encaprichado) to that dress. Innermost (más íntimo, más recóndito) → in your -- thoughts. Don't eat so fast or you'll choke (te atragantarás), he got a fish bone (espina) stuck in his throat (se atragantó con...), I can't stand this subject (esta asignatura se me atraganta).The rigging (tongo) of the elections caused quite a stir (mover, azizañar, despertar, aquí: fue muy sonado). A general mood (tónica) of cautious (=, relativo, prudente) optimism. I like all shades (tonod) of brown. Are you flirting (coqueteando, tonteando) with me? We're always arguing (discutiendo, exponiendo) about silly (tontas, ridículas) things. Talk nonsense (tonterías) =/= stop messing about/around (hacer travesuras). The wound isn't serious, you'll soon be alright. They quietly (con silencio, discretamente: discreetly) got their hands on a fortune. His reply amazed us (nos asombró). Act the fool, act dumb (bobo, mudo). I bumped into (tope con) my cousin, they bumped into each other in the street. An age limit (tope) for the competitors. We have been working flat out (a tope) for the last three months. I'm to my eyes (tope) at/with work. He filled the glasses to the brim (tope). Give three taps (golpes) on the wall. A hint (indicio) of irony in his words. Put the finished touch (toque). Give me a call before you leave. Peal (repique) of bells. I hurt my finger mending (arreglando) my bike. I hurt my neck playing rugby. The youngest woman bullfighter in Spain. A liberal who turned into a dictator. A basketball tournament (torneo). The press crowded round the player. Take the bull (toro) by the horns. You were really tactless mentioning... Contact (avisen) the control tower, (Electr.) pylon, (Telec.) mast, watchtower. Bloodstream (torrente). Smack (bofetada,V). Dike (lesbiana + =). Dove (paloma) → turtledove (tórtola). Tortuga: (tierra) tortoise, (marina) turtle. The smoke makes me cough. You are touchy (susceptible) today. Tan yourself! (¡Tuéstese al sol!). Drug addiction (toxicomanía). Lose your job → be out of work. A pig of a job (un trabajo de negros). Teamwork/shiftwork (trabajo en equipo). Hard labour (trabajos forzados). The news has reassured (tranquilizado) the police. He was waiting quietly, I live in a quiet area =/= calm down, please, he's so laid-back (parsimonioso, relajado, tranquilo) he makes me nervous. He failed, but she didn't seem bothered (se quedó tan tranquilo). Sth has passed since.., with the passing of time. In the course (transcurso) of the play (obra) the actor makes six appearances on stage. The police questioned (preguntó) the passers-by (transeúntes). The operation turned her into a beauty. Convert the power of wind into energy. Convert the garage into a gym. Score from a penalty. He's very compromised, accommodating (transigente, tolerante)/soft with the children. See through the blouse. An insect's transparent wing. Sudar: (pers.) perspiration/sweating =/= Bot.: transpiration (=). Blood carries oxygen round (por todo) the body. Carrier (transportista) → aircraft --, (Med.) portador. A street that crosses (es transversal a) the avenue. A cloth for polishing shoes. Wipe the table with a damp cloth. Make sb feel really small (como un trapo). My bottom (trasero) hurts me (me duele) from riding my bike, get up (levanta) your backside (trasero). The marchandise is valways coming around (vienen, llegan + volver en sí, pasársele el cabreo) in this factory + with all the rushing about/around (el correr de acá paras allá) I forgot... Move (trasladar) my things to... The opening date (inauguración) was moved to April, he moved to the number three =/= his transfer of players/to the other department/ to the University. A translucid (=) glass screen. The document has been misled(traspapelado). The bullet went through his liver; go through the sound barrier. The wine has soaked through the tablecloth. Go beyond the bounds (lím.) of credibility. He's going to have a kidney transplant. The boy is always up to mischief (hacer trastadas). I banged (dí un trastazo, golpeé) into the door. A lamp-post (farola). The new management (dirección) has ruined the business. The injury ruined her hopes. Trastero (boxroom). Take your things out of the sitting room (salón).

Pair up (liar, emparejar) your belongings. They're fighting (se tiran los trastos por la cabeza). He is upset, a gastric disorder has mentally deranged/disturbed (trastornado) him. All the suffering drives her out of her mind, the smoke will drive them out. This woman has driven him crazy (enamorado, lo sacó de quicio) =/= she is going crazy with so much work to do. Compensate for any inconvenience (todos los trastornos). The strike has seriously disrupted the international flights. White slave trade (trata de blancas). A medical treatise (tratado). Your treatment of the subject was very sound (acertado). Graphics & data processing. Treat this as if it were your own. The film is about (trata) show (del espectáculo) business. Deal with all kinds of plants, in my job I deal with... Try to get there in time. Treatment for an allergy. That cut (herida, corte) isn't getting any better. They haven't spoken to each other. Treat sb as an equal (de tú a tú). How do you address (tratas) the new manager? Call sb tú/Ud. They've always called each other Ud, be in familiar terms (tutearse). Treat sb well/badly. Ill-treatment (malos tratos). Childhood traumas. He got the job through his parents. He was running through (escapó por) the wood. Field of vision (campo visual). Transvestite (travesti). They are only childish pranks (bromas, travesuras). Most of the journey (trayecto). It's a very pretty (pintoresca) route. The trajectory of a missile/rocket. The direction your career is taking. A dangerous stretch (trecho). Fair: justo, bello, limpio, feria → It's a fair way from here to the school. A terrible blow (disgusto)/pain. This piece of news gives me tremendous pleasure. The play (obra) was a tremendous success. He is a real stunner: (pers.) estupenda, (cosa) maravillosa. Miss the boat/bus. Express/fast/slow/goods/local (cercanías)/high speed/through (directo) train travel. A climbing (trepadora) plant. I've got stand (tribuna) tickets. The court (tribunal) has found/ruled (fallado) in my favour. Examining board (tabla, junta, consejo; hospedar, abordar). Direct/indirect taxation. Trillion: un millón de billones. The police picked him up in the underground. Sledge/sleigh (pequeño/gran trineo) =/= sleight of hands (prestidigitación, juegos de manos...). Triple jump (salto). Nine is three times three. We've trebled our profits. Tripod (trípode), triptych (tríptico), triplet (trillizo). Crew men (tripulantes). A naturally sad & gloomy (deprimida) person → sadness (tristeza) + it makes me sad. Melancholy/sadness (melancolía). Waste disposal (deshacerse) unit: triturador de basuras. The winning (triunfador) film. He emerged triumphant. We shouldn't gloat (over sth.): no deberíamos regocijarnos de... The triumph of engineering. Trophy (trofeo). Give yourself a nasty knock (trompazo). It's thundering. Ascend the throne. A troop of schoolchildren. I stumbled/tripped (tropecé) & fell. We've encountered/come up against (topado con, enfrentado a) serious difficulties. Make the same mistake twice. Some chopped (molido) ham (jamón). This slip-up (equivocación) means that we'll lose millions. Globe-trotter (trotamundos). Troubadour (trobador). Several extracts (trozos sueltos) of a novel. Truffle (trufa). A pipe (tubería) has burst (reventado). That cheese stinks (hace tufo). He lurched (tambaleaba) from one crisis to another. Car wash: túnel de lavado. Tour (hacer turismo) around Africa. We haven't had any news lately. Be in the (last) throes (agonía, coletazos, pleno camino de) → America is in the -- of rebalancing foreign policy towards Asia. What a cheek! (¡Qué cara!). Be involved (implicado, involucrado) with sb. The aims (objetivos) that unite us. The wonders (maravillas) of the Universe. Quite a few (más de uno) ↔ no one (ni uno) survived. I haven't got money left (no me queda un céntimo). One on top of the other → muchos: on top of each other. Put cream (pomada) on a cut. Mancha: spot, mark, stain, (borrón) blot, smear → you've smeared (manchado, difamado,V) mud all over. They bribed (sobornaron) him to turn a blind eye (vista gorda). Grease sth (manchar con aceite, grasa). An asbestos (uralita) roof. Planning (urbanismo, planificación) → planner. Infringement (violación) of the planning laws. Develop: desarrollar, fomentar, urbanizar ↔ underdeveloped land. In case of emergency (emergencia, urgencia + urgency) → the emergency department (sala de urgencias). Second - hand clothes/shoes → shoes worn out (gastadas por el uso). When it was my turn to speak. Ever since I can remember (desde que tengo uso de razón). I'm not local (de aquí) but you are. Bemoan (lamentar) → he --ed his fate (suerte). Let's empty (out) the box (caja, arca, cofre). He drained his glass in one gulp (trago). The police cleared (despejó, aclaró) the premises (locales). Render sth meaningless (volver algo sin sentido). Walking unsteadily (tembloroso, parpadeante, vacilante). There is a gap in the law. A void in my life. The car went over the cliff (acantilado, precipicio). Be starving (hambriento). Wander around (vagabundear sin rumbo fijo). Be useless/worthless (no valer para nada). We'll meet at seve. Be worth his weight in gold. Sorry for repeating myself (valga la redundancia). She's proved her worth (valía). A person of great worth + a very valuable job (labor). You're very valiant/courageous/brave (valiente) + act tough (fuerte, duro): hacerse el valiente. Diplomatic bag (valija). Fence (valla en las casas) =/= barrier (vallas en las obras). Boarding pass (tarjeta de embarque). Attach importance (valor) to sth. The film has lost nothing with the passage of the time. The valuation of a flat. Boast about (vanagloriarse de) his artistic talent. A vain attempt/hope, empty promise, pointless (inútil, inmotivado). I like steamed (al vapor) vegetables. Cowherd (vaquero/a), cowgirl, cowboy. Variety shows are back in fashion. Motley (con muchos colores, variopinto: multiforme, diverso). Magic wand (varita mágica). Sailing ship (velero) → under full sail (a toda vela), he Works flat out (trabaja a toda vela), as quick as a flash (a toda vela + at top speed). Light ↔ put out a candle. Get up (coger) speed. Speedometer (velocímetro). Be in the mood (vena) for doing sth. He defeated his rival easily. I was overcome with sleep. The visiting team won. Plazo: within the specified (previsto) period, delivery date, the March installment (cuota, plazo) + buy/hire/purchase in installments. I don't give up (me doy por vencido) easily.They blindfolded me (me vendaron los ojos). For sale = to be sold (se vende). She likes hot cakes (churros). Poisonous (venenoso). Take revenge (vengarse). Improve in the coming (venideros) years. Tragedy came when we least expected it. Don't come to me with excuses. Have happy memories of sb =/= reminiscences of life 50 years ago. It amounts to the same thing (es igual, viene a ser lo mismo). Mail order (demanda por correo electrónico). The truth hurts (duele). The true (verdadera) history, it was a real (verdadero) pleasure. Rechazar: (Med., propuesta, invitación) rejection, (enmienda) defeat, (obligación, trabajo) turn down, (ataque) repel/repulse. Don't pick them, they are not ripe (maduros) yet. Rather: you need to practice, you're still rather (más bien) inexperienced; I'd – walk than... (prefiero andar a...), you'd go back to your home town. Bloodthirsty (sanguíneo). Executioner (verdugo). How embarrassing (embarazoso) → speaking in public makes me embarrassed. What a shame! Shameless, you have no shame! He was ashamed to admit it. He was grieved (apenado + saddened). Vet (revisar, examinar), checking/testing (verificación) → they checked the brakes. The thief jumped over the iron railings (verjas). Viajante: commercial traveller, sales man/woman; rep (representante). Have a right of veto ↔ lift the veto, he vetoed (rechazó) the idea. Take legal action. Free hand to hire new staff. Feasibility study. The accident left three deads + lifeless. The cost of living. A matter of life or death. At the death door (entre vida y muerte). Loose living (mala vida). He survived the explosion. Clairvoyant (vidente). Stained glass (de colores) window, pane (para puertas y ventanas). Carry the can (pagar los vasos rotos). Nightwatchman. Despreciable: vile, (pers.) despicable, nefarious (=, vil, malvado). Cruet (vinagreras). Bond (vínculo) of friendship, blood tie (vínculo de parentesco). Wine grower, wineyard (viña), water down the wine. Rapist (pers.: violador, =) =/= house breaking (invasión, robo). A sudden swerve (viraje repentino) of the car to avoid the rock. They play tennis really well (una virguería + amazing, fantastic). Your greatest virtue. A delightful (agradable) visit. Visiting hours. The visiting team. I'm longing (suspiro, tengo muchas ganas) to go to the islet/small island (islote) =/= the inland (el interior)/island (isla), en la calle (refugio) =/= inlet (ensenada, entrada) =/= inlet pipe (tubo de entrada) ↔ waste pipe. Left it ready (preparado) the day before. Be long-sighted (vista cansada), the sight (visión) of his eyes, I know her by sight, the view from the room has a good sight, a forward looking (visionaria) chairmanship (presidencia), a very far-sighted (mucha vista) politician ↔ political myopia/shortsightedness (falta de perspicacia). In the light of (a la vista de) what happened. With a view to... Not take the eyes off... (de encima...). I looked round to see if I was being followed. Have a look (echar un vistazo). Apparently (por lo visto). Bright (vistoso, brillante). Bed: lecho del río; oyster bed (vivero), vivero de peces: hatchery. Housing (vivienda). Know what they live on (de que viven), his work comes into effect/force, her work lives on (está en vigor). Their boss doesn't give them any peace (no los deja vivir). I've been worried sick (angustiado + distressed, anxious, worried) since he robbed me. Have a nice life (vivir bien). Be comfortable (vivir con desahogo) + make o.s. -- (ponerse cómodo). Live in a dream world (de ilusiones). Live on the income from your investment (de renta). Scrape (raspar, aprieto) a living: vivir muy justo. Live & learn (vivir para ver). Live beyond your means (possibilities). Verbal agreement. They operated on her without anaesthetic. Be the embodiment/incarnation (vivo ejemplo) of sth. Have a quick temper (genio vivo). Yell (grito, chillido, vociferar...). Take the wheel (ponerse al volante). The plane was flying very high. She vanished (ha desaparecido). Eat & drink as much as you like (a voluntad). Goodwill (buena voluntad). Be very determined (decidido) to. Iron will (voluntad de hierro). She volunteered (se ofreció volunaria) to prepare the party. Turn the mattress over (volcar el colchón), turn the garment (prenda) inside out. This chemical (producto) turns paper blue. He turned to me with tears in his eyes. He was sick over his jacket. Hurl (arrojar, lanzar) insults → -- o.s. at (avalancharse sobre) sb/sth, -- himself into his arms, --ed to the ground by the explosion, -- along (ir a toda velocidad), the car hurled past. Say sth in a loud/quiet (silenciosa, tranquila) voice. Give your brother a shout (pégale un grito para que venga). Raise your voice. In a low (media) voice. They are always shouting & arguing. A shout of protest (un grito de protesta). We have to make ourselves heard, even if we have to shout. The idea was going round in my head, he goes round (se pasea por allí) in a Rolls, go round barefoot/in torn jeans (vaqueros), there is a bug (virus, chinche, micrófono oculto, rumor) going round (dando vueltas). Is there enough food to go round (ir tirando)? Have no say (ni voz ni voto). Be quiet! (¡Calla!). Be hoarse (tener la voz ronca). Madrid-London flight. The sparrow & the swallow flew away (emprendieron el vuelo). He caught on immediately (lo cogió al vuelo). A high-flying (de alto nivel) executive. Direct/non-stop/low-level/scheduled (regular) flight. Put turn-ups (vueltas) on those trousers =/= they did three laps (vueltas) at the track (pista), do the lap of honour. The first round of the elections. We stopped in Madrid on our way back. There's an illustration overleaf (a vuelta de página). Summer is just round the corner (a la vuelta de la esquina). Go round sth. (dar la vuelta alrededor de algo) → go round the world (dar la vuelta al mundo), go round the (bull) ring: dar vuelta al ruedo (en la plaza de toros). Turn the record (disco) over. I always turn the key twice. Keep stirring (dando vueltas a) the béchamel or it'll stick. You're worrying too much about it. He turned round (dio media vuelta) & went off (se fue, salió, se apagó). I'll drop in (pasaré por tu casa) this evening. I'll arrive early. Straight away (desde ya). It's about time you called (que llames). That's quite enough (ya está bien). Yacht (yate). Grandad (yayo). Mare (yegua), burro/a: donkey =/= stupid/dumb. Deshabitado: (edificio) empty, vacant, (zona, ciudad) uninhabited. We must be quiet (callados). Everybody except me. If I were you... Ana doesn't want to go but I do. I practise yoga in the mornings. Low-fat (desnatado) yoghourt. Token: vale, ficha; muestra de apreciación, señal → as a token of friendship; this is just a small -- of your appreciation (agradecimiento). Solera: (vino) vintage wine, (país) a country with a long-established tradition, (barrio) it's a typically Spanish quartier. Social network ablaze (resplandece, en llamas). China' once drab (apagada, monótona, gris) and Mao-suited (apropiado, adaptado) interior. Muscle in on sth.: meterse por la fuerza (en el mercado, etc.). A modern shopping mall (centro comercial) has sprung up (brotado) → go shopping. In all likelihood China has just taken Japan to become the World's second-biggest consumer economy. It's striking (chocante, sorprendente) how much China spends. Local brands assortment (surtidos) of toothpaste, cosmetics, juices...; a surge (oleada) of people. Hard to pin down (concretar, identificar) to a strong brand loyalty (=, fidelidad), he pinned me down (me sujetó) by my wrists, I was pinned down (atrapado) by a fallen tree. A first/prime mover (promotor + =) advantage. The number of outbound (dirigidos hacia el exterior) Chinese tourists. Wry (irónicas) observations. The crowd even booed (abucheaba) them. Huge dust storms. The book angered (provocó la ira de) many farm owners. The acceptance speech for the Nobel prize. The valley was carpeted (enmoquetada, alfombrada) with spring flowers. Dry years, when the streams (corrientes) stopped & the earth cracked (se agrietó) =/= creaky/ squeaky (chirriante) =/= scrawl/scribble (garabatear)

=/= squiggle (garabato, retorcerse). Gullible (crédulo). The grass was scare & the dry wind blew dust down the valley. A machine for digging wells. He talked about the world outside the valley. He delivered (entregó) all of his own children. More people arrived penniless. Holding his head under the shallow (superficial) water of a muddy pool until he drowned (se ahogara). Express my sorrow. He did not punish him anymore. Mister's voice rose, he drove his fist (puño) into Adam's stomach. Once (antes, una vez) he swung (se balanceó) wildly at him. He heard rapid footsteps (pisadas) on the road. He pushed himself onto his knees. He grabbed (agarró) Adam by the arm & squeezed (apretó) it hard. Make sb angry (enfadar a alguien) → he got angry & he picked up his shotgun (escopeta), it was loaded (cargada). A closeness (fidelidad, proximidad...) grew that neither of them could have imagined. A sinless (inocente) boy. Pleasant pers., ease to live with. Overestimate one's strength. Engañar: trick/deceive/mislead sb about/over... He evaded, eluded the guards. Daily (cotidiano) =/= dairy (lechería/vaquería, lácteo). Approach the age with misgivings (dudas, recelos), -- of a scheme (proyecto, plan). Inquietud (worry, anxiety, concern, interest). Recoger: (levantar) pick up off the floor; clear the table, (dinero, firmas, deberes) collect, (trigo) harvest, gather/take in, (fruta) pick, harvest. Welfare office, tax office, customs desk, research (de estudios) consultancy, lost property office, employment agency, tobacconist shop, polling station. Paseo: walk, stroll + (en coche) drive, (en bici o a caballo) ride. Launderette (lavadora automática). Cake shop (pastelería). Tailor (sastre) → ladies' --. Overload (sobrecarga). Main lines (grandes líneas del tren). The roadwork is disrupted (interrumpido), the bus service has been suspended =/= temporary breakdown (en las negociaciones). Ahogarse: (en agua) drown, (estrangular) strangle, (sofoco en motines) stifle, a baby suffocated in its sheets, (espina, humo) choke + estárter), (fuego, llamas) smother + asfixiar. Airstream, air strike (ataque aéreo). Way out/exit (salida en edificios) =/= departure (en el transporte). You go first, stand in front (ponte delante), the bagpipers (gaiteros) are at the front, our house has a park opposite. Out of date/expired. Connection (correspondencia de tren, conexión/contacto de amistades) → I'll use my --s. Withdraw one's confidence. At once/right away/immediately. They are similar in character. Enjoy your meal! You too! A serious (grave) pb./offence (delito, falta, agravio, ofensa)/risk/illness/injury. Cementerio: (iglesia) graveyard, (municipal) cemetery. Become complicated, complex operation, complications during the labour. The piano sounds great (de maravilla, estupendo, genial). Ascender: rise, ascend ↔ descender: descend, the plane came down, be descended from. Full: (hotel) completo... =/= the complete works of Oscar Wilde. Medida: (unidad) measure → a glass as a measure + medición; measurement/measuring. Bannings (prohibiciones). Daily phrases (locuciones cotidianas). Price includes delivery; payable on delivery. Pull the alarm. Release the brake. Consignment (envío, remesa) → on --: en consignación). Make inquiries (buscar informaciones, investigar). Estar en: (pers.) stay, (agua, nieve) lie. Withdraw one's confidence in sb. Bellboy (botones) =/= waiter (camarero) =/= barman (el de barra). He was standing outside the house, stand waiting (esperar de pie). The wheels sank into the puddle/pool (charco). Young men never listen to their older brothers. I can't stay longer + if you want to dance, you can stay with us the saint's day (onomástico) =/= birthday. Sweet potatoes (boniatos). They arrived earlier than she usually does. He behaved badly (malamente). He left the house at six & has not come/returned yet. You are much better this year, even if you are a year older. Chapeau! (bravo!, well done!). I have a dinner appointment. I have to spend the day with him. He's Tina's bodyguard. Take these diamonds & think of me. He tried to kiss me but I moved away/stood aside (me aparté, me mudé). His shoulders were bent like an old man's. Some evil (malo, mal) I have done =/= devil (demonio). He was clever, difficult to trap (atrapar). He takes him back to the city. She folded (dobló) the (news) paper, the wings fold hydraulically, fold your arms (crúzate de brazos), fold away (plegar/doblar y guardar), a folding chair/table/bed. He pushed her sunhat back. She crushed (aplastó) them. He beats you? (¿Os pega?). He supplied (suministró) her... Their greediness (codicia) & cruelty, kindly (amablemente), kindness (amabilidad) & generosity. All novels, all poetry are built on the never-ending contest in ourselves between good & evil. They raised (criaron) nine children. California, the setting (marco, escenario) for his novels/conferences... An eventful (memorable, lleno de incidentes, crucial) period & many of the characters (personajes)... + it takes character (hace necesario tener --) to to that, a suspicious -- (tipo), the main -- (protagonista). He is eventually (al final) affected by jealousy =/= actually/in reality. A flat next to (junto a) the high street. A street off (que sale de) the square, they were driven off their land. Young people are sent away to fight. A timeless (eternal) question. Jealousy between the pairs of brothers (Cain & Abel). I was pretending to be someone else. I have to enter too early, without being seen. Tourists from wherever (donde sea) + sit wherever you like, whenever possible. You are not a little girl anymore. My mind is upside down (al revés, sin orden, trastornada). They have turned the whole house upside down (revuelta), stop fidgeting! (¡Deja de moverte tan nervioso!). The penalty is thirty years in prison =/= sorrow, pity. A film starring (protagonizando) James as Carl, a film starred by him, he has starred many films. After the war ended the country recovered & settlers moved west. He studied at Stanford but left without graduating & when he began a career as a writer he worked on ranches. Growing awareness (conciencia) of a young boy. Margen: (río) bank, see marginal notes, -- of error. Troublesome (molesto, penoso, fatigante). The information in his manual is believed to be accurate (exacta). Artículos: ítems, goods → knitted goods (géneros de punto), the itemize (desglose, detalle, enumeración,Vs) of a bill. Recycle bin tasks (tareas de la papelera de reciclaje) → empty the recycle bin. It floats faced down on the water. Then he lost consciousness. She didn't care what he did. With electricity running through his body. He looks like someone else. Did you see anybody else? He would do whatever she wanted. Problems can be left behind + leave sth aside/to one side. The mouse was caught (atrapada) in the trap (trampa). He was an only child. Leave our girls alone. Balancing (equilibrando) mind, body & spirit. A simple (sencilla) meal. Hernia (rupture) → rupture o.s. (herniarse). If you were married to an English man... She takes care (se cuida) of them. He swam back to the shores. Two wild cats came down & ran up to the mountains. Put the fruit to dry on the sun. I dropped the corn onto the sun. I saw sth that made me feel ill. Then he fell asleep. My hair is curly (erizado). She put their hands together & pretended to pray. He arranged (arregló, ordenó, planeó...) the murder of... Take the diamonds & think of me. Each of his marriages have followed the same patron (patrón; mecenas de arte....). Force the lock. It is useless (inservible, inútil...) to continue. Next term (mandato... sesión + session). If I fail my English test... Do you believe in ghosts? Ghost (escribir para) sb's book/speech. I'm sorry (lo siento) for being late. From morning to/till night. Go to hell! (¡Vete al diablo!). When it rains, the buses are crowded, the children are bussed to school. I think about you. Is it handmade? I always go away (fuera) at weekends. I wash my hair once a week. He lost consciousness. Nothing but work. Marco awoke & met again with Mª at the river. They understand each other. Slowly but surely. Lo acompaño en el sentimiento: my commiserations; it's a pity, he was...; please, accept my condolences. Desk (escritorio) + -- clerk (recepcionista).

Desktop publishing (autoedición). He shouted with relief (alivio). I just came up to... (sólo he subido para...). Councilman (concejal), consul (=). I beg your pardon, I'll make (haré) what you beg (pidas) to get in (entrar) here. Saying aloud (en voz alta) =/= a lonely (solitario) man. Speak from memory (de memoria). Faithful (fiel) to the memory of her husband. Fond (tiernas) memories of childhood. In his drive back. Could you wait a little while? The way your body stands (como se te ve). I never thought of you going (que te marcharas). The water was pleasant/nice (agradable). They climbed up out of the river/window. Light (iluminar) up the top of his head (por encima de su cabeza). The squareness (cuadratura) of Adam's jaw (mandíbula). Under the watchful eye of (bajo la atenta mirada de). He wanted to think of sth else. Why would he want to run away (marcharse)? Put away (aparte). Get lost (desorientarse). I was misled (conducido al error) by his instructions. Utmost: the -- (mayor) satisfaction for years to come, with the -- care (cuidado); with the ease (con facilidad). Hooter (bocina (+ horn). Troubleshooters: investigadores de conflictos laborales y empresa. Adjust the forward tilt (inclinación) of the seat. Use footrest to distribute your weight evenly (regularmente) & to relieve (aliviar) the pressure on the back of your thighs (muslos). Use a pillow (almohada) or cushion (cojín) to provide extra back support. Reach the mouse without stretching. Avoid discomfort (incomodidad) & injury (herirse, lastimarse) from repetitive strain (tensión, tirantez). The rope broke under the strain. I have no money with me/over = I'm run out. They were tired _of_ waiting. She is good at Math, but not at languages. Bill: (billete) → a $ -, pay your bill (cuenta, factura); cartel, anuncio; proyecto de ley. Run/get away from sth/ sb (huir de, escaparse de). He was hungry, but he listened to me easily patiently, =). He fought as a mad (menos loco que fool: en fool hay motivos para "encerrarlo"). Both players are vulnerable. He used to go to the theater. I have to (el "have" es para cuando hay mucha obligación) think of the future. You enjoy (disfrutas) a lot because... I haven't seen you for a long time. You have not finished yet. He is not Spanish but I am. Visit with a guide. We watch TV. I spent a very good time there (lo pasé bien allí). Twins (gemelos) → twin towers. Cherry (cereza), tulip, lily (lirio). You will sin (tú pecarás). Coffee maker (cafetera). The translations were fairly (justasmente, verdaderamente + bastante) close (próximas, casi iguales, minuciosas, estrictas). Draughtsman/draftsman (dibujante), commercial artist (dibujante publicitario). He leaned forward. Four of them met (se encontraron). He was ahead of me, our team was -- (llevaba la delantera). I guess it's funny (gracioso). Fresh (majas) women of the "whorehouse" have not time to enjoy. I have connections (soy un enchufado). Deep (sumido, hasta arriba) in a sticky (pegajoso) mud. Shaky (tembloroso). He said awkwardly (inoportunamente, incómodamente, torpemente). They were lean (flacos) & spotted (con manchas). His feets had thickened (se habían hinchado). The right-hand drawer (cajón, dibujante). Lo taché (I crossed it out from) de la lista (list). I was used to it. They were getting ready to celebrate... He made the other students laugh. I wouldn't worry if..., I shouldn't wonder (no me sorprendería), he lives at home, but I don't. + He doesn't drive the car, but I do. Does your boyfriend love you? I'm afraid he doesn't. What do you do in the evening (al atardecer)? Usually I go walking/for a walk. Do you think that the plane will be late? Pronóstico: prediction, forecast, (Med.) prognosis. Perversely (sin lógica, tercamente). Hang by a thread (pender de un hilo). Secretive (reservado) about our survival. There's nohurry (prisa), hurriedly (rápidamente) I said... A long haul between A and B. He managed it somehow (de una u otra manera). He was thankful (agradecido) to be alive + I was very thankful (me felicito) that he hadn't seen me. Tie (atar, amarrar) /tighten (tensar, apretar) them together with a rope. Put two & two together (atar los cabos). Open ground without trees. Opening: (ceremonia) inaugural, (pared) brecha, (árboles, nubes) claro; comienzo. Make pots (ollas, tiestos, tarros...) to keep in my food. You must take me back to England. Write down (anotar) my feelings. Meet me at the bridge. You are no longer my enemy. Kindly leave us alone. A lucky escape from death. Cave (rupestre) painting, cave dweller (cavernícola). A lovely (precioso) time. Useless (ineptas) ruins. Soon afterwards (poco después). Sum sth up (resumir) → it can be --ed-- in one word: rubbish! Turn off: (an appliance: aparato) desenchufar, (máquina) parar =/= bajar (T., volumen, calor): turn down. We spoke about the love we felt for each other. I will no longer keep the secret. I shouldn't wonder (no me sorprendería). Tied (atado) to a post (estaca, palo). From then on... I entered the house through the front door. Forming a U-shape. We reached the top of the road. The CNN (Cable News Network) kept me informed. The light bothers me. I almost cried. During the questioning (interrogatorio, cuestionamiento). Tape: (ropa, cassette) cinta → a blank (virgen) --, tape recording, record one's voice on tape (cinta). A tearful (con lloriqueo, triste) conversation. He had to pretend to ove her. He felt a little sorry (pena) for her, I'm sorry (lo siento) =/= I had a worry (preocupación) =/= sadness/sorrow (tristeza). He wants me to be his wife. He didn't behave as one (of a good family...). Badly burnt. He lives at number three. We walked through the night. An ambulance came & took the body away. Baggage in the boot & on the roof of the car. She was staying alone. He held her father's arms & said stop! There was going to be a flood (inundación) → the river goes higher & higher. Her business was getting better. He isn't getting any younger. They fell in love with her. We walked down through the garden to the river. You are so much older than me. My father wants me to become... I got in through a hole on the side. I ran with her down to the shore. We must leave for England today. We need to think of a plan. His success was largely (en gran parte) due to luck. He was someway/somehow (de algún modo) away from the Queen. Keep away from him! He had a lucky escape from death. Pum! Three soldiers dropped (cayeron) to the ground. Torch: antorcha → the Olympic -- + lámpara de bolsillo =/= lamp (l. de techo/mesa). All the walls (muros, murallas) were broken down. They took a long time (tardaron) to reply. Fool about/around (perder el tiempo). I believe in... The house he has rented. He was in no hurry to leave. No crime has been penalized. He was good at his job. He got a blood rush to his face. They were getting ready to celebrate... When he fell asleep he was troubled by dreams. Get it down to the sea... He will inherit my money. Without resorting (centro de vacaciones, recurso + options, resources) to violence. He felt ashamed. He answered at the first ring of the phone. People were waiting in line to get into. It was getting dark/late. Sent to prison for life. It improved the view of the house. I was away for three hours. Men & women alike (tanto hombres como mujeres) + they are very -- (se parecen mucho), think -- =/= he is likely (probable) to keep his promises. Shit (mierda) → we are in the -- (estamos jodidos), she's full of -- (es un mentiroso de --), no --! (¡No jodas!) They share the money between them, a secret shared among us. The waiter brought us the bill. Reduce the costs/the expenses (gastos). The murderer never confessed. Continue/go on making noise. Have you found the apartment you liked? I'm going to finish at (alrededor de) seven. Anybody who is homeless. What else can you say? I thought of my parents. All was instant: -- noodles, -- coffee, etcetera. Split up: (miembros) separarse, (multitud) dispersarse, (re) partir. I need to be on my own (estar solo). He lives alone/on his own + you're on your own from now on (en adelante te las arreglas por tu cuenta). The security guard let me in. Nearby their home to do some chopings; we go to a nearby restaurant. They were fully involved. He ran out of the house ←→ he came in &

fell to the ground. In the office people run in & out. Thirsty for revenge. The head & everything inside it. He stayed away from towns for a while. People trust me. They are angry (muy enfadados)/annoyed (en menor grado: enfadados) with me. He was good at poetry. Taxis are quicker. Don't send me away from you. When the sun comes up. He did extra well in the written exam. He's staying in Plaza hotel. In the subway (paso subterráneo) station. Climb over a wall/to power. Move the book onto the second shelf. The crowd ran onto the pitch (campo de Sp.). She st<u>ee</u>red me (me condujo) towards the bar =/= stir: mover, remover, estimular (→ --ed by the star), provocar, despertar...) =/= rummage (remover papeles, rebuscar en bolsillos/armarios/cosas viejas) =/= they turned the house upside down. They climb up towards the top of the hill. Do/wash the dishes; my favourite --. She peered out (miró afuera) through a slit (ranura) in the curtains. I lay in my sleeping bag =/= two sacks of corn. It's dangerous → he will get hurt. Harsh (áspero, duro; riguroso, severo, violento) → harshness (aspereza, severidad...). A deep voice. Leave me alone!, I drove through the dark. At work everything was grey (gris, sombrío). I left school early. This is our country, not theirs. I went to your flat when you were away. It's my duty to... An anxious (de inquietud/preocupación) moment. It was written in the teacher's own handwriting. A close friend of... He wanted to make her his wife. He makes me stand in front of the picture. Denso: (nube/líquido) thick, (bosque) dense, (pasta) stiff, (discurso, película) dense, weighty. My whole body froze with fear. His blood is black as if he had been beaten (batido + derrotado). I will join you there. We gave lectures on the street. He made the other students laugh. How had they found each other? Give the revolutionary support. Man of principles. A sleepless night =/= dreamless. There was no one around (allí). A depressed region. Awful: (horrible, atroz, espantoso) accident/weather... Badly: he did -- (mal) in his exams, he was --

(gravemente) injured, speak -- (mal) of sb, treat sb --, things are going --, -- (mal) explained. The rerouted (desviado) money: he wired it to Paris. An indictment (acusación, crítica) for capital sentence, bring a conviction against sb → with this evidence they managed to secure a conviction, he was sentenced to five months in prison. The restaurant is five blocks away. The doctor hopes he will get better with time. I can't accurately (con certeza) describe... A cell (celda) with prisoners. Claim an item (artículo) of lost property (objetos, propiedad). Arrangement: (disposición): the seating -- (distribución de los invitados), (arreglo): flowers -- (arreglo floral), (preparativos): the final --, (acuerdo): come to an --. You no longer have to take any pills. They asked where the poison hadcome from. The pain will soon go. He dropped the mail into a postbox. Looking at me scornfully (con desdén/desprecio). He laught at me/about... Turntable: (tocadiscos) plato, (ferrocarril) plataforma giratoria. The morning mist disappeared & the sun shined. Have I anything to receive? A partner of a business. Undo the wrong I have done. The house was pulled down (echada abajo) & the garden was overgrown: descuidado, lleno de hierbas (+ an overgrown (demasiado crecido) child. Work overseas, overseas trade, overseas students. An apprentice plumber. I wish to speak to you privately. Little money & no expectations + -- of life) + the holiday was beyond all our --. Duty: obligación, función, servicio, impuesto → do one's --, the guard -- (turno de guardia); allowance: complemento, asignación, prestación → duty free allowance (importación de mercancías libres de imposiciones aduaneras), luggage -- (permitido) + an expenses -- (subvención para gastos). I'm writing to you at the request (petición, solicitud) of... Full of praise (elogios) for him, I've been told about... Row up the river. I post the letters. He grew older, his breathing is weak. Excitarse: get worked up, get agitated, (sex) get excited. As time went by (transcurría). He beat him to death for no reason at all. He said cheerfully (alegremente, jovialmente, alentadoramente): it is useless to continue. Trespass: entrar ilegalmente, infringir, violar + (pers.) rape (violación), (ley) break/infringe, (principio) violate/breach. A brilliant crafter (artesano) of farces (farsas). Closed for lunch. They didn't find out (averiguaron, descubrieron) about him on time: no lo descubrieron a tiempo. I want to take you to the police. Wrestle (luchar) with a problem =/= wrest (arrancar) → -- back (arrebatar) control from..., -- gold from the roots =/= breast (pecho, seno), chest (pecho). Turning the corner I came face to face with a young man of my own age. Later on I will marry her. It's not music to enjoy, it is music to commune with (estar en íntima comunicación con) & to be transfigured by. She's just zipped (se fue deprisa) into a town; he -- the bag shut (cerró la cramellera de su bolsa), the morning -- by (se fue volando). She smiled at him. Guardar: keep your ticket, we'll keep your job open for you till September. Could you please keep my place in the queue? He keeps his opinion to himself. I have fond/happy memories (grato recuerdo) of my youth/friendship. I have put away all my winter clothes. Save your energy for the race on Sunday. I don't save a penny (ni un duro). Two soldiers guard the entrance to the barracks (cuartel). They have great respect for you. We are very fond of them (les guardamos mucho cariño). I give it to you as a memento (objeto de recuerdo). A souvenir of Majorca. Give him my regards, my mother sends her regards. He had failed at every work. He fed & clothed them. The iron bar slipped (resbaló) & the upper (superior) part crashed (se estrelló) hard into his forehead (frente). His wound healed. The scar began at his hairline. He stayed two days in Madrid & he was sleepwalking (sonámbulo). Clean the house from top to bottom. He did not reply right away (inmediatamente). He joined the army of restless (agitados) men. They camped outside the town at night. Sometimes he stayed with a woman. Arrested for vagrancy (vagancia + laziness, idleness).

Put in jail & sentenced to six months on a road gang (banda, grupo + en trabajo: cuadrilla). The guards would whip a man if he resisted or rebelled. Unpleasant (antipático), his dislike (antipatía) of him, we hated each other, we were shouting at each other. Worthwhile (loable, que vale la pena). Stem (tallo, tronco, pedúnculo de hoja, pie de vaso, tubo de pipa; contener; -- from... (provenir de ...). From rags (andrajos, periodicuchos, trapos + tomar el pelo) to riches (lujosas) tapestries + a dirty bundle (paquete, fardo, haz) of rags & mud was trying to crawl (arrastrarse) up the steps (subir lentamente por los peldaños). They got off the train at dusk (atardecer). She worked until she was of no use anymore & then he would throw her out. He grabbed (agarró) the purse out of her hand. They lost their temper (nervios). He was restless: (mar, viento) agitado, (pers.) inquieta. A muddy face with cracked (rajados, agrietados) lips & eyes. She fainted (se desmayó) & she was badly hurt. She was only partly conscious from shock & drugs. A fresh (en blanco) sheet of paper. She was rubbing (frotando) the scar & soon she was recovering well. He threw off (se quitó rápidamente) his clothes & tried to get comfortable. A kind of glory lit up (iluminó) his mind. We all have evil (mal) hidden inside us. A mudbrick house. The earth had a richness & a greenness (verde) foreign (ajenas) to this part of the country. The old house was lovely (preciosa). Barn: granero, cuadra + stable) → a -- for the animals he wanted to keep. Drive: penetrar, campaña; empuje, impulso; conducir, hacer funcionar; cavar, abrir un túnel,..., it's a long drive (se tarda mucho en coche). He knelt down & examined the animal tracks in the mud. He shook off (se liberó de + sacudió) the memories (=, recuerdo). Her baby is growing inside her. A lonely (solitaria) life. An I-shaped stick. It moved up & down. A terrible (insoportable, unbearable) headache. Dig wells & pump the water. After several attempts (intentos) at conversation, he finally gave up. I'll ride off (partir, alejarme de) home

↔ he rode back home in the moonlight. He showed true hatred (odio) in his eyes. Unforgiving (rencoroso, implacable) & murderous (homicida). Her eyes were unseeing (ciegos, con mirada perdida) & her body went stiff. He splashed (salpicó) whisky on his bleeding hand & rubbed (frotó) it. He was shaking (temblando) & he felt sick. A bundle (fardo...) in a laundry (lavandería) basket (cesto) =/= buckets (cubos) in the camp (campamento). The sound of tapping (golpecitos) from the bedroom. Nail (clavar, agarrar, sujetar) the blankets over the window. She rested & gathered (recogió, reunió, acumuló...) her strength (fuerza, valor). She had been standing (estado de pie) waiting. Leaning against a big pile of pillows (almohadas). His eyes were red around the edges, he wiped his streaming (llorosos, manando) eyes. My wife is away on a visit. Run away (escaparse) → -- -- with (llevarse con) → a runaway (fugitiva) girl. She really made a fool (engañó; bromeó, hizo el tonto) of him. Those boys have found out her mother is a "whore". She loaned (prestó) their money. Feed the girls. The most motherly (maternal) of women. She shook her head sadly. They sat in the warmth (calor, cariño, simpatía) for a long time before she moved. Her eyes grew watchful (vigilantes). A pool of wine spread over the table top (cima, parte superior, cubierta, superficie). Pouring sleeping medicine until the glass was half full. She talked thickly (copiosamente) for a while + a -- (densamente) populated área. He poured ammonia onto a handkerchief & standing as far away (lejano) as possible, held the cloth over Faye's nose. Blackness (negrura, tinieblas + darkness). She petted (acarició) & babied (mimó) her. He used a dropper (cuentagotas) to squeeze a few drops of poison onto the beans. I was out of breath & my heart started pounding (golpear, latir fuerte). He ran to the hallway (vestíbulo, pasillo) screaming for help. He was wiping (limpiando + platos: secar; trapo: pasar) the wound when the pain struck (alcanzó, golpeó) her. Take homemade beans alone. Her body had shrunk (encogió) to bones. Her heart just can't stand (resistir) the strain (esfuerzo, tensión). Wag: (cola) sacudida, meneo, movimiento, Vs =/= waggle: (dedos) movimiento, (caderas) contoneo, Vs =/= wage: (guerra) hacer, (campaña) llevar a cabo. They had to tie her up (amarrarla) to keep her from hurting herself. Adam withdrew (se retiró) into himself. She tried to bring him back to awareness (conciencia). He grew fond (encariñado) of these boys boys =/= be proud (orgulloso) of sth or sb. This is nonsense. A horsewhip: látigo de equitación. He looked stonily (fríjamente) at the threatening man. You have left them fatherless. He wore (lucía) a faraway (remoto, perdido) look (mirada; aspecto, aire, estilo). Am I my brother's keeper (protector + en el zoo: guarda, cuidador)? We're all descendants from Kain & his guilt (culpa) is in all of us. With rejection (rechazo) comes anger (ira). One of the twins woke up & joyfully (alegremente) began to cry. He hungered (tenía hambre) for learning. Her body was shipped home. Her fingers were all cracked (agrietados) & worn out (desgastados). Her clear eyes dulled (apagados) & her shoulders bent. The stony desert of the heartbreaking (angustiosa) hillside (ladera) =/= the rounded foothills (estribaciones). Carthorse (caballo de tiro). The twins stood shyly (tímidamente) staring at their guest. He stood there (estaba allí parado), he stood for a moment & then he turned & ran. Running & tripping (tropezando) until... His white hair shining with starlight. Sticky (pegajoso) mud. He went up the shaky (temblorosos, inestables) steps onto the dark porch (porche, terraza). The reception room was not well-lit. Her hands had aged & were lean & spotted with brown. He sat still as if he held her breath. He opened the right hand drawer of her desk & took out a gun. Loose (prisoner: soltar; suelta, floja, flácida) skin. The rain flooded (inundó) the countryside. A narrow stream twisted from one side to the other of its broad banks (orillas) of grey sand. They climbed up out of the river bottom to the level (llano) land. The width between his blue eyes gave him an expression of innocence. Through his gathering (crecientes) tears he could see his brother's eyes. He saw his trembling lips. I was just joking. You'd better go in. Her coat lay on a chair beside her. Her hands were folded (dobladas, cruzadas) in her lap (vuelta, regazo). A bunch (manojo) of flowers. Her mouth was sweet. He turned away (se apartó) from his cruelty. Disrespectful (irrespetuoso). He leaned on his shovel (pala). He climbed the crooked (torcidos, tortuosos) steps. The hailstones (granizo) beat against the window. He knocked on the weather-beaten (curtida, deteriorada) door. Aren't you tempted to get me sent away (despedido + dismissed, fired)? He stopped & turned & his eyes were thoughtful (meditabundos). Ugliness (fealdad). Her tightly-closed fists (puños anatómicos) in the folds (pliegues) of her skirt =/= cuff (puño de la camisa). Bung: tapón,V, meter → just -- it anywhere (en cualquier parte). Humans are caught in their longings (anhelos) & ambitions. A question left at the end of his life: was it good or evil? Dark-skinned & fair-haired (rubio). He holds (continuó) a position of leadership in the schoolyard (patio de recreo). Her reply puzzled me (me desconcertó). Not hide his prettiness (belleza) & his cleverness (habilidad, inteligencia, ingenio). A fearless (valiente, audaz) fighter. A tree with thin branches that hung down nearly to the ground. He parted (separó + separated) the branches like a curtain & went into the house of leaves. You could see out through the leaves & inside it was warm & safe. She stroked his cheek & wiped the flowing (que fluían) tears away with the edge of her skirt. He sat up (se incorporó, se levantó + got up) & said: "I hardly ever cry unless I'mmad". A gas stove (estufa, cocina). Live the way they used to. They aren't used to eating vegetables. The bottom left-hand corner, the bottom half of the page ↔ the top half of the page. Plums (ciruelas) are up to three cents → not surprised if they went up to ten cents. He made his great try (intento). Far-seeing/sighted (de largas miras) =/= forward-looking (con miras al futuro) =/= progress-minded. It was unbearably (insoportablemente) full. He lay hidden in the tall grass. He turned up (subió, apareció) at his gate (verja, portal) as usual. Freeze! (¡No te muevas!). It froze us in our tracks (nos dejó parados en el acto). A faintly (débilmente, levemente) remembered picture of him leaped into her mind. He removed her gloves, unwrapped loosely the bandage & held her crooked (torcidos) fingers under the light. He tried to tie me down (amarrarme, comprometerme) by making me grateful (agradecido). Then I broke out (me fugué) + (guerra) estallar, (discusión) producirse. A kind of realization (=, toma de conciencia) came over her. She thought of the only person who had ever made her feel this fear & hatred. His laughing eyes looked underneath her skin. She pulled (sacó) a chain which hung around her neck inside her dress. Safe-deposit box (caja de seguridad) keys. They unscrewed the top (tapón) from the tube & shook out (sacó sacudiendo) a capsule. He slid the capsule into the tube, screwed on (enroscó) the cap (casquete, tapón) & dropped the chain inside her dress. Oposición: competitive examination =/= entrance exam (examen de ingreso). Showroom (sala de exposiciones). I thought I might run the ranch + rancher (ganadero, ranchero). Give him back what he lost. He is very pleased (satisfecho) with the results. He felt a sudden warmth (calor, vivacidad, cordialidad) towards this boy & sensed (sintió, percibió)... He looked straight ahead (derecho hacia adelante). You don't want to farm (cultivar, ser granjero). Why does he want to save (salvar, ahorrar) a year? He put his arm around his shoulder to comfort (=, consolar) him. A very solitary existence. He's lonelier (más solitario) than you are because he has no lovely (precioso, encantador) future to dream about; loveliness (belleza, encanto). She looked ten years younger. He taped on his brother's bedroom door & went in. He wrapped them up (abrigó, disfrazó) & hid them in a drawer under... Red-ribboned (con cinta roja) package. Some will lie helplessly. I wanted to give you the money to make up for your loss. He stood up suddenly & his chair fell over (se cayó). He felt hate (odio) soaring through his body, poisoning every nerve. Her face was deadly (enormemente, mortalmente) pale. Inside myself I thought... When I was myself again... When I took my dose of drugs. I recovered my normal. Exhausted I slept heavily (pesadamente). Penalty (pena, castigo) for breaking the rules/for this crime. Rubbishy (sin valor, de pacotilla). I lost my temper (humor, estribos). Wait your turn in the queue. I do housework. He pressed tighter & tighter. The noise got louder & louder. Ann was pregnant. They were woken by the sound. Go & wake your sister up. Arose (despertar) the interest/suspicions of the neighbours. To my surprise.... Will Thursday/this weather/the course (plato) suit (convenir) me? He & his will are well suited (van bien, se corresponden). I can get the money back. I tripped/stumbled (tropecé) on a smooth (plano, liso, llano...) rock & fell forward. Around: I was sure nobody was --, she glanced -- (echó un vistazo a su alrededor), we're getting -- from (nos estamos alejando de). I remained quite still. What basis/grounds have you got for? (¿En qué te basas para...?). What was going on there? (¿Qué pasaba allí?). A memory suddenly flashed (transmitida) across my mind? Plenty of trouble. He felt the touch (tacto) of a hand. I will be in touch (te escribiré/llamaré) as soon as I can. His daily routine. Get into the army. They were high fliers: (Ind.) pujantes (pers.) con gran futuro, they treated ordinary people like rubbish. He was nasty (malo, desagradable) with the people giving them the most boring jobs. The house was badly damaged. He has been in power ever since then. Capital letters → OECD (Organization for Economic Cooperation & Development) for short, TV is short for television; stand for: tolerar, significar → OECD --s for (son las siglas de)..., fill in (rellenar) the application in block capitals; large print (letra/carácter grande) ↔ small --. Abreviar: (word) abbreviate, (text) abridge, reduce, (discurso) shorten. The Indians took over from (sustituyeron a) the Spanish speaking people. The wasted (perdidos) years. It reminded me of the bitterness (amargura) of my childhood. They were quiet/still (quietos, tranquilos, callados) for a while. They were careless (descuidados, negligentes) about that. Go to the nearby town to do some shopping. Else: anybody else? (cualquier otra p.? all -- (todos los demás), where -- could he go? He looked like s.o. --, does he need anything --? No one -- (nadie más) spoke, how -- (de qué otra manera)? What -- (¿Qué más?) + anyone (cualquiera), anytime, anything, anyplace, anyhow (de cualquier modo), somehow (de alguna manera), anywhere/somewhere (en alguna parte), no one (nadie). He was smarter & prettier than anyone else. Too possessive about him → possessiveness. I won't go to class any more. I saw rude (groseras) things. Front room/wheel/cover (of a book). Bring to the boil (que hierva) stirring constantly. He didn't stir (ni se movió) when I went in (entré), sth stirred (se movió) in the underground =/= undergrowth (maleza, monte bajo). He answered coldly. It will bring you nothing but sorrow (pesar, tristeza), express my -- for sth., my great -- was... Registration number + number plate. Stay here a bit longer. I am not on (de) vacation. Behind the sb's back. Laugh at him, laugh in sb's face. Appointed (designado) to be read in the church, appointment bureau/office (oficina de colocación). Let the Earth bring forth (dar) grass & herb yielding seed. Water bird, fowl (ave de corral), bird of prey (rapiña), night bird. Make man after our likeness (parecido). Behold! (¡Mire!) Behold servant! (¡He aquí tu servidor!) + behold the results! (¡He aquí los resultados!). Strive (luchar, esforzarse) to... → -- to do sth., -- after/for sth (para conseguir algo). The wickedness (malicia, crueldad) of men was gred. God said unto (a, hacia) Noah... The abated (amainadas, calmadas) waters turned from off the earth. He sent forth (mandó a buscar) a raven (cuervo). From this day forth (en adelante), they went forth (fueron, avanzaron) out of the ark. Enjoyable (agradable, divertido). Whispered gratefully (agradecidamente). Strong-minded (decidido, resuelto). My mind was upside down (revuelta), the children turned the room -- --. A young man with great expectations (expectativas, aspiraciones). He performed (interpretó + representó, realizó) his music here. On the French soil + rich/chalky (cretáceo) soil + potter's clay (arcilla de alfarería). A library card to borrow books. Be quiet! (¡Silencio!). They are good pals. I took a pill/tablet → I'm all right now, I feel better. Think of the blown bulb (bombilla). Write plainly (claramente), speak -- to sb. Her neat (cuidado, arreglado, bueno, hábil) handwriting. He sighed (suspiró) deeply when he called her. He brought coffee into and went out. He didn't have a weapon (arma) to fight it off (resolverlo, deshacerse de + enfermedad: combatir). The idea of sacrifice took hold of him (cogió de él) the way it does with a guilty-feeling man. The Germans smashed (hicieron añicos) everything in front of them & the war seemed hopeless. He wants to enlist (alistarse) → enlistment (reclutamiento). She held out (tendió, ofreció) a book. He was annoyed (enfadado) & angrily (furiosamente...) asked... A story that we made up (inventamos). He slept until late. The soldiers carried out their assignment (mission: misión, trabajo). Capture her on high ground (zona alta) looking over (visitando; revisando, inspeccionando). River valley. He swung (hizo oscilar) his head toward the table where the telegram lay. Heart attack =/= what a stroke (derrame cerebral + brain hemorrhage). A leakage (fuga, escape) of blood in the brain. He is nearly helpless/defenceless/powerless (indefenso, impotente). Aware of the danger. He held tightly (con fuerza) his arm with both hands. Only two children to look after. He is older than he looks. The disc was next to a computer. Send me to Spain for life. Hang him for murder. Turn of phrase (giro).

Pendiente arriba: slope → parking on a --, pendiente abajo: descend, going down → una cuesta con una pendiente del 25% (a hill with a gradient one in four). A gentle/steep (abrupta) slope. She was very attentive to her guests. We're waiting for his decision. The girls upstairs (de arriba). Do what you were taught. Write down his address & get in touch/contact with him yourself. He stayed (se quedó) in his room. Crooked (tortuosos, sinuosos, =) steps (pasos, peldaños, huellas) + footsteps, (vestigio) mark, take his fingerprints, (de animales) pawprint, hoofmark. The next step is to inform her. She rolled (hacía girar con el dedo) a pencil. Embargar: seize → the offenders'(infractores) accounts are going to be seized. A part of you is missing (me falta). Her body shook (se agitaba). Delayed (atrasado, aplazado) payment. When I was your age. As the saying (refrán) goes. We are towing (vamos a remolque) of... Black/ozone hole. Fortunately (menos mal/por suerte). The family/ancients's reunion. Roncar: (al dormir) snore, (mar) roar. During two weeks I was completely out. One person, two people. Stick: I go with -- (bastón), cera (barra), jabón (barra + bar) + give a lot of -- (una paliza + beating, thrashing), policy of big -- (mano dura). I'm lame in my leg. Vain: vanidoso + conceited, presumed; it was all in vain + a -- (vano) attempt. Coqueta (coquette, flirt, vain girl). Until noon/ midday ↔ since --/--. It's fully open, said he turning to me. Rectángulo (=), cuadrado (square) → 200 -- m., a – table. He made me stand in front of the teacher. What an ugly guy. Berlín: the crossroads between East & West. He has been in power ever since then. He didn't trust the lawyer. When they landed, officials hoped for him. I find her alone. He was not an only child + childless couple + I'm a self-made (hijo de mis obras) man. He got her pregnant. I won't dance with anybody. His magazine has a big circulation. Provide: proporcionar → this provides a basis for research, -- (prevenir) for sth. ↔ -- (tomar precaución) against sth. I became suspicious/jealous. A very pleasant meeting. To remember an outstanding (excepcional, pendiente) man + an ongoing (en curso) search for outstanding achievers (realizadores), outstanding citizen <u>minded (de mentalidad)</u> individuals + industrially minded + scientifically minded area. Be assigned for (ser asignado para); be rostered for (estar de turno), roster duty (lista de turnos). Archeological sites (emplazamientos, yacimientos). Make sure the rope is tight (bien tirante) → tightness: tirantez, (relaciones, ambiente) tensión. He's got a fever & he's started to shiver. Secretive: reservado + reserved, discreet, (asunto, documentos) confidential. Mandela addressed (dirigió) the meeting/rally/political speech. IMF (International Monetary Fund) experts spell out (exponen con detalle) policy flaws (defectos). Sorrow (pesar, pena, disgusto) → -- over/at sth, it was a great -- to me that... Sorry: I feel -- for him (le compadezco), I'm -- (lo siento), he said -- (pidió perdón), a -- (lamentable) sight. Awake/awoken (despertarse). Fly (mosca) =/= Fly, flew, flown (volar) =/= Flu (gripe). He got onto (se subió a) the table, we are onto them (les conocemos el juego), they were onto him at once (lo/la calaron enseguida). He was able to climb out (salir trepando). I poured the gasoline inside & outside the car. He rode away (partió). She'd handle (manejar, ocuparse de, comerciar con, tratar) the stock well. I was in a bugged (infectado) mall & I stayed there a couple of days. I went to the bank that the money was wired to. Race back (volver a toda prisa). A gun was pointed between his eyes. Check in: (aeropuerto) facturar, (hotel) registrarse, counter desk (contador de facturación/registro). A tearful moving/emotional (emotiva) conversation. Bowl (fuente, plato sopero, taza) → a -- half full, a fruit/salad--. Fairy story/tale (cuento de hadas). He spoke with superiority. Rashly (precipitadamente + very suddenly/quickly). The bell (campana, timbre...) rang. Incidentally: =, a propósito, por cierto, por casualidad. Reflect, think over/about (reflexionar) upon this pb. A branch (rama, sucursal) blocking the entrance. His tone was offensive. He looked severe (serio, grave) =/= he escaped a severe (difícil, rigurosa) matter. I was thankful (agradecido) to be alive. I tied them together. Work on them for a long time. The goat (cabra) went out every day. Go over sth in one's mind (repasar algo mentalmente). Put down: he was gorgeous (precioso, magnífico) & put down his gun + anotar, (Tf.) colgar, (carpeta) poner, (pasajero) dejar, (rebelión) sofocar, (suma) entregar. Cut the cancer out of his body. A fine for speeding (exceso de velocidad). Booth: (feria) puesto, (restaurante) reservado, (Tf., voto, intérpretes) cabina =/= Cabin: cabaña + (en el barco) camarote, (en el avión) cabina. A bug in the phone. He dropped all charges against him. I'm not working for him any more. Enter a plea (petición, Jur.: declaración) of guilty/no guilty. What's your plea? Guilty. A rope mark (huella) around his ankle. Servant (criado) → the servants (la servidumbre + domestic staff) → your devoted/humble -- (un servidor de Ud.), your obedient -- (su afectísimo, su atento y seguro servidor). The woman I love dearly (mucho). I paid dearly for... When he worked it up (consiguió) it, he went for a walk. He walked away leaving her crying. No one would find Eva, unless he wanted them to. Where else could he go? His journey (viaje, trayecto) is over. Race riot (disturbio racial). Race against clock (carrera contra reloj). Storage (almacenamiento). As/when dawn (alba) broke (despuntaba). A dine appointment. Fight to death. Richly (lujosamente, generosamente). He's gone. He speaks in private with her. He is about twenty. Pink (clavelines, color rosa), the rose. It fell out of my pocket. Her friends looked at each other. Take out (sacar) → you took me out of the darkness, I took out his mask. He flew away (salió volando, emprendió el vuelo) shaking with fear. Names carved on the stones. Fall down (caerse, fracasar, derrumbar una casa) → -- -- the stairs/into the darkness. Full of rooting (enraizado) people. He stretched out (se extendió) on the grass. Assailant (agresor, atacante). We saw each other every week. I look at the address/at the top of the letter. I felt him more alone than ever. He ran up the stairs. Hurry up! My heart was beating loudly. Only the mouth was unusual (fuera de lo corriente). Force the lock. He turned over a page. Face the unpleasant situation. He hurried off/away (se fue corriendo). Ring the bell of the door. Heavily (muy) loaded. I beg you to leave me alone. The habit of writing to each other. Reaching out (extendiendo) his arm & touching my hand. Her face was pale. They were having fun (divirtiéndose). I hurried back to my study. I blamed (culpé) myself. He allowed him to escape. Reparar: undo/repair the harm, (fuerzas) restore, (error) correct, (perjuicio) make good, compensate. It filled me with horror. He was silent for a while. He gave me a hard look. I said politely... Play the piano loudly & badly. At last I accepted. A guide book (guía turística). The stream (arroyo) became wider & deeper. It's me. If I were you, I... When I'm (sea) old... He made the theory on his own. He has money of his own (su propio dinero). A look of despair. A sad look (aire triste). I took two days off. I felt close to her. Take care! I fell a̱sleep (dormido), get to sleep (conciliar el sueño), are you sleepy?, be a light/heavy sleeper; he was wide awake (completamente despierto), a sleepless night. Could you recognize me in the dark? Creep (trepar, deslizarse) under the fences (vallas). They laid crying in pain. The flames lit up the curtain. The Berlin wall came down. Eyes shining with tears. A cheerful (alegre, jovial; agradable, servicial) voice. Extinguishers (extintores). Things get better as time. He steered (condujo, gobernó) → - --- clear of sth/ sb (eludió --/ --); he steered clear of controversial topics (temas de actualidad)/a high topica̱l talk (una conversación o un tema de gran actualidad). Entrance card (pase), -- fee, -- hall (vestíbulo, entrada), front/back --, gain -- to (conseguir entrar en, acceder a). I don't care what happens to me. I'm sorry to worry (preocupar, molestar) you. It's so unfair (injusto, desleal)... It was beginning to be light. They drop the charges against him. The evidence (prueba, demostración) is not good enough. The group approached me. She pushed him away from her. They hadn't spoken to each other since... You should have listened to me. Avoidable (evitable), I avoided him. Ivy (yedra) =/= ivory (marfil). He unlocked the dogs. Wildly (salvajemente). They were away (habían salido). Here lies (yace) the girl. They kicked (golpearon/dieron una patada a) the horse. Sudden (imprevista) death. He went to look for him (a buscarlo). Walnut tree (de nogal) hedges (cercas, salvaguardias). Angrily (coléricamente, airadamentre). Rather coldly (fríamente, indiferentemente). Unwell/sick (enfermo). He was holding (sostenía) the letter. Afterwards (después). If he is away... The lands (tierras) worth (valen)... Peaceful (pacífico) city, Sunday. He walked forward. He was shaken (agitado, afectado) by the scream/cry (grito...). He lit a match. Unexpectedly. I held up my hand. He ran away/escaped/fled (se fugó) to South America. The roof fell in. On the way back. The doorbell rang (sonó). He laughed loudly. I shot her a warning (de advertencia) glance (mirada). Cleverness (astucia, habilidad). I heard the sound of steps (pasos) behind me. A dull (apagado, soso) & foggy (brumoso) day. I won't break into (irrumpir) any house. She jumped up (subió de un salto) at once (inmediatamente). Heavy (fuerte) rain. Watcher (observador). I could check (frenar, controlar, comprobar)... Mark the mistakes. Wooden door. He pretended (hacía ver que) to play. Brand (marca,V, tildar) → be --ed as a liar. He fell down into a chair. He got off (se bajó de) his horse & went in. He laid down (dejó de lado, se echó, se tumbó) like a stone. You are very kind. You are unkind (duro, desagradable...) to your father. I'm glad (me alegro). I'm expecting (suponiendo, esperando) a baby. Unfurl/unfold (desplegar) the flag in response to sth. A decade - long peg of the peso to the dollar at parity. Kit out/up (equipar) → be kitted out in...: (ropa) llevar puesta =/= riding/tenis gear:

equipo/ropa de montar/de tenis. It was caught in a predicament (apuro, aprieto, dilema: dilemma). Stilettos (zapatos de tacón). Perch: percha, perca, posición privilegiada → come off your --! (¡A ver si te bajas del pedestal!), posarse → he --ed on the edge (borde) of the table, she --ed the child on her knee. We are still moving forward with the handbrake on. The focus on these four industries builds on (añade, construye) our existing emerging market platform across research/sales/trading. Foresight (previsión)ed: previsor. He broke into a run (echó a correr). Compound: compuesto, (pb.) agravar, (riesgo) aumentar, -- interest; -- a felony (crimen, delito grave): aceptar dinero para no ir a juicio, -- with (transigir con). The day was sunny. Trump (triunfo,V) → turn up --s (resultar bien), he always turns up trumps (no nos falla nunca), play one's -- card (la mejor carta). Cap - a - pie (de pies a cabeza). For full electric vehicles we need a breakthrough (avance importante). Without demur/objection → we have --ed/doubt (dudado); demure (recatado). Sheer: -- (puro) mud/rock, by -- (puro) chance (azar), in -- amazement (absolutamente estupefacto). Even though (aún cuando, a pesar de que). Senior (superior) certificate. HIV (Human Immunodeficiency Virus) prevalence (predominio) among adults. Off - stage (fuera de escena, entre bastidores, lo preparado en secreto). Whatever befalls you (te pase lo que te pase...) → If you keep your opinions to yourself, nothing untoward (adverso, desafortunado, perjudicial) would befall (pasar) you. Lift Ukraine out of the post - Soviet sump (sumidero, foso séptico, letrina). Sprinkle (rociar, salpicadura, Vs)r: esparsor, regadera; -- out (esparcir), a -- of rain; -- clear soup on the plate, -- (rociar) water on the plants, -- (espolvorear) sugar on sth =/= sparkle (destello, centelleo, chispa) → a pers. without --, a --ing (espumoso) wine =/= foam bath (baño de espuma) =/= froth (espuma de cava, de cerveza) → -- at the mouth (echar espuma por la boca), frothy: (liq.) espumoso, (hablar, escribir) banal. Vendetta (persecución) → pursue/carry on a -- (campaña) against sb. Venganza: revenge, vengeance; vengarse: avenge, take a revenge. Vindictive (vengativo, rencoroso) as anything that Ukrainian nationalists cooked up (tramaron + cook up an excuse). Rub up against: (gato) restregarse contra + raising Chinese prosperity rubs (frotar) up (pulir, sacar brillo) against Siberian dereliction (abandono), dereliction of duty (negligencia en el cumplimiento de su deber). Conveniente: advisable, suitable, convenient, proper. An upbeat (optimista + hopeful) world. Bankers would go to grips with (enfrentarse a) the weakness. G<u>r</u>anary (granero) =/= ga<u>r</u>ner (recoger, cosechar) =/= almacenar: (m.) store, (fortuna) amass. Tap into: (Comp.) acceder ilegalmente, (sb's ideas) aprovecharlas, (one's potential) aprovecharlo al máx. Flyover (paso elevado/a desnivel, desfile aéreo). Munch (mascar, masticar + =, chew). Amble (tranquilo, andar sin prisas) to their workstation. Tumulto: (=, turmoil + motín) → prison turmoil, riot disturbance, mutiny. Uproar (alboroto, jaleo) of rickshaws (carritos tirados por personas). Mill (fábrica de tejidos, acería, molino de trigo), milling (molienda). An outside (lado del pasillo) seat + go outside, outsi<u>de</u> (fuera de) their jurisdiction (=, competencias) =/= outsi<u>ze</u> (de muy grande talla). Reverse: dorso, reverso → are you upset? No, quite the --; in -- (al contrario, al revés); the -- side/face; -- gear (marcha atrás); in -- order, the roles are --ed. Heat up (recalentar comida, recalentarse). Gobbling (engullir) US mortgage bonds (bonos hipotecarios). Wean (destetar) + -- (alejar) sb from sth + -- off/away (from drugs...): desviar a alguien (de las drogas...), disuadir del mal camino. Chair (presidir) the meeting; preside at/over... Budding: (artista/genio) en ciernes =/= buddy (amigote), buggy (sillita de paseo, golf/niño: cochecito) =/= bogey (fantasma, duende) =/= boggle (pasmarse, quedar alucinado/helado/patidifuso) → China's ascend has been mind - boggling (increíble). They levy (imponen) on banks. A crowding - out (desplazamiento: ej.: exotic plants --ing the native species out);

this article will be --ed -- (excluido) from publishing/edition. Stocky (bajo y fornido) physique. The knock - on effect (repercusiones) on actions. He faced roadblocks (controles, barricadas policíacas). Head off (interceptar, atajar, cortar el paso, prevenir) a resurgence of Tamil militancy =/= set off: salir (---- on a trip), estallar; dar lugar a, hacer resaltar, separar. Bemoan (lamentar) the fact. A chunk (gran trozo) of flesh. Pillbox: (Med.) pastillero, casquete/pequeño sombrero redondo con pocas alas. Ice hockey (patinaje). The former operatives (agentes, operativos, obreros) → be operative/applicable (estar en vigor). Remain in detention (=, arresto). Half-heartedly (poco entusiasta). Abilities: talento → children of different -- (niveles). Foundation (de base) course, foundation stone (piedra fundamental). Individual: -- portions, -- (sueltas) enterprises, each -- member (cada socio), as a private -- (a título personal). Poach (cocer a fuego lento, cazar en vedado, birlar/quitar) airline (línea aérea) customers (clientes). Offload: descargar, (pers.) desembarcar. Pulse beat (latido), pulse rate (frecuencia). A customizing (adaptable al gusto del consumidor) solution. Sidestep (esquivar, eludir) the question. The cusp (cúspide) of development. He visits his relatives. Segregated (separados) accounts. Merienda (tea, afternoon snack/tea). Pretender to the throne, he pretended (fingía, pretendía) to pray for them. She held him in her arms. My hat jumped again. Hot & wet air. He spoke with an ugly (feo; crimen: horrible; noticias: inquietantes) look. I'm so glad you could come. The dog got out/loose/untied, came off. The traffic/negotiations were in a stand -still (parados, paralizados). Freeze: congelar → it will -- tonight + quedarse inmóvil → my body froze of fear. Dubbed (apodado) iPad + dubbing (doblaje) into English. TIC (Treasury International Capital) data. Coupon (vale, cupón, billete). IPO (Initial Public Offering) market has seized up (se ha agarrotado). Pick up (mejorar) recovery. Pick sb up (recoger a alguien) from the country house (masía). Discounting rate: a bank charges for billets to exchange. Rediscount: the discount of a bill of exchange or promissory note (pagaré) that has already been discounted for another holder. Wham: ¡Zas! (golpe fuerte y resonante,V). Prime (principal, de primera) commercial property. From peak to trough (depresión, punto bajo; canal, hoyo; comedero, bebedero) in early 2009. Prices are buoyed (flotantes, Ec.: en fluctuación creciente). He lost out (salió perdiendo). Restrained: moderado, sobrio ←→ unrestrained (sin trabas, desenfrenado), unfettered (sin grilletes). Frantic (frenético) lending (préstamo). Spin-off: producto secundario, consecuencia indirecta, beneficio indirecto → for instance the defence capacity to disseminate tech to other industries =/= fallout: lluvia radiactiva, consecuencias, secuelas. Clean-up (limpieza) of the book value (valor contable) of an asset. Swap in stock market (exchange of securities). Deferring (posponiendo) the € 4 bns cost of a new plant. Grey market (cuando la escasez conduce a mercados negros). Deduct (descontar) the whole pension deficit. Choppy (picadas, agitadas) market conditions. Affected by the outcome of a lawsuit pending (pendiente) against oligarchy. Waft (soplo, bocanada; flotar, llevar por el aire). Off - peak (fuera de horas punta...) holiday prices, off - peak train services. Defective accelerator pedals. 1867: toppling (basculeo) of the long - ruling Tokugawa. Parentage: ascendencia, familia → of humble (noble) --, of unknown --. The facing (de frente) page, South - facing (con orientación al sur). Rugged: áspero, escarpado, (máquina.) resistente, fuerte, (estilo) tosco, (facciones/condiciones) duras, (willpower) inquebrantable → rugged countenance (semblante, tolerancia). The chief jewel (el mejor regalo). The hotel doorman (portero). Dress (aliñar, vestir). Run away (huir, escapar). Break through (abrirse camino). Store up (almacenar) hatred. He was heavy → he has lost weight. Sitting next to him. Some stones were missing in the wall. Weeping (llanto, lloroso). Heater (calentador). Don't omit/neglect... Thoughtfully (cuidadosamente, contemplativo, =). Pen - holder (mango de pluma). Eviction (desahucio). Dear: querido, cariño, cielo, preferido → a very -- friend of us, everything I most -- (que más quiero), -- dady, my -- fellow (amigo), come along (ven) --! =/= darling! (¡Vida mía!), you'll always be my -- =/= dearth (escasez → in times of -- =/= dearly: mucho (I love him --), de verdad, caro (pay -- for his mistakes) =/= dread: terror, pavor, pavoroso, aterrador → use dreadfully (terriblemente) powerful tools =/= dreary: inhóspito, deprimente, monótono, (libro/discurso): pesado. Stretcher (camilla) → -- bearer (camillero). The light went out. A true story. Very friendly (simpático) with rich people. He looks/doesn't look his age. Under the cover (colcha, manta). Hunting ground (tierras de caza). He was having lunch. March: Marzo, marcha =/= marsh (pantano, marisma). Fashion parade/fashion show (desfile de modas o modelos). I fainted (me desmayé). The breezing (brisa) =/= breezy (ventoso, alegre, despreocupado, dinámico), --ily (alegremente). Go along (ir sobre la marcha) with (secundar, acompañar) your plan; I make corrections as I -- --. Quickly (de pronto) he ran down the hill. Be careful! (¡Atento!). Where can I hide...? The dog can't follow me up to a tree. He found a tall tree & went up. A sudden stampede (desbandada) for the door. Late into (entrada) the night. The midday meal. Look at you! (¡Mírate!). Her face went white. Bring him back dead or alive! He had run upstairs & hid (se escondió). Everybody hates her. He moved to the little back door. He said he was tired (cansado)... He went in quick, and went out through the back door! He opened the back door & looked out. The lorry slowed down, the lorry drove slowly south. He talked quietly (tranquilo). I can't stay longer. He got up from the bed & looked out the window. Police cars came & went. He is standing in front of the door. All of them began to talk at once (de repente), pay at once (de un golpe). He took the book away (se lo llevó) ↔ not to be taken away (es para consulta). Some helpful (amable, útil, servicial) advice. How can I leave (dejar, abandonar) him? He felt cold (se sintió helado). The chancelier (=) broke away from its ropes & crashed down the people below. Later it was back in place with new ropes. He took out (se quitó) his mask. Shriek (grito, chillido, Vs) → a woman screamed/shrieked: stop shrieking at me! (¡No me chilles!). The lights went out. He went down on the floor at Christine's Feet. Builder (constructor). Scorn (desdén, menosprecio/fully: desdeñosamente, con desprecio). A room lit by candles. My dream became true. Speak face to face. Take samples for testing. Sweet → bitter (amargo), sour (agrio), odourless (inodoro), insipid/tasteless (insípedo) → tasty (sabroso). The jury of the trial are behaving strangely. Serving time in prison. Aunts & uncles. When money changes the rules, they fall under its curse (maldición, lacra, palabrota) → the curse of unemployment, cursed/damned (maldito). FBI (Federal Bureau of Investigation) is not enough... He said they'd wait. His law firm. He swore that... He pushed Sam's upper arm (brazo superior). Read the sheet of instructions. He lost consciousness. Appearance (aparición, aspecto)s: las apariencias → the -- can be deceptive (engañosas); judge by -- (a juzgar por las apariencias). He pushed the lever (palanca) & electricity shot through Patrick's body. The robe (traje, túnica, bata) had rubbed (frotado) his skin =/= on the ropes (contra las cuerdas). The tape recorder was turned on. The money sent by wire (telegrama). Pray (orar) =/= say the rosary. Wait while she goes inside. Her thoughts weren't on money, but on him. Recuperar: (dinero, bienes, salud) recover, get back, (fuerza) get one's strength back. Make sure he's not hurt. He was back in the USA. They drank & argued (discutieron) a lot. There must be millions left (deben quedar...). Are you sure it's him? They both shook their heads. His life insurance. He won't go unless (a menos que) he's forced to. The law firm partners. District attorney (fiscal). By return mail (a vuelta de correo), many happy returns (feliz cumpleaños), the return home/to school, etcétera). How badly (gravemente) was he hurt (dañado, perjudicado)? Help her stay calm. He called her name aloud (en voz alta). I have to keep moving. Right now nothing else matters (importa). He paused & then asked. They tapped (golpeaban, pinchaban, agujereaban...) wires on my body until I talked. He leaned closer. He rolled over (se volteó) onto (sobre) his back & pulled the sheet (sábana) down to his waist. Look**!** **H**e said, pointing at two bad burns (quemaduras) on his chest. Whose prisoner am I? he asked politely. They got a little rough: áspero, (voz) ronca, (pers.) severa... I'm glad the chase (persecución) is over. Chase (correr) after sb. Lots of pbs are ahead. Money calms his fears (temores, miedos). He rode away (se fue). Parental guidance (consejos)/leave (permiso)/authority (patria potestad). A tearful (emotivo + moving, touching) meeting. They were anxious to see him. His first appearance. A steep (empinado, abrupto) hill 12 km. down the road. After the car burned, there was little left of the body in it. John's tent, gun & sleeping bag were not found. Burn the body to hide the evidence. He sounds scared (asustado) & his hands & knees shake. Bring it with you whenever we meet. Bring a lawsuit (pleito) against sb. Enter a plea (petición) of guilty (culpabilidad). He kneeled next to him. Handle (llevar) the matters before (ante) the trial (juicio), to make sure you are protected. Bit (bite, it, tten): mordió (his lip....). The front (1ª) row (fila). This hearing (audiencia) is closed. The defendant's (acusado) table. He has suffered through years afterwards (después). Overbilling (cobrar demasiado) & false claims (reclamos). He breathed heavily. Catch (coger, agarrar...; atraer): -- his attention about... He's gained weight steadily (constantemente). Amazed (asombrado) at how different I looked with my beard. Pottery (cerámica, alfarería) classes. Arch(a)eology of early (temprana) Britain. He wrote plays (juegos, obras) for TV. The book won the award. A mile away.

When he meets you... The girls stayed with their father. If the pills work, you will probably throw up (vomitar). He was puzzled (acertijo)d: perplejo, desconcertado. He didn't argue with her. Farewell (de despedida) dinner/party/gift/words. A storeroom (despensa, almacén) in the basement (sótano). He had to make him take the pills. He hated the books. Forgive me for the unhappiness (infelicidad, tristeza) that I'll bring to you. Put (one's) lipstick on. Check (control, chequeo,Vs) the blood pressure =/= security check ... Outer: the -- edge of the roof, the -- islands/garments =/= ledge: the stone --: saliente, (montaña) cornisa, shelf (repisa, estante), anaquel. I lied to you. He pushed her with all his strength. Away from Paris for a few days. She didn't want me to be upset (disgustado, alterado), he was upset about his parents' divorce. She's worried about getting married without telling me first. Repay (reembolsar, devolver) that money. He took out forty folders (carpetas) from a closet (armario). She smiled at her. He'd broken up with a girl. I broke up because she was getting too serious (serio, delicado, grave). He waved his arm at the taxi. He jumped into it. Don't shout for help. I swear on this Bible. She finished her meal. She smiled sadly. She was very possessive. He waited in the lobby (=, vestíbulo, pasillo) of the hotel. I won't have to talk with him for long. Did that little fall kill her? Her taste in music & books. They were alone for these weekly dinners. The mother'sdeath had increased Marion's dislike (antipatía) of him. The phone rang. That was kind of him. They didn't like each other/one another. She looks like (parece) she knows... A painting that hung on the wall. Silly (tontas, ridículas) stories. He'd been very careful. Interest in kingship (realeza). Far ahead I could see him. Come up (subir, aparecer) onto one of the catwalks/runways (pasarelas). He pointed up towards the roof/pointed us (indicarnos) the right direction. We wanted to make him confess. The sides of the pickup joint (puticlup) are not straight (en línea recta). The things they could be doing with him. He was chasing (persiguiendo) him. The lawyer referred (remitió, envió, derivó) them to him. Secrecy is vital → the meeting was held in --. He overcharged (cobró de más). Lead the whole file (carpeta, archivador) into the trunk (baúl, maleta, maletero) of his car. Throw out: (ropa vieja) tirar, (del equipo) echar, (proposal: proposición) rechazar, calor (despedir), (pers.) desconcertar, (oportunidad) desperdiciar. Tarry (enquitranado). Tablespoon (cuchara grande). Tabla: (de madera) plank, (de planchar) ironing board, (de ajedrez) draw, surfboard. Rough (áspero) to the touch (tacto), sense of touch. Get one's share (sacar tajada). Tajantemente (emphatically, categorically, sharply). Meanness/ stinginess (tacañería), crossing out/correction (tachadura,V + delete key: tecla de borrado). Tacitly (tácitamente). Taladrar (drill a hole, a bullet pierced his ankle). Tanto (so much, so many). Tartamudear (stutter, stammer). Tarugo: (de pan duro/ madera) hunk, (pers.) blockhead, dimwit. Tejido: (tela) fabric, (anatomía) tissue. Techo: (int.) ceiling, (ext., auto) roof →suelo: (tierra) ground, (casa) floor. There's nothing else left for him to try. Tejer (weave, o, o) y destejer: do & undo. Strictly (=, terminantemente) bad. I ended up (terminé) exhausted (rendido). Finish off all the supplies (suministros, provisiones). Tenderness (ternura), stubbornness/obstinacy (terquedad). Give ground (ceder terreno), terreno firme (safe/firm/solid ground), lose (perder) ground, on the -- (sobre el terreno). Tenacity (tesón). For a time (durante un tiempo). Through the ages (a través de los tiempos). Half: first --, the upper -- of the body, divide sth in --, we go halves on the rent (pagamos el alquiler a medias), do things by halves (hacer las cosas a medias). It's typical of him. Typical (lo típico) + a traditional (típico) costume. Discount rate. He scored (hizo) ten points in the first throw (tirada). Strained (tirantes) things between us. Demolish/pull down the house. The motorbike knocked her over (le atropelló). The wind has knocked the fence down. He tripped (tropezó) & dropped the tray (bandeja). You shouldn't waste (tirar) food. Don't throw away the leftovers in the bin. A donkey was pulling the cart. A tight dress. Shoot: retoño, (cine) rodaje, cacería, pegar un tiro → you'll get me shot (por tu culpa me fusilarán), the impact shot (lanzó) them forward, his shot missed (falló), you'll be -- for that! We heard a --, -- at goal, a fine (magnífico + magnificent, marvellous, wonderful) shot of Messi, shooting (tiroteo), be within range (a tiro), shooter (arma de fuego + firearm). Shoot! (¡Tira!), shoot at goal! Penalty, goal (=, portería, objetivo), corner kick. A book of Josep Capdevila entitled Pensología (the art of thinking). Throw in (tirar) the towel, a cruise including/throwing in (incluyendo) Cuba. They searched (registraron) the whole forest. The table is touching the wall. Sound (tocar) the retread (retirada). That issue (situación) closely (de cerca) concerns me. Wound one's pride (tocar el amor propio). The ball hit the post. Knock on/at the door. Not due to be down (aterrizado) until... It's our turn to pay. Be drawing to a close (tocar su fin). All the rest (todo lo demás). In all haste/with all speed (a toda prisa), do sth in -- (de prisa), make -- (apurarse), -- to do sth. By the way (a propósito), first of all (ante todo). Anyone who wants to (todo el que quiera). The prettiest (más bonito) of all. Rotting rubbish, perishable foods, advanced state of decomposition. Cadáver (body, corpse), (de un animal) carcass. It smells disgusting (un asco). Why (para qué) does he want it? How wonderful! (¡Qué maravilla!). Bonito (pretty, nice) =/= handsome (apuesto, bien parecido, magnífico, bello). You are awful! (¡Qué mala eres!) It's great (qué bien) living on your own (se vive solo)! That's a long way away. Ello queda por aquí (it's around here somewhere). He was second last, be left/fall behind in the space race. The coach (autocar) was wrecked (destrozado). Paralysed/paralytic. Disfigured face. The board (junta) has been elected. Orphaned/motherless. Make a good impression. He only did it to make himself look good (para quedar bien) ↔ get on the wrong side of them (quedar mal con ellos) + you made us look bad (nos hiciste quedar mal). So as not to cause any offence (ofensa, infracción,Vs). Is there any dinner left? The agency that looks after (cuida, se encarga de) his company's advertising. I look forward (miro hacia el futuro) to: espero con impaciencia. I look forward to hearing from you (quedo a la espera de sus noticias). There are none (ninguno) left, there is nothing left but rubble (escombros). If I take two from ten, leave eight. I've got € 5 left. I had to owe him (tuve que quedar debiéndole), he was left owing me € 25. The party is only a few days away. There's no harm in trying (por probar que no quede). Amable (kind, nice, pleasant). We have arranged to meet outside the cinema. Shall we meet at four? I stayed working until it closed. I'm going deaf (estoy quedando sordo). We've run out of coffee. Keep it as a memento (recuerdo). Keep the change (la vuelta). He kept my pen. Kid: cabrito, chiquillo, tomar el pelo → are you trying to kid me? Groan (gruñido, gemido) of pain. Moaning (gemidos, quejas). The sun is really scorching (quema). The curtain is getting burned. Pinewood (pinar). Be overexposed (salir demasiado) → -- -- in TV (quemarse). Bring (interponer) a lawsuit/an action (querella) against sb. They have set aside (rechazado, apartado) their old disputes (querellas). As long as the boss is opposed (no quiera). He did it on purpose/deliberately. We love each other. Mistress (querida, amante). Our beloved (querido) country + patria (fatherland, mother country, native land). The lady I was talking to (con quien hablaba). For anyone (quien) who knows it. Anyone (quien) who doesn't agree. To whom it may concern (a quien corresponda). No one can stand him (no hay quien lo aguante). Casually (con aires despreocupados, sin darle importancia) he moved closer to us =/= I found it by sheer chance. Who did you give it to? Whose turn is it? Who were you with last night? Whoever (quien quiera...). Quieto: still, motionless + keep still! Behave yourself! (¡Sé bueno!) + bueno de carácter (calm, placid), he lacks character, be good-natured, be open/have an open nature, a strong character. Three carat (quilates) gold. Chimera (=, monstruo imaginario, alucinación). A fortnight (quincena) → bimonthly → quarterly (trimestralmente). Do the (football) polls: jugar a las quinielas. Five year plan. Spokesman (portavoz). Severance pay (por despido). Quirúrgico: surgical; cirugía: surgery. Touchy (quisquilloso), stain (mancha) remover. Remove the rubble (escombros), remove him from his post. Snowplough (quitanieves). They took the flags down from the balconies. Get that away from there. Not take one's eyes off sb. He took the ball away from him. I had my licence taken away (me la han quitado). Steal sb's place. Relieve (quitar) the pain. It took my appetite away. Stop feeling hungry. It's filling (quita el hambre). I'm not losing any sleep over that matter. It takes a lot of my time. Apart/aside from the dessert we had a good meal. Get out of the way/of my sight. That wine stain won't come out. You look ten years younger. Have a tooth out. I can't get rid of her! What a relief! (¡Qué alivio!). Give up a bad habit. Let's stop being silly (dejémonos de tonterías). Radish (rábano). It makes me mad/infuriates me (me da rabia). A raging (rabiando) toothache. Tantrum (rabieta, berrinche). Racial hatred. A portion (=, ración) of ham/meatballs (albóndigas). Be rationed (racionados). As a result of (a raíz de)... Ramita: twig, sprig + bride's (de novia) bouquet. Broadly speaking (a grandes rasgos). Traces of blood on the floor. Vanish (desaparición) without traces. Bookworm (ratón de biblioteca). Talking for quite a while. A while ago (hace rato)... → he left -- -- --. Will you be long (tardarás mucho)? Quite a way to go (carretera para largo/y manto). So long! (¡Hasta otro rato!) = I will see you! After a while/in a while (dentro de un rato). I will stay a bit longer. He kept me waiting a good while. Shortly afterwards (a short while later). They called shortly after you left. In one's spare moments (a ratos perdidos). He knows quite a bit (bastante) of Maths. Overstep the mark (go too far). Dash in (entrar como un rayo) → -- out, rush past. Rightly or wrongly (con razón o sin ella). Agree that sb is right (dar la razón a alguien). Tell us his whereabouts (paradero). Reduce or cut the price. Rebasar: go beyond, (tiempo) exceed, (carrera/progreso/educación) overtake, leave behind. Reassessment (recalificación). Recargar (refill, recharge). Tributaries (afluentes). Terrible shock (susto). Welcome (recibir + receive) the guests with open arms + they entertain a lot (reciben mucho en casa) + the doctor doesn't see (recibe) patients on Fridays. Reciprocal, vice versa (a la recíproca). Recinto: enclosure, universitary campus, walled (amurallado) enclosure. Reclamar: (herencia, tierras, daños) claim, (derechos, soluciones) demand. Recoger: he bent down to pick up the spoon. I picked the paper up off the floor. If you spill (viertes) water on the floor... The mail (correo) is collected. Clear the table, clear up everything before you leave, gather up your things, put the plates in the sink (fregadero). Recolección: data capture, (dinero) collection, (fruta) pick up, (flores) pick up/gather, (cosechar) reap/harvest, (la cosecha en sí) crop; grow (cultivar), the award of her efforts,... We'll come & pick you up/fetch you/collect you at seven o'clock. He received nothing but condemnation (=, censuras), the last but three. The authorities seized all the copies (=, libros..., ejemplares). Asylum seeker. Two collections (de cartas, basura) a day. The border (borde, margen, orilla, frontera) is uneven/irregular (irregular, recortado). Reproach (recriminar). Empeorar: worsen, make worse. Recrudecer: worsen, intensify, recrudescence. Recoverable money, returnable canning/bottling. A resourceful (ingenioso, de muchos recursos) person. Red de alambre: wire mesh (mallas, engranar). Communication railway/network. Reducir: reduce, bring down → it's advisable to -- -- sth to the minimum, cut the journey by half/in two. He managed to overpower (vencer + al enemigo: defeat, vanquish) the robber. The last stronghold/redoubt/bastion (baluarte, reducto) of the imperial eagle. Reissue (reprint + 2ª edición). Replace (reemplazar) a man, a Brand... Reflexionar: reflect (on), thing over/about. Soft drink (refresco). He took refuge/shelter. A godsend (regalo del cielo). Whilst (while) → wait a -- (espera un rato). Irrigate/water/hose down. Birthday/wedding present. Regañar: scold, tell off, grumble, grouse, quarrel, (perro) snarl, growl. <u>Slim</u>ming diet. Full board (pensión completa). The statute (reglamento) which governs these cases. That law is no longer in force. Register mail in the consulate. Return trip, way home (regreso a casa), irrigation channel. It leaves a bad taste in the mouth. Rehacer: do again, rebuilt his life. Reign (reinado,V). Reintegro: refund, reimbursement, (lotería) return of one's stake. Don't make me laugh. Reivindicación: demand, (wage, attack) claim. A fair (justa) reappraisal (revaluación) of the politicians/currency. Be connected/bear relations with (tener relaciones con). Cause & effect relationship. It's put right or remedied/cured. Remit: remitir, perdonar (three months of the sentence were --ed) =/= remittance (pago, remesa, envío). Remendar: (ropa) mend/darn: zurcir, unir delicadamente), (parche) patch, (corregir) correct. Leave sth to soak (remojo). Remolcador: breakdown truck, tow truck; remolcar: (Náut.) tug, (Auto) tow. Remorse (remordimiento). Remoto: (en el tiempo) far-off, (en el espacio) far - away, distant (country, time...), (poco probable) remote. Unprofitable (no rentable), a close/hard-fought (reñido) game. Be on bad terms (en malas relaciones) with. They lashed out (repartieron golpes) to... Repeler: (enemigo) repel, repulse, drive back, (idea, oferta) reject. The play (obra) is being performed. He doesn't look his age. Sanctions against sb =/= sanctioned (aprobado) project, but with reservations. Responder: the project no longer meets (responde) market demands, meet sb's expectations, correspond to reality. I can vouch (responder, garantizar) for him... I don't reply that... I'm not responsible + a responsible boy. I'll do the rest. Resuelto (resolute, resolv<u>ed</u>, determin<u>ed</u>) to... Reticente (unwilling, reluctant). Retirar: (acusación, subvención, permiso, tropas, negociaciones) withdraw. Move away so that people can get through (pasar, llegar a destino sin dificultades...), move off (ponerse en marcha, camión: arrancar). Twist (enroscar, retorcer, torcerse, girar, enrollarse; (tergiversar) the memory + writhe (retorcerse) in pain ↔ double up with laughter =/= twirl: (hacer) girar/revolver → -- one's mustache/hair; (bailarinas) dar vueltas; give us a -- (date una vuelta para que te veamos). Return journey. Paint the portrait of... A badly paid post. Retroceder: move back a few steps, the crowd moved back. Unlawful (ilícita + illicit) assembly (reunión); briefing (reunión informativa; instrucciones, órdenes). He got his friends together to talk it over (discutirlo). Reveal/disclose his identity. It turned out to be (se ha revelado ser)... The house doesn't match up (no se ajusta) to requirements (condiciones). His <u>a</u>ccomplices (cómplices). Revender: (entradas) tout, scalp, (artic., alim.) resell. Flooding (inundado) valley. He can't stand (resistir) having to get up early. Split: descosido, abertura, rajadura, grieta, ruptura, división, (Pol.) escisión, (Rel.) cisma, escisión, Vs, -- up/separated from the rest of the passengers. Take those dirty clothes off. Do so at their own risk (por su cuenta y riesgo). Occupational hazard (riesgo profesional). Scientific precision (=, exactitud, rigor). Usual/customary (de rigor). Strict (riguroso, =) → rigorismo (strictness, severity). My lower back (riñones) hurt + it costs the earth (un riñón). He was funny (daba risa). Pay a pittance (sueldo de risa). I'll do it at my own pace (ritmo) ↔ flat out (a todo ritmo) with high risk. He was caught stealing. They broke into my house (entraron a robar). Fortaleza (robustness, strength, toughness). Make a detour (darse un rodeo). Surround (rodear) the field with barbed wire. The soldiers surrounded the home. He threw his arms around her neck. Gnawing/rodent (roedor). Rollo: (tela, cuerda fina) roll, (cuerda gruesa) coil, (de película de cine) reel, (de pergamino) scroll; what a pain! Pilgrimage (romería). Employers' organization (la patronal). Break a run (racha) of sth. Security cordon. He burst into tears/weeping/crying. Daisy (margarita). Windscreen/windshield wiper (limpiaparabrisas). Make sb blush (causar rubor). Rudo: (madera) rough/unpolished, (pers.) simple, (tosco) coarse. Roughness (rugosidad). Press conference (rueda de --). Background (formación, antecedentes, ambiente, fondo) → -- (de fondo) noise/music; against (sobre) a white --, the valley has faded into the background (quedado en segundo plano). + the -- (circunstancias) of the story (caso)/strike. Tacaño (mean, stingy). On the brink (borde) of ruin/madness. The venture (empresa, riesgo, aventura +Vs) ruined him =/= the spirit of adventure. Correct one's course (rumbo). Take off: quitar, cortar, sacar; despegar, irse → it has taken off to London. I savo(u)red the sweet taste of success. Break-off the diplomatic ties/family unit/with everything that went before (lo anterior). Air route/airway. Silk/air/sea route. Savanna(h). Go on/take a Sabbatical. I know you've lied to me. In a rut. Tosquedad: (objeto) coarseness, roughness, crudeness, (pers.) roughness, harshness, (lenguaje) crudeness. Just top ut it in one way (es un decir); manners! (¡Qué modales son estos!) → all -- (tipo) of things/people. Rutina (routine) →rutinario de cada día) ordinary, everyday =/= (persona) ordinary, unimaginative; ordinary people (hombre de la calle), out of ordinary (fuera de lo común). Namely (a saber)... Who knows! We haven't heard from him for 6 m. Saber hacer (be in the habit of doing). It tastes bitter (amargo). This tastes of... I don't mind (no me importa) a friend playing jokes on me. Wiser than Salomon. Tasteless, it leaves a nasty/unpleasant taste in the mouth, sabrosa (tasty, delicious) food. Eat one's fill (to satiety). Repeat ad nauseam (hasta la saciedad). Beat (sacudir) a carpet (alfombra) + Jump (salto,V)/jolt (sacudida,V)/lurch (sacudida, tambalearse) → the bus --ed forward (avanzaba dando tumbos/vaivenes violentos), lurch from crisis to crisis. The bomb blast (onda expansiva) could be felt here. Casualty department (sala de urgencias). Wage claim. If a suitable job/opportunity comes up/arises (surge). The water comes out of the tap (grifo), turn the tap off. Victorious in the elections. How did the performance (representación) go? Everything goes to plan, their plan didn't work out. The winning number in the lottery. How did your exam go? A celebration spoiled by the rain. Everything works out all right (sale bien) ↔ my drawing (dibujo) has come out very well. Be nice (amable) to her. This street comes out/leads to the square. He takes (salió) after his father. Get one's way (salirse con la suya). Vinegar coming out/leaking from the bottle. We came off the road, get off the point (tema). The plug (tapón, enchufe) has come off. Go beyond the limits/of what is normal. Swallow one's feelings (tragar saliva). Assembly room (salón de actos). Art gallery (salón de pintura). Ballroom. Break the ice. Healthiness (salud, salubridad). Savagely/brutally (salvajemente) =/= they hardly salvaged (salvaron)... + the firemen saved us from the blaze (fuego). Lifebelt (cinturón de seguridad), life jacket (chaleco salvavidas). Sanear: (ciudad, alcantarillas) clean up, (casa) upgrade, (economía) restructure, (deuda) write off. Annoy: molestar, fastidiar, irritar → get annoyed (hacer mala sangre, enfadarse), is this man annoying (molestando) you? Be --ed with sb. He got politics in his blood. In a flash (en un santiamén + quick, fast, rapid). We love each other, nothing can come between us (nada podrá separarnos). They write to each other. They try not to meet (encontrarse) each other. He is said to be very rich. It is believed that (se cree que)... It's nice here (se está bien aquí). Those concerned (interesados) are informed that... Served chilled (se sirve muy frío). Sebo (grease,V, fat). Dry up a well/the stream (arroyo), dry it near the radiator. Don't come in until the floor is dry. Cross: cruzar; (cruz): we all have our -- to bear, (santiguarse) cross oneself, (cruce): híbrido, (Sp.): pase cruzado (left/right --); crossed cheque; (plan) frustrar, (pers.) contrariar. A sharp (seco) bang (golpe) on the head. Brake sharply/stop dead (en seco). We survived on bread alone. Deposit → put down a -- of € 50; sedimento (=, deposit). He captivates (seduce) with his charm. Seguidamente (immediately after...). Next (próximo, siguiente, luego) we offer you... Five days in row (seguidos). The kidnapping received plenty of coverage (fue muy seguido) on all channels + pay coverage, cable/satellite --, news --, (en seguro) cobertura. Monitor (seguir, observar) events closely. His path (trayectoria) as film maker... The project is on course. The illness runs its course. Shall we go on? The road goes on as far as the town. Go on/carry on (siga adelante) looking at her... The Olympics went ahead despite the attack, a short distance ahead (un poco más adelante). We all agreed (estamos de acuerdo) on that point. Que siga Ud. bien (keep well, look after yourself). The murderer's cool-blooded nature. Warm/cold blooded animal. He belongs to the aristocracy (es de sangre azul). Con enfado (angrily, furiously, =). Sapiencia: knowledge, wisdom. This example stands out/highlights (destaca). According to the boss, act in accordance with one's instructions. Depending on what money we have/on the wealth. The way things are (según están las cosas). Question of road safety/self - confidence. We don't know for sure (con seguridad). There is no certainty (certeza) that. Don't go up that ladder. It's safer in the bank. He feels safe/secure close to his mother, he gestured to me (me hizo una seña) to move aside (me apartara), exclamation mark/point (signo de admiración), this death has set alarm bells ringing. Not at all (nada) secure. He is more & more (de más en más) sure of himself/confident on stage (escenario). Be pleased (estar contento, alegrarse). En el coche: lock the doors (pon el seguro), comprehensive (a todo riesgo) insurance, third party insurance. Unemployment benefit (seguro, prestacón, subsidio).

National health doctors. Two plus four make six. Postage (franqueo) stamp: sello de correo. Forest/jungle (selvático). Sow discord. They are alike/similar + look like + resemblance/similarity. Six-monthly (semestral). He dresses very simply (sencillamente), the simplicity/straightforwardness of the matter. The ageing (senescencia). A feeling (sensación, sentimiento) of pleasure. Sensibly (con sensatez, prudentemente). Emotional (afectiva) sensibility. Artistic feelings or sensibilities. Sensitize (sensibilizar) that it's liable (susceptible) to suffer damage. Put a sum down to sb's account. I took it for granted (dí por descontado) that you were in agreement. I want to make it clear (dejar sentado) that... That hairstyle doesn't suit her at all, it looks awful. White/black pepper (pimienta --/--) =/= green/red pepper (pimiento --/--) → -- disagree with me (no me sientan bien). Hot paprika (pimentón picante). Sit down/take a seat. Pronounce (en justicia: dictar) sentence. Sense of taste/of rhythm, business sense. He's self conscious (cohibido, acomplejado, afectado; con conciencia de la propia identidad): su sentido del ridículo + his sense of the ridiculous/absurd; self-consciousness (timidez + shyness; timidity (falta de coraje); inhibición; conciencia de la propia identidad). He was talking. Complain (quejarse, reclamar) to get what you can. Unconscious (sin sentido, inconsciente, involuntario). Barra: chocolate/jabón (bar), (armario) rail, (cortinas) rod; (Sp.): (cross) bar. Drive in the opp (opposite) direction. Sense: in a -- (en cierto sentido), he --sed (pre)sintió, percibió algo in the darkness, a -- (sensación) of space in the room, common --, the -- (sentido, significado) of the word. I didn't hear her come in (entrar). Love affair: amorío. It aroused (despertó) nationalistic feelings. Moving forward (avanzando) in the same direction. Guilty feeling. I suddenly felt cold. The effects of the crisis are beginning to be felt. Can you smell burning? I'm sorry to tell you that you haven't been selected/that you feel (piensas) that way. I was my mother's favourite. The robbers didn't leave the slightest trace. Her face has been left badly (gravemente) scarred/marked by acne. Leave a sum as a deposit. Leave your message after the beep/tone. As shown in the report. Personal description (señas personales). The needle shows the oil level. It's rude (mala educación) to point at people. Mark the mistakes. This mark of the decline/decadence. Point out (señalar) three fundamental aspects. All opinion polls point out at him as the favourite. A lady-killer (un don Juan). Young lady (señorita), feudal lord. Bookcases (estanterías + shelves). Cross the dividing line. At birth (al nacer). Work keeps her away from her family. The gulf (abismo) between/separating rich people & poors. I sorted them (los separé) into several piles. Put aside some (un poco de) cake. He gestured to me (me hizo una seña) to move aside (me apartara), this death has set alarm bells ringing. He retired/withdrew from public life. Sequedad: (terreno) dryness, (en respuesta/tono) curtness, he greeted (recibió) us curtly (secamente). Some lawyer other than (que no sea) him. In fact/actually (en realidad). He's the one who could do it. It's made of wool (it's woollen). It is to be hoped that... (es de esperar que...). Municipio: (territorio) municipality, (entidad) town council. The trophy went to him. The car isn't made for going very fast. He's a real gentleman (todo un Sr.), he is a real man (como debe ser), if this weren't the case we'd have to rid of him (eliminarlo). In case they get lost... Walk slowly so you don't fall over (no te caerás). We rid the house of mice (eliminamos una plaga de ratones en la casa), we rid the city of beggars. He may well be (an economist...), but still I don't trust him. My colleagues, that is (o sea) he and she... So (o sea) you're not coming... In case (no sea que) they get lost/they call. Put the keys here, so (así) you don't lose them. A raid (asalto) on a jeweller's. Her loved ones (sus seres queridos). He was moved (conmovido) by... Calmly, serenely =/= peacefully (=)/quietly (silenciosamente). Serenar: calm (down), (pb.) settle. The ordinary series of articles about serial killings, mass (en serie) production. Speak seriously/in earnest. Sense/lack of responsibility. You are looking (pareces) serious. He looked at me seriously. She became serious when... Take the matter seriously. Get cross: enojado (+ angry, annoyed, mad). This is getting serious. He's not very reliable (fiable + trustworthy). Not responsible for them to back out (echarse atrás) now. Black is too severe/serious for a girl. A very formal suit (traje). The seriousness of the report/information/account. What a lecture (clase, conferencia) your dad gave us! Serpentear: (animal) wriggle, creep (+ vegetal: trepar), (camino) wind, twist, turn, (río) wind, meander. They availed (aprovecharon + took advantage) themselves of the darkness to escape; of what avail is it to? (¿Para qué sirve?), to no avail (en vano: in vain), it is of no -- (no sirve para nada). Subsidize (subvencionar). Reckless/rash (temerario). Get one's bearing/orient oneself (orientarse). Hectic: (viaje) agotador, (actividad) frenética, (vida) agitada =/= (mar) rough, choppy; (pers.) agitated. Session time (sesión de control al gobierno). Rack (devanarse) one's brains + be --ed (atormentado) with guilt (culpabilidad, remordimiento + remorse) =/= guild (gremio, asociación). Cream (crema, nata) → the cream (la flor y nata) of society. Let me know (avísenme) if you can come. I wonder (me cuestiono) if it's worth it (si vale la pena). We have been paid (nos han pagado). I ought to do it. Oh, it's you, I didn't recognize you. One finger up means yes. It's a nice flat but it's a bit dark. I'm not a betting man (no me gusta apostar). I bet you anything..., don't bet on it! (¡No estés tan seguro!), I bet you can't. They hardly (apenas) have enough money. She will certainly come (ella sí vendrá). Betray? No, absolutely no. No se puede aguantar (that's unbearable, I can't stand that). I think so (creo que sí). He nodded in agreement. Rotundo: (respuesta: categorical; éxito: resounding; a definite (definitivo, seguro, rotundo) yes. Bad temper (mal carácter). They have to take a lot of risks to get rich. Why me? (just)

Because! (¡Porque sí!). He found it hard (le costó mucho) to agree to the project. The majority of nine votes (in favour) was needed. He won't be able to do it on his own. She has a tract (rastro, trayectoria) record that many actresses would be envious of. The product itself (en sí) is inoffensive. He is talking about himself. He has given his all (lo mayor de sí) to the project. Learn things by himself. They are very confident/sure of themselves. The facts (hechos) speak for themselves. They are identical to each other. They shared the inheritance among themselves. The two solutions are mutually incompatible. She is gone forever (para siempre). Siempre que (whenever, as long as) → as long as he agrees; provided (that)... I go whenever I can. Whenever I go out it rains. Water them down (diluir; críticas/Pol.: suavizar) them whenever necessary. He means (significa) nothing to me. That will mean the end. Syllable (sílaba). He conveyed (transportó, condujo, transmitió, expresó) the family's sympathy. Silencer (silenciador). Silence!/ Quiet! -- in court (en la sala)! Keep quiet (mantenerse en silencio), remain silent, suffer in silence. Silently/quietly. It is quiet here! (¡Qué silencio hay aquí!). A deadly (sepulcral) silence. Policy of the empty chair: not taking one's seat =/= folding chair/armchair (butaca). A swimsuit that shows off (resalta) your figure. Status (de prestigio, =) symbol; marital/civil/ financial --. Similarity (parecido). It's a show (muestra) of sympathy towards the victim. Likes & dislikes (aficiones y manías + lo que les gusta y lo que no). Take a liking (simpatía) to sb. Win everybody's affection, I did it without anybody's help, they left without anyone realizing. We don't like it at all. We were charmed (cautivados) by her friendly nature/friendliness (simpatía). Simpático: nice, pleasant, likeable, congenial she was very nice to everybody. Ingratiate himself (hacerse el simpático, congraciarse) with. Get on (well together) with: llevarse bien con. We are just amateurs. Simulate (aparentar, simular, fingir) → --ed attack/pearls (perlas artificiales)/fur (piel sintética, =). Go in pairs (por parejas), live together (vivir en pareja). Alcohol free beer. Still (sin gas) mineral water. Run out of (quedarse sin) sth. The Price of the bath (bañera) not including the taps (grifos). We'd like to remind you that...We haven't been paid for two months. The beds still hadn't been made. A pile (montón) of rubble, he made his -- (fortuna), my desk was --d high with boxes. I'm sick of doing unpaid overtime (h. extras). Without him knowing (sin que él lo sepa). I can't do it unless they ask me to. Not only... but... Jokingly (en broma). Only he would have dared. Sinvergüenza: swine, scoundrel, crook, rascal, naughty (travieso), brazen, shameless. Once at least, just once. Lest (para que no) → -- we forget; -- (por si acaso) he be a spy. He didn't even (ni siquiera)... Aunque (even if, even though). Invoicing (facturación) system. Database management (gestión), he administers... Tax (impositivo) system. Nowhere better than here. You will get nowhere like that (así). I've saved (guardado) you a place. Located/sited in the city centre. In a superb location (ubicación, lugar, posición). The building is in a state of ruin. A lot of food left, this money will be more than enough. Settle an income (pensión, renta, ingresos) on sb. =/= disability/retirement/war pension. There is too much on this side. The surplus (exceso, sobrante, (Econ.) superávit) of talent. Sobrecogedor (imposing, impressive). What you say is quite unnecessary. We have plenty of time. Jumped on/fell upon (se abalanzaron sobre) him. I have to stand over him to make him do it. It fills ten pages. On top of all (sobre todos) my duties I have a new one. In nine cases out of ten. One out of every three smokes. Superabundance/overabundance. The lights shone overhead (por lo alto) =/= overheat (recalentar). Overload/extra-burden (extra carga) =/= extra charge (sobrecosto) → install it at no -- --; charge extra for sth. Be overshadowed (eclipsado) by anybody else. Through sheer carelessness (por simple descuido). Superhuman. Sobremesa (sitting on after a meal). Sobrepasar:

(esperanzas) exceed, (récord, rival) beat, excess weight, overpopulation, pay a little extra for that + an extra pay. Fly over (sobrevolar). Sober (sobrio, frugal), soberly (con sobriedad/con moderación) dressed. The consumer society. Benefit association, benefit concert. Lifeguard/life-saver (socorrista). Crush (aplastar) the rebellion. Sleep therapy (sofrología). Sojuzgar/someter (conquer, subjugate). At sunrise ↔ at sunset. Always so pleasant. The rising sun. Nine hours of sunshine. It is sunny. Sunbathe: tomar el aire + lie in the sun. The receptionist was very solicitous/attentive (atento) in dealing our claims/complaints (reclamaciones). Submitted (presentada) application; it was rejected. A very caring (solidaria, =) person) → uncaring. An act of solidarity. Very sympathetic (comprensivo, favorable, receptivo) to our country. Declare my support to. Talk to himself. Leave sb alone. He was left alone/in an orphanage at seven. He feels very alone. It's better to be on your own than in bad company, he feels very alone. At the touch of a button. Let me go! (¡Suéltame!), Don't let go of the rope. He released a dove (paloma) as a token (señal) of peace. She hit him (le dio un golpe/puñetazo). Solvent: disolvente, (Ec.) solvente. Take one's hat to (ante) sb, top (de copa) hat, straw (de paja) hat. He managed to free himself/get free. Someter: subjugate/conquer one country, (rebeldes) subdue/put down. Entirely subjected/subordinated to her will/to external stimuli. They have held a referendum on joining the EEC. Subjugation of the Celts. The princess made her suitors (pretendientes) undergo a test. Put sth to the vote. Submit (=, presentar) the agreement for the approval of the ministers. Submit a work (obra) to the censor. Submission to the plenary session for approval. Sleeping pill. Sleepiness/drowsiness (somnolencia). A much talked-about (sonado) scandal/divorce. It was strange coming from him. Isn't the name familiar? (¿Te suena el nombre?), his face isn't at all familiar to me. Smile at sb, he didn't even smile at the hike (caminata, excursión a pie). He has a bright future ahead of him. Her name is always coming up/being mentioned in connection with... I dreamed about you/of becoming rich. I'd never have dreamed of it. Me go by plane? In your dreams! (¡Ni en sueños!). A mink (visón) coat. Talk in one's sleep. Stop dreaming & get on (ponte) with some work. They dreamed of victory/having a washing machine/of being a singer. A new pack of proposals. The week flew by/was over (pasó) in no time (como un soplo). Quejido de dolor (moan, groan) =/= without a murmur (queja + complaint). Aguantar: (clima, dolor) bear, (pers.) put up with her husband, he can't support pain, stand that idiot, the beams bear (aguantan, soportan)/ carry the weight of the ceiling. Support (soporte) to her parents. He was deaf to her entreaties (súplicas + request, (Jur.: petition). Drop/put sth. in the post (poste, correo). Keep the club going (sostener el club). Gain enough to support a family. The skier swerved (sorteó/viró bruscamente) skilfully round the flags. Get in (hacer entrar, meter, entregar...), get on (seguir), -- --! → -- -- your work, please! Going on with just a sandwich. I was getting on (me iba) fine till he came along (se presentó). Keen (entusiasta) → he's keen coming on (quiere progresar). My legs could barely hold me up/support me. The opposite direction/side/opinión. As the judge maintains/ holds... Go on & on (enrollarse como una persiana). Catch: coger desprevenido → they caught him stealing. The delicacy (=) of her poetry (poesía) =/= pottery. He got angry. He got a surprise for me. I've the feeling they don't belong. I suspected as much, his behaviour is very suspicious, suspicious-looking types. Dubious (sospechosas) acquaintances (amistades). He's suspected of murder. He had a clash (enfrentamiento, choque) with the president. Stand upright/on one's feet (de pie). The sculpture stands on four columns. He can support himself on his income. The mining industry is kept going by subsidies. He persists in her refusal. Sustainable situation in the long term. Maintenance of democracy, -- worker: encargado del servicio de mantenimiento. Sótano: (habitable) basements, (almacén) cellar. I must get a move on (cambiar de trabajo) to a bigger company. High-ranking: de categoría, (oficial) de alto grado, (piso) luxury, (woman) of high standing. A bear (oso) & his cub (cachorro + perro: puppy, pup). Look after one's own business. Stay (quedarse) in his room. A balloon (globo) ascent/rise. Subvención: export subsidy/grant, agricultural subsidies, sick/unemployment/maternity benefit, old age pension. Underground (subterráneo), undervaluing/underrating (subestimar, infravalorar). Subyugar: (país) subjugate, subdue, (enemigo) overpower, (voluntad) dominate. Suceda lo que suceda (come what may come + whatever happens). Succeed sb in a post. Her smile vanished (se desvaneció), my savings -- (desaparecieron). Dirty shoes/words. They flat out (van a toda máquina) to get that prize. A marble floor. Echarse un sueño: get a nap, have a kip. Sweet dreams, the house of her dreams. The bandits/dogs are on the loose (andan sueltos), your shoelaces are undone, loose hair, the book has two pages loose, loose change (dinero suelto), they aren't sold singly/separately, a separate extract from the novel. Luck wasn't on our side. This is my lucky number, a lucky man, be in luck, try (probar) one's luck. For better (bien) or for worse (mal). Suffer the same fate as sb. Universal suffrage. Complaisant (sumiso, servicial) husband. Undergo (sufrir) a proof/an exam. What do you suggest? Hypnotic powers. The archeological findings (hallazgos) suggest a previous settlement. Suggestive (provocativo, que sugiere). Peg (sujeta) the clothes properly, so the wind doesn't blow them away. Staple (sujetar con grapa; prod. de 1ª necesidad). Hold his trousers up. An elastic band (banda, tira) to hold my hair up. Is the rope secure? The wheels are held/secured by three nuts. What ares the total expenses? He added up (sumó) everything they spent. Lump (terrón, pedazo…) → lump sum (suma total). Add (suma) these two accounts. The bill adds up/ comes to € 60. The disaster filled him with sadness. Submissive (sumiso), with the utmost (mayor) care. The greatest/utmost difficulties. I'm going to give in (supeditarme) to her whims (caprichos). Dead (muy) expensive. He got over (superó) his parents' divorce. The closest (el más cercano) rival. She overtook the other runners. Sales have far exceeded our expectations. They outnumbered us. She is the cleverer of us, you think you're so clever! Don't try to be -- with me. The team did not get past the first round (vuelta). At the top of the age. The top left quadrant. Be superior to sth/sb. A higher-ranking (superior) post (cargo) than yours. High-fashion dress. The surviving (que me quedan) relatives (parientes), survivors. Replace: nobody can ever -- you, my darling; -- incompetent managers. Beg/implore sb... → I beg you to stay. Assuming/presuming (suponiendo) everything goes to plan. The move (mudanza) won't mean/involve more expenses than... The trip turned out (resultó) as I had imagined → I thought so (me lo suponía). I took it for granted (lo dí por descontado/supuesto). Not to be qualified (no tener título). In the supposed (supuesto) police report. In the event (caso) of the authority requiring proofs. That is further south. The southern cities/part of the city. The assumption (suposición) that it was true, let's assume they.... Surgir: arise, emerge, appear (unexpectedly). Various problems have come up. Be well-supplied (surtido) with... Large assortment (surtido, colección). Take out a subscription to a magazine. The above- mentioned. They have called the wedding off (cancelado la boda). Suspicacia (suspicion, mistrust). Grasp (captar) the substance of his speech. The flat tyre is replaceable. They want him replaced. Can you stand in for me (substituirme)? Take my place while I am away. Home-produced goods. Asistencia: (escuela...) attendance, (ayuda) assistance, help, (ayudante) assistant. Demand: solicitud, exigencia, (Com.) demanda,V. Purpose (propósito). Review (revisar, repasar). Usually (por lo general). No pasó del susto: it was less serious than was at first thought. Sustracción: (acto) removal of contents, (resta matemática) subtraction, taking away, (descuento) deduction. Extract water. Several books of theirs (several of their books). This book is hers (el suyo de ella). Reservas: (vitaminas, armas...) reserves, (booking) reservation, (agua) supply, (en almacén) stocks. Gas supply (suministro). Go one's own way (a lo suyo) → get one's way (salirse con la suya) ↔ we will never get out from this one (de esta no salimos), the plan worked out well. Hold back (retener), stop him from escaping, hold back from (refrenarse de), hold back (ocultar) information. Without delay (retraso), --yed (en diferido) broadcast (transmisión), -- our departure, --ed action bomb, we --ed going out until... Give your coat a brush. Pick/choose (elegir). Be awake ↔ be asleep/slept. Check (control, inspección, comprobar...). Career (vida profesional). Impressive (impresionante). Revival: (custom, usage) recuperación (=), vuelta, (old ideas) resurgimiento, renacimiento, (Med.) reanimación. Easel (caballete de artista). Trend (tendencia + =). Ideal doll (muñeca, preciosidad). Registered post (correo certificado) =/= recommend sb/sth ("recomendar a alguien"). Cup (taza). Plant (planta). Living room (cuarto de estar). Incomplete. Specially (sobre todo). Duration. In favour of... Attend (asistir). Unfair (injusto, desleal), it's so --! (¡Es una injusticia! ¡No hay derecho!), unfairness (injusticia) =/= unfaithful ("infiel"). Account: cash or account (a cuenta) → charge to sb's --, open an --, render (pasar) an -- (factura), settle (ajuste de) --s with... Coincidence (=)/ chance (casualidad). Primary/literary ... education. Educationalist: pedagogo, + =, educator. Aloud (en voz alta). We can't afford (permitirnos) such things. Business trip (viaje de negocios). Confident (confiado), convinced (=). Defective (defectuoso). Assistant (dependiente, ayudante) =/= attendance (asistencia). The hospital is starved of resources (recursos), a woman of considerable --. Clear: a -- case of murder, make -- that, do I make myself --? (¿Me explico?), as -- as crystal, a -- sup, -- eyes, be -- in one's support for..., a -- (llamativa) jacket. Attend: assistir a, prestar atención, (waiter) servir. By the way (a propósito), it is devoted (dedicado) to... Gesture (gesto, detalle). In charge of (responsable de + responsible of). The entry is free (gratis). Since when (desde cuándo)...? Appearance (apariencia + aparición). Key (claves) economic indicators (indicadores) =/= this car is very economical (barato) =/= political economics (economía política). It doesn't make sense (no tiene sentido). Pipe (tubería, cañería, flauta, pipa). Apart from (aparte de). Beneficial (beneficioso). Freely (libremente). Location (ubicación). Respectable. Statement of account (estado de cuentas). Deal (tratar) with... A well/badly brought up child; bring a problem up (sacar a relucir un problema). Regret (sentir). Hopeless (sin esperanza). Atrasado: (con retraso) late, behind, (pago) overdue, (reloj) be slow, (pers.) be a bit behind, (en pagos) be in arrears, be short of resources. As usual (como de costumbre). On purpose (a propósito). Request (pedir, solicitud). Requirements (requisitos). Basis (base, fundamento). Discuss (hablar, tratar, conversar un problema) =/= (contradecir) question, (disputar) argue, (gritar) shout. Watermelon (sandía). Grow up (hacerse mayor). Valuable (valioso). Lately (últimamente). Quite a few/lot (bastantes) mistakes/friends/help), etcétera. Call (convocar) a meeting (reunión)/elections/a strike. Get back (llegar de regreso) =/= get off (quitar, salir, rescatar) =/= undress/take off (quitarse la ropa). Grateful (agradecido). She devoted (dedicó) his life to helping the poor =/= devotee (devoto). Get better (mejorar). Prove (demostrar) → -- sth right/wrong (cierto/equivocado). Quit (abandonar, irse), I quit! (¡Me voy!). On time, punctual (puntual). Get ready for (prepararse para). Traffic light. Enjoy (disfrutar). Remove (quitar, extraer). Weekday (días de trabajo). Stage: tablado, escenario, escena (the political --), etapa, tramo (+ stretch). Department store (gran almacén). Strength (fuerza, solidez, resistencia, potencia; convincente). Get (conseguir) results. The ruins of a castle, the prospects (perspectivas) of a financial ruin, drink is his ruin. A ruined dress. A two-way street. Adversary, adversity. Impress (impresionar). Uncommon/strange/odd/funny (raro). Affectionate/warm (cariñoso). As well as (así como). Cage (jaula, enjaular) → like a --ed tiger (como una fiera enjaulada). Pay in advance, the solutions --d, -- in tech., --d age. In the meantime/meanwhile (mientras tanto). Predictable (predecible). Fulfill: cumplir con, llevar a cabo, satisfacer. Bossy (mandón, autoritario). Known mainly as recording artists (por sus grabaciones). Don't speak with your mouth full, she is -- of fun (muy divertida), full time (plena jornada) =/= Overtime (horas extras). Initially/at first (al principio). At present (en estos momentos). On foot. So what? (¿Y que?). The influence on sb forgetful (olvidadizo). It's a done deal (es cosa hecha). Our ancestors (antepasados, antecesores), cut deeply (profundamente) into the wood, -- indebted to her. Preferable. Shortcut (atajo). € 6 apiece (cada uno), at time (a tiempo). List (lista, catálogo,V). Briefly: por un momento (pensé...), brevemente, en suma, en síntesis. Exciting: emocionante (+ moving, thrilling). Inventive (ingenioso, con inventiva). Apply for a job (solicitar un empleo), appliance (solicitud) =/= reply (respuesta, reacción) for sth. =/= request/petition (petición) → by popular request/demand. Shape (forma, configuración). Campaign (campaña). Cashier (cajero). Genuinely (realmente, sinceramente, de verdad). Collect: (documentos) reunir, (gente) recoger → I'll collect you at 9, -- the mail, (renta) cobrar → be paid, can you take for this? He charged me € 19, collect/draw the pension. Enclose (adjuntar a una carta). Depressed (deprimido, abatido). The price of seafood (mariscos) is prohibitive. Prohibir (ban, prohibit, forbid; caza: no hunting). Unpopular. Though (aunque) it was raining, -- small... Involve: (suponer) how much work would it --, be --ed (involucrado) in the scandal, --ed (envuelto) in an accident. Lower: bajar, hacer descender. Mature: maduro, adulto, (Ec.) vencido. Proceed (avanzar, continuar, proceder). Impolite (maleducado, descortés). Envidia (envy, jealousy) =/= codiciar: desire, covet (lo ajeno), greed. Persuasive (=, convincente). Get together (reunirse). Hairstyle (peinado). Press: prensa, (botón) pulsar, insistir, (olivos) prensar... Vary (variar). A prerequisite (*sine qua non*) → requirement (requisito). Hardworking (trabajador). Plenty: abundancia, it takes -- of courage, they have -- of money, I've got -- of work to be getting on with (para empezar). Advertising campaign. Gorgeous (magnífico, delicioso, precioso). Profitability/return/yield (rentabilidad). Acceptance (=, aprobación + approval, passing). Accountant/countable (contable), accounting accountancy (contabilidad). Checking/current account (cuenta corriente). Fraction (=, porción). French fries (patatas fritas). Reading (lectura). Shipment (envío de m.). Source (fuente, origen). Switch (interruptor): the -- is on/off, -- the conversation to another. The management (la dirección). Provide (suministrar, proveer; estipular). Left handed (zurdo). Proof: prueba, demostración + =). Willing/ready/prepared (dispuesto). Accomplishment (logro). The current month, her -- boyfriend, a word in -- use, this method is still quite --, go with/against the --. Indefinitely. Proper (adecuado, suitable). Be worthwhile (valer la pena) → it's -- getting there early (llegar temprano). I was so embarrassed (avergonzado)! → people are --ed about... I feel so --ed when I have to speak in public... Search (búsqueda) for (buscar)... Triplicate. Hold on! Wait! (¡Espera!). Hostess (anfitriona). In writing (por escrito). Tiny (muy pequeño). Be familiar with (estar familiarizado con). Holy week. Prompt: dar lugar a, a -- (rápida) action is needed, he's always -- (puntual), -- a bill through the parliament (sin discutirla), -- (inducir) sb into doing sth. Connection: (=), relación → it's not -- between two facts. Railroad (ferrocarril). Housework (tareas domésticas). Rating (nivel de popularidad, valoración, opinión). Tank (depósito, cisterna, tanque). The content (contenido). Be willing (dispuesto) to. Make waves (causar sensación + cause a sensation), the hair with natural waves (ondas), (terreno) undulating, the recent waving (oleada) of bombings. Bulletin board (tablón de anuncios). Dealer (comerciante, proveedor, concesionario). Pending (pendiente). Get in trouble (meterse en un lío) → be -- --. Amazing (extra, asombroso). Unlikeable (improbable + =). Located (ubicado). Have a secure (firme) foothold (punto de apoyo) in the market + gain a -- (lograr establecerse). For no reason (sin motivo), lose one's --, within -- (dentro de lo razonable). Trust: (=, confianza, fondo de inversiones/fiduciario,V), -- in God, entrust sth to sb (confiar algo a alguien). Charming/delightful (encantador). Decadencia: (proceso) decline, (estado) decadence + declining/decadent (=) + be/fall on the decline → the -- of Roman Empire. Fall (rehusar) to do sth. Go ahead! (¡Adelante!). Graph (gráfico). (News) stand/kiosk/stall: kiosco. Short/long/medium term (plazo). Hall (way): pasillo + corridor, (en avión y teatro) aisle. Murder (asesinato +V). Demanding/exacting (exigente). Go sightseeing (hacer turismo). Despiadado: (pers.) ruthless, heartless, (crítica, ataque) savage, merciless. Dated (fechado). Guapo: (hombre) handsome, good-looking, attractive; (mujer, niño) good-looking, attractive; (bebé) beautiful, lovely. The "weather'man". Cement =/= reinforced (armado) concrete (hormigón). Effectiveness (eficacia). Meeting (de encuentro) place. Terrific (fabuloso, genial, tremendo). The oven has a timing (reloj automático) mechanism. Fortunate: (pers.) afortunada, (coincidencia) feliz. Hard-boiled egg (huevo duro), plain omelette (tortilla a la francesa), fried eggs, scrambled eggs (huevos revueltos). Individual: -- cases, -- telephone, -- rights, -- style. Uncomfortable (incómodo). In slow motion (a cámara lenta). Leadership (dotes de mando, autoridad, liderazgo). Pressure group. Self-restraint (dominio de sí mismo). Undergo: sufrir, experimentar, (trato) recibir, (operación) someterse a. Unforgettable. Please accept my apologies (disculpas). In compliance with (conformemente a). Leisure (ocio) → have the -- (disponer de tiempo) to do sth. Procedure (=, trámites). Revenue (rentas públicas; --s: ingresos → oil –s. Sloppy (chapucero, descuidado + careless, neglected). Botch: chapuza, fastidio,Vs =/= batch: hornada, tanda, lote, (libros) pila, remesa, (pers.) grupo. Stuffy (ambiente cargado). Lyric: (poema) lírico, the lyrics (letra de una canción). Appraise/value/assess (tasar, valorar). Commit suicide. Run/manage (dirigir) the show. Loud (alto, fuerte, enérgico; llamativo) mouth: bocazas. Blend: (gente, ingredientes, colores) mezcla,V, (sonido, colores) armonizar. Compliment (cumplido, piropo). Lenient (permisivo, benévolo). Profile (perfil). Upcoming (venidero). Appreciate (=, agradecer). Comply (cumplir) with. Orient = oriente =/= get one's bearing (orientarse: orientate o.s.) in the city. Appetizing (apetitoso). Underrate (subvalorar). Blessing (bendición). Easy-going (tranquilo: =, quiet, calm, relaxed). ¡Tranquilo! (Relax!). Lik(e)able (agradable). Rewarding (gratificantes). Congratulate (felicitar). Get undressed, outlive (a una persona). Sued (demandado) for libel (difamación + slander), sue for (pedir) divorce/peace. A reminder: notificación/aviso; un recuerdo, -- of old days. Be concerned (muy interesado) with sth. Assertion (aseveración, afirmación). Set an example (dar un ejemplo). Untie (desatar). Vacuum cleaner (aspiradora). Likelihood (probabilidad); (un) profitable: (no) rentable. Superb (soberbio, excelente). The plague (la peste). Settle down (sentar cabeza). Unwrap (desenvolver). Valuable (valioso)s: objetos de valor. Appreciative (agradecido + grateful). Bothersome: (cuestiones) molestas, (niños, reporteros) pesados, fastidiosos + annoying). Conscientious (concienzudo). Effective/efficacious/efficient (eficaz), effectively (eficazmente, con eficacia), effectiveness (eficacia + efficacy). Notepad (bloc para notas). Promising (prometedor). Rivalry (rivalidad, competencia) between them.

Easy does it (despacio y buena letra). Settler (colono, colonizador). Softness (blandura). Support/back (up) respaldar. A trouble maker (incordio). In the flesh (en carne y huesos). Helpful (servicial) ↔ helpless (indefenso, desamparado). Prospects (perspectivas + =). Route (ruta). Overlap (solaparse, sobreponerse). A town surrounded by hills. Appropriately. Ingenuity. Octopus (pulpo de menos de 10 m). Cut back (recorte, reducción + reduction). Vicious circle. Arabic (idioma árabe). Let us pray God for strength (fuerza), prayer: oración, plegaria. Contest (contienda, concurso, rebatir)ant: concursante, candidato, competitor. Deaf–mute (sordomudo). Embarrassing (embarazoso). Old age (vejez). Vintage wine (añejo). Accordingly (en consecuencia). Bureaucracy. Delighted (encantado) + delightful (encantador). Encouragement: aliento/ánimo → (animar): cheer up + (a. el espíritu): boost + estimular, fomentar). Foam rubber (goma espumosa). Hesitant (vacilante, titubeante). Shameful (vergonzoso). Swan (cisne, chulear, fanfarronada + swank, boasting, bragging). The parcel is overweight (pesa más de la cuenta). Deem (considerar + try, judge). Pass away (desaparecer, fallecer + die). Work out (resolver, salir, resultar, calmar, idear....). Insane (loco) → --nity (locura), -- asylum (manicomio, hospital mental. Long-range (de largo alcance) misiles. Ruler (regla), ruling/judgement (fallo, resolución). Spicy (picante, muy condimentado). Sign up for (apuntarse para). He volunteered (se presentó como voluntario). Endurance (fondo, aguante). Demoralising/disheartening. Thick-heated (tozudo). Accuracy/precision (precisión). Convenience (=, comodidad + comfort), live in comfort (con holgura). Exigir: demand, call for, ask; exigencia: (=, demand, requirement → demanding (exigente); demand: petición, solicitud, exigencia,V → final --/call (último aviso, last notice). Vulture (buitre). Convenient (=, cómodo, oportuno). Be engaged (ocupado, prometido de matrimonio); keep one's promise/word. Lousy (chapucero, piojoso, asqueroso) → -- with (tener mucho) money. Overpopulated. Slap (abofetear) → -- sb's face, he ran -- into (se dio de narices contra) the tree. Achilles heel. The asphalt (la ciudad). Spine (espina, púa) =/= backbone (espina dorsal, columna vertebral). Thickness (grosor). Ceasefire. Convincing (convincente). Hostage (rehén). Involvement (involucración). Loyal (leal). Reassuring (tranquilizante, Med.: tranquilizing). Shortage (escasez) → in times of --. Spokesman (portavoz). Deploy: (Mil.) desplegar, (recursos) utilizar. Keep fit (mantenerse en forma). Warrant (cédula, justificación, permiso)y: garantía + guarantee. Acoustic nerve (n. auditivo). Forte (punto fuerte) ↔ weak point. Preach (predicar). Smell a rat (sospechar algo). Deserving (merecedor). Take steps (tomar medidas). Recreation (recreo + entertainment, break). Advance (avance,V, adelantar). Detrimental/harmful/damaging (perjudicial). Stack (estantería, cañón de chimenea, montón) → a pile/stack of books, --s of work =/= loads/masses of people. Thoughtful (considerado)ness: consideración. Tease (tomar el pelo, coquetear). Toothpick (palillo). Advantageous. Stagnant (agua/Ec.: estancadas). Bluff: prosaico, francote, directo; embaucar, farolear. Provide (proporcionar). Solve (esclarecer, solucionar) a crime. Think out loud (pensar en voz alta). It's about time! (¡Ya era hora!). Regardless of (independientemente de). It left a deep scar (cicatriz, huella) on his mind =/= scare (susto, miedo, asustar) → scarecrow (cuervo): espantapájaros; -- off/away (espantar, ahuyentar) =/= spare: pieza de repuesto; escatimar (-- no effort), perdonar, sobrante → -- industrial capacity meant (mean, t, t: significar) that Russia's firms did not have to invest to produce more =/= mean: mezquino, miserable, humilde, media (the -- annual rainfall), promedio (geometric --). Sickening (repugnante, nauseabundo). Tangerine (mandarina). Blush (rubor, sonrojarse...). Do sth willingly (con gusto). Laugh heartily (cordial, efusivo) → please accept my congratulations. At the very least (como mínimo) the corporate tax (impuesto sobre sociedades)... Banking relationship can sour (agriar, deteriorar) overnight. The judge examines a request (demanda, solicitud) to be dismissed (rechazada). It will have taken heart (cogido ánimo) from Catalonia. Gladly (de buena gana). Really (en verdad). Please: do as one pleases, -- the customers, you're very hard to --, you can -- everyone (todos), she is easily --ed ↔ reluctantly (a regañadientes). Think over (reflexionar sobre). Checklist (lista de verificación). Costly (costoso, suntuoso). Payroll (nómina) → be on -- (estar en plantilla). Regretful (lamentable + regrettable). Drop: gota,V, caída/bajada (of 10%, of ten m.), dejar caer, soltar, bajar... Punch: empuje, garra; punzón, perforar, (dar un) puñetazo) → pull one's punch (andarse con miramientos). Whimsical (caprichoso + capricious). Affable (=, atento, agradable, cordial). Counselor (consejero + adviser). A states (de estado) man + estadista). Affluent (rico, acaudalado, acomodado). Imbalance (desequilibrio). Reliability (fiabilidad). Bounce (rebotar) → the ball went --cing along the road. Qualify: terminar la carrera, clasificarse, capacitar, reunir las condiciones... Christmas Eve (Nochebuena). He stands out (sobresale) for his modesty. Be on the roll (en racha). Indonesia's fuel (combustible, abastecer) subsidies are wasteful (derrochadores) & poorly targeted (fijados, dirigidos). Triturar: grind, crush, triturate. Lap: regazo, (Sp.) vuelta, etapa, lametazo → -- (up): beber a lametazos. Degression (divagación). Escurridizo: (nudo) slipknot, (pers.) slippery, (idea, respuesta, actitud) elusive. Carry: -- the tray (bandeja), llevar encima, transportar m. → --away: llevarse, entusiasmarse, -- along: llevar, arrastrar. Play a prank (broma) on sb. Sofocar: (por calor) stifle, (por fuego, humo) suffocate, (apagar un incendio) smother/put out, (achicharramiento) broiling, (rebelión) crush, put down. Sofocarse: (por esfuerzo) get out of breath (aliento) =/= breathe (respirar). Apretar: (tornillo, nudo) tighten, (interruptor, tecla) press, (gatillo) squeeze, pull, (zapatos) be too tight... Down-to-earth: natural, (política/perspectiva) práctica, realista → -- - -- ways: since the cash-laden (cargado de dinero) trend to have more, diverting (desviando) incomes (ingresos, rentas) to penniless people...

Segunda parte: el inglés más técnico, incluyendo muchas explicaciones útiles redactadas directamente en inglés

Se ha procedido al día a día, anotando cuanto de las lecturas de revistas técnicas y serias iba pareciendo conveniente, para alcanzar un más complejo grado de conocimientos y de soltura (*fluency*).

Dividiremos el capítulo en dos secciones. Primera sección: sustantivos y adjetivaciones variadas complejas; segunda sección: palabras y frases de nivel superior.

Primera sección: sustantivos y adjetivaciones variadas complejas

Aunque algunos en principio parecen rebuscados, con constantes neologismos, no dejan de ser también necesarios para las lecturas cotidianas en una sociedad cada vez más tecnificada. Empezaremos también con la dirección español → inglés

Alargar: (cuerda, goma) stretch, (vestido, pista) lengthen, (mano) stretch out, (visita, discurso) prolong, extend.

Altura: (pers., edificio, posición...) height → what -- are you? At the -- (en el punto álgido) of recession, at a -- of 2,000 m. above the sea level; flying at an altitude of 5,000 m.

Ampliar y amplitud. Ampliar: extend the living room, enlarge/ampliphy the photo, extend/expand his vocabulary, expand the period for enrollment (matrícula), broaden his studies, increase the number of teaching posts, (foto) enlarge, ampliphy. Amplitude: (habitación, casa) spaciousness, (calle) width, (facultades, garantías) extend, (proyecto, reforma de gran valor, criterios) wide ranging/far-reaching reform, de miras/criterios (range) → a broad -- (gama) of courses.

Ancho y amplio. Ancho: (alfombra) width, (camino, manga, habitación, río, margen) wide, broad + abroad back (espaldas), (chaqueta, pantalón) loose, (sonrisa y manos) broad, three m. broad (=/= in broad: generales) terms, (habitación) roomy. Amplio: spacious room, wide area, in its broader (más amplio) sense.

Animado: in very high spirits, be keen to do sth + alegre: lively, (bar, mercado) bustling, busy + animadamente: animatedly, they danced merrily, in a lively way + lust (codicia, lujuria + greed) ily (animadamente), con mucha energía.

Contrario: the opposing party's lawyer. The other or opposing side's goal. The opposite opinion/direction/of tall/of the desired effect. Are you bored? No way, quite the opposite. He put his jumper on inside out. She always has to be different to everyone else. Unlike him, she... Until proven otherwise. It all appears to be going well, when in fact... On the contrary (al contrario). Contrary to what we thought. Why do you always have to be so contrary? He always contradicts me. They came out (se mostraron) against the agreement. Her shoe on the wrong foot.

Cuidado: ¡--! (Look out!), mind the ceiling! Watch out for the pickpockets! Take care over sth, be careful what you do!/of sth! Be aware of the cars when you cross the road! Tread (entrar, pisar) carefully/warily (andarse con cuidado), watch how you go! Wash delicate garments with care, she received medical care, she left her daughter in the care of a friend, formerly (antes) women had to stay at home & look after the house.

De cuando en cuando; día sí, día no...: one out of every three months, every other day (día sí, día no), every now & then/once in a while (de vez en cuando)/from time to time/now & again... =/= year in, year out (año tras año).

Empatar en fútbol: they were level-pegging (empatados), the score is still level, the score is two-all, they tied two-two, they have just levelled the score, after drawing two matches, nil-nil draw =/= (en política): they are neck & neck, they won for four-two/by ten votes.

Escaso: food is scarce, the chances of finding him are slim, poor visibility, short of food (víveres). The recital was poorly/sparsely attended, little information, a programme of little interest, a thinly populated region, a short staffed factory, there are barely/scarcely two towns + he is --/-- fourteen.

Longitud (length): what -- (largo) is it? The tail was twice the -- of the body, they range in -- (longitud) from three to six m., I've travelled the -- & the breadth of the country, -- (años) of service.

Llevar: (en brazos) carry: -- the tray (bandeja), transportar m., -- away: dejarse llevar, entusiasmarse, -- along: arrastrar, (en coche) transport, (-- puesto: vestido...) wear, (aportar) bring: she brings home the money, (inducir) lead sb to think that... (soportar) bear misfortunes patiently, I've only got € 6, it has a label (rótulo), he has a beard, short hair, she will be named after her mother, the book has the title of/is entitled..., this road takes us to Madrid, he allowed the waves to carry him away, she drives the car very well, be taken in (dejarse llevar por) the appearances can be deceptive (aparente, engañoso: the appearances are --) =/= deceitful: falso, engañoso), run a business/an estate (finca), how long have you been here? The train is an hour late, live/lead a quiet life, the bonds pay/bear interests at 8%, it has no fruit this year.

Mancha: (borrón) blot, (de suciedad: en el suelo...) spot, mark, (sangre, comida) stain; spread like a wildfire (extenderse como una mancha de aceite/ reguero de pólvora), (Zool.): (grande) patch, (redonda) spot → manchar: get dirty, stain, (honor) tarnish.

Pista: track, trail... (scent: aroma) → be on the scent; give me a clue, false trail, runway, (Mil.: landing strip: pista de desembarco), athletics track, ski slope/run, ice rink, dance floor, skating rink, grass court, tennis court, tennis clay (tierra batida).

Rayo: ray → -- of sunlight; beam → sunbeam, dash out (salir como un rayo) ↔ dash in; rush/flash past (pasó como un rayo), damn him! (¡Que le parta un rayo!) the tower was struck by lightning (rayo), the news hit him like a bombshell (bomba, obús) =/= a real -- (bombón).

Recordar: (a) recall (recuerdo, memoria,V): those days are going beyond -- (pasaron al olvido), he does not -- what he did, (b) remember (acordar**se** de): not to -- these days, I -- that one day..., (c) remind (<u>traer</u> a la memoria): these boots -- me..., what does that photo --? -- sth to sb.

<u>Reflejar</u>: refle<u>c</u>t (the nobel --s...), refle<u>c</u>tion of the light/in the water..., this refle<u>c</u>ts/is a refle<u>c</u>tion of people's unease; he had a refle<u>c</u>t in his eyes (le chispeaban los ojos), they have good refle<u>x</u>es, metallic glint, chestnut (castaño) hair with blond highlights (reflejos).

<u>Revestimiento</u>: coating, covering, (forro) lining. Non-stick (antiadherente) → adhesive. Cork tiles (láminas de corcho). Lined (revestido) the ceiling with fibreglass. A steel frame (armazón) clad (re)vestido) in concrete (hormigón). The trees are coming into leaf (se revisten de hojas).

<u>Revolver</u>: (líq.) stir, (papeles) go through, (tierra) turn over/up, dig over, they have turned the whole house upside down, it turns my stomach just thinking about it, the civil (populares) disturbances (revueltas). Revuelto: (objetos) mixed up/in disorder, (agua) turbid/cloudy, (mar) rough, (tiempo) unsettled.

<u>Ritmo</u>: rhythm, he moved to the -- of the music, sense of the --, flat out (a todo --), I'll do it at my own pace, pace of life in the villages, fast pace (ritmo intenso), keep up (mantener, seguir) with this lifestyle, heart rate.

<u>Rozar</u>: I brushed past her (la rocé al pasar) ↔ she -- -- me, these boots rub my ankles, your skirt is trailing (se arrastra) on the floor, the table has scraped the wall, the ball shaved the post, the arrow grazed the ear, the seagull skimmed over the sea. (Pol.) friction.

<u>Sacar</u>: he drew his revolver & fired, take the rubbish out, remove the wrapping from the present, get me out of here!, released from jail, I took the dog for a walk, I've had a tooth out, stuck your tongue out, report (denunciar) him to the police, we won the jackpot (premio gordo), she got the nursing post, where did you get such a girl? Get sth out of sb, take the

cover (funda) off a rifle, she got us out of a bad situation, the opposing team kicked off (sacó).

Subir: (brazo, pierna, objeto) lift, raise; (pantalones, contraventana, shutter): pull up; take up the cases (maletas), bring the picture up from down there, they put it up on the rack, she went up the stairs two at a time, get up, climb the stairs, the cap/taxi driver put their fares up/raised their fares, turn the radio/television up, go up to the third floor, come up, the fly move up (sube por) the window, petrol has gone up again, share prices (en la bolsa) are still rising, the child climbed up onto her knees, zip (sth) up → zip open; she blushed: se le subieron los colores a la cabeza.

Aim: objetivo, propósito → his one (único) --, achieve one's --, I achieved the -- I set myself (me propuse), have a good/poor -- (puntería), miss one's -- (tiro), he took careful -- (apuntó con cuidado), he --ed the pistol at me.

Assert: afirmar, (derechos) hacer valer, (autoridad) imponer → assertive (firme, enérgico), assertively (con energía), assertiveness (firmeza, afirmación, imposición) → stand up to (hacer frente a) its territorial assertiveness. Reassert (reafirmar).

Bachelor: the single/unmarried people = solteros + (soltero) confirmed bachelor ↔ (soltera) bachelor girl, spinster; bachelor flat (piso), bachelor party (despedida de); bachelor of Science degree (licenciado), -- of arts.

The bedrock (base, fundamento) of hunting, go to the -- (ir a lo fundamental), tinker with (jugar con) data & simple models come up (surgen, aparecen) with the ideas that form the bedrock (base) of modern economies.

Blame: bear/take the blame (asumir la culpa). Lay/put the blame (for sth.) on sb. Be to blame for (tener la culpa de). I'm not to blame (yo no tengo la culpa). Who is to --? Blameworthy: (acción) censurable, (pers.) culpable.

Blow: (a) soplar → -- one's nose (sonarse la nariz), -- smoke in sb's face/eyes, -- smoke up sb's ass (lamer el culo a alguien), stop --ing smoke into my face; -- the whistle on sth/sb (alarmarse sobre algo/alguien), the wind blew (llevó) the ship towards the coast; the plane was --n off course (el viento lo sacó de su curso), her hat was --ing out, (b) golpe → at one -- (de un --), cushion/soften (amortiguar) the --, it's a cruel -- for everybody, that's a --! (¡Qué lástima!); deal a blow to an unsolved pb, at one -- (de un golpe, a la vez),

Board: tablero... → on -- (a bordo); comida → --ed with (hospedado en casa de), waterboarded prisoners, full -- (pensión completa); junta, consejo, comisión: -- chairman (presidente del consejo de administración), -- meeting (reunión de la junta directiva).

Booze & binge: Booze (bebidas) → go on the " – " (darse a la bebida). Binge: exceso → -- on debt + borrachera, atracón → go on a " – " (ir de juerga), -- on chocolate, -- drinker (se emborracha con facilidad).

Breach: Be in a -- of a rule (incumplir una ley), fill the -- (vacío), heal the -- (hacer las paces + make (it) up), a -- (abuso) of confidence, -- of peace (perturbación del orden público), -- of promise (de matrimonio), -- of security.

Break down: analizar, desglosar, descomponer; derribar, acabar con, estropearse =/= breakdown: (sistema, Electr.) fallo, (negociaciones, matrimonio) fracaso; colapso, crisis nerviosa.

Bring: -- (poner) the infrastructure up to a scratch (arañazo,V, rascarse, cancelar, garabatear + scrawl, scribble: poner la infraestructura en buenas condiciones ←→ she is simply not up to a -- (simplemente no da la talla).

Cast: molde, escayola; lanzamiento, reparto en teatro y TV → she was -- as the princess; mudar la piel, moldear; echar, arrojar → never -- an anchor in shifting (movediza) sand + cast out (expulsar), cast aside (descartar).

Chip: (electrónica: =, pedacito, astilla, muesca, ficha, french fries); -- (away): (pintura...) desconchar, descascarillar → -- -- at: (terreno) ir usurpando, (autoridad) ir mermando/debilitando; -- in: intervenir, contribuir.

Chunk, hunk/snuggle, chuck...: Chunk (queso, pan, carne...) pedazo,V, (dinero) mucho, ruido metálico seco =/= hunk (queso/pan...: trozo)er down: agacharse, pasar desapercibido, acurrucarse + curl up, snuggle → snuggle up against sb: arrimarse a =/= chuck (tirar, lanzar, botar) → get the -- (ser despedido), -- away (tirar), (oportunidad) desperdiciar, (dinero) despilfarrar.

Comfort: the mastermind (genio, cerebro; planear y organizar) finds solace/comfort (consuelo) now + seek -- with (procurar consolarse con), live in -- (desahogadamente), he likes his home --s, words of -- (palabras de consuelo).

Come off: (botón) caerse, (mancha) quitarse → the stain -- --; does this lid -- --? The play (obra) -- -- (dejó de figurar en cartelera) in January, tener lugar/éxito; -- -- (salir) well/ badly, -- -- best (salir ganando) ↔ -- -- worst (salir perdiendo); the car -- -- the road =/= come out: we -- -- of the cinema at ten, -- -- on strike, he -- -- (sale, aparece) fighting.

Cripple: cojo, minusválido; lisiar, mutilar, (barco, avión...) inutilizar, (producción, exportaciones) paralizar; crippled with (por) arthritis/ (barco, avión...) averiados. Crippling: que conduce a parálisis, defecto muy grave, deudas abrumadoras; agobiante, feroz, catastrófico → the cost is so crippling (tan severo, atroz, agobiante) that...

Dash: (gota, chorro, poquito) → with a -- of soda, there was a mad -- for the exit (todos se precipitaron hacia la salida), he made a -- for freedom (intentó escapar), the 100 m. -- (lisos), -- (tirar) sth to theground, the waves are --ing (rompen) against the rock, -- in/out (entrar, salir disparado), she --ed the plate to pieces, I --ed (me lancé) to their rescue.

Dire: nefasto, (situación) desesperada, (pobreza) extrema; be in dire need of sth (necesitar algo desesperadamente), be in dire straits (estar con la soga al cuello) =/= dare (atreverse).

Ditch: cuneta; deshacerse de, desechar, botar → he's --ing of an association agreement with the EU; stop --ing over her/it (deja de amargarte pensando en ella/ello, de darle vueltas al asunto); defend sth to the last -- (encarnizadamente).

Dread, dreary & sorrow. Dread: terror, --full (terriblemente lleno), fill sb with dread (terror), I -- (tengo pavor) going to the dentist. Dreary: (tiempo) gris, (trabajo, vida) monótona, (libro, discurso) pesado. Sorrow: overcome your -- (pesar, dolor), to my -- (con gran pesar mío).

Drive: it'd a long drive (se tarda mucho en coche), one hour's -- from London, can (sabes) you --? He drives (viaja) alone, he --ed me to the station; have/lack -- (empuje, dinamismo), a recruitment -- (campaña), a sales -- (promoción), four-wheel --, put the car in a -- (en marcha), -- the cattle to new pastures, the wind drives the clouds, -- (clavar) a post (poste) into the ground, -- one's fist straight (justo) into the face, I was --ed to it (me ví forzado a ello), -- (volver) sb mad, -- away (ahuyentar, quitarse de encima).

Dump: vertedero,V, basuras, basurero =/= (garbage collector, refuse (desperdicios) collector, dustman); (Mil.) depósito, a real -- (auténtica pocilga); (Comp.) volcado de memoria, (carga) descargar, (paquete, pasajero) dejar, (pers.) deshacerse de, (novio/a) plantar.

Each other, one another, & themselves. Each other: America & China are vying (vie: disputarse) with -- -- for..., Unionists hugging (abrazándose) -- --. One another: talk directly to -- --, cars avoid -- -- at road crossing, many cars communicate with -- --. Themselves: the leaders devote -- (se dedican) to...

Ecosystems: -- (in the startups): finance department is replaced by venture capital funds, legal d. by law firms, research d. by universities, & so on. Sizeable (considerable) startup colony (ecosistema), startup schools (aceleradores). Working spaces with a lot of human toil (trabajo humano duro) hunched (encorvados) over their laptops. All these ecosystems are highly interconnected. Things are awesome (imponentes, abrumadoras, formidables). The prevailing model will be platforms with small & innovative firms operating on the top of them.

Edge & hedge.... Edge: it --s (bordea) towards 5% level at which the Fed (Federal Reserve Board)..., his performance lacks -- (mordacidad), wind with sharp -- (cortante), -- out (derrotar por muy poco), competitive -- (ventaja), leaves --ed (con bordes) with red, he --ed the car into the traffic (con cuidado) ..., she --ed her way (se abrió paso) through the crowd, an --y (crispado, de vanguardia) innovator =/= hedge (seto, cercado) → -- (lucha) against inflation + -- funds (fondo especulativo).

Enlarge: (círculo de amigos, socios) aumentar, (habitación, foto) ampliar, lengthen one's stride (paso), (colas, pantalones) alargar + lengthen; (silencio) prolongar =/= (plazo, contrato, línea, calle) extend; vacaciones, negociaciones: prolong, extend).

Even: incluso, justo, equitativo, todavía, (superficie) plana, ej. the floorboards (tablas), (velocidad,T., progreso) constantes, (respiración) regular, (distribución, color, trabajo) uniforme, (facciones) regulares, that makes us -- (así quedamos empatados), get -- with sb (vengarse) → I'll get -- with her one day (algún día me las pagará), con (-): he didn't even (ni siquiera) kiss me.

Fix: -- (atar) better the load (carga), sujetar, grabar in one's memory, he --ed his eyes/gazed on me, --ed (concertado) at 3 p.m., -- (arreglar) one's hair, be in a -- (aprieto), -- the mirror on the wall, -- the hose (manguera) to the tap (grifo), -- two pieces of bone together, a legislative -- (arreglo, aprieto, solución;V); fijar, clavar. A quick fix (fijación, el asegurar; preparación, currency pegs (vínculo), rather than, say...

Float: flotador,V + en baños: rubber-ring; (carroza) procesión; -- plane, seaplane, hydroplane + hidroavión, (barco) sacar a flote; floating (emitiendo) shares (acciones), -- a company (introd. una empresa en bolsa), -- capital (activo en circulación), (acciones) emitir; (dinero) reserva, (moneda) hacer flotar, the flotation (issue new shares/loans) of initial public offering.

Flush: cisterna, a slight -- (colores) in his cheeks, resplandor de salud, belleza, a -- (arrebato) of excitement (emoción)/of anger (arrebato), (Med.) hot --es (sofocos), the first -- of youth (flor de la vida), -- the lavatory/toilet (tirar de), -- before using.

Front: (edificio) fachada, (camisa) pechera, (prenda) front, (libro) portada, (automóvil) parte delantera, the car in --, be in -- (llevar la delantera + be in the lead), cold/warm -- (frente).

Further: have you much -- to go? How much -- is it? Let's go -- north, move it -- away (apártalo un poco), we're getting -- away from..., they live even further away (aún más lejos), it's -- down the street (bajando un poco más), push it -- in (hacia dentro), a bit -- forward (un poco más adelante), let's look a little -- ahead, get -- into a matter (estudiar más un tema), you will get -- (lograrás más) if you are polite, without -- delay (demora), we have not -- need of your service, -- education (extensión cultural para adultos), I have nothing -- to say, have you any -- question? -- up/ under the river, the -- end of the field, until -- notice (nuevo aviso), a -- stage (una etapa más)...

Grande: (casa, dimensiones...) large, big; demasiado grande (too big), (alto) tall; (edad) old, big; (empresa) big, (maduro) a mature woman; (excelente) great man/artist/wine; (familia) large, big.

Grip, grim, grind, grin y grunt. Grip: apretón de manos, asidero; asir, adherirse; fascinar → he has a tight -- (agarra con fuerza), keep a firm -- (rígido control) of the expenses, he lost his -- on the rope, he was --ped by the panic (el pánico se apoderó de él) =/= g<u>ri</u>m (duro, sombrío, lúgubre, espantoso...) → the -- reality, I feel pretty -- (fatal), -- times for industry =/= g<u>ri</u>nd: moler, triturar, -- (incrustar) the cigarette end into the carpet, afilar; -- to a halt (pararse en seco); funcionar con dificultad, estudiar mucho, trabajo pesado =/= g<u>ri</u>n (sonrisa burlona, mueca, reír abiertamente → -- & bear it (poner al mal tiempo buena cara) =/= g<u>ru</u>nt (gruñido,V).

<u>Harsh</u>: (tiempo, condiciones, castigo, sentencia) severos, (palabras, observación, críticas) duras, (luz) fuerte, (color) chillón, (contraste) violento, (tono, material) áspero, (detergente) fuerte → --ness: (trato) severidad, (palabras) dureza, (clima) rigor, (sonido) estridencia, (textura) aspereza...

<u>Heed</u>: take (no) -- of sth. (tener algo - o no - en cuenta), --ing (teniendo en cuenta) calls for reform, the warnings have been --ed (escuchados). Directives from the top often go un--ed (desatendidas) at the bottom. Inattentive/rude/heedless (despreocupado, descuidado) ly: sin prestar atención.

<u>Hit</u>: golpe, (Sp.) tiro, (on target) acierto, (Mús., teatro) éxito; pegar, golpear, dar con, dañar, (bomba) impactar, dar/chocar contra → be in a -- (tener éxito), -- the front page/the headlines (salir en primera página).

<u>Horde</u> (pers.: multitud; insectos: plaga) =/= ho<u>ar</u>d (acumular, (dinero) atesorar) → cash --ers (acaparadores); when the -- (tesoro; amontonar, acaparar) finally emerged; hoarding: acaparamiento anticipándose a una escasez (shortage), valla publicitaria =/= h<u>u</u>rdle (barrera, obstáculo), 100 m. --, fall at the first -- (fracaso a la primera de cambio).

<u>Inch</u>: pulgada (2.54 cm.), not an -- (palmo) of territory, -- by -- (palmo a palmo) + every -- of it was used, he didn't give an -- (no hizo la menor concesión); -- forward (avanzar muy lentamente), -- up (subir poco a poco), -- out (derrotar por muy poco).

Jockey: jinete (+ horseman/woman, rider), -- (convencer) sb into doing sth, -- (competir, maniobrar) for a position ↔ -- out (disuadir de, quitar) → he was --ed out the chairmanship (le quitaron la presidencia a base de maniobras).

Lead (plomo) → -- paint, -- poisoning (saturnismo) =/= (lead, led, led): ocupar el primer puesto, have two minutes -- (ventaja) over sb, (Sp.) take the -- (delantera), give sb a -- (mostrar el camino a), the police have a -- (pista), play the -- (tener papel principal) → with G. Garbo in the --, sing the -- (llevarse la voz cantante, dirigir, encabezar, mandar), -- the field (llevar la delantera), they -- us by 30 sg., -- a full life (llevar la vida muy activa), (teatro) papel principal, primer actor.

Leave: -- of absence (permiso para ausentarse), be on -- (de permiso), -- (abandonar) one's post (su puesto), ask -- (permiso) to do sth, by your -- (permiso), I take the -- to doubt it, -- the rails. There's nothing left (no queda nada), how many are left? Nothing was left to me but to sell it. There are three left over (sobran tres). We would have nothing left. All the money I've left.

Let down: (window) bajar, let one's hair -- (sueltos), (vestido) alargar, (neumático) desinflar, the weather -- us -- (nos defrauda), we all are felt -- -- (defraudados); the country feels -- -- by America reluctance (reticencia).

Let up: (tiempo) mejorar (→ the time --s up), (tormenta, viento) amainar → in spite of his health, he did not -- -- (no aflojó el ritmo de trabajo), she can't afford to -- -- (permitirse aflojar) on her studies, he never --s up (no calla nunca).

Miss: he scored three hits (aciertos) & two --es (fallos), the arrow --ed the target, that was a near miss, we had a near miss with the truck (no nos golpeó de poco), the shot missed me, we missed the tide (marea), she doesn't miss the trick (no le escapa nada), don't miss the Louvre! Does anybody miss me? They are missing one another, he narrowly missed being killed, I do miss París, he won't be missed.

Nip: pellizco, mordisco + there is a -- in the air (hace mucho frío); -- into (acercarse), -- inside (entrar un momento), -- at sth (mordisquear algo), -- in & out of the traffic (colarse por entre el tráfico), -- down (bajar un momento), -- one's fingers (cogerse) in a door.

Past: she walked slowly -- (pasó despacio), we went -- (por delante) your house, we drove -- (por delante) her shop, she run/rush -- (ella pasó corriendo), just -- the town hill, get -- (vérselas con) a fierce dog, he is -- 40, her -- & present pupils, the -- few weeks, what's -- is --.

Pit: hoyo, foso, abismo; the -- (boca) of one's stomach, mina de carbón, cantera; picar (a car --ted with rust, the tarmac (calzada) was --ted (marcada) with craters; his argument was --ted with flaws (defectos), -- against (enfrentarse con), be on the -- (estar por los suelos), pepita, hueso de fruta.

Pitch: campo (-- inspection/invasion), (baseball) tiro, (mercado) puesto, to such -- (extremo), emotion at a high -- (rojo vivo), he stood up & made his -- (soltó su discurso), lanzar: it must be --ed at the right level of the audience (es necesario se ajuste al tono del público), -- the camp (montar el campamento), how important is it to -- in (arrimar el hombro).

Plea(d): despite pleas (peticiones) from their governments → plead sb's cause (interceder por), I --ed & --ed (supliqué mil veces), he --ed for mercy (misericordia), he --ed the rights of the oppressed (oprimidos).

Pluck: desplumar, arrancar (-- from the bosom (seno) of his family), it takes real -- (coraje) to..., maritime refugees plucked (rescatados) from the waves by a passing vessel/the helicopter.

Point: there was no -- (no tenía sentido), with a sharp (puntiaguda) --, -- of departure, up to a -- (hasta cierto punto), that's not the -- (no viene a caso), gain/carry/win one's -- (salirse con la suya), tact (discreción) is not his strong --, (fusil) apuntar, (dedo) señalar, the -- at issue (el tema en cuestión).

Premium: -- (prima de seguro, recargo) for quality, sell sth at a --, put a -- (valorar más) at sth, -- rate (precio elevado), danger premium, be above -- (por encima de la par), incentive bonus/productivity -- (-- a la producción).

Prickle, prick, pickle, picky: Prickle: espina, picor, púa, pinchar → the French are prickly (enojadizos, quisquillosos, espinosos, que pican) about criticism in Brussels =/= prick (picar, pinchar, escocer) =/= pickle (encurtido, V, conservar en vinagre, lío aprieto → be in a -- (estar metido en un lío) =/= picky (criticón, quisquilloso) =/= fickle: veleidoso, inconstante, versátil, variable.

Rack: estante, escurreplatos → dish/plate --, (documentos) organizador; (tren) portaequipaje; perchero (hat --, clothes --), (tortura) potro, be on the -- (pasar las de Caín), sacudir (be –ed by doubt), sufrir atroces dolores/atormentarse por sus deudas + -- up (acumular) debts.

Raise: -- windows, flag (izar), water level, weigh, (precios, embargos, salarios, impuestos), (construcción, cría de animales), (provocar, plantear, recaudar, conseguir un préstamo).

Rally: (coche) =, (Med.) mejoría, mitin/ concentración, V → political --, (soporte) conseguir, (fuerza, espíritu) recobrar, congregarse → -- behind sb/support sb (solidarizarse con), they --ed outside the embassy.

Rattle: agitar; traqueteo, ruido de cohetes → get sb --ed (poner nervioso a alguien), the hail --ed (golpeaba) on the plastic, he --ed (golpeaba) the door until I opened it, -- off: recitar de un tirón.

Rise: (hola, río), (tasas, número, valor), (presión, T., cantidad, tensión, tono), ascenso (voz, tono, hola), development: meteoric -- of fame, the -- & fall of the empire, give -- (nacimiento/origen) to..., sublevarse + ascenso, cuesta arriba, pendiente, levantarse =/= sesión: the court is adjourned (se levanta la sesión).

Scare: be --ed (asustado), cause a -- (sembrar pánico), give sb. a -- (susto), bomb -- (amenaza), you --ed me (me has asustado), the invasion -- (da pánico), don't be --ed, are you --ed of him? (¿Les tienes miedo?). I'm--ed of spiders (arañas), be --ed (tener miedo) of doing sth, know how to -- (tener dotes de mando), --monger (alarmista), -- off/away (espantar, ahuyentar), bomb -- (amenaza de bomba), --head/ headline (titulares sensacionalistas) =/= sensationalist press/yellow press/tabloid press (prensa sensacionalista).

Scramble: motocros, -- (pelearse) for sweets, hurt (doler, hacer daño) in the -- (lastimados en el barullo), escalada difícil, we --ed through the bushes (nos abrimos paso entre los arbustos), -- through/in/up/along/away: atravesar/entrar/... dificilmente, trepando ↔ unscramble: descifrar, descodificar.

Screw & hélice: Screw: he's got a -- loose (le falta un tornillo), put the --s on sb (apretar las clavijas a alguien), -- sth down (atornillar), -- sth on the board/wall..., -- sth. tight (bien fuerte) ↔ unscrew, -- off. Hélice: (Náut.) propeller, screw, (Aér.) propeller, airscrew.

Set: juego (de llaves...), serie, a -- of dishes/crockery (vajilla + service) =/= cutlery (cubertería), 5 - 2 in the first --, the jelly (gelatina) is -- (cuajada), at a -- (señalada) time (hora), radio/ TV --, in their -- (pandilla), be -- against (opuesto a) sth., be all -- (listo) to do sth., -- a plan before (ante) a committee (comité, comisión), I'll -- your room, the sun was setting, -- apart (separar), -- aside (poner aparte).

Settle: points to be --d (resueltos), the terms (condiciones) were --d, acomodar (an invalid...); saldar una deuda, ordenar, asignar; colonizar, instalarse/establecerse, (dust) asentarse, (sedimento) depósito, (líquido) reposar; reach an agreement, -- down (ponerse cómodo) in a chair, calmarse, (situación) normalizarse, weather (establecerse).

Shift (mover, correr, cambiar...): -- the responsibility onto us, he --ed uneasily (con intranquilidad) in his chair, he --ed onto her back (se puso boca arriba), the focus of attention has --ed to Europe, (-- over): correrse hacia) → can you -- a bid toward...?

Shrug (off), head off & fend off. Shrug: encogimiento de hombros (shoulders) → shrug off (hacer caso omiso) of GDP (Gross Domestic Product) shrinking (encogimiento) =/= the new politics head off (cortan el paso, interceptan, previenen) the populists =/= fend off: esquivar, rechazar.

Sign: -- (suscribir) a petition/a control → -- up: registrarse, matricularse; firmar un contrato, reclutar; sign (firmar) sth with one's initials; -- off: (final de carta + TV) despedirse, the stop sign/traffic sign, a sign that things are improving, sign of surprise/nervousness, they shook hands as a sign of friendship, a sign of health, a sign of the cross, plus sign (+), equal sign (=), minus sign (--), star (zodíaco) sign,

(actividad) terminar → -- the arms deal, communicate using --s, the turnoff (desvío) was not properly signposted (señalados), signpost (señal, poste indicador).

Signal: the signal to take off (partir), a whistle was the signal for them to keep quiet (se callasen), warning (de alarma) signal, signal (hacer señas) to the helicopter, distress (de dolor/angustia/fatiga/miseria) area (área deprimida), the signal has gone.

Slam: atacar violentamente, cerrar de un portazo, apalizar, -- a door (dar un portazo), -- the book down on the table (tirar el libro sobre la mesa), have most to gain from slamming (vapulear) him, he slammed his fist through the door (atravesó la puerta de un puñetazo), they --ed (criticaron) the government.

Slap: -- sb's face, a -- (palmada) on the back, he ran -- (de lleno) into the tree, he --pped (tiró) a book on the table, the judge --pped (aumentó) the fine, -- (incrementar) a storey (piso) on the house, restrictions were slapped (aumentadas).

Slip: -- (resbalón,V, error,V, he --ped into the bed; poner/deslizar → the dog --s its leash (se suelta); let -- secret information; Japanese officials & servicemen let -- (dejaron escapar)... It completely --ped my mind (se me olvidó por completo).

Smelt (fundir), --ing work (fundición), --ing furnace (altos hornos) =/= furnace (industria: horno; calefacción: caldera). Fundición: smelting; fábrica: foundry; lingotes/joyas: melting down =/= meltdown (fusión de un reactor nuclear) =/= horno culinario: oven, stove.

Smooth: (piel) suave, (carretera) llana, (salsa) sin grumos, (transición) facilitar, sin problemas + alisar, pulir, suavizar → -- down: alisar, pulir, (pers.) aplacar; -- out: alisar, allanar, (pb.) resolver → -- -- the flapping (agitada) situation.

Snap: golpe seco, romper, it --ped shut (se cerró de golpe), -- (chasquear) one's finger, it is a -- (esto está tirado), he --ped into action (se echó a trabajar enseguida), take a photo of sb, a cold -- (una ola de frío), the dog made a -- at the biscuit (se lanzó sobre la galleta), a -- (sin pensar) answer, -- (regañar) at sb, a -- (repentina) election, -- back (hablar/contestar bruscamente) at sb.

Sneak: -- sth into (entrar algo a escondidas) ↔ -- sth out (sacar algo a escondidas), -- in/out (entrar/salir a hurtadillas), soplón, (visita, ataque) sorpresa, → some sneaky (chivatas, cucas, que ocultan su pensamiento, taimadas. Sort: things sort (clase, clasificar, arreglar) themselves out: se arreglan, se resuelven... por sí mismas + there are two details to -- -- (concretar), -- -- (quitar) the bad ones, -- -- (arreglar) their problems.

Sprawl: (a) tumbarse: send sb sprawling (tender alguien en el suelo), he lay (estaba) sprawled across the desk, sprawled out in front of the fire (chimenea), (b) extensión: urban -- (crecimiento urbano desconocido), a large sprawling city.

Squeeze: apretón, (crédito) restricción, estrujón, (fruta) exprimir, (salario) recortar... → official visits to squeeze in (buscar un sitio para) the president's four day trip; -- in (buscar un hueco para), -- into (introducir: into the car...), technicians who <u>squeezed</u> (apretaban, exprimían; extraían, financiaban, restringían) high inflation <u>out</u> (<u>suprimieron</u>) of the rich countries; --d (apretado, metido) between beefier (más fornidos) turbulent neighbours; a credit -- (restricción de), squeezing out (echando) weaker staff.

<u>Stall</u>: establo, casilla (for a single horse), puesto en el mercado, emplazamiento en un parque; the talks are --ed (callejón sin salida)/in a standoff (ídem + punto muerto); set out (exponer) one's -- (m., etcétera), we --ed (quedamos parados) on a step (abrupta) hill (cuesta); entretener, andar con rodeos.

<u>Stand</u>: puesto, estante, stand, -- on one's two feets (valerse por sí mismo/defenderse solo), take a firm stand (actitud) in sth, the -- (resistencia) of Paris, the cold --, make/take -- against sth, make <u>a</u> -- (hacer parada, plantarse), make <u>the</u> -- (prestar declaración/subir a la tribuna de los testigos), -- (poner) a vase (florero) on a table, I can't -- (aguantar) him, I can't -- (soportar) carrots, he could hardly -- (ponerse de pie), the home is still standing, all --! (¡levántense!), then they stood up, it --s beside the town hall, my objections still -- (siguen de pie), nothing --s between us (nada nos separa), let it -- (en reposo) for three days, -- aside! (¡sepárate!), please, -- back (más atrás), please, he's --ing down (se retira) in favour of sth, you may -- down (puede Ud. retirarse), MP --s for (significa) member of the Parliament. He stood over me (me vigilaba) while I did it, stand on the sideline (fuera del terreno): ver los toros desde la barrera.

<u>Standing</u>: you are standing (de pie, parado, permanente, arraigado; rango, reputación → Mr. Cameron --) on the frontiers of Science → What is his -- locally? Financial -- (solvencia), be in good/high -- (reputación).

<u>Stick</u>: trozo de madera, bastón, batuta, porra → policy of -- & carrot (incentivos y amenazas); use/wield the big -- (amenazar con el garrote), live out in the --s (vivir en la Cochinchina), I can't -- him (aguantarlo) any more; pegar, encolar: he --s the

envelope down, -- stamps into the album, -- a poster on the wall, -- no bills (carteles); meter: -- the hand into the pocket, -- it on the shelf, -- a knife onto the table; clavar: -- a needle into my finger, -- an advert (advertisement) into the paper; it --s out a mile (salta a la vista); -- up for (hacer valer) one's rights. Stuck (bloqueado) in the lift/window, a -- (encallado) car between two trucks.

Stir up: remover, agitar; despertar, provocar → don't -- -- the past, they --red up the mob to violence, -- -- trouble (armar lío), she is --ring things up again (ya está otra vez armándola).

Strain: break under -- (presión, tensión), -- relations with, a -- (carga) on the economy/his purse (bolso, cartera), the -- (esfuerzo) of one's eyes/of climbing (subir) the stairs, -- (esguinzar) a muscle, (Ec.) debilitar; raza/variedad.

Stream: arroyo, chorrito, manar, (flag, hair) ondear, --ing (llorosos) eyes, blood streaming from a cut, people --ed into the hall, light --s through the window, flags --ed (ondeaban) into the wind, water --ed from a cracked (agrietada) pipe (cañería).

Strike: huelga, descubrir (a big oil --: un descubrimiento de petróleo en gran cantidad), golpe,V, ataque aéreo, dar la hora, acuñar moneda, alcanzar un acuerdo, (actitud) adoptar; strike off (borrar de la lista); --uck down by (afectado por) paralysis; he --uck down in his prima (su vida fue segada en flor).

Stuff: sustancia, materia → -- in the bucket (cubo), the good -- (cosas buenas) of this book, the -- (historia) about how..., rellenar, (animal) disecar, embalsamar, -- (meter) sth. into sth., -- you! (¡Vete al carajo!).

Swing: movimiento, oscilación; columpiar, balancear → a sudden -- (cambio de opiniones), walk in a -- (rítmicamente), be in full -- (pleno apogeo), he was given full -- (carta blanca) to make decisions, the door swung back (se cerró), the car swung into (viró y entró en) the square.

Tackle: -- (abordar, enfrentar) the knottiest (más espinoso) issue of all: a process of post-conflict justice. It will take patience to tackle (abordar) so called bedrock (lo fundamental, lecho de roca) regulations on sensitive areas such as health care & labour market.

Take away: llevarse, sacar los niños de la escuela; quitar (un privilegio...); restar (seven -- -- three is four =/= give away: obsequiar, revelar (secreto) =/= give up: (sitio) ceder, (alcohol, trabajo) dejar, (estudios, proyectos) abandonar, (ticket...) entregar; entregarse, rendirse.

Tap: (micrófono de escucha), Tf. (pinchar), (situación) explotar, (Med.) punción, toque (on my shoulders), golpear (-- one's foot: taconear), stop --ping (para de dar golpecitos), -- into (acceder, aprovechar) sb's ideas, turn off the -- (grifo), -- wires in my body.

Through, thorough & throughout. Through: he is -- (ha aprobado) the exam, does this train go -- (directo) to London? We'll be -- at seven, are you -- criticizing? they have been -- a difficult decade. Thorough: -- (riguroso)fare (vía pública)/ breed (raza pura), concienzudo, esmerado, meticuloso, a thorough (rigurosa, sólida, minuciosa) reform of the country, a -- (total, absoluto) waste of time, a -- (verdadera) nuisance (lata). Throughout (total...): the house is carpeted --, the emphasis has been on teamwork (trabajo de equipo) -- (de principio a fin).

Thumb: -- (pulgar, manosear) → be all -- (ser un manazas), be under sb's -- (estar dominado por alguien), -- a lift/ride (hacer autostop), the rule of -- (la regla general + generally as a rule (por regla general), well-thumbed (muy manoseado, muy usado) =/= thump (golpear) their chests (pechos, cofres) → thumping (descomunal, enorme; derrota: aplastante) speech; -- (descomunal) majority =/= big toe: dedo gordo del pie.

Tip: (a) (dedos, zapatos) punta → he stood on the -- of his toes (dedos del pie), -- of an arrow, the -- of the iceberg, southern --s of Madrid, filtro del cigarro, from tip to toes (de pies a cabeza), (b) inclinar: he --pped the soup bowl towards him, -- the cat off the chair, -- one's hat (saludar con) to sb, -- the balance/scales (in/ against) sb's favour, -- back/forward a chair, (c) echar: -- vegetable into a bowl, -- rubbish into a river; rubbish -- (vertedero), -- out (vaciar, verter): -- her things out of his suitcase, he --ped up (alzaba) his chin defiantly, tipper truck (volquete), (d) varios: propina,V, consejo,V, her horse was --ped (se pronosticó) to win; -- off (dar un chivatazo) → the police had been --ped off; the parrot's wings were --ped with red.

Treat: tratar (algo especial), -- sb like a child, gusto, little -- (cosillas) for children, it was a -- (placer) to see him, the garden is coming a -- (va de maravilla), everything worked a -- (todo salió a las mil maravilla).

Trip: visita, viaje, excursión, tropezón,V, hacer la zancadilla → his first -- abroad, he brought the other player down with a -- (zancadilla), he --ped (tropezó) & fell, he --ped on/over sth (con algo), take a -- down memory lane (revivir el pasado).

Tuck (pinza, pliegue)ed: metida, plegada, pers.: arropada) → underperformance tucked away (escondida, guardada, zampada) in corners of sprawling (que crecen rápidamente) multinationals.

Turn: -- the page, he gave the handle (palanca) a --, no left --! (¡prohibido girar a la izquierda!), give a screw (tornillo) another --, Russia turns alluringly (de manera seductora), we missed our -- back there (nos hemos pasado la salida), at the -- (fines) of the century, a surprising -- (giro) of the events, -- of the tide (marea), things took a new -- (cariz), it's her -- next, give up (ceder) one's --, take one's -- (llegarle el --), events took a tragic -- (rumbo), take a -- in the park, it's done to a -- (está en su punto), -- it through 90º, -- a dress inside out, -- (apuntar) a gun on sb, -- one's head, have --ed the corner (haber pasado lo peor), the goal --ed the game (dio la vuelta al partido), -- the land into a park, nothing will -- him from his purpose, the earth --s on his axis, -- & go back (dar la vuelta y regresar), the game --ed after half-time (descanso), the milk has --ed (se ha cortado), his admiration --ed to scorn (desprecio), -- nasty (antipático, repugnante), -- red.

Complementos de turn:Turn the light down (bajar la luz), turned down (boca abajo); they were --ed back at the frontier; -- about/around: (pers.) dar una vuelta, (viento) cambiar de dirección, (Ec.) recuperar; -- aside/away: apartarse, desviarse; -- off (doblar) at the next exit, the oven (horno) --s itself off; -- on (sb) volverse contra alguien; how are things --ing out (salen)? It's --ed out nice again (vuelve a hacer buen tiempo); -- over: (coche) volcar, (estómago) revolverse, (lectura) pasar a la siguiente página, -- over one idea in one's mind (darle vueltas a una idea en la cabeza); as soon as I --ed round (cambié de rumbo, dí un giro radical)...; I could hardly -- round (volverme); he --ed up (apareció) two hours late.

Wake field: shrinking (encoger) their machines using a phenomenon called the wake field (campo de estela) effect: en un acelerador de *wake field*, con laser y plasma (gas ionizado) aceleran partículas como si fuese surf en una onda. Como resultado se consigue un acelerador de partículas más pequeño con la misma potencia.

Wriggle: mover, retorcerse → -- one's way through sth (avanzar con dificultad a través de algo), -- about/around: avanzar serpenteando, (de pena) retorcerse, (serpiente) serpentear, (pez) colear; -- (away) escaparse + France --s free (se escapa) from hard (duro, fuerte, severo, difícil) taskmasters (muy exigentes tiranos).

Segunda sección: las palabras y frases de nivel superior

Realmente, a medida que avanzamos descubrimos cómo disfrutan los periodistas y cómo avanzan las ciencias, aportando novedades sin cesar. No soslayemos esta riqueza técnicoliteraria, en la que incluimos un gran repertorio de frases prácticas. Algunas son difíciles, pero también rentables:

Conjunto: combined operations, form a whole, overall impression, all embraced view, (ropa) outfit, combined effort, joint operations. Enchufar: fit in, fit together, (Electr.) plug in. Learn by practice, put sth into practice, she's out of -- (le falta práctica), (en laboratorio) experiments. Many would pick (elegir, fruta: coger) Italy, a few finger France, which has yet to come to terms with (asumir, asimilar) the failure of its statist model. Use the crisis to trim (recortar) the state. Coming (a) round: -- -- (llegando) to the long-held British view that the European Union should be smaller; convencerse; she'll soon -- -- (ya se le pasará). There is talk of deepening the single market in services, a huge boom (estruendo, auge) for Britain. Britain attracts nearly twice as much FDI (Foreign Direct Investment) as the rich countries average. Britain excel (destacan) at turning new arrivals into productive, integrated members. Smudge: a -- (mancha) of grease; emborronar, difuminar → --d (manchados + dirty, stained), (reputación) tarnished. Arrepentido: contrite, reformed terrorist, (Rel.) repentant. Fewer immigrants than drop out of (abandonan) the school. Whose most worrying neighbourhoods (barrios) are white &

poor. Straightforward (honrrado, franco, sencillo) =/= straight: (nariz, carretera...) recto; (cuadro, sombrero) derecho; franco, directo, claro =/= outright (rotundo, indiscutible) =/= upright (vertical, derecho, erguido). A country that cannot hold itself (mantenerse) together (unido) can scarcely lecture (dictar clase, sermonear) others. Shape (formar) the bloc that takes half its exports. Law-abiding & tracing: one – in five illegal fish are often sold by otherwise (de lo contrario) law-abiding (que cumplen las leyes) firms, that have no way of reliably tracing (localización, ubicación, seguimiento de la pista,Vs) them back to the vessels that caught them. The plebiscite could break up (disolver, desintegrar) the conservative party. Bring in less skilled workers, crimping (obstaculizando) the ability to export. British stick together (se mantienen unidos) but some of them don't want to stay in Europe. Cravenly (cobardemente + cowardly). Bear down (aplastar, empujar) on: hacer presión sobre. Hold on (esperar, conservar, resistir, agarrarse, mantener ventaja) to most of the Northern Sea oil. For their own sake (bien). Curl up (acurrucarse, hacerse un ovillo) & hide. The inflation is 1.5, down from 2.2 in 2012. In America it has stubbornly (tenazmente) stayed at 1.2. Indicios: (droga...) traces, (Jur.) evidence + pruebas. Inkling (presentimiento, insinuación) of a looser (más relajada) monetary policy. Clip: tijeretada, esquileo, (cine: secuencia); golpe, cortar, (ticket) picar → -- out (periódico: recortar) + at a -- (a toda pastilla). Once: una vez, antes → at --: inmediatamente, al mismo tiempo. They put off (aplazan, disuaden; apagan) buying things. The deflation in Japan did not set in (no se declaró) until seven years after the asset bubble burst. Central bankers are reliant (dependientes), trusting, over-confident (demasiado confiados en sí mismos) on unconventional measures to loosen (relajar) money conditions. Too little inflation will undermine (socavará, debilitará) CB (Central Bank)'s ability. Rich countries would be better off (les valdría mejor) if consumer prices... How should central bankers go about (deberían emprender) nudging (codeando, empujando suavemente) prices upwards. The Fed (Federal Reserve)'s motto (lema, divisa): in God we trust. He bows (se somete, se inclina...) to stop the police from frisking (cachear, registrar) so many Hispanic men. His crushing (aplastante) victory. The city is indeed (de verdad) staggeringly (asombrosamente) unequal. Bashing (agresión, ataque, paliza) the rich will not change. The top 1% of taxpayers fork out (sueltan la pasta de, desembolsan) a whopping (enorme) 43% of the income taxes. The wealthy Manhattanites will quit the dazzling (deslumbrante) metropolis for dull (gris, apagadas, aburridas) areas. Like his chuns (colegas) in the teachers teachers Unions, he wants to block school choice. He took a robust approach (acercamiento, enfoque) to crime: being stopped & frisked may be irksome (fastidioso, pesado). If he cares (cuida, se preocupa) about affordable (asequibles) homes... Keep a lid (tapa) on spending. His union backers want retroactive pay hikes (incrementos). Left wingers who sound alarming on the stump (pequeño trozo que queda, muñón, tocón; campaña electoral) can prove pragmatic at home; stump up (apoquinar). Briefing (instrucciones, reunión informativa) → press -- (rueda de prensa). Under the spell (hechizo; racha, turno; deletrear, significar) of Sunni fanaticism → spell out: explicar en detalle =/= speak out (hablar claro, expresar su opinión). The odds (probabilidades) of success are long. Fuelling (alimentando) the combat. Sponsoring countries need to cut off funds & arms to their proxies (apoderados, autorizados, representantes). A mutually hurting (que lastima) stalemate (en tablas, paralizado) between two states... That would be tantamount to (equivalente a) accepting defeat. Tantalizing: (offer...) tentadora, (aroma: =; flores: scent; vino: bouquet) incitante. At the very least (como mínimo) means admitting Iran as a full partner to the diplomacy. He is shut out (excluido) from... Turn up: aparecer, descubrir, volverse hacia arriba, desenterrar, (a clase) asistir, (gas...) abrir, (manga) subir. Succour (socorro), a cry/ask for help. Bluster: fanfarronada, intimidación, (viento) bramar, soplar con fuerza. Dirty money distrust (desconfía) the trusts (confianzas, fondos de inversiones). Hide the proceeds (lo recaudado + avanzar, proceder, continuar) of crime =/= tax collector. Be<u>late</u>dly (con retraso). Money launderers (que blanquean + que lavan y planchan). Those who abet (instigan, incitan) them/a crime. Spurred (espoleado, incitado) by complaints from the police & pressure from campaigners (general) partidarios, (del medio ambiente) defensores, -- against sth.). British shield (blindaje) coax (persuade, =) its offshore dependencies into greater openness. Proper (correctos) purposes such as safeguarding (protección) assets for children & opening bequests (legados). Conceal: (objetos, noticias) ocultar, (emociones, pensamiento) disminuir. America is tiptoeing (ir de puntillas) in this direction. He convened (convocó) representatives to alter (modificar, falsificar) a lot of haggling (regateo, discusión). Ongoing (en curso) → the -- (no resueltos) problems. Bloodletting (derrame de sangre). The civil wars kick off (empiezan) every year in 1-2% of countries. As y so en las comparaciones: As... as (tan... como) ↔ not as....as/not so... as → I'm not <u>so</u> young as you. The outcome (resultado, consecuencia) of the war. Frantically (desesperadamente) → I'm -- busy (estoy agobiado de trabajo). Underlying (subyacentes) dynamics. America fuelled (alimentaba) internecined (destrucción mutua o intestina) fighting. More conflicts in the fifteen years after the fall of the Berlin wall than in the preceding century. Back away (retroceder + move back, go backwards), back down/off (echarse atrás). Wreak (hacer, causar) preventable (evitables) havoc (estragos) → the storm wreaked havoc (hizo estragos) on the area. Factious (faccioso, rebelde, sublevado; argumento: contencioso) Pakistan =/= bolshie: revoltoso, rebelde, indisciplinado. This genocide spreads murder across a swath (franja, banda) of neighbours =/= swathe sth (envolver algo) in sheets (sábanas). In Mali a brawl (camorra) involving a mutinous (rebelde, amotinada) army. The charms (encantos) of a victory can be overstate (exagerados). Talks towards the end were brokered in Lebanon. Pummel (aporrear, apalear) ↔ take a --. Rife (corrupción...: abundar + microbios/paro: hacer estragos) =/= madurar: (fruta) ripen, (plan, p.) mature =/= rip (desgarrar) out/off: arrancar → populations are mobilized by grievances (quejas, reivindicaciones) that have ripened (madurado) over decades. The drawbacks (inconvenientes) to partition are well rehearsed (ensayados). Saddle (silla) → be in the -- (en el poder); ensillar, -- sb with sth (cargar a alguien con algo); be --ed with (tener que cargar con). Kerfuffle (jaleo, follón). Blooming: (árbol) floreciente, (salud) radiante, -- peace. Carve (trinchar, tallar, esculpir), carve up (dividir/repartir, rajar). Tricky (complicado), (pers.) astuta. Blood trickled (salía a chorros) out of his nose. Limb: miembro, rama: → tear sb -- from -- (despedazar algo). Bombs rained down on (llovían sobre) his capital. Curtailing (cortando, interrumpiendo) the flow of money, outsiders can engineer a mutually hurting (hiriente, perjudicable) stalemate (tablas, punto muerto; paralización; chess: ahogado); Lazarus blame for the partisan (parcial; partidario, partidista) deadlock (punto muerto en las negociaciones) that grips immigration reform raising the ghastly (fatal, espantoso, horrible) prospect. Knowing that the enemy is under the cosh (porra,V) can tempt embattled (asediados, Mil: en orden de batalla) combatants to hold out (durar, aguantar). Legitimacy seeps through/in/out/(se filtra a través/adentro/afuera), seeps away (escurrirse). He is not in tune with the piano. Consumption soared. Simply unlock (abrir; secretos: desentrañar) the capacity that had been sitting (sentada, colocada...) unused. The state driving investment is tapering off (se apaga poco a poco, decae)... Private investment is flat (apagado, flojo). Require tenure (ocupación, tenencia, titularidad, ejercicio) to be informed of whether a teacher is any good. The past layoffs (despidos)... =/= layouts (distribución, trazado, plan) were simply by seniority (años de trabajo), the new hired <u>dumped</u> first. It had an outsize (enorme, de talla muy grande) impact. A mooted (planteado, sometido a discusión) bombing, a -- (discutible) plan. They pay less heed (atención) pledging (prometiendo) to reform the EU for the good of all & most to the referendum for the pull out (salida). Leer (mirada lasciva, con recelo,Vs). Singapore draws all their teachers from the top third of the academic pool. In America three quarters of teacher-training colleges accept students who graduate in the bottom half of their class. Anoint (ungir). British economy is 16% smaller than if it had kept spending at its trend rate before the crisis. British population is going up, flattering (halagando, favoreciendo) its GDP figures (=, cifra, datos). The tide (marea) of foreign students is flooding into (inundando) its universities. Scottish nationalism was in headlong (precipitado, echado de cabeza) retreat (retirada). Quibble (objeción de poca monta, quejarse por poca cosa) with the details → quibbler (quisquilloso). Bashing (golpear) → union-bashing (ataque contra los sindicatos). A global trade at which Britain excels (destaca). Take on (recoger, adoptar, asumir, encargarse de) ballast (lastre, contrapeso); few governments seem minded to take on vested interests (derechos adquiridos, interés personal). When the Pound dropped by a quarter in trade weight terms, economists assumed that exports would surge (oleada, hincharse, aumentar...). Gradual depletion (reducción) of North sea oil. British strength is in service. Export performance remains dismal (pésimo, triste). There is a political disappointment (decepción) too =/= deceive (engañar). Manufactures are in fine/good fettle (en buenas condiciones/humor) ↔ in bad --. Emulate (=) the successful German model. BAE (British aerospace) systems derives (proviene, proporciona) over half its turnover (facturación, volumen de ventas) from after-sale services. The state meddles (se entromete) excessively in the broadcast market, meddling with sth (manosear, estropear algo) =/= muddle: follón, desorden + what a --! -- through (arreglárselas), -- along (ir tirando). It renews BBC (British Croadcasting Corporation)'s royal charter (estatuto) & sets the licence fee that is levied (impuesto, recaudado) on all TV owning households. It lacks bureaucratic heft (peso, influencia) in Brussels. The Dutch drew a red line against further integration. Britain wants to move the line so that (para que) powers are repatriated. Eurosceptics tend to shuffle (remover, traspapelar, arrastrar los pies, barajar) at that question. Britain is exceedingly (sumamente, extremadamente)... =/= excessively. They are at ease (relajados, aliviados) with the idea. Some people have fallen (out) (caído) of mainstream (corriente principal/dominante) life. The union is fraying (se irrita, se desgasta). Soon prams (cochecitos) & backpacks (mochilas) sprouted (brotaban) alongside (al lado de, junto a) union flags. The Labour Government devolved powers of some public services to Scotland in 1999. Even in Wales most people want the assembly to be given new powers over policing (mantener el orden público) & welfare. A public service reform binge (borrachera, comilona). Bachelet, clad (vestida) in a shawl (chal) of... Heading back (volviendo) to La Moneda. She will win outright (completamente, al momento, sin reservas) or be taken to a runoff (segunda votación) → run-up (período previo (a las votaciones...). Confidence oozes (rezuma, irradia) from her campaigning team. Ease (aliviar) recession through emergency handouts (donativos) & infrastructure projects. Chile is experiencing a seething (burbujeante, que hierve, con furia) undercurrent (tendencia oculta, corriente submarina) of dissatisfaction. The growth rate of 5% under her stewardship (administración). Fully (enteramente, en total) taxpayers funded (financiaron) higher education to be rolled out (desplegada) over the next six years. A state funding (fondos, ayuda económica) to rich & poor students alike. It has drawn howls (aullidos, bramidos, pitidos) of protest. Sl*a*nder (difamación, calumnia (=) =/= he can hope for (esperar) a sl*e*nder (delgada, escasa) majority in both houses. She would govern from farther to the left than she did in her previous term. A sort of low-key (discreto) pragmatism. Sitting: sesión, (lunch) turno) → -- member: miembro actual/en funciones. The bottom fell/dropped out of his world (se le vino el mundo encima). The port L. Cárdenas is the second biggest in Mexico & a thriving (próspero) Pacific hub (centro, eje) for N. America trade with Asia; hub airport (aeropuerto principal). The surrounding (circundante) area is the stronghold (reducto, fortaleza) of a messianic gang (banda, cuadrilla). Pitch (Sp.: campo...) =/= whose turf (césped, zona de influencia) with rival mobs (multitud, banda, populacho; acosar, asediar) have turned the state of Michoacán into one of Mexico's most lawless. Ortega, waved on (animado) by his lackeys in the Supreme Court. Recognition of a ruling (fallo) by the ICJ (International Court of Justice), that awards (otorga) Nicaragua fishing & oil rights in waters that Colombians have considered theirs from 1929. The long-cherished (valorado, querido) dream. Quick sand (arena movediza). Drum: tambor → beat the -- for sth (pregonar con bombo y platillo), (mesa, suelo) golpetear. The hardliners (de línea dura, radical) within the motley (variados) ranks of the revels. Syrian national coalition has been a flip-flop (giro de 180º, chancleta). The ensuing (subsiguientes) deals have bolstered (reforzado) Assembly's legitimacy. The west's sole (único) focus is not his overthrow (derrocamiento). G*a*ggle (manada, pandilla) =/= g*o*ggle (mirar con ojos desorbitados) =/= g*i*ggle (risita,V) =/= chuckle → (a) reírse: she --ed to herself (entre dientes), (b) risita: it might raise a -- (puede que haga reír). The fickleness (sin objetivo, irresponsabilidad) of the coalition. The Saudis see an axis of Shia mischief (daño, diablura,Vs).

Linchpin (eje de un factor vital), =/= (Geogr., Astron., Hist.) axis, (ruedas de coche) axle → rear/front axle. Prop (apoyo,V), -- up: sujetar, respaldar, (Arquit.) apuntalar. His acquittal (absolución) could shake up (agitar) its politics. Business tangles (enredo, enmarañadas,Vs) allegations (acusaciones) that had swirled (arremolinado) around (alrededor) for many years. Angling (pescando; orientando, dirigiendo) for the role of prime (principal) ministerial heir. Cheering (alentador, esperanzador) on the peace. Shroud (sudario)ed (envuelto) in mystery/secrecy. He was crestfallen (cabizbajo, débil, alicaído). Outbreak: (guerra) declaración, (enfermedad) brote, (violencia) arranque, (granos) erupción. Troubles brewed (elaborados, tramados) by the disenfranchised (privados de derecho de voto/de representación) majority. They jockeyed (maniobraban, intentaban colocarse) to exploit... The talks of reform denied/refuted (desmentidos) by such enduring (duraderos) woes (infortunios) as a yawning (enorme) wealth gap (hueco, espacio, intervalo). Heavily state-managed (dirigidas, orquestadas) politics. Relent (transigir) ↔ unrelenting (implacable, despiadada) violence. Jordanians are so relieved (aliviados) that their king has kept them out of neighbouring conflicts. The troubles have driven a wedge (han sembrado la discordia) into Jordan's political opposition. The Muslim brotherhood in its guise (apariencia, forma) as Islamic action front, under the guise (bajo pretexto) of..., in that guise (manera). Opposition clout (tortazo, influencia). Weeny (pequeñito) → enact (llevar a cabo, Jur.: decretar) deeper reforms, such as reining (llevar las riendas) in the overweening (presuntuoso, arrogante, soberbio) power. Stability is not a turning point (punto decisivo) but merely a reprieve (indulto, respiro, aplazamiento). Mozambique has made enormous strides (pasos). A darling (querido) of aid donors. A spate (racha) of mutual accusations & charges. Río Tinto was pulling out (sacando, retirando) its expatriate workers' families. Troubles have been brewing (elaboradas, tramadas) for at least a year. They are sore (doloridos) at its narrow election defeat in 1999, which they put down (han atribuido) to fraud. People want to travel without delays or hassle (follón, jaleo, fastidio,Vs). The lion's share (la parte del león). Dole out (repartir) building contracts. Investors snapped up (se llevaron, no dejaron escapar) a bond worth $ 800 m. issued by a new state-batched (lote, hornada, grupo...) tuna-fishing venture (empresa, arriesgar, operación). As things are/stand (tal como están las cosas)... IMF called for non-commercial activities. Slosh (echar líquido)ing about/around: chapotear. Snag (pega, pb, obstáculo) → I don't see what the -- is. He loses sway (balance, dominio) over the choice of his successor. Placards (pancartas, letreros). Turmoil (confusión, trastorno). Hardly (apenas, casi) anyone/anything =/= the government badly (malamente, miserablemente) misguided the public mood (humor, aire) & the strength of the forces arrayed (dispuestas, desplegadas, en formación) against it. The establishment twice saw off (despidió) subsequent (posteriores, subsiguientes) popular governments loyals to... Rabble (chusma, gentío) → -- - rousing (demagógico, agitador, enardecedor) speech. Soldiers are incensed (furiosos, encolerizados) that the bill (factura, billete, proyecto de ley, anuncio) let off (perdona) anyone accused. Crackdown (medidas energéticas, duras) on the drugs. He gave a climbdown (marcha atrás). Get on (tener éxito, seguir adelante) with (llevarse bien con) the rest. In response to a thug (voyau, ganster + --ing: matonismo, brutalidad)'s demise (desaparición, fallecimiento) Pakistán wrings its hands (retuerce sus manos) in distress (con aflicción) + -- -- -- nervously. The swaggering (arrogante) leader loosely (poco rígido, libremente, ligeramente)... You should be thankful (dar gracias a Dios) you're fit & well (con salud). The government hauled (arrastraba) the Administration in for a ticking-off (bronca), the fishermen hauled in (recogieron) their nets. The remote-controlled aircraft prowling (rondando, merodeando) the skies. The rebels never wavered (flaquearon, vacilaron; luz/llama: temblar) from its aims of overthrowing (derrocar) the state. The bickering (que discuten) groups. He remains worried about being outflanked (aventajado, (Mil.: flanqueado). At least (por lo menos) =/= not least (sobre todo) reacted to John's killing. Government's tub-thumping (demagógico, =) triumphalism. An excuse for the drab (monótona, triste) capital to get a makeover (maquillaje), hairdresser's (peluquería). Glitzy (esplendoroso, de lo más espléndido) hotels development. Navy (flota, marina de guerra), navy-blue (azul marino) =/= na<u>vv</u>y (peón caminero) =/= laborer (peón de construcción) =/= agricultural -- =/= pawn (de ajedrez). Some car-carrying ships have been ordered to divert (desviar) to... There are trains chugging (resoplando en marcha lenta). Once (antes) torpid (aletargada), the city... Car's showrooms (salas de exposiciones). The building boom has pushed up (ha hecho subir) inflation. Corruption has blossomed (florecido) along with padded (reforzados, que cobraron de más) contracts. A common quip (ocurrencia, salida, bromear) is that new roads are narrower than planned, because politicians pocket money (dinero de bolsillo, para gastos generales) meant (significa) tarmac (asfalto). He bridles (se pica, se molesta) at any suggestion of graft (soborno, injerto). Weakened by defections (deserciones) & infightings (luchas internas). Triumphalism after a war has emboldened (envalentonado) a hardline (línea dura) political right. Stop picking on me (meterte conmigo) =/= they picked on me (me eligieron)... Peremptory (=, autoritario, imperioso) sacking off (despido de) the chief. It is muzzled (amordazado, puesto el bozal). The president routinely calls up (llama a filas a) publishers to issue directives. Attacks by goons (matones + -- squad: la policía). They bar (cierran) a couple of papers. Retrenchment (disminución de gastos) =/= tatty (gastado, estropeado) envelope. A sweeping (radical) victory. A mass conviction (declaración de culpables) of mutineers (insurgentes). A bloody mutiny broke out (estalló), I'm broke (sin un duro), he went -- (se arruinó) =/= (cosecha, proyecto) be ruined. Their bodies dumped (vertidos) in sewers (cloacas) & makeshift (provisionales) graves. A high-profile (perfil) trial: a criminal court handed down (dejó en herencia, (maleta) bajó, (Jur.) pronunció (dictó) sentence... Boost: estímulo, empuje; fomento, promoción, (moral) levantar. Street violence is likely in the next months. With so much (tanto) in common. Relations are at their lower ebb since officials (=, funcionarios) expect worse to come. Having snubbed (desairado) Abe, she said she saw no point (sentido) in meeting him; there is no point in complaining. America is infuriated by the incessant squabbles (riñas) between Japan & South Korea. Each side's diplomats ooze (irradian) exasperated contempt (desprecio) for the other. Stir up (provocar) historic disputes. Willfully (deliberadamente) ignoring..., scratching (rasguñando, borrando, tachando; arrancando, retirando) old sores (llagas). Japan has not atoned (expiado) for its wartime crimes. Compensate the women who had been dragooned (obligadas/presionadas a hacer algo) into working for it. They expressed remorse for wartime excesses. None of this, in Korean eyes, amounted to (equivalía + cifras: ascendía a, significaba) a formal government apology. Spur (espuela, estímulo...,V) → win/gain one's spurs (pasar pruebas, demostrar su valía) → Korea's president won his spurs in Japan's imperial army. The direct costs of falling out (caída, riña,V) are bearable (soportables). S. Korea's tourist industry has taken a hit (ha sido afectada) but trade & investment flows continue. The lack of face-to-face (cara a cara) economical relations with Japan matters less than... A strong trilateral alliance causes China to rethink the backing it provides to N. Korea. A slide into sharper acrimony (=, acritud, disputa enconada) seems unavoidable. The rail network climbs (trepa, escala, sube) onto the Tibetan plateau before... Will be by far the world's longest high-speed rail network by one-fifth compared with its current length. In just five years the high-speed track (huella, vía) in service has reached 10,000 km. more than in all Europe. Bordering on (lindando con) central Asia. A recent incident has been blamed on Uighur terrorists. Tibet is likely to be the only province without a high-speed line. Plummeting (cayendo en picada) on a 16 km. stretch (tramo) of tunnels, joined (unido) by a bridge at an altitude of... Gusts (ráfagas, rachas) hurled (lanzaban, proferían) grit (arena) so violently that it chattered (destruía) the windows. Japan's more regressive companies shudder (vibran, se estremecen) at all this. They will dedicate the old line to freight (flete, transporte de m.); freight charges (gastos de transportes). A sport-utility (deportivo utilitario) vehicle ploughed or plowed into (chocó con, se estrelló contra) pedestrians. It is in Xinjiang that the reverberations (resonancias, repercusiones) of the Tianammen incident will be most evident. Uighurs grumble (refunfuñan) about Chinese rules. They ascribe (atribuyen) outbreaks of violence more frequently to pent-up (contenidas, reprimidas) grievances over repressive policies. Government offers rewards for deals related to terrorist incidents. They are filling (empastando, rellenando) potholes (baches, cuevas) & prettifying (engalanando) pavements =/= petrifying (aterrador)... =/= when I described the loopholes (escapatorias) his eyes lit up (se iluminaron) + tax -- (agujeros), legal -- (lagunas) → every law has a -- (hecha la ley, hecha la trampa). Scribbler (escritor de pacotilla). Shell: cáscara, concha; obús, proyectil, armazón; desconchar, pelar → shell hole, -- shock (neurosis de guerra). Reporting restrictions (restricciones informativas). Set out (expuestos) in twelve bullet points (puntos importantes). Cordiality & secrecy/secret (secreto). Media gluttons (glotones) can devour the content (contento,V, contenido) without charge as long as they sit through (aguanten) the advertisements (anuncios); advertising (publicidad). The boss is confident (seguro de sí mismo). The software firm sees a sluggish (lento, Ec: flojo) economy as an opportunity. Brazil's two billions-a-year market. Folly (locura) to be reliant on (depender de) an economy where growth slowed to 1% in 2012. It also brought in (introdujo) a turnaround/turnabout (giro radical, operación de carga y descarga) + --/ -- time: tiempo de devolución o de respuesta. Europe's performance is dismal (pésimo, deprimente): it ranks (rango) fourth (ocupa el 4º lugar), rank among (figurar entre) → Spain ranked 125th out of 140. Kitchen appliances (aparatos eléctricos): electrodomésticos. Nestled (enclavado) in the green hillsides (laderas). The praise (elogio) of Mondragón as a shining alternative to shareholder capitalism. Its sales have fallen sharply because of Spain's property (=, inmueble) bust & low-cost competition from Asia. Its business ranges from finance to car parts. Britain's even (aún, todavía) older cooperative movement (founded in 1844) is undergoing (sufriendo, experimentando; trato: recibiendo) a similar harsh (riguroso) encounter (choque) with reality. A lower yen has turbocharged (=, alimentado) exporter's profits. Mr. Abe is hectoring (es autoritario, amedrenta, intimida) to raise their game (negocio, juego) & boost their firm's performance. They want to serve out (servir; sentencia: cumplir) their turn in top management + give it another turn. The elephant in Japan's boardroom (sala de juntas) is the country's ageing & shrinking population. Slack (flojos, negligentes) energy prices contributed to recent declines in overall (global, total) inflation. Across the G7 (Grupo de los 7) core (núcleo) consumer-price inflation has been stuck (atascada) over the past year at 1%. Trying to escape the shackles/fetters (grilletes, trabas) of deflation. Bit: trozo, parte, un poco de → do one's -- (aportar su granito de arena, hacer su parte), -- by -- (poco a poco). A painfully (dolorosa) double-dip/digit (de dos cifras, más del 10%) recession. A levy (impuesto, cobro,V) on the sales of internet devices (aparato, estratagema...) & an increase in duty (impuestos) on diesel fuel. The tax on high income still looms (asoma, amenaza). A swipe (golpear, birlar), lector de tarjetas, pasar la tarjeta) at profits in S. Korea + swipe card (tarjeta de banda magnética) =/= stop spooks (espías, fantasmas; aparición, asustar) attempting to slip (resbalar, pasar desapercibidos, pasar, meter) unreliable (informal, poco fidedigna) technology beyond (más allá de) its vettings (exámenes, investigaciones) procedures; they were incensed (encolerizados) by leaks (filtraciones), which suggested that American spooks, helped by their British counterparts (homólogos), had been working quietly (silenciosamente) for years. That elusiveness (carácter esquivo, fugacidad) is unusual. Digital banking: with its catchy (pegadizo, fácil de recordar, con gancho) punctuation represents one of the most voguish (en boga) trends (tendencias) in banking. Debt-ridden (agobiados) countries have been ringing (sonando) with an ungodly (impía, tremenda, intempestiva) phrase: debt restructuring. A one-off (único, excepcional) forgiveness (perdón). The emerging markets have flopped (fracasado, desplomado) & then bounced (re)botado) in the past six m. The Fed comments sparked (suscitaron, provocaron) a rout (derrota aplastante). Foreigners dumped (vertieron, abandonaron) emerging market assets & locals shipped cash abroad. The edge of the cliff (borde del precipicio). Very low inflation could be a harbinger (presagio, heraldo, precursor) of deflation. Internet security besieged (asediada): programmers ponder (reflexionan, consideran) how to fight back (contraatacar). Keep tabs (etiquetas) on (vigilar) particular targets, but also to snoop (fisgón,V) about/around: fisgonear, entrometerse en... The NSA (National Security Agency), the most munificently (generosamente) funded (financiada) electronic system agency whose researches sat up (colocaron, constituyeron)... Instead they try to work around them. One way is to subvert (trastocar, socavar + undermine; minar, subvertir) the standards & software which implement (llevan a cabo, realizan...) cryptography: besides trying to defeat (derrotar) the cryptographic efforts of others, the NSA also helps produce ciphers (claves) for America to use. Warns to users against employing anything that might have been tampered with (manipulado, falsificado). Technology championed (defendida) by the NSA. Get in (entrar, hacer entrar) → America's government is getting in on (tomar parte en) the act =/= log on in (entrar en el sistema). Display: exposición, muestra; presentar, manifestar, (plumas) desplegar, lucir → a -- (alarde) of generosity, a program that ciphers (cifra) a user's hard disks but which displays (expone) some odd-looking (aspecto singular) behaviour. America's spies have bugged (pinchado) private, unencrypted fibre-optic cables. Google has brought forward (adelantado, presentado) a programme to encrypt traffic between its data centre. They run ahead of legal ones. Leaked (infiltradas) slides (diapo). It's worrying that they can be thwarted (frustrados, desbaratados) without too much trouble (problema, dificultad, molestia). Baffling (desconcertante, incomprensible). NASA (National Aeronautics & Space Administration)'s exoplanet-hunting space telescope Kepler. They orbit stars other than the sun. The release (liberación) of the most recent data from the spacecraft (nave especial). Whose presence is inferred (inferida, deducida, insinuada) by the tiny dimming (atenuar, oscurecer...) they cause when they pass in front of their host star. Mr X having crunched (crujido, nos: devorado) the numbers, told the meeting that around the fifth of sun like stars in the Milky Way are likely to host planets roughly (aproximadamente, más o menos) the size of Earth. Sun-like stars are a fifth of the total. Asteroseismology. Pimp (chulo, proxeneta) for sb. May I borrow a car from the lender (prestamista)? Clash: estruendo, choque... → a -- of wills (un conflicto de voluntades). The hatstand (perchero para sombreros) was tilting/leaning (inclinado) under the weight of the coats + he tilted his plate, he reclined his seat. Bajar: (persian, precio) lower, (fiebre) bring down, (mano, cabeza) lower, put down, (radio) turn down; they lowered their heads before the altar, he leaned his head forward, he nodded in agreement. Obama seemed blithely (alegremente, despreocupadamente) unaware that anything was amiss (pasaba), sth was amiss (falta) in his calculations, he said sth amiss (inoportuno). Few succeeded. Projects often go awry (fracasan) + be awry (estar mal puesto, al revés). The cash-strapped (escasos de dinero) receive big subsidies. Disdain (desdén, desprecio) for business. Insurers have set their premium (primas) on the assumption that people would be compelled (convencido, fascinado) to buy their policies (pólizas). Americans took their president at his word, their old policies could be cancelled. Conservative forces seeking to stifle (ahogar, suprimir, sofocar) conservative voices have been quieted (silenciadas). Travel where they want in China, albeit (aunque) with varying degrees of hassle (fastidio, lío, pb) for those from the countryside (campo). Opposition to a global trade deal risks hurting the very (mismas) companies India claims it is protecting. Words & deeds (hechos). India stands (se encuentra) in the way of a deal. A non-negligent percentage of Moldova's GDP consists of remittances. Cheerleader (animador). Next of kin: familiares o parientes más cercanos. The longer it takes to fix the website, the greater the Obamacare will fail. Be stuck with (tener que aguantar) a far more expensive pool of customers. The law could make bare-bones (muy limitados, justos, esenciales) plans illegal → they made a -- - -- living (vivieron con lo justo). At home he seldom schmoozes (chismorrea, habla para crear contacto) with his political opponents. Business moguls (magnates + oilman, shipping magnate/tycoon, the press barons). This announcement is a sham (farsa, simulación, ficción). He is open to tackling (abordar, emprender) it piecemeal (poco sistemático, poco a poco), rather than in a comprehensive bill (programa completo). The Obama brand (marca) is less tarnished (deslustrada, sin brillo). Having over- reached (ido más allá de lo posible) in Asia & with a string (cinta, cordón, cuerda; serie, hilera) of problems at home... Change is bubbling (burbujeando) up from the bottom. The gestures (ademanes, gestos; demostraciones, detalles) towards reform were barely (apenas) visible. Whatever he says (diga lo que diga); linking the economic reforms to whatever putative (=, supuesto) future, political reforms might come. Dare (reto, atrevimiento) to ford (vadear + wade across) dangerous waters. Mr Xi is inclined to wobble (temblar, tambalearse, bambolear) =/= falter: titubear, tambalear, balbucear, flaquear =/= halting (titubeante, vacilante, entrecortado). Slim: esbelto, delgado, escaso; adelgazar, racionalizar → slimmed-down (saneado, reconvertido, racionalizado) deal: simplify customs & rules which almost everyone can support. Tangling up (enmarañando) the talks & threatening a breakdown (fracaso) in Bali. Richer countries are pushing forward (están siguiendo adelante) with ambitious new regional talks. A binding (vinculante) schedule (horario, inventario, programa) for the elimination of rich countries farm subsidies. Grid (rejilla) → national -- (red de suministro de electricidad n.); to overcome the gridlock (colapso, embotellamiento, paralización total del tráfico) he struck (alcanzó) a pact with the opposition. He dropped (abandonó) his plan for thorough (riguroso, total, concienzudo) overhaul (revisión) of the tax system. Clobber (dar una paliza) =/= cobble (up): adoquinar, remendar zapato =/= he cobbled together (hizo apresuradamente, improvisó) deals with the opposition =/= club (garrote) → clubbed: aporreó + con el puño: beat, thump, pound, punch. Pemex decline in oil production (down by 20% in a decade) & proven reserves (down by a third). They pay around twice as much for power as their competitors north of the border. Fumble (dejar caer, buscar a tientas, meter la pata) it & Mexico's moment is a fleeting (efímero) one. Europe's dilatory (lentos, tardíos) regulators. Some wounds go on hurting (siguen doliendo) for years after they were inflicted (inferidos, ocasionados). The financial trauma is as row (puro, crudo, abierto; fila, serie; remar; riña) as if it had just happened. It has spanned (abarcado) the World, overseen (revisado) in America =/= overview (visión de conjunto) =/= overlook: (dar a, dominar) → the room --s the valley, a room --ing the see; (pasar por alto) he was --ed for promotion, (vigilar, examiner) → -- the tear (rotura, desgarro) of the duct (conducto). Arrebato: (ira) rage, (éxtasis) ecstasy; rapture. Britain has been allowed to snatch (arrebatar) $ 90 m. from its operation just days before the bankruptcy (bancarrota). The Bundesbank saddled (cargada) with defaults (impagos). Europe's tardiness (lentitud) in cleaning up its own banking system: still undercapitalized compared with their American peers (iguales; en el tiempo: coetaneos). It fragments global finance & provoks trim (reducido, cortado, recortado; arreglado, delgado, adornado) global growth. Freeports: an attractive new breed (variedad) of tax haven (paraíso fiscal). Cluster (grupo) of cranes (gruas) near the runway (pista de aterrizaje). Skylight (claraboya). Loading bay (área de carga, muelle). A spillover: derrame, excedente de población, (Ec.) incidencia indirecta en el gasto público =/= spill over: rebosar, derramarse. Site: emplazamiento, yacimiento → burial -- (necrópolis), site for the cargo (cargamento) terminal. Will be soon home of billions of $ worth of fine art & other treasures. Whisk off/away (quitar con movimiento brusco) → they whisked him off (se lo llevaron volando) to a meeting + the children whisked off after school to yet more classes. Repository (depósito, almacén). The value of goods stashed (escondidas) in freeports is unknowable. Fuel this buying binge (borrachera): growing distrust (desconfianza,V, recelo) of financial assets. Steady growth of the world's ultra wealthy population. As the contents have grown glitzier (más ostentosos, glamorosos), so have the premises (establecimientos, locales). Provide with (dotar de) vibration-detection technology. Taint (mancha, contaminar)ed (sucios, corrompidos, manipulados, contaminados) treasures. Objects plundered (pillados, saqueados) from tombs in Italy are tracked down (localizados + localized) in Geneva. Uppish/Uppity (engreídos, presumidos) Social democrats veering (virando) in the wrong direction. Even a 3% drawdown (bajada) implied an expansionary impulse of the economy. Poland championed (defendía) the eastern partnership. Kiev was the cradle (Med: cabestrillo; cuna, mecer) of Russian statehood (categoría de estado). Opponents are scornful (desdeñosos, despreciativos). Turn down: poner boca abajo, (T., vol., gas...) bajar, rechazar (+ reject, repel, repulse). Salvaged (salvados; rescatados) slops (lavazas, líquido de desecho). Cull: (flores) escoger, (información, hechos) seleccionar, matanza selectiva. Swill (comida para cerdos). Britain swiftly (rápidamente) banned feeding animals with any kitchen waste. Hand out (repartir). A watery (aguada, floja) consolation to backbenchers (diputados sin cargo) rejected for preferment (promoción, ascenso, nominación). They are slyly (astutamente) encroaching (avanzando, usurpando derechos) on power =/= pluralistic democracy is well entrenched (arraigada). Traipse (andar penosamente, patearse un recorrido) from public administration to culture & home (=, hogar, patria), it's a bit of a traipse (existe un buen trecho/caminata) to the shops. Their berths (camarotes, literas; atracaderos, atracar; eludir, puesto en el trabajo) under the old patronage (patrocinio, apoyo)-based system. The attention of members prone (propensos) to wander (deambular, vagar, desviarse). Political groups of every stripe (lista; tendencia) =/= people of all political stripe enshrine (engloba) equal voting rights regardless of race in S. Africa. Hardliners (partidarios de la línea dura) hunker down (se agachan, pasan desapercibidos) in all-white cultural villages. Blacks complain about feeling shut out (excluidos) in Cape Town. Many whites are disgruntled (descontentos + dissatisfied). They have spawned (engendrado, generado) vile harmless (inofensivos) extremist groups. A showdown (enfrentamiento) with the militias may mark a turning point (punto de inflexión, momento decisivo) in Libya. The country's fledgling (novatos) official security forces → full fledged (adulto) parliament. The public anger (ira) boiled over (rebosaba, perdió el control). For once, the militias backed down (se echaron atrás). The more extreme rebels/prices are on the rise. He is laughing loudly (fuerte). Despairingly (desesperadamente) passed (a)round (de uno a otro, entre todos) photographs on their mobile Tf. Build a rebel army at breakneck (vertiginosa) speed. The strength failed him, he gave me the strength to carry on (continuar adelante). Snatch: arrebatar → make a -- at sth. (-- algo), hurto,V; trocito; he whistled snatches of Mozard. He defected (desertó) from Poland & will give/swear his allegiance (lealtad) to western Governments/the king. They are in a quandary (dilema, =). He should reach out to (llegar a) groups tied to X, whose vision harks back (evoca) to the days of the Prophet. The high-flying (ambiciosos, de altos vuelos, prometedores) emirates... The fully automated Dubai crashed (se estrelló, quebró...) in the wake (estela) of world slump (depresión) whose oil riches (abundancias) anchor (anclan, afianzan) the federation of seven statelets (pequeños estados). The World's tallest building & a symbol of what looked like heedless (despreocupado, irresponsable) excess. The number will rise as news *t*rickle (chorrito; gotean, fluyen, hilito) in (vayan informando); people *t*rickling in (entrando poco a poco), we received a *t*rickle of (algunas que otras) news; the stream (arroyo, corriente, chorro) of missions to the outer planets turns into a *t*rickle) =/= a patch (mancha, parche, remendar; parcela, territorio, pedazo) of dust now *p*rickles (espina, púa,V; picor,V), even in the sparkling (centelleante) high-rise blocks (edificios de muchas plantas). Dismissed (despachado, rechazado) on its opening as a costly dud (invendible, estropeado, birria, cheque sin fondos), the system is spotless (inmaculado). Property prices have to regain their pre-burst (quiebra, ráfaga, reventón) hug, but have surged (oleaje; hinchado,V, aumentar vertiginosamente) as much as 40%. A region with the world's fastest growing volume of air traffic. Dubai will host the new world expo. Boosters (promotores) think it would bring profits in the long term. Rising rents could make corporate tenants (inquilinos) scuttle (cubo para el carbón, plan: sabotear, Náut.: hundir; -- away/off (escabullirse) for cheaper climes =/= he needs to fix his reform or risk scuppering (barco: hundir; plan: echar por tierra) his second term. Pampered (mimada). The second term will be wretched (desgraciado, miserable, horrible). Mitigate (aliviar) → --ed (atenuantes) circumstances ↔ Obama has been flayed (despellejado, hecho trizas, recibir una paliza) with headliness (titulares) like unmitigated (rotundo) disaster. Voters are gobsmacked (alucinados) at how badly he has bundle (bulto, haz, fardo, V, liar...)d: guardado sin orden (his health reform...) =/= it costs a bundle (cuesta un dineral), make a -- (ganarse un dineral), bundle (paquete) of software. The law still inspires expletives (expletivos, palabrotas). (Technical) glitches (problemas técnicos). The law bars insurers from rejecting sick patients or charging them higher prices. This could spark (chispa, provocar) a dreaded (terrorífica) death spiral of soaring (montantes) premiums, a flimsy (ligera, poco sólida) promise for the 12 m. -odd (extraños, desparejados, que sobran) people on the individual insurance market. This insurance barely (apenas) works. America's staggering (asombrosos, sorprendentes) healthcare costs & mediocre outcomes (resultados). Obamacare tries to mend this, but it is a flawed (defectuoso) patch placed on a flawed system by a flawed president. The affordable (asequible) Care Act runs to 2,400 pages & has spawned (engendrado) a vast labyrinth of explanatory (explicativas) regulations. The average length (extensión) of new laws has increased. Personal consumption has crept up (subido) 2%, while real growth has fallen by 12%. Free tax repatriation of profits. These perks (beneficios) lured in (atrajeron) textile. Comparative advantages began to wear out (desgastar, agotar). The downturn (disminución, deterioro económico) occurred just as the government was cracking down on cross-border drug routes. A third of people receive food stamps (cupones para comida). Small communities are becoming ghost (fantasma) towns. The bond market sopped up (absorbió) paper that was fully exempt from taxation in all fifty American states. Young Americans are walking away (se alejan) from the stern (severas, duras) measures that have held such sway (dominio, influjo) over post-war American life. Humans & chimpances share a common ancestor. Petty (insignificante, mezquina) mindedness → industrial minded (inclinado a la industria). The partnership (asociación, sociedad, el ser socio) never really stopped at the water's edge & the NWO (New world order) gives emerging powers more say in the World affairs. Even Britain at the height of empire was repeatedly distracted (trastornada) by the need to stop any country dominating Europe. Flair (estilo, elegancia, don) for languages =/= the system would begin to fray (nervios: crispar; lucha deshilacharse) =/= revered (venerado) but frail (débil, frágil) → the 1930s frailty (fragilidad) in the finances was followed by populist anger (enfado) at banks. China scours (friega, registra) the world for raw materials & sends out manufactures of every kind in return. Putin chafes (se irrita, se impacienta) against America primacy (primacía) & the values that come with it. American tech., people & finances are geopolitically more potent than mere headcount (plantilla, recuento del personal). American military spending far outstrips (aventaja, sobrepasa) anyone else's. Russian economy does well when energy prices are rising. Russia-China border is an abiding (permanente) source of tension. Russia is by far China's most useful ally. America, by contrast, has a world-beating (liderazgo mundial) list of supporters: 60% of the 150 largest countries by population. China's challenge (desafio, competición) to America is not over global primacy. States like India, Turkey, Brazil & Indonesia are also acquiring a taste for power: they seem to want to compete rather than overturn (volcar, derrocar, ruling: anular) it. Shrinking the army by up to 110,000 troops from its current target of 490,000. America should aim (apuntar, marcarse como objetivo) to fight them less often & more wisely. American capitalism is as spirited (enérgico, fogoso) as ever. Clinch: abrazo,V, (elecciones) ganar, afianzar, (clavo) remachar, firmar/cerrar un contrato; clincher (factor decisivo) → debt will be a clinching problem. The $ is still the world's main reserve currency & is likely to remain so. The weary (cansados, pesados) theatrics of Congress's furloughs (permisos + licences, permissions) sequestered (=, aislaron, confiscaron) fiscal cliffs (precipicios). The huge expansion of TPP (Trans - pacific partnership) & the new TTIP (Transatlantic trade & investment partnership). A bigger worry is that the deals will fall (+ temperatura: descender). TPP presents all twelve countries with big problems. Obama observed wryly (irónicamente) that America chastised (castigaba, reprendía) for meddling (intromisión) in the region. The removal (supresión, extracción, eliminación; traslado) of S. Hussein was meant to eradicate weapons of mass destruction & demonstrate to rogue (pícaro, villano, grosero) states they would not defy the world's only superpower. Bush swept insurgences & jihadist movements into one worldwide war on terror. This galvanized the American public into supporting the campaigns in Afghanistan & Iraq. Misunderstand the significance of the unipolar moment/unrivalled power. He & his officials belittled (menospreciaron) international institutions like UNO (United Nations Organisation). Countries with overwhelming power mistakenly come to believe that force will solve everything.

American primacy is helpful rather than threatening. Obama has made a stab (intento, navajazo) at setting a new balance. Some governments crimes will be so egregious (=, famosos, célebres, insignes) that other nations must act. Institutions that they claim to cherish (apreciar). In anyone of its closest allies have dispatched (=, enviado, expedido) forces with the unanimous backing of the UN Security council. South America feels alternately ignored & intruded (importunada, molesta & inmiscuida). America is smarting (se escuece, se resiente) from the anxiety of decline. The armed forces are peerless (sin igual) & will remain so, even if they are financed less lavishly (generosamente)... America doesn't count those two threats as decline. China is sneering (despreciativa y burllona) at the disfunction in Washington. The main advisers are stretched too thin (exigidos al máximo esfuerzo). Many years could elapse/pass (transcurrir). Oil & terrorism are core (centro de, núcleo de) interest for America. Iran wants sanctions to be lifted. A breathless (entrecortado, jadeante, sin aliento) programme. When in office he made downs, but more ups. A raft (serie) of reforms that he has launched. Mexico remains in the grip (bajo control, en la garra/empuñadura) of monopolistic business & unions. An autonomous trust (=, confianza,V, fondo de inversión, fundación) that could curb (frenar) the dominance of Telmes. A be<u>late</u>d (atrasado) attempt to..., a banking reform to boost lending. The stripping away (desmantelamiento) of the monopolies of Pemex & FEC (Federal Electricity Commission). Whether or not energy firms flock (rebaño, ir en tropel) to Mexico will depend on the fine print (letra pequeña) of the contracts & the fairness (justicia, imparcialidad, belleza) of regulators. It worries that the word "Concessions" would break one taboo to many. Instead it may accept licences. Security remains fragile, with nerves twitching (tirantes, contraídos,Vs) after a spike (punta, aumento brusco; púa; espiga, clavar...) in kidnapping & extortion. Lingering (persistente) drug-related violence in the poor South & West. Chile's election: we thought this would be an eight-month pregnancy but in the end it's going to the full term. Few Brazilians believed he would be charged, let alone (aún menos) convicted or jailed. He quietly fled (huyó, escapó) to Italy, where he also has citizenship. Acquittal (absolución) on those charges is possible, saving several years from sentences (=, fallos, condenas). The court recently dismissed (despidió, Jur: anuló) a flurry (racha) of arcane (misteriosas) appeals (apelaciones) as merely delaying tactics. He executed (cumplió con las formalidades) last year's expropriation of Repsol's controlling stakes. Ridden (cargado) with debts/doubts → Ms Fernández would moderate her control-ridden (muy controlada) economic policy =/= conflict-ridden (muy conflictivo). Boot up (cebar) =/= boot out (poner de patitas en la calle) governments. Some billions of people now live within democracies, however imperfect. The news was met stonily (severamente + coolly: friamente) in... Elections to refresh (refrescar, actualizar) that assembly were twice put off (pospuestas + postponed). Voters were not cowed (acobardados) by threats of violence. Televisions advertisements (anuncios publicitarios) touting (pregonando) the victory. Bristle: (of brush/animals) cerda + erizarse → -- with anger (enfurecerse). The public approves of the government taking aim (dirigiéndose) at welfare recipients. Amid a din (estruendo) of slot (ranura) machines & air thick with smoke. Grim (sombrío, lúgubre, desalentador) -faced punters (apostadores, clientes) in the parlours (salones). A law that orders citizens to inform on anyone found (encontrado) squandering (derrochando) welfare money on pachinko. The economy is picking up (mejora). Thanks to Abe the stock market is sharply (bruscamente, claramente, de repente) higher & property prices are rising. This has benefited the better-off, though not noticeably (sensiblemente): a 2.2 m. draw livelihood (sustento) assistance for the poor. Sweeping (excesiva generalización, cambio radical, victoria arrolladora)s: desechos, escoria. The criticism is unfair (injusto). Mr Aquino is under fire (atacado) for seeming (aparente) complacent (satisfecho de sí mismo), somewhat unfeeling (insensible) & for trying to pass the buck (escurrir el bulto). Accused of being <u>dismiss</u> (destituir, descartar)<u>ive (despectivo</u> + contemptuous, disparaging) towards the suffering of some victims. He finds unalloyed (puro, no mezclado, absoluto) respite (respiro) from his troubles at home. The outpouring (efusión) of international sympathy & generosity the disaster prompted (dio lugar). Niggardly (tacaño, miserable). Philip's temerity in standing up (hacer frente) to China over... The hard power America can bring to bear (ejercer) in the Pacific + bring influence to bear. Chary (reacio, cauteloso) of meddling (intromisión). Swamped (inundado, agobiado) by a typhoon. Thailand donated X tonnes of rice from the Government stockpiles (reservas, almacenes), swollen (aumentado) by an expensive Price-support scheme. Scrap: trocito/pizca (of truth...); pelearse, descartar (the € zone --s its rules) =/= scrap<u>s</u>: sobras =/= scrap<u>e</u>: rozar, raspar, rascar, pelar; apuro =/= scrappy (deshilvanado, irregular, luchador) outsiders (pers. de fuera). A system to protect depositors: smaller banks might get into trouble if interest rates on deposits are freed. Key resources: oil, water, gas, electricity, transport... hail (aclaman...) steps in predictably (previsible + foreseeable) effusive language. The cookie (galleta) crumbles (se desmigaja). She is pressing ahead with sth. (sigue adelante con algo). Tout: pronosticar, ofrecer, revendedor,V → -- for business (captar clientes), -- even wholesome (sanos) products to children is to exploit his naivety. The bounceback (recuperación + recovery; democracia: restoration)... Within reach (a mi alcance) ↔ out/ beyond --, -- cruising (de cruceros) altitude. The law is mightier than the words. A shrunken (encogida, reducida) head. Asian shipyards (astilleros): the deeper, the better. Churn (lechera, mantequera; batir, agitar;

ruedas/hélice: girar rápidamente) up: revolver → he capped (coronó y puso tope a) a stomach-churning fortnight =/= -- out: producción en serie. Plenty of behemoths (monstruos) are welded (soldados, unificados) in S. Korea. Thrust (empujón, ofensiva, propulsión) → the most advanced bits (trozos, partes) of the kit are the six th̲rusters (cohetes propulsores, arribistas). The most convoluted (enrevesados) cold war spy games/ nobel... Run into (tropezar con) last-minute problems. Run into debt (contraer deudas). The car ran into (chocó con) the lamppost (farola). Australia, as common transit points, would benefit. Motorist (automovilista), cyclist/moped (ciclomotor, bicimotor), motorcycle (motocicleta). Portfolio management (gestión de cartera). What was once marshy (pantanoso) wasteland (yermo, inculto). Schema̲ (esquema) =/= a pension scheme̲ (plan) that is not fully funded (financiado). Implicitly depends on future workers & taxpayers to make up (compensar) the shortfall (déficit, =). A system to deal with higher pension costs. Retirement income is linked to final salaries. The falcon/heron (garza) took flight. The collapse of a sprawling (desgarbado, crecimiento rápido) bank. The only thing they don't want to be blamed for is if a big foreign bank blows up (estalla) in their market. The sea water houses algae, bacteria & plants that generate about half the oxygen in the atmosphera. It also provides seafood. Its well being (bienestar) is therefore (por lo tanto) of direct concern (inquietud, incumbir). A fall of one pH point is thus a tenfold rise in acidity. A 26% rise in oceanic acidity since the beginning of the industrial revolution, 250 years ago. This figure will be 170% by 2100. Shells made of aragonite will not tend to dissolve. Acidification may help cyanobacteria to fix nitrogen & turn it into protein. 56 m. years ago, carbon dioxide levels rose sharply, the climate suddenly warmed & the seas became a lot more acide. The increased acidity was more to blame for this than the rise of T. Some think the planet is entering, as it did

56 m. years ago, in a new epoch, the Anthropocene. The handheld camera (máquina de fotografiar portátil) appalled (consternó, horrorizó) the 19th century society as did the Kodak keen (aficionados) snapping sunbathers. A device perched (encaramada, colocada) on a person's nose. Cameras on the dashboards (tablero de mando) that film the road ahead. Collar cams (cámaras) help anxious cat lovers keep tabs (etiquetas) on (seguir de cerca) their wandering pets (mascotas). Offender (infractor, delincuente), offence/se (infracción, atentado, ataque, delito), offend (ofender) → -- against sth. (atentar contra algo). A small band (banda, tira, cinta, faja) squirrels (ardilla) away (almacena, guarda) years of footage (imágenes, secuencias) into databases of e-memories. The web thronged (atestada) with furtive photos. Wearable (ponible) cameras will make such surreptitious (=, furtiva) photography easier. The looming (inminente, amenazante, que surge) issue is the growing sophistication of face-recognition tech., to enable Governments & business to extract information about individuals by scouring (registrando) billions of images online. Japanese digital cameramakers ensure their products emit a shutter (de obturador) sound everytime a picture is taken. Existing laws to control stalking (el acechar) or harassment (acoso) can be extended to deal with peeping (asomarse, echar un vistazo, mirar rápidamente) drones. Victims drowned (ahogadas), hit by debris (escombros, desechos, detritos) or trapped into rubble (escombros). Plucky (valeroso, bravo, valiente) ↔ feckless (débil, incapaz, irresponsable). Plight: situación grave → the country's ec. -- + jurar, prometer → plight one's troth (hacer promesa de matrimonio). Gauge (calibre, ancho, indicador; medir, juzgar) → they are --ed (medidos, estimados, juzgados) without compassion; key -- (indicadores) of the strength =/= gear: engranaje, cambio de velocidad (a -- change), equipo, orientar → stuck (atasco) in the --, they are gearing (se preparan) to provide more aid. Landslide, often

triggered by deforestation, have pushed more people to the low lying (baja) coast, where many eke out (escatiman, hacen que alcance) a living (el ganarse la vida) by fishing. There is much more than it can do to build resilience (resistencia) in the face of natural catastrophes. Shanty (chabola) towns by the shore. Sustained by pork-barrel (dinero para electoralismo) spending. Encroach on/upon (invadir algo) → I don't wish to -- in your time; Taiwanese worried about Chinese encroachment (invasión, usurpación), -- of your liberty =/= it entrenches (arraiga, afianza, consolida) powerful families with little incentives to improve the lives & breeds (cría, engendra) endemic corruption. The government writ (mandato, orden) remains pitifully (lastimosamente) small =/= regrettably (lamentablemente). Early-warning system (sist. de alarma temprana), drills & better zoning (división por zonas) all help. Bang (cerrar de golpe, estallido, explotar) together: hacer que un acuerdo se establezca. Oversee (supervisar) reforms... Mandatory (obligatorio) - sentencing (fallos) laws. Kingpin: kingbolt (eje, pivote de dirección) =/= cornerstone (piedra angular). Bust: busto, redada, estropeado,V); go -- (arruinarse). The punishment disgraces (deshonra) every American oficial who has collided (confabulado, tramado) in it. It is getting ever easier to record anything. A wide-angle camera around his neck which snaps several pictures of his field of view every minute. Cloud the issue (complicar el asunto). A lens cover provides seclusion (aislamiento). Headband (cinta para la cabeza), headboard (cabecera). It helps the wearer to take pictures & to see data on a tiny screen held just above. Disclosure (revelación). Google executive chairman (presidente ejecutivo). Another step on the way to a world where those who wish to can record, rewind (rebobinar) & rewatch more. Adding a run-of-the-mill (común y corriente + perfectly ordinary) camera to a phone. Drivers can defend themselves against fraudulent insurance claims. Some patients with impaired (dañadas) memories should wear such devices. Such approaches (=, enfoques) could alleviate some symptoms of dementia & Alzheimer. Run counter to sth (ser contrario a algo) → that proposal runs counter to/is at odds with... Record masterclasses (clases magistrales). The technology is clunky (maciza, anticuada, tosca y pesada) & overhyped (exagerada, recargada de bombo publicitario). Cage bird (pájaro de jaula). It is ludicrous (absurdo, ridículo) to believe it can be solved easily. Far out (extrañas, de vanguardia) ideas. Samsung earns from their sleek (lustroso, impecable) machines. Slipping (metiendo, deslizando) them ever more seamlessly (sin soldadura, impecable, sin que se note) into the wearer's life. A camera that would keep track (pista) of what notices (se da cuenta). Face recognition could be a boon (gran ayuda) to all sorts of surveillance. The ability to greet (saludar, recibir) everyone cheerily (jovialmente). There are rampant (galopantes) possibilities for phoniness (falsedades) & for a loss of frankness (franqueza). An unapproved software hack (corte, pirateo) allows glass users to take photos simply by winking (pestañeo, parpadeo). A touchy (susceptible) lot (=, terreno, destino) & new collaboration could be doomed (condenada, muerto, de destino funesto/fatal) to... =/= deemed (considerado, juzgado) wayward (indócil, rebelde + rebellious)ness (rebeldía) =/= a vote on the new property tax is looming (inminente, que amenaza). The wilder's courtship (cortejo, noviazgo) of Le Pen could founder (ir a pique). Harbour (puerto, albergue, dar refugio) → she harboured (abrigaba, escondía) not a millimeter of racism or anti - Semitism. It was Germany's turn to face a possible ticking-off (bronca). Buildup: urbanizar, (empresa) crear, (stock) acumular → -- área (zona urbanizada). According to a scorecard (tarjeta para apuntar resultados) of eleven indicators, ranking from current-account imbalances to export performance & pre-debt burdens (cargas). A system of surveillance & coordination that is both cumbersome/

cumbrous (pesado y torpe) & complicated. Euro area lacks a common budget & a single finance Minister to give economical & budgetary direction. Skittish: versátil, variable, voluble, (animal) asustadizo =/= even before the skirmish (escaramuza, refriega) between Brussels & Berlin, the German government had little confidence in its ability to police (vigilar, controlar...) the public finances. Germany insists on the fiscal compact (=, conciso, sólido...; pacto, convenio): obligation of the countries to write stern (severas) budgetary disciplines into their national laws. Defectors (desertores) =/= detractors; deflection: desviación, refracción =/= defection: deserción → the Greece's bailout: the coalition scraped through (lograda por los pelos) after a deflection of Pasok lawmaker. It should be replaced by a sweeping (amplia, radical, aplastante) wealth tax. The Greec shortfall (déficit) is only € 700 m. & can be covered by... With 4,000 civil servants due to be sacked, the government wants to avert (desviar, evitar) more job cuts. The fatal stabbing (apuñalamiento) of an anti-fascist rapper (músico de rap) by a self-proclaimed supporter of... In 1999 the Swedes had made it criminal to pay for sex. Pimping/procuring (proxenetismo) was already a crime. Buckle (hebilla, abrochar, torcer) → as the Spanish capital buckles (se dobla) under the weight of a cleaner's strike. Tussle (lucha) over proposals to lay off 1,400 cleaners & to change working conditions. Face punishments such as corrective rape (violación, rapto, expoliación + colza), torture, jail & death. As a tourist destination is fading: visits were down by 10% in the summer months, whereas tourists boomed across the rest of the cheap-rate (índice, precio...) Spain. Officials blame high airport fees & fewer long-haul (de larga distancia) visitors. There is more underused high-cost infrastructure, such is a network of new toll roads. Gay's law repeal (abrogación, revocación), gays can be hounded (perseguidos). On the fringes (fleco; margen, periferia) of French policies, populists are surfing (=, explorando, Comp.: navegando) this sentiment with zeal (entusiasmo). Mishandled (maltratado; asunto/caso: mal llevado). Hollande's poll rating has dropped. Policies will be bickered over (discutidas) by secret committees. A pile of unfinished laws teeters (tambalea, titubea) over Britain's next government. The hung parliament (no hay mayoría) the Tories feared. The other items in the in-tray (bandeja de entrada/de asuntos pendientes) are just as hefty (corpulentos, fuertes, pesados) as an in/out referendum. Nuclear deterrent (disuasión) is uncertain. Three things are jamming (atascando, aglomerando) this motor. Young men lounge (salón; gandulear, estar arrellanados) on wooden (=, rígidos) benches (bancos + escaños en Tory/Labour). Upmarket (de categoría, de calidad superior). In the grottier (asqueroso, cutre) end of the informal labour market. Most Spanish people find the British schools baffling (difícilisimas, desconcertantes). Check out (irse; cuadrar, verificar; cobrar, pagar) =/= checkout (caja), -- assistant (cajero/a + cashier). Correspondingly (por consecuencia, en la misma medida) grumpy (malhumorado). Gambit (táctica, estrategia, =) → a conversational/opening --: una táctica para entablar conversación. The populist bidding (oferta, puja) for votes. The blandishments (halagos, lisonjas) of the right-wing party. Tantalising (tentador, incitante) → six world powers & Iran came tantalisingly (tentadoramente) close: estuvieron a punto de entenderse. Constraining (obligando) Iran's ability to produce nuclear weapons in exchange for relief (alivio) on debt sanctions. Even J. Kerry flew in (llegó en avión) to clinch (abrazar, afianzar, cerrar...) the deal. Iran's existing stockpile (reservas) are just a short step from being turned into the weapons-grade (de uso militar) stuff. Anything that falls short of (no alcanza) Iran giving away (obsequiar, revelar) in full to their demands must be rejected. Foreigners in S. Arabia: they will soon be packed off (mandados, despachados), joining an exodus... Trimming (adorno, recorte) of foreign workforce will free jobs for locals. Those of menial (servil, de baja calidad) kind, which kingdom tend to shun (rechazar). Since (desde entonces, desde que, puesto que) women are banned from driving. The recruiters (reclutas, socios del club, miembros del personal) boldly advertised (anunciaron)... Most Saudis endorse (endosan, respaldan) the crackdown. The Gaza strip (franja): mothers wake at midnight when the electricity flickers on (destella), to flush (cisterna, funcionar, tirar de la cadena (+ pull chain), descargar agua) toilets & iron clothes + flush (colores) on his cheeks, resplandor; arrebato: a -- of anger (ira). Much of the mess is of Hamas's own making (trato, fabricación, ingrediente). Missiles lobbed (lanzados, volaban alto) at Israel from Gaza. Children in Israel's border sleep not in shelters, & no longer go to school in armoured buses. Israel stops most Gazan foods from being exported. Chuck (tirar, lanzar, dejar un trabajo) <u>away</u>: (dinero) derrochar, (oportunidad) desperdiciar =/= a growing number of Gazans wants Hamas chucked <u>out</u> (despedidos, tirados) of power. Egyptians are grooming (preparando) a comeback of Abbas's former strongman in Gaza. Harshness (rigor, dureza) towards dissent (disidencia, disconformidad). Gaza could again become a free-for-all (pelea, discusión) for extreme militants. Private health in Africa: insurers have spotted (notado, reconocido, salpicado) an opening for no-<u>frills (adornos, florituras)</u> (sencillos) life-saving (socorrismo) health care. Cut closing date (fecha límite) payments. Pundits (expertos). Counterfeit (falsificación) medicines & unlicensed outpatients' departments (dispensarios para los de afuera). Play hide-&-seek (jugar al escondite) with sparse (escasos) health inspectors. The Republicans are getting shirty (se cabrean) about it. He was mauled (apaleado, herido, arruinado) by a fighting bull (toro de pelea). In his teens he got hooked (enganchado) on drugs, trespassing (entrometiéndose, entrando sin permiso) against (violando)... His undoing (ruina, perdición). The judge had to lock him up (cerrar con llave) forever. A hefty (enorme, pesado...) 83% of such sentences were mandatory (obligatorias). Slur (mancha, calumnia, pronunciar mal): a cowardly (cobarde) --, a --/affront (afrenta, insulto, =) on my family's name (al honor de...). Convictions for battery (=, agresión, violencia). Blacks are twenty times more likely to receive such sentences. Skew/distort (torcer, sesgar) → -- the plans, these features skew (desvían, tuercen) parents's attitude to their offspring (cría, prole), in some states the number is yet more skewed (torcido, desviado). Stingy (mezquino, tacaño + miserly, mean) =/= evidence (prueba) of reducing crime is skimpy (dinero: escaso; comida: mezquina...). Long sentences have not made drugs harder to buy or Americans less likely to get high ("colocarse"). The sums spent would surely reduce crime more if spent instead on detective work. Tough: resistente, duro, severo, exigente, estricto → several states have started to retreat from ultra - tough sentencing. Probation: libertad condicional, período de prueba. Others lose public benefits such as food stamp & housing assistance. Patching up: (ropas) remendar, (relaciones) salvar. Two numbers give democrats the jitters (nervios): los pone nerviosos =/= get -- (ponerse nervioso). The deadline (fecha límite, plazo de entrega) may be missed: the site (lugar, escenario, yacimiento) sends insurers garbled (confusa) information. Foreign students in America have risen by 40% over the past decade to a high of one million. The Saudis make up the fourth-largest group. Americans poach (birlan) foreign brainpower. Those who venture on (lo emprenden) tend to choose... The numbers are leveling off (se están nivelando). Abashed (tímido) → the unabashed (descarado) pursuit (búsqueda, persecución) of profits. Lovingly (cariñosamente + affectionately, fondly). Candlelit (alumbrado con candelas) lanes (caminos). Gawking/gawping (mirar boquiabierto) at the replica (reproducciones) of the three ships. Crisis is brewing (se avecina, se elabora...) in

America's relations with Israel. Wicke*d* (malvado, pícaro, cruel + evil, villain) =/= wicke*t* (palos de cricked, terreno de juego) =/= whack: parte → they all want their --; intento: have another -- at it, colossal; porrazo, golpe Vs → a -- with the book; including likely contenders (competidores) for the White House have dodged (esquivado) initiatives to whack the president with the cudgel (porra, defensa) proffered (ofrecida) by Netanyahu. Take up the cudgel for sth/ sb (salir a la defensa de --/--). It's flaky (raro, descabellado) on national security. Bumper (parachoque) car: auto the choque, bumper-sticker (pegatina de parachoques). The Israeli lobby loses leverage (=, influencia, apalancamiento): to those whom brood (empollar, nidada/prole; están melancólicos) about Israel's influence in American politi*cs*, the bogeyman (coco, fantasma) of choice has been the American-Israel foreign entanglements (enredos, líos amorosos, Mil: alambrada); stop brooding over her/it: deja de amargarte pensando en ella/de darle vueltas al asunto. Netanyahu is stuck (pegado) to Obama. Colombia: spin out (prolonga) the process as cover for... The plot gave ammunition (munición, argumentos) to conservatives. They are going to turn into a party. The discussions remain vulnerable to derailment (descarrilamiento). After serving two terms he is constitutionally barred from running away (fugarse, perderse) for president. Shops besieged (asediadas) by bargain hunters (cazadores de oportunidades). Looters (saqueadores) ransacked (saquearon) an outlet (desagüe; liq./gas: salida; toma de Electr., tienda...). Price slashing (navajazo fulminante, disminución). Hoard (tesoro) → they were defeating (derrotando) hoarders (acaparadores) & speculators. Daunt (intimidar)ing: intimidante, abrumador, desalentador, alarmante (=) ↔ Maduro is undaunted: impávido, impertérreo. Pérez was brought down (derribado). Bring down the prices of publicity (de un tema)/advertising (en marketing) will have an impact on the figures (cifras). Panorámica (general view, survey). A sustained (constante) speed of 200 km. per hour. The scale (escala, magnitud) of the damage left in the wake of the revolution was shocking (pésimo, espantoso, escandaloso); the tornado left/brought a trail (estela, rastro) of destruction in its visit (a su paso). Man-made climate changes are heightening (aumentando) the risk of typhoons. Their backwardness helps to account (explicar) for the slowness of the rescue effort. Aid is being flown in quite easily (con toda la facilidad) to the tourist hub in Cuba. Amid (entre, en medio de) the devastation of fallen trees, flattened (arrasó, aplanó) crops. Toppled (caídas) power lines & houses blown away. Children hold up (sostienen) crudely (groseramente, de modo rutinario) written cardboards (cartones) signs (señales, letreros, símbolo): "Please help". Thousands have been trooping (ir en tropel) to the wrecked (destrozado...) airport to get out (marcharse...). A port so prone (propenso) to terrible storms. With two days notice (aviso) + notice to appear (citación jurídica). The reinforced roof of the indoor (cubierto) stadium stayed on (quedó)... Five m. high surge (oleada) of water. Foundation: establecimiento, fundación, cimiento) → the weight of waters & the weight of the foundations + the story is without foundations. The rickety (tambaleante, Med.: raquítico) & corrupt political system. Chide: (--ed/; --ded/--id/--dden) → Vietnam's government is chidden (reprendido, censurado) for its tight repression. Well-meaning (bien intencionados) plans drawn up (redactados, elaborados) at the centre are ignored. Economic planners are grumpy (gruñones, malhumorados) that the World Bank always ranks (=, °, clasifica) India as a rotten place to do business. Investors look giddy (atolondrados, mareados). Bad sampling (muestreo) methods often mean respondents (demandados, que llenan el cuestionario) are not picked at random. Japan's participation in talks to the TTP membership will require slashing high import tariffs on farm products. Schowcase (vitrina, exhibir) → -- (escaparate) for capitalism, the series (la serie) is simply a -- (vitrina de lucimiento) for its stars, deregulation will be --d (exhibida) in the special zones before being extended to the country as a whole. Since 1969 the government has held down (mantenido bajo, reprimido) the nº of acres (0.405 Ha) devoted to rice. Rice-growing area (zona arrocera). Part-time farmers, whose presence makes much of agriculture inefficient, would be squeezed out. Contract part-time workers & full-time position. The Fukushima clean-up (limpieza). Cover the damage from a hydrogen explosion that blew its roof off days after a massive earthquake & tsunami hit the plant. Pluck (tirón, ánimo,Vs) → the government will start plucking out (arrancando) over 1,500 radioactive rods (barras) from the pool. Rule with a rod (vara) of iron. The government efforts to <u>switch back on</u> (volver a encender). Abe is pushing for the 150 usable reactors to restart as soon as possible. Koizume has stepped in (entrado, intervenido), calling for an end to nuclear power. The shrill (chillones, agudos) peeps (ojeadas, vistazos,Vs). The political divide looks as unbridgeable (infranqueable) as ever. Turf (césped, hipódromo, zona de influencia) out: echar de casa + they turfed him out (lo plantaron en la <u>calle</u>) in a coup in 2006. Scotch: (rumor) acallar, (plan) frustar + =), -- tape (cinta scotch), scotch tape (pegar con esta cinta). The crown Prince (príncipe elector) is feared & reviled (injuriado, censurado, abucheado, vituperado: reprobado). King's death would jeopardize (arriesgar, hacer peligrar) the stability that they may even (aún) have made it likely. Wide-ranging reforms. Have a good grip of a subject (entender algo a fondo). The China's state-controlled media has hailed (aclamado, llamado) the meeting. The pace (=, ritmo) of the reforms will pick-up (continuar, reanimar) & will outstrip (dejar atrás)... An upsurge (recrudecimiento, fuerte aumento) of reformist zeal (entusiasmo). Pave: enlosar, pavimentar, (-- the way: preparar el terreno para) → the market-opening measures (1990's) have paved the way for accession to the WTO. Sovereignty in Antarctica is disputed: States assert (se afirman, se imponen) themselves by building bases. The choicest (más electos) spots (sitios) for research stations were already snapped up (agotados, agarrados). For a planet's lasting (duradero) unspoiled wilderness (desierto, jungla, tierra virgen) an updated framework is needed. Bare (sin hojas) branches. All around (en todo el alrededor) are blasts (ráfagas, tempestades...) from heavy ordnance (artillería) & too chatter (charla,V, cotorrear, machine guns: ametralladoras, V; máquina de escribir: tabletear). Air-defence missiles shriek (chillan) across the leaden (plomizo, oscuro) sky. Russia has targeted (fijado como objetivo) political refugees. An activist stranded (encallado, plantado) in Estonia. Abuse (abusar, insultar) → -- of trust (confianza)/power, sexual --... A write down (anotación, amortización,Vs) on the investments. Cheap energy will prompt (dar lugar a) invest more. America will overtake Russia & S. Arabia to become the world's largest producer. The long-term decline in jobs has merely (simplemente) bottomed out (tocado fondo). Buccaneering (aventurero, pirata, piratería). Orient has forty trophy (trofeos, que exhiben) properties. Grading their staff ruthlessly (despiadadamente). Clear off! (¡Lárgate!). The pros & cons (contras) + con (estafa,V) → I've been conned. Corrupt connections to control the government. For the time required to get a licence. It ranks (=, se clasifica) near the bottom. Forklift (truk): (carretilla elevadora)... Plastic parts for the likes (gustos) of Siemens. He bills (anuncia, presenta) it as... He leases (arrienda, alquila) the machine. Current rules let the firm keep both assets & liabilities of its balance-sheet (balance). Branch office petty (insignificante, mezquino) expenses. Put a "Tap" on sb's phone + spinal -- (punción). Piano Basching (<u>ataque, paliza</u>). M. Weber credited (reconoció, dio crédito a) the protestant ethic with giving rise to capitalism + I'd credited you with more common sense (le creía...).

Bullish: optimista, (Ec.) tendencia alcista. By rote (de memoria), rote learning (memorización, aprender con mucha repetición) may be waning (menguante, decreciente). In the fullness (abundancia, plenitud) of time: con el correr del tiempo. Be mindful of (tener presente, en cuenta). Buddhist & mindfulness: taking time out from the hurly-burly (alboroto, tumulto) of daily activities to relax & meditate. An excuse to unplug & chill out (relajarse). In today's corporate World you are more likely to hear about it than self-restraint (control) + self-awareness (conocerse bien). Google course (rumbo, curso...): search yourself. Apple's co-founder had visited India on a meditation break. Zen influenced the design of these products. Three things are making the wheels roll faster: a) Omni-connectivity: the pinging (sonido metálico) of electronic devices drives people to the end of their tether (soga, atar, ronzal): no aguantar más. They overload the senses, invade leisure time & feed on (se alimentan) themselves, b) Rat race (la competencia, lucha por la persistencia): the single-minded (resuelto, firme) pursuit of material success has produced epidemic & corporate scandals & a widespread (generalizado) feeling of angst (angustia), c) Shelling (bombardeo de) mindful has become a business in its own right. A website that urges people to turn off (desconectar) for 60 seconds by visualising a dot. Yoga health-care costs. Get ahead (progresar, tomar la delantera) in life. Dwelling (vivienda) =/= China's swelling (aumento, hinchazón) middle class: from shoddy (chapucero, baja calidad) housing to fancier (más caprichosos...) flats. Shot up: disparó, creció mucho → she's really -- -- (ha pegado un gran estirón), sales shot up by 35% versus the same period a year ago. In slightly (ligeramente) smaller cities prices rose by around sixteen %. Valuations (tasaciones, valoraciones) + make a valuation (tasar). People from all over China buy trophy (trofeos, que les gustan exhibir) apartments making their market as resilient (pers.: fuerte, con capacidad de recuperación; material/mercado: elástico) as those of Manhattan & central London. Policies aimed at squelching (aplastar, sofocar, despachurrar) speculation. The sale of a second home incurs (contrae, corre el riesgo, provoca) a 20% capital-gain tax. Not always enforced (hecho cumplir) in other cities. The stock of new housing is soaring towards the oversupply. A growing overhang (sobresalir) of unsold homes. Indebted for a decade. He bought a stake (participación) in NY's G.M. (General motors de Nueva York) building. He reportedly (según se dice) outbid (ofreció/pujó más alto que) him to secure (conseguir; proteger, garantizar) a $ 20 m. townhouse (residencia urbana). Sting: aguijón, picadura, timo → -- in tail (algo no tan agradable al final): return the bail-out (fianza). The bank will have cost French taxpayers 990 m. in all. He took over (tomó el poder, adquirió) dodgy (poco fiables, arriesgados; inestables) assets from a company & tried to dispose (deshacerse) of them =/= dodge (esquivar) a blow. The process bolstering (reforzando) the banks balance-sheet. B. Tapi was cheated: he sold Adidas at a modest price & promptly (inmediatamente) it was resolt at whacking (enorme) profit. Argentine peso: heavy-handed (torpes, severos) controls on foreign exchange spawn (engendran) dodges (regateos, trucos). A pedestrianism (peatonizado) shopping spot in downtown (centro) of B. Aires. The increasingly controlled & farcical (absurda) manner. The use of Argentinian credit cards to make purchases abroad is subject to a tax of 20%, worsening the exchange rate to 7 Pesos/Dollar. Recruitment (reclutamiento). Banks try to assuage (calmar) the misgivings (dudas, recelos) of the brightest (más brillantes/fuertes/inteligentes) institutions. Banks have cottoned on (caído en la cuenta). A more restful (descansado) capitalism. A hundred applications for eleven slots (vacantes, ranuras, huecos). One guest (invitado) at a recruiting event admitted attending solely for the free booze (bebida) → go on the -- ↔ be off the --.

High-minded (altruista, de nobles pensamientos). Insurers'health. The NYSE (New York Stock Exchange) highlights (destaca...). Regulators did away with (suprimieron) that in 2000. At the crack (romper) of dawn ↔ get dark, at nightfall (al anochecer). Splashing (salpicando) out: derrochando. A breeding (crianza, cultivo, reproducción, educación) experiment. The animals' coat (pelaje, abrigo, cubrir) developed patches of color, ears became floppy (flexible) & their faces flattened (allanadas, lisas). The most beautiful women had up to (hasta) 16% more offspring. The beholder (observador)'seyes. It looks plausible (=, convincente, verosímil). New Guinea singing dogs & their offshoots (vástagos, retoños, empresa: filiales; familia: ramas) are descendents of the first pooches (perros). Their forebears (antepasados) accompanied the first American colonists (colonos) to cross Bering before the sea level rose to flood it at the end of the last ice age. Finicky (maniático, demasiado delicado), melindroso + affected, squeamish (delicado, aprensivo) & prudish (mojigato: hace escrúpulos de todo, santurrón) attitude. Either domestication happened more than once, or each group is descending from crosses of dogs with wolves. Pinpoint (precisar, localizar) where the dog comes from. Earth & Mars lie within the sun'shabitable zone, being far enough from it for liquid water to exist on their surface. Only Earth is inhabited. Venus, which skirts (rodea) the zone's inner edge..., wrapped in a thick layer of planet-heating dioxide. Mars is the opposite: a frigid desert almost bereft (desprovisto) of atmosphere, with all its water locked away (encerrada) as ice. Early in his history, four billions years ago, it was wet. A NASA spacecraft, Maven, will blast off (despegar) in an attempt to work out (calcular, resolver) where that early atmosphere went. Magnetised minerals on the surface would have helped protect its atm. From the full force of the solar wind (a stream of charged particles), by deflecting (desviando) them away. The wraith (fantasma, espectro, aparición) which remains. Outlying: remoto, periférico, alejado, circundante. Cloud computing: software & services delivered over the internet... Emergency big data: computer software that can analyse special masses of information. Financial tech enterprises to entrust (confiar) your savings... I'm very glad to make your acquaintance (conocerlo). We're old acquaintances. I don't have the honour of her --. Queja: (reclamación) complaint, (refunfuñar) grumble, (con rencor) grudge, resentment. I'm tired of your complaining. Behold, (o, e, e): contemplar → be --ing to sb. (tener obligaciones con alguien) =/= beget (e, o/a, o), otten (engendrar, provocar) =/= befall (a, e, a) (acontecer). Nostril (orificio nasal). Till (labrar la tierra, caja). Art (arte, destreza). Cain slew (slay, e, ain: matar) Abel. Nakedness (desnudez), Sem & Hafet took a garment & laid it upon both their shoulders. Backward (atrasado, hacia atrás). Look upon/on (considerar). Womb (matriz, útero). Philistines: filisteos (incultos). Joseph commanded the physicians (médicos) to embalm his father. Deposition: (ley) deposición, (Geogr.) sedimentación, (presidente, dictador) destitución + overthrow, (rey) destronamiento. Stool: taburete, banco. In the midst (medio, pleno) of a battle. Covenant (pacto, Bibl.: alianza). Deafening roar (rugido) =/= rear (parte trasera; criar, erigir) the Tabernacle. Ye (vosotros), thou (tu, tus). Righteousness (rectitud + rectitude, honesty). Stumbling block (tropiezo, escollo + pitfall). Cancel/rescind (anular). Grudge (rencor, envidiar). Whosoever (cualquier, quien, todo aquel que) unite/join together carnally... Her father betrothed (prometió en matrimonio) her to a rich merchant. Scourged (azotada) → a region --ed by famine. Thanksgiving (acción de gracias) =/= agradecimiento: with our more sincerest thanks, in appreciation of all you have down. Wherefore (el por qué, la razón) =/= therefore (por lo tanto). Depart (partir, marcharse) from the evil. Void the enticing (tentador, atractivo) of sinning. Gladness (gozo, alegría). Perish (perecer). Perverseness/

perversity (obstinación malsana) =/= persversely (sin lógica, tercamente, con obstinación). Sadden: make sad (entristecer). Transgressor (infractor + offender). Startups: computing power & digital storage are delivered online... Applicants are rigorously screened (tamizados). Slate (pizarra,V; lista de candidatos/ofertas) → he is --ed (candidato) to replace the director; put it on the -- (apúntalo en mi cuenta). Roller-coaster (montaña rusa). Long-standing (antiguo) employee. Slog (afanarse, sudar tinta, esfuerzo; golpe,V) → it's a hard -- to the top (cuesta años llegar a la cumbre), a hard -- ahead (arduo camino por delante) =/= slop: (alimentos) porquería; derramar(se), volcar(se) → -- about/along: chapotear, deambular. One-track (de vía única) → be a -- - -- mind (tener sólo una idea a la cabeza). Knob (nudo, botón, pomo). A feeling of drowsiness (modorra, somnolencia) overcame (invadió) him. Tracker (rastreador) dog. Circuit boards (tarjetas de circuito; notice board (tablero de anuncios). Add-on (componente adicional, accesorio). Biological machines can be quite scary (espeluznantes, que dan miedo). Felt (fieltro: en el sombrero...) =/= filter (filtro). Vending (venta, distribución) machine: expendedora automática. Landfill (entierro de basuras) work → landfill site (vertedero de basuras). Unpredictable (imprevisible). From this time forward (en adelante); let's sit further --. Mismatch (mal emparejado). Disposable (desechable) batteries. Showcased (exhibido, mostrado) in the front page headlines of a daily. Eavesdropper (fisgón)ing: fisgonear. Implementation: ejecución, puesta en práctica. Self-demeaning (autodegradante) prejudice. S. Africa's transformation from a byword (sinónimo, =) for nastiness (gravedad, lo repugnante) & narrowness (estrechez) into a rainbow (arcoiris: de muchos colores) nation. Banal Marxist ramblings: (veget.) trepador, (excursionismo) laberíntico, (libro, discurso) por las ramas, inconexo, =/= flib (con mucha labia, insincero) =/= garrulous (parlanchín + talkative) =/= a waffly (rollo con mucha paja) document =/= swagger (fanfarrón, arrogante + haughty) =/= scheming (intrigante, maquinador) =/= skulduggery (embustes, trampas, tejemanejes) by mainland's agents =/= loudmouth/bragger (fanfaron). Shrine (santuario, sepulcro) =/= the myth of racial superiority was enshrined (englobado, encerrado) in law + consagrado por la ley. Utter: total, completo, absoluto; pronunciar, proferir, decir → an -- disaster; utterly (completamente) without prejudice. I have had my say (he dado mi opinión). The bloodshed (derrame de sangre) to become... Perk (beneficio adicional) → while the rest of Africa has perked up (se ha animado). The racial animosity that he so abhorred (abominaba)... Harshly (duramente, ásperamente) judged. The ANC (African national council)'s failings (defectos, faltas) are not his fault. Lethal misguidedness (desacierto, torpeza). Outweigh: (disadvantage, risk) ser mayor que, → the rewards far – (compensan) the difficulties, do his qualities outweigh that huge stain (mancha) of dishonor (de deshonra)? Congress was deservedly walloped (apalizado, golpeado) =/= walloping (paliza; enorme, descomunal). These titans are besotted with him (locos por él). Fire up (enardecer) the economy. Skull-caps (gorros, casquetes). Feature: rasgo/facción característica, (cine) actuar; mostrar, figurar; película, artículo, documental → politics that featured the toppling (vuelco) of a statue of Lenin & a rapturous (entusiasta + =) reception for EU officials. The WTO'll all or nothing approach of seeking a jumbo (grande) deal... Leaving out (omitir + miss out, omit) more difficult topics: farm trade & intellectual property. The law that aims to pare (cortar; fruta: pelar) financial risks + pare down: reducir. Insurers pension funds may take up (recoger, continuar con, retomar una cuestión, ocupar el tiempo/el espacio, retomar una cuestión...) some of the slack (negligente, flojo, poco activo) in the economy: utilizar toda la capacidad productora de la economía. The heady (excitantes, embriagadores) days for the country. Handsomely (espléndidamente, hábilmente) his audiences bellow (rugen, braman) their scorn (desprecio, menosprecio). A springboard (trampolín) to become prime minister. He host a big summit for investors. His big rallies (mitins). The communal (común, comunitario) violence is connived (confabulada, con vista gorda) by some politicians =/= conniption: ataque de pánico, rabia, histeria. Run down a steep (escarpado) hill...The protesters struck up (entablaron, empezaron a tocar) the chorus (coro) line: "souls & bodies we'll lay down (dejar, deponer, liberarnos) all for our freedom"... The flags fluttered (aletearon) alongside each other (juntas, codo a codo). Skirmishes (escaramuzas) with the police floundering (debatiéndose, revolcándose; speech: perdiendo el hilo). They were standing (permanentes, arraigados, de pie, estancados) in the way of a police state (estado policial). Size/take hold of (apoderarse de) =/= a perception took hold/root (se reafirmó) that this party catered (ofrecía servicios) to rich people & favoured cliques (camarillas). Fillip (estímulo,V + stimulus, encouragement) to the party. All this is puzzling (curioso, desconcertante). They published reams (resmas: páginas y páginas) of other sensitive evidence. Bonus (prima, bonificación, ventaja) → bonus scheme (plan de incentivos). Coddling (consintiendo, mimando) the banks. Rearguard (retaguardia). Leeway (margen, libertad de acción) to save them if a systemic crisis comes. The most glaring (resplandeciente, flagrante) flaw (defecto, fallo). Brainchild (invento, creación). They are moving beyond the menial (lo servil, de ínfima importancia). The crowd greeted (saludaba, recibía) Obama's arrival. Breaking down (derribando, descomponiendo) lethal chemical agents into sludge (fango, residuos). Hurry/speed up/hasten (apresurar). The debate has rolled around (llegado) again. The hourly minimum wage. Saver (ahorrador), salary/wage earner (asalariado) → between 1979 & 2007 the incomes (ingresos) of the top 1% of American earners rose by 275%. Those of the bottom 20% Officials toiled (se esforzaron) to patch up (remendar) health care. Holiday tinkling/jingling (tintineo, musiquilla). Leafleting (reparto de folletos: leaflets/panfletos: pamphlets) for selected homes. The slow decline of marriage is upending (mesa de trabajo/pecho: puesto vertical; volcando) American politics. Boffins (cerebritos). Campaigns might have blanketed (cubierto, envuelto) majority-black city blocks. Strengthen (aumentar, consolidar, reforzar) his grip (empuñadura, agarro) on power, but undermine (minar, socavar) both democracy & economy. A humpy (agitado) year. In a three stooge (títere + =, personaje burlado en una comedia) episode, a bungled (chapuza, metedura de pata) attempt to find uranium. Merrily (alegremente) sitting on top of a gushing (efusivo, animado; chorro) oil well. Reforms are clumsier (más torpes) than expected. Rowdy (alborotadas) protests. An epoch (época + age, period) making (que hace época) give up of an oil monopoly. The ring (sortija) is a family heirloom (reliquia), the relic of a saint. A burst (estallido; tubería: reventar) of enthusiasm. Book (contratar, anotar, reservar) oil reserves. Revenue streams (fuentes de ganancias). Strip (off) quitar ropa de la cama, arrancar, quitar pintura, despojarse de algo,... → -- the powerful & murky (sucio, turbio, tenebroso) oil-workers union of his five seats on Pemex' member board (junta). He arm-twisted (presionó) his way to a multilateral deal in Bali; after a bit of an arm-twist (presionando un poco), I got him to agree. Cosseted (mimados) farmers. Even swingeing (durísimas) tariffs cannot keep out high-competition. Three blo<u>c</u>s (Pol.: bloques) → Western bloc which Mercosur left out (ha omitido) =/= bloc<u>k</u> (madera: bloque; calle: manzana; papel: bloc; obstrucción). Footwear (calzado). Brazil's new-found (recién descubierta) determination to strike (huelga..., adoptar, acuñar) a deal with the EU (European Union). A stopgap (medida provisional) =/= a makeshift (improvisado, provisional) stage (escenario, teatro, representar; fase, etapa; organizar). A push (empujón, esfuerzo) to oust the government. Affray (alteración del orden público, pelea, refriega). Singapore relies (depende, confía) on cheap migrant labour. No marrying Singaporeans or fleeced (esquilados, desplumados) by unscrupulous agents. Fleece (vellón de lana). Uninhabited islands. Backward - looking (retrógrado). A stunning (deslumbrante) debut for a left - leaning (inclinación). Hinting (at): hacer alusión a... → he gave us no hint of what was coming. In Delhi he would have won had it not been for the new party. Making N. Korea even scarier (más espeluznante, da más miedo); a scary (de miedo/terror) film... It has long baffled (desconcertado) N. Korea's leaders. He cloaked (cubrió, encubrió) his wicked (malvadas) intentions in the most deceptive (engañoso) of disguises (disfraces). Mr. Jang's downfall (caída). Western policy boils down (se reduce) to the hope... Mourning (duelo, luto) because a tousled (despeinado, alborotado) psycho-killer. Yet in the brinkmanship (política arriesgada, suicida) & chicanery (embuste) he did. Public unease (malestar). People of very political hues (colores). Before their visit expires. Glee (júbilo) =/= Glow: -- with (rebosar de) health, --er at sb (fulminar a alguien con la mirada), --ing (brillante, resplandeciente) in the dark: when trafficking in radiological materials. A tame (dócil, fiable, sumiso) people =/= a tame (soso, anodino, insípido) report. These materials slipped out (salieron un momento de + escaparon de) the regulatory control. Not overseen (revisados) with terrorism in mind. Undercover (clandestinos, + =, secret) cops (policías). Terror groups will pay dearly (caro, de verdad) for dirty bomb ingredients (=, components). What may be a nuisance in a rich country can be truly (realmente) crippling (agobiante, abrumador, paralizante) in a poor one. Not visually impaired (dañado) ↔ sighted (vidente) people. Forthcoming (próximos) legal wrangles (disputas, pleitos). Set-top box (decodificador de señal digital). Comcast is becoming more like the firms it is battling against for the attention of couch potatoes (teleadictos). Jolly (alegre, gracioso; muy): -- glat (muy contento), you did jolly well (lo hiciste muy bien), -- mood (muy contento, con muy buen talante). Mudslinger (difamador), the mudslinging (insultos, injurias + slander, insults) have been restrained (cohibidos, contenidos, reservados). Effigy (efigie, muñeco). She keeps improving GM's line-up (alineación, reparto) of vehicles if it is to take on (asumir, aceptar, encargarse de, enfrentarse a...) the contract. India is grappling (confronta un problema, lucha contra) with high inflation. With his trim (bien cuidado) moustache he struts (se pavonea de) past (más) hundred-<u>odd (y pico)</u> tractors & trucks laden with endives, escaroles & lettuces. Have a trim (cortarse el pelo). Farmers hurl (arrojan) armfuls (brazadas, montones) at his feet. A gaggle (manada, pandilla) of auctioneers (subastadores) & scribes (escribientes) follow him. Bickering (discusiones + =, arguments) =/= squabbling (peleas, riñas + fights) & yanking (tirando) each other's hair. The food supply cannot keep up (sostenerse) with booming demand. His forefathers/forebears (antepasados) have grown onions near the hamlet (caserío). Wastage (pérdida, merma) rates of up 20%. Verbiage (verborrea). Jettisons (echar al mar, deshacerse de, prescindir de) scores (resultados, puntuaciones, puntos) of flawed (erróneas) assumptions (suposiciones). Its powwow (asamblea, consejo, reunión) rose (se levantó) to applaud → a family -- (un consejo de familia). Chip away (pintura...: desconchar) → -- -- at (ir usurpando, debilitando) America'sembargo (+ seizure, sequestration). India spearheaded (encabezaba, era la punta de lanza de) an effort... Wring: retorcer, escurrir → give the clothes a --, -- one's hands (retorcerse las manos), -- out (escurrir; dinero/verdad: sacar): eventually we wrung the truth out of them. He confided to me that... (me confió que...). Day-to-day (cotidiana + daily) relationship. Financial globalization helped wean the dollar off (desligar el dollar de) its link to commodity prices. They fume (echan humo, están furiosos) about the €. An endorsement (respaldo, aprobación) of the battered (maltratada) single currency. Mint: menta, acuñar, (dinero, sellos) sin usar → in -- conditions (como nuevo). Kindle (encender, despertar) → it is likely to rekindle (reavivar, volver a despertar) calls in Germany. He ended up paying $100 m. less than what he would have had to pay to hand over (traspasar, entregar, ceder) under the new scheme. Hordes (multitud) of advisers poring (escudriñando, estudiando muchas horas) over their books. A lack of folate (vitamina 6) damages the reprogramming of the sperm. The process of methylation (=) alters the behaviour of gens. In the aftermath (secuelas, período subsiguiente) move uphill (hacia arriba). Credit-rating (tasación) agency. These models are no doubt better than the clunkers (cacharros, trastos, fracasos) put out (dispuestos, sacados) by Mody's. The more money follows black Ec., the more money is to be made betting against it. This single-minded (resuelto, decidido) focus on mastering risks is to be commended (elogiado, recomendado). It's not the West's interests to allow Afghanistan to fall apart (caer a trozos, desmoronarse, fracasar) & become once more a base for extremists. Al-Qaeda, holed up (escondida, refugiada) in Pakistan's tribal badlands (regiones yermas). Goon (matón) squad: la policía. Teetering (que se balancea) economy, ominous (de mal augurio) deficit. Scoundrels (sinvergüenzas) & oligarchs placemen (hombres de confianza). Dollops (cucharadas, porciones) of debts to spice up (estimular, condimentar) returns. Bubble-wrap (envolver en plástico con burbujas). All monetary bond-buying loosening bolsters (refuerza) an economy. Food crops are more resistant to droughts & floods. Vagaries (caprichos) of climate change. Shoot off (salir disparado). Single-handedly (sin ayuda, ella sola) she manages almost as much money as... He delights (deleita) in drawing (trazando) contrast between the flashiness (exhibicionismo: =) of Wall Street & his nondescript (anodinos (ineficaces); sosos, indefinidos) Manhattan offices. The police pummelled (apalizó) them, sprayed them with tear gas & chased up (buscó, averiguó) a hill to beat them more. Unlike the 2004 upheaval (trastorno, Pol: agitación)... Appease (pacificar (=), calmar, satisfacer) the protesters. Break-up: (contrato, acuerdo) disolución) =/= breakaway (ruptura; disidentes; Sp.: escapada) terrorists. Leaving the country vulnerable to outside pressure. The new generation feels European & shakes off (se deshacen de) the post-Soviet legacy. Grapple (asir, agarrar, luchar cuerpo a cuerpo) → --ing with (confrontando) a visible pb. Homeless people pull down their trousers & underwear (ropa interior) in full view of startled (asustados) tourists before relieving (aliviarse) themselves (orinar). Smears (manchas, calumnias) across advertising billboards (carteleras). Small piles of human excrement dot (punto,V, salpican) the back wall, where the destitute (indigentes) huddle (pers.: se apiñan, se acurrucan; cosas: montón) at night. After cleaning themselves on bus stop shelters (refugios) & defecating. Playground (patio de recreo). A strike for ten days without an end in sight. Undergraduate (estudiante) unable to register for courses, let alone (y para que hablar de) attend classes + short course (cursillo), take/do a --, a -- in, on..., main (principal) -- (plato), (en hipódromos) lista para carreras. Work is winding down (se relaja + disminuye poco a poco) ahead. Drag: arrastrar → the turf (territorio, zona de influencia) battle could drag on (durar mucho, hacerse pesado) for month =/= drag away (llevarse a la fuerza), drag in (sacar a relucir). Britain wants to renegotiate membership & repatriate powers. Dutch would like the European institutions to take a vow (hacer voto) of self-restraint (auto-control) & national parliaments should have more scope (libertad, alcance) to block initiatives. Jig: plantilla, criba, bailar dando brincos → rejigging of priorities + keep jigging up & down (no poder estarse quieto). Pin: alfiler, prender con alfiler; insignia; (Electr.) clavija, (ropa) pinza, sujetar, culpar, depositar sus esperanzas en); they --ned him (lo arrinconaron) against the wall; I don't -- (me importa un bledo) what... → National leaders too often pin their failures on Brussels. The € needs a more hand-off (de no intervención) means of stabilizing the economy. Kingmaker (persona muy influyente). Fret: preocuparse, corroer → don't fret! (¡No te preocupes!); -- about immigration. Winch (torno, levantar con torno) onto lorries. They gathered round him. They round them up (los acorralan) & shepherd (pastor, hicieron entrar) them into lorries. Shear (esquilar, romper) audacity. A cameline snort (resoplido, V) as he races for the water's edge. Prone (propenso) to blunder (meter la pata) & rarely inconvenienced (=, incomodado). His usual good humour & thunderous (estruendoso) optimism. Plum<u>b</u> (plomo, a plomo, sondear, dilucidar) =/= voters are more likely to plum<u>p</u> (relleno, regordete, rollizo; dejarse caer, plantear, planificar) for (optar por) upper class, -- for tolerance, -- for sth: decidirse por algo. Aloof/distant/far all/remote (distante). Slap (palmada) → by slapping down (bajar los humos a) his more popular rival. Straightfaced (serio, sin reír). Resumption (reasunción) of old ways. Landlocked country. The former coup (golpe, éxito) leader is dragged to court. They frogmarched in/out (entraron/sacaron a la fuerza) the strongman to court. Bank <u>notes: billetes</u> de banco, pagaré. Commodity prices have wobbled (tambaleado). Franqueza (frankness, familiarity). It's worth it (vale la pena) reading (leerlo); a museum which is well worth a visit or which is worthy of a visit. A statue of a stern (severo) -faced man in a <u>frock</u> (vestido, hábito) <u>coat</u> (levita). One clenched (apretado) fist at his side. Whip (látigo, azote,V) → he whipped up (preparó rápido, improvisó; montó, exaltó) sentiments against her. Nor can they portray (retratar, describir) him as a hapless (desventurada, desafortunada) egghead (lumbrera). Burial mounds (túmulos funerarios) containing likeness (parecidos) of mythical animals. Airwaves: (radio, TV) ondas.

Crackles (crepitaciones, crujidos, chisporroteos; interferencias) & shrieks (chillidos, gritos,Vs). Cruise: hacer un crucero, navegar, patrullar, -- ship: transatlántico. Leaving entrenched (arraigados) regimes running shody (chapuceros, de pacotilla) states. They deny this stoutly (sólidamemente, rotundamente). Market for sluggish (floja, lenta) western economy. Assertive (enérgico, afirmado) approach of territorial disputes. Domestic economy in the doldrums (abatimiento, estancamiento). The days of derision (burla) are long done. Geeks (obsesos, gansos/ personas socialmente ineptas) → computer --: obseso de la informática) are Gods. An old explanation for economic drift (cambio, deriva) gains a new following (audiencia). A lurking (vaga, indefinible) suspicion =/= the party lurked (merodeaba, estaba al acecho de) reviled on the far right of politics. List (lista, catálogo; enumerar, cotizar)less: apático, indiferente, lánguido. British pressure gradually cracks (desmorona, raja) open service markets. The party comes in many blends (mezclas, combinaciones) but the members share three convictions (=). The elite at the top & the scroungers (gorrones) at the bottom → -- a ticket, -- on/off sb. (vivir a costa de alguien). Bulge (bulto, abombamiento, incremento) → pockets --ed with apples, the postwar -- in the birth rate (explosión demográfica). Mainstream (corriente principal) → -- parties in Europa, the -- has done so badly this work that it diverges not sharply (radicalmente) from the -- of fiction, the -- of American life (el americano medio). Come to naught (malograrse + intento, proyecto: failed; persona: ill-fated). Under Le Pen'sthuggish (desalmado, matón) father. Squat: agacharse, rechoncho y bajo; ocupar un inmueble ilegalmente. She has recruited three graduates of ENA (Ecole Nationale Administration). So it has signals of seriousness. Fully (completamente, por lo menos) 55% of French 18 – to - 24-year-old would not rule out (descartar) voting for the FN (Frente Nacional). When she speaks, she is heard by the public at large. Sleaze (sordidez, desaliño, desaseo). Slick (hábil, impecable + skilful). Downsize (recorte de personal). Headscarves (pañuelos de cabeza). Roll back: (enemigo) hacer retroceder, (autonomía, precios, salarios) disminuir. The conflict of northern Caucasus is the most deadly (mortal, certero, enorme) → in -- (sepulcral) silence. Over two decades the crisis has mutated from fight separatists into a global jihad aimed to establish Islamist sharia law across the region. The money lavished (suntuoso, espléndido, abundante) on building offshore wind farms (parques eólicos) leaves the country. Bungalow (=, casa de una planta) or other low density housing. S. Sudan is criss-crossed (entrelazada, surcada) with battle lines. Arab media looks back on 2013 with almost unremitting (incansable, continuo, devoción aboluta) gloom (melancolía, oscuridad). Arab spring's toppling (derrocamiento, caída) of dictators has split our flimsy (muy ligeras, poco sólidas) nations into clashing (de choque, estruendosas..., discordes) sects & tribes. NAFTA (North America Free Trade Agreement): two decades ago got off to a flying start (empezó a volar). México potholed (con brechas) roads & blaring (estruendosos) horns (cuernos, bocinas,V) ... No pungent (acre, áspero, mordaz) oil smells, no whining (con quejidos/chirridos) drills (taladros), no soul-stirring (conmovedor) hammering. Blooper → bloomer (metedura de pata,V). Chopper: hacha pequeña, helicóptero =/= shopper (comprador). Rummaging: buscar revolviendo, hurgar (escarbar con el dedo...); ropa usada, objetos usados → -- sales (cuando se mercadean para obras de beneficencia). He called off (abandonó, anuló) a visit. Racial tokenism (formulismo). Support for free trade may founder (=, hundirse, fracasar) unless they gave concessions to foreigners on spying. Front-runner: -- - -- (favorito) in the opinion polls, (Sp., empresa) puntero, the company is a -- - -- (puntera, en vanguardia) in research. Site: emplazamiento, terreno; the -- (lugar que ocupaba) a Roman temple; the -- of a battle; (Arqueol.) yacimiento → a spoof (burla, parodia, truco, trampa) calendar circulating on networking (conexión, red de contactos) sites. Hearsay (rumores) for the next tournament (torneo). Clog (zueco) → a clog (up): atasco,V) of one-km. grocery aisle (nave lateral, pasillo + aisle seat: asiento del pasillo) =/= hall (way): =, entrada, vestíbulo, pasillo, corredor. The fares (billetes, pasajes) have gone up a 65% increase. Researches for the appositely/suitably (apropiadamente) named Sigma have fingered (tecleado, delatado, acusado) a culprit (culpable). The spirits of fourteen high-ranking war criminals. Rebuke (reproche) to China. Its ministers are <u>crawling</u> (gateando, arrastrándose, andando lentamente) <u>with</u>: estan atestados de (foreign policy,...). The gulf (=, abismo) between America & India. Mangled (estropeados, mutilados) messages: plenty of boulders (cantos rodados) have blocked the path to closer friendship. Swa<u>b</u> (estropajo, algodón) → -- down: limpiar la herida con algodón/estropajo =/= swa<u>t</u>: aplastar, matar → give a -- (zurriagazo) to sb. Zurriagazo: (azote) lash, stroke (of bad luck...), severe blow. Fly-swats (matamoscas). Handcuffing (esposas). Petty (insignificante, mezquino, ruin). Tit-for-tat (ojo por ojo) → a -- -- -- killing (ajuste de cuentas). The security roadblock (control, barricada, rechazo del enemigo) outside the American embassy. Fan (abanico, ventilador, abanicar, avivar) → thousands of auditors fanned out (avanzaban en abanico) across the country. Excise (extirpar) a tumour. Enable (permitir) sb. to do sth. + web-enabled (con conexión a la web). The NAO (National Audit Office) notes tartly (ásperamente, de manera cortante)... Honey pot (mielera). Support for Nabucco fell away (se desmoronó). They are hung upside-down, divided into two & shaved of their beard. The slaughterhouse, ten football pitches (campos) along with 11 km. of conveyor (transportador) belts. Its managers attend to the tiniest detail. Carve (trinchar, esculpir) the flesh where the various parts will fetch (traer, ir a buscar; venderse por) the highest qualities. Keeping inflation at way (acorralada). The cent<u>r</u>epiece (eje, atracción principal). Automation accounting for about 60%. Work, wrought, wrought → changes have been -- (causados) by the computer revolution; destruction wrought by the floods + G. Eiffel unveiled (descubrió, dio a conocer his wrought (forjada) iron tower. Get over: atravesar el camino, superar un pb. In a single week F. Hollande notched up (se apuntó) two continents. Traffic wh<u>oo</u>shing (con ruido al pasar el tráfico, el agua a presión, el viento fuerte...). Tight knit (punto): muy unido, integrado. Smash (choque, golpe, aplastar; rotura, quiebra). Gonna: going to → she's gonna take... Snarl (gruñido,V) up: atasco, enredo, maraña,Vs. Flickering (tembloroso, parpadeo; vacilante, oscilante) squabbles (riñas,V) are often involving star-crossed (malhadados: infelices, desventurados) results... The situation has been ebbed & flowed: con flujo y reflujo, con altibajos. British slapdash (chapucero, descuidado) approach to... Outdoor<u>s</u> (de fuera) man once summed up (resumió) his vision for America as a doctrine of the strenuous (agotadora, árdua, intensa) life. Blast (tirar, derribar, acribillar, marchitar; ráfaga, chorro, sacudida) a bear (oso) tied (atado) to a tree by his hosts (anfitriones, multitud, hostias) on a 1902 hunt (caza, cacería) + blast out (emitir a todo volumen); a nice blast (una ráfaga de aire frío). The spawning (el desove, el engendrar) ground (lugar de desove). Teddy (bear): osito de peluche. Roosevelt crafted & promoted a credo of fair (justa, bella) chase (persecución): keep men hardy (fuertes, resistentes), so that at need be fit for strife (conflictos) in their native land. Woodcutter/logger (leñador). Bag: bolsa..., cazar, pillar, embolsar. A freezer (congelador) full of venison (carne de venado). The action is in trophies (trofeos), in the slaying (matanza) of mighty bucks (ciervos) with 10 or 12 antlers (cuernos) for point racks (percheros). Ma<u>dd</u>eningly (de forma exasperante). Insurance policy (póliza de seguro) gives blanket cover (total cobertura + comprehensive insurance). Uncharted (inexplorado, desconocido) fourth amendment. Firms have called for curbs (restricciones) → put a -- on the snooping (fisgoneo, husmeo)... Lose customers if the public thinks they hoover (aspiradora,V) people's personal information & hand it to spooks. Pupils tossing (sacudiendo, echando) peanuts at each other in the back of the bus ended up charged with felony (crimen, delito grave) assault. One of the nuts (chiflados) hit the driver. Yet partisans seem unruffled (serenos) ←→ ruffle (rizo, arruga; agitar, erizar; despeinar, alborotar). Obama promised that it would bring new or improved coverage to millions left outside traditional schemes. Swoo<u>n</u> (desmayo, desvanecimiento) =/= swoo<u>p</u>: descenso brusco, redada (de la policía) → at one full -- (de un solo golpe). Republican ideas are at once (inmediatamente, a la vez) too ideological to win broad support & too small to tackle the problems that anger (enojan) many voters. Delivery (entrega, reparto; expresión oral,Vs, liberación). Museums are showcases (vitrinas) & repositories (depositarios) of scholarship (erudición, beca). Sleepovers (que pasan la noche en el lugar de trabajo, estancia nocturna). People look on (mira, considera) in awe (pavor, asombro, temor reverencial) → she is in -- of (se siente intimidado por) her superiors. China is racing to catch up with America. Bring blighted (desertizadas, deprimidas, arruinadas) city areas back to life. Blockbuster (exitazo, bestseller). Shafts (astiles, mangos, varas; joder) → (vulgar) give sb the -- (joder a alguien). Escalators (escaleras mecánicas) on the outside of the building. Spain public spending has been slashed. Non-for-profit municipal art gallery (museo, galería). Humidifiers to create sweet-smelling (fragante, con fragancia) mist. Showrooms to show off (presumir, hacer resaltar) ancient culture to locals & foreigners alike. Rough (áspero) neck: chulo, matón. Script: escritura, (cine) guión, (radio) argumento. Imprisoned or enslaved. The statues of their Gods are returned to their original shrines. Doff (quitarse) → escaped from the most Godforsaken tract (extensión, panfleto) of the desert, doffed (se quitó) his hat & said... A hook (percha, gancho,V) up (enganche, conexión,V). Fracking turns America into the world's largest oil & gas producer, outstripping S. Arabia and Russia. Natural gas curbs (mengua) greenhouse-gas emissions, since gas is cleaner than coal. Gold rush arguably (posiblemente, podemos decir) led to creation of Silicon Valley =/= allegedly (presuntamente). It doesn't lack skilled workers. The statistics institute is likely (probable) to cheery (alegremente, jovialmente) pick (recoger) items (artículos, temas). Bachelet duly (como previsto, debidamente) trounced (derrotó, apalizó) her opponent. Laughing ruefully (tristemente, con arrepentimiento). Work out (encontrar, entender, idear, calcular; resolver, resultar) → things will work themselves out... India: more than 8,000 women were murdered over dowry (dote) in 2014. An emotional numbness (entumecimiento, atontamiento) in society. Holiday entitlement (derechos), be entitled to sth (tener derecho a) =/= a well endowed (dotada) girl =/= endowment (donación, legado). A boy is coddled/pampered (mimado, consentido), & made to think... God-<u>fear</u>ing (temeroso), quarrelsome (pendenciero, peleón). She wipes (limpia) a metal plate with the end of a grubby (sucio, mugriento) sari (=). A hazardous (peligroso) drinking habit/pb. of alcohol intake. Expanding love of country & security education in Japan. In practice many doctors turn them away (los desvían, los rechazan) because the government's reimbursement rates are too low. Medicare does not cover the full cost of treatments. A growing number of elderly (ancianos) Americans are switching to a medicare plan, managed by private insurers, the government paying the premiums (primas de seguro); Bonus: prima, bonificación, pago extra, dividendo adicional. (Riding) breeches (pantalones de montar) → wear the -- (llevar los pantalones). Stewardship (administración, gobierno) =/= stewardess (azafata). A central bank run by bankers would keep too tight a grip on the supply of money, and so appears the starving business. During the Great depression the Fed reverted (volvió) to its original passivity, allowing thousands of banks to fail (fracasar, suspender; frenos: fallar). Caged (enjaulados) banks & an activist Fed kept the economy humming (canturreando, zumbando, ir viento en popa). Albeit (aunque) wanly (lentamente, lánguidamente). Rock-bottom (muy tirados) prices. Growth picked up (reanimado) & budget deficits declined. Recede: alejarse → -- from danger, -- from view: ir perdiéndose de vista. This lacklustre (deslustrada, deslucida, mediocre, apagada) performance is underpinned (respaldada) by the banks' loose policy. Print money to purchase bonds. In the hope of driving down long term interest rates. Bumble (andar a tropezones) → a bumbling (inepto, torpe) Mr has a mascot. In Candide Voltaire mocks (se mofa de) the folly (locura) of looking on (=, consider) the bright side of the face of unimaginable horrors. They never got over (superaron) the failed promise of the May 68 students uprising (sublevación). The upshot (resultado) was a sense of doom (destino funesto...) & decline. Petite & sprightly (enérgica, vivaz). Jet-set (alta sociedad) → the globe-trotting president is an inveterate (=, arraigado, viejo, empedernido) jet-set_ter_. Bafflement (desconcierto, desorden, confusión + uncertainty) & proc_r_astination (indecisión → his -- cost him...). Dithering (vacilando, estando nervioso) at home & show decisiveness (firmeza) abroad. A lukewarm (tibio, poco entusiasta) 51%. Loveliness (belleza + beauty). Civilisation after civilisation have been brought down (derribadas). The pier (embarcadero, muelle) of Waterloo bridge became the nuclei (Pl. of nucleous) of islets (isleta, islote) of recifs (arrecifes) & cast (lanzó, arrojó) the jagged (dentado) shadows of their broken arches (arcos, puentes). Brood: clueca, empollar; nidada, prole) → broody (melancólico, meditabundo); brood on/over: dar vueltas a (you musn't -- over it). Pelted (apedreado) with stones. Hulk: armatoste (lo que es más estorbo que útil, casco de barco abandonado). The hounded (acosados, perseguidos) rulers. Ramses II was never surpassed (superado) in his mastery of the violin. The British drove the French out of Egypt & picked out (eligieron, reconocieron, destacaron) their antiquarian loot (botín). Thebes, with its 100 gates is populated by a dark & woolly (lanosa, confusa)-haired - under - race. Hiss (silvar, abuchear) an actor. His left arm is severed (rota, cortada) at the shoulder & the top right side of his head is sheared (esquilada, rota). His toppling (caída, derribo) into the sand. The cockup (lío, fastidio) tends to be wrongly judged. Tug: arrastrar, tirar de algo, (Náut.) remolcar, --gish (desalmado + heartless) president. Lone (solitarios) egomaniacs (ególatras). Crossbreed (híbrido, cruce) of starry-eyed (idealista, soñador) dreamer & hard-nosed (duro) businessman. A rocket (cohete)-plane to carry passengers to the giddy (mareado, vertiginoso) height of 100 km. above Earth. The inner edge of outer space (espacio sideral: de los astros). Passing: (ojeada) rápida, (moda) pasajera, fallecimiento; a – (que pasa) car; (costumbre) eliminación, (Parlamento) aprobación + passing traffic would drown (out) (ahogar, inundar) with the splash (chapoteo, salpicadura). They were slip - ups (deslices, meteduras de pata). It pained him (le dolía) to imagine... He abhorred (abominaba) work. A thick crossbar (listón, (bicicleta) barra; goalpost: larguero...) of the upper caste. Floating along (circulando) in a small skiff (esquife: barquito) on the Thames. The revolt was a doddle (pan comido, estar chupado) → this is a --! Bust: busto, caída, descalabro; romper, agarrar; dejar sin blanca, degradar, dar un puñetazo → the last -- began in 1970's =/= burst: reventar, ráfaga → -- into (entró de sopetón en) the room, -- into tears (echarse a llorar); filled to bursting point (a reventar). A Christian backlash (reacción violenta, contragolpe). Toyota will swiftly (rápidamente) be followed by... Prone (propenso) to electricity shortage. Oily droplets (gotitas) called liposomes. The onrushing (creciente) wave of immigrants. Triggered (provocado) by local gripes (quejas), pull/squeeze the trigger (gatillo). Hurl: S. California -- (arroja, lanza) more money at its footloose (libre y sin compromiso) film industry → foot loose & fancy (caprichoso, lujoso...) free: libre como el aire + hurl back: rechazar + push away, repel, beat off, (idea) reject; -- along: ir a toda velocidad → the car --ed past (pasó como un rayo) =/= hu<u>r</u>tle (precipitarse) =/= hu<u>s</u>tle: bullicio, ajetreo; trabajar duro, empujar → they --ed him in/out (lo hicieron entrar/salir a empujones); --er (pers. dinámica, timadora). The luminaries (=/ luces de adorno, lumbreras) of the film <u>flock</u> (rebaño) <u>ed</u> (fueron en tropel) to Los Angeles. Virtual realm (campo, reino). Sizeable (considerable). Hunch (corazonada, presentimiento); hunch back (encorvar)ed: jorobado =/= hump (encorvar, joroba). Shut (down): (apagar, desconectar, cerrar) the government district. At his behest (petición). On staging (escenificando) the event. The conspicuous (=, insigne, ilustre) dazzle (deslumbrar, resplandor) of the games masks a country in deepening trouble. A flawed (defectuoso, (teor.: errónea) country. Sinfulness (pecaminosidad) that entitle it (da derecho...). Government accountability, independent judiciary. Chime (repique, campanada,V+ stroke) → the clock --ed six + -- in with (estar en armonía con) the feelings of the middle class. Dough (masa, pasta) filled with meat. Unseat: (ridder) derribar, desarzonar, (pasajero) echar de su asiento, (diputado) hacerle perder un escaño. Flip: tirar → − one's lid (perder los estribos) + he --ped the book open (de un golpe). We'd have to reapply (solicitar de nuevo). The Labour party will raise the top rate of income (renta) tax from 45 to 50. The sturdy (robustos, fuertes) supporters are drifting away (se dejan llevar por la corriente). Sullen: (pers.) huraña, (ambiente) triste. Saudi officials see themselves as having vested (vencido) such rivals for regional influence. Avoid competing head-on (de frente). The biggest banks team up (se asocian). Far from the thrum (repiqueteo, vibración, =) & bustle (bullicio, ajetreo) of Manhattan. Argentina stood out (destacó) as country of the future. The best - looking (de major aspecto) people of the planet. Emporium (lugar comercial con gente de muchos países). Protectionism has undermined (minado, socavado) Mercosur. The Supreme Court has been repeatedly tampered with (manipulada, forzada, falsificada). Populism stalks (acecha, acosa; tallo, caña) many emerging countries: constitutions are being stretched (violentadas, forzadas; estiradas, exigidas). America by 2020 should overtake S. Arabia as the largest pumper of oil, the more valuable fuel; events have overtaken us. Thus (así) will create twice as many jobs than car making provides today. In Cyprus after years of foot dragging (tácticas dilatorias) by Greek-Cypriod leader have been keener (más entusiastas) to block the Turkish's efforts to join the EU. China is emitting almost twice as much carbon dioxide as the next biggest polluter: 500 billions tonnes carbon dioxide between 1990 & 2050. In Spain the bill would replace the woman right to abortion. A system requiring proof of potential damage to mother's mental or physical health. The top income tax rate in the cash-strapped north eastern region of Catalonia is 56%. Spain's income from tax & social contributions is well below the EU average. He wends his way home (se encaminó hacia casa). Manufacturing in Africa: an awakening (naciente) giant. Manufacturing's share of GDP in sub-Saharan Africa has held steady at 10-14% in recent years. Set up workshops (talleres) to fill the gaps in local markets. China trades more goods across its international borders than any other country. Panama canal: A € 1.3 billions row (flujo, fila, ruido, pelea) will have ripple (onda, rizo, murmullo,Vs) effects (reacción en cadena, onda expansiva) on global trade at sea. Overrun: be -- (invadido, plagado) with sth, the meeting overran (se prolongó más de lo previsto) by half an hour; it's the cost -- (invasión, exceso, prolongación) on their € 2.8 billions portion. A sandbagging (saco de arena) to protect... Many of them are merely estimates based on incomplete information from unregulated & illiquid markets. Putative (supuestas) regulations. Hito: (acontecimiento) landmark; an historical milestone + señal, mojón. Libor (London interbank offered range) → scandals involving financial benchmarks (cotas, precios de referencia) such as Libor, which purportedly (supuestamente) track (sigue la pista de) the prix of loans between banks in London =/= students interact with each other & submit assignments (misiones, tareas) by e-mail. Universities have joined various startups in the rush (apuro, ráfaga, ataque, avalancha: of orders...) to provide stand-alone (autónomo, independiente) instruction online. Modern education is dear (querida, cara). One of the few upsides (ventajas, lado positivo) of war is that it frequently gives technology a boost (incentivo, estímulo, Ec.: fomento) =/= bolster (reforzar, moral: levantar) =/= foster: acoger en el hogar, (sospecha, talento, competición) fomentar, (reconciliación) promover, (odio) alimentar. The self-proclaimed mission of Putin to rebuild the Russian empire. In the next decade, more emerging markets firms will snap up (agarrar) rich world assets. Teetering (tambaleantes) banks. Irrelevance (=, sin importancia) → it's irrelevant to be disposed of (era superfluo, se podía prescindir de ello). Quantum computers: by harnessing (enganchando, aprovechando) the strangeness (novedad, rareza) of quantum machines they should be able to perform some calculations far faster. Block/stymie (bloquear) → we're really stymied (la hemos pifiado). Vague (vagas, imprecisas) & overly (demasiado) broad patents. The innovation act is a bill aimed squarely (directamente, como es debido) at neutralising so called patent trolls (un tipo de duendes): buy lots of patents (todo lo existente) & then use them to extract payments from unsuspecting (confiadas) victims. The most contentious (polémico) issue: which inventions are actually eligible for patent protection. The legal bullying (matonismo, amedrentar, intimidación) is a symptom of a wider complaint: the poor quality of many patents granted by the UP & 500. As it becomes harder to cram (meter) more transistors into a slice of silicon, alternative ways of making ships are being sought). Transistors tininess (ser minúsculo) turns against them. Spintronics use the spin of subatomic particles to make a chip from five transistors. Neuromorphic computer looks to biology for inspiration. A transistor connects a handful of peers (coetáneos). A transistor may switch on & off many times a second ↔ neurons are many times slower. Making whole organs for transplant remains elusive (esquivo). Bioprinting: cells are cultured & then seeded into biodegradable moulds whose shapes resemble that of the organ. Conductive fibres: from lighter aircraft to electric knickers (bragas). Intelligent textiles to deliver power to the equipment of soldiers & to do away with (suprimir) the battle dress being swathed (envuelto) with cables & batteries. Electromagnetic launchers hurling (arrojando) objects with electric energy. Bacteriophages that could be genetically engineered to bind to other organic materials. Bind,(i, ou, ou) atar, rodear, (libro) encuadernar, (cement) cuajarse, unirse, aprieto, apuro =/= bend (d, t, t): torcer, (rodilla, vara) doblar; curva, ángulo de tubería =/= reverenciar: revere, venerate. The virus that can find tumours & light them up (iluminarlos). Freedoms that Hong Kong has enjoyed under Great Britain & China are slowly whittled (tallados) away (disminuidos, mermados). Debt burden incurred (contraída). Executives latched on (comprendían, se daban cuenta)... Footprints (huellas) in Asia & Africa from colonial times. Most European firms have not a motley (multicolor) collection of emerging-markets assets. Mug (taza, tarro; bobo, ingenuo)'s game: cosa de idiotas. A madcap (tarambana, alocada, descabellada) idea. Humming (zumbido) of bees. Collbert: plucking a goose (ganso) with the smallest hissing (silbido, abucheo). Sidling in/out: (entrar/salir furtivamente). Iran wants all but (todo menos) quadruple sales. It is rumoured that...; rumou<u>rmonger (propagador de)</u>. Long been deadlocked (en punto muerto, estancados, en un impasse) between... Commended (elogiados, recomendados). Lagos disgorges (vomita, arroja) 10,000 metric tonnes of waste a day. Only 13% of recyclable material is salvaged (reutilizado, teoría: rescatado). Kenya: charges (tarifas) for state primary schools in East Africa's biggest country were abolished. Gruesome (horribles, atroces, crueles) sketches (esbozos, bosquejos). They crave (ansian, reclaman; comida: tienen antojo de)...; may I -- your attention for a moment? Cyber-security: law-abiding (cumplidores) hackers are helping businesses to fight off (repeler, rechazar) the bad guys (tipos...). Crook (pillo, ladrón; doblar, cayado)ed: torcido, sinuoso; deshonesto =/= spooks (fantasms, agentes secretos; asustar) are finding plenty of chinks (grietas, tintineos) in digital armour (blindaje) too. Target's catastrophic breach (brecha, infracción,V). Weather (capear) the storm + the world's four most populous country is weathering (aguantando) the emerging market turmoil (confusión, agitación). Turn around (cambiar de dirección, sanear, recuperarse) to timing (ritmo, hora fijada). Solar cells are made of semiconductors, every type of them has a property called "Band gap": it defines the longest wavelength of light a semiconductor can absorb; fix the maximum amount, del anochecer (twilight), del amanecer (down light). Padded -shoulders (hombreras). Spry (ágil, activo). The uptake (consumo, aceptación) of robots + be quick on the uptake (coger las cosas al vuelo) ↔ be slow - - -- (ser corto de entendederas). Go bust (quebrar), busting (combate) → inflation/crime --. Freeing up (liberando) airspace. Sumatra's haze (bruma, neblina) + a haze of smoke + be in a haze: andar atontado. Fur (piel) -trimmed (arreglado, corte elegante, recortado, adelgazado); velvet (terciopelo). Put off: aplazar, disuadir; desanimar (with her manners), distraer (stop putting off!), (aplazar pagos

+ defer); (luz) apagar, (put sb off with an excuse) dar largas. Ominous: amedrentador, de mal augurio. Pettifogging (=, insignificante) details. The European central bank was undermined (minada, debilitada, socavada) by the Karlsruhe court. The excessive legalism has messed (estropeado) the banking union, which will not live up (cumplir) the promise to sever (cortar, romper) the doom (fatalidad...). Meeting (reunión, sesión, mitin) in Catalonia. Be mindful (tener en cuenta) of the risk. Stateless (apátrida). Relief (alivio, auxilio, relieve; liberación, relevo). Misreading (mala interpretación). In compliance with (conforme a). Bouteflika looks set (fijo, forzado...) to hang on (esperar, depender de) grimly (gravemente, tristemente, denodadamente)... Wretchedness (miseria, desdicha, desgracia). Opencast (a cielo abierto) mining. America & Europe alike worry about losing out (salir perdiendo) to Asian rivals. Peel off (quitar, separarse, salirse) → my skin's --ing off. Russian firms are casting about/around (buscando) Asia & elsewhere for new customers. Be unfriendly (antipático) to/towards sb. Banking is spluttering (ranqueando, chisporroteando). John Wayne: lidded (con tapa, párpados) almond-shaped eyes, high cheekbones (pómulos) & lopsided (torcida) smile. A minister's downfall (caída, ruina) spurs (espuela, estimula) unhealthy debate. Tough (fuerte, duro)en: fortalecer, endurecer → attempts to tough it out (no ceder, aguantar el tipo + put on a brave face). Dumb/mute (mudo) =/= dump (verter, vertedero) the giant rocks into the waiting (que esperan) cruchers (trituradores). Underline (subrayar, destacar (+ point sth. out), remarcar (+ emphasize) =/= underwrite: asegurar contra el riesgo, Ec.: suscribir, aprobar; soportar, respaldar. Remorse (remordimiento)less: implacable, despiadado. An economic powerforce (fuente de ideas, centro neurálgico). Be in arrears (estar atrasados) with the rent. Conundrum (enigma, acertijo) → there remain a few --s surrounding... (relacionados con, de alrededor de...). Welding (soldaduras) fumes (humos, gases, vapores; echar pestes) =/= wield: (espada) blandir, empujar, (influencia) ejercer, (cuchillo, cadenas) manejar → -- chains at the police ↔ unwieldy (difícil de manejar) =/= yielding: (mat.) blando, flexible, (pers.) flexible, complaciente + yield: ceder, producir, rendir → rental -- are high. Puncture (pinchazo,V) his popularity. A run (racha) of good luck. Dwarf (enano) variety of wheat. Short-stemmed (de tallo corto) crops ↔ leggy (piernas largas). A second green revolution is stirring (despertando...) movers (en debate: ponente) + the movers (los de la mudanza) are already here. Music screeches (gritos, chirridos,Vs). Whistleblower (que desvela una situación interna ilegítima). Sap (savia, inocentón; minar, debilitar, socavar) trade surplus. Blow torch (antorcha): soplete. Hand off (rechazar) payments. Pockmark (picadura, agujero, hoyuelo, marca de smallpox: viruela)ed with coal mines. Make off (largarse) with sth: llevarse algo. A sleek (impecable, acicalado) smartphone. Intake: (gas, Electr.) toma, (food) consumo. Blatant (flagrante, descarado) attempt. Wrecked/ruined (destruyó, arruinó) certain industries. Eye-catching (vistoso, emotivo). Grudgingly (de mala gana). Grandstanding (demagogia, pavoneo). Tepid (poco entusiasta, tibio). Nag (fastidiar, gruñón)ging (acuciantes, persistentes) doubts. Eating away (corroer + corrode). Backsliders (reincidentes). Trails (estelas, sigue) the separatist group. General dismay (consternación,V). Fluff (pelusa; pifiada, pifiarla); pelts (pellejos, cueros) of fluffy (plumosas, esponjosas; suaves, fluidas, esponjosas) creatures + pelt sb (acribillar a alguien) with insults/questions, at full pelt (a toda máquina)... Clean-up (limpieza) of banking. A ghost (fantasma) bobbling (moviéndose de un lado a otro) idle. Busker (músico callejero) on a clapped out (desvencijado) bus. Spurt (chorros) of investments + final -(esfuerzo final) + work in --s (por rachas). Mincing (menuditos) rascals (granujas). Quit: parar, irse, abandonar; call it quits (hacer las paces, rendirse + make peace); quit while you're ahead (retírate ahora que ganas), don't quit now (no abandones ahora). Unshakable (inquebrantable) + he has an iron constitution (una salud inquebrantable). Protracted (prolongada) Ec. war. Sober (sobrio, serio) up: (borrachera) despejar, volverse más serio. Trendsetter (indicador de una moda). Shy (huraño, vergonzoso) away: rehuir, tener miedo + be frightened). Cutting-edge (de vanguardia) tech. Hidebound (aferrado, rígido) by tradition: conservador por tradición. Adornments (adornos, embellecimiento) =/= decorations (condecoraciones). Satellites launchpads: plataformas/rampas de lanzamiento, (ideas, carrera) trampolines + springboards. Shoot down a hostile missile after take-off. Scale back (recortar) its power. Nimble (ligero, hábil, diestro), nimbly (ágilmente, con destreza) =/= nimby: quien aprueba establecer un vertedero, pero no en su vecindad. Cosy/cozy (íntimo, acogedor). Ir tirando/arreglárselas (get by, manage to). Onslaught (arremetida, ataque) → -- of summer visitors. E-tail (venta por Internet). Tetchy (irritable) relations. Rake (barrer) in (recoger) Ec. uplift (animación, sostén, inspiración). J. Carlos swift (rápido) squashing (dar al traste, escape, aplastamiento) of an attempt coup. Britain's tides (olas, corrientes) → tidal (marea) power: maremoto. Miss out (saltarse) on (dejar pasar, perder, desperdiciar) several good deals (ocasiones, acuerdos). Filled with gravel (grava). Shenanigan (chanchullo, travesura, artimaña). Niched (de nicho) market. Mash (mezcla, moler; puré de patatas). Shirk (esquivar) the problems. One snag (inconveniente, problema). Etch (grabar en vidrio/cobre, en la memoria) =/= engrave (en metal), record (sonido, imagen). Uncoil (desenroscar + unscrew). Natty (elegantes) pleats (pliegues,V). Makeover (sesión de maquillaje y peluquería) =/= make over (reorganización, transformación). Sniff out: encontrar husmeando, fisgonear + sniffer dog (perro rastreador). Aloft (arriba) → he held (levantó) the cup -- (en alto). Payload (carga útil/explosiva). A tragic sequel (consecuencia + continuación, secuela). He takes a knock (recibe un golpe). Petty (insignificante, pequeño, ruin, mezquino). He comes out (sale, se muestra, florece) fighting. Party leaders jockey (maniobran) for position + political juggles (malabarismos) → juggle the demands of work & family (hacer malabarismos para compaginar...). Rigger: (Náut.) aparejador, (aéreo) montador. Between the cradle (cuna) & coffin (ataúd). Defeat: vencer → alter the -- (derrota) of the rebels; -- one's own purpose: ir contra sus propios intereses. Anger & folly (locura). A rich man hated & a poor man scorned (despreciado). Laden (cargado) with gold. A babe (criatura de pecho) in arms. Well (bien, pozo, manar, brotar...) → a (well)spring (fuente) of pleasure =/= fountain (artificial). Strife (conflicto, lucha) → a country torn (destrozado) by civil (intestinas) --. Critter (bicho). Irritable (=), (quisquilloso) touchy, (perfeccionista) pernickety. Power supply, source of income. Bait (cebo de pesca) + decoy (señuelo, reclamo). Beware (tener cuidado). Torpor (letargo). Buoy (boya, aboyar) ed up: animado, mantenido a flote + --ant: flotante, optimista, (Ec.) tendencia a la alta. More than 1% of the € stands (resiste) or wobbles (tambalea). Push through (hacer aprobar, introducir) reforms. Epitomize (personificar, resumir, tipificar) → her situation --s that of the others. Coughed (tosió) up (arrojó, expectoró, soltó el dinero) close to € 50 billions. Abetted (instigó, secundó, fue cómplice). It's rather tricky (astuto; difícil, peliagudo). Chutzpah (fresco, cara dura + sassy, cheeky). Breach: infracción + infringement, offence. Mire (fango) → France is mired (enfangada, atrapada) in stagnation. A keen (aficionado, entusiasta; fuerte, vivo, agudo, afilado) photograph + (estudiante) aplicado. Suspend (colgar, aplazar, flights: suspender +-- sb from office. Critically injured people. Masonry (albañilería). A defence's radar can register incoming objects, but only a fraction contains warheads (cabeza explosiva). The blast (ráfaga) demolished (demolió, echó abajo) a disused (abandonado) ship. Cartridges (cartuchos) → -- belt (cartuchera). Barely (apenas) notices (avisa) as the car slows down or speeds up. A smartphone checks the battery/instructs the vehicle to park itself. Infotainment (=), (información concebida como espectáculo) programme. Smart infrastructure (sensors...) to make traffic flow (flujo) more smoothly & safely. In-vehicle services, hardware & connectivity will rise to a staggering (asombroso) $ 400 billion by 2022. Poison =/= venom (v. de serpiente). Encubrir: (ocultar) hide, (delincuente) harbour, (delito) cover up, (ayudar) be an accomplice in, (encalar) whitewash. Lock & unlock remotely (a distance). It calls for help in the event of a crash & will be fitted to all new vehicles. Trackers (rastreadores) to reduce theft. They avoid one another at road crossings. Connectivity will bring customers & carmakers closer together & safely spaced. It let cars talk to cars. Monitored (controlado, supervisado) by traffic controllers. Serve (up) the ads (advertisements) to them. Glean (inf.: recoger; Agr.: espigar) where users visit. Sweep: barrer, (elecciones) arrasar, (emociones) invadir, (fuego) apagar. Data leakage (gotera, escape). Put the squeeze on (apretar las tuercas). Xenophobic innuendo (indirecta, insinuación). Spill: derramar(se), verter + -- over (derramarse, rebosar, desbordarse); clear up (resolver, esclarecer, ordenar) oil spills (vertidos...); -- the beans (descubrir el pastel). Pickup (aumentar) wages/sales/prices. He is unpicking (descosiendo, deshaciendo) a rent-control law. The run-up (período previo) to the elections that he is contesting (rebatiendo). A slit (corte, abertura) in a stone. An outright (rotunda, absoluta) majority. Cared (preocupado) for... The quirkier (los más raros). He has drawn up (redactado) contingencies (=, eventualidades) plans: medidas para emergencia. Ofimática (Office automation), manager's office, outside office hours, office junior (auxiliar de oficina). Demeanour (conducta + Unwittingly (sin darse cuenta). Publicly chastised (castigado, regañado). Driving (abriendo) a wedge (cuña, pedazo; brecha; wedged in (encajado) between two lorries. IS (Islamic State) leaders are secret agents for Iran. Hong Kong: the most politically galvanized (=, animado, -- sb into action (movido, impulsado alguien para que haga algo) city in China. Pro-shia brass (latón, Pol.: jefazo). Complaint: queja, reclamación, denuncia. Tax hike (aumento). He extolled (alabó, elogió) the notion of... rounding up (acorralando, cogiendo) activists. Affluent (acaudalado) → the -- society (la sociedad de consumo). He's prone (propenso) to getting angry; drought prone regions. Ozone layer (capa). Henchman (secuaz, guardaespaldas). Runaway (desenfrenada, fuera de control) epidemic. He eschewed (evitó + avoided; un derecho: renounced) state action. Sideline (marginar) the shareholders. Pliable (flexible, maleable) venue (local, lugar de reunión; jurisdicción). Lashings (azotes, montones; cuerdas, ataduras) of sugar. Sickly (enfermizo, débil, empalagoso + cloying) sweet (dulce, agradable, melodioso). Doughnut (donut)-shaped vessel (barco, vaso, vasija). Bash (golpear) with enough oomph (brío) to fuse (fundir) sth → blow a fuse (fundir un fusible). At the very least (como mínimo). Swamped (inundado, abrumado) by the disorder. Steady (continuo, firme, seguro; formal, serio; estabilizar, calmar, apaciguar) the World. The World spinning (girando) out of control. Intervention requested (solicitada) by Iraq. Poorly thought out (elaborado, meditado a fondo, encontrado una solución). Typified (=, representado) by the rash (temeraria, precipitada) "mission accomplished" banner (pancarta). Syria rose up (se sublevó, se revoltó). Cut off (cortar, aislar) heads on social media. Strike (dar, golpear) a blow. Carry off (llevarse, premio: alzarse con, elección: ganar). Unionists hugging (abrazándose) each other. Wrench (torcedura, tirón; arrancar; llave inglesa). Constituency (circunscription, distrito electoral). Embarcadero: jetty, pier =/= muelle: wharf, quay =/= puerto: port, harbour =/= dock: dársena, dique; atracar. I'm not accountable (responsable) to sb, -- for English policies, ending up feuding (disputando, peleando) the clout (peso, influencia) of... Be cajoled (camelado, engatusado) into parting (separación, despedida) + parting (de despedida) words. Banking relationship can sour (deteriorar, agriar) overnight. Slue → slew (montón, patinar, girar bruscamente). Claw back (volver a tomar, recuperar). Straintened (difíciles) circumstances. Sluice gate: esclusa, compuerta. Beijing is ringed (rodeado) with waterhungry golf courses (pistas). Governments entice (tientan, seducen) water-intensive firms. In my early years. Mesmerize (hipnotizar, fascinar). Almost twice the usual evening TV news audience turned in (sintonizaron) on September 21st. Alpha male (macho dominante) Sarko. Restore French confidence. Whirl (giro) → the French are brazing (se vigorizan) themselves for a political whirlwind (torbellino). Landslide (arrolladora) victory. Rejuvenate (rejuvenecer) its crusty (pan: crujiente; malhumorada, arisca) image =/= creak (chirrido, crujido,Vs) =/= rustle (susurro, V). The alleged (supuesta) influence. Spruce (pulcro, arreglado, acicalado). Pilfering (robo), pilferer (ratero). Sprightly (enérgicos) migrants. Ailment (problema, enfermedad). Shrimp (langostino, camarón/gamba) trawler (pesquero de arrastre + trawling fleet, flota de arrastre). Jumpy: nervioso, asustadizo. $100 m. cargoes (cargamento) siphoned off (desviadas) into smaller vessels. Socialism comes to fruition (cumplimiento): se cumple, se realiza. The crisis ebbing; ebb & flow, rise & fall; ebbed (decaído). Trek (expedición,V, caminar) beside (junto a) the upper (superior) river; trekker/hiker (senderista). China flounders (se debate, pierde el hilo en discursos) in its effort to combat text-messaging spam (en internet: correo basura). A roaring/thunderous/(estruendoso) business. Startle (sobresaltar, asustar + frighten) → --ling (extra, alarmante) cost. Bonded (vinculado) labour (trabajo, tarea, obreros). Interspersed (intercalado, incluido). Foil (frustar; lámina de metal, espada. florete, culinario: papel de aluminio/plata); frustrar: (pers.) =, (proyectos...) thwart, (operación) foil.

Reward (recompensa,V) caution (cautela, advertencia). Shedding: (ropa, piel: deshacerse de, despojar, (trabajo) recortar, (lágrimas, sangre) derramar, (calor) dar, (luz) echar; cobertizo. Spring uprising (sublevación). Wanton (libe price hovered (about) (rondaba) € 40. A decade-long glut (superabundancia, inundación de...) market. Overstretch (forzar, exigir demasiado). Bespatter (salpicar) shale oil reputation. Shake out (sacudir) =/= shake out: reorganizar, racionalizar, (trabajos) disminuir. Hardly (apenas) tactful (discreto). Keep up (sostener; tradición: mantener) with: seguir el ritmo. Enthusing (entusiasmando) her. His appointment caps (tapas, coronas; completa) Poland's journey to Europe's core. Provide villages with technical training (capacitación, entrenamiento). Delivering (entregando, asestando, rutina, sin sentido) destruction ↔ vie for sth (dispuesto a algo)/with sb (competir, rivalizar). Hong Kong increasingly chafing (irritando, impacientando, rozando) Chinese rulers. Think aloud (pensar en voz alta). Relations marred (estropeadas) by fraught (tenso) public disagreement. Liken (comparado) to... Oil & gas extracted from underground rocks by blasting (chorro, bombardeo) with fracking. Chips are fabricated in batched (lotes) on silicon wafers (hostia, Comp: oblea de Silicio). Knock out: dejar sin sentido, extraer, vaciar, (competición) eliminar. Toner (tonificador). Enamel (esmalte). Foothold (punto de apoyo del pie) → gain a -- (establecerse). Hunt down (dar caza). The batteries when idle (vacías, flojas)... Hold their breath (contener su risa). Robots to inspect cracks (golpes, crujidos, grietas) instead of workers kitted out (equipados). A tracking (rastreo) device on your wrist. Supportive (de apoyo) fiscal policy → she'sbeen very --, very -- parents. Stroppy (borde, insolente). Headgear (gorro, sombrero). Skulduggery (trapicheo, embuste). Lenient (benévolo). Plume (pluma; a -- of smoke: columna de humo). Alien (extraño, extranjero) → illegal --, that's -- (ajeno) to him. Golden calf (becerro de oro). Blink (párpado + eyelid) + eyelash (pestañas), eyebrow (cejas), in the blink (parpadeo) of an eye (en un abrir y cerrar de ojos), blink at sb (guiñar el ojo a alguien). Excoriate (vilipendiar (desdeñar), excoriar (corroer el cutis). Revive (reanimar), garish (chillón, llamativo). Lampoon (sátira,V). Hack attack (pirateo). Crow (cuervo)ing: cacareo, pavoneo, → -- over sth. Cesspool = cesspit = septic tank (pozo negro, ciego) =/= oil well. Roaming: (animal) vagar, vagabundo; excursión, (Telec.) itinerancia. Amble (andar sin prisa). Sworn: (enemigo) declarado, (testimonio) jurado. A pesky (latosa, molesta) clause. Hover (rondar, planear) over sth/sb: cernirse (elevarse, mantenerse) sobre --/--. Spate (avalancha, racha, serie) of accidents. Agitation (agitación, inquietud) → their arrival caused agitation, a great -- (revuelo). Rustle (susurro,V). Shell out (soltar dinero). Rutted (llenas de baches) roads. Fling (i,, u, u) (arrojar, lanzar; aventura amorosa). Rustbeld: cinturón industrial = industrial beld. Outdoor (al aire libre). Spine-tingling (hormigueo, cosquilleo): emocionante + moving, inquietante. Slippery (resbaladizo). Junkyard patio) (chatarrería). Ráfaga: (llevar por el aire, bocanada, olor a...) waft, (meteo) gust, (de tiros) burst. Debauch (depravar, alterar, corromper)ed: depravado, libertino. Oscilar: (péndulo) swing, oscillate, (precios,T., peso) fluctuate + the distance ranges between 100 & 200 m. Fiddle (trampa)→ tax --, (enredar) → stop --ing!, violín, play second -- (papel), -- about/around (perder el tiempo con), -- with (juguetear con), fiddly (complicada) download. Quejarse: complain, grumble, moaning (quejica). Take heart (coger ánimo). Rouse (despertar, provocar: the lion is dangerous when --ed). Slumber (sueño, dormir). The ideas of statehood (independencia, categoría de estado) led to a daunting (gigantesca, desmoralizadora) task. The officials strained (forzaron al límite) to avoid... Relieved (aliviado) by the outcome (resultado). Hitch: obstáculo, =), problema, tirón → he gave his trousers a -- (se los subió de un tirón), to – (enganchar algo a algo.

Biafra sought (seek, ou, ou): buscó, ambicionó, pidió) to break off (partir)... Ethnic groups lumped (se agrupaban) crudely (groseramente) together. Quail (temblar, codorniz) → she --ed at the idea (la idea lo aterrorizaba) + her heart --ed (se le encogía). The Polisario, egged on (incitado) by Algeria. Waiting in the wings (entre bastidores). Leader in his industry by revenues (+ rentas públicas). Priceless (inestimable) pills. Status markers (indicadores), danger/warning sign, marker buoy (boya indicadora). One out of every three smokes. Penance (castigo, penitencia), ugly duckling (patito feo). Tie up: atar, amarrar, inmovilizar; be tied up (ocupado) to..., (deal) cerrar =/= tie-up: acuerdo (entre empresas...), enlace, vínculo. Strong track records (antecedentes) elsewhere & trip up (tropieza, se equivoca) in China. Quotas will cap (restringir) the flow of funds. The controls are heavy-handed (severos). I put a high on privacy (valoro mucho la intimidad). Stock turnover (renovación de existencias, movimiento de mercancías): individuals account for 80%, institutions for 20%. Accomplice, conspiratorial (cómplice), complicity. Corporatestingines/miserliness/meanness (tacañería). Lovers' vows (promesas). Filed (archivado) a decade ago. Break one's vow (faltar a su compromiso). Vow of poverty. Scatter: (papeles) esparcir, (semillas) sembrar esparciendo, the flowers were --ed about on the floor, (nubes) dispersar, --brained (atolondrado), his relatives were --ed around the world. Overconfident (exceso de confianza). Fireside (chimenea) tales: cuentos íntimós... The gringos riddled (acribillaron) the land with petroleum-laden (cargados) pits (fosos). Filed a class-action (querella colectiva) suit (pleito) → file/bring a suit (pleito) against... Wrangling (riña, discusión). The award (recompensa, sentencia) was enforced (ejecutada, hecha cumplir). The sleuths (detectives) reached (alcanzaron, contactaron) the plaintiffs (demandantes). Turncoat (chaquetero) → become a -- (cambiar de chaqueta + change sides). Nightlife springing up (surgiendo) in new places. Blare: (Mús., sirena) estruendo, trompetazo → -- out (vociferar, tocar muy fuerte). They have risen at double the rate of those doing so during the day. Laca: lacquer, hairspray, nail polish. Shirk (gandulear, eludir). Write/describe poignantly (de modo conmovedor). Fasten (acelerar) a deal. Rohmani's message gives us a little slack (período de inactividad, relajación; flojo, negligente) on nuclear file & things flow from it. The upheaval (trastorno) was harsh (duro). Catch up: (-- sb --) alcanzar a alguien, (growth, one's sleep) recuperar, caught up in (atrapado en) the traffic. Scapegoat (cabeza de turco). The events have moved swiftly. Swiftness (rapidez, velocidad). Onslaught (arremetida, ataque + attack). Agotarse: run out, (pers.) exhaust o.s. + peter (out): irse agotando/acabando → the road --ed out (se perdía) in the dunes. Profits/crowd funnelled (encauzados)... Call in: hacer entrar, pedir la devolución. Masquerading (farsa + sham, farce) as a patriotic duty. Saborear: relishes the opportunity, (food) savor. S<u>ee</u>mly (decente + =, respetable) ↔ <u>un</u>seemly (indecoroso, impropio) =/= seemingly (aparentemente) =/= se<u>a</u>mless (sin soldadura)ly: sin que se note. Duly: (debidamente, como previsto) noted in the minutes (=, actas). Lifeless (sin vida) affair. They long for (anhelan) a Budget commensurated (que se corresponde) with their ambitions. A piddling (insignificante, mísero) 1%. It turned out that (resultó que) a grumpy (malhumorado, gruñón)... By hugging (ciñiendo, ajustando) sth close (apretado) + figure - -- (ceñido al cuerpo)... Mushy: blando, pulposo (fleshy), sentimentaloide. Mingle (mezcla). Hoodie (jersey con capucha). Mascar: chew, chomp; masticar: chew, masticate. Revel (ir de parranda, deleitarse) → late night --ing. Gaze at (mirar fijamente). This truly (realmente, verdaderamente) is the heart of Africa. The case was put in hold (en espera) while judges examine a request (solicitud, petición) to be dismissed (rechazada). Expiry date. Roar: rugido, carcajada, estruendo, fragor,Vs; a roaring (crujiente) success (un tremendo éxito); a roaring trade (un buen negocio). Vidente: sighted, clairvoyant, viewer, (profeta) seer. Impressive (impresionante). Misgivings (reservas, dudas, recelos). Pinch (coger, apretar; pellizco,V, robar...) → penny pinches: tacaño, pesetero. Steep (abrupto, empinado). Income tax (impuesto sobre la renta), tax return (declaración de la renta, de impuestos). Embrace (abrazar), a coalition --ing six parties. Throw out (tirar, echar; expulsar a otro país). Rave (delirar, elogio,V) about sth (entusiasmarse por) → they raved about the film (pusieron la película por las nubes). Property (propiedad, inmueble) development (promoción inmobiliaria). Improper (inapropiado, indecoroso, incorrecto). Physical fitness (buena salud física), a fitness centre open round the clock, be at the peak of the --. Bring up (vomitar, criar, educar). Tickle: pers.: hacer cosquillas (tickling), animal (acariciar) → my ear --s: siento cosquillas/hormigueo en la oreja. Evolve: desarrollar, evolucionar. Expense account (cuenta de gastos). Misunderstanding (malentendido). Skillful (mañoso). Tempting (tentador). Tin (estaño, lata). Crab (cangrejo). Vergonzoso: (pers.) bashful, shy; (acto) disgraceful, shameful =/= Shyness/timidity: timidez. Removal (eliminación, mudanza). Screwdriver (destornillador). Skinny (flaco, estrecho, angosto). Excel (destacar, sobresalir). Make a fun of... Expertise: pericia, expertizar. Renowned (de renombre). Line one's pockets = make a fortune (forrarse). Call off: cancelar, (huelga) desconvocar. Start from scratch (a cero). Cr_a_sh: choque, estruendo, quebrar, estrellar, (Ec.) crac (29...) =/= cr_u_sh (aplastar, aglomeración) slaves =/= crack; golpe, crujido; abertura, raja, grieta,Vs. Greedy: codicioso, (comida) goloso. Pitf_all_: trampa, escollo, peligro =/= pitf_ul_: lastimoso, lamentable. Terrific (genial, fabuloso, increible). Calmar: (nervios) calm, (dolor/picor) relieve. T_ou_ghen (fortalecer, endurecer) =/= ti_gh_ten: tensar, (seguridad, disciplina) reforzar =/= strengthen (fortalecer, reforzar, aumentar). Draft (boceto, borrador) out: redactar, (contrato) draw up. Extension cord (cable alargador). Mostly (mayormente, la mayoría) =/= plenty (de sobras, muchos). Slant: inclinación/pendiente, punto de vista → what is your --? Make trouble (causar problemas), family/financial --, get sb. into --. Accomplish (efectuar, conseguir, llevar a cabo). Carry out (llevar a cabo, efectuar, orden: cumplir). Tuition: matrícula → -- fees (tasas académicas de matrícula), private -- (clases particulares). Bathrobe (albornoz). Simpático (amiable, nice, pleasant). Patron/sponsor (patronizador, en arte: mecenas) of arts. Mother tongue. In charge of (responsable de). Lamb chops (chuleta de cordero). Slave driver (negrero). Crossword puzzle (crucigrama). Stink (apestar, hedor)... → the -- of curruption; (follón) → make a -- (armar escándalo). Trap (trampa, atrapar; gas/calor/luz: retener). Colleague (colega). Guinea pig (cobaya, conejillo de Indias). Decline (declive, deterioro, descenso, decadencia). Resolute (decidido, resuelto). Self-centered (egocéntrico). The plan fall (a, e, allen) through: se viene abajo. Beforehand (de antemano). Commercial (anuncio en TV). Inconvenience (molestia + bother, trouble). Dry cleanee's (tintorería). Fair play (juego limpio). Hangover: (bebida) resaca; de guerra: vestigio; reliquia + relic). In depth (en profundidad). Mountain climber (alpinista). Finish line (meta). Address: your home --, change of --, -- book, e - mail --, dirigirse a. Retreat: (militar) retirada + (general) withdrawal; jubilación: retirement). Try on (probarse). Faithful: (pers.) fiel + (traducción, balanza) accurate. Mountain pass (paso). Dumb/silly/stupid: tonto. Self-conscious (tímido, cohibido, afectado, autorreflexivo). Revise (reconsiderar) → -- (cambiar) one's opinión, -- sth upwards. Turn down (rechazar, bajar el volumen) ↔ turn up: aparecer, subir el volumen. Unease (intranquilo, preocupado) → sit --ly on his chair. X-ray: (radiografía). Cut back budget (recorte presupuestario, de inversiones). Harmless (inofensivo). Resumé (CV, resumen + summary). Rub shoulders with (codearse con). Press-clipping (recorte). Self-reliant: independiente y seguro de sí mismo. Apply for (solicitar) → -- in writing: dirigirse por escrito. Clear up (aclarar + color: lighten; pb: clarify). Misplace (perder, traspapelar). Estropear: (ascensor, lavadoras, juguetes) break, (automóvil) damage, (ropa, zapatos, vista: eyesight) ruin, (actuación, plan, cosecha) spoil, ruin. Faltering: (voz) entrecortada, (paso) vacilante. Unsettle: (oponente) desconcertar, (relaciones) desestabilizar, (pers.) intranquilizar, (materia) pendiente, (tiempo) se desestabiliza. Opening up yawning (enormes) gaps (huecos). Tontería: silliness, foolishness, that's nonsense/rubbish, a silly thing to say, let's be serious (dejémonos de tonterías). He scratched (rascó) his head, just a -- (rasguño), stop --ing! The dog --ed (arañó) at the door. Look round (volver la cabeza), be snowed (ir de cabeza) with work + It's up to my eyes/eyeballs (globo ocular) in work. Go bareheaded (a cabeza descubierta). Rush headlong at (lanzarse de cabeza). Attorney general (ministro de justicia). Testing governments beset (acosados) by new offers; he will be sorely missed (lo echaremos mucho de menos). The technology increases productivity only after a long lag (retraso, intervalo, lapso). Those baffled (desconcertados) by these instructions. Protected by swingeing (muy severas, drásticas) import tariffs. Underwhelmed (poco entusiasta/satisfactorio) by what was on offer. Acrimonious: reñido, (disputa) mordaz, (palabras) ásperas, (riña) enconada. Fast track (vía rápida), fast-track executive (ejecutivo que llegará lejos). The bus stalled (paró + ahogar, estancarse). A dismal (sombrío, deprimente; lúgubre, poco prometedor) tale. Be on the rocks (no tener un céntimo). Dancers in fluorescent uniforms writhing (retorciéndose) to the national anthem (himno). Google grapples (se confronta) with the controversial ruling (fallo) on the boundary (límite) between privacy & free speech. One of the thorniest (más espinosos) pbs. Dwarfed (eclipsados, empequeñecidos) by... Does this lid (tapa) come off (se puede quitar)? German firms are on the rampage (pasan arrasando) across the pond (charco, estanque). Probar: (teoría, acusación) probe, (alim.) taste, (intentar/método/por 1ª) try, (ropa) try on. Desktop (ordenador de sobremesa), laptop (portátil). Bulging (muy lleno, a reventar) order books. They are rubbing (frotando) their hands. The ship was outward-bound (iba, salía) for London. An inward looking (introvertido) boy/country (cerrado en sí mismo). I can't endure (soportar) being corrected a moment longer =/= an enduring (duradera) friendship (amistad)/affection (cariño). Ravine/gully (barranco) → it went into (cayó en) the --/--. They devote themselves (se dedican) to... Bound: límite,V, rodeado, salto,V; atado, obligado; dirigirse → set -- to one's ambitions; groping (tanteando, toqueteando) towards inward-bound courses (rumbos, cursos). Big ideas are becoming as much of a status (situación, rango) marker (=, señal, jalón) in high-tech hubs as cars are in the oil belt (zona, cinturón). The commodity boom of the 2000's was a big contributor. When the financial crisis took hold in late 2008... Restricting fees (honorarios) & card (tarjeta) transactions has not worked out as planned. Debit balance (saldo deudor), debit card (tarjeta de cobro automático). A promising recipe (receta), devising (concibiendo) new recipes. Streak: (carne/mineral) veta, (luz) rayo, (luck) racha, → -- along (correr a gran velocidad), like a -- of lighting (como un rayo), -- in/out/past (entrar/salir/pasar como un rayo). Push ahead (seguir adelante) & pounce on (lanzarse/avalancharse sobre) the prey (presa)... Dreadful (espantoso, terrible). Many firms were being squeezed (en aprietos) due to rising wages & increased competition or had got bloated (hinchadas, abotargadas) but few could pass on cost increases. He could speak to him... The coffee/noise keeps me awake. Be aware/conscious of sth. (ser consciente de algo), wide-awake (completamente despierto). He is but a child (no es más que un crío). Had I but know... (de haberlo sabido...), all but nacked (casi desnudo), anything but that, anyone but him. He honked (tocaba la bocina) through the streets. Live on charity. Blackout (apagón). Curfew (toque de queda). Barbed wire fence (cercado de alambrada). Snazzy (vistosos, distintivo) features (rasgos). Embed (enterrar; incrustar, insertar) sound & video inside e-books. Stubbornly (obstinadamente, con tesón, tercamente). A chance of breaking out: (prisioneros) fugarse, (guerra, epidemia) estallar. Stumble on (avanzar dando traspiés)/over/against (tropezar con) + -- along/in/out: ir/entrar/salir a tropezones. Get bookstores/shops to display the pictures. Flesh out (desarrollar) his prose. Cliffhanger (situación tensa, película de suspense + thriller). Longish (bastante largos) texts. A storytelling (cuenta cuentos). Conveyed (llevaron, transmitieron) kind (clase, amable) regards. Resourceful (ingenioso + clever, ingenious, witty). Patch up (hacer las paces, remendar) with the South. A resort (recurso, recurrir, lugar de reunión/de vacaciones) shut off since 2008. Fief (dom): feudo. Burnishing (mejorando) its image. Rumbled (rumoreaba, retumbaba...) on (coleaba) the scandal while he was out of view. The number is dwindling (mengua). Plug (tapar) a huge outflow (efusión, fuga de capital...). On the back (a consecuencia) of growing trade. Gem: joya, gema, piedra preciosa. Beauty parlour (salón). Brand-new (flamantes) necklaces/string of pearls (collares). We are halfway there (a medio camino); halfway up/down the hill (a media cuesta). Submarino: underwater, submarine =/= submarinista: scuba diver, submariner. Patrol (patrulla) boats. It was towed back (remolcado hacia atrás). Bruise (magullar, moratón, magulladura). Long-standing (antiguo, que viene de largo) ban. The embargo is dismal (sombrío, pésimo, funesto). Go with/against stream. Come (properly) on stream (entra en funcionamiento). Overstate (exagerar + exaggerate). The reserves inched out (salieron poco a poco), inch forward (avanzar lentamente). Treasured (preciada) autonomy. A lifeline (cuerda de salvamento, cordón umbilical) in terms of swaps to Mongolia's central bank. Keep sb out of trouble (evitar se meta en líos)/out of cold (protegerse del frío). A ragbag (mescolanza + hotchpotch, hodgepodge) of smaller parties that surrounds (rodea) the main two. Scuffles (refriegas) with protesters/police. Screw up (arrugar, apretar, poner neurótico) one's eyes (el entrecejo) + -- - one's courage (armarse de valor). Restrain (refrenar, reprimir, disuadir) → -- sb from doing sth, -- o.s. (contenerse). He does not get on (sigue, va bien; subirse) with the central leadership. The project got awry (fracasó). Blazer (chaqueta de sport) =/= blaze (fuego, llamarada, brillo,Vs) + blazing (ardiente, brillante). The Hong Kong's return to China didn't get off (partió, salió) to a very good smooth start; the ideas promoted in Hong Kong might catch on (cuajar, tener éxito) elsewhere. The spoiled (mimados, consentidos; estropeados, arruinados, dañados) brats (mocosos, niños mimados) of democracy. Ten-lane (carril, camino) highway. The disgruntled (descontentos) of affluence (opulencia, bienestar económico). Fob off/cajole (engatusar, que da evasivas, excusas). The (long) touted (pregonado) health care. Even tablets (pastillas) have failed to usher in (acomodarse a; anunciar) a new reign, the telemedicine revolution. The declining predictability (previsibilidad). He filed (archivó) a € 50 m. tax claim (reclamación). The cushioned (protegidas) firms. Ben Alí was swept away (eliminado, barrido) along with other cronies. There are downsides (pegas, desventajas) too =/= downsize (tamaño, plantilla) disminuir =/= downbeat (pesimista) ↔ upbeat. House (alojar) troves (tesoros, treasure troves). Tax break (amnistía fiscal). International push (empujón, esfuerzo, Mil.: ofensiva). Close loopholes (lagunas) to massage (=, manipular números) down their tax bills. Doomsday (día del Juicio Final). Beef up (reforzar) their presence. Tax-compliant (sumiso a los impuestos). Shady (turbia, sospechosa, sombría) activity. Funds have become Luxembourg's flagship (buque insignia, punta de lanza) → the newspaper is the -- of his media empire. Either underestimate their earnings or fail to disclose (revelar) them to the taxman altogether (por completo, en total). Peru in the 1990s tackled (abordó, se enfrentó con) tax evasion. A rosy (rosáceo, prometedor) dusk (atardecer) settle on (escoge) the X strait. Deplete (mermar, agotar) → stocks --ed by overfishing. Groups lined up (preparados) to dip their bread in the gravy (salsa de carne, dinero fácil, ganga). The reaction is a stoic nonchalance (despreocupación, indiferencia). Lousy: (pésima) economy, a -- (pésimo) driver; (comida, tiempo) asquerosos. Shame: vergüenza, deshonra, pena → --ing (vergonzoso). Tight (tirante, tenso; escaso, ajustado; difícil, reñido) → it will stick to -- budget. Mas is on a tightrope (cuerda floja). He takes on (acepta, asume) the new party. Undertook (emprendió, asumió) to uphold (sostener, defender, confirmar) religión - rights =/= withhold: (información) ocultar, (dinero) retener, (decisión) aplazar → -- the truth from sb (no revelar la verdad a alguien), -- one's consent/help (negar el --/la --). Downplay (restar importancia a). Swayed (balanceó + dominó) from side to side + -- his sway over the party; hold sway (gobierna, domina) the faltering (vacilante) parliament. Duck (pato) → he may duck out (escabullirse, aludir) of... Liberal consensus. Give/lend sb a hand (echarle una mano) =/= they gave him a big hand (lo aplaudieron calurosamente). Bloodletting (sangría) + blood money (dinero sucio). Running out of (quedarse sin) time... He is matter-of-fact (prosaico, práctico, realista) to a fault (defecto, culpa). The submarine ran aground (encalló). Runt (animal: el pequeño de la camada; pers.: mequetrefe) → Greece is the runt of the € zone litter (desorden, basura). The machine is gummed up (paralizada). The unemployment within the € area stands (resiste, aguanta...) at 11.5%. The lessons that the government drew from... The height of one's fam. Be in top form. Abe's plan to raise the profile (=) of a woman in his cabinet is in tatters (hecho trizas). Along the causeway (calzada). The tiff (pelea) began + a lovers'-- (una pelea de amantes). Smack: -- (sabor, manotazo), smack of sth. (oler a algo) → the whole thing --s of bribery, it --s of trichery (traición), give to a child a -- (bofetada). Oil producers are in turmoil (confusion, agitación). Upheaval: (en casa...) trastorno, (Política) agitación, (Geog.) levantamiento. Courtier (cortesano, cortés, comedido). A smidgen (un poco, una pizca) resentful (rencoroso). His psychological damage can only be guessed (supuesto, adivinado). Carcass (=, res muerta, armazón) → save one's -- (salvar el pellejo). Abide (aguantar, soportar) → I can't -- the cowards, two abiding (permanentes, pertinaces) fixations (obsesiones). Bombastic (pomposo, grandilocuente). Of no help (inútil: useless). Of little avail (poco provechoso). His intervention brought (provocó) those things about. Procrastinate over a decision (aplazar una decisión). Harried (acosado, hostigado; agobiado). Rabble (gentío) → the -- (la chusma) had deceived (engañado) German people into betraying them. The Prophet Muhammad rubbed (frotó) shoulders (se codeó) with Christians, Jews, Zoroastrians & Pagans. Scholar (erudito, estudioso, alumno, becario). Works by artists whom Picasso collected (reunió) & cherished (apreció, acarició). Dabble (salpicar, mojar, chapotear) → -- in sth (interesarse superficialmente en), -- in politics (politiquear), -- in shares (jugar a la bolsa). Locked up (cerrar con llave, encarcelar) & tortured citizens. The country is seething (hirviendo, furioso). Hard to fathom: (Náut.) sondear, (misterio) desenterrar. Drone (zumbido) on: hablar monótono. A political lodestar (estrella polar, guía, fig.: Norte y guía). Cage (jaula,V) → I feel caged (me siento como enjaulado). In my lifetime (vida): durante mi vida; once in a --. Put out (sacar fuera, expulsar, publicar) statement (declaración, comunicación, Ec.: estado de cuentas). The cleric's power has waned (se puso pálido, decaído, lánguido). Cordless (sin cable) headphones. Grievances procedures (sistema de trámite de quejas). Face veils: banned after three men wearing them entered the school & groped (toquetearon) girls. He left a trail (estela, rastro, sendero) of litter/ debts (basura/deudas) behind him. He despised (despreció) the state structure. Skimp (escatimar, economizar) =/= skim: pasar rozando, echar una ojeada, leer por encima, desnatar → -- across (deslizarse a través de), -- along the ground (pasar rozando la tierra), -- off (separar) money for the kit. Barter (trueque) deal. Diehard (intransigente) with alcohol abuse. Trading partners could peel (pelar, piel, cáscara) away: desplegarse, desprenderse, desconcharse (quitar parte del enlucido o revestimiento). Deceive (engañar)r: impostor =/= deceit (fraude, engaño)ful: engañoso, fraudulento. A house off (una casa un poco apartada de) the main road; red crosses (cruces) are hoisted (izadas, levantadas) off the building. Western allies heaped praise (colmaron de elogios) on the pro-european anti-american rant (vocifeo, despotricar,V). Foremost (principal, en primer lugar) credit. Leash (correa) → the devastation unleashed (desatada, desencadenada) across the € zone put paid (acabó, puso fin) to all that. Sue: demandar, (Jur.) poner pleito → -- (llamamiento), -- for peace, -- for libel (difamación,V) -- over the health-care law, -- for divorce... He states/declare (declara, expresa) the terms (períodos, plazos, condiciones) of... Broach (abordar/mencionar un tema) it. Lighten (aligerar, iluminar) up (relajarse). He is beholden (tiene obligaciones) to them; behold the results! (¡He aquí los resultados!). Cut out (recortar, suprimir + abolish, remove, suppress). Shrouded (envolvió) in uncertainty his pledge (promesa) to renegotiate the terms of Br's EU membership. Veto in all EU edicts (edictos, decretos). Show up (verse, aparecer) → he --ed up late as usual. Pay up (pagar lo debido) → in the end the country --ed --. Steadfastness (firmeza) in upholding (sosteniendo) rules. His ruddy (rojizo) -cheeked fussy (meticuloso, quisquilloso) friend. Solace oneself (consolarse). Such mishap (contratiempo) would outlive (sobrevivir) the memory of... Enthuse about/over (entusiasmar con...). Taiwan president has conjoined (unido) Taiwan's Ec. ever closer to China. They screamed (gritaban) & waved (agitaban, blandían, ondeaban...) at the rally (mitin) in Taipei. They played them down (les disminuyeron la importancia, les minimizaron...). Parochialism (lo provinciano, lo pueblerino) + bumpkin (pueblerino, paleto). Outrageous: idea estrafalaria, precio exorbitante, acto atroz. A back–to-back gathering (el adosar, consecutivo). Loud: fuerte, enérgico, llamativo. He took a back seat (se metió en segundo plano). Dissent (disentir)er: disidente. China is the rising (que sube) power & America is the waning (que disminuye) one. A lengthy (extenso, largo y pesado) document. He talked up (exageró, Ec.: infló, habló claro, etcetera)... A party mouthpiece (portavoz + spokesman; micrófono, protector de dentadura). A chance in the offing (en perspectiva). Few enterprises have refreshed their product line-up (alineación, reparto) so often. The Silk road demise (muerte, desaparición). A flop (golpe seco, dejar caer, fracaso) crushed (aplastó) three artists; she flopped down into thechair. A never-ending (interminable) barrage (presa + lluvia) of questions, fines... He punctured (pinchó, destruyó...) its share price/on the motorway/the pride (+ bajó los humos). Spurring (espoleando, estimulando) Japanese firms to expand abroad. Which have skimped (escatimado) on investment. A hoard (montón) of € 500 m. he has pledged (prometido) + as a pledge (señal, garantía) of sincerity, it pledges (garantiza, promete) to throw out the lot: mucho, grupo, he took the -- (todo el lote), divide by --s, his -- (destino) was different. Penny-wise (mirar mucho el dinero). Pull-off (conseguir, arrancar) a spectacular feat/exploit (proeza). The hover (planeador, que ronda)kraft (aerodeslizador) has a niche (=, mercado especializado, concavidad para colocar algo) applications. SpaceX & Orbital: the only American outfits that ferry (transbordan) supplies (reservas, suministros, ofertas) to the international space station. By acquiring their lift (ánimo, propulsión) from aerodynamic interaction. Cruise (navegar) as high as 6 m. above H2O level. A crucial breakthrough (adelanto importante). Horse-trading (chalaneo, trafiqueo). D. Cameron is imperilling Britain's place in Europe by making promises he cannot keep. Young Nepalese toil (esfuerzo, trabajar duro) in Qatar & S. Arabia: € 4 bns each year remittances. Donors: if they are not looting (saqueando), they connive (hacen vista gorda, se confabulan) in graft (soborno, mordida). Stint: limitar, restringir → without -- (libremente), do one's stint (hacer su parte), a two years --... (fue miembro dos años)..., he did not -- (escatimó) his praises ←→ unstinting: pródigo → be -- in one's praise (prodigar alabanzas) =/= by instinct, the -- for self preservation. Splutter: echar saliva, (Máq.) ranquear. Outsiders (forasteros) will be baffled (desconcertados + disconcerted). The people that trust it is a wretched (miserable, desgraciado) 7%. America faces a host (anfitrión, huésped; receptor, presentador, multitud, (Comp.) servidor, Rel.: hostia) of ailments (enfermedades, achaques). Money splurged (derrochado) on elections. Balance: (=, equilibrio de mente, out of -- (desequilibrado), what's my -- (saldo). Filibuster: obstruir, obstaculizar. That has taken the politicians by storm (por asalto). The Civil guard was on the take (dispuesto a dejarse sobornar). Patronage (patrocinio, mecenazgo, clientela) → -- system (clientelismo). Roll: rollo, lista, panecillo; liar, hacer rodar → be on a roll (estar en racha); roll over: voltearse, volcar, (deuda) refinanciar. High-handedness (despotismo, arbitrariedad). Clamp (abrazadera) down (medidas drásticas, restricción, prohibición) on foreign - owned media. Defraudar: (=, disappoint, dash). Bash (golpe, pegar, abolladura; juerga). Misty (neblinoso, lloroso) -eyed: sentimental + haze (neblina) from its cobbled (adoquinada) (court) yard. Itching (inquieto, irritado, picor) to wield (manejar, ejercer) American power. Moonlight (pluriempleo). Squalid (miserable, sórdido, sucio, indecente, avaro) =/= squalls (borrascas, tempestades, chillidos,Vs) in places like

Hong Kong. He defected (desertó) to Spain. Playground (paraíso, patio de recreo, lugar preferido). Crafting (artesanía, astucia) of the rules in contention (discusión, opinión). The lopsided (desequilibrada) inversion has been stuck (pegada, atascada, soportada). Stake (participación) holder: accionista. Shore up (apoyar, reforzar) the system. The devolved (delegado, descentralizado) country. The policies laid down (establecidas; ser liberadas de, dejadas de lado); lay o.s. down (tumbarse). Ensnared (atrapados) by corruption. The weird thing is that... (lo raro es que...). Agog: the country was -- (muy emocionado), I was -- (tenía mucha curiosidad) to hear the news; he is deeply moved/stirred. It will be his downfall (ruina, caída, perdición). Catalonia peel off Spain. Clutch: embrague; garra, asir, agarrar → make a -- at sth (tratar de arreglar algo), be in/fall into sb's -- (garras); put in the -- ←→ depress the -- =/= choke (starter, Mec.: obturador; atragantarse...). Breach: (ley) infracción, -- (incumplimiento) of a contract, it caused a -- (puso en peligro a) the national security. The executive suite (séquito, serie, grupo) are male-dominated. Maternity leave (permiso). Rules hemmed (cercadas, arrinconadas) in banks, to let them fall (fallar, caída, apagarse, T: descender,...). Touchdown (aterrizaje). Pigeons use gravity to get a course back to their lofts (desvanes, pajares). Distant sound (sonido) of the ocean. Preserved in aspic (gelatina + jelly). Steeped (impregnado, remojado, abrupto) in the European Enlightenment; too -- (empinado) for the tractor. Fanciful (caprichoso) & ramshackle (destartalado) empire. I'll see you in a bit. Arrow (flecha, señalar con una --) =/= dart (dardo). Hitting the target/bullseye (diana): dar al blanco. Sham (falsas, fingidas) elections. Honest/honourable (honrado). Deplete (mermar, agotar) → relentless (implacable, incesante) air attacks have --ed, -- our savings/stocks, --ed (empobrecido) Uranium. Errant (errante) =/= errand (recado, mandado, misión) → run --s (hacer recados), -- boy (recadero),

-- of mercy (misericordia): una misión de caridad. The common (llano) people. Taiwanese are fed up (hartos) with bickering (riñas, discusiones) between the two main parties. Eyes twinkling (centelleo,V, brillar) → in the -- of an eye (en un abrir y cerrar de ojos). A sluggish (lento, perezoso; Ec.: deprimido) 2015. Warlords (caudillos, líderes). Bliss (dicha: ser feliz) → ignorance is -- (ojos que no ven, corazón que no oye) + blissful (maravillosa, dichosa) impunity as displayed in the protracted (prolongado) theft. Relish (sabor,V, entusiasmar) his task + I don't -- the prospect; with relish (gusto, placer). Retrial (revisión, nuevo juicio). Villains (maleantes). Learned (erudito). Right-minded (honrado). Gobbledegook (líos, galimatías, lenguaje confuso). Half-backed (mal concebidos) experiments. His critics advocated (abogaban), music critics (críticos), be critical of... (criticar)... Chaff (cascarilla, pienso, forraje) =/= protesters chafed (irritados, impacientes) at the meek (sumisa, dócil) response. Rogue: pícaro, Bio: solitario, animal apartado de la manada → -- state (estado villano). Financial-messaging (mensajería) network. Backroom: (equipo) que trabaja a la sombra, (negocios) entre bastidores, preparado en secreto. Bulging (abombadas) waistlines (cinturas, tallas). Shockingly (terriblemente, pésimamente) bad. Mostly (en su mayoría) unappealing (poco atractivo). Breeding ground (caldo de cultivo). Overturn: (mesa, barco) darle la vuelta, (Gobierno) revocar, (decisión, juicio) anular, (teoría) invalidar → -- the mobile-telecoms operators. Newly minted (recién acuñados)/salidos de la universidad + mentolados). Let's not get carried away (entusiasmados) in... Wary: -- (cautelosos) of easing (relajar) monetary policy, --ness (cautela), un-- (imprudente + --less, rash) → tread warily (andarse con cautela) → investors will tread (pisar) warily (cautelosamente) as they wait to see if rekindling (que despierta, que se enciende)'s Indian growth will be given higher priority than securing the Government's hold (aguante) in power =/= weary:

cansar (se), aburrir (se) → Oxford found the ideas wearisome. Doggedly (tenazmente) pursued. The damned (maldito, condenado) book, do one's damnedest (lo más imposible) to succeed. Toll (peaje, número de víctimas, efectos graves, provocar daños) → rust (óxidos...) have taken their toll, the severe weather has taken his -- (ocasionado pérdidas) on the crops. Mow (segar, cortar) the lawn (césped). Buccaneering (piratas) oligarchs. Staying out (quedarse fuera) at night; he usually stays out late. Sucking (chupar, aspirar) money out of the state. Tunnelling (escavando) through seemingly (aparentemente) insuperable barriers. Workaday (rutinario, monótono). Frog (gabacho/franchutis, rana). Kooky (majareta, chiflado). Britain & France carve up (se repartieron) the non- Arab peninsular provinces of the Ottoman Empire. Be in tatters (andrajos): estar hecho trizas, (Ec.) por los suelos. IS: a redrawing border is on the card (tarjeta, ficha, fichero, carta de juego, programa). Swell the United Nations membership from 51 countries (1945) to 193 today. Grazing (de pastoreo) land. If Russia thinks it can get away (irse) with (llevarse) its Ukrainian land-grabs, other ex-Soviet neighbours may be at risk. Making plain (claro, evidente) the conditions of any separation. Spear (lanza, arpón,Vs) a fish. Once Slovenia has secured its independence, the Yougoslavian Federation fell apart (se desmoronó: collapsed) =/= fall away (desprenderse). Step up (aumentar) efforts to... Homophobia has been relegated from a legally buttressed (reforzada, apuntalada, apoyada) norm... A risible (que causa risa) canard (bulo). A court struck it down (mató, ley: revocó) but others have pledged (han prometido) to revive (reactivar, reanimar) it. To emulate (copiar) a move (movimiento, jugada, mudanza) from... Noxious (nocivo) populism. The rhetoric draws on (se inspira en) cold-war enmities. It enlists (alista, consigue) the mantras of anti-colonialism. War-torn (destrozada/desgraciada por la guerra) eastern Ukraine. Forcibles (forzadas) mass conversions.

Ghastly (horriblemente) law → how --! (¡Qué horror!) + aghast (horrorizado). Stir up (agitar) racial prejudices. Skating (patinaje) =/= scathing (mordaz: áspero, que corroe; feroz) against... A more enlightened (progresista, inteligente) stance (postura, actitud). Seize on/upon: aprovechar, (idea: fijarse) → ideas --ed on by the opposition. Bias: sesgo, parcialidad → this paper has a left wing -- (tendencia), she was accused of --, his scientific -- (inclinación), influir en, afectar. Misfire (fallar, encasquillarse), the plan backfired on him, his trick misfired. Rights it upholds (que mantiene, que defiende) at home. Act (acto,V, ley...) which target (diana)s (se dirige a) officials implicated in offences (faltas, ofensas, delitos) for visa bans & asset freezes. Impair (dañar, afectar) → unimpaired (intactos). Inquests (investigaciones). In proportion to the degree of his offence. Husbandry: agricultura, cría de animals (animal --), good gestion/thrifty management). Mercy (clemencia) → beg for -- (pedir clemencia), have -- on sb (tener clemencia para alguien)... Kin (pariente) → his next kin (su más cercano pariente), be no -- to sb. Pending tray (bandeja): cajón de asuntos pendientes. Lawful (legal) =/= loyal (fiel, leal). At length (por fin, con mucho detalle, detenidamente). Scrums (melée, avalancha). Net phone (teléfono por Internet). Not once since the second World war has any political party won over 50% of the vote in Britain. Obsess (obsesionar) over/about foreign phantoms (=, imaginario). Another airport runway (pista de aterrizaje) near London & scrap (desechar, descartar) others. Face about (dar media vuelta); face up to: hacer frente a → -- -- -- the overseers (supervisores). The gravel (grava) pit (hoyo, foso, cantera): gravera + gravel bed). Argue (sostener, discutir) flatly (rotundamente) for staying in. A caveat (advertencia). Barge (abrirse paso a empujones) their way to the top of the European Union's agenda; -- through the crowd. The likes of him (gente como él) → the enmity (enemistad) of the likes of Poland & Baltics. Putin plays the trump (triunfo) card of friendliness (simpatías) with Germany. Hungary, Cyprus & Bulgaria have usually been pro-Russian. Juncker wants a three year € 300 billions investment splurge (derroche). The fighting has abated (aplacado, amainado, mitigado)... He bemoans (lamenta) its inability... A renegotiation ahead of an in-or-out referendum in 2016. On the governments to-do (follón) list... Work council (consejo de empresa). His tough-guy (tipo duro). Sarkozy is loathed (detestado) as wildly (locamente, desenfrenadamente) popular. Steal the limelight (centro de atracción) from his rivals. His main obstacle is not other contenders so much as pending judicial investigations. Distrust (desconfianza)ful (receloso, desconfiado) & doubtful (dudoso). He junked (se deshizo de, tiró a la basura) his social policies. It should put on a good show (debería hacer un buen papel). Cling: (ropa) agarrarse, (pers.) pegarse, (opinión) aferrarse → she was clinging to her mother's skirt, they clung (se pegaron) to one another, a dress that clings to the figure, the smell clung (impregnaba) her clothes. Piffle (tonterías, estupideces). Harangue (arengar: hacer un discurso) when sth goes wrong. Shirk (eludir, rehuir) → the shirker (gandul) of International Community. Cue (ejemplo, entrada de teatro, momento adecuado) → East Berlin took its -- from Moscow, that's your --, miss one's -- (no salir a escena en el momento adecuado). Germany's elite took on (asumió, aceptó) the nagging (quejas/críticas, gruñidos) by western peers to be assertive (enérgico, firme) abroad. Demostrators' falseness/falsehood (falsedad). He acts reassuringly (tranquilizadoramente). The likes (gustos) for bricks & mortars (construcción). So thoroughly (a fondo, minuciosamente) is the Labour leader reviled (insultado, vituperado) that... Spain was held up (mostrada) as a model to reform laggards. The smug (engreídas, petulantes) talks. A country that goes over & above (va más allá de, además de) its economic power... First-past–the-post (sistema mayoritario uninominal). Boundary (límite) → -- line (línea divisoria). Bounce back/recover (recuperar) to power. Surge: oleada → a -- of people, -- of power (subida de la tensión), the crowded into the building (entró en tropel)/they --ed round him. Its splinter (astilla)ing (fragmentado) vote & likelihood of coalitions. Lingering (persisten) effects of the downturn (deterioro, disminución). Rare boons (grandes ayudas, favores). The sapping (minados, socavados) drains (desagües; drain: drenar; agotar, consumir). His erstwhile (antiguo) hero F. Hollande. They didn't last long. A lovable (adorable, amoroso) boneshaker (armatoste, carraca, cacharro). Doughty (aguerrido, valiente) people ↔ effete: (civilización, institución) decadente, (persona) agotada + exhausted =/= (libros...) ídem + sold out, out of stock. Dearth (escasez) of spares. Dampen (humedecer, frustrar, hacer perder) voters' enthusiasm. Winding-up (liquidación, conclusión) & other upgrades (mejoras). Jar: jarro; sacudida, choque, (Vs); sorpresa, conmoción, desentonar →it seems -- with América. Dazzling (deslumbrante, resplandeciente) rate of improvement (mejora, Med.: recuperación). Throughput: rendimiento, producción, (Comp.) capacidad de procesamiento. Human lifespan (tramo), for a brief -- (durante un breve lapso). Internet gateway (puerta, acceso) → -- to success. Feedback (reacción, retroalimentación), (Comp.: bucle). Borg: short for cyborg (organismo cibernético). Look up (buscar en el diccionario), a -- - (de consulta) dictionary, (pers.) visitar; (en general.) mejorar. Packet switching: (informática) comunicación de paquetes. From 2008 onwards he has suffered a setback (revés); mishap (contratiempo, revés); upset (vuelco, desbaratar planes, altercado,Vs); turmoil (confusión, desorden). Hasta: as far as, up to; to date (hasta la fecha) → their land stretch <u>up to/as far as</u> the mountains; as far as the eye can see (alcanza la vista) ↔ later, from now on. His ball is three times as large as that of our nearest relatives. Humans & delphines are very close. Until further notice. Disappear from sight, know sb. by sight, loose one's sight, keep sb in sight. See

295

you! (¡Hasta la vista!). See you in a minute, see you soon! (¡Hasta pronto!). Stare (fijar la vista) at... Bird's eye view. These pictures are very similar; he bears some resemblance to his brother ↔ I can't see any family resemblance. Your consciousness/awareness transcends your brain. Endless (interminable) stimuli of the world. Emotional realm (reino, esfera, campo). Emotional addiction. Psycho-neuroimmunology. Although it produces a biochemical reaction. Plausible (=, verosímil, convincente) experience. Our repetitive unconscious thoughts produce automatic, acquired patterns of behaviours that are almost involuntary. We can reinvent ourselves. Relationship brain/mind. Our self-conscious (tímida, afectada, cohibida) identity: la conciencia de nuestra propia identidad + self-consciousness (timidez, conciencia de la propia identidad). Be mindful (tener presente, ser consciente) of risks. Neocortex (area of free will: voluntad, libre albedrío). The invisible quality of self -- reflexion & self-contemplation defines the subject. Conscious mind (mente consciente) afford us the ability to process conscious thought. Phrenology (the archaic mapping system): the regions covering the surface area of a skull. Neuroplasticity: the glial cells & astrocyte enhance (realzan, mejoran) the speed of neurological transmission & help form simpatic (la parte encargada de la vigilia ↔ parasympathetic: para tranquilidad, buena digestión...) connections. Mirror neurons: they facilitate information of behaviour. Personality: a set of memories, behaviours, values, beliefs, perceptions & attitudes that we either project into the world or hide from it. Travel enables us to plot (parcela, argumento, conjura, fraguar) our future more clearly. Uplifted (levantado, en alto, exaltado) → feel -- (by sth): sentirse animados (por algo). Woe (desgracia)ful: lamentable, deplorable. Some questions lurk (merodean, están al acecho) about our ability. Some costlier gas-fired power stations will be mothballed (a la reserva). Long-winded: (procedimiento) interminable; (discurso/artículo) denso, prolijo) → a -- - -- overhaul (revisión, adelanto a, puesta a punto,Vs) of subsidies. Demand outstrips (aventaja, deja atrás) supply. The crowning (supremo) point of the process. A meatier (más sustancioso) range of power. War in Bosnia: France & the U.K. were the prime movers (promotores). The stalling (paro) of European integration. Tie (atar), tying (atadura). Leave no loose ends (cabos sueltos), leave everything properly tied up (dejar algo bien atado). Lame-duck: (pers.) caso perdido, (proyecto) fracasado. Despise (despreciar + look down on, spurn, reject, disregard). A bumpy (accidentado, agitado) year in office/journey. While these contests (concursos, competiciones, impugnaciones) play out (ocurren, se realizan). Encounter (=, tropezar con) Obamacare... Repeal (revocar, abrogar). Luring (atracción de) the remaining holdouts (que se resisten) will be a tougher task. He pay lip service to (defiende de boquilla) an ideal... Pay cash/down (al contado) the pre crisis debt. A dearth (escasez) of investment. Flood (inundar) the market with products. Plough (arar, invertir dinero) → they ploughed the excess into bonds market. Bludgeoned (aporreado, coaccionado) by austerity. A lid (tapa) on interest rates. Slump: sufrir bajón, (precio, producción) caída, (Ec.) depresión, crac (29...), (precios) caída, desplome (over her desk) =/= the devastating slumps (suburbios, barriadas). Boredom (aburrimiento). Slacker (vago, holgazán + idle, lazy) & shirker (flojo/gandul). Devi_s_e: idear, concebir, inventar =/= devi_c_e: mecanismo, aparato, artefacto; recurso. Crop-dusting/crop-spraying: fumigación. Upcoming (próximas) rules. Boomerang (contraproducente, da lo contrario de lo esperado) =/= more success will beget (e, a, o) (engendrar) more hope. Chincheta: drawing pin; thumbtack + tachuela. Pent-up (reprimida) demand. Sky-high (por las nubes) youth unemployment. Pump: bomba, bombear → the gas is --ed from under the sea, -- money into the project, -- up (reactivar, inchar) the economy. Despite fire-ups (enardecimiento, riñas) in the South & East chinese seas. More bluster (fanfarrón) than searing (agudo, ardiente; mordaz, abrasador). China could <u>lash</u> (látigo, azotar) <u>out</u> (arremeter, atacar) abroad. Progress has stalled (parado) owing to snags (problemas) in Japan. Soothe (calmar) popular irritation. Provided (a condición de que) oil prices... Tories have held sway (dominado) since early 2006. His tactics have ranged from the subtle (flavour: suave; pers.: sutil, perspicaz) to the blatant (flagrante, descarado). Downplay (disminución de importancia) of the peacekeeping tradition. Change the country's default (falta, omisión, no pago, de incumplimiento) mindset (actitud) =/= mindful (tener en cuenta). Stamp (sellar, imprimir) their brand on... Conc<u>ei</u>vable (possible, imaginable) rebound. Turning-point (punto de inflexión, momento decisivo). Wellbeing (bienestar) of citizens worldwide. Indonesia's fresh (reciente) start. The flood-prone (propenso) riverbank (orilla, ribera) → it is grown along the banks of the Ebro. Impromptu (improvisadas, espontáneas) neighborhood visits. The estate's immense fuel subsidies. A more likelyscenario is a multi-year taper (astilla + estrecharse, disminuir, afilarse). The continued European sluggishness (flojedad, pereza) has dampened (humedecido, amortizado, frustrado) demand for raw (crudas, sin tratar) commodities (materias primas). Capital outliers (desembolsos). President's steadfast (firme, resuelta) opposition to graft/bribe (soborno), opposition looks crushed (aplastada). Drumming up (despertar, Com: fomentar) foreign capital to give the economy a lift. Underwhelmed (poco impresionados) observers. India scuppered (echó por tierra) a WTO plan to make headway (avance) in preparing the ground for... Compiling (recopilando) into one online process the ten forms (impresos) needed to open a business. India dismal (sombría, pésima) place in the World bank's ranking. Strikingly (sorprendentemente) bold promises. Glitzy (ostentosos) ads (advertisements) lure (cebo,V; encanto, atraer...) students. So outcomes (resultados, consecuencias) will disappoint (decepcionar). Roll out: (masa) estirar, (nuevo producto, sistema) introducir, lanzar =/= roll<u>o</u>ut: (nuevo producto) lanzamiento público, presentación, rodaje por la pista de aterrizaje. The club has billed (facturado, proyectado, programado) 2015 as... It sounds (suena,V; sólidos, formales) as if an EU-style in SEA (South East Asia) union is in the offing (en perspectiva) =/= it is in the making (fabricación, confección, preparación). Come to naught (malograrse). Unassailable (inatacable, irrefutable). Unravel (desenredar). He spent much of 2014 basking (disfrutando) in international acclaim (aclamación). Forward-looking (previsor, (Pol.: progresista) statement. Taiwan's vivid (=, intensa) culture melds (fusiona) traditions from indigenous tribus with those from... Quest (búsqueda) of holy (sagrados) temples or lively (alegres) local celebrations. It's not all hushed (silenciosa) → in – tones) reverence (=, veneración). Light-footed (rápido, veloz) & sure-foodness (seguro/ conocedor de lo que se pisa) of his foreign police. No dumping! (¡Prohibido echar basura!), dumping ground (vertedero). The dumping dredging (dragado, culin.: espolvoreado) spoils (se estropea, se echa a perder) inside the reef (arrecife)'s waters. Outraged (ultrajado) by the dumping (=) plans. Stamping (sellar, estampar) out: erradicar (such practices). China rise unsettles (descontenta, intranquiliza) some in the West. Frictions will not subside (bajar, hundirse; apagar, amainar). Galimatías (sandeces): (asunto) rigmarole, (lenguaje) gibberish. Scale down (disminuir) its efforts to take out (sacar, eliminar, retirar; obtener) his job. Outbound (hacia afuera, hacia el exterior) investment from China. Happily (felizmente, sin problema) the leaders have changed tack (rumbo, táctica...; tachuela, chincheta) → try a different --. Afterthought (idea adicional). At daylight (luz del día, cosas claras): al amanecer + I'm beginning to see --. I owe you € 50. The spectacular success of IS owes as much to the awfulness (lo terrible) of rulers in Damascus & Baghdad as to the prowess of IS's fighters. Both multi-ethnic states ruled by minorities espousing (adoptando) ultra-nationalist Baathist ideology. A spiffing (estupendo, sensacional) underground, tube, subway. The caveats (advertencias) are in order + with the -- (salvedad) that. Israel bucks (se opone a) the regional trend: va contra tendencia. Israel must beware (tener cuidado) of its own incompetence. Dubai's current balloon might pop (reventar) if greed (avaricia) again blinds (deslumbra) better judgment. Spin (vuelta, hacer girar, dar efecto...) → put spin (efecto) on a ball, go for a -- (dar una vuelta) + -- out: alargar, (dinero, bebida) estirar. Stampede (desbandada) of customers. Pinch: pizca, robar; pellizco,V), agarrar, apretar; at a -- (en caso de apuro, si fuera necesario). A built-up (acumulación) of borrowings. Booster: (radio, TV) repetidor), (Med.) vacuna, refuerzo, (Aerosp): -- racket (cohete propulsor). The world's most far-out (extraño, muy moderno, genial) frontier economies are snapped up (agarradas) by hungry investors. The trip to London is already oversubscribed (sobrevendido); the issue was oversubscribed four times (la demanda de acciones superó a la oferta 4 veces) ↔ the offer was --. From the outset (desde el principio). The record -breaking sale. Carry on: (conversación) mantener, (tradición) continuar. The lifeblood (alma, sustento) of Africa's rise. Efforts to negotiate a global climate treaty crashed (quebraron). Titubear: vacillate, hesitate. USA could abide (soportar) by (acatar, cumplir) the terms of any likely (probable) climate treaty. Flagging (que flaquea, enfría, decae) a rise in social unrest =/= flog (azotar, vender) their prized assets. Yardstick (patrón, criterio, medida). He maps out (planifica) both the gains. He's the sole breadwinner (sostén de la familia). It is not good for the bottom line (mínimo aceptable) either. Followers have been drawn to its blendy (mezclado, armonizado) charm (encanto). American products, from trendy (de moda) attire (atavío,V) & mats (esteras) to studio class. Be bonkers (chalados, como una cabra) to attract followers → go -- (perder la chaveta). More staid (serias, sobrias) clothes/pers. They questioned a bloated (hinchada, con exceso de funcionarios, abotargada) situation with pride; be bloated with pride/after all that food. Revenues plummeted (cayeron en picada). Attendance figures (número de espectadores). Live up (animar). Walk out (salir). Dropping (soltando) two bombs. Signatories (signatorios, firmantes) from the non-alignment movement are grumpy (gruñones, malhumorados). A pledge to hold a conference has not been met. The growth of IS has begun to stoke (up) (atizar; esperanzas: cebar) from... Flashpoint (punto crítico) for a war/social movement. Astounding (asombrosa) transformation. Resources extraction underpins (sustenta) growth. Hit the -- on the head (dar en el clavo), -- down (sujetar con clavos, obligar a concretar), -- - bitting (angustioso, con mucha tensión). The debt overhangs (sobresale) from the 2008 housing bust (quiebra...). Too broad (ancho, extenso, amplio) to plot (conspirar, trazar, fraguar, determinar). In broad (general) terms. Crunch: mascar; hammered by the credit crunch (crujido, crisis), -- sth up (triturar algo), when it comes to a -- (a la hora de la verdad). The policy is a given (determinada) austerity. It is in the making (fabricación, confección, preparación). Occasional splurge (derroche) to mollify (aplacar) a weary (cansado) public. Veer (round): virar, torcer. Proponents (defensores) of discipline are to the fore (van delante, en proa) after the president. Faint (débiles) signs of life. Held back (refrenado, retenido) by an electoral willing... Fitful: (progreso/brillo del sol: intermitente; dormir: irregular). Thumb (manosear) its nose: hacer burla. The economy is saddled (cargada) with unemployment. The government will make inroads into (recurrirá a) the country's high-tax environment. It may edge (abrir) its way into power. Once the icon (icono) of post-Soviet stability, the country has been battered (estropeada; reputación: maltrecha) by scandals.

While the politicians scrabble (pelean) the economy will begin a slow climb (subida, ascendencia) to growth. With the economy out of the woods (fuera de peligro) → the Ec. in the full blush (rubor) of recovery. A sole mandate/owner. Eye (observar) a bubbly (burbujeante, lleno de vida) housing market. A pump (bomba, bombeo) priming (preparando) the budgeted fuel subsidies. A hand-picked (cuidadosamente seleccionado) cadre (delegado, (Mil.: cuadro). Toe the line (acatar la disciplina), a "stick" with which to beat those who want toe (conformarse) with Mr Xi's line + be/keep on one's toes (estar/mantenerse en alerta). Help all$\underline{a}$y (calmar) headwinds (vientos en contra). Extending paid parental leave (permiso) & get welfare recipients back to work. Entice (seducir, atraer) investors. Have a penchant (predilección, inclinación) for... A drag on (alargado, que se hace interminable) business/speech. Quell: (revuelta) sofocar, aplastar, (crítica) acallar, (miedo) disipar → -- dissent (disconformistas...) → a potent brew (fabricar, elaborar, tramar; variedad de cerveza, té; infusión) to quell the thirst of loans + quench (sed: quitar; deseo: satisfacer; llamas: apagar; acero: enfriar). Blocka$\underline{d}$e (bloqueo,V) =/= blockage (obstrucción). Be in the doldrums (en zona de aguas ecuatoriales, abatido). Peña pushed reforms onto (sobre) the statutes (=, ley). The last full year of his term. Run up: ir acumulando, (deuda) contraer, (bandera) izar + hoist. His tenure (tierra: posesión; puesto asegurado) has brought stability. The catch-up (puesta al día) growth is no longer on the cards (programas). The contest for succession will take centre-stage (primer plano). Iran is charting (trazando) conciliatory course (=, rumbo). Iraq: having escaped break-up (separación) once before, it is again coming/falling apart (deshaciéndose) at the seams (costuras, junturas). The Sunny constituency it has championed (defendido, abogado) will remain hostile without a shared stake (participación) in running the country. Israel tough stance (postura). Kenya: a full blown (hecho y derecho, a gran escala) insurgency alongside (al lado de, junto a) locals malcontents. The economy is rallying (recuperándose) from a slow patch (remiendo). Syria: the beleaguered (asediado) president hold off (rechaza) the attempt... The economy is in dispiriting (desalentador) shape (forma, configuración,V; estado físico...). Easy money unleashed (soltado, desencadenado) by Fed's bond-buying program will be over. The biggest hazards (riesgos) will lurk (acechar) in debt-ridden (cargada) Europe. Sales of purely electric vehicles will lag (retrasar). Car firms will polish (pulir, refinar, perfeccionar) performance of tarmac (asfalto) -bound vehicles. The EU is phasing (escalonando, organizando) in trend-setting (que impone la moda), fleet (flota, veloz) -average carbon emission standards. Geopolitical runctions (tensiones, jaleos). Shale-gas revolution will spawn (frezar, engendrar, producir...) a batch (hornada) of American plants. The nuclear plants could clear (aclarar, despejar, desatascar) safety checks (controles) by late 2016. Chart (trazar) an altogether (total) surer course (rumbo, curso). Money-making rolls on (pasa, continúa)... The target, which looked unlikely to be hit (alcanzado, afectado). Devilishly (endemoniadamente) complex. Mild (templado) weather & bumper (años: récord; ediciones: extra; parachoques) harvests. A full-blown (gran escala) route(derrota aplastante, fuga desordenada) in emerging markets. Average life<u>spans (tramos, extensiones)</u> will reach 73 years. A web's remorseless (despiadado) advance (=, sugerencia, (dinero): anticipo...). America accounts for big chunks (pedazos) of the fast-growing bits (partes) of the market. Outlays (gastos) in computing programs =/= google's Android operating system will outdo (superar) the rest of the competition =/= undo/untie (deshacer). The rise of mobile internet will give felons (delincuentes) a hackable (piratizable) user-base =/= felony: crimen, delito grave. Admen (profesionales de la pub.). Facebook outshines (eclipsa) google in advertisers' affections (afecto, cariño).

Money-backed guaranties. Abating (disminuyendo) ructions (tensiones, jaleo, follón). The chief (principal, jefe) mover (promotor) of commodities market. Long-haul (de larga distancia) market. Overturn: volcar, zozobrar, (ley) anular. Stainless (inox)-steel. Loud (altos, fuertes) complaints. Dig the stuff up (desarraigar el material, arrancar) =/= desenterrar (disinter, unearth). Succour (socorro). Saving money is a spur (espuela, estímulo). Edge up (subir poco a poco). Indoor (interior, cubiertas) ski slopes (pendientes). Bump (chocar) into fences. Downloads (descargas) at speeds approaching 50 megabits per second. Telecoms revenues dragged down (decayeron) by price competition. Globe-trotters (trotones). Curdle: leche/salsa: cortar, cuajar; sangre: coagularse; (clot) coágulo. Mind-readers (adivinos). The case for prosecution ↔ -- -- -- defense. He was on his way (en camino). The case could drag on (alargarse) for months, the drag for prosecution (la acusación), the drag for defence (la defensa). Retrieve (recuperar, rescatar) documents. Band (franja, tira, banda... grupo) → an attention-grabbing (atrayente) Chinese superband. Hair-raising (horrifying). The payback (restitución, recuperación) time (plazo), it's time to face the consequences. It may seem far-fetched (inverosímil, descabellado). This squeeze (restricción) will intensify. Western Ecs. climb out (salen trepando) of the slump (bajón). Companies are scouting (explorando) lagged (rezagados) people. Swivel round: girar, volverse sobre los talones + -- chair. Leaps & bounds (pasos agigantados). Our mind can be warped (pervertida, deformada, combada). Bulky (corpulento). Marauding (merodeador: intruso + intruder). Tread (huella, paso), mill (dar vueltas) → running on a treadmill (rutina) is uncool (anticuado, conservador). Borderline (dudoso, frontera) case. Insane: loco, descabellado, insensato, the insane (los enfermos mentales). Be snowed in/up (aislado por la nieve). Be all the rage (hacer furor) → going home will be all the rage (hará furor). Lie about/around it (estar sin hacer nada, por ahí tirado). Simplicity (=, sencillez) as a core value (valor central). Fewer pointless (inútil, inmotivada) initiative. Memo (memorandum). Parting (de despedida) words, -- (de gracia) shot (tiro), parting of the ways (encrucijada, momento de separación, despido definitivo). Fun (alegría, diversión) run: maratón corto/popular. Embark on (emprender, lanzarse en)... Reacquaint (reconocer). Grilling (interrogatorio + questioning). Bedtime (hora de acostarse) stories. Time lie ahead in corporate boardrooms (sala de juntas) as the dull (soso) leader stages (escenifica) a comeback. Brag (about): jactarse de, fanfarronear. Name dropping: dárselas de conocer gente importante; name-dropper. Heartily (a carcajadas, encarecidamente, efusivamente) embraced the new shorter-hours culture. I slept through (sin oír) the alarm clock. Puff: (aire) soplo, (wind) racha + -- smoke (bocanada, calada), --s (soplos) of bacterias, out of -- (sin aliento), -- out (arrojar, despedir), off-puffing (desalentador, desagradable). Stringent (rigurosas + strict, severe) emission regulations. Rev (revolución) up: girar rápidamente. Mass-market (mercado popular). Coated (cubierto) with a thin layer of gold. Petrol-powered saloons (turismos, salones, cantinas). Internal-combustion (motor de explosión) engines. Nowhere will match (igualar, emparejar, ajustar) the hefty (fornidos, robustos) subsidies. Bulli*sh* (optimista, Ec: alcista) =/= don't bull*shit* me (no me vengas con sandeces). Toyota ramps (rampas, desniveles,V) up production to tens of thousands in the early 2020's. Adaptor: adaptador, enchufe múltiple. Paperback (libro en rústico, para el gran público, de bolsillo). There's a stream alongside the garden (hay un arroyo al lado del jardín). The car stopped alongside me (a mi lado). Long-running (mucho tiempo) in TV program. A battering (bombardeo, paliza) from the critics. My primary (principal, primario) purpose. Tail fins (aletas). The congestion is tamed (amansada, dominada). Envision (prever + foresee, anticipate; imaginarse, =). Avoid rear-impact crashes. Stop & go (alternancia, restricción y expansión) growth. How prescient (clarividentes) they were. Squall (borrasca) → --s of rain: chubascos, aguaceros. Storm (tempestad, =, irrumpir, tomar por asalto, salir precipitado) → crisis 2008: it looks like a sudden storm sweeping away (arrasando) a pond (estanque, laguna). Bull the market: hacer subir el mercado comprando acciones especulativamente. Abutting (colindante, adyacente, junto) Israel. Africa's rugged (accidentado, tosco, con facciones duras) South. Enloquecer (drive mad, madden) se: go mad, go out of one's mind. In the wake of (trás, a raíz de) the revolution. Get sucked (aspirado, arrastrado) to overseeing (supervisar) Libya's hoped-for (esperada) transition. Be mindful of (tener en cuenta)... There is too much at stake not to try. Fast (rápido; firme, sólido, inalterable)ness (fortaleza, lo más intrincado, inalterabilidad) of Syria. Wholeheartedly (incondicionalmente, =). In escrow (en depósito, en fideicomiso: en custodia de un tercero). Ensconced (acomodado, instalado) → -- in the capital's prime (primordial, de primera) properties; ensconce o.s. Hand in: (homework) entregar, (resignation) presentar. He claims their premises (=, establecimientos, locales) → licensed -- (local donde se permite vender bebidas alcohólicas). They harked back (recordaron, volvieron a) the time... Reproach (recriminar) to sb. Raid (incursión, ataque aéreo, asalto,V) to her apartment. Sack (saco,V, botar, saquear) critical hacks (cortes, pirateos). The government uses the judges as a rubber-stamp (aprobación sin cuestionar con carácter oficial) =/= rubber stamp: tampón, visto bueno. Perkiest (más alegre) economy. Bookish (estudioso). Sideshow (atracción secundaria). Readily (fácilmente, de buena gana) transfer... Flicker (vibrar, vacilar, parpadear) → the candle --ed & went out. Outspend sb (gastar más que alguien). Relentless (imparable + unstoppable) courtship (cortejo) of centrist voters. Country's surfeit (saciar, en exceso + =) importations. They will force a terrorist backward movement/withdrawal/

backing down (retroceso). Spring chickens (polluelo joven y tierno) → she is not a -- -- (ya no es ninguna niña). Batsman (bateador de cricket). Sibling (hermanos) rivalry. Balk (impedir, evadir, no aprovechar) at: plantarse, resistirse. Scaffold (ing): andamio, patíbulo (of the Capitol's dome (cúpula)...). Celebrating with a leathery (correoso, curtido, áspero) kiss. Unpicked (desecho, descosido + unstitched) Congress. Disclaims (desmentidos). Line up (hacer cola) early to vie (disputarse) the public gallery (=, tribuna, museo de arte). Seemed buffeted (golpeado, castigado) by the storm. A trying (dura, difícil) task. The swirl (remolino; girar, dar vueltas) of the skirts. Circling (rodeando) the starting-line of that contest (contienda, concurso, combate). Daydream (ilusión, soñar despierto) about... Undertake: asumir, emprender; -- to + inf (comprometerse a) → biggish (bastante grande) undertakings (tareas, empresas; garantías, promesas). Aggrieved (ofendidos)... They sullied (mancharon) their cause. The capitalist drubbing (paliza, derrota). The phasing out (retiro progresivo) of subsidies. Infrastructure upgrades (mejoras). In Indonesia they can move on (hacer circular, seguir adelante) the thornier (más espinoso) pb of streamlining (racionalizar) a tangled (enredado) tax regime. Kim Jong could bask in (sol, favor...: disfrutar de) the cowed (intimidada, =) admiration of his benighted (ignorantes, =) people. N. Korean old nemesis (justo castigo). The most gall (bilis, hiel)ing (mortificante, que domina las pasiones) of all. "No", he sobbed (dijo sollozando)... Titter (risa tonta/ahogada,V). Bride (novia) ↔ groom (mozo de cuadra, cepillar, acicalar, novio) → his grooming (acicalamiento + dress up) features (rasgos, características). Curtailment (disminución, restricción). Delusional (delirioso) despotism. Falso: (billete) counterfeit, (cuadro) forged, (joya) fake, (dato/declaración) false, (queja, documento) bogus; false testimony (=): jurar en falso, commit perjury. Seem fanciful (caprichoso, fantástico, =) to his advisers. He disposed on (se deshizo de) his mentor (tutor). Cussedness (terquedad + obstinacy, stubbornness) → cussedly unmalleable. An attempt to defect (defecto, desertar)ion (deserción) & cross the Chinese borders. Rag (trapo, periodicucho, broma pesada) → I was only --ging (tomando el pelo). Ragpicker (trapero). He set out (salió, expuso, presentó) a row of plastic cups on a bare floor. Toss (sacudida, tirada,V) rings around the cups. The chirp (decir alegremente; gorjeo, chirrido,Vs)y: alegre + (pers.) happy, cheerful. He did her chores (tareas) without prodding (instarlo, empujarlo). Share parenting (participación a la vida familiar); parenting is a full-time occupation. China's <u>secretive</u> (reservado) space programme. A deadly (mortal, funesto, terrible) stampede (estampida). Muzzle (bozal, mordaza,Vs, hocico + snout) → the government muzzles public crisis =/= fuzzy (velloso, idea confusa) =/= huffy (enojadizo, irritable) ness toward Kim =/= thug(gish) desalmada) rule. Onlookers (espectadores) who lingered (persistían, tardaban en marchar). Overwhelmed (aplastado, arrollado, abrumado) → sorrow --ed him, she was --ed (sumida) with grief (en la tristeza)/with joy (rebosaba de alegría). Firework (artilugio pirotécnico, fuego artificial) =/= firefight (tiroteo) =/= firestorm (tormenta ígnea) =/= fireproofing (a prueba de fuego) as banks. Covering up (ocultando, cubriendo completamente, abrigando; disimulando) criticism. Cynicism is warranted (garantizado). Villain (maleante + crook)'s sidekick (secuaz). Keep (guardar, reservar, llevar) a tally (cuenta) of... I doubt whether... Throw up (llevarse a la cabeza) their hands. Top-up loan (préstamo adicional) + can I give you a top-up? (¿Te sirvo un poco más?). Mc Donald's is floundering (se debate, en discurso: perder el hilo) & activist (=) investors are circling (rodeando) it; the lion circled its prey. High speed rail has clawed (arañado...) a market share from airlines. Extoll (alabar, elogiar). The public carping (quejas constantes). Its central tenets (principios) are outlandish: (conducta, ideas) extrañas, (vestidos) estrafalarios.

Usefully (provechosamente, útilmente). Checklist (lista de control). A furious (violent) onslaught (ataque) on a critic (crítico)... Window-shoppers (miradores de escaparates). Spit: saliva, escupir, chisporrotear → -- it out! (¡Escúpelo!), I spat it out (lo escupí). Not as scary (espeluznante, que da miedo) as science-fiction. Firm's inhouse (organización) data. Reap (recoger) the benefits. Venues: the -- (locales) for the match, a change of -- (lugar) for the research. See the quarry (cantera, extraer; víctima, presa). Miniskirts are back in fashion. She has a slight T. (fiebre), she walks with a slight limp (cojera, cojear): cojea ligeramente; the chances are slight. Glance (mirar) → at first -- (a primera vista), the starlight glancing off (rebotando en)... =/= it produces a glint (centelleo). Alongside (al lado de) the offline (desconectado, autónomo) World. A debt-addled (confundida, aturullada) economy; her brain's addled (confundido, aturullado). Financial products have gone belly up (al garete). Growing bearishness (pesimismo; mercado: tendencia bajista) toward emerging markets. Bond-market jitters (nervios) could return. Inroads: all -- lead to Rome, -- (avances) into Chinese territory, the -- (efectos) of mass tourism, make -- into sb's time (robar tiempo), make -- (echar mano) into savings, make -- (adentrarse) into enemy territory. Lift-off: quitar, levantar, (avión) despegar. Rut (surco, rodera, Biol.: celo) → the wheels leaving thin --, be in/get into a rut: ser/hacerse esclavo de una rutina ←→ get out of the --. Litigation (litigio). Savvy (inteligencia), computer savvy (con conocimientos de). Easy money has led to runaway (fugitivo, sin frenos, galopante) prices. Loosen: aflojar → I had to -- my belt, it --s the bowls (tiene efecto laxante + laxative). A pool (reserva) of untapped (sin explotar) labour. Risk that its government's' debt gets downgrades (decae) → be on the -- (estar en plena decadencia). Just a sliver (tajada, rodaja, astilla) away from junk (baratija, trastos, basura) status. Stumping up (aflojar, apoquinar + fork out). The miss-selling (mala venta).

Interlopers (intrusos + intrusive, intruders). Trigger-happy (pronto a disparar). Class action (querella colectiva) suits (pleitos) are a sure-fire (seguro, infalible) success. Sobriquet (apodo + nickname). Improper/wrongful (indebido). Undue (excesivo) → it will unduly (excesivamente) trouble (dificultar, molestar, preocupar)... For all-singing (por todo lo alto). American banks got out (salen) of perish (perecederos) business. Vengeful (vengativo). At the height (cumbre) of his career. Makes it all the more (aún más) important. Credit rating (clasificación crediticia) agency. Britain falls in-between (en medio). Divest: -- sb of sth (despojar), (Ec.) desinvertir (from oil...), -- (renunciar) one's rights. The challengers (aspirantes, desafiadores) are nibbling (mordisquean, muestran interés a una oferta). Humdrum (rutina,V, monotonía) of the incumbents. Miscreant (malas, ruines; sagaces) firms have instilled (inspirado, infundido) fear. To a lesser extent/ degree (en menor grado). Keep your shirt on! (¡Cálmate!). Weigh down: sujetar con piedras, pesos + agobiar, abrumar → -- -- with debt, -- -- on sb (a alguien). Ec. growth is measly (mezquino, miserable). They piled into him: se abalanzaron sobre él + -- into the car, -- on (meterse a empujones). Earn more than the paltriest (más ínfimo, miserable) of returns. Finance leeway (libertad de acción) to... Asset managers hunted (=, buscaban, perseguían) desperately... A poor trade-off (compensación). Hoovering up (pasar la aspiradora). The investments furthest (más lejanos) up the risk curve are the ones... There will be no letup (pausa, descanso + rest; relief: alivio). By the same token (razón); as a -- (motivo, razón) of respect. Inflation - proof (resiste a) income. Sound: tocar, hacer sonar, sonido, ruido, (Med.) auscultar; sano, robusto, de confianza, razonable. I'm friendly (simpático, cordial) with... The index funds (fondos indexados) replicate (reproducen exactamente) the S&P500. Go for: (atacar): the dog went for me, (gustar): I don't go for these films. Little scope (alcance, posibilidad) for fresh: =, lozano, reciente, nuevo, (pers.) impertinente, (agua) dulce... Uncharted (inexplorados) oceans. Discutir: discuss, question, argue. Span: abarcar → wingspan (envergadura + importance, scope, magnitude). You stay right there (no te muevas de ahí). Stay aloft (arriba). Top up (llenar, recargar + recharge) batteries. Overcome (vencer, dominar) misfortune (desgracia). Eking out (escatimar, hacer que alcance) the power... Try out (probar) the jet (reactor) fans (ventiladores). Swallow the bait: morder el anzuelo/cebo, fifty pellets (gránulos) of poisonous bait. Den: guarida; gabinete, estudio =/= sett: madriguera de tejón, adoquín + paving stone) =/= burrow: madriguera, -- into the rock (excavar la roca), --ing: cavando (one's way...), -- a den (madriguera) of species found nowhere else. Fur (piel, pelo, sarro) → -- coat. Wiped out (limpiado, aniquilado) within fifty years. This is irrelevant: intransigente, no viene a cuenta, no tiene relación con. New Horizons blasted off (despegó) in 2006. Harpoon (arponear). Lump: trozo → a -- of sugar, -- (grumos) in the sauce; hinchazón, bulto (→ in one's throat), zoquete, aguantar → if you don't like it, (you can) -- it (te aguantas); -- together (agruparse). We went past your house (pasamos por delante de tu casa). A mottled (moteado, jaspeado, manchado) World =/= demoted (degradado, con menos categoría). Striking (llamativos) geysers. Alien (extraño, extranjero, extraterrestre, =). Trundle (empujar, tirar) on: avanzar con mucho ruido, pesadamente. It flew round & down (volcó dando vueltas). Sedately (seriamente, formalmente). A covering of frost (escarcha). Updraft/updraught: corriente ascendente. Superbug (bacteria asesina/transgénica). This does away with (suprime) the need. Beyond the seas (más allá/allende los mares). A refrain summed up (resumido) in... Headline-grabbing (que salta a los titulares). Telling: (argumento, crítica) contundente, (golpe) certero, (signo, observación) revelador/a, elocuente; (tellingly) eficazmente, efficiently, effectively. Astronomers will relish (saborear, hacerles gracia) this close-up (primer plano) glimpse (destello, vislumbre) of Pluto. The bleached (blanqueada, descolorida) atmosphere of the desert. Philandering (mujeriego), flirt (flirtear). A sand<u>bar: barra, obstáculo</u>. Centerpiece (eje, atracción principal). Performing (de la interpretación) → -- arts. Laugh off (tomarse a risa). A taster (catador, muestra) exhibition. A. Dhabi was feeling slighted (ligero, menospreciado). Memento: recuerdo, regalo + souvenir → happy memory, my warmest regards. Unravelling (desenredando) politics. Once stingy (tacañas, escasas) websites are putting cartoonists (dibujantes de chistes, humoristas) on their payroll (nómina). Highlight: poner de relieve, the --s (los puntos más interesantes) of the game, the elections are the highlight (punto culminante, plato fuerte, lo más destacado) of their calendar. Before "Alice in wonderland" (1865) children's books tended to be dull (aburridos, apagados...). Worthy (digno, merecido, respetable) → -- opponent, -- of attention, -- of her father. He lectures (da clases) & smokes a hookah (marguila). It's on loan (está prestado). Seek (out): buscar → -- -- the operatic (operística) version. Gargantuan (gigantesca) collection. Bombshell: obus, (informaciones) bomba, (a real --: un bombón). The onlookers (espectadores) were gripped (emocionados). Dangling (colgando) from a skyscraper. Will-power (fuerza de voluntad). Exposure: (light, heat, risk) exposición, (impostor/que finge/ que engaña) desenmascarar, a house with a southern --. Trap: trampa → lay (tender) a -- to sb, keep one's -- shut, shut your --! atrapar/cazar, trampilla, (teatro) escotillón. Drove people out (expulsó + expelled, sent off). A hum (murmullo, canturreo, zumbido) of conversation. Pine: pino, pine cone (piña + pineapple); (pers. kernel) piñón, p. for sth/sb: suspirar por --/- -. Flee to a wilderness (desierto, jungla) free of temptations. He teetered (tambaleó, titubeó). Be on leave (permiso), take (one's) -- (of sb): despedirse de alguien, I'll-- you at the station, the car -- the road. Stir: give sth. a -- (conmoción), -- (incitar) sb to sth, excitar, -- up (remover) the past, meter cizaña. Build things anew (de nuevo). Racy (picantes, animadas, briosas) novels. Lounging (gandulear, salón) =/= roaming: vagabundo, itinerante (de un lado a otro). Good riddance! (¡Adiós y buen viaje!) for them! ¡Que se pudran! Oblivious (inconsciente + unconscious) of/to... (ajeno a...). Track: pista, huella, sendero → be on sb's --, he keeps – (lleva la cuenta) of expenditure, he lost- (hilo) of the argument (discusión) =/= leaving trail (rastro, estela) behind us. Ten or thereabouts (más o menos, allí cerca). Customer (cliente + client, shopper). Partygoers (asiduos + asiduous). Get enmeshed (enredarse + estar cogido) into a net... Slimness (delgadez) =/= sliminess (viscosidad + thickness) =/= slimy (viscoso, (pers.) falsa. Peeks (miraditas), no --ing! (¡sin mirar!), -- over (por encima) the fence (valla), -- in at the kids (echarles una mirada). Buff: lustrar, pulir, aficionado ↔ Rebuff (desaire, rechazo,V). Of unknown authorship (autoría). To a great/certain/lesser (menor) extend. Plentiful (abundante). Who reaps (cosecha, recoge) the rewards (recompensas)? =/= beneficio: profit, benefit. Collision (colisión) =/= prices collusion (confabulación) by producers. Acosado: hounded, harassed, pestered (+ molesto), beset → -- with questions about political troubles. Fossil-fuel (hidrocarburos + hydrocarbons). Wrongheadedness (desatino + foolishness, tactlessness + falto de tacto). The green energies bits (partes) are wilting (marchitando) under the impact of oil price. Modern coal-fired plants, though pricey, are cleaner. The agreement is fatally flawed (con defectos que lo condenan al fracaso). Solar flare (llamarada). The new generations are eating away (desgastan, corroen) the ancient models. Sightly (agradable a la vista) ↔ unsightly: feo + ugly, nasty, unpleasant. Solar new tech stacks (amontona) layers of photovoltaic materials to capture a much broader section of the spectrum. Sewage works (estación depuradora). Maim: mutilar, =). Flatten (allanar) the peaks. Such assortative (concordante, conveniente) mating (apareamiento). Today's rich people pass on (pasa, da; contagia) an asset to their children that cannot be frittered (away) (malgastada). Nine % of college-educated mothers who give birth each year are unmarried, 61% of high-school dropouts (no completan los estudios, marginados). Live on welfare (bienestar, asistencia social). Pull strings (mover palancas) to get junior (7 - 11) into a top-notch (de primerísima categoría) college. Splash out (derroche de dinero, darse un lujo). Back: trasero, (animal) lomo, (silla) respaldo...; espalda → my back (espalda)'s trouble (molestia). At the top of the pile (montón). Pointless (inútil) bureaucracy & flashy (ostentosos) buildings. Middle-class students have to rack up (acumular) huge debts. He played handsomely (espléndidamente). State-of-the-art (lo más moderno, la vanguardia). Tilted (inclinado) to favour the poor; the tilt of the earth's axis, he --ed his back in his chair; -- at/against (arremeter contra). Grown-up (desarrolladas) alternatives. Blood<u>lust (set)</u>. Wanton (sin sentido, terca, desenfrenada) destruction. Shirk (gandulear, esquivar una obligación)er: gandul. Senior officials skim off (separan) money for the kit (equipo). Repressed (personas: reprimidas). Give sb a piggyback (llevar a alguien a cuestas). Over-tough (duras, fuertes) rules. Pageant: festividades → beauty --: concurso de belleza; espectáculo histórico al aire libre; the -- of history (el desfile de la historia) + pageantry: pompa, esplendor. Prosecuted for holding a placard (pancarta, letrero). Turkey is a champion locker - up (encarceladora) of journalists, but its shameless prime minister turn up (aparece, descubre, desentierra)... He valued (valoró, tasó, apreció) her freedom, all the more so (tanto más en cuanto que)... He sto<u>k</u>ed (avivó, atizó el horno, agudizó una tensión) extremism rather than soothe it (calmarlo), he --s extremism to present himself as the only bulwark against jihadists. Slights (ligeros, escasos; desaires, desprecios) against Islam. Disparage (despreciar) another's faith. The safeguard (resguardo, protección,Vs) afforded to ethnic groups by hate-speech laws. Flippantly (con poca seriedad, ligeramente)... Zealots (fanáticos) to decry (criticar) its decadence. Advocacy (defensa + =ce). Caveat (advertencia + warning, advise). Chiller (refrigerador, película de terror/de suspense). These reserves increase catches (tomas), provided (con tal de que) no one cheats (estafa, haga fraude) by plundering (saqueando) them. Opportunity is slipping away (se va, se escurre). Bootlegging: contrabando, (música/edición) pirateo). Something else (otra cosa) is now afoot (planeada, tramada) → plans are -- to create... Assortment (surtido). Competition is farcically (ridículamente) intense. Surmising (suponiendo, conjeturando) that the people at the top are a rotten crowd. Bone up ("empollar") on (sobre) how to make the right impression. In public school, the advantage of living in a well-off neighbourhood that kick in (derriba la puerta, contribuye con dinero, apoquina)... He got onto (se subió a) the table. Dirigir: (pers.) direct, (tiro) aim, (hotel) run, (orquesta) conduct, (auto) drive. The legacy (legado) of the previous government. Tier: (estadio, anfiteatro) grada, a two-tier (que distingue entre dos grupos) health service. Stories crop up (surgen) of parents of academically borderline (línea divisoria, límite, caso dudoso) students. Endowment (dotación, donación) fund: fondo de beneficencia. Enticing (atractivo, tentador, apetecible) =/= enacted (decretado), enjoyed (disfrutado) =/= endeavour (intento) → -- to do sth (procurar hacer algo)... It ran (estuvo en cartelera) for three years. Varsity (equipo universitario). He presses on (continúa, sigue adelante), he swept into office (arrasó y cogió el poder), he snatched (arrebató) the power. Waist-deep (hasta la cintura). Cantankerous (cascarrabias). Dissidents grouse (urogallo, se quejan) that the bill (proyecto) confer... Be neck-&-neck (ir parejos, a la par), a -- - -- finish (un final muy reñido). The typical marcher (manifestante) is a middle age. A wobbly (flojo, débil; cojo, tambaleante) pudding (=, pudín, postre) →

chocolate -- (crema de chocolate). They likened (compararon) him to... Manhunt (búsqueda de alguien desaparecido/delincuente). Bombastic: (estilo) ampuloso, persona pomposa. Preserve (preservar, conservar, proteger) → Heaven -- us! Ec. upturn (aumento, mejora). She mishandled (maltrató, manejó mal) her response to the terror attacks. Single out (elegir, hacer resaltar). Dot: dot, dot dot (puntos suspensivos), at 7 o'clock on the dot + deep craters dot (puntean, motean + se esparcen en) the runway (pistas de aterrizaje). Pound: perrera, depósito de coches; martillear, (tabla, puerta) aporrear, (especies) machacar → the IS's income is taking a pounding (fuertes latidos, palizas). Dislocated (dislocados, trastornados) plans. Cop (policía) =/= ca<u>b</u> (driver): taxista =/= the Swiss francs ca<u>p</u> (gorra, tapón, funda; selección, restricción,Vs, tope) against the $. It shot up (T., valor...: se disparó; creció rápidamente) by 30% provoking howls (clamores; animales: aullidos). Take off: (avión) despegar, (mancha) eliminar, (ropas) quitar, (miembro) amputar, (precios) descontar. The impending (inminente) announcement. Among the most fret (preocupante)ful: inquieto + anxious, worried =/= faithful (fiel, digno de confianza). He is now even dearer (más querido, más caro). Upscale (calidad superior). Podar un árbol: prune, lop; lop off: cortar, podar, eliminar un párrafo. Azotar: whip, flog + (lluvia, olas) lash. Trash (basura, gentuza; destrozar, poner verde) =/= t<u>h</u>rash (golpear, retorcerse, apalizar) out: discutir a fondo, idear, acordar. Hardship (privación, miseria) clause: cláusula de salvaguardia; suffer hardship (pasar apuros). Test the staying power (aguante, resistencia) of the new upstart (arribista, presuntuoso) left-wing party. Mas: his original plan for a single list uniting all the separatist parties has been dropped at the insistence of his rivals from the ERC (Esquerra (izquierda) republicana de Cataluña). The Catalonia's national day, which campaigners (defensores) have turned to a mass (de masas, misa) event. Catalans are distracted (distraídos) by a flurry (racha, ráfaga) of activity (un frenesí de actividad). Be distracted with anxiety (estar loco de ansiedad, trastornado). Roadmap (hoja de ruta). The slim (delgada, escasa) majority for independence found in some polls. His political party is read<u>y</u>ing (se prepara) itself for bruising (dolorosa, penosa, durísima) defeat. His sight (vista, mira) set on the general elections. Spain's mainstream Socialists go the way of Greece's ailing (debilitado) Pasok. An alternative outlet (salida, toma de corriente). Flick: (cola) coletazo, (dedos) capirotazo, (muñeca) movimiento rápido → -- through (hojear rápidamente). Whatever: -- it may be (sea lo que sea), -- he says, -- it costs, -- the weather. Europe's economy is in the doldrums (abatida, estancada). He downplays (disminuye la importancia) of the deflation threat. Backtrack (retroceder) as soon as the bank intervention had cut interest rates. Scratch (rasguño, chirrido, raspar, rascar)y: que rasca o pica, áspero, (escritura o dibujo) garabateado. The anti € groups are furrowing brows (fruncen los ceños). The political damage could turn out (aparecer, resultar) to outweigh (pesar más que) the economic benefits. The Ulster had an Irish recession with a British twist (enfoque, giro). Wiping out (limpiar, aniquilar, cancelar) jobs & force indebted households to cut back (recortar) economy. Ulster's grant (concesión, otorgamiento, donación, subsidio,Vs) has been cut. He likens (compara) Ulster to a moody (variable, temperamental, malhumorada) society. Grievous: (pérdida) dolorosa, (golpe) severo, (dolor) fuerte, (crimen) grave, (tarea) penosa. His right to lobby (=, vestíbulo, presionar) Muslims. Set aside (puesta aparte) the drivel (tonterías, chorradas) put out (presentadas, sacadas, expulsadas) by British media. He tutted (chasqueó la lengua en señal de desaprobación). Stand out (sobresalir) among other role models (modelos a imitar). Surveyor (topógrafo, perito). Crack: grieta, golpe,V, rajar, intento, (en informática) descifrar un código, (tropas) de primera → failure to crack on (ponerse en marcha). Whose relish (sabor; entusiasmo,V)... The suddenness (repentino, inesperado; brusquedad). A sketchy (incompleto, sin detalle) grasp (entender...) of their religion. Training militias deemed (consideradas) helpful (útiles, eficaces, serviciales). Syria has fallen ever more (cada día más) under Iran's spell (encanto). Iran's secret activities. Prop (puntal) → --ping up: apuntalar, respaldar. Iran largesse (generosidad) to Hezbollah. A dress trimmed (decorado) with feathers (plumas) =/= trim (quitar) excess fat from chops (chuletas). Abrasive (=, áspero, pers.: brusca). Stockpile (reservas; acumular, almacenar). House (domiciliario) arrest. Rato was released (liberado) from police detention. Snatching (secuestro, arrebato, robo) of striking (llamativa, sorprendente) peace. Hand in (entregar, presentar) its weapons. In their stead (lugar). Riven (desgarrado, hendido) by factionalism (enfrentamiento entre facciones)/by grief (dolor, pena, tristeza) → come to a grief: fracasar; -- - stricken: apesadumbrado. Stamp (sello, impronta, timbre,Vs, señalar) out: erradicar, acabar con, sofocar, apagar con los pies. Cram: repleto a reventar, aprender/preparar apresuradamente. Move on: (tiempo): pasar, (multitud): (hacer) circular, cambiar → things have --ed on; move out: (pers., objeto) sacar, (tropas) retirar, -- -- of a flat (piso). Overrun (u, a, u) (invadir, exceder). Bicker (discutir) the details of a plan + initiatives have been floundered (debatidas + floundering in the water: debatirse para salir del agua), -- around in the ice (tambalearse), the economy is --ing. Politicking (politiqueo). Slapping (palmada, añadir) a new levy (impuesto). The play (obra) has an upbeat (optimista) ending. Snort (resoplido, ronquido, gruñido,V). Pay for sick leave (baja de enfermedad). Rastrear: (zona) search, (pers.) track, (pescadores) trawl, (policía) drag; rastreo: (zona) thorough search, (río, lago) trawling, (satélite) tracking, (causas, origen) investigation, search. Poke: pinchar, atizar, introducir → -- a rag (trapo) into the tube, -- about/around (fisgonear, curiosear). He did not fl<u>u</u>b (no metió la pata; examen no lo pifió; no echó a perder una oportunidad) or commit any gaffes (planchas)... Race: carrera → they --ed vintage (antiguos) cars, competir (-- against sb.), we --ed (nos dimos prisa); raza. Disrupted (alteraron) the marble - pillars (pilares de mármol) courtroom. Relatives in lockups (calabozo + cell) =/= prison, jail. Revamped (renovado, modernizado). This reduce the likelihood of an inmate (enfermo, preso, internado) reoffending (reincidencia). Did not return request (solicitud) for comment. Snow<u>mobiling (moto)</u>. Declared void (nulo + (pers.) useless/hopeless). The House (sesión de la cámara) sat (duró) all night. Humdrum (rutinario, monótono, + =, tedious). Gestures & gait (modo de andar)... He is fidgeting (se inquieta). Spot: (mancha, lugar → (on the --: en el acto), pizca, dar cuenta, precios del momento. You have been mislead (engañados, despistados, corrompidos) to reveal c<u>o</u>ncealed (objetos/novedades: ocultados, Jur.: encubiertas/disimuladas) emotions. Swaggering (fanfarrones, de pavoneo, arrogantes) speeches. Their dependants (personas a cargo). Be on roll (de racha), the rise in the rolls (inscritos) + inscribirse (register, enroll). Get into a trouble (molestia, preocupación) =/= muddle/mix-up: lío, confusión =/= fuss (alboroto, escándalo). Figure hug (ceñido al cuerpo). Sealing (cerrar) a pact. The deck (cubierta) of the warship. Mule (mulo, testarudo). A blip (problema pasajero, accidente). He may dent (abollar, hacer mella a) America's idea. Shop (comprar) on the world market. Bankrolling (recursos económicos, financiamiento) imams to preach (predicar) loyalty to the king. Nakedly (manifestamente) self-interested (interesado personalmente). Lay out (exponer, disponer; planear, arreglar) evidence. Hur<u>l</u>: lanzar, tirar, arrojar =/= hur<u>t</u>: lastimar, perjudicar, doler → the papers were unhurt/unharmed (ilesos). Akin (semejantes) to those that thronged (atestaban) the streets. Strew (esparcir, desparramar) → it snakes (serpentea) around the dusty, rubbish-strewn (cubierto, regado, esparcido) back lot (lote, solar, parte) of a giant supermarket. Squarely (directamente, justamente) → the blow hit him on the nose. A trade spat (disputa) has sprung (brotado, nacido). The terminal's run-down (débiles, en decadencia) moorings (amarraderos) =/= run down: descargar, ir reduciendo, agotar, (pedestrian) atropellar. Moras (cenagal, lugar pantanoso). On an equal footing (en pie de igualdad). Thereafter (a partir de entonces), thereby (así, de ese modo), affront (ofensa) to sove<u>reig</u>nty. Fast-tracked (rápido, por la vía rápida). Heaven knows (Dios sabe). Namesake (homónimo, =). Wasp (vispa), hornet (avispón) → stir a hornet's nest (armar mucho revuelo). The sole reason. Men languishing (languideciendo, consumiéndose) on the "death row" have been executed. The only sitting (en funciones) American president to visit India twice. Their underlyings (subyacentes, subordinados) hardly have time to... Servant/maid (criada, sirvienta) =/= virgin/mai<u>den</u> (doncella, soltera) =/= midwife (comadrona). A tour of Abe was knocked sideways (dejado de piedra/patidifuso) by the news. Stage: escenario, organizar, representación,V); etapa, tramo. Snub (desaire, rechazo,V). Executed by firing squad (pelotón de fusilamiento). Aloofness (actitud distante). Autopista: motorway, (USA) freeway, (de peaje) toll road/tollway. Central-planning mindset (actitud, disposición). Leaps & bounds (pasos agigantados). Lust: codicia, sexo: lujuria, poder: ansia). Digging (excavación). The cities engulfed (tragaron, sumergieron) their villages (aldeas). Licence number/plate (matrícula, placa). The outpost (puesto avanzado, reducto civilizado) of the city has all the trappings (ceremonias) of the office (que conlleva el cargo); trappings (símbolos) of success. The scenery (paisaje; teatro: escenografía, decorado) is less grand (grandioso, imponente; espléndido, solemne). Hinder (impedir, estorbar) → -- sb from doing sth, hindrance (obstáculo, =). One issue in which China & the West stand shoulder–to-shoulder is the fight against Jihad. China criticized the Paris attacks unreservedly (sin condiciones). China's officials loftily (con altanería/altivez) ignored the slur (mancha, calumnia, el pronunciar mal). Acquiescence (consentimiento, =) in religious extremism. The Uighurs have long bridled (embridado, frenado, detenido) at the influx (afluencia) of Hans. Sporadic revolts have been harshly (duramente) put down + (bag, pen) dejar, colgar el Tf., (parasol) cerrar; anotar, reprimir. Blasphemy laws carried (llevaban, transmitían, aprobaban) death penalty before 1789. The president's public utterance (declaración, expression,Vs). Wavering (indeciso, vacilante, que flaquea) ideal. Startle: sobresaltar, asustar → --tling: (descubrimiento) inesperado, (apariencia) llamativa, (noticias) alarmantes. Razed (to the ground): asolados. A lecherous (lujurioso, lascivo) thug (matón). The ease (alivio, facilidad, relajamiento, soltura,V). Unmet (insatisfecho + dis/ unsatisfied). Put paid (poner fin) to that. Put boots in (emplear la violencia). An unrest (que molesta, que inquieta,Vs) rumbling (ruido sordo, rumor,Vs); civil unrest (malestar social). Draft bill (proyecto de ley). Mandatory (obligatorio). The law could usher in (hacer pasar) a welcome (grato) change. A sweeping (barrido, amplio, arrollador) free-trade agreement. Upgraded: (mejoradas, reformadas) operations. Outsize (enorme, de talla muy grande). Conning (de mando) tower. Haul: botín, (peces) redada, (drogas, armas) alijo; arrastre, trayecto, transporte → haulage (transporte), hauler (transportista). A scruffy (desaliñada) town. A man squint (mira de reojo; estrabismo) → --s up at a telecoms mast (mira entrecerrando los ojos) al mástil that has sprouted (brotado, surgiido) next to a mud (de lodo) track (rastro, sendero). A brash (chillón, presuntuoso) outfit (traje, equipo; grupo, empresa). A leaner (más magro) approach. Snag (problema, inconveniente; tocón, madera: nudo; enganchar → he --ged his sweater on those brambles (zarzas). Outwit (burlar, ser más listos que) → they had been --ed by... Souped up: (coche) trucado, (film) mejorado. The debate heats up (se calienta). A free-trade deal encompassing (cercando, englobando, abarcando) China & Japan. Jig (criba; dar brincos, bailar). Array (formación, orden) → in a battle --, a fine -- (serie) of flowers; atavío, V, disponer, desplegar. Wake (estela), (a, o, a) (despertar) → in the wake of riots/storm (tras la tormenta). Cook up (inventar, tramar) new stances (actitudes). Sizzle: crepitar (al freir), chispa → the idea doesn't have any --. Mindful (tener presente) of tight (ajustado, ceñido, estrecho) credit. The bias (propensión, predisposición) → right - wing --; -- (prejuicio) against. Thread (hilo, enhebrar) → --bare: (ropa…) gastada, (argumento) trillado. Dwindle (disminuir) away to nothing (ir disminuyendo hasta quedar en nada), -- in importance. Boom (estruendo, (empresas…: auge) market. Vastness (inmensidad). Have a stab (puñalada,V) at it: intentar hacer algo; a -- of pain (una punzada de dolor), --bing (apuñalamiento). Stamp (sello, timbre, impronta, dar patadas) → --ed it out (lo/la erradicó) → we must -- -- these abuses. Crosscheck (verificar) information → you'd better (sería mejor) --. Regardless/whatever conditions. Zigzagging (serpenteante). Purport (significado, intención, pretender)ed to be... Nature's bounty (generosidad, munificencia). Blob (gota, mancha, borrón) → --by: borroso. Outermost (exterior) layer (capa, estrato; gallina ponedora) → the outermost island in the archipelago. Tantalising (tentador, incitante). Charred (carbonizados) papyres. A field of study has been tilled (cultivado). Scan (explorar, registrar, escanear). Mastermind: genio/cerebro; (robo, crimen: planear y organizar) → he --ed the robbery (asalto). Airtight/tight-lipped: hermético → be --ed on sth (mantener la boca cerrada respecto algo). Entumecerse: (dedos) get numb, (pierna, músculos) get stiff ↔ loosen (relajar, aflojar, desentumecer). Up & down (de arriba abajo). Township: pueblo, (USA) municipio. Convenience: comodidad, ventaja → do it at your own -- + -- foods (fáciles de preparar). Engrossing (absorbente, apasionado) book, become engrossed in (dedicarse por completo a).

Cussedness (terquedad + obstinacy, stubbornness). Bring forward: presentar, exponer, adelantar, hacer comparecer =/= pay in advance. Secondhalf (2ª parte) =/= second-guess (anticiparse a (+ anticipate to), cuestionar a posteriori ←→foresee (prever). Potty (chiflado) for sth. Run up to the house. The tide (marea, corriente) of the events, high tide, go against the tide ←→ swim with the --. The quake (temblor) that struck Haiti. Compounded: (interés, frase, palabra) compuestos, (problema) agravado. Realm (reino, campo) → beyond the --s of possibility (totalmente imposible), it belongs to the -- of metaphysics =/= kingdom. Spurning (rechazo, desdeño). Mistrust (desconfianza) of officialdom (burocracia). Battered (magullado, estropeado), (mujer) maltratada. Lived up (cumplió, estuvo a la altura) to its history. The attacks rocked (sacudieron) France. Cartoons lampooning (satirizando) politicians & religions. More surprised by this outpouring (desahogo, efusión: an -- of emotion) than the French themselves. Belated (tardía) attention. Nice salute (saludo). A grumpy (gruñón, malhumorado) electorate. Fuss (alboroto) → make/kick up a -- about sth baby-sitting (canguro). A breathtaking (imponente) landscape. Elusive (esquivo, escurridizo). Rugged (escabrosos) trails. Political hue (matiz, color) → <u>-- & cry (revuelo)</u>. Duck (pato, tío; sumergirse, zambullida,V; esquivar). Plausible: verosímil, convincente; loable, meritoso. Blokeish/blokey (machote, tipo/tío). Compelling (convincente, persuasivo) =/= appalling (espantosa, atroz) communal (comunitaria) violence =/= boggle (quedar atónito) → we take on (aceptamos, asumimos, contratamos) missions of mind-boggling (increíbles, alucinantes) protests. Labour's failure (fracaso) is more abject (abyecta/servil, deplorable). Miliband's campaign to slam (tortazo; vapulear, apalizar) the tories as state-wreckers (destructores). Call-in: (Med./experto) llamar, (Com.) retirar los malos → -- -- on sb (pasar a ver), -- -- any times (ven cuando quieras). Pigmy (=, enano + dwarf). Be lovelorn: perdidamente enamorado. Britain is superseding (desbancando, suplantando, cambiando de sentido) European countries. Chinese businessmen seem unfaced (tan panchos) by the contest (lucha, competición, impugnación, contradicción,Vs). Most fast growing African nations hew (cortan, labran; se ciñen) closer to western free-markt ideas. With high-octanes (con mucho carácter). The drugs were dumped (descargadas, desechadas) overboard (por el borde). Considerable scope (gran alcance), the scope (campo de aplicación) of new measures. Obama wants Congress to bolster (cabezal, cojín; reforzar, moral: levantar) cyber-security. Swot (empollón) up (empollar) for an examen =/= data will be scooped (up) (recogidos) by NASA. Buccaneer (bucanero: corsarios del VI y VII, emprendedor + enterprising). Manliness (virilidad). Muck (estiércol: suciedad,V; echar a perder). Glares (deslumbra, mira ferozmente; miradas) of disapproval directed at loose (sueltas...,V) women. Multi-storey (piso) building. Ease (alivia, facilita) the political crisis, the ease (facilidad, comodidad) of doing business =/= assuage (calmar, aliviar, suavizar) American grievances. Warring (en guerra, enfrentados) politicians. Undercut (vender más barato, debilitar) its manufactures. Raucous (chillones, estridentes), if peaceable (pacíficas) protests... Harebrained (descabellado, disparatado). Foreign Office, Home (interior) Office. We draw on (nos inspiramos de)... Show off (presumir, hacer resaltar, destacar). Churlish (maleducado, grosero → -- not to thank him. Blood<u>shed (derrame,V, despojar de, recortar, cabaña)</u>. Flout (ignorar, incumplir) government policies. She whisked (batió, sacudió, agitó) away (sacó rápidamente) the plates/the cloth off the table. He panders (consiente) sb's desire for sth. The contentious (conflictivos) are shunned (rechazados). They are ming<u>l</u>ing (se mezclan) with the crowd =/= mingy (tacaño, mísero, agarrado). Highwayman (asaltante de caminos). Go out for a good time (ir de juerga). Pilar (poste, pillar. Izar la bandera: raise, hoist, run up. U-turn (cambio de sentido en UV). Contender (competidor). Gas - guzzling (consumir mucha gasolina). At his behest (a su petición). Disparaging (despectivo). Uncool (anticuado; nervioso, excitable). Discern: distinguir, percibir → --ing (exigentes, con criterio, educados) experts. Help keep afloat (a flote)... He resent (le molesta) being duped (engañado). Ticketing (emisión de billetes). Schmoozing (estar de cháchara, hablar mucho). It's just a knack (truco) → get the -- (don) of doing sth. Draw: lotería, empate, (dientes, bala, petróleo) extraer, (atención, clientes) atraer, dibujar, (conclusión) sacar. Get carried away (entusiasmarse). Shibboleth: dogma, rasgo característico. Pet: mascota, preferido → he is the teacher's --. He is briefed (informado) on people he is about to meet. Brown-nosing (lameculo). Guidebook (guía turística). As markets slide (deslizan, bajan; bajón + diapo). Lore (saber popular) → in local -- (según la tradición local), French peasant -- (las tradiciones rurales francesas. Funnel: chimenea, embudo; (tráfico...) canalizar, (ayuda, finanzas) encauzar. Savvy (conocimiento, inteligencia, espabilado, sentido común) to surf (=, oleaje, explorar, navegar) → surf the Net (navegar por Internet). Rout: derrota aplastante, huída, desbandada,V; buscar. Tussling (luchando, discutiendo, peleándose). Argentina severed (cortó) its decade-long link with the $ in 2002. Groves: arboleda, -- of poplars (chopos, álamos): alameda. The academe (mundo académico), academy (academia). Child-rearing (cría). Brainteaser: rompecabezas. A bird's flapping (aleteo). Unduly (excesivamente) worried. Airborne: en el aire, volando → become -- (elevarse en los aires + aerotransported). Onto: sobre, en, arriba de, be onto sth (encontrar algo, seguir una pista). Lift (propulsión, ánimo) → give sb a -- (levantar el ánimo a alguien). Undergrads (estudiantes no licenciados). Hackles: pelo erizado del lomo del perro → have one's -- up (estar furioso), his -- rose (se enfureció). Hunted down (cazado). The finding: resultado, (Jur) fallo. He sparked (despertó) a furious debate. Un<u>daunt (intimidar)</u>ed: impávido, no se inmuta. Administered partway (parcialmente, a mitad) through... The avoidance (el evitar) fatty foods. Overstep (sobrepasar, rebosar). Peers (compañeros), -- (mirar fijamente) at the photo, -- out (sacar la cabeza), he has not -- (igual), RU: Lord, -- to -- lending: in which institutions extend credit to people/business directly. Bitcoin: electronic cash; it also exists as entries in a giant electronic ledger (libro mayor: the blockchain); blockchain: programa para buscar datos, asegura que un mismo bitcoin nunca sea gastado dos veces. Hazard (peligro) → -- warning lights (luces de emergencia), a fire --, a health --, -- of stagnation → --ous: peligroso, arriesgado → -- wastes (residuos). Shale (esquisto) - oil. The state's role in the economy is less heavy-handed (torpe, inepto). France has grown painfully (dolorosamente, terriblemente) accustomed to seeing its countrymen taken hostages (rehenes) abroad. Painstakingly (laboriosamente). They were freed & arrived safely (sin problemas) at home. In broad daylight (en pleno día). The execution took place in cold blood (a sangre fría). Pickup truck (camión), delivery (de reparto) van (furgoneta), the pickup truck broke down (averió) before being dumped (tirada, abandonada). Target → he missed the -- (blanco), (objeto): prime (perfecto) -- for blackmail (chantaje), production --s (meta) for 2017, the enterprise is targeting (dirigida) to children. The upshot (resultado final) is a sense (sensación) of less security, the -- was that he resigned. In your senses (sano juicio) ↔ out of your --. The Nazis derided (ridiculizaron) most avant-garde arts as degenerate. Dereliction on duty (negligencia en el deber). As the cops (policías) entered the trove (tesoro + treasure) their jaws dropped (quedaron boquiabiertas). Buried treasure. Experts carted off (se llevaron) the artworks & hired an art historian to evaluate the find (hallazgo). The proceedings (acta, proceso) were kept secret. Sold & resold under duress (bajo coacción). He remains at large (en libertad). Charge him with crime. The state had turned on (vuelto en contra de) its own citizens. Outlawing sexual intercourse (coito) between jews & non-jews. The head of Turkey's national spy agency ousted (ha expulsado) twelve Iranians working for Israel to his colleagues in Iran. Part of a purported (supuesto) Zionist conspiracy. The prime minister's dovish (blanda/o) pronouncement (declaración, dictamen). Turkey's western friends are as alarmed as Shia leaders in Iran & Iraq about its coddling (mimo, consentimiento) of jihadists fighting Syria's president. Erdogan's sycophantic (serviles, adulatorios) advisers. Erdogan will go ahead (seguir adelante) with chinese deal. Turkey picked (eligió) the chinese missile because it was vastly cheaper. The alliance remains of utmost (de mayor) importance for us. The desirable America stood for (significaba) blue jeans, chewing gum, but also democracy & welfare. Germans were America's most eager (ávidos/ansiosos) pupils =/= America's military aegis (tutela, patrocinio, auspicios, =). America practices incarceration at home & unlawful (ilegales) practices (prácticas) in Guantánamo. Its demeanour (actitud, conducta) towards allies is arrogant. When he eavesdrops (escucha a escondidas) from them he becomes exasperated. Merkel embodies (encarna) the clash (choque, estruendo; contraste, =) of these sentiments. He yearned (suspiraba, anhelaba) for American freedom. Merkel feels betrayed as many ordinary Germans do. Her rage (cólera) is largely impotent. They will continue to love-hate (amor y odio; amar y odiar) them as they always had. The outer (externo) London boroughs (municipios). The poshest (más lujosas) streets in Mayfair. Almost 73% of new central London flats are sold abroad. Gentrify (aburguesamiento) places that were once poor. Without further ado (sin más ni más). Plenty of spare (no utilizado) land & little oposición to interlopers (intrusos). Private consumption may stutter (tartamudear) & remain meagre → stutterer (tartamudo). Britain's firms can cope with (arreglárselas) paying workers up to Pounds X. Unemployment is down because hiring is up, not because firing is down. Forcing wages higher & making controls more rigid put the society at risk. Britain needs stronger competition enforcement (aplicación) in cosy (acogedores, de lo más conveniente) markets. It needs R & D (Research & development) & better education to lift productivity. The disclosure (revelación) of its dock-yards (astilleros). They lugged (arrastraban) the boulders (cantos rodados)/the cases (maletas). Match: cerilla, partido, enfrentar (dos equipos); hacer juego con, estar a la altura de, igualar; casamiento, emparejar, ajustarse a una descripción. A satisfying clunk (sonido sordo metálico, golpeteo,V). Britain's highest award for gallantry (=, valentía). Ambush (emboscada). Wrath: cólera, ira + anger, rage =/= wreath (corona, guirnalda) =/= wreath*e* (adornar, ceñir, coronar, engalanar). Ambassadors will lay wreaths (coronas) of paper poppies (amapolas) at the Cenotaph (=: monumento sepulcral vacío en memoria de alguien). Remembrance (memoria, recuerdo) day + in -- of sth. Refrain (estribillo) =/= as the saying (refrán) goes. Bluntly (llanamente, sin rodeos). Trenches (trincheras). In the outpouring (desahogo) of a tormented soul. Fulsome (exagerado) praise (elogio). I've been here albeit briefly. The lopsided (torcido, desequilibrado) result: 73% to 24%. Democrats outnumber republicans six to one in NY. He exudes (=, irradia) empathy for those who struggle to pay the rent. The contrast to middle class's pain is telling (revelador). He seems aloof (distante). Manner*s*: modales, educación =/= manner: manera, actitud, estilo → Blasio has a warm manner; decoration in the French --. Payback (restitución + return). Her neighbourhood, once gritty (arenoso, enérgico) has seen an influx of hipsters (aficionados al jazz, con pantalones de tiro corto) & soaring rents. He vowed (prometió solemnemente) to tax the rich to pay for universal pre-school. Curving taxes up by half a percentage point may not, in itself, cause them to flee to Florida. At least sixteen terrorist attacks have been foiled (frustrados). Crime has fallen twice as far in NY as in the rest of America. The NY police department crunches (cruje, chirria, números: devora) data & send officers where needed. Young men in the roughest (más ásperas, violentas) áreas are stopped & frisked (cacheados) to deter (desalentar, disuadir) them from carrying guns. High-crime areas are largely black & Hispanic. A fifth of students dropped out (se retiraron, dejaron los estudios) of high school before graduating. Not one city public school was in NY state's leading twenty five. Today twenty two to twenty five. A system that allowed some charter schools (independientes pero con fondos públicos) to operate. He made principals (=, escuela: directores) accountable (responsables) for test scores (puntuaciones) & tried to make it easier to sack bad teachers. Buscar las cosquillas a alguien: rile (irritar)/annoy sb. Almost 20% of NY's people were proficient (competentes) or better in Maths. Caer: get into a bad habit (vicio), fall badly (mal). Agencies tracked (seguían las pistas) of complaints (denuncias...) & linked them to tax irregularities. To pinpoint (precisar, identificar) illegal building conversions (=, remodelaciones) which are fire hazards (peligro de fuego), quickly & fairly accurately (con precisión). Blasio will face challenges as soon as he takes office. He will raise salaries & backdate (dar efecto retroactivo, poner fecha anterior a) the increases. American politics can be distilled (=, reducidas a lo esencial) into this: where is the Republican party heading. Archetypal (arquetípico) backroom (trastienda, cuarto trasero, anónimo) politician. None of the twelve largest has a republican mayor. But can abide (soportar) the zealots (fanáticos). A huge polling (votación) deficit to see off (despedir, deshacerse de, derrotar) a proposal for compulsory labelling of most genetically modified foods. Take away (apartar, llevarse) the first two agreeable/pleasant perks (ventajas, beneficios). Perky (animado, alegre). Burlarse de alguien (mock/make a joke of sb).

Insularity: (=, estrechez de mente). Seal (foca, sello,V) off: (building, room) cerrar, (área, calle) acordonar. Inhabitant/resident/denizen/dweller (habitante, morador). Bump (choque)y: (superficie, camino) accidentado, (viaje, vuelo) agitado. Kite (cometa, cheque sin fondos). Steadier (más firme) hand (pulso) in conducting foreign affairs. Un<u>noticed (darse cuenta)</u>: desapercibido. Iran's nuclear deal was clinched: abrazado, (acuerdo) cerrado, (argumento, clavo) remachado. Spools (carrete de foto, bobina de cine). Skewed (desvió) medical science. The crusty (arisco, malhumorado; pan: crujiente) regime. Slough (off) (deshacerse de) their habit/tax farming. Mismatch (emparejar mal): there was a -- between the skills offered & needed. Mangrove (mangle), swamp (pantano, ciénaga, inundar) → mangrove swamp (manglar); swamped with work (agobiados de trabajo). The streets & canals will be teeming with people (atestados de gente) & craps (porquerías, estupideces, mierda...) respectively. Be dredged (dragado) through (por) pristine (inmaculado, impolite; prístino: original, antiguo) lake & rain forests (selvas tropicales) will be uprooted (arrancadas, desarraigadas). The shady (sombreados, frondosos; sospechosos; negocios: turbios) palm trees buttress (apoyan, refuerzan) K. Lumpur soutermost (más extremo) sprawl (expansión, despatarrarse + urban --: expansión urbana). Secreted/segregated by the corals. String (cuerda; ensartar, colgar) together: coordinar, hilar (ideas...). Overly (demasiado) concerned. Receding line (entradas de calvicie). Play up: dar guerra/coba, exagerar, entretener con engaños/halagos. Convincingly (convincentemente) thrown into extreme shadow (sombra, oscuridad; sospecha). Warmth (calor) of a smile (sonrisa)/of greetings (recuerdos, saludos). Greater degree of completion (terminación). Wash: limpiar, (barco) estela, (pintura) capa... Arrebato: a run of luck, a gust of wind, outburst of anger (cólera), a sudden fit of enthusiasm; ecstasy, rapture. A rachas: I sleep very fitfully, it's raining on &

off, by fits and starts. Rabia: fury, anger → it's annoying to have to leave so soon, she was in terrible pain all night. Beep: (emitir) pitidos, llamar... We are outbound (dirigidos hacia fuera) from Pluto. Unpacked (desembolsado). Whet: (instrumento) afilar, (curiosidad) estimular, (apetito) despertar → whetting of scientific appetites. Discount (=),V), descartar + reject, rule out. (Sheep)fold (redil). Eating with your fingers is a no-no (algo que no se debe hacer). Parish (parroquia), priest (párroco), curate (ayudante de párroco) =/= chaplain (capellán), chapel (capilla). The coffee berry (baya) borer (taladrador) is an annoying (molesto) beetle (escarabajo). Hands -off (de no intervención) approach (enfoque, propuesta...). Be cranked out (producido penosamente) by using a template (plantilla). Strut about/around sth (pavonearse, jactarse de algo). Playful (festivo, juguetón). Gritty (arenoso, enérgico) backcloth/ backdrop (telón de fondo). Molluscs/ks: with shell as mussels or without as slug (babosa) or squid (calamar) =/= squad (pelotón) =/skid (patinar). Sketchy (incompleto, sin detalles) bill of rights (declaración de derechos). Germany's nuclear plant is to be switch off by 2012. Combined/joint operations. Enchufar: (Electr.) plug in, (objetos) fit in/together, (en trabajo) set/lined her up for secretary..., get a cushy job, wangle o.s. a job (arreglárselas para un chanchullo). Arriesgar: (una oportunidad) endanger, (dinero) stake, (multa) risk a fine, (una empresa) venture upon an enterprise. Charcoal (carbón vegetal). Hauled up in court (llevado ante los tribunales). Be released (libres, liberados). Upshot (resultado final). Backsliding: (reincidencia + recidivism), (recaída,V) relapse. Bludgeon: cachiporra, aporrear; forzar, coaccionar. Timing (fijar el tiempo). 4G will be both wireless & wireline. Buffer: parachoque, amortiguador; proteger. It has equivalent capabilities. Unforeseen/unexpected (imprevisto). Reliance on (dependencia de) → I'm relying/depending on you, he depends on his parents financially. A rival paper (periódico) brought out a spoiler: un periódico rival publicó una exclusiva para disminuir<u>le</u> las ventas. Overstretched (estirado al máximo). Canvases (lienzos), lithographs & prints (grabados) → under the -- (en tienda de campaña) =/= canvas: (Pol.) hacer campaña, sondear, (órdenes) solicitar, (idea) proponer. Corral: (farm)yard, poultry yard, (de vacas) slum. Spanish firms have been bruised (magulladas, contusionadas,V). I could climb (the) trees/<u>on</u> the trees. Hoarse/husky (ronco), I'm voiceless (afónico), my throat/vocal cords hurt(s) me. Unpleasant experiences. One of them wants her to die. It's regrettable that... Please, tell people you have few friends in common with. Nothing but the truth. Crime story collection. A tagged (etiquetada) web. The partner (compañero, pareja, socio). A kiss before dying. Great expectations/the result has exceeded our expectations/life expectancy. I'm not completely helpless. Your enquiry (averiguación), complaint or suggestion have been received properly. Date of receipt + recibo. This message has been generated automatically. Start/begin the countdown (la vuelta atrás) → in the -- of (los días que precedieron) the Olympic Games. Request (solicitud/petición,Vs). Fellowship (compañerismo) for lifelong training & career development. We're not getting much feedback (reacción, retroalimentación). The helicopter vibrates as it hovers (planea). The officers scan (examinan, escanean) the crowded city for any signs of danger. Two satellites flying in precise relative locations (ubicaciones relativas) to one another. They all rallied around (se reunieron) when their mother was ill. Purchase of moisturisers (hidratantes) relies on (dependen de) online. Clouds of black smoke mott<u>l</u>ed (motearon) the snow covered ground. Pemex tussled (luchó) with Repsol, in which he has a stake (participación). Despite these hiccups (hipos, dificultades, tropiezos) South America has acted as a shock absorber during the Spanish slump. The clashes (conflictos, estruendos, enfrentamientos) show vividly (vivamente) the refusal to heed (tener en cuenta) such laws. He cold-shouldered at (volvió la espalda a). Russia foiled (pers.: desbarató; intento: frustró) Ukranian's European plans & bought out (compró, sobornó) Mr... Flare-up: (violencia) brote, (enfermedad) recrudecer; altercado, llamarada → hardly a day goes by (pasa) without a flare-up in the war of attrition (desgaste) fought out (resuelta, competida) by China and Japan. The economy is held back (contenida) by heavy private debts. Shedding (despojarse, liberarse de) their debts, keeping money out of the economy. Turkey is turning away (se separa) from... If both energy sources die down (decrecen).... Britain is going all-out (con máxima fuerza) for shale gas + all-out (general) strike. Britain isle (isla) of Wight is an idyllic spot off (lugar algo apartado de) southern coast. The Isle's six state secondary schools are stuck in the unhappy middle: just 23 % of people entitled (con derecho) to free school meals for poverty. The island (isla, refugio en calle) endured (soportó) a muddled (confusa, hecha un lío) transition from three-tier (3 grupos) school system to a two-tier. Receive dollops (dosis) of government cash... Egypt: a turnout of 38% & a walloping (paliza, colosal...) 98% yes vote. Even as it snuffed (out) (apagó, extinguió) dissent (disidencia). Punters (apostadores, clientes, público) in the stock exchange. Keep: -- (away) mantenerse a distancia, (off) no acercarse), (back) retener, (in) no dejar salir, (out) echar a patadas, (to) limitarse a, (up) continuar. Kick (coz) → the police kicked the door open (abrió la puerta de un golpe). Move: (cambio de sentido, de trabajo) -- around, (avanzar) -- along, (retroceder) -- back, (instalarse) -- in, (seguir adelante) -- on. Llave: under clock (bajo llave), lock a door, ignition key, skeleton (1)/master key (maestra); llave de paso: (agua) stopcock, (gas) mains tap =/= in the main (en general, = + in the whole) =/= skeleton (2): =, armadura, estructura, armazón) → they don't want the skeletons in the cupboard to come out: no quieren que salgan a la calle los trapos sucios ←→ at the dinner party (cena) they washed their linen in public (sacaron a relucir los platos sucios) + they were raking up (sacando a relucir) his past + wrap up the past (remover el pasado). QE (Quantitative earnings): creating money to buy financial assets including sovereign bonds. Deduce/deduct/infer. Infringement (violación). Inhabit = habitar = live in = occupy. Prevent/impide/inhibit. Indicios: signs, indicators, (Jur.) circumstantial evidence. Role reversal (inversión) in the family. Inquest: investigación Jur. Insight (idea, novedad, nueva percepción sobre algo): a book full of remarkable (excelentes) --s, a person of -- (perspicacia). Plazo: period, (cuenta/depósito a -- fijo) fixed term account/deposit, (de pago) installment → pay in installments (a plazos). Asegurar: (sujetar) secure, (una zona) make secure, (derecho) guarantee, (casa, coche) insure. Intake: consumo, entrada, (Mec.) toma. Intimacy → be intimated with sth. (estar familiarizado con algo). Laboured: (respiro) pesado, (estilo) fatigoso, (texto) farragoso. Ladylike (elegante, fino, propio de una dama). Fetch (llamen) the owner (propietario + landlord, landlady, madame of a brothel). Lanky (larguirucho). Lash out (arremeter contra, tirar la casa por la ventana). Lasting (duradero), lastly (finalmente). Sweat (sudar) → be in a -- (estar sudando), be in a -- about sth (estar preocupado por algo). His shirt was soaked in sweat. Slog (sudar tinta, afanarse) your guts out/slog it out (luchar hasta el fin). Lay (poner, instalar) → -- aside: ahorrar, dejar de lado, -- down: liberarse de, deponer, -- (off): despedir, -- on: proporcionar, -- out: diseñar, disponer; exponer. We assumed he would have told it to you. Be soft in the head (estar tocado). Tocar: touch, can I feel the fabric (tela)? (campana...) ring, (bocina, sirena) sound, (hora) strike. Run (u, a, u) → Morsi ran/rode roughshod over (pisoteó) political opponents. Egypt's weary (cansado) public is fearful (temeroso, tremendo, horrible). Nag: fastidiar, dar la lata, gruñón → nagging (gruñones, persistentes) troubles. Egypt's press has largely degenerated into a cheerleading (animado) booster (estímulo, repetidor de TV, elevador de tensión...) of the regime. Prosecutorial (procesantes) summons (Jur.: citaciones) & harsh court sentences. Liberally: generosamente, con tolerancia. Prosecutors slapped (dieron manotadas/palmadas, dieron de lleno, arrojaron sobre la mesa, añadieron...) travel (viaje) bans on a score (veintena) of people. Drag on (hacerse largo/pesado), drag in (sacar a relucir), drag away (llevarse a la fuerza) → an American activist has languished (=, se ha languidecido, se ha podrido) in jail since being dragged away. He ran slap into a tree (dió de lleno contra un árbol). The civil war in Syria is scaring away/off (ahuyenta) big oil companies. The pipeline might have to pass through officially recognised Greek Cyprus & the Turkish-ruled north of the island. An alternative route, under Syrian & Lebanon waters, would be trickier (más difícil) still. The magic of truffles (trufas) is their scent (perfume, fragancia): a savoury, drowsy (somnoliento) smell. Disclosures (revelaciones) that the CIA (Central Intelligence agency) had tried to assassinate them. Diet pill (píldora para adelgazar) & posh (elegante, pijo) shoes in Virginia. The meeting (encuentro) of the UMTS (Universal Mobile Telecommunications) in Barcelona. The UWB (Ultra-wideband) irrefutable (incontestable) solution. Broadband wireless: possibility to combine *ad hoc* (para el caso) networks neighbours campuses with public cellular networks. ITU (International telecommunications union) dictionary look up (consulta)... Biochemical sensors: utilising molecular or atomic structure can selfasemble, replicate & repair themselves. P2P (peer 2 peer): a type of network where each workstation has equivalent capabilities & responsibilities. Aerosols offset (compensan) part of the overall warming trend (tendencia). Backsliding (reincidencia + relapse, recidivism). Monger (pers. dedicada a) → rumour-monger (gente dedicada a difundir rumores), fishmonger, a man reviled (insultado, vituperado) for being warmonger (belicista), etc. In such a rush/hurry (precipitadamente) =/= Musharraf rashly (temerariamente) returned from self-imposed exile. Row: fila, paseo, remar; ruido, regañina, pelea,Vs. This trove (treasury) of data is fiddly (difícil, complicado) to download (Comp.: descargar, bajar) =/= offload: desembarcar, descargar, (pers.) hacer bajar + -- sth onto sb (endilgarle algo a alguien). Thatcher used privatization to curb the power of the unions & Eastern countries did the same to dismantle commanded economies. Public indebtedness at its highest peacetime lived in advanced economies. During the electric storm unplug both. Slide (deslizar, correr) the voltage selection switch (interruptor) to the correct voltage position. A power-saving mode (modo, Comp.: función, modalidad) called standby. Waking up (despertando) your computer ↔ turning it off + unplugging it. Press & hold the power button five seconds, then release it. As a part of the regular start up (puesta en marcha) process, a programme to check the disk status (categoría, situación) runs automatically. Use left & right on the mouse to select objects on the display (expo, aquí: pantalla). Shut down your computer → the power turns off but some electric current still flows. Use a damp (húmedo) grease free (sin grasa) cloth. Not use abrasive, economic solvent (disolvente) cleaners. Remove dust & grease trapped under the keys (=, tecla). Turn your keyboard upside down (patas arriba). If the mouse pointer (indicador, puntero) begins moving erratically or becomes difficult to control precisely, cleaning the mouse will likely improve its accuracy (precisión). Its reputation was burnished (mejorada; metal: dado lustre). A loosening of fiscal targets elicited (suscita, provoca) a predictable response. The effort is unsuccessful/ fruitless =/= inepto (useless, hopeless). Genetic defect (defecto, desertar + desert). Blight: arruinar, infester, asolar, (Bot.) plaga → (urban --) los pbs. de las zonas urbanas. Designer (diseñador). It also heralds (es heraldo/precursor, anuncia) the distant prospect (posibilidad, perspectiva, panorama). Awashed (inundados) with applicants =/= abashed (avergonzado(s). Discernible (apreciable) progress. Biology has a tenuous (=, endeble) grip (dominio) on the origins of complex traits (rasgos) in humanity. Grapple: (asir/agarrar) with: luchar cuerpo a cuerpo, confrontar un pb. He stands out (destaca). Throwback (vuelta atrás) to the styles of the twenties. Ask the hotel staff for an early wake-up call (te despierten pronto). Comb (peine,V), registrar a fondo) the countryside looking for celebrities. Clear up: (dificultad...) aclarar, (crimen, misterio...) resolver, (habitación...) ordenar, (duda...) disipar... =/= -- out (vaciar, quitar, hacer salir) rebels. The Koran sanctions (=, autoriza) the marriage of up to four wives. Comilón: glutton, greedy → be -- of sth (tener ansias de algo). This political party clears (salva) the 5% hurdle (valla) to get into Parliament. Literate (sabe leer y escribir). Embedded (encrustados, empotrados) computers. Appliances (aparatos, aplicaciones). Knock-on effect/impact (repercusiones, =) of banks funding (que financian) costs. Come (a)round (venir/llegar, volver en sí), -- -- (aceptar) the point of view, -- -- & see us (ven a visitarnos), don't scold, he will come round (se le pasará). Exon compete (rivaliza, compite) with Apple. The source of friction is the artificial underwater reefs (arrecifes) made of concrete blocks with metal spikes (púas). Work long hours for a pittance & with no time off. IWO (International Work Organization) reckons (considera) more than o. 5 millions S. Arabia runaways (fugitivos) find it hard to leave the country. Kickback (soborno, mordida). The army conscripts (reclutas). Sunstroke (insolación). A confinement (reclusión, prisión) to perform harsh regime of push-ups (flexiones) & jumping (saltos) in a sweltering (stifling, suffocating) heat. Splash (chapotear, salpicar, manchar) → splashed all over the front page (salió en los grandes titulares) + make a -- (causar sensación). Kindle (suscitar) interest/hopes in sth. Vengarse: avenge, take revenge. Farmer (agricultor, granjero), till (cultivar, labrar, cajón)er: timón + ridder; en el mando: helm. Rude

Word (taco). Anointed (ungido) with oil. Cain was furious & angry/cross (cruz, enojado,Vs). Make an atonement (expiación) for... Creditworthiness/solvency (solvencia económica). Edge over sth (ventaja sobre algo) =/= be on edge (con los nervios de punta). Badly (gravemente) damaged. Jumble (mezclar; revoltijo, confusión → the clothes were all --ed in the drawer; -- sale (artículos de segunda mano) =/= grumble (refunfuñar, queja) =/= bungle (chapuza, echar a perder, meter la pata). Bog (ciénaga) → get bogged down (estancarse, quedar empantanado). A cluster (grupo) of start-ups. Striking (llamativo, sorprendente) =/= stricken: afligido, dañado, enfermo → -- with guilt (culpabilidad). The beefiest (más fornido) party survive its founder demise (fallecimiento, desaparición). Back down (retractarse + retract, recant). I withdraw the accusation. En voz alta (aloud), think (soñar) aloud ←→ in a low voice. Wrench (tirón, torcedura; arrancar, llave inglesa) off/from/out of: arrancar de un golpe, -- a door open (abrir una puerta de un tirón). Foist sth on/onto sb (endosar/endilgar algo a alguien) =/= endorse: (cheque) endosar, (Pol.) refrendar, (plan, decisión) aprobar, (producto) promocionar. The voters find an annoyance (fastidio, molestia), get annoyed. Crank: manivela, V; cascarrabias, excéntrico). Blaze: resplandor, llamarada,V; fuego, derroche → in a -- (arranque) of anger (cólera). Entice (tentar, atraer, seducir) wealth funds to bankroll (recursos económicos, financiar...) + entice sb with an offer. Unfulfilled (no cumplida) pledge (promesa). Lifesaver/lifeguard (socorrista). A commuter (de cercanías) train slammed (entró de golpe en) a wall. Abe's popularity is uncannily (astutamente) (asombrosamente, increíblemente)... Booze (bebida alcohólica)er + boozy (aficionado a ella). Trace (huella, rastro,V, dar con algo) → tracing messy (desordenado, complicado) people is a grim (severa, macabra) task. Berlin is a stand out (sobresaliente) among the start ups. Standoff (mantenerse a distancia, apartarse) =/= stand-off (punto muerto, callejón sin salida) =/=

stand sb up (dar un plantón a alguien). Hype: exageración, bombo publicitario → a "media" --; -- their productos. The country oversized (descomunal, con más de lo normal) trade surplus. Stamp out (erradicar, apagar, aplastar) corruption. Spotlight (atención, poner de relieve, teatro: foco) → be in the -- (centro de atención). Funds that pay out (se gastan) when catastrophe strikes. Mettle (valor) → a man of --. Profiteering (especulación + =). Tease: bromista, tomar el pelo, fastidiar → -- out: desenredar, (información) sonsacar. Merciful (clementes, compasivos) doctors. Clutter (atestar, abarrotar). Obamacare from its inception (inicio) to implementation (ejecución)... Uplifting (inspiradora, edificante) story. Partisanship (partidismo). Prong (diente, punta); three-pronged (de tres puntas + attack: por tres flancos). He did such (tal) thing. Inútil: (esfuerzo) fruitless, (inepto) useless → there is no point in keeping on trying (seguir intentándolo) = it is of no avail (es inútil)... + to no -- (en vano), -- o.s. of (aprovecharse/valerse de). The policy wonks (tambaleos) favoured... + wonky: cojo, tambaleante; torcido, estropeado. An espoused (adoptado, defendido, apoyado) plan. Botched (chapucero), a --ed job (una chapuza), a --ed blood sample. Ascribe (atribuir) sth to sb/sth Wintry: (glacial, invernal). Delusion (engaño, falsa ilusión, delirio) → a -- reception (recibimiento). Handy (a mano, hábil, práctico). Bless (s, st, st): (bendecir). Bleakly (en tono sombrío, con desaliento) comical. Brittle (precario, quebradizo) deal. His overarching (general, global) aim. Tantrum: berrinche → fly into a -- (coger un --) = have a fit. Lopped (off): podado. Wilfully (terca, deliberadamente, obstinada + =). Throttle (regulador, acelerador; ahogar, silenciar, estrangular) tax rises →full -- (acelerar al máximo), -- down/back the engine (moderar la marcha). Stranglehold (dominar completamente) → she has an -- on him. His coterie (círculo, grupo, peña)'s greed (codicia)..., a cultural --. Cast-iron: de hierro fundido, sólido, férreo → a -- - -- constitution (una salud de hierro).

Sullying (que mancha la reputación) =/= sulky (malhumorado). Mishmash (revoltijo + mess, jumble). Wishy-washy: sin gracia, insípido, endeble, sin personalidad. They must be buttressed (sostenidos, apoyados). Putin squeals (chillidos,V). Contempt (desdén, desprecio). Notch (corte, muesca, desfiladero + defile, gorge) up: apuntarse (puntos, victoria) its own record. Disrepute (desprestigio, descrédito + =) =/= disparagement (menosprecio + content). Alumni (graduados, ex-alumnos). Xi is <u>bringing (sobreponiéndose a)</u> a corrupt army <u>to heel</u>. So secretive (reservada, callada) is China's army that... A basement (sótano) stacked (amontonado) with cash (dinero en efectivo). Shirkers (gandules) strive after/for sth: se esfuerzan para conseguir algo. America is bent (empeñada) on China's destruction. Their relations built on (agregan) stronger foundations (bases, fundamentos). Carrier (transportador, (enfermo) portador, portaaviones. Clash (conflicto, enfrentamiento; choque, estruendo) of ideas. At its apex (cúspide; Geogr.: summit, peak). A slapdash (chapucera) campaign. They hail (aclaman; granizo,V) he as leader. Spirits (duendes + a magical/enchanted village). Garrison (Mil.): guarnecer, guarnición =/= (en alimentos) garnish. Feed (alimentar, suministrar). Devious (tortuoso + (camino) winding. They benighted (ignoraron) Government policies. Seesaw (oscilante; vacilante, vaivén). A set-up (montaje, sistema, organización). Pimping/procuring (proxenetismo) =/= soliciting (abordar los clientes). Perp (perpetrator): autor, responsable. Being torn (desgarrado). Pooh Pooh (despreciar, menospreciar). A secular creed (credo). Scratchy (picante, que rasca, irregular).The back seat driver (pasajero que aconseja al conductor). The fighting <u>flare</u> (llamarada, destello, bengala) up: (fuego) llamear, (protesta) estallar; (pers.) explotar + lose the temper) =/= he helped <u>fire</u> up (a enardecer) campaigns. Bust: romper, degradar, destrozar; hacer una redada → sanctions/ inflation busting =/= bl<u>u</u>ster (fanfarronada, rugir, bravuconear)y: tempestuoso, blustering (fanfarrón) =/= blister (ampolla, burbuja,V)ing (achicharrante, abrasador, virulento) attack =/= bustle: ajetreo, bullicio, ir y venir → Madrid --ing (animado) Chueca district. Feisty/live up (animado + lively, cheerful, in good spirits). Lurid (escabroso, morboso; color: chillón) details. Purloin (hurtar, sustraer) a phrase to fathom (sondear, descifrar, llegar a entender)... Tin (estaño, bote, lata,V). Excoriate (vilipendiar, despreciar). An elongated (alargado) rant (vocerío, despotricar, V, diatriba/injuria) on behalf of (de parte de, a favor de) the disillusioned. Spend oodles (cantidad, montones) of... The job was foisted (endosado, endilgado) on me. Disjointed (inconexo, desilvanado) speech, writing. Wooliness (lanosidad, imprecisión). The tories should be streets ahead (adelantarse por mucho). Flicker: parpadeo, vacilar, vibrar, (llama) destello; (de diversión) expresión; flickering (vacilante, parpadeante). Gag (mordaza) → the Gulf statelets gagged (prisioneros: amordazaron)... Airing (espacioso, aireado). Hart-hit (muy afectado) → -- - --ing (contundente). Wannabe (imitador; amateur, aspirante) journalist. (Be)wildering: desconcertante + disconcerting. Gourmet (gastrónomo) → -- cooking (gastronomía). Craggy: (roca) escarpada, (rasgos) curtidos, arrugados. Blended (mezclado) into a light dough (pasta, masa) that is fried (frita). Unabridged (resumido): íntegro. Hoax (engaño, V) call: llamar a los servicios de emergencia por falsa alarma. Stalwart (robusto, fuerte; leal, fiel). Tied-up (atado) & flogged (azotado). A run-down (gastado, ruinoso, agitado) district. Disposable (desechable). Fritter (buñuelo) away: malgastar, desperdiciar. Steelworks (siderurgía). Commandeer (apropiarse, expropiar). Wads (tacos, tapones; -- (billetes: fajo) of money: un dineral. A revolution at bay (bahía, muelle de carga, aullido): acorralada, mantenida a raya. Excel (superar) at (destacar en), -- as (destacar como). Surfaced (emergió, salió a la luz/a relucir). Shore/prop up (apuntalar, reforzar) his support. He sidelined (marginó) several powerful ministers. Rulings: dirigentes, dominantes, (precios) vigentes, (Jur.) fallos. Newsprint (papel de prensa). Stubble (barba incipiente, rastrojo). Winning over/round (convencer) many disillusioned. Without ressort (recurrir) to the force/violence + as a last -- + you -- (acudes) to me for help + holiday (turismo) -- (lugar). Constrain (obligar, constreñir)t: coacción, limitación, represión → budget -- =/= restrain: contener, dominar → -- o.s. (contenerse) --t: restricción, control, moderación, reserva. Temper (suavizar, atenuar, templar) the system =/= tamper/interfere with: (máquina) manipular, (papeles, pruebas) falsificar, (testigos/jurado) sobornar, (coche...) manosear, manejar... =/= he has trampled (pisoteado, atropellado) all over. The electoral system he bequeathed (legó). The winning (ganador) candidat → the runner-up (subcampeón). They were given more weight than they warranted (merecían, autorizaron, garantizaron). Offender (delincuente, infractor) + previous -- (reincidente). Back off/away (ir marcha atrás, retroceder) = backtracking, back-pedalling, go into reverse =/= at full/top speed: a toda marcha. Bloom (flor, florecer, prosperar) → in the -- of youth. Bouquets (ramos) to sell briskly (enérgicamente, con brío). He blew (desperdició) his opportunity & flopped (fracasó). Line-up (alinear) too many candidates. Embroiled (enredado) =/= embroidered (bordado) with his name. Known as high-handed (despótico, arbitrario) & aloof (distante). Golden pinstripes (traje de rayas diplomáticas doradas). The wild-eyed (mirada) radicals. Graze: raspar, pastar, rozar → --ing (pastoreo). Overturning (derrocando, derribando) it. Graveyard (cementerio) shift: turno de noche = night shift. Back paw (garra, pata). Down: abajo, write -- (apunta), the tyres are -- (desinfladas), it's -- (le toca) to him, the computer is -- (no funciona), derribar/abatir. Sauté (salteado) feline in one eatery (restaurante). Pup/puppy (cachorro) → a terrified –'s eyes stare out (miraba fijamente) from a metal cage. A victim yells (chillido,V) as a butcher raises his knife.

Get through: the staff got -- (se abrió paso), (libro) acabar, (dinero) gastar, (examen) aprobar, conseguir. Legal travails (esfuerzos penosos legales). Rank (rango) & file = soldado raso, tropa + the -- - -- (de las bases del) party/union. Flexes his muscle (alardea de poder, hace ejercicio muscular de calentamiento). Commissioned (encargado), (Mil): --ed (nombrado) officer. Hidebound (rígido, retrógrado) by tradition (conservador por tradition). Scuttle: (planes) echar por tierra → -- away/off (escabullirse). Cutting down (suprimir) middlemen (intermediarios). The staging (escenificación). Well-timed/timely (oportuno). Sidestep (eludir) them. Court (tribunal; patio, pista de tenis; pretender)→ -- favour with sb (intentar congraciarse con alguien). Soar: (aves) levantar el vuelo, (esperanza) aumentar, (precios) dispararse, (popularidad) aumentar. Chart: mapa, tabla de materias, gráfico, carta,Vs, (Mus.) lista de éxitos. Get onto = get on to: (moto, caballo) montar, (tren) subirse, we -- -- to the motorway at the junction (acceso) 15; ocuparse de, meterse en contacto con =/= ... to getting on with (para empezar). Tom succeed, authors must be more businesslike (serios, formales, eficientes) than ever. Books that fly off (salen volando) from the shelves. Drum up: despertar, (comercio) fomentar. Compile (recopilar + collect together). Tracking (seguir el rastro de) sales. Salesmanship: arte de vender. Splurge (derroche,V). Add-up: sumar, cuadrar, tener sentido. Zumbido: (insecto, oídos) buzz (ing), (máquina) hum, whir. Wayward (caprichoso, rebelde, incontrolable). Stopped dead (se paró en seco). Scared off (espantados, ahuyentados) investors. Dealership (concesión, representación). Preemptive (preventiva) defence. Hassle (fastidiar, causar problemas) → No --! It's not worth the -- (no vale la pena). The nimble (ágil, hábil) firm. Lumber: maderos, trastos viejos; cortar árboles, moverse pesadamente → speed (apresurar) the lumbering (torpe, pesado)... The surface is pitted (picada) & ridge_d_ (estriada) =/= the ice thaws (deshiela) forming ponds (charcos) between ridges (caballones, cadenas de montañas). Primary (primarios, fundamentales, principales) products. Moult: mudar piel/pelo/plumas. Breeding (cría) ground (lugar). Awakening (despertar) → the raise in primary products which sustains biological awakening may suddenly be capped. Delve (escarbar) into (ahondar/buscar en). Wed (casarse)ding (boda) → be born out of wedlock (matrimonio). Riña (quarrel, argument) =/= lucha (fight, crawl (pelea), wrestling (lucha libre); contest (lucha, contienda). Rough: (superficie, piel) áspera, rugosa, (terreno) accidentado, (voz, sonido) ronco, (conducta) brusca, (pers.) ruda; roughness (agitación/embravecimiento del mar, aspereza de una superficie) + tumble (caída, tropiezo,Vs) → become rough & tumble (vaivenes) of life, -- & -- (avatares) of politics + the ups & downs (altibajos) or the vicissitudes (=, avatares) of politics. Desmentir: (acusación, teoría) deny, refute. Entrants (participantes, =), competidores, =). The bespoke (hechos a medida) screens. Award-winning (premiado) film. He was full of praise for her, he spoke in -- of her staff, songs of -- (de alabanza). He pushed back the chair & stood up + stand up for (respaldar, defender) sb → stand up to (hacer frente a) sb =/= stand in for sb (substituir a alguien) =/= Mandela's achievements to stand out (sobresalir)... You can tell it a mile away (eso se ve a la legua). She was nothing but the clothes she was wearing up (llevaba). Feel a bit low (estar bajo de moral) → raise sb's spirit/morale, my heart sank (se me cayó por los suelos). Soulful (conmovedor + moving, touching). Lash out (atacar, golpear a diestra y siniestra) at (contra): arremeter contra. Coin/piece → he paid me in coins (monedas), pay sb back (devolver) in his own (misma) coin, paying in kind (especies); national currency. Tarnish (deslustrar, manchar la reputación) with accusations. Expelled migrants in the delusion (ilusión, engaño)... Capital offence (delito capital). Shall I have to go? (Pruebo?). Have another go (probar otra vez). Be full of go (energía), have a go at sb (atacar a alguien). Pretzels: galleta (biscuit, cookie) salada. Rebuke (reprochar + reproach). Cumbersome: voluminoso, incómodo, engorroso. Dying cities: some are doomed to fade away (apagarse, consumirse). Bench (banco): be on the bench (ser juez) + (Sp.) estar en el banquillo. Skulk: esconderse + hide → I saw him skulking in the background: lo vi al fondo, tratando de pasar desapercibido. China is saddled (cargada) with polluting. Tree-huggers (fanáticos del medio ambiente). Robbers/raiders (asaltantes). Jackals (chacales). Consoling (consolador, reconfortante) profits (beneficios). Depose (deponer/destituir + dismiss, remove). Breach: violación, infracción; brecha, abertura) → a -- of peace in the stuffy (sofocado) World. Gravitas/seriousness (seriedad). Diddle/swindle/rip off/defraud (estafar). Overreach o.s. (ir más allá de sus posibilidades). Extraterritorial forays (incursiones + (Mil.) incursions, raids). Mistrust (desconfianza)ful: desconfiado. Hailed (aclamados) as heros. Freak: (victoria, resultado) inesperados, anomalía, (pers., animal) monstruo/fenómeno → a -- of the nature; fanático → peace -- (fanático de la paz), freaky (estrafalario + odd, eccentric). Stem the tide (marea, corriente) of events: detener el curso de las cosas, go against the tide, from bow/prow/stem (proa) to stern (popa: detrás). Heartland (interior, zona central). Electoral outing (vuelta, excursión, paseo). Tatters (andrajos + rags). Dazed (aturdido + stun). It was once backwater: (agua) remanso, (lugar) atrasado. Flinty (de sílex, duro) =/= not even flinch (estremecerse + shake (a, o, a) at the sound of a rocket fire. Team up (asociarse). Fault (defecto, culpa, avería) → with all their --s. Foremost (principal, destacado, en primer lugar). Firewalls (cortafuegos). Teeter (titubear, tambalear). Fetter (trabar, encadenar) → unfettered (sin trabas). Leviathan: (=, buque enorme). Scale down: disminuir a escala, make proportionally smaller. Cast aside (desechar, descartar) austerity. Backtrack (marcha atrás) reforms =/= climb-down (retroceso) that spells (representa, augura, significa) an early end. Sulky (a los malhumorados) voters resent (les molesta) stumping (apoquinar) any more for Greece. Recoil: rollo, rizo, espiral; bobinar, enrollar (-- sth around sth), (screw: tornillo,V) enroscarse, (humo) subir en espiral. Tear (lágrima, rotura, rasgar; ropa/papel: romperse) up: carta/papel: romper; árbol/poste: arrancar; terreno: abrir. With painful (dolorosas) consequences all round (completo, en todos los aspectos). He tuned (afinó) his skills. Freeze: helada, congelar, quedar inmóvil. Creditors were at loggerheads (a matar, picados). Derrocar: (edificio) knock down, demolish, (ministro) oust, (gobierno) overthrow. Forbearance (tolerancia, paciencia, =) toward fiscal sinners. Opresión: (sensación) oppression, (de situación, lugar) oppressiveness, (opresor) oppressive. A rat (=) he had cornered (acorralado) had nowhere to go & jumped out (saltó) at him + it jumps out at you (eso salta a la vista). He has shattered (hecho añicos, quebrantado, frustrado) a fragile cease fire. Black leather-clad (vestido de) bikers (motociclistas + motorcyclist). Put the country on a war footing (pie de guerra) would spoke (fastidiar) Ukraine + put a spoke in sb's wheel (fastidiar los planes de alguien). Lose/keep his balance (equilibrio). Being greeted (recibido) with howls (aullidos/clamores/gritos) & rotten tomatoes. The friendship of Germany & Israel is fraught (tensa, difícil), a -- relationship → -- with (lleno, cargado de) danger. Give fodder (pienso, forraje) to anti Semitism. For Germany, living up to (viviendo de acuerdo con) the exhortations (súplicas, consejos, invitaciones) of the past are becoming ever trickier (más delicado, tramposo). The theme is touted (tratado, ofrecido) as a spur (estímulo) for tackling (abordar, afrontar) World hunger =/= bestow (hacer, conferir, otorgar, ofrecer) generous benefits, -- (hacer) a gift. Spain has a much larger economy than Greece. Unnervingly (que pone nervioso, desconcertadamente + disconcerting) quiet/calm. Poor children fare better (se lo pasan mejor) in poor neighbourhood. Refugees endure (resisten, soportan) appalling (horroroso) joblessness. The well-to-do (las clases acomodadas) neighbourhoods. The grass was frosted over (cubierta de escarcha). Drilling (perforando) a well is noisy & disruptive (perjudicial, perturbador). No sooner had he taken the crown. The government first move: gestión, mudanza, movimiento, proposición,Vs. The S. Arabia's ageing rulers moved no nimbling (ágilmente, hábilmente), Salman is 80. Power would have to be handed to the next generation, but what prince would be worthy (merecido, digno, honorable)? The smooth transfer of power belies (defrauda, contradice) the view that S. Arabia must collapse due to its contradictions. Truculent (malhumorados, agresivos) princes. Oath of allegiance (juramento de lealtad). Put up: (ventana) subir, (mano) levantar, (cuadro) colgar, (edificio) construir, (satélite) lanzar, (resistencia) oponer, alojar, presentar un plan → -- -- with (aguantar, soportar) MrAbe provocation. Relate: he --s. sth with sth, related by blood; be --d to sb (ser pariente con), distantly --d (pariente lejano), the two incidents are --d (relacionados), drug --d crimes. It has no equal (semejante). Despreciar: look down on, spurn, disregard. Sliver (tajada, astilla) of land. Read out (leer en voz alta). Subplots (intrigas secundarias). Relationship/kinship (relación, parentesco, similitud). A bombardment of London akin (semejante, afín) to Israel's devastation of parts of Gaza. Apartheit's killers are vilified (vilipendiados, despreciados...). Freewheeling (alocado, irresponsable). It has suffered plunder (saqueo, botín), both organised & freelance (por cuenta propia, independiente, francotirador) =/= filibuster (obstruccionista) =/= sniper (francotirador, guerrillero) =/= gunman (pistolero) =/= Moscow's moles (tipos, espías). Some swear by (son entusiastas de, creen ciegamente con) debunked (desacreditados) studies. Goddam (¡Maldición!): a -- (una puñetera/maldita) stone. Stalwart: robusto, leal, fiel, (creencia) empedernido. Bleeding (hemorragia). Futile (=, vano). He panned (dejó por los suelos) the film

=/= he jabbed/gave a jab (pinchazo, codazo, golpe,Vs) → I --bed myself with a needle. More pleasure in the killing than his on-screen (en pantalla) character (=, personaje). Outwardly (por fuera, aparentemente). A previous round-up (rodeo, redada) of undercover (secretos, clandestinos, =) illegals. Play down (minimizar) the threat. A sort (especie) of amicable/friendly relations. V2x: una técnica inalámbrica en coches. Vacuous (vacío, bobo, insustancial) starlet (aspirante a estrella). Parents (padres) who skip (saltan) vaccines are portrayed as swayed (balanceados, influidos, dominados) by conspiracy theory. Gag: mordaza =/= --gle: (pers.) grupo, pandilla, (ocas) bandada =/= hogged (acaparó) the limelight. Avocado (aguacate) will be mashed → mashed (molidas) potatoes (puré). Lay a trail (estela, rastro; camino). Super Bowl (liga de fútbol americana). Let-up (descanso, tregua, disminuir) → don't -- - -- in the fighting. Cheerleaders (animadores) + (de un equipo) encouraging, (de un programa) presentar. Girlie (chiquilla). Dogfight (combate aéreo confuso, pelea de perros, refriega). Actuaries (actuarios: peritos de seguros). A running back (volver corriendo). Trickle (up) (chorrito, escurrir, gotear) down economics: filtrar riqueza de las capas altas a las bajas, -- away (our money): consumirlo poco a poco. Bubble (up: burbujear). Tight-lipped (hermético, silenciado, expresión de rabia contenida). They are remotely related (parientes lejanos), isn't remotely (ni por asomo) Canadian Ec. Gruesome/horrifying (truculento, cruel, atroz). Largely (en gran medida) due to... Canada is the fifth-largest producer. Shamelessly (descaradamente). Petroleum-spattered (salpicado) prime minister. Enacted (promulgaron) them late last year. Fleet: armada, flota, veloz → --ing (fugaz, breve)ly: fugazmente =/= fleece: vellón, forro polar; desplumar, esquilar. For an explosion occur several circumstances are needed. The fingerprints match with those of the murder. Take off (despegar) =/= set off (provocar, desencadenar) a rash (erupción, avalancha) of killings. It needs a shakeup (reorganización, remodelación). Wheelchair-access (acceso)/ bound (atado a). Misguided (insensata, errónea) enough to believe in him, a -- (torpe) attempt (intento). A furor(e): protesta, ola de entusiasmo. Ally (aliado: -- with sb.) =/= allay (calmar, aliviar) =/= alley (callejón) =/= alloy (aleación, mezcla. Mishandling (maltrato). Wiretapping (escuchas telefónicas). Coupled (unido, asociado). Rant (echar pestes, despotricar. Ache (dolor) → achingly (increíblemente) slowly. Glimpse (vislumbre, V, visión momentánea) → a fleeting -- (una visión fugaz), a -- into the future, he glimpsed (vislumbró, alcanzó a ver) the end of its ascendance (=). Supremacy (supremacía). Glitz (ostentación), glitzy (deslumbrante) =/= glare: mirada feroz, luz deslumbrante → install a glare screen filter on your monitor =/= glint (destello, centelleo (in his eyes...). Quible (queja, objeción de poca monta → legal --. Headgear (casco, gorra, sombrero). Sickening (repugnante, horrible, asqueante) footage (metraje; cine: secuencia, imagen). Cleavage (escisión, división) between leaders. No longer long (anhela)...; longing (nostalgia, añoranza). Matchmaker (celestina, casamentera, (Sp.) promotor). Ploy (estratagema, astucia). Hatch: incubar, salir del huevo; idear, tramar. Snow-covered bluff (acantilado, escarpado; francote, farol, V). Plough/plow: arado,V → --shares (rejas). Maker (Creador) =/= maker (artífice, fabricante) of lavatories/ bathrooms... Allotted (asignado, repartido) time. Fraternities (hermandad, círculo estudiantil) & sororities (hermandad femenina). Cabbage (col) =/= sprout -- (col de Bruselas) =/= sprout (brotar) new shoots (retoños). Cad: canalla, sinvergüenza + swine, scoundrel, (estafador) crook, (pícaro) rascal, little devil =/= cod (bacalao) Interlocking (entrelazado, engranado) system. A bungle (chapuza) operation/job = botched job =/= fumble (manosear, remover, hurgar (en bolsillos). Encubrir: (delito) cover up, (delincuente) harbor. In cramped (estrechos, apretados, incómodos) mouldy (mohosos) quarters (barrios, cuarta parte/un cuarto). Ringing (anillado; sonoro, enérgico, repique, toque...) tone: señal de llamada. Peacenik (pacifista + pacifist). Decommissioning (desguace, desmantelamiento nuclear). He run up to the house. A blond boy went up to her (se le acercó). Waste products (desperdicios). Average span (duración) of life. Brick <u>kilns (hornos para cerámica)</u>. Staging: escenificación, organización, montaje. They agreed to show up (poner en evidencia, aparecer, verse). Singled out (elegido). Be<u>littl</u>ing (menospreciando, minimizando)... The issue rankles (duele + hurt) in S. Korea. Plug: tapón, V, → -- this cloth into the hole; enchufe, toma de corriente; give sb/sth a -- (hacer publicidad de --/--). Circumventing: (burlar, salvar) the control. Dad (papá), mum/mummy (mamá). Fiend (diablo, malvado)ishly (terriblemente) complex. Mirage (espejismo). Alluvium of letters/bills. Upgrade (pendiente hacia arriba) → be on the -- (prosperar), (sistema) reformar, (Comp.) expansión, (softw.) actualización. Tosh: paparruchas (noticias falsas esparcidas entre vulgos, obra literaria insustancial). Too brittle (quebradizo) to be useful. Crystals shearing (esquileo, el partirse). What time the shop shut? After<u>glow (resplandor</u> crepuscular). Underwent (sufrió, experimentó) knotty (espinosos) problems. Chimera/fiction (ficción). Adrift: desorientado, a la deriva =/= drift (movimiento, cambio de dirección, navegar sin rumbo a causa del viento, ir a la deriva) → -- from the lands (éxodo rural), the -- of events, -- downstream (dejarse llevar por la corriente), --ing apart (separarse poco a poco, distanciarse de). Plundered (saqueado). Loosely (ligeramente, libremente). Mercurial (=, vivo, inestable, veleidoso, caprichoso + capricious, fickle) =/= fluke (chiripa) → by a -- (por casualidad, de chiripa). Weeping (lloroso) over her son's death. Palleness/pallor (palidez). Un<u>settl</u>ing (desestabilizante). Acomodador: usher(ette) → usher in: acomodar, hacer pasar a + he --ed us to the door. Public spending spree (derroche de dinero público). Ask/beg forgiveness (perdón). Face value (valor nominal).

Vent (respiradero, chimenea; descarga, desahogo + give --: dar rienda suelta a) his leftist urges (impulsos, ánimos,V, (sexo) deseos. Repercutir: have repercussions on, affect, (sonido) eco. Fudge: eludir, esquivar la cuestión. Onset (principio) of the crisis. Blistering (feroz, devastador). Harshness: dureza, rigor del clima, (sonido) áspero... Sycophancy (adulación, servilismo), sycophantic: servil, adulatorio). False alarm. Gold-braided (con galones/trenzas) gown (toga). It was not welcomed (bienvenido). Stud: clavo, tachuela, V, cuadra → decorated with --s; --ded (lleno) with sth; stud horse (semental). Core business (actividad principal), core subject (asignatura principal). Undemanding (poco exigentes, que exigen poco esfuerzo). Power befitting (apropiado) to an economy of its size. Say one's farewell (despedirse), his parting (de despedida) words/thoughts. Fritter away: (dinero) malgastar, (fortuna) dilapidar, (tiempo) desperdiciar. Valedictory: discurso de despedida. Churlishly (groseramente, sin educación) deprived (privado) of... Air -brushed (pintado con aerógrafo). He forced themselves onto the corner (los arrinconó). Waterboarding: (en tortura) "submarino". He looks ever grubbier (más sucio/repugnante). Beckon: -- sb in (hacerle señas para que entre), he --ed me over to this table, I'm sorry: work --s (me llama), she –ed & he wet over to her. Heartwarming: grato, reconfortante, emocionante. Unveiling (descubrimiento, inauguración de un monumento) =/= (de teatro, expo) opening. Pep (energía, dinamismo) up: animar, estimular. Do away with (suprimir) costly services. Worthwhile (valer la pena) → it's -- getting there early, not be <u>worth</u> banking agents <u>while</u> to hold cash. Flat: apartamento; plano, llano, liso; desinflado, soso, apagado, (rechazo) rotundo, (TV, Comp.) pantalla plana. Caer en la cuenta de algo (realize sth). Financial cr<u>u</u>sh (aplastar, triturar..., aglomeración, abatimiento...) caused by mortgage excesses (excesos) result in deep recession. Particle physics: creating exotic particles means cr<u>a</u>shing (estrellar, quebrar, chocar) the quotidian ones (e-, p+). Seaweed (alga). Pipes (tubos) interspersed/intermingled (entremezclados) with cavities filled with electric field. Pull one's punches (andarse con miramientos). A new awakening (despertar). Pin: alfiler, clavo; sujetar, pb.: identificar → -- down (sujetar, inmovilizar; identificar) an ineffable (=, inexplicable) taste...; they pinned him down. Their political paymasters (pagadores, mecenas) balk (impiden, pierden, no aprovechan) at: se plantan ante... Flavoursome (sabroso) stuff. Be a branding (imagen de marca) exercise rather than a scientific one. Propensity for frequent weighting (pesajes) → -- machines (básculas). Predict how much weight s.o. who stayed the course (terminase la carrera) would lose. Ceres has a core & a mantle (manto, capa), it was quietly (discretamente, silenciosamente) demoted (degradado, disminuido de categoría). Junkyard (depósito de chatarra, chatarrería) of rock & ice called asteroid belt. Wailing (lamentando, echando gemidos) & gnashing (rechinando) the tooth. Quarry: cantera, extraer → -- for marble (abrir una cantera en busca de mármol). The leftover turkey (el pavo sobrante). Probes approach (se dirige a) a pair of former planets & five truly (realmente, de veras) Worlds turn up (aparecen). Scorchingly (abrasadoramente). The exhilaration (alegría, excitación, vigorización) of scruffy (descuidado, desaliñado) people. Voice (expresar) concerns about corruption, hit back (devuelve el golpe) at tycoons who tried to bully around (intimidar) him into doing sth. Chivvy (apurar, meter prisa a) sb into doing sth. Lambast (fustigar, azotar, vituperar, arremeter contra) =/= lambent (que brilla con luz tenue). Downfall (caída, ruina) of his investments. Wipe out: (déficit) cancelar, (taza) limpiar, (especies) exterminar, (ventaja) eliminar, (enfermedad) erradicar, (pers.) aniquilar, (memoria) borrar. Pieced together (reconstruido). Mammouth (=, descomunal). Swanky: (pers.) presumida, fanfarrón, (coche) despampanante. Strike (ike,uck,uck): (huelga, ataque, golpe,V; descubrimiento...); stru<u>c</u>ken (afligido, dañado) → drought --; str<u>i</u>ke out: arremeter, -- -- widely (dar golpes sin mirar a quien), -- -- for the shore (andar hacia la playa), for the summit (hacia la cumbre), -- -- on one's own (volar con sus propias alas). Extradited to Russia on trumped-up (inventadas) fraud charges. Timorous (temeroso, huraño, asustadizo). Unanimously (por unanimidad). Ably (hábilmente) gh<u>o</u>st (fantasma) written: escrito por otros. Holy Gh<u>o</u>st (Espíritu Santo) =/= gh<u>a</u>stly/dreadful/hideous: horroroso, espantoso... =/= agh<u>a</u>st (horrorizado) → we were – at the very thought (sólo pensarlo). He has befr<u>ie</u>nded (hecho amigos con) human right activists. Hitler's airborne (aerotransportador, volando en el aire) Condor Legion. Bonfire (hoguera). Obnoxious/disgusting (repugnante). Strafing (ametrallamiento, bombardeo) of civilians. Screenwriter (guionista). Air raid (antiaéreos) shelters (refugios). Astoundingly (asombrosamente) good. Search a quieter life. Loop: curva, meandro, lazada/boucle, (calle) serpentear; it loops forwards & backwards, keep sb. in the -- (mantener informado a alguien), be in/out of the -- (estar dentro/fuera del circuito de información). Yearns for (añora a), -- to do sth. Fun-loving (amigo de diversión). Sideway (lateral, de lado) → look -- (de reojo). Witness (testigo) =/= a witless (tonto, estúpido + stupid silly) hero =/= wit<u>t</u>iness (ingenio, agudeza). Playfully (de broma, alegremente + happily, cheerfully). Strong follow-up (seguimiento, continuación). Make mincements (conservas de picadillo de frutas, de carne picada). The police is baffled (desconcertada), the pb --es me. Be <u>out of kilter</u> (estar estropeado) → business are -- - -- (desorganizados). Bewitching (cautivador, encantador, seductor) → I find the place – (para mí el sitio tiene magia). Altarpiece (retablo). Disq<u>uie</u>ting (inquietante). Vividness (intensidad, viveza). Vividly (vivamente). He stood (se quedó) transfixed (paralizado) with fear. Sinuous/winding (sinuoso). Unbridled (desenfrenada) sensuality. Set upon → set on (agredir, atacar) with glee (júbilo + rejoicing, joyfully).

Primal: (primero en el tiempo) original, (en importancia) principal. Primarily (ante todo, principalmente). Raw: crudo, puro, sin refinar; (sewage, rubber) sin tratar; sewage disposal (depuradora). Belabour: (atacar, fustigar (criticar); asediar con cuestiones) =/= bereaved (afligidos, desconsolados) → the -- (los familiares del difunto). A puny (enclenque) sword. Fling (arrojar, lanzar) → -- sb into jail, go on a -- (echar una cañita al aire), -- one's arms round sb, -- o.s. into a job. Soliloquy (=, monólogo). Winding down (disminuir poco a poco). By striking (alcanzando) an agreement. Build up: urbanizar, labrarse una reputación, levantar un negocio, -- -- a lead (tomar la delantera), -- -- a picture (una imagen) in his mind, -- -- one's strength (fortalecerse). The generals seem bent (empeñados, inclinados, curvados, dirigidos) on eradicating.... A bout (ataque) of E. Coli. Ticket: (tren...) boleto, billete, (museo...) entrada, (tienda de reparación, parking) ticket, de compra (receipt) + a big-ticket item (compra importante), a big-ticket reform. Tone down: disminuir/suavizar/atenuar. A warm glow (brillo, sensación) of their country. A country with expansionist mindsets (actitudes, disposiciones). Chuffed (contentos, satisfechos). Timeless (intemporal). Manufacturing what has lain fallow (dejado en barbecho). Honking (claxonando + blowing a horn). The tingle: (ears) zumbar, (piel) hormigueo, (emoción) estremecimiento → -- with excitement (estremecer de emoción). Restaurants are popping up (aparecen inesperadamente). Pungent (acre: áspero; mordaz, cáustico) fish. Braziers (braseros). Crammed: lleno a reventar, (examen) empollar → -- food into one's mouth, the hall is --. Gild (d, ed, il_t_/ed) dorar. Hilltop (cumbre, cima). Assuage (calmar, aliviar...): he was not easily --ed. He precludes (excluye, impide) easier fixes (aprietos, intenciones, posiciones, arreglos...). Instead: I couldn't go, so she went instead (a mi lugar). Stocks depleted (mermados, agotados) by overfishing. Sewers (cloacas) have hardly been upgraded (reformadas, mejoradas,

Comp.: actualizado. Brought-down (bajado, derribado). Disgruntled: descontento, malhumorado. Massage (masaje, V, maquillar) + -- parlour (sala de). He writes beautiful, as befits (corresponde) to a poet. Cow (intimidar) friends & foes alike. Face-saving (salvar las apariencias) → take the easier -- - -- (más fáciles soluciones). He mocked (burló) hopes. Avowed (declarado) nationalist. Outmaneuvered: (oponente) se mostró más hábil que, (coche) fue más maniobrable que). Grudge (resentimiento, rencor, envidia, V) → give the president --ing (reticente) credit. The scourge (plaga, azote,Vs) of poaching (caza y pesca furtiva/en vedado) by foreign fishermen/hunters. I'll be with you by & by (enseguida). Step up (intensificar) efforts + -- -- (acercarse) to sb. Jettisoning (deshaciéndose de) its GDP projects + (Aér.) vaciar, (Náut.) echar.por la borda. Waver: vacilar, tambalear, titubear → unwavering (firme, inquebrantable). Public lavatory (aseos). Bolshie (volchebique). Iron - ore (mineral de hierro). A snub (desaire, rechazo, Vs). Steamed into (entró echando vapor). Flagpole (hasta de bandera). Selling at gross margins (márgenes brutos). Ballyhoo (bombo, propaganda estrepitosa), --hooed (tan cacareado). A terse (lacónica, seca) letter. Changes are afoot (plan: tramándose, en proyecto), what's --? (¿Qué se está tramando?). A maker of air coolers. Unsung: (pers., logros) no reconocidos, (héroe) olvidado. Sidestep (eludir, esquivar). He spotted (observó)... Ward: pupilo, distrito postal, tutela, sala de hospital. Stock: surtido, (teatro) repertorio, acciones. Onlookers (espectadores). Vs) → -- (rozar) with failure, -- with death: ver la muerte cerca. Bothersome (molesto). Kit (útiles, bártulos, indumentaria, equipo) =/= kid: cabrito, chiquillo; engañar, bromear → he's kidding you on/along (te está tomando el pelo). The rationale (base, fundamento) for the emergency. Can practise (ejercer) both Chinese & foreign law. Blue-chip: (categoría) de primera, (inversión) asegurada, -- - -- securities (fianzas fiables). Pick up: (mejora, subida) in demand. Cheerful: jovial, feliz, alegre → be -- about (alegrarse de) sb. Increasingly far-flung (extenso). Ongoing (en curso) costs. Workforce: población activa, plantilla, mano de obra. Savior (Salvador), salvation (salvación). Swiftness (velocidad, rapidez) of the departure... Moan: gemir, quejarse → she's always moaning about sth. He was dogged (seguido) by ill luck (mala suerte). Allow (permitir, aceptar) his awareness (conciencia, conocimiento) of what he is about to be numbed (adormecido, entumecido) =/= nimble (ligero, hábil) → nimbleness: destreza + dexterity. He sought for/after (buscaba) animal spirits. Contemplate one's navel/belly button (mirarse el ombligo) → Paris isn't the center (ombligo) of the Universe. Lifeline (cordón ombilical). Pool (fondo, charca, reserva, Vs) $ 500 m. gasping (jadeando) for liquidity. Cloister (claustro) → lead a --ed (de ermitaño) life. Chequered/checkered (accidentado, con altibajos + (terreno) rough, uneven. Financial transactions: a century-old stamp-duty (impuesto de timbre). Dust down/off (desempolvar). Obama pressed for tax increase but Republicans have hampered (lo impidieron); we were hampered to see it. Stay away from (no acercarse a) my daughter/that machine. Militar rule, the rule (imperio) of the law; rule of the roost (percha): llevar la batuta, rule (gobernar). A simple (sencilla) manner of speaking. Sencillo en el trato (very natural or unaffected). Put on one's make up (maquillarse), put on weight/three kgs., put the heating on, put a clock on one hour ↔ put it back one hour. He is pretending to be asleep. Play dead (hacerse el muerto). His mastery (maestría) on the football field. Gain the mastery of (llegar a dominar, hacerse el señor de). Claim (demanda, reivindicación): wage claim, she lost her -- for damages (daños y perjuicios), make a -- (reclamar), he renounced his -- to the throne. Spoil: dañar, estropear, (voting paper) invalidar, the coast spoiled by development (urbanizaciones); mimar. Drown: ahogar → -- o.s., -- out by demand, (tierra) inundar, his cries were --ed by the noise of the waves.

Error is human. Blackballing (votar en contra de, exclusión). Bump (choque, sacudida, abolladura) off: liquidar a alguien. Stuffy: mal ventilado, (pers.) miras estrechas. Strain: (rope/leash: correa) tensión, (on the economy...) presión, (on heart, of climbing the stairs) esfuerzo. I'm indebted (estoy muy agradecido) to you for... Causally (causalmente) → they are -- related (guardan relación causa - efecto). Shred: (papel) tira, a -- (mínimo) of decency (honradez)/of evidence (prueba), tear sth to --s (hacer algo trizas). Inquiry (pregunta, investigación). Locate: situar, ubicar → central (céntrica) location near the sea. Renounce to a right/violence, abandon a plan, resign (dimisión). Estropearse: break (down), damage a car, ruin/spoil the crop/a plan, (pers.): he has aged really badly. You are really (muy) mistaken; it was really hot (hacía mucho calor). Pick up the tab/bill (pagar la cuenta, asumir la responsabilidad). Irrelevant (intrascendente, indiferente). Surreptitiously: subrepticiamente (a escondidas). Desideratum (desiderátum): parte de la ciencia no tratada y que merece más atención). Dissent: =, discrepar, disidir. Disagree/differ (discrepar). Baby crèche/nursery (guardería). Constituent (constitutivo, Pol.: elector). Peevish (malhumorado + bad tempered). Trustees (administradores, fiduciarios). Polish: pulimiento, lustro, refinamiento, Vs). Surmise (suponer, conjeturar). By & large (en general). By & by: de pasada → he mentioned it -- & --. Lecture hall (aula de conferencias). Nigeria has woefully (lamentablemente) failed to defeat an insurgency by B. Haram. Unwilling (poco dispuesto a). Cravings: anhelos, ansias, antojos. Bereavement (pérdida, duelo, pesar) → counselling (apoyo psicológico). Meal (comida) -skip (saltar, pasar por alto)ping during the pregnancy. Unbothered (no preocupado, no molestado) by the world sneers (desdeñar, desprecios + disdains, disregards) → he --ed of my attempts (intentos). The rating (popularidad) of the PS. The PS stuck (atascado) near his tally (concordar, coincidir; cuenta) → keep the -- of (llevar la cuenta de). Fightback (contraataque). Encroachment (usurpación) of our liberty. Rallying (de encuentro) point. A song about lynching (linchamiento). The floundering (que se debate/se revuelca) government indulgences (=, complacencia, tolerancia) calls for toughen Islamic law. Grinding (absoluta) poverty (=, miseria). Scream (chirrido, chillido, grito)ing (divertido) match between…; they were --ing with laugher (se reían a carcajadas: guffaws) =/= chillar: (pájaro) screech, (cerdo) squeal, (ratón) squeak, (de dolor y de miedo) scream =/= quejarse: grouse, complain, grumble, protest, moan, groan =/= (lamentar) regret. Hive (colmena, enjambre) off (privatizar, vender; escindir, enajenar) → a -- of industry (donde se trabaja mucho), a -- of activity (un hervidero de actividad). Overdraft (cuenta al descubierto) → -- facility (préstamo). Wiring (cableado eléctrico, conectar, comunicar) the world. If you are so minded (si quieres hacerlo)… Fair-minded (justo, imparcial), an industry-minded nation, scientifically minded. Minder (guardaespaldas + bodyguard). Sequence (orden) → in --, in historical (cronológico) --, a -- (serie) of events. Bid, bad (e), bidden (mandar) → -- sb to do sth =/= bid (i, i, i,): (a) puja, oferta, Vs → the highest --, raise one's --, (b) intento: a -- for freedom/power =/= b<u>e</u>t (apuesta, V) → I had a -- with him (le hice una apuesta). Upstart (arribista + ambitious). Tinker: calderero, pícaro → -- with (toquetear, jugar con → he's been --ing with the car + they're only --ing with the problem of buoyancy (flotabilidad, Ec.: en alta). Scoop (recoger, hacerse con, (provecho) sacar → --ed data for scientists to pore over (estudiar; escudriñar, investigar, averiguar). He will sit atop (encima) it. Beacon (faro + lighthouse) → a distant twinkle (centelleo). Boom & bust-ups & downs (con altibajos). Fare: billete, pasaje, -- well/badly (pasarlo bien, mal). Apocryphal (fingido, supuesto, falsamente atribuido). Dragnet (red de arrastre, policía: emboscada) that ensnares (atrapa) everyone. Back up: respaldar, (Comp.) hacer copia de seguridad. He was within a whisker (le faltó un pelo) of disabling emergency services. Dryly (drily): (irónicamente, con sequedad) can muster (reunir, congregarse)...; muster up courage (armarse de valor). Coarse (áspera, basta, ordinaria) wool. Prevent the stains from spreading. He's a real cheat (es muy tramposo). Mop (fregona, estropajo + scourer, steel wool) → mopping up (limpieza). Slick: hábil superficialmente, impecable (a -- performance), oil slick (marea negra, capa de petróleo en el agua), slicker (tramposo) =/= sleek: pelo lustroso, apariencia impecable. A vial (frasquito, ampolla) containing... Air-freighted (transportado por). Groove: surco, ranura; estriar, acanalar, Mús. (ritmo) → be in a -- (rutina), be in the -- (estar en forma), --ed (acanalado, estriado). Unravelled (desenmarañado). Revs. (revoluciones). Spark (chispa, chispear) plug (tapón, toma de corriente): bujía de auto. Wallop (golpe fuerte, V)ing (paliza) → give sb a -- (paliza). Rover (vagabundo, trotamundo + wanderer). Novel (novedoso, original), after hurtling (arrojarse violentamente) six billion km. through space... Elation: júbilo, euforia (=). Hamburger patty (empanada + de carne picada: hamburguesa). Vegan: veganoestricto. Jubilee: jubileo, aniversario → silver/golden -- + (de un hecho: ej. wedding, birthday... Sci-fi (ciencia ficción). Randomize (aleatorizar). Wizardry (brujería, hechicería). Jaywalk (cruzar la calle imprudentemente). Bone (hueso, espina)head: estúpido =/= bane (ruina, pesadilla)ful (funesto, nefasto + terrible effect). The new party is not yet pulling away (arrancando). He scoffed (se mofó) at the idea... Crib (cuna, plagio, chuleta) → -- (copiar) sth from sth., he --bed the whole paragraph. Overall/overarching (global, general) goals (=, portería, objetivo) & tarjets (objetivo, diana). Sustainable development goals. Pre-empting (anticipándose a) the next crisis. Lick (lametazo,V) → a -- (mano) of paint, -- sb's boots, -- one's wounds. Flinched (estremecido) at the pain... ↔ the unflinching (impávida, inmutable, resuelta) rivalry... Trample (pisotear). China left America looking churlish (grosera, mezquina, maleducada) & ineffectual (inútil + unsuccessful, fruitless, useless, hopeless) =/= ineffective (ineficaz) =/= disabled (invalidado, discapacitado, minusválido). Rumble: ruido sordo, (trueno) estruendo. Tangle: enredo, maraña; -- streets (laberinto), a -- of resulting claims & counter-claim is being litigated (=, en pleito → untangle (desenredar, desenmarañar). Soldiers of the Jewish underground (subterráneo; movimiento/periódico: clandestino). Marauder (merodeador, intruso). Dismiss (despedir, destituir). He bankrolled (financió) & seconded (=, apoyó) fifty men to its ranks (rango, Mil: filas). Lightness (suavidad, ligereza). Engaged in crass (craso, grosero, estúpido) anti-Semitism. Hamstrung (i, u, u) (paralizado, atado de pies a cabeza) by American support for Zionism.; the project was – (frustrado) by lack of funds. Growing apace (rápidamente). Armaggedon (=, guerra del fin del mundo, apocalipsis). Banks are in no mood (sin humor) to quibble (quisquilloso, objeción de poca monta,Vs, hacer problemas con nimiedades). Rowdy (pers.: agitadora, alborotadora, escandalosa). Quiescent (inactivo). Losing out (salir perdiendo). Hand off (rechazo) ←→ hand on (transmitir) =/= hang on: -- - (agarrar) his arm, -- - (agarrarse) to the branch, this --s - (depende de) his decision, -- - (aguanta) a minute. Sagga (=: leyenda de Eddas: en la mitología y leyendas escandinavas). Grimly (gravemente, denodadamente, con valentía) → -- hurt. Splutter: resoplar, ranquear, chisporrotear. Pettifogging (pedante) details: detalles insignificantes. Foreclose: (loan, mortgage) ejecutar → foreclosure (ejecución). Conundrum (acertijo, enigma). Tokenism (acción simbólica, formulismo). Whitewash: tapadera,V, encubrimiento, blanquear =/= cover up: cubrir, tapar, ocultar, disimular. Make off (salir corriendo) with sth (llevarse algo). Pockmark (picadura, hoyuelo)ed (picado de viruela, lleno de agujeros) with coalmines. Stare (mirar fijamente) down (hasta lograr que aparte la vista). Avert (apartar, evitar, prevenir). Pelts (pellejos) of feathery (plumoso)... Eat away (corroer). Dismay (consternación, =). Spurt (chorro, chorrear) of investments. Protracted (prolongada) Ec. War. Uplift (inspiración, animación; espíritu: elevación,Vs). Sober (sobrio, serio, formal) up: despejar (se), volver (se) más serio. Fiat (autorización; decreto, orden) → the governor's --. Pent-up: (emoción, odio) contenido, reprimido, (energía) acumulación. Tepid: (agua) tibia; poco entusiasta ←→ nagging (persistente). Scale-back (recortar, disminuir el nº). Rickshaw (carrito oriental tirado por humanos). A snazzy (vistoso) dress. Yank out (arrancar de un tirón). Tetchy (irritable, =). Tidal (marea) power: maremoto. Missing out (soltarse, perderse). Hairspring: muelle muy fino en espiral, espiral de un reloj. Shirk (esquivar un deber, hacer el gandul). It is etched (gravado) in my memory forever. Snag (inconveniente, problema) → I don't see what the − is. Mainspring (motivo principal) =/= mainstream (corriente dominante). Whiff: tufillo, olorcillo, (corrupción) indicio, go out for a -- of air (ir a tomar el fresco). Natty (elegantes) pleats (pliegues). Hose out (regar con manguera).Vintage (vendimia, cosecha; añejo, excelente) car: coche antiguo. Handle/operate (maniobra) for a position. Manoeuvre (maniobra,V). Political juggles (malabarismos). Folly (locura). A rich man scorned/despised (despreciaba)... A poor critter (bicho). Torpor (letargo + letargy). Labour dispute (=, conflicto + =, strife) → cease from strife (deponer las armas). Fuss: mimar, consentir, molestar por poca cosa; escándalo, alboroto, conmoción → --y (quisquilloso, escrupuloso) about details. Take in: (harvest) recoger + pick up, (stray dog...) acoger, (pers.) hacer entrar. Rake (rastrillo,V) in: (fichas de juego) recoger; sacar dinero de un negocio. By its own bootstraps (por sus propias fuerzas). Chisel (escoplo). Beguile (cautivar, seducir + sharm, captivate, attract) a nation. They caught up (alcanzaron: a alguien, recogieron, agarraron) close to fifty $ m. Chutzpah (cara dura, descaro). Suspend (=, colgar, aplazar) → -- from office, licence --ed for six month, --ed animation (constantes vitales al mínimo). Infotainment programme (información concebida como espectáculo). The traffic flows smoothly & safely. To a staggering (asombroso + astonishing, amazing) $500 billions by 2002. Rígido: (material) rigid/stiff, (incondicional) staunch, (moralmente severo) strict, harsh. Rizado: (pelo) curly, (superficie) ridged, crimped, (terreno) undulating, (mar) choppy. Llorar: weep, cry → crocodile tears, (difunto) mourn, (desgracia) bemoan. Spoof (parodia, trampa, burla, broma + fun, joke). Raspar: scrape off, scratch. Cercar: (terreno) enclose, surround, (con vallas) fence in, (pers. & Mil.) surround, besiege. Prop (sostén, puntal, apuntalar) → -- a ladder against the wall, the door --ped open with a bucket (cubo). Shy away: -- -- from (rehuir del) emotional...; tener miedo (+ get frightened, scared) → we musn't -- -- (no debemos tener miedo) from making a decision. School year (curso escolar), a course in business administration, I'm doing a degree in economics =/= career (carrera professional) =/= course of a river/the life/a ship (rumbo). Relish (entusiasmo, sabor,Vs) → do/ eat sth. with --. Ticket: billete, pasaje, round -- (de ida y vuelta), (multa en estacionamiento): get a parking --, run a republican -- (presentarse como...), -- counter/ desk, -- machine. Torpeza: (movimiento) clumsiness, (inteligencia) dimness. Abduction (rapto, secuestro; plagio). Playwright (dramaturgo). Japan's companies are sitting on (ocultan, forman parte de, retienen) $ two trn. in cash. Leapfrog (pídola, saltar por encima) → a whippersnapper (mocoso/a) leapfrogs (=, deja atrás) a more experienced worker. The shortages of Electr. are holding back (retienen) growth. Abatement (bajada, disminución), it abet (incita) financial crisis. Old-age dependency ratio (=, proporción). Flunk (exámenes: suspender + fail). Putin concocted (confecciona, trama) plots. The party makeover (modernización, cambio de imagen). Rickets (raquitismo) =/= rickety (destartalado). Abhor (aborrecer, abominar) → abhorrence (repugnancia, aborrecimiento, el detestar). Highbrow (intellectual (=); hard-headed (realista, práctico, testarudo). Scotland severance (ruptura, despido) → -- pay: indemnización. Desenlace: (film, libro) ending, (aventura) outcome. Rajoy bungle_d_ (ejecutó mal, hizo chapuza de) the corruption issue + blun_d_er (grave error, meter la pata) in economy + blunder on moral grounds, --rer (metepatas). Alienated by stale (duras; añejas, rancias, pasadas, marchitas) politics. Retain some high fliers (ambiciosos, de prestigio)... frequently lobbed (echaba algo a alguien, volaba por alto, lanzaba) shells (obuses). Raise the school-leaving (escolaridad obligatoria) age. Watchfulness (vigilancia, =). Donors are prescriptive (legales, preceptivos). A middling (regular, mediano) S. Korean. Run on: you -- -- (continúa adelante), I'll catch (agarrar, alcanzar, coger, tomar; contagiar, transmitir + pass on)... Global downturn (deterioro). A loss-making (deficitario) national... Be comfortably off (vivir holgadamente). Top up (llenar, recargar) the batteries. Pinpoint (precisas/identificadas) areas. Fire (disparar, incendiar; despedir) volley (descarga) of weighty (pesada, importante) ordnance (material de guerra, artillería). Enthralling (cautivador + captivating). Bluffing (engaño, faroleo). Pouring rain (lluvia torrencial). Aimless (sin propósito), calls for America to shore up (sostener, apuntalar) its allies confidence. Cocking up (fastidiar, joder) all over (integralmente, completamente, sobre toda la superficie de) the world. Un_rewarding (gratificante)_: (finanzas, bancos) improductivos, =), ingrato. Fevered: calenturiento, (Med.) febril + feverish. Fester: enconarse → the Ottoman empire created the f_e_stering (situación degradante, que se encona) resentment & the sore (llaga) that is today's Middle East; a festering sore (una llaga purulenta). Nasser embraced (abrazó, abarcó) Africa, f_o_stering (fomentando, alentando, niño: acogiendo) leaders who sought to emulate (imitar) his Egyptian revolution. She was misguided enough (insensata) to believe in him; Sisi often misguidedly (equivocadamente) conflates (combina, refunde) with terrorism. By stifling (agobiante) debate. At loggerheads (a matar, en desacuerdo). Forebears (antepasados + ancestors) kitted out/up (equipados)... =/= forbearance (paciencia + =). Swell: hinchar, oleaje; arrebato de ira, oleada de emoción. (Hand) span: palmo; lapso de tiempo, abarcar: a story --ing generations; wingspan (ave, avión: envergadura + importance, magnitude). First leg (pierna, etapa/tramo). A psychiatrist & a balloonist (aeróstata). Bob (meneo, sacudida, reverencia, inclinación, Vs) → -- up (aparecer). Unchallenged (incontestable) master of suspense. Splinter (astilla, fragmento,V) → a --ed (dividido) group. His crisp (fresco, limpio, crepitante) record shows how Thatcher was nudging (codeando, refrescando la memoria a) the African parties. Courtship (cortejo) → cortejo nupcial (wedding party). Wo<u>o</u> (galantear, cortejar, buscar) the disgruntled (descontentos, de mal humor) Sunnis; (inversiones) atraer =/= wo<u>w</u> (excitar, enloquecer, cautivar → fans --ed by the speed. Séquito: entourage, (Rel.) procession, (funeral) cortege/procession. Bond (bono, fianza, enlace, vínculo) → friendship --, in bond (bajo fianza, en depósito). Figure: a -- in a blue dress + a nice -- (tipo), a key (clave) -- + cifra. Attend (asistir, prestar atención). Rugged (áspero + rough; escabroso). Prenda usada: (ropa) worn out, (diccionario) well-thumbed. Fast track (pista, trayectoria): por la vía rápida. Hobbling (cojeando), disability (invalidación, discapacidad). They tussled (lucharon) with the police. Crime-buster (el que esclarece los crímenes). Stoke/stir (atizar) an already blazing (abrasador, en llama) fire. China is awash (inundada) in cash. Contrive (idear)d (artificial) nod. Flybys (desfiles aéreos). A surface covered in craters scorched (quemada, abrasada) by the nearby sun. Gash (raja, cuchillada, hendidura,V). Gravitational kneading (masaje,V) from the sun. Boil away (evaporar por ebullición). Greening: concienciación ecológica. Clearheaded (lúcido). Gutsier (más valiente). Eschew (evitar, abstenerse de).

Aglow (radiante, brillante) with happines. The length of the gallery gently entices (seduce) the visitors. Courtly (cortés, elegante + courteous, polite). Sawtooth (diente de sierra) roof. The vista (=, panorama) at either end opens up new vistas (abre nuevas perspectivas) =/= view: vista → the hotel comes into view, a -- over the lake/bay; parecer → what's your --? A particular -- of things; mirar, examiner, considera; the operator lays the wireless device on a patient's arm & views an ultrasound image on a nearby (cercano) computer screen. Smallish (más bien pequeño). Tumble down (desplomarse, venirse abajo). Stem (tallo, vástago, detener) the tide (corriente, marea, curso) of events. Struggling: lucha, forcejeo,V, pasar apuros. Bilked (estafado + swindled, defrauded) =/= bulky (corpulentos) ministers. String-pulling (enchufismo, amiguismo). Hob (quemador) of an oven (horno)/heater (estufa). Putting on an apron (delantal, mandil) → leather --. Islam is incorrigibly flawed (mercancías: defectuosas; teoría: errónea). She's doing economics at the university. Tuck (pliegue; meter, arropar) → tucked (puesta) between Paris & London, under the mattress, etcétera. Blink (parpadeo, destello) → in the -- of an eye (en un abrir y cerrar de ojos) → go on the -- (estropearse); be on the -- (estar averiado). Statues of Lenin dotted (esparcidas en) the wide streets. Both are running (dirigiendo, llevando a cabo) drearily (tristemente + dreariness: lo deprimente) predictable campaigns. At odds with (en desacuerdo con). Brandishing (weapons...: brandir) sunflowers + a grassroots (de base) campaign has been wide ranging (de gran alcance); grassroots politics (donde se tratan los problemas corrientes). They tottled up (sumaban) income from salaries & alimony (pensiones alimentarias) payments. Chime (campanada, tocar, sonar) with: estar en armonía/de acuerdo con; chime in: meter baza/la cucharada. Those twiddling (girando, dando vueltas) with (jugueteando con) the fiscal deals should mull on/over (reflexionar) these findings (descubrimientos, resultados,

(Jur.:fallos). Phase in (introducir progresivamente) ←→ phase out (eliminar progresivamente). Be bereft (estar desprovistos, faltos) of... Flock (bandada, rebaño, multitud) of helium balloons. They stay (permanecen) over (pasan la noche en, se quedan a dormir en) a fixed point on the Earth. Fall off (empeorar la calidad, (de)caer; desprender, disminuir en número). Stay aloft (en el aire) for months; the balloon remained --. Mar<u>c</u>h (marzo) =/= mar<u>s</u>h: pantano, ciénaga; salt -- (marisma) =/= marsh<u>a</u>l: mariscal, (soldados) formar, (hechos) ordenar, (pruebas) presentar: -- them around the world... One in ten Americans are stricken (dañados) by... High-flying (de altos vuelos) curator (comisario/conservador de museos). Bisque (sopa de mariscos) → crab -- (sopa de cangrejos). Mingled (mezclados) with the millionaires. Pattern (patrón, dibujo) → tapestry made from patterned (estampados) fabrics (telas). Droll (graciosos, curiosos) paintings + oh yes, terribly --. It ails (aflige + afflict) Africa, what ails you? (¿Qué te pasa?). African potentates (potentados). Spiral: a -- staircase (escalera =/= stairwell), the inflationary --, a -- of violence, a -- bound notebook. A gritty (arenoso, enérgico) candidate. Tug: tirón, remolcar; ánimo, valor → it takes -- to do that, plenty of -- (agallas). Drudge: trabajo pesado → work as a -- (trabajar como un esclavo). Bridge a gap (espacio, separación, distancia, laguna) that bedevils (sufre) all AI (Artificial Intelligence) research + be bedeviled (plagados) of problems. It's necessary to approximate how minds (mentes) equip humans with autonomy, interests & desires. Despite a century of poking (hurgar, remover). <u>C</u>ringe (encogerse) at seeing... + --with fear/with embarrassment (de vergüenza). The dog snarled at us (nos griñó). He has failed (suspendido, fracasado, luz: apagado). He performed dismally (pésimamente), the play was bad performed. Bent (doblado, inclinado) on doing down (menospreciando) his country. Cash (dinero efectivo, cobrar) hoards (montones, tesoros,Vs). Hinge (bisagra, girar sobre). Grocers team up (se asocian). Make a sally (hacer una salida) into America. Weld (soldar, unir) the twelve quarrelsome (peleones) states. Forge a nation out of an inchoate (embrionaria, incipiente) nation. Falling (que flojean/decaen) Gallic (galos, franceses) contenders (competidores). Bear the brunt of sth (soportar lo más duro de algo), the brunt of the work (-- la mayor parte del trabajo). The ousted (echado, obligado a renunciar) crown prince is 69. Slug (babosa; puñetazo, pegar) → two heavy weights are slugging it out (se pegan, se aporrean). In tandem (conjuntamente + jointly). Lattice (enrejado, celosía, en ventana: reja). Beneath (debajo) the bonhomie (afabilidad, atención) lies the unease (malestar, inquietud). They are grudging (son reticentes, están de mala gana). Western economies sweeten (endulzan, facilitan, temperamento: aplacan) the cost of borrowing. The warping (distorsión, deformación) of the Ec. Sail: vela, velero; zarpar, gobernar/manejar → cast/drop anchor (anclar) ↔ weigh anchor (levar anclas). Move back (regresar, retirarse), move away (apartarse) from the door. Shrink (encoger) back (retroceder) from a danger. Back pedal (pedalear hacia atrás, dar marcha atrás) on reforms. Hum (zumbar, canturrear, ir viento en popa). Grizzly (gris, canoso, quejumbroso) parties are non-events (fiascos). Harp (arpa) on: insistir sobre. Pesky (molesto, latoso). Diversity into cash crops (cultivos comerciales). Undisclosed (no reveladas) donations. Ice-breaking (rompehielos) + -- - -- chit-chat (habladurías). Jet lag (desfase horario en un viaje en avión). Sw*o*t (empollón) up: estudiar como un loco. Bracket: soporte, paréntesis (add sth in --), categoría → the best car in this -- (gama). Bulge in the birth rate (explosión demográfica), they --ed at the sight (se les saltaron los ojos al verlo). Pair (pareja,V, par) the token (ficha, muestra; obsequio, recuerdo). Rely on (contar con, depender de). Distraído: be miles away, be absentminded → I wasn't paying attention... Lackadaisical (apático, displicente, perezoso). Spook: asustarse; policía secreta, fantasma) → most fish spooked & some jellyfish avoid bubbles (burbujas) lest they (para que ellas no) fill their umbrella. The combo: (Mús, ropa) colección, conjunto (+ conjunto de jazz). Come along! (¡Vamos!) Presentarse: you -- -- at the right time (en el momento preciso). Wholeheartedly (con entusiasmo, incondicionalmente). Renew (renovar, (negocio) reanudar, (componentes: cambiar. Restoration (restablecimiento; poder/monarquía: restauración) =/= refurbish (renovar, hacer reformas, restaurar + restore). Drawing board (mesa de dibujo). Fly off (alejarse, salir volando). The fretting (desgaste, preocupación). Run down (agotar, atropellar) before recharging... He hands out (distribuye) welfare =/= the international law Putin says he upholds (mantiene, defiende) in Syria =/= hold up (levantar, sostener, asaltar, retrasar) =/= hold out (tender, ofrecer, presenter, resistir: the strikers are --ing out for 5% salary increase) =/= holdup (retraso, atasco; atraco) → a bank -- =/= hold to (atenerse a) the account (cuenta, factura, informe) =/= hold on (agarrarse, asirse) → -- -- tight (agárrate bien), hold (on) tight to the rail (barandilla)! This car holds the road very well on bends, hold (on to) your handbag firmly (agarrar bien el bolso) =/= hold sb to/for ransom (rescate): exigir un rescate por alguien =/= abide by (acatar)/comply with the rule. Heist (golpe, atraco a mano armada). Mr Modi's blushes (rubores, sonrojos, vergüenzas). Japan: looking after 5.7 m. very old people will overwhelm (abrumar, aplastar) the already stretched (forzados, distorsionados) services. They boarded (hospedaban) 40 people. Animosity (=, rencor + hard feeling). I bear you no malice, don't bear any grudge (rencilla); she bears me a grudge (no me perdona) for having her. Filtering goodies (beatucos, golosinas + the --: los buenos) =/= do - gooding (hacedor de buenas obras). Denial: denegación, rechazo → self-denial (abnegación, generosidad) =/= wrapped in a cloak (manto, capa) of selflessness (desinterés + lack of interest). Boardwalk (paseo marítimo entablado). Knick-knacks (chismes, baratijas) such as prayer beads (collares, rosarios). Faned: excitado, abanicado, (llamas) atizadas. Tourists are dazzled (deslumbrados) by the glitz (ostentación) of China's ersatz (sucedáneo). Extortionate (exorbitante, excesivo) prices. Incense joss sticks (varita de incienso, pebete: pasta de perfume). The bank lending is still subdued (suave, apagado). Weasel (pers.: rata, Zool.: comadreja) words: ambages, palabras equívocas. Make a splash (causar sensación). Quizzical (socarrón, burlesco, astuto, sin formalidad). Brazzen (descarada) claim... Retroceso: backward movement. Story: historia/cuento (tell a --), chiste, argumento, artículo, a likely -- (puro cuento). Drink to the health of sb. Executive search (registro, búsqueda, inspección,V) firms. Fall by the wayside: quedarse en agua de borrajas, (pers.) a medio camino. Astounding (asombrosos, pasmosos) claims. Depleted (mermado, agotado, reducido). Nigh (próximo, cercano) → the end is -- + -- on (casi) → it's -- -- finished/impossible. Round: -- tower (t. redonda), (golf) partido, (drink/negociaciones) ronda. Unbearable lightness (ligereza, sencillez; tráfico: fluido). Magpie (urraca). Divide up the cake (repartirse el pastel) =/= pie (pastel de carne, tarta de fruta) → it's easy as pie (es pan comido). Desmentir: (rumor, acusaciones) deny, refute. Deny a charge flatly (rotundamente). Put off (aplazar) pesky/awkward (molestos) pbs. Bear: oso; aguantar, sostener; traer, llevar; devengar intereses. Contradict (llevar la contraria). Economic blemish (mancha, imperfección, estropear) ↔ unblemish (sin mancha). Becalmed (estancado, inmóvil a falta de viento). Forego (go, went, gone): preceder → --ing (precedente) =/= forgo (es, ing, forwent): renunciar a, privarse de. At his behest (petición). Plateau: meseta; estancamiento,V. Stub (colilla, talón de cheque/recibo, tocón) out: (cigarro) apagar. Imperturbable: =, impassive, unruffled (sereno). Hogtied (atados de pies y manos) by old rules. Hog (cerdo, monopolizar) the limelight: acaparar toda la atención =/= gag (amordazar).

Bang: estallido, explosión, golpear, justo, bang in the middle (justo en el medio), -- the drum (anunciar algo a bombo y platillo). Years elapsed (transcurridos, pasados). Quandary (dilema, apuro). Buy cheaply (barato) in more exacting (rigurosos, exigibles) countries. Dismal: (día, pensamiento, lugar) sombrío, (noticias) funestas, (tiempo) malísimo, (rendimiento, condiciones) pésimos. Pick (eligir + choose, Elect.) one new. Graphene usher in (se acomoda en) radios (radiofrecuencias) that do not use radio waves. Demeaning (degradantes) terms. Muddy (llenas de barro, confusas, turbias) outposts (avanzadas) → the shelling (bombardeo) of its --. They are dying in droves (manadas, multitudes, tropeles). Heretics (herejes). Snippets: (papel) recortes, (información) fragmentos. Wistful (pensativo + thoughtful; melancólico + (=); nostálgico). He refused (rechazó) once more/again. Mood swing (cambio de humor). Indulgence (=, tolerancia). Cheer up (animar, alegrar) =/= --less (triste, sombrío). Ironwork (obra de hierro, herraje del mueble). Potted: (historia, versión) resumidas, (comida) en jarras de conserva, (plantas) en tiestos. Snort: resoplido, bufido, (whisky) trago, (cocaína) esnife. The € zone needs shoring up (ser apuntalada) against downturns (deterioros, bajones, empeoramientos). Throwback (salto atrás) → this year's styles are a -- to the twenties. Russia supports Cuba. Assad deems (juzga) IS illegal. Chechnya dispatch (=, envío, expedición,Vs; informe, reportaje). Almost everywhere new turbines are mooted (discutibles + a mooted question). Drawbridge (puente levadizo). Hack off (molestar, mosquear) → cabreado: furious, livid. Severe: (daño, pb.) grave, serio, (tiempos, condiciones) duros, rigurosos, (pers.) severa. IS franchises: (Pol.) ayuda, sufragio, (Com.) concesión + =. Men in suits (trajes) swarmed (pululaban, iban en enjambres) everywhere. Lid (gorro, tapa, párpado) → take the -- off (exponer a la luz pública). Yearn to + inf.: anhelar → he --ed to go back =/= yearns for sth. (añorar): -- -- foreign success.

Australia's north: once a haven for misfits (inadaptados) & fortune-seekers. Islam & punishment: the killing & maiming (el mutilar) will continue. The lift-off (despegue) passed without hitch (obstáculos) =/= given the glitches (fallos técnicos)... → this -- leave people with goggle (mirando sin comprender). Abyss/chasm (abismo). Arrest: (pers.) detención, (cosas) secuestro,V; atraer la atención → arresting (llamativo, fascinante, deslumbrante). Lampoon/satire (sátira,V). Have a nose job (operarse la nariz). Meld (unir, fusionar; mezcla, combinación) & the brainy (inteligentes)... A flair (don, instinto, elegancia) for self–promotion... Curmudgeonly (arisco, cascarrabias). Mr Smith's brittleness (crispación de la voz, lo quebradizo + fragility, frailty). Surprising panache (garbo, gracia). Personality quirks (rarezas + rarity, oddity, peculiarity). Feint/jink (regate en Sp). =/= dodge: (golpe) esquivar, (pb.) soslayar/eludir, (trabajo/ responsabilidad) eludir, rehuir, (impuesto) evadir. Overly (demasiado) fixed ideas =/= overlay (revestir). Informal: (pers.) unreliable, (cena, charla) informal, informal meeting (reunión). The unofficial sector of the economy. Iran devoted (dedicó) resources to Syria & Iraq. Play down (disminuir la importancia) to Iran's antagonism to America. Forgive any debt outright (total, rotundo, franco). Dangle (colgar, dejar colgados; hacer oscilar). Conformarse: be satisfied, accept a fact. Relay: (información) transmitir; relevo → wok in --s. Afterthought (idea adicional, ocurrencia más tarde) → as an -- (por si acaso + just in case). Part: separar (se), abrir (se). Uptick (repunte + recovery, upturn) =/= uptight (tenso, nervioso) ↔ loosen (aflojar) up: entrar en calor, relajarse, desentumecerse. Orderliness (orden, método, disciplina), orderly (ordenado). Slippery slope (terreno resbaladizo). Fractious (irritables, quisquillosas, rebeldes) relations. Coal less deadly (mortal, mortífero) to extract. Winning (ganadoras, encantadoras, cautivadoras) manners (modales, maneras de ser). Disgruntled (descontento, contrariado). Hotly (con pasión, con vehemencia). Gut (visceral, instintiva) hostility. Old mindset (actitud) of full control. Sag: combadura, caída; the --ging (que se hunde) international oil market, --ging breasts (pechos caídos), (tejado, cama) hundirse, (espaldas) encorvarse, (ropa) aflojarse, (precio) disminuir, his spirits --ed. Demerge (dividir, fragmentar + fragment) =/= divided (up): repartió (activos...). The City is a mainstay (sostén principal) of British economy. Grandee (grande, pez gordo), its grandees (grandezas). Rout (aplastar rotundamente, derrota aplastante). Malware (software malicioso). $50 m. to have the attacks called off (cancelados, anulados). Further (más, además..., fomentar, promover) scams (chanchullos + racket, fiddle). Creak (crujido, chirrido,V, poco sólido) → Cuba's --ky revolution. Power grid (red). Inc. (included, incorporated). Step down (renunciar, dimitir). Corral (acorralar) them. A peppy (lleno de vida)... Get a seat on the board (estar metido en la junta directiva). In a flash (en un santiamén). It's a dazzling (deslumbrante, resplandeciente) sight (vista, espectáculo). Heist: golpe, atraco/ robo,Vs + armed robbery, hold-up. A zombie (poder sobrenatural para recuperar un cuerpo muerto; ese mismo cuerpo) programmed to behave as if it was conscious. Tuck (meter; pinza, pliegue,V) → cells tucked below the cerebral cortex. Ineffability ((=, indescriptibilidad). Beneath the outer (exterior) bank of the superhighway (autopista de muchos carriles). Earthwork: trabajo de preparación del terreno, terraplén + embankment. Plot: trazar, fraguar; parcela; complot. Cave (cueva, caverna) system in S. Africa + cave painting (pintura rupestre), cave in (derrumbarse, patrón: ceder). Caveat: advertencia → with the -- that: con la salvedad de que... Despise (despreciar). Scientists slim (delgados; escasos, insuficientes) enough to crave (ansiar, suplicar) crawl into (entrar gateando) + crave (anhelar) <u>for sth</u> (tener antojo de). The specimens (muestras, ejemplares) of the femur have ridges (protuberancias, crestas, cadenas). It fits in (cuadra, encuadra).

It's all up for grabs (está a disposición de cualquiera). Grab bar/rail (barra de apoyo). Underscores (subraya, recalca) a shift in the timeline (calendario, =, de trabajo: schedule). Dug up (arrancados, desenterrados). It is rare to catch (coger, comprender) this transition. Mainland kin (parientes). Stagger (tambaleo, dejar estupefacto)ing: asombroso, sorprendente. Shake up: agitar, conmocionar, espabilar, reorganizar. Chop (cortar) one's way through (abrirse camino con un machete). F. Great of Prussia is buried in a tomb next to his dogs. He got up (cobró) speed. Farrago: =, conjunto de cosas superfluas y mal ordenadas =/= the aristocracy had to forgo (renunciar a, privarse de) the lusts/lecheries (lujurias) that emasculated (castraron, debilitaron) the French nobility. Parade (desfile) ground: plaza de armas. He bullied (intimidó) him. Eventful (lleno de incidentes, azaroso). The geography is jaw-dropping (alucinante). Paved (asfaltado + asphalted). Shanty (chabola) towns that cling to (se pegan a) the slopes (cuestas) above..., the car got stuck (se atascó) on a slope, there is a slope down to the town. He commissioned (=, encargó, puso en servicio; --ed officer) portraits of... The victim encased (encerrada) in car tyres. Lawlessness (anarquía + anarchy). Russia grumpily (tristemente, melancólicamente, sombríamente) cooperated... Enthuse over/about (entusiasmarse por) the technical challenges. He noted drily (secamente)... The country is spineless (débil). Pun (juego de palabras). Plunge a prisoner headfirst into a large water vessel, gripping (sujetando) his twisted leg. Every work can be read as eye-<u>candy (golosina)</u>: como regalo para la vista. It can show froth (espuma,V, banalidad) or fury. Convey: (mercancías) transportar, (corriente) transmitir, (olor) llevar, (gracias) comunicar, (significado) expresar, (Jur.) traspasar, transferir. Preempt (anticiparse a, apoderarse de) its sale =/= prescient (clarividente, profético). It reveals its hidden depths (profundidades). Laughing-stock (hazmerreír). A dismal (deprimente, pésimo) prospect. Wheeler-dealer (chanchullero + fiddler, racketer). Scoff at sb/sth (burlarse de), scoffed (mofado) → his remarks (comentarios) were greeted (recibidas) with –s & jeers (burlas y abucheos). Goblin (duende) → un pueblo con duendes: a magical/enchanting village. Stake (estaca, apuesta) out (marcar con estacas) → -- -- your place early (asegurarle un lugar pronto) + -- -- your position (afianzar su postura) on social policy. He will deport eleven m. Boorishness (groserías) → be coarse/crude (decir groserías). Trip: viaje, visita,V, excursión; zancadilla, tropezón,V + trip up: meter la pata, equivocarse → she tried to trip him up (que se equivocase). Cameron, nonchalantly (despreocupadamente)... He creamed off (separó lo mejor). Rooftop (techo, tejado) → proclaim it from the -- (proclamar a los cuatro vientos). Lap: falda, etapa, (Sp.) vuelta, beber a lengüetazos → the Russian press lapping up (deleitándose con) rumours laden with nationalist longing (nostalgia + de casa/patria: homesickness). A motorway that cuts through (atraviesa) the town. It enjoyed cross-party (entre partidos, multilateral) support. He has a fixation (obsesión) with Islam. Postings (mensajes) on facebook. Lookalike (pers. doble, imitación,V) mainstream parties. Eventful (azaroso). Toothless (ineficaz + ineffectual, ineffective, inefficient). Favoured insiders (empleados de la empresa favorecidos). Mobster (gángster). Chumminess (amiguismo) → a chummy atmosphere (un ambiente de camaradería). Underworld: infierno, infernal, delictivo, mundo del hampa (pícaros que roban). Hearse (carro fúnebre). Areas of municipal authority are vulnerable, including rubbish collection, park management & housing (vivienda). German is hip (al día, al tanto, enterado; cadera). Trustworthy (formal, fiable) =/= thrust: empuje,V, estacada, ofensiva; sacar, clavar)ers: propulsores, dinamizadores. It discomfits/disconcerts (desconcierta) Germans. Officials mutter (murmullo), mutter of voices. He seems blasé (indiferente). Claim (demanda, reclamación → my – for a disability allowance (prestación por invalidez) was rejected) =/= complaint (queja, protesta) → an unjustified --, I'm tired of your --ints =/= (refunfuñar) grumble, grouse, (con rencor) grudge/resentment. Assembly (asamblea, reunión; ensamblaje). Pull off: quitar, arrancar; (plan, acuerdo) llevar a cabo =/= America should pull back: tirar hacia sí, (Mil.) retirarse, (enemigo) rechazar, (amenazas) apartar; aplazar, ponerse a distancia). Edging up (subir poco a poco) a mountain path. It mollifies (aplaca, apacigua) the other party. Palatable (apetitoso + appetizing). Throwing a ball about (jugando con una pelota); throwing one's arms about (agitar mucho los brazos). Infighting (lucha interna, intestina) → political -- (peleas políticas). Music journalism follows suit (sigue el ejemplo). Avoid adverts (advertisements); advert to (aludir a + allude to, refer to). Elusive (esquivo, insociable...). Readership (número de lectores) → a wide/large --. Give out: distribuir, anunciar → it was given -- that; repartir, emitir, (energía, paciencia) agotarse → my legs gave out. Apply it thus (así, de este modo), I was only 16, thus unable to vote. In the flower of one'syouth. He profess (manifesta, declara) to dislike. Miff (disgustar, ofender + offend) → they feel miffed about the free distribution. A city teemed with (abundante en) life. The gabble (balbuceo, murmullo) of middle-aged couples. Disparage (menospreciar + scorn, despise) the museum. Brave (aguantar) the storm (tormenta), take a town by -- (asalto). Vociferar (yell, shout). So it is in labour at large (en general) =/= if he were still at large (andase suelto), would he... Propel (propulsar) sb. toward disaster. Ideological clashes (estruendos, choques, disconformidades) that burn in his mind. Spurn (rechaza) displays (exposiciones, demostraciones) of sincerity. Sardonicism (=, burla), everyone's jokes (burla de todos). Royal (real, espléndido, personaje real) the royals (la realeza). Voters have outgrown (crecido más que)... =/= overheads (gastos generales) =/= overdue (atrasado, vencido y no pagado) =/= the Scottish effect was overdone: (papel/ drama) exagerado, (culinario) recocido =/= override (anular, cancelar, invalidar, hacer caso omiso de) + overriding: primordial, prioritario, preponderante, (cláusula) derogatoria. Bemused: perplejo, desconcertado, aturdido. Straight out: directamente, sin rodeos. Morsel (bocado, pedazo) of hope. Upwardly mobile: pers. ambiciosa, =, de movilidad social ascendente. That pile (montón, dineral) has cushioned (amortiguado) against serious fallouts (lluvia radioactiva, secuelas). Fears of sustained depression (=, recesión). Upper-management (los altos cargos administrativos). Properties (inmuebles) at the upper end (sección más cara) of the market. Persons in the upper income bracket (nivel de ingresos superiores). The upper Nile/chamber/house/classes/Egypt/jaw/lip. Decimating (aniquilando, causando la muerte) & exhausting (agotando) Islamist opponents. Exhaust o.s. (agotarse). Relapse (recaída: -- into bad habits). A public rebuke (reproche). Kosher (autorizados) devices (aparatos, dispositivos). New bout (ataque, asalto, racha) of protectionism. Munched (masticado) merrily (felizmente). On the sly (astuto, pícaro, travieso): a escondidas + secretly, by stealth. Tuck (pliegue → put a -- in a skirt), V) away: ocultar, zamparse. Abridged (resumidos, compendiados) → un-- (íntegros). Unintended (involuntarias) consequences. Demise (muerte, desaparición; transferir en arrendamiento: the –ed premises (el inmueble arrendado). Bombastic (=, grandilocuente) ideology ↔ mild (moderado, suave, dulce, afable) → -- mannered (apacible, afable, de modales suaves). A bounty (generosidad, recompensa) of $ 8 m. on his head. He tosses (lanza al, sacude al) congress a challenge. Apagar: turn/switch off, (ira) appease, (incendio) put out, stinguish, (sed) quench. Beset (acosado) by dismal (pésimos, deprimentes) economic data. Single-figure (< de 10%) approval ratings. Play hardball (mostrarse implacable). He was shaking (sacudía para que hiciesen algo...) legislators into making hard decisions rather than simply blocking... Reinstate a tax that would have brought $ 80 m. Parish (parroquia)ioner: feligrés. Unrepentant (impenitente). Canadian indigenous faiths (fes, creencias) use sage (sabio, Bot.: salvia) in their rites. Brown<u>outs</u> (voltios: oscilaciones) & power cuts. Chemo (químico)therapia. A long haul (un buen trecho). Bump into (chocar contra). How long the devices would stick around (quedarse) =/= joystick (Aviac.: palanca de mando; Electr. y Comp.: mando). Scroll (rollo, pergamino + parchment) → the Dead sea --s (los Manuscritos); -- up & down: hacer avanzar/retroceder el texto de la pantalla; --ing (desplazamiento). With some utilities in all–to-often overcast (cielo nublado) Britain has limited the amount of solar electricity which can be fed into the grid (red). Propeller (hélice) with a flapping (que aletea, que se agita) fin (ala). Getting the craft (destreza) to ride up (subirse) onto the hydrofoil (hidroala, hidrodeslizador). Gusty (borrascosos) winds. Render useless (inútil) the device. Distinctive (característico) feature (rasgo). The operation was code-named (dado nombre clave) Alberta. Covert (furtivo, secreto, encubierto) weapon. Impair (afectar, dañar) efforts to detect... Fiend (diablo, desalmado, malvado) ishly (terriblemente, diabólicamente) difficult; drugs fiend (maníaco), sex fiend. Grapadora: staple<u>r</u> =/= staple: grapa,V; asunto principal, prod. de 1ª necesidad =/= top-notch (corte, muesca): de primerísima calidad. A company spun out (alargada) by a furniture maker. Temper (carácter, genio): she's got such a temper! (¡Menudo genio tiene!), be in a -- (estar furioso), keep one's -- (no perder la calma), a quick --ed woman (que tiene genio), be bad --ed ↔ be good --ed. Truco: trick, gimmick → advertisement -- + get the knack (coger el truco). The fuel nozzle (boquilla, pulverizador, inyector) will be 25% lighter & should last five times longer. Put forward: proponer, presentar, (reloj) adelantar =/= put back: volver a poner, reloj/proyecto: retrasar. Be secretive (reservado) about... Contest (contienda, concurso) → beauty --; rebatir: I -- your right to... That clock gains two minutes a day, Widespreaded (generalizada) adoption. Quizz: interrogar, (TV...) concurso. Cebar: fatten (up) animals; get/grow fat (engordar). Feeder: (Mec.) alimentador, (Geog.) afluente. Jet propulsion (a reacción). Dairy farming (industria láctea). Moo (mugido,V). Outside the birthing (centro de partos) barn. As cows step onto a slow-motion merry-go-round (caballitos). It runs through sieves (cribas, tamices) to capture the long fibres. Lavish (suntuoso, generoso, espléndido) gifts. Terco/obstinado: obstinate, stubborn, tenacious, dogged. Military spat (riña,V, disputa). Resumption (reanudación) of the sitting (turno, sesión). Political posturing (pose, fingimiento). Broach (abordar, mencionar, espitar) it implies... Pointless (inútil) workaholism (trabajo adicto). Ordeal (terrible experiencia). Dish out: (comida) servir, (dinero) repartir, (consejo) dar. Pomp (pompa, fausto + pageantry) → -- & circumstance (y solemnidad) =/= bomb (bomba de guerra) =/= pumb (bomba para fluidos, bombear, surtidor de gasolina). It's not up to me (no es cosa mía) whether you... China gets along (se las arregla) with its neighbours. He worries about losing out (salir perdiendo). Urging Russian companies not to bedependent on western ones. Shoot down a hostile missile after take-off. The bloated (hinchado) civil service. Replace those they fear... Driverless future. A model whom he married while in office. Driving (abriendo) wedge (cuña, brecha) between Muslims. Russian companies are casting about/around for (buscan) =/= cast out (expulsar). Raise funds/collect taxes. Keep/break a promise/a vow → lovers' vow (promesas solemnes de los enamorados). Vow of poverty, of chastity. Overconfident (con exceso de confianza). File/bring a suit (pleito) against sb.: demandar alguien en justicia. Judging & ruling in his favour... Failure: the plan is doomed to end in -- (fracaso), -- (quiebras) rate, engine (mecánico) failure (fallo) =/= the award (premio, fallo) was enforced (impuesto, Jur.: ejecutado). I worked it out in my head (lo calculé mentalmente), I worked out a plan (idea). Firms with huge (enorme, inmensa) valuation (valoración) & hardly any staff. The point was duly (debidamente) noted in the minutes (acta, minuta). It turned out that (resultó que)... A budget commensurate with (según, que se corresponde con) their ambitions. He prepares to stand down (dimitir + resign). Keen (entusiasta, aplicado + enthusiastic) photographer. A plea (súplica) for mercy (clemencia, =, Jur.: leniency (indulgencia). Hint (indicación, alusión, indirecta...) → broad (inconfundible) --. Emphasis on teamwork (en trabajo de equipo). Log: leño, logaritmo, anotar, registrar. A backlog (atraso, pedidos pendientes) of aircraft is worth $1 trillion. Don't make me laugh, burst out laughing. Burst out of the room (salir de la habitación rápidamente). There is so much work to do, I've so much to do, <u>so many/such a lot of</u> tourists. You were very assertive (firme y enérgico). Not so confident (confianza en sí mismo) as he looks. We must be getting out (tenemos que salir) → get on with your work, please! We can get away (nos bastará) with just repainting it. It would be inappropriate (=, inoportuno) to complain. When oil prices drop America pulls back (se retira) from shale. His conviction (=, condena) that the Jewish rabble (gentío) had deceived (engañado) into betraying him. He has conjoined (unido) Taiwan's Ec. ever closer to China in 2015. China: innovative private entrepreneurs are suffocated (asfixiados) losing out (perdiendo) to state enterprises. Blatant (flagrante, ostensible) attempts. Russian firms are casting (buscando) elsewhere for new customers to replace those they fear losing from the West. Make traffic flow more smoothly & safely. Go down in <u>hi</u>story as (pasar a la historia como)..., know the inner history (secreto, historial) of an affair =/= <u>s</u>tory (cuento, relato...) → another -- (cantar), it's a long -- (es largo de contar), the -- goes that (se dice que), tell --s (contar embustes). You can depend on me (cuente conmigo), he depends on her for everything, your success depends on how... The tones of the painting. Meet (encontrar...): -- for lunch, --

her in downtown (centro), I'll -- you outside (a la puerta de) the cinema. In easy (fáciles de superar) stages (etapas). Make rapid progress (quemar etapas). Development in stages (gradualmente). A phased (gradual) takeover (adquisición). Up there (allí arriba), in the freezer. Higher up (más arriba). The people three floors up. Halfway there (a medio camino), halfway up/down (a media cuesta subiendo/bajando). Up in the mountain (monte arriba), the jug (jarra)'s up there. We are up at 7. At what time you will be up? At any rate (en cualquier caso), while you are up (puesto que estás de pie)..., so that (para que)... Forever (para siempre). By any means (de cualquier manera), by these means (medios) to do it. It's worth reading/effort/having (tenerlo)/mentioning that... Something like (algo así como)... Handy: a flashlight (linterna) -- (a mano) in case of power cuts, the shops are very -- (cerca) here, it's quite -- (nos va bastante bien) that he can't come, the money came -- (vino bien) to... Get mixed up (confundirse); be mixed up (estar hecho un lío). Little impact on events in either Hong Kong & Taiwan. Give in (ceder, rendirse; entregar, presentar). Deal with (tratar con). Provided that (siempre que). Wrap up (envolver, poner punto final); -- - (cerrar) a deal. For the time being (por ahora). Sit up (ponerse derecho, incorporarse + join). Aside from (aparte de). Keep up with: mantenerse con (el ritmo...). At all costs (a toda costa), at least (al menos). It doesn't make any sense (no tiene sentido). Kick out (echar a patadas). At best (en el mejor de los casos), at length (detenidamente). It's a good thing! (¡Menos mal! + just as well!). I guess so (supongo que sí). Leave out (omitir, =). He pulled springs (recurrió a enchufes) to do it. It's not worth it (no vale la pena). Drop out (darse de baja). Lay down (tumbarse), look into (investigar). Tie loose ends (atar cabos sueltos). Call for: (cuenta, auxilio) pedir, (acción) exigir, (pers.) ir a buscar. To a certain extent (punto). In any event (en cualquier caso). In short (en resumidas cuentas). Get ahead (salir adelante). You will get over it (ya lo superarás). Get used to the new regime. Alike: think/dress -- (parecido), they are very --, you are all --, they all look -- to me (me parecen iguales). Terms of trade (condiciones de transacción). Be in good terms with sb, in real terms incomes have fallen. Be as solid (firme) as a rock (roca). He blew his top (se le fundieron los plomos). Down from 70% a year earlier ←→ down to 38º. Putting taxes up by half a percentage point. Crime has fallen as far in NY as in the rest of América; the fallen (los caídos). The line will extend (=, alargar) by one fifth compared with its current length. The production was down by 20% in a decade. Home (domicilio) of 5 billions of $ worth of fine art (bellas artes). After Argentina's economic crash in 2001, the ranks (=, ºs, filas) of informal workers grew along with (junto a) those of unemployment. He revealed how we would like to conduct elections. She lay spread out (estaba tendida) on the floor. Float away/off: ir a la deriva, irse volando en el aire. Wormhole (agujero de gusano/polilla). Embaucador: (estafador) trickster, (impostor) swindler, (farsante) humbug. Plonk: (dejar caer) → to -- o.s. down, she --ed herself down on the sofa, it fell -- onto the floor: cayó ¡Plaf! (al suelo). The artists demur (objetan, ponen reparos), they mock (mofan) Japanese mothers. Let off: perdonar (anyone acused), hacer explotar, (soltar) steam, dejar salir (let the children off). Bar: -- (association): colegio de abogados, the -- (la abogacía)...; -- of soap/chocolate; mostrador, atrancar puertas o ventanas; barra, (fútbol) larguero. Picking (recolección + harvesting)s: ganancias, sobras de alimento. The rain flooded (inundó) the countryside/the market with products + swamped with offers/work/applications... Illegal logging (explotación forestal) + the loggers (leñadores) were nailed (agarrados). The soldiers raided (asaltaron) & swooped (hicieron una redada, bajaron en picada) upon...; in/at one fell swoop (de un solo golpe/de una vez). China is more amenable (dócil, flexible, responsable). A ham (jamón, cómico) actor libbing (liberando) his way. Disturbed/unhinged (trastornado mental). Jerk (sacudida, dar un tirón; imbécil) back into autocracy. Escrúpulos: scruple → no -- about saying it. Brass (mandamases) fanfare (fanfarria): jactancia de los jefazos. Black tie dinner (cena de etiqueta). Eye-catching (llamativo). Do piecework (trabajar a destajo). The cost & hassle (molestar, lío, pb.) of preparing regular meals. Upgrade: cuesta arriba, actualización, mejora. Contractor (contratista). Poster (póster, afiche, cartel) → poster - child: icono (=), poster - girl/boy... Moving containers around (de un sitio a otro) between them (entre ellos). Add-on (accesorio, dispositivo adicional) of various sorts. Spreadsheet (hoja electrónica de cálculo) for big piles of data. China's e-commerce giants (Alibaba, Tencent) provide smaller firms with low-cost launching pad (almohadilla, plataforma). The World trade is becalmed (estancado). Keel (quilla) → solidity of a bank: amount of money it can afford to lose without keeling over (volcar, derrumbarse). Gut: intestino, panza, tripa, testículo → he's balls & guts (es un tío con cojones); limpiar, vaciar, destripar, destruir el interior. Basel IV: a big & intemperate (inmaduro, excesivo, bebe en exceso) change in the rules of banking & an underhanded (turbio, poco limpio) way of forcing them to raise (movilizar) yet more capital. Regulators' attempt to reduce complexity & weed out (arrancar, suprimir) wilfully/on purpose (adrede) distorted risks weightings (ponderaciones, primas) → London --: plus salarial por vivir en L.) are welcome. Foolproof (infalible, sencillo de manejar). Incentives (=, estímulos). The lot (todo), improve their lot (destino, suerte). Piecemeal (poco a poco, poco sistemático) → a -- (de compromiso) solution. Mad-looking (aspecto), strange (raro) looking. In-flight (de a bordo) emissions, meal, movie... We are cruising (navegando) at an altitude of... Crafty (astuto, hábil), foxy (astuto/a + mujer sexy). Faster-acting materials can seal (foca; sello; cerrar, tapar) holes in any emergency. Be on display (expuestos). Come into being (nacer), bring into being (llevar a cabo + carry out). Holey (lleno de agujeros) veil. Drape: (cubrir, colocar) → they draped a flag over the tomb; he draped his legs over the chair. Vault: bóveda; panteón, cripta, sótano → wine --/wine cellar (bodega); saltar → -- over the fence (valla, cerca). Puckered: (labios, cejas) fruncidos, (piel) arrugada. Daylight-saving time (horario de verano). Repossessions (recuperaciones de artículos no pagados) =/= (Ec., salud) recovery. Linger (rezagarse, persistir, durar; sobrevivir, tardar en morir) long on issues of mortality. Poke: empujar, remover, introducir; atizar, pinchar → Roosevelt enjoyed poking fun at (se reía de) Churchill, while Stalin chain-smoked (fumaba empedernidamente) & doodled (garabateaba) wolves heads. Rum (ron, extraño/raro + rare) collection of arguments, some of them arcane (ocultos, misteriosos; reservados) in the most ludicrous (ridículas) navel-<u>gazing (mirándose)</u> traditions. Plagiar (plagiarize, copy, pirate). Vignettes (dibujos de portada). Warping (alabeo: torcer; urdimbre: urdir antes del telar) machines are creating spider webs (telarañas, Comp.: araña) of yarn (hilo de lana; (historias: inventar). The seam (costura)stresses (costureras). Chinese firms are mere copycats (imitadoras) that cannot innovate. Onset (aparición, comienzo) of the slowdown (Ec.: relentización). At first blush (a primera vista) this model has run out of steam (quedado sin fuerza). The stirrup: en saddle (montura): estribo. The clockwork (de relojería) mechanism. Oddball (raro, excéntrico + eccentric). Brainchild (creación, invento + =). Valuations have been bid up (ofrecido/pujado más) by competition. Accolade (honor, premio, galardón, elogio). Powerhouse (central eléctrica, centro neurálgico). Some may grow tired of bling (i, i, i) (en modas: adornarse con joyas, vestidos... muy llamativos y caros) offerings. Scrabble (escarbar) in the dust (tierra) for the coins, -- frantically (desesperadamente) for a foothold (donde poner el pie), -- about (buscar) in the dark looking for the key. Tight spot/corner (situación apurada). Delantera: (Sp.) forward line; take over the lead from sb, be in the lead. Pests are on the move (de un lado para otro). Uncompensated (no indemnizado). The European Union is groping (tanteando, andando a tientas) towards... He alighted (encendió, se apeó) on (caer en la cuenta de) a new tactic; set sth alight (prender fuego a algo), be alight (estar ardiendo). The easterners saw off (vencieron, despidieron, acabaron con) an attempt... Nay (no) → the naysayers (los que dicen lo contrario) will struggle to muster (reunir) the votes needed to block it. She roasted (asó) an ox. Four hallmarks (contrastes, sellos) of the era stand out (sobresalen). Sludge (lodo, residuo) that filled the water ways (vías fluviales). The hankering (anhelo, añoranza) after more of a say + have one's say: dar una opinión + have a say: tener voz y voto). The city that greeted (saludó, recibió) her. Hacking/piracy (piratería informática), at which China excels (destaca, supera) is one of the main threats to America. Recall (recordar, retirar) cars ignition-switch (interruptor) defect. Muck (suciedad)y: sucio. Prospects of shut (down). The holdout (resistencia, negación) to negotiate/in trying.... Caseload: nº de encargos asignados a un profesional. Hew, hewed, hewed/hewn: (carbón) extraer, (árboles) talar. Demeaning (degradante), demeaned women. Hardcore (incondicional, duro) porno. It starts with vanilla (=, estándar) fare (tarifa, precio) & clung (se pegó, se aferró) through the more outré (extravagante) stuff. Naked (desnudo, visible; patente, manifiesto) capitalism. Brim (borde), brim over (rebosar, desbordarse), brim with (rebosar de) potential... Gloat over sth. (regocijarse/recrearse en algo + enjoy o.s.). They moved into its plain (evidente, claro, franco) lookalike (imitación, doble) homes to man (tripular, hacer funcionar) its state-owned textile mills. It blends (mezcla, armoniza, combina) ersatz (sucedánea, reemplazante) European architecture. Drones to scout (explorar, escuchar, buscar, reconocer,Vs) houses to burgle (robar casas). Snatched (agarraba, arrebataba) breath (aliento, soplo) samples from sprouting (emanaciones) of whales for DNA (Desoxyribonucleic acid) analysis. Canopy (toldo) → A canopy (manto) of leaves. Hover: (pájaro) planear, (pers.) rondar) in a way that gulls (gaviotas) & other soaring (planeadores; precios, esperanzas...: en alza) birds do. The space will be abuzz (ocupado + engaged, busy) with machines → the whole office was -- with the news (toda la oficina comentaba la noticia). A drone keeps itself airborne (volando en el aire). The global movement from which IS emerges as a sprawling (espatarrado, crecimiento rápido) extended family. Cowards flinch (se estremecen, se inmutan...) & traitors sneer (desprecian + expresión desdeñosa)... Infamia: infamy; infame: loathsome, despicable, horrible; the loathing (odio) I felt for him, the -- of Westminster that he represents. Dour (adusto, arisco) → a -- (muy reñida) struggle (batalla). The quip (ocurrencia + witty, funny, remark; bromear) by G. Brown =/= crazy idea. China, the locomotive to which many are still hitched (atados). That saps (mina, debilita) the domestic economy. In Mexico, where tacos (tortillas) sizzle (chisporrotean al freírse, chispa) alongside every bus stop. Drug-related crimes stalk (acechan, tallo) Mexico's scruffy (destartalado, descuidado) barrios (areas, districts). Push on (continuar) to (hasta) our country. Momentum (=, impulso, ímpetu). Snazzy (elegante, vistoso) car... =/= snappy: irascible, brusco; alegre, vivaz, elegante =/= punchy: (artículo) incisivo, (campaña) con garra, (nº musical) brioso =/= zippy: estilo vigoroso, coche brioso/veloz. Clusters: (edificios, casas) grupos, plátanos (racimo), (estrellas) grupo, (plantas) macizo; apiñarse, agruparse =/= clump: grupo de árboles, macizo de flores, terrón de tierra, amontonar. Pisada: footstep + footprint (huella). The din (estruendo, alboroto) of the streets. Inimical (adverso, hostil) to those ideas. Hopper (tolva), grasshoppers (saltamontes). Razor wire (alambrada de seguridad). Sealed off (cerrado) behind his Iron curtain. Power stations would mar (estropear, echar a perder) unique (excepcionales) landscapes. Slippage (deslizamiento, patinaje, (schedule) bajón → the -- seems inevitable. Unresponsive (insensible, indiferente) =/= irresponsible. Steep: (escarpadas, poco accesibles) terraces. Beam: viga, (láser) rayo; emitir, brillar, sonreír) → a middle-aged widow beams under an orange head cloth. The people slurped (sorbía ruidosamente) coffee. Not to mention... (y no digamos ya...). They are not ripped off (estafados) by the first buyer to show up (que aparece). He tops (cubre) his billowy (ondeante) white *boubou*, the traditional menswear (ropa de caballeros), the turban (=). He scoffed (se zampaba, se mofaba)... Prepared for the pilgrimage, which Koran enjoins (impone, exige) every believer who can afford it to perform at least once in a lifetime. Bereft (despojado) → be -- of (desprovisto de). He excites more hoopla (bombo y platillo) than is the looming (inminente, que amenaza) prospect (perspectiva) of Pope Francis. It brought into focus (enfocó) the wearsome (aburrido + boring, tedious) degree to which the church main split (it, it, it) has become a proxy (poder, apoderado, representante) for America's wider political brawl (pelea) =/= poxy (puñetero) =/= pox (sífilis), smallpox (viruela). Pope's every utterance (expresión, declaración, palabra). Admirers called J. Serra a champion of the underdogs (los más débiles, desvalidos) who denounced Spanish troops for raping Indian women. Revered (venerado) by some. A bountiful (generosa) source of product. A painted sign from the 1960s welcomed visitors, where trod (pisaron) the daring (atrevido) redskin (un piel roja) spirited Mexican. Alegre: (carácter) happy, cheerful, be in a good mood; (fiesta, música) lively; merry; (por el alcohol) tipsy; (color) bright. Deserters were hunted down (cazados) & beaten or chained. That fight will outlast (sobrevivir) his canonization. He sorrowed (se afligía) over excess, but supported flogging (flagelación), which he likened (comparaba, =) to stern (severa) parental discipline. Rust belt (cinturón industrial): the drug epidemic is ravaging (asolando, saqueando) the once idyllic communities. Illinois is lagging behind in efforts to fight it. It is the least equipped state in the Midwest. War-path (estar en pie de guerra, en búsqueda de camorra). Brazil's sagging (hundida, floja) economy. Canada: after years of abstaining, aboriginal people could be swing (basculantes, que balancean) voters. Pipe (tubería, flauta,V, canalizar con tuberías). Outvote: (partido, pers.) vencer en las votaciones ↔ be --ed. Mistrust (desconfianza). Middling (regular, mediano) net contributor. Blasting (mina: voladura). Loiter (perder el tiempo, rezagarse) → don't -- (no te entretengas) on the way! Inward-looking: (pers.) introvertida, (empresa, país) cerrados en sí mismos. He is waking up (despertándose). Stewardship (administración + management). Premiership (1ª división en fútbol, puesto de primer ministro). Tamp (down): (tabaco) apretar, (tierra) aplastar. Play down (minimizar, disminuir la importancia). Crack troops (tropas de primera). Seaborne (transporte marítimo) trade. Stand-alone: (autónomo, independiente). Retrieve (datos: recuperar; joyas, muebles: rescatar) data. Have one's head on the cloud (estar en las nubes). Ease (aliviar, relajar) China's curbs (frenos, restricciones) on internal migration. Rubbish-strewn (esparcida) beach. Ghastly (horrorosa) scene + how --! (¡Qué horror!). Expelled (expulsados) immigrants. A wide ranging (una gran variedad) of bilateral agreements. Pamper (mimar, consentir). Burner (quemador) → Crimea is in the back -- (pospuesta, dejada para más tarde) diplomacy. Well-heeled (ricacho + rich guy/woman). He noted approvingly (con aprobación)... Douse: mojar con agua; fuego: apagar → the EU doused the Greek fire, though the embers (brasas) still glow (brillan) + glowing: brillante, (pers.) rebosante, (descripción) entusiasta. Ejercer: practise, exert, exercise → he no longer practises. Plug (llenar, tapar) the current account gap. Inherited land & tenures (posesiones, ocupaciones, puestos de trabajo asegurados). Ministers pillory (ridiculizan + deride) them. Constabulary (policía). Without demur (objeción). Receipt (recibo, poner el sello de pagado); the --s (ingresos) frittered (away) (malgastados, derrochados) on middle-class giveaways (regalos). The committee crushed (estrujó, aplastó) a proposal. At checkpoints (puntos de control). Spread dissent (sembrar la discordia), dissenters (disidentes). Phoney (farsante, falso + false) communism frets (preocupa) about it. He cut a dash (destaca, llama la atención). Banking funding may be squeezed (recortado, restringido). A prank (de broma) call → play (gastar) a --. Sloppy (aguadas, desaliñadas, descuidadas) assumptions =/= snooty (presumida, altanera) rejection =/= have a snooze (echar una cabezada/siestecita). That idea tallied (concordaba) with observations that in aggregate (conjunto, total) consumption looked smoother (más flúida...) than income. Ambicioso: =, (over)ambitious, self-seeking, enterprising, careerist). Poke: (fuego: atizar; pegar; asomar: the shoots (brotes) -- out of the soil) → sell sb a pig in a poke (dar gato por liebre). A baboon (babuino) heart as a stopgap (recurso, provisión) until a human donor... Tawdriness (chabacanería + vulgarity). Crap: estupideces (talk --s); mierda (the film is a --); gilipollas + jerk). Corporate tax avoidance (evitar). Enliven (animar). Deepen (incrementar, agudizar, intensificar, profundizar). The likes (los semejantes). Vividly (vivamente). Dumb (mudo, bobo) → as -- as an ox (más bruto que un arado), dumbed down (embrutecido, empobrecido intelectualmente). A flair (don, instinto, estilo) for improvisation. AIDS (Acquired Immune Deficiency Syndrome) carries off (mata, se lleva por delante) fits (sanos), young & adults. Merkel faces a <u>backlash</u> (reacción violenta) on asylum seekers =/= we are not getting much <u>feedback</u> (reacción, respuesta, realimentación): no nos tienen demasiado informados; in England of two m. people eligible to give feedback on devolution only a hundred replied =/= our democracy is <u>backsliding</u> (reincidente, de recaída). The process power is crumbling (se desmigaja, se desmorona).

Endorse (=, aprobar, respaldar) powers the executive has awarded himself. By stealth (sigilosamente, a urtadillas). In a nail-biting (angustiada, emocionadísima) election. The Government grappled with (confronta un pb. de...) law enforcement. Drape (cubrir, poner sobre) =/= a drab (color apagado/soso, vía monótona) office block which is home of hundreds of multinational companies. Inflow (afluencia, entrada). A shake-out (reestructuración) is hitting debt-strapped (correa, azote, V) shale producers. The Almeida theater shakes up (agita, conmociona; reorganiza) the Classics. Sixty percent of the world's output lie (está en reposo, se encuentra...) within a de facto $ zone. The system that the Dollar anchors (ancla, afianza, sujeta) is cracking (agrieta) + get --ing (ponerse manos a la obra). China has balked (at) (se plantó) helping... Putin blamed America for unsettling (desetabilizar) the Middle East. Clear (despejar) the area of IS. Redeemed (redimido). Trudeau is impulsive & doesn't like the scripted (aceptar guiones/lo preparado de antemano). The lead-up (período previo, pre- campaña). Stewart: robusto, fuerte de espíritu, (creencia) empedernido. Holmes's sidekick (secuaz, compañero). Nitty-gritty (lo esencial, el meollo) → get down to the -- -- (ir al grano, a lo esencial). Biome (biomedio). Brand (tildar) sb (as) a racist. It was scrubbed clean (fregado hasta que quedó limpio). Run of good luck (buena racha) ←→ -- of bad luck. Dry-up (desecar, deshidratar). Frozen (congelado) soil. This seemed wax & wane (crecer y decrecer) with martian seasons. The walls of certain martian craters. The latest research bolsters (refuerza; moral: levanta). Salmuera: brine =/= pickle (encurtidos, escabeche). Rough & ready: improvisado + improvised. Clinging (pegándose) on dwindling (menguantes) pockets of dampness (humedad). It has two revers (solapas) trundling (avanzando lentamente, empujando) around the surface of... To-do (lío, follón) history → make a to – do about sth (armar un lío). Disown (desconocer, repudiar, negar). Scathing (mordaz, feroz) scepticism. Spew (arrojar, vomitar) fire & brimstone (azufre + sulfur). Laughable (irrisorio). Meaty (carnoso, sustancioso). Seedbed/nursery (semillero) + (semillero de delincuencia: hotbed/breeding ground → --/-- -- for crime). Protagonista: star, main figure, hose who played a central/leading role. Glitter (brillo,V)ati: celebridad del mundo literario y artístico. 100 mile trek (caminata,V). Hit-or-miss (al azar + at random, by chance). It's my turn to pay. It's not up to me (no depende de mí), everything depends on you, will you come? It depends, if it were up to me... That rings a bell (eso me suena). Cashpoint (cajero automático). Molluscs branched off (se desviaron) to form... + -- - to the left. Batter (bateador en cricket, mezcla para rebozar. Alien (extraños, extranjeros) planets. A tasty morsel (pedazo, comida: bocado). The city became eponymous (toma el nombre) of his ideas. Monument, war memorial (monumento a los caídos) + monument to the unknown soldier. Op-Eds (page): opposite (enfrente) -editorial → página de tribuna → The -- - -- decried (criticó, menospreció) German bull headedness (terquedad). En el Mall (en Washington): American front (fachada, parte delantera) yard (patio, jardín)... Surfeit (exceso) of media. Data collection. Intimidad: (amistad) intimacy, familiarity, (en privado) privacy. Toddler (niño que empieza a andar) =/= tiddler (pececillo, renacuajo) =/= minnow (pequeño pez de agua dulce). As a feat (hazaña) of brawn (fuerza muscular) is impressive (impresionante), he's all -- & no brain. Hand-picked (muy seleccionado) speaker. Fate (destino, suerte)d: predestinado, condenado → it was -- (inevitable) that... → fateful (fatídico + ominous). The dreamboat (bombón, sueño) next door. Summon: llamar, convocar, (ayuda) pedir, (justicia) citar. Comfy (cómodas) chairs. Colmillo: (pers., perro) fang, (elefante, morsa, jabalí) tusk =/= trunk (tronco, trompa de elefante; baúl, maletero). Ordenado: tidy, (oficina) well - organized) ↔ unravelling (desordenado + untidy, messy). Miscreant (sinvergüenza, ruín

\+ rotten, brazen, rogue, shameless, scoundrel). Flash: destello, arrebato de ira..., in a -- (instante), ráfaga (of inspiration), enfoque de luz. Newsflash (noticias de última hora). Offbeat (excéntrico, original) investment. The Arab spring unleashed (soltó, desató, desencadenó) more than hopes for change. Rumble (ruido sordo/de tripas) →your stomach's --ing; estruendo, retumbar, murmullo → a -- of disapproval. The spate (serie, avalancha) of tragedies. Desdeñoso/despectivo (scornful, disdainful). Retrenchment (recorte/racionalización de gastos) of army-backed rule in Egypt. Un<u>abashedly (tímidamente, avergonzadamente)</u>: descaradamente. Refugees & dropouts (marginados). Flit (revolotear) in/out: entrar/salir, --ting (mudanza) between A & B. Omar's eye: he was said to have extracted the remains (restos) himself & stitched (cosió) the wound. Brilliant marksman (tirador + shooter). The 2008 miasma (=, efluvio (emanación) maligno que exhalan los cuerpos enfermos, las materias corruptas...). His piety (=, devoción, beatería) was not learned or bookish (libresco). Unseen (oculto, inadvertido) & unknown haunted (rondó, apareció, frecuentó; obsesionó) the scene. Browbeat/threat (intimidar + =). Global market rout (desbandada, fuga desordenada; derrota aplastante,Vs); vencer de forma aplastante). Give sb a drubbing (paliza). The chug (motor: resoplar)ing (ir tirando resoplando) at 7% provokes (=, suscita) derison (mofa). Stunned (atontados, aturdidos) investors. Be on the tenterhooks (ascuas: inquieto, sobresaltado). The official data is iffy (dudoso, incierto). Taper (afilar, estrechar) → the stick --s to a point (el palo termina en punta). She had a tantrum (le dio un berrinche). Scoop: (harina) pala, (crema) cucharón, (diario) exclusiva, (Com.) ganar un dineral, (beneficio) sacar; recoger. Drag (arrastrar) down (arrastrar, debilitar, hacer fracasar) → you are not going to drag me down with you (cargar con las consecuencias), drag down the entire party; be --ged down (arrastrado) to your level. Contrive (inventar, idear) arrangements. Artimaña: trick, (caza) trap, (ingenio) cunning. Puzzle (rompecabezas) → puzzling (=, desconcertante) weakness of manufacturing; puzzled (perplejo). Stamp out (erradicar) corruption. Drifter (vagabundo + =, wandering, vagrant). Mock (mofa, fingir) campaign placards (carteles, letreros). Tufts (pelo: mecha; hierba: mata) of grass... Mull over (meditar, reflexionar sobre) new rules. Campaigners (partidarios) → environment -- (defensores). Trestle (caballete + (de arte) easel =/= adulterous trysts (citas) → trysting place. Compliant (sumisas) courts, compliance (sumisión, conformidad). Shortchange (no dar % del cambio, defraudar, tratar mal un proyecto) governments through artful (astuto) use of loopholes in national levels. Chunned (evitó, impidió) to give them a try (probarlos, darles una oportunidad). Dip: baño/sumergir, chapuzón; bajada de precios; pendiente/inclinación/bajar en pendiente, depresión, baño de desinfección de animales; a -- in the stream of consciousness. They are venting (desahogando, descargando) their fury → be in a fury, she blew (se puso) into a fury. Her underlings (subordinados, subalternos). Spy (espía) → spy story (novela de espionaje), spy out (hacer un reconocimiento de) the land; attempts to slip (pasar desapercibido de) the spyware (espía de software). Power outages (apagones). Wheelbarrows (carretillas) to the rescue (rescate). Bane: ruina → foxes are the -- of farmers, baneful (nefasto, funesto); nefasto: ill-fated, unlucky, unfortunate, pernicious, harmful; funesto: ill-fated, fatal, disastrous, baneful. Meneo: (cola) wag, (cabeza) shake, (líquido) stir, (caderas) swing, (sacudida) jerk, jolt. Curl: bucle, (pelo) rizo, (humo) espiral, (papel) ondularse, (leaf) abarquillar, (waves) encresparse → he --ed his lip in scorn (hizo una mueca de desprecio). Keep sb at ray (a raya). You'll be the envy of your friends, make sb envious/jealous. Be green (morir) of envy. By a roundabout (alternativo, indirecto) way. Tapering off (disminuir/amainar poco a poco). Experts carted off (se llevaron)... The truck broke down (averió). Break through (abrir camino). The desirable Americans stood for (significaban, representaban, permitían)... He stood down: (oficial) dimitió, (candidato, testigo) se retiró. Democrats outnumber Republicans six to one. Draw up: (testamento, contrato) redactar, (plan) elaborar, (tropas) ordenar, (agua) sacar → draw up contingency plans (redactar medidas de emergencia). Waved on (animado) by his lackeys (lacayos) =/= cheer up/liven up/encourage: animar, (Ec.) estimular. Whisper: rumor, susurro,V) =/= mutter (refunfuñar, hablar entre dientes, no estar de acuerdo) =/= gossip (murmullo, cotilleo,Vs). I've an empty feeling inside. He was told (le ordenaron) to register his pockets. Reach (alcanzar, llegar a) the groups... Strip down/away (desmantelar) the monopolies. Sit through (aguantar hasta el final) → I sat -- two boring lectures (conferencias). Sell out: lleno, éxito de taquila. Hark (escuchar en imperativo) back to: recordar, volver a → he's always --ing back to that (siempre está con la misma canción). They passed (a)round (de uno a otro, entre todos) photo (graphs) on their Tf. Run into (tropezar con) debt: contraer deudas. Ejercer: (oficio) practice/practise, (un derecho) exercise, (influencia) exert, exercise. Inveigh (vituperar, arremeter/lanzar invectivas) against. Trespass (entrar ilegalmente) upon: abusar de, -- against: infringir, violar → no trespassing (prohibida la entrada). Do away with (suprimir). Hang about (esperar) = hang around + holgazanear. Bring down: (gobierno) derrocar, (oponente) derribar, (precio) disminuir. Our stock was snapped up (se lo llevaron) at once (al instante). The decline in jobs has bottomed out (tocado fin). Chill out: relajar(se) + relax; calmar(se). Get ahead (progresar, tomar la delantera). Look upon/on (considerar). Lock up/away: (casa) cerrar con llave, criminal (encarcelar). Come up: (pers.) ascender, (sol) salir, (dificultad) surgir, (en justicia) comparecer; come up against (tropezar con), come up to (llegar hasta). The Nasa spacecraft (Maven) will blast off (despegar) & work out (resolver, calcular)... Pare:

(nails) cortar, (fruta...) pelar → pare down (reducir) to a minimum. A marginal note, win by a narrow margin, safety margin, margin of error. Plenty of scope (libertad, ámbito, alcance) for fraud. Its erstwhile (antiguo) enemy. Molasses (melazas). Flog (azotar) → give sb a flogging. Manhole (boca de alcantarilla) cover (tapa). The shaming (vergüenza, bochorno) of tax havens is fraught (tenso, difícil) with (cargado de) folly (locura)/danger... Aerobatics (acrobacia aérea). The height of elegance (el colmo de la elegancia). Suffuse (bañar, teñir, inundar). Data to shore up (sostener, apoyar) or shoot down (derribar, echar por tierra). Skewer: pincho, broqueta; ensartar, espetar (clavar en el espeto: asador), --ed by a claw (garfio, garra...). Hart to rebut (rebatir + refute; refutar) =/= contest/ challenge/impugn (impugnar). As conflit roils (se agita, se enturbia) in the M.E. (Middle East) some are gazing (miran fijamente) fondly (con cariño, ingenuamente). Towering (muy alto, imponente) sillies (tonterías). Skyline: horizonte, (ciudad) contorno. Bland: (pers.) afable, (comida) insípida, (libro, film) soso, fácil de digerir, anodino. Coax (engatusar, convencer) sb into doing sth. Interior decoration (interiorismo). Condominium: bloque de pisos, (Pol.) condominio. Square sth with sth (conciliar algo con algo). Handlers (comerciantes, adiestradores) grow more jittery (inquietos, nerviosos). Click: golpecito seco, taconeo, chasquido de la lengua → the door --ed shut (cerró de un golpe seco), -- with sb (gustarse, congeniar). Drivers & couriers (guías turísticos, mensajeros). Backtrack: retroceder, (en explicaciones) ir más atrás, (decisión) echarse atrás =/= backward → fall/walk --; -- looking (retrógrado). Break out: (prisioneros) fugarse, (guerra, epidemia) estallar, (lucha, discusión) producirse + -- -- in a sweat (empezar a sudar). Apostasy (apostasía, desvío, reniego). Mendacious: mendaz (mentiroso, falso). Be in cahoots with (estar conchabado con: confabulado, asociado con). Munificiencia (esplendidez, generosidad). The pretence (pretensión) that she leads Europe. Teller: (cuento) narrador, (banco) cajero, (elección) escrutador. Dither (indeciso, titubear, ponerse nervioso). Fellow: compañero, hombre, tipo → he's an old -- countryman (compatriota), -- inmate (compañero de cárcel), -- student... Without pandering (consentimiento) → pander sb's whim. He spurned (rechazó, desdeñó) the risk sharing... Her staunch (leal, firme, incondicional) refusal. Overblown: (estilo) pomposo, pretencioso, (flor) demasiado abierta. Onrush (oleada, avalancha) of immigrants. The refugees were drown or dying of exposition (a la T., al frío...). He was principled (basado en fuertes principios). Leave in (no omitir) Mr Cameron's promise of in/out referendum. Mo<u>b</u>: multitud, pandilla; the -- (el populacho) =/= mo<u>p</u>: fregona, estropajo, fregar → -- up: secar, (suelo) limpiar, pasar la fregona, (Mil.) acabar con. Gamble: Market's gamble (riesgo, apuesta, jugar); -- (jugarme) my reputation. Rock bottom (bajísimos) approval ratings. Remnants (restos, remanentes) of Chiang-Kai-Shek's army. Trust (confianza) → the trusty (leal) defence minister. The latest briefing (informe) on Russia's military campaign. Bring to bear: ejercer → abroad France <u>brings</u> its military might (influencia) <u>to bear</u>. Germany earns accolades (elogios, entusiastas, honores, galardones) as the european humanitarian spirit. <u>Cherry-pick</u> (seleccionar cuidadosamente) the benefits (=, ventajas) of integration =/= <u>fringe</u> (al margen; supletorios, complementarios) benefits/advantages. Britain might flounce (moverse haciendo aspaviento: demostración excesiva de espanto o admiración) → flounce in/out: entrar/salir indignado, airado. The disruption: (comunicaciones) interrupción, (planes) alteración... Horde (multitud) of yuppies (young upwards mobile professionals) move in (llevan hacia dentro, se ponen manos a la obra)... Stilt: zanco, (cosas) pilar, soporte. Hillary: the hostile Congress is shaping (forma, determina) her pitch (campo, puesto...). Her warm-up (preparatorio, Sp.: de precalentamiento) act. He was prosecuted (procesado). She gamely (valientemente) was playing along (siguiendo el juego). He nips (pellizco,V, mordisquea) colonial nostalgia in the bud (brote, capullo): corta de raíz. He unseated (derribó, echó del asiento) him. Prince Philip: the British-style gongs (condecoraciones, medallas) played a big part in his downfall (caída, ruina, perdición). He revived (reanimó) them. Ethos (espíritu de grupo, escala de valores) → the middle class --, the -- of free enterprise. Llevarse bien con: I get on/along (well) with my sister ←→ we don't get on well, we get on very badly. A talent spotter (cazatalentos). Today is regarded as a has-been (vieja gloria). A guesstimate (cálculo/estimación aproximada). Pranksters (bromistas) → who's the – who did this? Pavonearse: swagger (+ arrogante)/strut along with a blonde; pavonearse de algo: brag/cow about sth. Bafflingly (desconcertante, incomprensible). Lurk (acechar, merodear). Pot: cazuela, jarro, (flores) tiesto/maceta + flower pot; teapot, "chocolate". Kettle: caldera + boiler, cauldron. They dog (siguen) one of them. Maple syrup (jarabe de arce). Hell's grannies (abuelos). The oncoming (que viene en sentido contrario, se aproxima) → the -- winter/car. Sabre-rattling: alarde de un poder militar que no se tiene. Come to fruition (realizarse el plan). Head-on (de frente) → a -- - clash with the union. Efforts have foundered (fracasado). A hitherto (hasta ahora) obscure... The rough & tumble of life (los vaivenes de la vida)/of the ocean waves/of politics (avatares)... A glamorous raiment/clothes (vestiduras). A natural history they like to think they have cracked (rajado, golpeado, pb.: resuelto). Both sexs are equally showy (ostentosos + ostentious). Eerie (inquietante, extraño, sobrecogedor), eerily (de manera inquietanteextraña/sobrecogedora). Study afresh (otra vez, de nuevo). Seize on/upon (suerte: aprovechar; idea: fijarse en) by a beleaguered (asediado, atormentado, acosado) president. Snarl: gruñido,V; (lana) maraña, (tráfico) atasco. A glittering (brillante) throne (trono) overlooking (dominando, vigilando, pasando por alto) red-leather benches (bancos, escaños). Snug: (habitación) acogedora, confortable; ceñido, ajustado. Punter (jugador, apostador). Sod: suelo, césped; cabrón, pobre diablo, coñazo. Rickety (desvencijado, destartalado). Bulk (bulto, masa) → the -- of (la mayoría de). The rules are far from set in stone (inamovibles). All it purports to be (pretende ser)... GPS (Global Positioning System) signals are jammed (atascadas). A down-at-heel (de mala muerte, venida a menos) town. Pithy (concisas, sucintas) introductions. We move between metaphors, without ever mixing or belabouring (apalear, atacar con insultos, asediar con cuestiones) any of them. Mr Xi has been more of a hardliner (más radical) than even his two immediate predecessors. China's companies go abroad, Brazil has them aplenty (en abundancia)..., there was food aplenty. Kowtow (saludar humildemente, doblarse ante alguien). Attending a babyshower (fiesta con regalos a la madre y al futuro hijo). County town (capital de condado). Many parliamentarians are aggrieved (ofendidos) → in an -- (de queja) tone at how far trade has come to trump (superado, triunfado) the concern (asunto, preocupación, interés, empresa) over human rights. A drumbeat (redoble) of criticism. Even if it's bollocks (huevadas, cojones)... An American icon covers up (oculta, tapa completamente, disimula emociones)... A bunny (conejito, tía buena). Titillating (estimulante, sexo: excitante) notes (=, comentarios) on scores (gol, resultado, puntuación) of women. The creaking (crujiente, poco sólido) empire. A gargantuan (gigantesco) repository (depósito) of books. Deft (hábil, diestra) campaign =/= deaf (sordo) =/= dumb (mudo, bobo), mute =/= (máquina/pers.) silenciosos: quiets, silents. Angle: ángulo, punto de vista, componente; orientar, dirigir, torcerse. The plant's radioactive plume (pluma; smoke: columna) headed (encabezada, dirigida) north-west. Scathing (mordaz: áspero, sarcástico, picante al gusto; feroz) ↔ unscathed (ileso + unhurt, unharmed). Terms: (términos, plazos, períodos) →

winter/spring/summer/autum (or fall) terms: (primero...trimestres); -- (condiciones) of the contract. Vexed (enfadado, confuso). Jejune (cándido, sin astucia, aburrido, insípido). Pent-up (contenida) agony. The purge has steered (conducido, mejorado, dirigido) the private sector. Lash out: pegar golpes, arremeter contra. Slavishly (servilmente). Encompass (cercar, rodear; abarcar, englobar). Local officials scurry (se apresuran) to adjust their rethoric to fall in line with the plan. Coin: (moneda) acuñar, (palabra, plan...) inventar. Post-traumatic stress: symptoms of hypervigilance, nightmares & flashbacks (escenas retrospectivas). Sc*e*nt: perfume,V, aroma, olfatear; (peligro) presentir → be on the -- (sobre la pista) =/= a brief footnote containing sc*a*nt (escasos) details. A snazzier (más vistoso) dress. Coo: arrullar para enamorar, adormecer un niño, divulgar cosas secretas → she enjoyed cooing press reports. Aboard (embarcar..., a bordo). Vessel: barco, recipiente, (Bot.) vaso. Sweetheart (amor, novio). Tepid: tibio, (recepción) poco entusiasta. Clamber (trepar, subir gateando) out of inflation (salir con penas de la inflación), they --ed over the wall/into a car. Be a show-stopper (que causa sensación), show -stopping (sensacional). Tax avoidance (evasión). Favourable tax tantamount (equivalente) to government subsidies. Caucus (junta directiva, comité central, asamblea local, grupo). The Fed is set (resuelto, decidido)... Core business (actividad principal). Fine-tune: (máquina) ajustar, poner a punto, (plan, idea) afinar, poner a punto. By shoving (empujando) rates upward. Lopsided (desequilibrado, torcido, asimétrico, desigual). The bond markets have priced (cotizado) in a slower pace (paso, ritmo). Rely (depender de, contar con) foreign capital + a doctor relying on (confiando con) leeches (sanguijuelas) & bloodletting (sangría, carnicería). Get off (bajarse de, salir, mancha: quitar), -- -- my land/foot! Voters rebuked (reprendían, reprochaban) a repressive regime. He squanders (derrocha) the earnings. Will subvert (=, trastornar) the new N. Assembly. Delusional (de engaño, de ilusión, de delirio) policies. A farrago (conjunto de cosas desordenadas, ideas inconexas) of controls: prices, foreign exchange & production. The bumbling (ineptos) Bolivarians. Spot the pattern (darse cuenta del patrón, del molde). Many bristled (se resintieron, se erizaron) at what they saw. The upstanding (de pie, honrado) future citizen → the court (sala) will be -- (se pondrá de pie). A nurse winkle (saca) the sperm out of the testicles. Trolley: carrito, trolebús, tranvía. Pop: pequeño estallido, refresco; hacer reventar, ropa: ponerse deprisa → he pops on his woolly hat; -- your coat up (ponte el abrigo); popping up (emergiendo, apareciendo) a brawl (pelea) in partnership. Byword (sinónimo, =). The fertility rate has fallen blisteringly (Sol, calor): de manera abrasadora/vertiginosa; crítica: devastadoramente...) fast. Coa<u>c</u>h (coche, vagón, entrenar, entrenador)ing: entrenamiento, preparación, ayuda (on public health...) =/= cou<u>c</u>h: sofá, expresión, formular =/= cou<u>t</u>h (buenos modales) ↔ uncouth (groseros, torpes) accents... While shushing (acallando) fussy (nerviosos) babies. A cardboard cut-out (figura de cartón) of a sleek (impecable) smiling (sonriente) urban couple. So that clinics in remote areas never run out (se acaban). They flog (azotan, venden) discounted hairspray & nail varnish. Regional elections are just a steppingstone (pasadera). Ms Le Pen has racked up (acumulado) electoral successes. She railed (clamaba) against radical mosques & leaky (con fugas...) borders. Gather strength: cobrar fuerzas, solidez, resistencia, Mil: efectivos. Ostracised (aislado, excluído, condenado al ostracismo) by mainstream (corriente principal) politicians. Scramble (revolver) the European project. Put up (alojados...) in school halls. Acidly (mordazmente) demanding how many migrants the Vatican City has accepted. Expressing obnoxious (repugnantes, asquerosos) prejudices. Dampen (apagar, humedecer + moisten; frustrar esperanzas, enfriar ilusión) their support. Yet attempts flopped (fracasaron). The West is getting tired of nagging (regañar) Ukraine. The folksy (rústico, campechano) J. Biden. German soldiers to relieve (calmar, liberar, relevar) the French. The EU is punch-drunk (aturdida, tocada) & gasping (respirando con dificultad, decir jadeando). Mr Cameron can override (hacer caso omiso de...) the objections of pettifogging (pedantes, insignificantes) bureaucrats. His watchword (contraseña) was flexibility. A much-ballyhooed (de propaganda estrepitosa) breakthrough (gran avance). Its focus is at ease (cómodo, relajado) with free markets. Clashing (conflictivas, con choques) strands (facetas, tendencias) within the party. Prisoners in orange jumpsuits (monos)... It snaffled (birló) a pipeline network. Cottage (casita <u>artesanal</u>), cottage industry (industria artesanal). A restraint (control, restricción, moderación) of its finances is needed. S. Africa's bows (lazos) in the continent. Its wobbly (cojo, flojo, poco firme) credit rating (credibilidad, clasificación crediticia). Muggy (bochornoso) evening. Dapper (atildado, pulcro). Renowned (famoso) by his sartorial elegance: por su elegancia en el vestir. Seedy (cutres, sórdidas, de mala muerte) rooms... Plush (afelpados, de mucho lujo) flats. A roaring (estruendoso) business. Man: (barco) tripular, (fortaleza) guarnecer, (fusiles) servir. He had shepherded (llevado, acompañado...) legislation through the Senate. The Chicago gangland (mundo del crimen) boss (cabecilla). Shoot-out (coser a tiros.). However bonkers (chalados)'storylines (argumentos)..., arrange the furniture however you like. Under a cloak (capa) of secrecy, be --ed (envuelto) in sth. The solution they have devised (concebido, ideado, inventado). Sniggering (risitas tontas) from some rivals. Grandee (grande, pez gordo). His thuggery (brutalidad). Some residents unfurled (desplegaron) the stars (estrellas) & the stripes (franjas, tiras...) alongside the Cuban flag. Diplomatic thaw (deshielo). Sparing (moderado) ↔ un-- (incansable, despiadado) pursuit of suspects. Treat convicts (reclusos) leniently (indulgentemente)...

Expansionist mindset (actitud, disposición). Nanny (niñera, abuelita, yaya), nannying (profesión de niñera, protección excesiva) migrants... Prudish (mojigato, santurrón). Censors' shockability (que se escandalizan por poca cosa) has varied over time. Viewer (telespectador) → for home viewing. Re-edit shots (tiros, tiradas, intentos...) that include plunging (muy profundos) necklines (escotes muy bajos). Big-head (engreído). Dripping (empapados) corpses; be dripping wet (chorreantes, empapados). The film was heavily (muy, pesadamente) censored. The desperate bunch (racimo, grupo): the ultra-poor. Trap (trampa, boca, atrapar, cazar)ped (atrapados) in poverty; they lived by --ping fish. It lifts people out (sacar la gente) of deep poverty. Its motto: stay open-minded (libre de prejuicios, de miras amplias). Midwifery (partería, obstetricia). The professions Europeans spurn (rechazan, desdeñan). The dressing (el vestir), hairdressing (peluquería). Trainee (aprendiz de, hace prácticas) → -- manager, -- hairdresser. Losing their rags (estribos). Tarnish (deslustrar) the image of China rather than burnish it (mejorarla). Reps (representantes). Ding-dong (=, bronca, pelea). Bespeak (ea, o, en/ e): indicar; encargar, reservar. Pop-up (emergentes) schools. Sophistication to bear (cargar con, aguantar, soportar). Buckle (hebilla, abrochar) up: ponerse el cinturón de seguridad. Chalk (tiza)s up (apunta, escribe) the shortfalls to (a la cuenta de) a strong $. Peter out (irse agotando). Horizon-gazing (mirada). Sulk (estar enfurruñado: de mal humor). Excruciating: (aburrimiento) terrible, (dolor) atroz, (arte) mordaz, (situación) feroz. Some growth had dimmed (debilitado, oscurecido) memories. Weed out (plantas: arrancar; errores...: eliminar). Embezzlers (malversadores). What tickles (hace cosquillas, divierte) petrolheads (fanáticos del automovilismo). Probe: cohete, sonda, space -- (sonda espacial) → NASA's probe + sond(e)ar, investigar → money "Laundering" probe (investigación). He rocks (se balancea, mece) backwards. His sidekicks (secuaces, compañeros)... Impinge (incidir, afectar, vulnerar) on sb's rights/privacy (intimidad). Bug-eyed (que mira con ojos saltones). A flawed (defectuoso) impeachment. Wrong-doing (maldad, delincuencia). Leniency (indulgencia). Be in the dock (dársena, banquillo de los acusados). Fiend (diablo)ish (feroz, muy travieso)ly (terriblemente) hard. A wired-up (con servicios de punta conectados a Internet) society. Spiv (gandul, chanchullero, vivales). Far-off (lejanos, remotos) profits. Talking guff (chorradas). Straw poll (sondeo informal de opinión). Frock (hábito, vestido de mujer). Outsource this function to fickle (inconstantes) outsiders (pers. ajena, de fuera) =/= foreigners. Frantic (frenética, desesperada) flight (huida); the thieves took -- (emprendieron la huida). The Minister tried to axe: (hacha,V), (presupuesto) recortar, (servicio) cancelar, (staff) despedir. Highbrows (de intelectuales) theater/book... Mirth: alegría, regocijo, risas, júbilo + rejoicing → joyfully (con júbilo). Pool table (mesa de billar). Posh (elegantes) neighbourhoods. Damp-proofing (a prueba de humedad). Custody (custodia, detención). The eye-swivelling (giratorio + swivel chair) world of the organisation. A squashy (fruta: blanda; terreno: húmedo y mullido) pacifist. With thee (contigo). He stymied (bloqueó) Mr Maliki's bid for a third term. Hulk (armatoste)ing (grandote, pesada) statue. Afrikaners splutter (balbuceo, chisporroteo,Vs) at being told that... Traffic lights are often on the blink (averiadas). Impervious (impermeable, inmune, insensible, que no entra en razón) reading of the speech. A finicky (melindroso, excesivamente delicado) work. D. Trump is a long-shot (desconocido; en cine: toma a distancia) for the Republican nomination. Movable (móviles o movibles) feasts (fiestas). The flunkies (aduladores, lacayos) placed it, baaing (balando), in the boot (maletero; botas, patada). Repatriate blacks to the smallholdings (parcelas, minifundios) given to some ex-slaves. Self-serving (egoísta, interesado) political class in full swing (en pleno apogeo). The argument laid out (tendido, expuesto) by the lawyer. His name has cropped up (aflorado, surgido) repeatedly. Quash (sofocar, rechazar, anular) hyperinflation. The longer downturn (deterioro, disminución) since the 1930s. Self abasement (auto<u>degradación/humillación</u>). Snitch on sb. (chivarse a alguien + squeal, grass). Eulogy (elogio, encomio). Even muggings (atracos) are vanishingly (en desaparición) rare. Shoplifter (ladrón)ing: latrocinio, el rateo. Mind-numbing: soporífero, que inclina al sueño. Grinder (afilador, amolador, molendero) → a knife --, a coffee --: molinillo). Pall (hacerse pesado, paño mortuorio) → a -- of smog (una cortina de humo). A raft (serie) of reforms. Cart (carro, llevar, acarrear) → carted away (llevado) by the anti-corruption commission. Plants are pulled up (arrancadas). Poised: (1) (sereno, ecuánime, preparado) → he is -- to approve..., to win the presidency, -- to cash (cobrar, canjear) mightly (vigorosamente) the control; (2) (suspendido) → -- in the air. Possum (zarigüeya (ave) → play -- (fingir estar dormido). Bugger (hijo de pers., cabrón...) about/around: hacer pendejadas/gilipolleces. Crowd out (desplegar, hacer salir) the natives. They clog (zueco, atascan) water-intake pipes. Good marksmen (tiradores). Stifle: sofocar, agobiar, (ira) contener, (pers.) ahogarse, (expresión) reprimir → Burmese found China's embrace (abrazo) stifling; stifle whistleblowing (denuncias internas de prácticas ilegales) to harm the business =/= stiffly (rígidamente, fríamente) starched (almidonados y tiesos). Conceited (consentidos, mimados) lots of people (mucha gente). Articulación: (Bio., Mec.) =, joint. Great store (reserva, repertorio) of expertise: muchos hombres competentes. The credit bender (borrachera, juerga) =/= involved in bootlegging (en contrabando; Mús.: grabación pirata) booze (bebida, juerga,V). Disparate (dispares) currencies. Yardstick (patrón, criterio). A bevy (grupo, bandada) of co-operatives. As the horseman (jinete)'s mouth snorts (resopla)... <u>D</u>iddle (estafar) =/= <u>r</u>iddled (acrivillado, plagado) with loopholes =/= ripple:

rizo, oleada, onda, (agua) rizarse, -- effect (onda expansiva, reacción en cadena), a -- (oleada) of excitement, rizar (se), → rippling (tensas,V...) distortions (deformaciones) in space given off (despedidas, emitidas) when... Mind-set (modo de pensar). The warping (deformación, alabeo, torsión) of the fabric (tejido, estructura). Subserviently (con sumisión). Images beamed out/up (emitidas) nightly (todas las noches). Scale back (recortar, reducir) talks of formal coalition. Drum up: (entusiasmo) despertar, (soporte) movilizar, (comercio) fomentar. This solidarity has rankled (dolido, herido) Russia. The butt (extremo, colilla, culata; blanco; topetazo, cabezazo) of European jokes. Brussels is enduring (resistiendo, aguantando) its own threat. Labour opposition ambushed (agarró por sorpresa/hizo una emboscada a) him. Chucking (tirando, botando, desperdiciando) pensions + get the chuck (ser despedido) ↔ give sb the chuck (plantar a alguien). Ultimate: (destino, decisión) final, (poder) máximo, (causa, verdad, fuente) principal/fundamental. It strays (se extravía) into its territory. This view holds sway (se impone) → -- -- over (dominar) a nation/sb. Flabby (fofo) state. Obama's words sound cloying (empalagosas). Forgiven for muttering (murmullos, comentarios, quejas). A merciless (cruel, despiadada) campaign. Faze: desconcertar, perturbar → Mr Obama is unfazed (tan pancho, como si nada) by his critics, he considers them disingenuous (falsas) & deluded (ilusas, engañadas). Nonchalance (despreocupación). Nunnery (convento de monjas). Both resented (molestos) but now extolled (alabados, encomiados); resentful (resentido, rencoroso). A hunch (corazonada, presentimiento) that the evil (maldad, mal...) walks among them. A hash (embrollo, hachís: hashish) of plans → make a -- of sth (hacer algo muy mal). Unlikely (insólito, increíble, improbable) president. Aloof (distante) & inarticulate. Ms Fernández snubbed (hizo desaire, rechazó) the relations with the EU in favour of friendship with authoritarian regimes (Russia, Iran, China).

Depleted (mermados, agotados) by debt payments. Airbags (bolsas de aire). Mr Kim purged a clique (camarilla) of officers. Pursuits (persecuciones, búsquedas; actividades) such as reading were frowned on/upon (desaprobados). Myanmar's swift (rápida) transition is heartening (alentadora). Exhilaration (euforia, júbilo) → exhilarat<u>ing</u> (estimulante, vigorizante, excitante) turnaround (cambio de rumbo, giro radical). Sham (falsa, farsa, fingir) democracy whets (aviva, estimula, despierta) people to win fake (falsas,V) elections. This democracy may be stillborn (nacida muerta). A los making (deficitaria) startup. Lofty (elevadas, altas, altivas) valuations (valoraciones, tasaciones). <u>Dual</u>-ownership (<u>con</u>dominios). Parochial (=, provinciano, de miras estrechas; Rel.: parroquial) financial centres on the chinese mainland, unlike the Hong Kong's bastion (=, baluarte) of global capitalism. Business acumen (perspicacia, sagacidad). The benefits are fully passed on (pasados, dados, comunicados) to governments. Foothold (punto de apoyo) → get/gain a -- (afianzarse, establecerse). Insuring lorry-loads (camionadas) of banknotes trumps (supera, triunfa) the smallish (más bien pequeña) charge of... For every yuan of loans he takes out (saca, obtiene)... Relieve (aliviar) banks. Offsetting (compensando) the pain of the recession. Nugatory (ineficaz, baladí) role played by... Be on tenterhooks (estar sobre ascuas: inquieto). Dingy (deslustradas, sombrías, deprimentes) back alleys (callejuelas). Hip: cadera, en la onda → be --pped (estar al día, enterado, al corriente (de algo) + know (about sth.). In quantum theory everything is bitty (sin conexión, deshilvanado). A follow-up (de seguimiento) theory. Scared (cicatrizado, marcado) by violence. One-size-fits-all: no considerar las diferencias individuales; ropa de talla única; Jur.: solución para dejar contentos a todos. Tossed around/about (lanzado de acá para allá) but not sunk (perdido). After Paris, where drawbridges (puentes levadizos) up? Cockpit (Aér./Náut.: cabina de mando). This attire (atavío) for a startling (alarmante, llamativo) 99% of Egyptian women. The viciousness (brutalidad, malicia, salvajismo) of attacks. The blighted (con plagas, marchita, arruinada, frustrada) city. Bereft (desprovista) of hope. Crank (excéntrico, cascarrabias; manivela) up: intensificar (monetary policy...), (Mús) poner más fuerte. Desencadenar: (prisionero) unchain, (perro, ira) unleash, (crisis) trigger, set off. Fend for (arreglárselas) themselves (solos). Tender: tierno, delicado; ofrecer sus servicios, proponer, presentarse a concurso. Be hard-pressed (en apuros). Sneaky (cuco, taimado, astuto) =/= sneak, uck or eaked: soplón, chivato, acusar; sorpresa + -- in/out (entrar/salir a hurtadillas), -- away/about (escabullirse a hurtadillas). Slang (jerga, argot). Sexual intercourse (relaciones). Catch-all (general, que sirve para todo) charge (acusación, instrucción, carga) & hooliganism (gamberrismo). Counterfeit condoms. Shoddily (chapuceramente) made sheaths (fundas, cubiertas, preservativos) being passed off (hechos pasar) as popular brands → sheathe: envainar, enfundar =/= a gentle swish (silbido agitando una caña, susurro de agua, agitar la cola, muy elegante) sound. Scourge (plaga, azote) of our times. Live up (darse a la gran vida) to: vivir de acuerdo con. Stuffed (lleno, disecado...) with steering (de dirección) commitees. Defaulter (moroso). Fritter (buñuelo) (away): malgastar, desperdiciar. Headline-grabbing (que salta a los titulares) sums (of money...). People read the freebies (regalos + gift, present). Far-flung (extensas) communications. Heady (embriagador, vertiginoso). A queer (extraño, raro + marica) thing. Tailor (sastre, confeccionar) products more snugly (bien) → the door close --, it fits --, wrap him --. They dawdled (se entretuvieron) on the way + andaron muy despacio. Fetishized (=, obsesionado). Mooted point (punto discutido). Tether (soga, cadena,V)ed: atados, amarrados. Whatsoever = whatever: sea como sea ↔ none/nothing -- (ninguno/nada en absoluto). It hoovered up (aspiró) all the profits. The treasure has been feasting (se ha dado un banquete, festín) on their capital. Spotter (Aér.: observador) plane to feed him with information. Actuator (impulsor, accionador). Sweltering (calor sofocante, abrasador). Stanching (restañar: detener su curso) bleeding. Embossing: repujar = dibujos (en piel...) grabados desde una placa metálica. Trawl (rastreo, red de arrastre). Low oil prices ratched up (incrementaron) the pressure on indebted miners. Yet relying (dependiendo) on... With no say (sin voz) in drawing them up (preparándolos, redactándolos)... ←→ have one's say (tener voz y voto). A rolling (agitada, tambaleante) debt crisis get them restive (inquietos). Screenplay (guion + script). Depart (salir, partir) + depart from sth (apartarse de algo) → his version --s from the truth. Gang (banda, pandilla, grupo) → The euro zone will not gang up on (tenerla tomada con) non-euro members. Do a favour by quashing: (protesta) acallar, (rebelión) sofocar, (proposición) rechazar, (verdict) invalidar. Who owns this pen? (¿De quién es...?). My time is my own (dispongo del tiempo como quiero), he made the theory his own. Untimely (inoportuno, prematuro) demise (fallecimiento, desaparición). Grimly (gravemente, denodadamente) determined to succeed. Milk (ordenar, exprimir, sacar partida de) the historic importance. Bonhomie (afabilidad). He ditched (se deshizo de) its relations. Some oil barons are ducking (se zambullen en, están esquivando) the issue of global warming. Scale back (recortar, reducir) their loss-making (negocio no rentable) green energy. Warrior (guerrero). Firm (firme, sólido, estricto...). Collective nemesis (=, castigo). Restrained (cohibido, reservado, sobrio, moderado). Department store (grandes almacenes). Perky (alegre, animado). Splurging (derrochando)... Flit (revolotear) → as customers flit in/out (entran y salen precipitadamente).Verbose (hablador). Real <u>ale</u> (cerveza): cerveza de elaboración tradicional. Badges (insignias, distintivo) of quality. Well-grounded (adulto, maduro) value. The market is bullish (optimista, con tendencia alcista). Scintillating (chispeantes, brillantes) bibliographies. Droop (ponerse mustio, flaquear)ing (marchito, lánguido) brands. Swill (comida para cerdos, basura, lavar, beber a tragos) → beer --ing (borrachos) sightseers; alcohol is --ed in parlours (salones)... Gruel: gachas (alimento blando compuesto de harina, leche y miel). Gruelling (duro, penoso). Welter (mezcla confusa, revoltijo). Extol (ensalzar, encomiar), fluffy (suave y esponjoso). Japanese rave (delirio, desvarío). Strained (tenso, crispado, Ec.: debilitada) =/= stra_it_ened circumstances (condiciones difíciles). Lifeblood (sangre vital, alma). Elusive (esquivo, escurridizo). Top-of-the-line/range: de primerísima calidad =/= the top-of-the-model (el mejor modelo de la gama). The say-so (visto bueno). Chew the matter over (ruminar, considerar). Fingertips research (investigación exhaustiva). The plain speaking (de hablar con franqueza) practicality (utilidad, sentido práctico). Upfront (abierto/franco; inicial, por adelantado). Go by (pasar por... transcurrir, guiarse por) → he used to -- -- the position of the sun. Shake off (sacudirse de encima, librarse de). Hazy (neblinoso). Sludge: fango, residuos, aguas residuales → toxic --. Land área, beneath which lie vast reserves of oil, gas, minerals; oil-rich north gets a quarter of its government revenue from well-managed estate companies. Shore up (reforzar, sostener) the single currency. If Hollande allows the Ec. to slide (bajar, caer, deslizarse), he will spoil the chances of reelection. Talgo (1942): a system of axles (ejes) to avoid wear (desgaste por el uso) & tear on wheels. When it encounters the guides (guía, corredera), its weight transfers, freeing up the wheels & unlocking the bolts (cerraduras) that hold the wheel system. It has some challenges ahead. Centralised project management. Collaborative engineering: it studies the interactive process of engineering collaboration, whereby (por lo que)... Bargain for individual or collective advantages. Agree upon (sobre) joint (común) action. Go off course (desviarse de su curso).

Outcomes (resultados/consecuencias) which serve their mutual interests. Is quickly becoming a topic of great interest. This upsurge (recrudescencia) is partially due to... Once & forever (de una vez para siempre). In the opposite extreme of this spectrum... Thus it has a hard time (lo pasa mal) delegating responsibility. The backbone (CV) of any online collaborative efforts is security. Provide & update more meaningful (significativo) usage. Framework: armazón, estructura, marco → within the -- of the constitution, within the same collaborative --. The mapping of appropriate data. DKT (Distributive Active Knowledge) can notify interested parties on available (disponibles) objects, processes & services. Critically acclaimed (=, reconocidos) librarians (bibliotecarios). He recognizes your individual accomplishments (logro, realización) & dedication. Sanctioned (autorizado, sancionado) with the official ABI seal. All pieces are unconditionally guaranteed. The information is deemed (considerada) confidential & will only be used for Institute correspondence, orders fulfilment (cumplimiento, servicio) & shipping (transporte) purposes. Deteriorar: (damage, (relación, imagen) affect. Your standing (prestigio) as a professional with whom the Institute is proud to associate. It backs (apoya) Spain, the back row (la última fila). Potential risks of harmful (nocivas, perniciosas) substances must be assessed & legislation drafted (redactada) to ensure... Nano risks get minimal media coverage. The commission explorations to industrial pressure on nano definition leaves people & environment at risk. Nanotech inequity (injusticia) help or hindrance (obstáculo): rather than overcoming inequity could mean existing inequalities worse. Exposure to nano-silver, commonly used in odour-killing socks & clothing, triggers microbes to release (liberar) a lot of nitrous oxide (potent greenhouse gas). Workers ill-advised regarding nano risks. Nan- sunscreen safety debate heads up (dirige)... Unaskable (no formulables) questions. Nanoparticles found in ten top brand cosmetics. Companies failing to disclose (divulgar, revelar) use of nano for fear of consumer backlash (reacción adversa). Carbon nanomaterials delay (retrasa) rice flowering & reduce seed set. Fails to back tough (fuertes, duras, severas) measures on nano risks. UK inquiry (investigación) hears expert evidence, but nanofood risks remain largely unknown. Frustration with pointless (vano, inútil) stakeholder dialogue. Britain is the odd one out (único desaparejado) in Europe; which is the odd one out (el que no pega)? Sociology is a reflection (reflejo) of gradual spread (propagación). As such (como tales) each attendee (asistente) bears the title of ambassador. He's forever (sin cese) complaining. The relationship is tenuous (ligero, endeble, frágil) & fraught (tensa). It affords shade (da sombra). Eye-catching (vistoso, llamativo). Sandez: foolishness, stupid thing. Frustrar: (pers.) frustrate → I was –ed in my attempts to obtain justice, (proyecto) thwart, (atentado, operación): foil. Ráfaga: (aire, viento) blast, (de tiros) burst, (viento) gust. Atracador: (calle) mugger, (tienda, banco) armed robber, raider. Bochornoso: it's mugg/sultry/sticky. Transitorio: (medida) provisional, (situación) temporary; (período) transitional, (efímero) transitory, fleeting. Erizo (hedgehog). Prompt: rápido, pronto, puntual; dar lugar + cause, spark off, induce. Desdeñar/rechazar: spurn, push away, repel/repulse (repeler), drive back, reject, refuse. Charlatán: talkative, gossipy, quack + curandero (folk healer). Maul: (tiger) atacar, malherir, (writer, play) vapulear, (text) arruinar, (team: equipo) apalizar =/= attack (atacar en general). Perplejidad/desconcierto: perplexity, puzzlement. Plucky: valiente + brave, courageous, valiant. Avert: (ojos, pensamiento) apartar, (sospecha, golpe) desviar, (posibilidades) evitar, (accidente) prevenir. Disfrutar: enjoy (o.s.) + disfrute: enjoyment. Lush (lozano, opulento, suntuoso). Bootleggers (contrabandistas + smugglers). Joint: articulación, junta, unión, a -- (trozo) of pork, they are -- heirs (son coherederos), a -- (de equipo) effort (trabajo), -- owner (copropietario), jointly (conjuntamente). Taxing potency (fuerza) + sexual potency. Alluring (atrayentes, seductores) packages. Wrought: the innovations -- by the computer revolution, the devastation -- by the war, -- iron (hierro forjado), they -- fresh omens (augurios). Bank shares plumped up (hincharon) their core (meollo, esencia) equities (valores, acciones ordinarias). A mossy (musgoso) green buds (brotes, yemas, capullos). Demand for tobacco seems to go up along with demand for cannabis. At a later (más tardía) date. Get tougher on its unruly (rebelde) client; rebel, rebellious. Fatty (graso) acid. He looks (mira, parece) ineffectual/useless (inútil). Business<u>wise (en cuanto a)</u>... Policymakers (politólogos) sneer (hablan/comentan con desprecio) that... Asian diplomats crow (cacarean)... They have been rounded up: rodeados, reunidos, (animales) acorralados. The violence flared (estalló) amid rumors... Intricate (=, complejas) pink (rosadas, felices, entusiastas) structures stand out (destacan) amid contortions (=: actitudes forzadas) & turtles hover (rondan) above. Looking (pinta, aspecto) → bleached (descoloridos)looking (aspecto) skeletons. Enduring (resistiendo) the high waves. The sun cream soaks in (penetra).Thorns (espinas) of starfish (estrella de mar). Coranchompers (mascadores) have proliferated. Giant clams (almejas) crushing (aplastando) some reefs without possibility of recovery. Sediments from construction cloud (enturbian) waters. Kill the reefs that snorkellers (buceadores) like to swim over. In such MPA (Marine protected areas), activities that are deemed harmful... Tracking (rastreo) tagged members. Its upkeep (mantenimiento) will require... Repopulate ravaged (hecho estragos, saqueados) reefs. Their shells are cut into trinkets (chucherías, baratijas). There are skippers (capitanes, patrones) & rickety (desvencijados) wooden fishing vessels with provisions for a month... Barrels of water are lashed down (amarrados, sujetados con cuerdas) at the stern (popa, severo/

duro) & pigs led to pens (corrales + =, (farm) yard...) at the bow (proa + bow, prow). Long propeller (hélice) shafts (astiles, ejes, mangos). Chew up (mastica bien, estropea) submerged corals. When the murk (oscuridad, tinieblas) clears (se despeja, se aclara...) divers (submarinistas)... Clam-harvesters will be chased off (ahuyentados)... The showiest (las más ostentosas). The Almighty (todopoderosos) bosses. The firm's returned (regresado, devuelto) boss has to turn it around (cambiarla completamente). Stave off: (derrota, desastre) evitar, (peligro: conjurar) + I --ed -- (no fui a trabajar) today; he --ed -- (no volvió a) drink. The climate parching (que reseca). The chummy (de muy amigo) relations. Labour markets are hotbeds (semilleros + seedbed) of inequality. Double-edged (con segundas) words + -- - -- (de doble filo) swords. High-handed (prepotente, arbitrario). Women are chatty (habladoras). Spirited (fogoso, animado). A pot-bellied (panzudo). A newfangled (de moda) language. Afilar: sharpen, (instrumento) tune, strategies honed (afiladas) over millennia to meet & mate (aparejar). Club (cachiporra)bed (aporreados) to death. Males snuggle (se acurrucan) up (se arriman) & release their sperm. He winced in pain (hizo una mueca de dolor). Ammo (ammunition: munición). Central bankers are running down (reduciendo, agotando, hundiendo) their arsenal. Stock markets in bear (oso, bajista) territory. A build-up (acumulación) of debt & unwind (relaja, desenrolla)... The bazooka (bazuka: arma para lanzar cohetes) boo-boo (mete la pata). Pack a punch (pegar duro). This ideas fuse (fusible; funden, fusionan) fiscal & monetary policies. The state-licensing (autorización) laws. America's political establishment is riven (desgarrado, hendido, dividido) → -- by in- fighting: -- por luchas internas). It stokes (atiza, aviva; esperanzas: ceba) worries. Ensnared: atrapado en una trampa/by the law. Be chicken (acobardarse). Fake (falsifica) an illness: fingirse enfermo. The justice grind (muele, afila, funciona con dificultad) slow. Shoving (empujando) it back into the campaigner (combatiente, defensor)'s hand. Shovel up (quitar la nieve con pala). Hand anti- EU leaflets to the cliques (camarillas). They are growing fearful (temerosos, espantados) about... Throw "Colonial" art on the pyre (hoguera). Clad (vestido,V): scantily -- girls (chicas ligeras de ropa), -- in his trademark (marca de fábrica, sello característico) bright shirt, then ambled (andó sin prisa) to the marquee (entoldado, marquesina) to listen to the tribute (=, homenaje). The interest in the affair has gone off the oil (ha dejado de hervir, decayó). A spokeswoman/man (portavoz) denied (negó, desmintió) the report. A bus towed away (remolcado). Fold: pliegue,V, fracasar → his operation folded. He has made a filing (archivó los documentos) of his finance. Conventional (=, tradicional). His wealth may have been overstated (exagerada). He has outperformed (superado) the S&P 500 index of big firms. Tipplers (addiction to the booze, borrachín). Draught (de barril) beers. A hiss (decir entre dientes, silbido,V)y fit: rabieta + tantrum. Walloping (apalizar; enorme, colossal) tax-dodgers (evasores). A horn like protrusion (protuberancia). Media companies can stream (agrupar, clasificar) films with ever higher resolution (=, Comp.: definición), so IOT (Internet of things) firms don't need much bandwidth. Upgrade (atender, mejorar, Comp.: actualizar) their 5G network to comply (=, acceder) to a global standard. The radio spectrum used by 4G (below 3 gigahertz) is running out (acabado). He pinned (sujetó) his treatise (tratado) to a church door. Snap (chasquido, ruido seco; energía, brio; foto) =/= crackle (crujido, chisporroteo,Vs) =/= pop (pequeño estallido, refresco...). The taxmen did not repay (reembolsan, devuelven) the kindness (amabilidad, favor, detalle). Inauspicious (inoportuno, poco propicio) place to meander (deambular). A production freeze is likely to be a non-starter (imposible, fracaso). Pump up: inflar, -- -- (reactivar) the economy. Suspension (=, exclusión) the disbelief (incredulidad),

-- of payments. Starchy (con fécula, almidón) roots: mandioca + cassava, manioc. Such imports fall foul of (se enfrentan a) cassava mosaic (mosaico) disease. Turbocharging (turboalimentación). Stick around (quedarse, no irse,Vs) in... That was his undoing (ruina, perdición). At the very least (como mínimo)... A courtly (cortés, elegante) song. Syria bleeds (sangra). A chilling (escalofriante) encounter. Self-harm (automutilación + self - mutilation). Hold out (ofrecer, tender) sth to sb as an inducement (aliciente, incentivo). Wiretapping (instalando escuchas telefónicas a) a phone line. The deal will lapse (caducar). Britain would have to try to replicate (reproducir exactamente) them. Heading (encabezamiento, título, membrete) for Brexit. An oldie (cosa anticuada). The weather vane (veleta) whipped around (volteada rápidamente) by the prevailing political winds. Needling (pinchándose, fastidiándose) each other. Hit the jackpot (sacar el premio gordo, ser un exitazo), win the first prize/the lottery. Hanging out (pasando el rato) with friends. Parts of Asia are racked (sacudidas, atormentadas) by low-level civil wars. We're still a long way short of our target, the world's poorest not far short of (no lejos de alcanzar) the population of India. Custom (costumbre, clientela) → they've lost --, as -- dwindles (disminuye) =/= customs: aduana. His ideas cause a flutter (revuelo), be in a -- (estar nervioso). Naturalness (naturalidad) in painting. Heavenly (celestial) bodies. His work is rooted in the everyday life (vida cotidiana). Oblivious (inconsciente, ajeno) to what is going on near them. He presents a Christ who is bowed (inclinado, reverenciado) & lacerated (=, lastimado) with whippings (palizas, azotainas) & dripping (chorreando) with blood. Earthly delights (deleites, encantos) → -- in sth (disfrutar con algo). On the brink (borde) of the new times, in the brink (a punto) of doing sth. Scenes of hell (infierno) & damnation (condenación) + damn it! (¡Maldición!). Overbearing (autoritaria) American mother, first female member of parliament. Eating rubbish, living in a sett (madriguera de tejón) as a bear, cowering (encogido de miedo) naked on a moor (páramo, amarrar un barco) as a deer, pretending to be a otter (nutria). The author hones (afila) senses (sentidos, sensaciones) long neglected. He slinks (se escabulle) into the rubbish dumps (vertederos). A caterpillar (oruga)'s grunt (gruñido,V) as it noses on (olfatea). Nenúfar (water lily). The linguistic prowess (valor, capacidad, habilidad) as a proxy (poder) for intellectual agility. Broadsheets (periódicos de gran formato). The holdouts (los que se resisten) to give in (entregarse, rendirse). Germany was more at ease (más tranquila) with itself/her... The pointy-headed (intelectualoides) reformers. Rail: rail de tren, barandilla, valla → -- against sb (recriminar a alguien), -- against inefficiency. The practices are slipshod (descuidadas, chapuceras). Other terminals must slip (meter...) stevedores (estibadores) & crane operators (operadores de grúa). Berth: atracar, amarradero. That is the pb in a nutshell (en pocas palabras), the far - flung (extenso) east. Cajole (camelar, engatusar) & hector (intimidar de palabra) =/= hectic (agitado, frenético). Bottom trawling (pesca de arrastre de fondo). Glad-handing (estrechando la mano con entusiasmo fingido, para conquistar su voto) & anodyne (insignificantes) statements. Upgrade: prosperar, mejorar, (Comp.) actualización, (pers.) ascender. Allegiance (lealtad) to the organisation. Blanketed (cubierta) by the haze (neblina, calina), this forests grow on peat (turba). Slash-land-burn (talar y quemar). Ruthless: (acto, pers.) despiadados, (persecución, oponente) implacable. It introduced a host (multitud) of overdue (vencidas) reforms → such measures are long overdue (debían haberse tomado antes). India is a better template (plantilla) for the e commerce battle in other emerging markets. Its diverse population gives its zest (entusiasmo) & vim (energía, brío, empuje). Hollande applied the 75% tax rate & then binned (tiró, rechazó) it. Elusive (esquivo, escurridizo) to these actions. Hooded (encapuchado), hooded eyes (de párpados caídos, de matón). Boomed (hizo estruendo, resonó) her dissent (discrepar, disconformidad): No, no. Europe has since transfixed (traspasado, paralizado) & sundered (roto, dividido) the Conservative Party. Barely (apenas) veiled (encubiertos) attacks. Sheepishly (tímidamente, con vergüenza). He was piqued (interés: despertado; resentido + painful). Tonterias: silly/stupid things, foolish/stupid remarks; warning the risks of Brexit as baloney (tonterías). Vitriolic (violenta) confrontation. The conservatives belie (defraudan, desmienten, ocultan) the reality. Britain's humiliating crash out (deja hecha polvo, queda fuera) of the Exchange rate mechanism. Engañar: (embaucar) deceive, trick, (despistar) mislead, (estafar) cheat, swindle. Arrimar (move nearer/ closer)se a: come nearer/closer to; he snuggled up (se arrimó) to some Lebanese; + -- (up) (acurrucados) on the settee (sofá). Bumpy: (roads...) accidentadas, (journey) agitado... Hook (up): -- (gancho, percha; enganchar, abrochar) to the grid, he's off the -- (se ha librado). A stepping stone (peldaño) to America/ success + a springboard (trampolín) to get job. The fence is tattered (destrozada, (pers.) andrajosa, (reputación) hecha trizas. Shop fronts (fachadas de tiendas). The catalyst for foreigner-bashing (ataque, paliza). Glimmer (luz trémula, espejeo del agua) + a -- of hope (un rayo de esperanza) =/= glitzy (glamoroso, ostentoso) =/= glossy (brillante, lustroso) → -- (de moda, ilustradas) magazines. Burla (fun, mock, joke) → everyone makes fun of her/mocks her, this makes a mockery of the regulations (reglamentación, normas, reglas...). Tedious (pesadas, aburridas) intricacies (complejidades, lo intrincado). Hiccup (dificultad, hipo). It's a follow-up (continuación) of the meeting + subsequent -- - -- (seguimiento) is a part of the program. Animar: cheer up, liven up, encourage, animate. It sparked (suscitaba, desencadenaba) elation (entusiasmo, euforia), the market was jubilant (jubiloso), recovery flags/flanks (flaquea) + weakens, slackens). The upturn (mejora, Ec.:

repunte) has failed to live up to the promise. Boggy (pantanoso), bogged (empantanado) in bureaucratic twaddle (pendejadas, tonterías); bogged-down (ahogado) with work =/= twiddle (dar vueltas, girar) with sth.: jugar con algo =/= twirl (hacer) girar, revolear el bastón, pirueta, retorcer el bigote; -- a finger in a clockwise circle. Offenders (infractores). The ECB (European central bank) could introduce tiered (con gradas/niveles, escalonados) negative rates. The state sponsoring (fiador, avalista, patrocinador) of the SOES (State-owned enterprises). Dud: (m.) invendible, (Máq.) estropeada), (pers.) desastre, (cheque) sin fondos, (moneda) falsa) → --s swamped (agobiaron, inundaron) the banking system. Bad debts are written down (amortiguadas) & bankrupt SOES shut. The paragon (modelo, dechado: ejemplo digno de imitación) of cold-blooded (de sangre fría, desalmada) rationality/of virtues. The acme (colmo, cima) of communication. Posting: destino, (Internet) mensaje. Take as unflattering (poco halagüeño/favorecedor) a self-portrait as possible. A doe (cierva, coneja, liebre) → -eyed Indian girl. The world art zeros in on (se centra en, apunta a, se dirige a) a new region. Churn (mantequera, lechera, batir, agitar) → the continent perma-churn (agitación permanente) of alliance-building that forges decisions. Bash: porrazo, abolladura, pegarle a, despotricar contra → the bank-bashing mood (humor, atmósfera, clima). The geopolitical vortex (torbellino, remolino). A fib (mentirijilla, bola) blows up (vuela, hincha, explota) into an international incident. An unruly (rebelde) ally ruffled (agitó, alteró, alborotó) Germany. Farcical (absurdo, ridículo). A safeguard (salvaguardia, garantía) against their steamrollering (su apisonar; oposición: aplastar) by single-currency members. Living it up (pasárselo en grande). Vilify (vilipendiar, menospreciar) the court. The only hint of anything untoward (adverso). Protect from logging (explotación forestal). Anchor: ancla → be/lie/ride at -- (estar anclado); cast/drop the -- (echar el --); sostén (faith was his --);

anclar (sujetar, asegurar). Bulge: bulto, aumento pasajero (of the population...), sobresalir: her eyes --ed at the thought (sus ojos se le salían de las órbitas con sólo pensarlo), bulging with sth. (estar repletos de). How bust-ups (riñas, roturas) are handled (tratadas). The rearguard (retaguardia) action. I googled (googleé) five universities. In the grand (=, magnífico, imponente, fabuloso) manner: a lo grande → they live in a -- style. They are torn apart (hechos trizas) by pointless (sin sentido) disputes, they tore the place apart (lo destrozaron todo) looking for the money. Leery (receloso, cautelosos) of globalisation. Beethoven's string quartets (cuartetos de cuerda). Overreach (ir más allá de, sobrepasar, ser demasiado ambicioso) followed by remorse. Jarring (discordante) → strike a -- note (nota). He is too picky (quisquilloso) & sleeps in a bunk (camastro: lecho pobre) & uses a bucket to wash in. Students rack up (acumulan) heavy debts. Call centers (centros de atención al cliente). Putting the tyke (persona pilla, perro de calle) near a tycoon (magnate). Tertiary education (enseñanza superior). Unaccountable (inexplicable, irresponsable). Attainment (logro, realización) in Science & Maths. Unskilled migrants depress (deprimen, reducen) pay for locals. Back-breaking (deslomador) toil(esfuerzo, trabajo duro). A clear-headed (lúcida) choice. The apps (aplicaciones) to arrange dates. Hook-up (abrochar, enganchar, TV: transmisiones en cadena). A roughed-up (apalizado) man, despite the blistering (calor: abrasador; crítica: feroz; velocidad: frenética/con frenesí) point of view. Strife (conflicto) → -prone (propenso) + strife ridden (conflictivo), a horse ridden (montado) by... He is jobless & broke (penniless: sin un duro). The troops treat females as spoil (estropear, invalidar; botín). Deluded (ilusos, engañados) narcissists. The discovery was hailed (acogida) as a major (importante) breakthrough (avance). Responsive: sensible, receptivo → the orchestra was -- to the conductor (director). Economic imprint (imprimir, impresión, huella) of Walmart.

Taiwan roils (agita, enturbia) waters. Under the UNCLOS (United nations convention on the law of sea) Itu Aba is a rock that cannot sustain human life. The smuggling has encroached on (invadido, usurpado) a state monopoly & has encouraged the border blockage (bloqueo). Cut a dash (destacar, ser el centro de atención) from Madrid to... Moss-clad (vestidos de musgos) tree =/= moho: (metal) rust, (alim.) mould =/= mushroom. Downplaying (quitando importancia a) the far-flung (extensa) bureaucracy. They are all the more (aún más) unwilling to inhibit/restrain action + all the more because/as/since: tanto más cuanto que. Twelve notched up (conseguidos, apuntados) by their predecessors. Glaciers retreated (retirados) by about 20%. The current vogue (moda). In a hit-&-run (los que producen el accidente se fugan) road he was smitten (i, o, tten) (golpeado, castigado). The pillory (puesta en ridículo). A reminder (recuerdo) of his party's tolerance to help pad out (inflar) budgets & defray (sufragar) costs of... A gouty (gotoso: afectado de gota) gait (modo de andar). Size him up (evaluar cómo es él) → she --ed him up straight away (lo caló enseguida). Cherry-pick (escoger cuidadosamente) the least risky customers. Tax avoidance/evasion (evasión de impuestos) + avoidance of physical contacts. Claw back (recuperar) lost taxes. A digital dust-up (pelea). By shuffling (arrastrando, relegando) intellectual property to tax havens. A raft (balsa; montón, serie) of anti avoidance (contra el evitar) measures; rafts (montones) of troubles (problemas). Alluring (seductor, atrayente) country in tax terms. Rouse sb's ire: suscitar/provocar la ira de alguien. Touchscreen (pantalla táctil). Flip: tirar, volverse loco, flip a coin: echar a cara y cruz, -- through (hojear) new options. The control panel (tablero). Jab (clavar) sth into sth, jab sb with one's elbow (dar un codazo) → I jabbed the knife in my arm. Famously finicky: (pers.) melindrosa, escrupulosa, (trabajo) complicado. Satellites sent up (lanzados) during the deliveries to the International space station.

419

Avenger (vengador). Quaint: (costumbre) curiosa, (pers.) poco corriente, peculiar, (edificio) pintoresco. He is writing his memoirs. A delaying (dilatoria) tactic to allow him to prepare for... I took out my boot & shook out a stone. Ingratiating (alegrándose, congraciándose) himself into foreign surroundings (entornos, alrededores). Be in a haze (bruma): estar aturdido. Speakeasy (taberna clandestina). Rumble: ruido, rumor, estruendo,Vs, pelea... → the war has --ed on (coleado) since... The war on drugs has far overshot (oo, o,o) (rebasado, excedido, ido más allá de) the ills; you can't overshoot your deadline (no puedes pasarte del plazo establecido). It's scary (da miedo) here in the dark. (At) full tilt (inclinación): a toda velocidad; -- at sth/sb (arremeter contra --/--). It ought to be..., I ought to do... Explore in out-of-the-way (remotas, poco comunes) provinces. State of emergency (excepción). Tear up (romper, anular) wasteful subsidies. Hoe (azada,V). A vine (vid, parra, enredadera) that is rooted... The roughnecks (trabajadores en pozos petrolíferos; duros, matones) obtain the oil gushing (efusión, chorreo). Some members of OPEC (Organization of Petroleum-exporting countries) are pumping at record levels. Bear market (mercado bajista). The partners are restive (inquietos). It has gamely (valientemente) advanced. Snowden infuriated digital-privacy advocates (defensores). He will lose out (saldrá perdiendo). Beset: (acosar, acuciar) → -- by fears of terrorism; (plagados) the way ahead is -- with difficulties. Scoffing (mofándose) at the idea... Pay up-front (por adelantado). Oil will be less of a cash cow (actividad/producto muy rentable). He eyes (observa) the Holy land. A brisk (enérgico) business in safeguarding (que resguarda/protege) guns → as a -- (defensa) against... Be available: disponible, libre; be easily/ readily -- (ser fácil de conseguir). Ship that loiters (se rezaga, se entretiene en) international waters. The Kenya's breadbasket (panera, the -- (granero) of Europe). It is anything to go by (guiarse por + (tiempo) transcurrir, pasar). By flaunting (alardeando) its national flags. Duty roster (lista de turnos), be --ed for do sth. (tener asignado hacer algo), be --ed (estar de turno). Tear-stained act of contrition (arrepentimiento). A shoot-out (tiroteo) with the police. The army-tainted (contaminadas, manchadas, deslucidas) policies + his writings are --ed with racism. Be on the move (estar de viaje). They raced down the hillside (bajaron corriendo por la ladera). The hardy (potentes, resistentes) faithful (fieles). An earlier push (empuje, esfuerzo, dinamismo). Foundry (fundición, fundidora). It was a slog (me costó trabajo), -- away at sth (afanarse para hacer algo), -- it out (luchar hasta el fin). Barely budged (movido, cambiado de opinión). They are coining (acuñando, inventando)... Bumper: parachoques; record, abundantes (earnings...). Carried away (entusiasmado). The benefits of being hands-off (no intervenido). It's so cut-throat (asesino, feroz). Pass on (pasar, dar; comunicar, poner en contacto). The flabby (soso, fofo) state sector is a let-down (decepción). Godliness (piedad + pity, mercy, Rel.: piety). A wavy-haired crooner (cantante melódico). The Ec. is sliding (cayendo) into recession. Add up (hacer el cálculo). Newsworthy (de interés periodístico). Flipped (enloquecidos, tirados, burlados) from hawkishness (dureza) to dovishness/leniency (blandura); blandura de cama (softness), de carne (tenderness). The rock that rocked (sacudió, estremeció) the world. A grinding (estancando; plan, negociación: llegando al punto muerto; agotador) movement + come to a -- halt (detenerse en seco). The city harried (hostigaba, agobiaba) drivers. Hold back (ocultar, retener). Batter (apalear, magullar) → clutching (dando embrague; agarrando, cogiendo) battered (magulladas, estropeadas) engines. Stifle yawns: contener bostezos. Brush (maleza, broza) & sand. Farfetched (descabellado, exagerado) stretch (tramo...). Endanger (poner en peligro) → a critically endangered (en peligro de extinción) bird suggests the logging (madereros, tala de árboles) wars are not over. Crash: estrépito, accidente, crac, (banco) quiebra, (-- into sth) estrellaese contra algo), the parrots' habit of crashing (pasar la noche…) into the office windows + can I crash at your place? (¿Puedo quedarme a dormir a tu casa?). Songbirds (pájaros cantores). The fairy (hada, homosexual) land: el país de las hadas. Stray: extraviarse, vagar sin rumbo fijo. Dummy (maniquí, muñeco, maqueta, de juguete, testaferro) interlopers (intrusos). Testaferro: front → a -- company, figurehead, straw man. Untutored (poco instruidos). They circle (se rodean) one another. The first chink (grieta, tintineo, sonido metálico,V) in relativity's armour (armadura, blindaje). Prescience/clairvoyance/discernment/sightedness (clarividencia). The reform has yet to follow through (continuar). Berlin's aftershok (réplica). Barriga: stomach, tunny, undernourished children with swollen stomachs/bellies. They formed a huddle (grupo; acurrucarse, apiñarse) around women. Fell short of (no llegó a la) rape (violación) in Cologne. A lopsided (inclinado, desequilibrado) migrant sex ratios. Sleazy (desaseado, de mala pinta). Scorn/disdain (desdeñar). Avow: reconocer, confesar → an avowedly (declaradamente) confrontational government. Forebode/betoken: presagiar + =) =/= presagio (omen, portent, premonition). His gambit (táctica) flopped (fracasó). In the EU nobody wants a Federal law trumping (superando) state law. Europe's voters hooked (se engancharon) on the rush (prisa, apuro; ráfaga, ataque) of direct democracy. Voters stroppily (con insolencia, de manera borde) used referendums to punish governments. It is hemmed (hecho el bordillo) in: cercado + (terreno) enclosed, (ciudad) surrounded. Sanction illegal snatch (arrebato, agarrar) squad (pelotón): unidad de arresto. Seat's headcount (plantilla) has grown. Additional investment to jumpstart (arrancar empujando un coche, o haciendo puente) its potential. Harried (agobiado, preocupado) by theft (robo) of natural resources. Chinese firms that rushed to expand are now gasping (respirando difícilmente). The IEA (International Energy Agency) finds lots (muchos, grupos; lotes, terrenos...) in the oil market to be bearish (pesimista, tendencia bajista). The geo profiling (perfiles) software. The squander (derroche) of energy may be dimmed (atenuado). Trounce (derrotar/zurrar de forma aplastante) → give sb a --ing (paliza). Burp/belch (eructo) of ruminants; flames belched from the mouth of the cannon. Homing (buscador, volver al hogar) pigeon: paloma mensajera. Larva: grub, (de mosca) maggots, (de mariposa) caterpillar + the grubs (larvas) that hatches (incuban) eat its host alive. Gum (encía, goma de mascar) =/= chewing gum (chiclé). Piercing (perforantes) bullets. Snowstorms, avalanches & crevasses/crevices (grietas). Flab/fat(ness): gordura. The war is a morass (cenegal, pantano) + a -- of pbs. (un laberinto de problemas/reglamentos...). The spear (lanza + lance) & dagger (=, puñal) of tradition. The homilies (=, plática sobre asuntos religiosos, sermones) of the jihadists. Compact (=, sólido, compacto). Gunpowder (pólvora). A sardinian (sarda: de Cerdaña) villa. They have a listing (cotización) on the stock. Cox (timonel: el que gobierna el timón,V). He sang before a spellbound (embelesada, hechizada) audience. The region bellwether (barómetro + =). The revolution was hijacked (secuestrada) by Islamists. A jumble (revoltijo, embrollo, cosas usadas) → -- sale: mercadillo de beneficiencia de cosas usadas. The revolutionary hotheads (exaltados). They are in shattered (destrozada) abeyance (desuso) → fall into -- (caer en desuso). Sliced (en rodajas) onions/lemons... The 250 ethnic groups in Nigeria can divvy up (repartir) oil money & government jobs. My home is in jeopardy (peligro)ize (arriesgar). Fitful: intermitente, irregular → the dialogue pursued fitfully (irregularmente). Festering (que se enconan, que degeneran) issues can't be solved soon. Sound: sonido,V, pronunciar; parecer; sano, formal... → he had --ed powerless/ helpless (impotente) =/= Med.: impotent. Less racially segregated, thanks to suburban (de clase media, zonas residenciales, aburguesadas) sprawl, extortionate (excesivos, exorbitantes) house prices &

immigrants. Light shining off (brillando/deslumbrando desde) a puddle (charco) is harmless. Profits may seep (filtrarse) away (escurrirse + fuerzas: abandonar) towards the producers. It spun out (alargó, estiró) the work of geneticists. A tech luminary (lumbrera). A bedraggled (desaliñado, enmarañado) rack (perchero). From lucky to plucky (valeroso, valiente). People hankering (que añoran, anhelan) for privacy (intimidad, privacidad). Competition is phoney (phony): falsa, postiza. In sooth (en realidad, en verdad) =/= soothe (calmar, tranquilizar) =/= swath (banda, franja)e: envolver → -- in a furry (peluda) gauze (gasa). Various lash-ups (arreglos provisionales). Rocket scientist (Ing. astronauta). The universe'sdarkest denizens (moradores). The galaxias bash (golpean) into one another & merge. Many people have done Africa a disservice (perjuicio): la han perjudicado. S. Sudan shuffles (pies: arrastra; papeles: traspapela, revuelve) paperwork (papeleo, trámites administrativos). It is cleaving (se parte, se surca, se abre camino) itself away from the rest, cleave through the throng. Americans grew stubble (rastrojo, barba incipiente) → a three days'--. He nosed (olfateó) out (averiguó, descubrió)... Nefarious (=, indigno de trato humano, vil). Modernist turret (torreta, de castillo: torreón). Even innocuous (=, inofensivos) projects can incur (=, contraer, provocar) the wrath (ira). The household chores (tareas). Contentious (polémico), the contentiousness (conflictividad,V) of the Catalans. Bedfellows (compañeros de cama). CiU (Convergencia i unió) political party party has been plodding (lento y pesado, más aplicado que brillante) towards secession. Vocational (professional) or academic systems, vocational guidance (orientación), -- training (formación). Remorselessly (despiadadamente). Water gushing down (sale a grandes chorros en) the streets. The gusty (valiente, con agallas) case for cooperation. Morale-boosting (estímulo, inyección de). Expunging (eliminando, suprimiendo) the memory of the fight. Feed up: (pers.) engordar, (animal) cebar.

He said Nativity scenes were a charade (farsa, payasada). Bossy (mandón) → --iness (autoritarismo). Belly (del vientre) → -dancers. Berate (regañar) women for wearing too flirty (coquetas) dresses. A cloaked figure (silueta envuelta en una capa). Conceal (disimular, ocultar) their wrists & bottoms (traseros). Peinado: this hairstyle suits you, her hair always looks nice ←→ unkempt (+ desarreglado), dishevelled, uncombed, with the hair on a mess. Refrigeration is rop(e)y (flojo, poco convincente). Play a prank (gastar una broma) on sb. Perversely: =, tercamente, sin lógica. Fight (pelea) → a closely (estrecha, de cerca) fought (reñida) battle. Supply-side (de oferta) economy/ strategy. The battles of attrition (desgaste) engulfed (tragaron, sumergieron) the European powers. Crisol: crucible, melting pot. British & French fomented Arab nationalism to undermine Ottoman empire & staved off (evitaron, aplazaron) German attempts to promote a pan -Islamic *jihad*. The baneful (funestos + fatal, disastrous) results... They spirited (animaron) Tibetans. Both claim the mantle (manto, capa, liderazgo) of Vladimir the Great: he accepted Christian baptism for his unruly (rebeldes) Slavs & Vikings. Be short of sth (quedar sin algo) → Ukraine was -- - its elites. Range: ámbito, campo; variedad; alcance del tiro; deambular → he shot at point-blank range: a boca jarro. Largesse (generosidad, liberalidad) of small municipalities. Civil servants wants to have cast iron (inquebrantables) job guarantee. The FN (Front national) drew 6.8 m. votes in the second round, up from 6 m. in the first. Newlyweds (recién casados). Dolphins feed humans & throw fish up onto the jetty (muelle). Porthole: (aviación) ventanilla, portilla en los lados del barco. During the courtship (cortejo) the <u>hunch/hump</u>back (jorobado) male whale sings songs. Manipulate ten implements (herramientas, instrumentos): clubs/sticks (porras) to beat with... A pitch (lugar...) -black (oscura) street in a run-down (agotado, ruinoso) district. Baseball in Cuba is a badge (insignia) of honour.

425

Snitch (chivarse) on sb. He is prone (propenso) to muffle (amortiguar)d (sordo, apagado) shouting (vocerío). Bleach: lejía, decolorear)ers: tribuna descubierta. Patient care (cuidado de pacientes). Have the right to light up (iluminar..., encender un cigarrillo). Canadians get creakier (más crujientes, chirriantes)... With suicide vests (chalecos, camisetas), the crowd rampaged (se desmadró, pasó arrasando). Islam used to rile (molestar, irritar) India. Avow (reconocer, admitir, confesar)edly: declaradamente; avowal (reconocimiento). Be rude/disrespectful (faltar al respeto de). Winsome/charming/delightful (encantadores) N. Korea rock chicks (pajaritos, chicas). Cause ruckus/ructions (follones, tensiones) with America. The overbearing (autoritario) Mr Kim & the <u>band</u>leader (lider de banda). The spotters (observadores) of the shrubs (arbustos, matas) & the scraggy (flacucha) vegetation. The show will be a crowd-puller (una gran atracción). The pillars of social control are fla<u>k</u>ing (se desmenuzan, se desconchan) at the edge =/= flagging (que decae/se enfría) growth. She fell for (se enamoró de, se tragó/se dejó engañar por) the scam (estafa, timo), handing over (entregando) Yuans 1 m. to the crooks (cayados, maleantes). He rubs (frota) his armpit (axila) while patting (acariciando) his head → rub up (pulir + polish). Twig (ramita, darse cuenta) to sth (de algo). Broom (escoba) cupboard/closet: armario para artículos de limpieza. It drowns (out) (ahoga) a nearby (cercana) melody; I turned up (subí) the radio, to drown (out) the traffic (ahogar el ruido del tráfico). Jogger (corredor de footing). Shoulder (cargar con) the child care. Frolic: juguetear, travesura, aventurilla. Equipment for grown-ups (adultos). A soppy (sentimentaloide, tonta) tune (melodía). Pitch in (echar una mano, ponerse a trabajar) if they can afford to (si se lo pueden permitir) =/= he refused to chip in (contribuir, intervenir). The bearishness (pesimismo) that pushed oil prices below... A notional (teórica, hipotética) offsetting (compensación). They were greeted (recibidos) with amazement (asombro). A newly (recién) maroon (granate)ed (abandonado, aislado (by floods...) sailor. The harrowing (angustioso, conmovedor) tale of the castaways (náufragos). The brackish (de salobre) well slaked (aplacó) the slave's thirst. The investors bat (murciélago, golpean) around (discuten acerca de/superficialmente sobre) ideas. Musty (anticuados, que huelen a moho/humedad) corners of the Ec. It seems barmy (chalado) until you realise... Frantic (frenético), sloppy (descuidado, sensiblero, sentimentaloide) & smallish (más bien pequeño)... Hop (lúpulo) =/= a hop (brinco) across the rue. A one-off item (un caso único) held up (alzó, sostuvo, mostró) it best. Fraudsters (defraudadores). The onset (inicio) of the credit crunch (crisis). A spasm (=, acceso, ataque) of coughing. Investors have soured (agriado, deteriorado relaciones) on equity investment. A parlous (lamentable, crítico, calamitoso) state. The soldiers kitted-up (equipados) with. An exoskeleton that a worker straps (venda, ata con correa) to his buttocks (nalgas), thighs & calves (pantorrillas). Tow (remolque) lines (=, cuerdas, cables) made of fabrics (tejidos)... A startling (alarmante, llamativo) painting. <u>Goose</u> (oca) <u>flesh/pimples)</u>: carne de gallina. He learned to draw by scratching (arañando, improvisando + improvise) pictures on birch (abedul) bark (corteza) using a pin (alfiler). His look is wry (irónico), humorous (divertido) & forthright (franco). Bereaved (afligiido) senator. It seems quaint (curioso, pintoresco) in this era (=, época). Deluded (ilusos) or dispirited (desanimados). Confiding (confiado) in a stranger & be titillated (estimulado, excitado) by... Cresta: (Biol./ola) crest, (gallo) comb, (monte) crest. Purse one's lips (fruncir los labios). Broach (abordar) the topics. Some snappy (rápido, enérgico, vigoroso) advice. Crocus (azafrán + saffron). Whisker: bigote de animal, pelo, patillas (+ sideburn), barba (+ beard) → by a -- (por un pelo) → a victory by a --; he was within a -- of falling down. Mindbites: share knowledge, skills & passions through audio & video lessons. Interface: interface, interrelación, punto de contacto, Comp.: interface/interfaz, conexión entre dos componentes de hardware, cara visible de los programas que interactúan con usuarios. A serendipitous (serendípico: arte de descubrir cosas sin proponérselo) trawl (rastreo, red de arrastre).The destruction has cast (lanzado, echado...) the current lot (grupo) in unflattering (poco halagüeño/favorecedor) relief (alivio, auxilio, liberación, relieve,Vs). He is a quisling (colaboracionista) with martial valour. The bosses of Banks would once (antes, una vez, inmediatamente) have cringed (avergonzado) at releasing these kind of results. Tuck shop (en una escuela: tienda de golosinas). Low-key (discreta) entrance belies (defrauda, contradice) with a home placed between a chemist & a clothes shop. A gloomy (lúgubre, pesimista...) pundit (experto). Bot (robot) → Botnets (utilizados en cibercrimen): vast network of compromised (comprometidos) computers. Reckoning (cálculos: by my --; opinión: in my --: juicio). Holography (=: técnica fotográfica a base de luz coherente producida por láser). Hash (embrollo, lío, hachís). Heuristic (heurística: arte de inventar). Stellar (estelar, sidéreo). Modem (=). Quantum (cuanto: unidad de radiación según Max Planck). Uptight (tenso, nervioso). Wholesome (sano, saludable). Wholly (totalmente)... Reckon (calcular, considerar). Reel (hilo/pesca: carrete; cine: rollo, cotton --: carrete de hilo; reel off (recitar de un tirón). Widget (artilugio, aparato). Land grabbing (apoderarse, compra de terrenos). Blog (blog → bloguero (tiene una página web). Geomancer (geomántico: creador de un sistema de números y líneas). Snug (acogedor, confortable, ajustado). Scrapers (raspadores, espátulas). Gopher (gofer: técnica para organizar la información en Internet). Bust: romper → the door was locked, so we --ed it open; busto; descalabro; go -- (quebrar); trust busting (el hacer cumplir la legislación antimonopolio). Implode (implosionar: explosión hacia el interior, gracias a una menor presión...). Buck up (animarse, espabilarse; -- --!

(¡Date prisa!). Spaniel (=: una raza de perros). Recoil (retroceso,V). At the risk of one's life, at one's -- (por su cuenta y riesgo). Release (liberar, ceder, desatar, arrojar, hacer público) → be –ed (puesto en libertad) on bail (bajo fianza), they –ed him (lo condonaron) from the contract, he –ed his grip on her (la soltó). Whistle stop (visita relámpago, apeadero). FDI is wilting (debilitándose, marchitándose). Nudge (codear ligeramente, empuje suave, rondar: -- 38ºC) =/= elbow (codear más fuerte) =/= relentless (implacable, despiadado, incesante) tweaks (pellizco,V, pequeños retoques) =/= tweet (un tejido de vestir; gorgear, piar + chirp). Rejuvenating (rejuvenecedores) reefs. Aboveboard (legítimo, limpio) business. Boisterous (bullicioso) + brouhaha (barullo, revuelo) + hullabaloo (jaleo, escándalo → raise a --). Brazenly (descaradamente). Biff (puñetazo) → -- sb on the nose. Buffet: =, bar, golpe, sacudir. Can-do (dinámico), co-opt (nombrar) sb onto sth. Conflate: refundir, combinar. Chortle: risa, carcajada, reírse de satisfacción. Circumvention (sorteo) of the obstacles, (burla): the -- of the law. Diffident (tímido, poco seguro de sí mismo). Decimate: diezmar (causar mortaldad en una multitud, pagar el diezmo a la iglesia). Despondent (desanimado + downhearted, dispirited). Ludicrous (absurda, ridícula) election. Nary a (ni una) word. Endearing: atractivo, simpático. Elated (eufórico) → they were in an − mood (estaban--). Enturbiar: (agua) cloud, (relaciones) mar, cloud. Enraptured/captivated (cautivado). Expendable: prescindible, dispensable, fungible (se consume con el uso). Hardy (fuerte, resistente) → fool--: insensato, imprudente. Flout: incumplir/desacatar) the law. Flummox: desconcertar, dejar cortado. Frazzled (reventado, hecho polvo); so tempers can easily frazzle (la gente anda muy irritable). Fusty (olor cerrado, ideas falsas). Gapping: herida/boca: abiertas; abismo/agujero: enormes. Gormless (idiota, corto de entendimiento). He acted with guile (malicia) & deceit (engaño) ↔ guileless (cándido, sin malicia). Gutted: (ciudad) destrozada, (pez, conejo) destripado → be/feel -- (estar/sentirse hecho polvo + knackered). Gore: cornear, sangre =/= gory (sangriento). Mark up: anotar, incrementar el precio. Mugger (atracador). Hands-on (práctico) approach. Headship (dirección) of a club/a college → this is my first --. Pinch/swipe/snaffle (birlar) → I had my umbrella --ed. Risk-averse (reacio al). Reek: hedor, apestar. Timbre: (door) bell. Ringing: repique de campana; categórico, rotundo, sonoro; grandilocuente (sublime, eminente). Stitch: punto, coser, puntada; punzada (al costado...) → I've got a --; bordar, (Med.) suturar; → -- up: traicionar + (en delito) treason, (en acto desleal) treachery. Shudder: (pers.) estremecimiento, (máquina) sacudida,Vs. Swanky (pers.: fanfarrón, estilo: chic) centres/centers. Sheming: intrigante, maquinador. Shoo → I --ed the birds off/away (los ahuyenté), I --ed the children into (los hice entrar en) the house; it's a shoo-in (coser y cantar) → he once thought to be the shoo-in (candidato favorito) for a party leader. Send-off: enviar + echar, expulsar. Seminal: fundamental, de mucha influencia. Slant: inclinación, pendiente,Vs + --ing: (tejado, letra) inclinados), (ojos) almendrados. Shoot-em-up (película de pistoleros) =/= (del Oeste) Western. Surrogate: sustituto, sucedáneo. Toss out (botar a la basura). Tacky (chabacano, hortero, de mal gusto). Thrum: (guitarra) rasguear, (máquina) producir sonido vibrante. Dim: oscuro, débil, tenue,Vs → a dimly lit (poco iluminada) room ←→undimmed: (intelecto) claro, (entusiasmo) duradero. The unintended (no planeadas/buscadas/deliberadas) consequences. Wisp: (paja) brizna, (humo) voluta. Sunni anger (ira, enojo,V) → words spoken in -- (palabras dichas en un momento de ira). A region racked (sacudida) by earthquakes, be --ed with pain (sufrir dolores atroces). Tolerate (tolerar) the unpalatable (desagradable). Pricing (fijación de precios). Latch (pestillo) onto (agarrarse; hacerse con, conseguir) a rich widower. Wire up (conectar) to sth. The quintessential (por excelencia/antonomasia) Sunni.

Wiretap (escucha telefónica). One-upmanship: arte de colocarse en una situación de superioridad respecto a los demás. Helipads (pista de aterrizaje de helicópteros). Custombuild (hechos de encargo) ships. Upshot: resultado final + a machine able to represent & process-vast amounts of data at once (de una vez). Dandle: mecer sobre las rodillas. Show up: evidenciar, poner de manifiesto → the incident –ed him up to be a coward. Africa is strewn (esparcida, desparramada) with hurdles (obstáculos). Stash: esconder, alijo; ir ahorrando, acumulando. The endgame (final) of Chinese rule. He greets (recibe) visitors. A close scrutiny (un riguroso examen). Backsliding (recaída, reincidencia) on the reforms. Germany's loony (chiflada, disparatada) right. Befuddle (aturdir, ofuscar) them. I joke (chiste entre nosotros). Breaches: infracciones, violaciones, brechas. Guardedly (cautelosamente + cautiously). Dodder: tambaleante, con paso inseguro; doddery (temblequeante). Flaunt (alardear + boost). He dozes off (dormita) in meetings. A wash (capa) of greenery (vegetación)/painting. Strike back (contraataque) at sb. Bring deals to fruition (a buen término). The veneer (enchapado,V) is beginning to chip (desconcharse) + chip away of sth.: (autoridad) socavar, (pintura) desconcharse. Relish: salsa, guarnición, (pasear) hacerle gracia, with -- (con gusto), (proyecto) ser entusiasta. Debase: (idea, principio) degradar, (lenguaje) corromper, (pers.) rebajar, degradar. The meddlesome (indiscreto, entrometido) army back to the barracks. Staffers (pers. de plantilla) with trays (bandejas) of pastries (masas, pastelitos). It progressively depletes (reduce, Med: drena) nutrients from... Equipaje (baggage, luggage) → check in (facturar) one's --/--; he travels light (con poco equipaje); hand --/--; excess --/--/ weight. Graft (injerto, chanchullo, trabajar mucho)→ -bustling (animada, bulliciosa) S.K. =/= bust (degradar, quebrar, estropear...). A bleak (triste, funesto) view of the cataclysm. Poor countries are playthings/puppets (juguetes) of the imperialists. Oil money sloshing (borrachera) through the region; be sloshed (como una cuba). Rightful: (hijo/partido Pol.) legítimo, (recompensa) justa. Taking no sides (no participa) in the conflict. Hive off (separar, escindir; vender, enajenar) 2 m. Palestinians. Pander (consentir) sb's whim + hacer el juego → she is accused of --ing to these pressure groups. We reached a provisional or temporary arrangement. The $ squeeze (restricción). Blinkered (de miras estrechas) commentators. Egg on to + inf. (incitar a algo). Ace: as → have/hold all the --s (tener todas las de ganar); de primera → an – driver/pilot, destacar, sobresalir en... Perfidious: falso, pérfido (desleal). These hopes are not panning out (resultando) as... Craze: manía, moda. Randomized: fortuito, aleatorio; randomly (al azar). Xi spars (discute, se entrena) with crusty (crujientes, malhumoradas) girls. The trial was put on hold (en suspenso). An alternative to the stiffness/rigidity (rigidez) of the college. New rules baffle (desconciertan, frustran) humans, the –ed panel of experts. Stark: duro, crudo; severo, austero, -- (patente) poverty; in -- (marcado) contraste; agreste, inhóspito; desnudo, descarnado; escueto (libre, descubierto, claro, sin ambages). You're under no compulsion (coacción, obligación) to do it. Mesmerize (cautivar) → I was --ed (me quedé pasmado, boquiabierto). A stroke of luck. It is a doddle (pan comido, está tirado). He singled out (eligió, señaló, hizo resaltar) ten mental hospitals/lunatic asylum (manicomios). Breathtaking (impresionante, increíble) pace (paso, ritmo). Carer (cuidador/a) =/= caress (caricia) =/= charity (caridad) =/= caries (=). Bearing (demora, relación, porte, modales) → lose one's -- (desorientarse) ↔ get/ find --; that has no – on the subject (tema) The road skirts (bordea) the lake. The well-meaning (bien intencionadas) parties (partes). It's decked out (engalanado) in fairy (de colores) lights bulbs (bombillas). Stick: the tower --s up (sobresale) above the housetops (tejados) + -- up for one's rights (hacer valer los derechos de uno) + -- out for (defender, sacar la cara por) democracy. Remission:

remisión (perdón). The OAS (Organisation American States) dithers (titubea). For your own good (por tu bien). The president's veto is ringingly (categóricamente) overturned (anulado) by the Congress. His brothers ambushed (tendieron una emboscada a) him & gouged (aguj.: abrieron) out (le sacaron) his eyes. Crushingly (terriblemente, de manera aplastante) thick atmosphere. Disruption (trastorno) may be the buzzword (palabra de moda) =/= watchword (lema, contraseña). Two miles downriver (río abajo) from here. He will not endure (soportar) this treatment any longer. Excruciating (atroz, terrible, espantoso) toothaches. Arousing (suscitantes, que despiertan) perorations (perorata: discursos inoportunos). Pore over: hacer un estudio minucioso. The taint: mancha, contaminación, deshonor,Vs. Scout: explorar, patrulla de reconocimiento → have a -- around (the area); talent -- (cazatalentos), -- for sth (buscar algo). Brainwave: idea genial. Regulators never kept up (estuvieron al corriente...) with latest news. He hones (afina, pone a punto) new ideas. Hotshot: (personaje científico) célebre =/= bigwig (pez gordo). Drench: empapar → he get –ed, (culinario) macerar. He croons (canta suavemente) the psalms. He dons (asume) his role. Make fun of... (burlarse de...). Dampen: (a) humedecer: -- sb's spirits (desmoralizar o entristecer a alguien), the news --ed (aguaron) the mood (clima, ambiente, humor), (b) hacer perder las esperanzas → it was a final -- on their hopes (lo que les hizo perder las esperanzas). Grippingly (apasionadamente) retold (contado de nuevo). The book is timely (oportuno) in an era... Elusive: (presa, enemigo) escurridizo, (pers.) esquiva, (memoria) fugaz, (acuerdo) difícil, → the cities brash (gran desparpajo, color chillón) is frustatingly elusive. Forbid (i, a, idd): prohibir → --ding: (mirada, persona) severa, intimidante, (acantilado, paisaje) imponente, (tarea) difícil. Soup (sopa) =/= sop (concesión) to conservative factions → -- up: rebañar (recoger sin dejar nada). Other problems befall (ocurren). Hatch: incubar + incubate), (complot) tramar; trampilla; (barco, avión) escotilla.They blew themselves up: estallaron, saltaron por los aires. Preclude: excluir, descartar → your decision --s further action on our part (no nos deja hacer nada más). Galore (en cantidad) → opportunities & bargains (gangas) --. S. Africa love to splash out (darse un lujo). Russia may have piqued (despertado) European interest for... Profiteers (especuladores + =). Diluted: =, atenuado (ej. tax) to make it more palatable (aceptable, agradable). Sync. (sincronización) → be in/ out of -- (estar o no --do). Heft (peso, levantar con esfuerzo, sopesar)y: robusto, fornido, corpulento, fuerte, (salario) alto. He's rather fearsome (aterrador, de temer). The mobs (muchedumbre) got roudier (más alborotada). The one-party system is brittle (frágil, expresión: crispada). Reboot (reiniciación,V). Undisclosed (no revelados) loans. A hefty dollop (buena dosis) of sarcasm. Trendy (modernos) buildings. Faff about/around: ocuparse de bagatelas, dar vueltas perdiendo el tiempo. Sitting down (acomodarse, apaciguarse) after dinner. A traffic snarling (gruñiente) cavalcades (=, desfiles). Bin liners (bolsas para basura). Imprudente; =, careless, reckless + it was rash or imprudent of them (fue imprudente de su parte) to accept. Students won over (conquistados) by the speech. Stomp in/out (entrar/salir pisando fuerte) to/of the WTO. Hard won (guardada con esfuerzo) wisdom. Running mate: compañero de candidatura, candidato a la vicepresidencia. Buck the system (ir contra el sistema). Cold-hearted (insensible, frío) code. Trusted (de confianza) record (=, registro, anotar). Live up to (estar a la altura de) the hype (publicidad). Deprecation: desprecio, desaprobación. The progressive (progresistas) embraced religious exemptions (=, exoneraciones). Pawn (peón, empeñar) emeralds ring. Not part with (deshacerse de) the painting for 20 years.They leafed through (hojeaban) piles of... Who the heck (quién diablos) can do a deal with? The question is apt (apropiada, oportuna) =/= apto: suitable, fit. The low-hanging fruit has been plucked (arrancada, desplumada). He was half-hearted (poco entusiasta). Turfed out (pers.: echada; ropa: botada) by his parents in law (suegros). The users (usuarios) of the public transport. Outraged (ultrajados, indignados) netizens (usuarios de Internet). Saloon: bar, taberna, salón de barco. Please everybody (contentar a todos) =/= fulfill (cumplir con, llevar a cabo, realizar) =/= satisfy (=) =/= chuffed (contento) =/= scuffle (enfrentarse, escaramuza) → the police --ed with the protesters. He disclaimed (descargó, negó) all responsibility. He holds great allure (atractivo, encanto,V; el cautivar). He rubbished (puso por los suelos a) China, the carpenter's – (es un desastre). Dongle: =, dispositivo de protección del software. Whinger (quejica). This deplete (reduce) the ozone that protects Earth. All fell through (quedó en nada). An act of defiance (un desafío). Disillusion (desilusión,V), disabuse (desengaño,V) Germans of homegrown (local) quackery (curanderismo). High-tech wizards (brujos, magos). Chopping (cortando) business into ever smaller chunks. Lithe (ágil + =, lively) → the presentation needs to be livelier or more dynamic. Soggy: (terreno, hierba) saturados, empapados, (verduras) pasadas. Juggernaut (jigante, camión grande). Mis (demeanour (conducta): delitos menores. Sentry (centinela). Legal system: overburdened yet overactive. Unobtrusive (molesto, prominente, (olor) penetrante: discreto + discreet. Well-liked (muy querido) by... Vendetta (=) → A gangland (hampa, gangster)/political vendetta: pugna vengativa entre --/--; carry on a vendetta (campaña) against sb. Slur: difamación,V, manchar, dificultad en hablar → that's a -- on my family's name (afrenta al honor de mi familia). Drugs racket (tinglado, asunto)/dealing/trafficking. Chump/silly/dimwit (tontorrón). Brush scandals aside: apartar, no hacer caso de... Tribal or in-group (camarilla + cronies, cliques). Muse (reflexionar) about... The pings (sonidos) they emit. Courtly (fino, distinguido). Rue: lamentar, arrepentirse de. He bears some resemblance to his brother, a similar experience/colour/customs; our fellow men (semejantes), they're as much alike as people say. Grove: bosquecillo, arboleda → an olive -- (olivar). Mindset (modo de pensar). Join-stocks firms (empresas por acciones). Rumbustious (ruidosos) shoutings (voceríos). Take head (tener cuidado) & pay homage/court (rendir homenaje) to Trump. Bondage (cautiverio, esclavitud). China's deep-seated (profundamente arraigada) bureaucratic tradition. Trump yarns (inventa una historia) about... Defuse: (bomba) desactivar, (situación) distender, (crisis, peligro) calmar. Lurking (acechando) traffic wardens (guardianes, encargados). Less jeer (abuchear, mofarse) than cheer. American exhaustion (agotamiento) at bearing burdens it took up (cogió, aceptó, levantó) 70 years ago. The payoff (liquidación, compensación, ajuste de cuentas; soborno) reduces an all-out (total, global) conflict. Words of endearment (expresión de cariño). Low-cost regime leavens (alegra) the industry's otherwise wafer-thin (finísimos) margins. Maximum employment is in the eye of the beholder (depende del cristal con que se mira). Equate sth with sth (equiparar, identificar...), -- with sth (corresponder a algo). I search for a face-saving (que cubra las apariencias) deal to avoid an unsettling (inquietante, perturbante) referendum. Grovel (humillarse) → -- for mercy (implorar piedad), I'm very sorry; grovel, grovel (mil perdones). Make headway (hacer progreso). Draw inferences (sacar conclusiones) from sth. Markup (margen de beneficios) firms can charge over their production costs. Rein (rienda) in: frenar → Nasser --ed in the clerics by nationalising their endowments (legados, donaciones). Extricate sth/sb from sth.: sacar algo/a alguien de algo (ex. de una dificultad). Void (vacío, inválido, nulo,Vs) → be --ed (desprovisto) of sth Scoop (sacar) business from London hard taskmasters (muy estrictos y exigentes). Tease (tomar el pelo, burlarse de, fastidiar; bromista)→ -- sth out of sth/sb (sacar algo de algo/alguien), ex: I managed (conseguí) to -- it out of her + tease out at least one strand (ramal, filamento, tendencia) of the debate about Islam. Backfire (petardeo,V, fracasar) → his plan --ed at him (les salió el tiro por la culata). Subside: (terreno) hundirse, (tormenta) amainar, (fiebre) disminuir, (excitación) decaer, (odio) calmarse. An allout (total, global), the blanket (globales) tariffs. He yanked (tiró) at my air/on the rope. Happiness is fleeting (efímera). The underdogs (desemparados). Touch: sense of --, a -- (toque, unas gotas) of vinegar, a nice -- (detalle), stay in -- with me. Keep/lose (guardar/perder) the count of sth. Bottom out (tocar fondo). In compliance (conforme a) your wishes. Zealotry (fanatismo, fervor ciego). Overlay: -- (recubrir) sth with sth; revestimiento. Prong (diente, punta)s (flancos) of the attack. Meek (dócil, sumiso). Scrawny (esquelético, canijo). Tether (atar, amarrar). Swell: hincharse, (stream) crecer, (población) aumentar; --ollen with pride. It adds to (amplia) the volatility. Confined: limitado/restringido. Steppe (llanura extensa con vegetación herbácea) + uncultivated land (erial). Pork-barrel (dinero oficial para beneficiar a un grupo) policies. Keep the riff-raff (chusma) out of politics. A racy (brioso, animado) content (contenido). Staid: seria/formal culture & tech. The chastening (lo aleccionador, lo que hace pensar) of a firm. Forfeit: multa, confiscación; (honor, derechos) perder → -- large chunks of equity to the Banks. Shards (fragmentos) of metal. I singled out (critiqué, acusé; eligí, señalé) him for blame. Money lenders & borrowers have the whip (azote) hand (voz cantante) in credit market. Bristle: pelo, (animal) cerda, erizarse → a place --ing (repleto) with tourists. Mistrust/distrust/suspicion (desconfianza). Any goals were barely (apenas) met. Boated: (cara) aletargada, (presupuesto, IMF) inflado. América has earmarked (destinado) funding (money) to help people adjust to trade-related shocks. Bonnet (sombrero, capó). Flutter: revoloteo, V, (por pánico) revuelo, (bandera) ondear, agitar; aleteo, mostrar nervios; pequeña apuesta

→ turn a -- at the bookies (corredores de apuestas) into an investment class =/= fl<u>atter</u>/ fawn (adular) =/= flatte<u>n</u> (allanar, aplanar, echar abajo, arrasar una ciudad). 2012: the Ec. was a vortex (torbellino) threatening the €. Full-bodied (aroma: intenso; vino: con cuerpo; ...) → the transformation of a -- -- -- to a gaunt (pers.: descarnada; campo: adusto, desolado). The downtrodden (oprimidas) masses. Whipping boy: cabeza de turco, chivo expiatorio. Firebrand (activista, agitador) leader. Cock-a-hoop (muy contento) about sth. + his plans were knocked all -- -- -- (se le desbarataban). A tradeoff between prix & quality (sacrificio de calidad a cargo de un buen precio); the missing -- between inflation & unemployment; the side effects are a reasonable -- for long-term recovery. Elephants hold a scientific mirror (reflejo) up to human beings. Politicians gush over (elogian mucho) him/international accolade (honor, galardón). Let out (revelar, soltar/eximir, alquilar). Abduct: raptar, secuestrar. China is no longer beholden (en deuda) to Hong Kong for its economic welfare. Foist sth on/onto sb (endilgarle, endosarle) → protests stopped a move to -- -- schools a programme... The kingdom that bankrolls (financia, costea)... Argentina has defaulted six times in the past 100 years. Presentador: presenter, (radio, TV) broadcaster. Heavy handed (torpe) blockade (bloqueo). Emit wearisome (aburrido) stream (corriente, chorro...) of announcements. Biased: tendencioso, parcial, partidista → -- toward(s) sb/sth (predispuesto en favor de alguien/algo). Equate (equiparar, identificar) sb with sb... Hand out (distribuir) losses... Cuddle (abrazar) & kissing, she just needs a -- (que le hagan mimos)... A fulcrum (fulcro: punto de apoyo) between America & Europe. An undercover (secreto) journalist aired (manifestaba, transmitía) footage (secuencia filmada) of justice. Buff (up): pulir, sacar brillo → -- laws to woo investors. Spike: punta, púa, pincho; espiga,Vs → --ed: tratado con alcohol, droga o veneno para acallar/silenciar algo. Hold sb to ransom (exigir un rescate). Unreadable gibberish (galimatías, sandeces, lenguaje confuso). Slapdash (chapucero). Lump (trozo, agrupar) the top 1%. Shortlisted (preseleccionado). Abutting (colindante). Damning: (hecho) condenatorio, (apreciación) crítica. Sexually coy (tímido), a coy little smile (una sonrisa tímida y coqueta). Cherry-picked (eligido las mejores) images. Military drills (instrucciones). It cloaks (mantiene, cubre) Russian military exercise. Forthcoming: -- books (edición en preparación), -- exercise. Scrub (matorral; restregar, fregar; cancelar) electronic devices. Trump's bluster (bravatas: amenazas arrogantes) may be thwarting (fracasados) efforts. It has abetted (inducido, instigado) this revolution. Sober (sobrio, serio, formal) ing: aleccionador. Ferret: hurón,V, hurgar, husmear. A Boorish (grosera) comedy. Highrise: alto, de muchas plantas. Be in escrow (fideicomiso, custodia de un tercero). Platforms to take down (bajar, quitar, desmontar) hate speech. Heckle (interrumpir)r: la pers. que interrumpe un orador para molestar. Bring sth to fulfillment (cumplimiento): llevar algo a cabo. Illfated: infortunado, desventurado. "Write off (cancelación, declaración de siniestro) → tax --. Laundromats (lavandería automática). Yucky (asqueroso). Lime: cal, lima, limero. Embattled: asediado/acuciado de problemas =/= entrenched (afianzado, consolidado) dictador. Ragtag (mezcla, variopinto) side/camp (bando) of fighters. Peal: repique,V → the city's clock --s, -- of bells. Breach (violación) of Constitution. Sloppiness/ slovenliness/laziness/slackness (dejadez). Tidying (ordenando, arreglando) anomalies. Hands clasped (agarradas) as if in prayer. It has heeded (considerado, prestado atención a) one lesson. Malfeasance: administración desleal. Dredgers: (en el mar) dragadores. Acumen: perspicacia, sagacidad → business -- (visión). Boggle (atónito, patidifuso,Vs) the mind: quedar pasmado, alucinado. Other states are catching up (nos alcanzan). Space travel, coastal navigation. Blunder: metedura de pata, error garrafal, -- around (andar dando tumbos), -- in/out (entrar/salir dando tumbos, (atolondrado), I --ed into a wrong room. Skills honed (afilados, puestos a punto). Throw/ launch/ bowl (out): lanzar. Canniness (astucia). Bound: límite, brinco, atado. Make strange bedfellows (extraña pareja), the crises bring together -- -- (forja peculiares alianzas). Ta<u>b</u>: etiqueta; (Mil.) insignia; cuenta → I run a -- on my own, keep --s on them (vigilarlos), -- what we spend, pick up the -- (correr con los gastos) =/= ta<u>p</u> (llave, grifo, espita...). Fester: inflamar, irritar, enconar; a --ing (purulenta) sore (llaga), anger (ira) --ed into deep resentment. Shelter: refugio → air raid --, a -- for battered (maltratadas) women, a wall provide -- from the wind, -- (proteger) sb/sth from sb/sth; we need food, -- (albergue) & clothing; he --ed behind his diplomatic immunity. Charter: (Universidad) status, (ciudad) fueros, (empresa) escritura de constitución), (Constitución) carta, (transporte) contrato defletamiento. Lock (cerradura,V, mechón): I --ed myself out, my money is --ed up in the business, investors committed to -- up their money for the duration of the work, he has the appointment --ed up (asegurada). Practitioner: profesional → general -- (médico de medicina general). Chafe (rozar, irritar) → he --ed at the shackles (lo irritaban las trabas/ grilletes). The straitjacket (limitaciones) of the party. Asset: the city greatest -- (atractivo), this knowledge will be an -- (se valorará), living so centrally will be a -- (ventaja), your degree (carrera) will be an -- (punto a favor) =/= asset<u>s</u> (activos) → current/fixed --... Wherewithal (medios) to seize & hold disputed territories. Typing Chinese characters is fiddly (difícil). Footage from roadside cameras. Chinese breakthroughs are mute by data protection. Poland resumes (reanuda, reasume) efforts to dismiss judges from Supreme Court. Of paramount (primordial) importance. Plinth: (edificio) zócalo, (estátua) pedestal. Strip down (desmontar) the health reform. Five days of looting (saqueo) & arson (incendio); the fire was started deliberately (fue provocado). FARC (Fuerzas armadas revolucionarias de Colombia) was fond (tenía cariño) of bombing & torching (incendios). Gladly (con mucho gusto) took it. India's transport infrastructure was shoddy (chapuza, mezquina) =/= tardiness (lentitud, demora) & scheming (intriga). Hope for hours in a shirt-drenching (empapada) extreme situation. That is galling (mortificante) for India. It rates (ritmos, índices, considera) its progress by comparing itself... Russia's access to international capital market, severed (cortado) as a result of sanctions... Putin, shunned (rechazado) by the West. Low-profile (poco prominente). Pay full whack (parte) for the music they listen to ↔ streaming (acceso sin descarga). Achieve self-fulfillment (llegar a sentirse realizado). Blip: pitido, señal luminosa; problema, accidente pasajero. Storefront (frente, fachada). Foreshadow (anunciar, prefigurar). Acting out (representando, demostrando) their lowly status. I can do mischief (causar daño) or heartbreak (desengaño + disappointment). Atracador: (pers.) mugger, banco (robber). A thoughtful (atento, pensativo) chap (tipo). Put the coin in the slot (ranura), a -- (puesto) in the city/bar... A three-tier (tres niveles) education system, a second-tier (actor...: de segunda fila) tournament. Technology to revamp (reformar, modernizar) education. Brimming (rebosando) with ideas. Money mostly dressed up (disfrazado) as research funds, criticism -- - as advised. It dispenses with (prescinde de) the EU's four freedoms. S. Arabia: a TV show which pokes fun (se burla) at his kingdom's royal highness (alteza). An *Al Jazeera* journalist said: London remains the channel backup (respaldo, refuerzo). Poke: (fuego) atizar, -- (codazo) in the ribs (costillas), -- (asomar) out of the sheets, -- (golpe) in the nose. Fleck (mota, salpicadura + splash) → blue fabric with green flecks (moteada de verde), the skirt was --ed (salpicada) with mud. Chair: silla, cátedra, presidencia,Vs; topple: caerse, inclinarse; derrocar, derribar → a chair topple fight. The microphone cajoles (engatusa, camela), hectors (intimida) & wheedles (sonsaca, adula) customers. Peaceful ejections (=, expulsiones). Sewing/nail scissors, nail clippers (cortauñas), secateurs (tijeras de podar + lop, trim), nailbiter (que angustia, que provoca tensión). Plug (tapar, rellenar, hacer propaganda de) the family's products. A cuddly (adorable) sideshow (puesto/barraca en la feria). A struggle to reckon with (vérselas con, tener en cuenta) the stories... The stink (olor, apestar; escándalo) of 1858. Concoction (mejunje, trama, excusa, cuento) of herbs. Barraca: (puesto) stall, (caseta) booth, (Mil.) barrack hut. Ramp: rampa, (Aviac.) escalerilla, hydraulic -- (elevador) → -- up: (precios, producción) incrementar. Fetch: traer, ir a buscar → -- my cigarettes, go & -- help! -- the washing in (entrar la ropa), -- him from the station; the appendage (apéndice, añadidura) of rhino's horns -- (se vende) at thousands of $ kilo. The heading back (regreso) into government. It is heightening (aumenta, recrudece) the debate. Twelve towns have held drills (taladros, (Mil.: instrucción, simulacros) for N. Korea missile attack. Streak: a missile carrying a nuclear warhead (cabeza, ojiva) --ed (pasó rápido) over Northern Japan; a -- (reflejo) of light, a --/run/spell (racha) of luck. Bullshits (sandeces,V, tirarse faroles). Quagmire: atolladero, impedimento, cenegal. Do-gooding (hacer buenas obras). India demonetisation: no windfall from stashed (ahorrado, acumulado) cash. An upmarket (gran categoría, que atrae pers. pudientes) grocer =/= oversell: (m.) the market is --old (con promoción exagerada). Bay: muelle/dársena, espacio → parking --; aullido,V, bahía, at -- (acorralado) → bring sth./ sb to --, keep ídem. Manchar: mark, get dirty, stain, (reputación) stain, tarnish. Step up: (exportaciones, poder, volumen) aumentar, (producción, campaña) intensificar. Sloshing (echando) tides (mareas) of money. Offset: compensar; any overpayment (saldo a su favor) will be -- (deducido). Politicians want to grab more of the spoils (estropear, malcriar; mimar, botines) that the multinationals have come to control + the spoils of the war (el trofeo de la Guerra). Payoff:

pago, liquidación, compensación; ajuste de cuentas, soborno, V. Terms (expresiones)/words of endearment (cariño). Boondoggle/waste (despilfarro). Blazing (en llamas, resplandeciente, violento) → trail--/groundbreaking (pionero, innovador) + the cutting-edge (de vanguardia) technology. His longtime (de toda la vida) enemy. He gave him the heave-ho (lo rechazó, le dio calabaza). Roast: asado,V; gastar bromas pesadas, ridiculizar. Istanbul has always lent itself (se prestó) to rioting. Carve out: (reputación) forjarse, (a career for o.s.) labrarse un porvenir. Draw inferences (=) (sacar una conclusión) from sth Damp (húmedo) down (=, sofocar, apagar) cyclones. Disruptive: perjudicial, perturbador. They balked (evitaron) a shelling out (apoquinar) ↔ freeloader (gorrón). Merci (misericordia)lessly (despiadadamente). Howitzer (obús), shell/mortar bomb (proyectil, =). An itchy (picante, insidioso) trigger (gatillo) finger (índice). Far-fetched (exagerado, rocambolesco). Aficionado: keen, enthusiast, amateur, buff. Ancillary (auxiliar) → be -- to sth (estar subordinado a algo). The main drag (lata, coñazo, resistencia al avance). Furious (furioso) → he has a -- temper (tiene muy mal genio). Dispense with (prescindir de) intelligence. They clapped (aplaudían) & stamped one's foot (daba patadas en el suelo). He pulls rank (abusa de autoridad, hace valer privilegios) on him. Balk (obstáculizar, evitar) at: rehusar (+ refuse). Stoking (avivando, alimentando) tensions/hatred/discontent quell (sofocar, acallar) the outcry (protesta). Burly (fornido, corpulento, feroz). A discomfiting (desconcertante, frustrante) experience. Trainers (zapatillas de deporte, entrenadores). Weakling (debilucho, pelele) → the – of the herd (lo debilucho de la manada). Greeks will follow suits (se adaptarán, seguirán el ejemplo). Subdued: (precio) dominado, (pers.) sometida, dominada, (pasión) contenida, (espíritu, atmósfera) apagados. Fluid (incierta) political situation. Let things slide (se vengan abajo). Run up (acumular) debts. Misdemeanours (fechorías, delitos menores). Sede: (gobierno) seat, (Rel) see, (organización internacional, empresa) headquarter, (feria, congreso) venue. They're joking/teasing/pulling your leg: le toman el pelo. Disparage (menosprecio). Reckless (imprudentemente). Stalwart: fornido, robusto, inquebrantable, incondicional. Rumbustious (ruidoso) shouting (voceríos). Acrimony: =, acritud, aspereza, (disputa) enconada. Bland (soso, insípido, anodino) functionary. Sundry (varios, diversos) political groupings. Awestruck (atemorizar). The commonality (pueblo llano). Fall back (perder terreno, quedarse atrás) on: recurrir a, echar mano de. Implausible: inverosímil, poco convincente. A long-slumbering (dormido) notebook (libreta, cuaderno; ordenador portátil) awakens. Lowly (humilde) soldier. Thunderstorm (tormenta eléctrica). Caution (cautela)ary words/remarks. Infer: =, deducir, insinuar. A sideshow (secundaria) campaign. Its underlying (subyacentes) genetics. Climbing (trepadora) planta. Misnomer: nombre poco adecuado. Cowered (encogido de miedo) in caves. Bully (acosar, intimidar) firms into saving (salvar) jobs. The workers are cock-a-hoop (muy contentos). Buy off/ brive/suborn (sobornar). Two a penny (a montones). Snug (acogedor, ropa: ceñida) sanctuary =/= snub: desaire, desdeño (desprecio) =/= snap up: no dejar escapar (foreign rivals...). Exhausting/ gruelling (agotador) journey. The mainstay (pilar) of the business. Agree staunchly (incondicionalmente) about the leadership. Zippy (briosa) Spain. Upstaged (eclipsado) by... The economy is picking up (despunta). Sulkily/bad tempered/in a bad mood (malhumorado). He won by a narrow margin. Bring about (ocasionar, provocar). Heyday (himno) =/= heathen (pagano) → the -- (los infieles). Heighten: agudizar, incrementar, realzar, intensificar (+ --fy), destacar, acentuar. Bottom line: balance final. He was scathing (mordaz, feroz) about my efforts (intentos) ←→unscathed (ileso). Public spats (rencillas, discusiones) =/= online ranting (despotricar, sermón; vituperio: afrenta, censura, reprobación). Earn only razor-thin (muy finos/escasos) margins =/= skin - deep (superficial) Japanese westernisation. Roll bad loans over (refinanciar), four years to foreclosure (ejecutar) a loan. War in drugs is impending (inminente). Outspoken (franco, directo). N. Korean's lack of squeamishness (escrúpulos). See through: anyone couldn't -- -- (nadie se creía) that history, his support saw me -- (me mantuvo a flote). Mangy: (perro, gato) sarnoso, (abrigo, sofá, manta) raído, usado, gastado. Spurt: he works in --s (rachas), --s (llamaradas) of flame (fuego), a final -- (esfuerzo, sprint) won him the race, put on a -- (acelerar, pisar el acelerador), (líquido) salir a chorros + the blood poured gushed out. Understate (subestimar, disminuir la importancia) → --ed (sobrio, sencillo, discreto)..., it is --ment (es quedarse corto). Stark: (climate) severo, (landscape) inhóspito, (truth) escueta, sin adornos, (realism) crudo → --ly: representado/interpretado de forma descarnada, crudamente, (clear, obvious) absolutamente. It panders (consiente) to the pious, he -- her whim. Flak (críticas)e: copo, escama, astilla; descascarillarse. Equate (equiparar) sth with sth Shirk: eludir una obligación/responsabilidad. For aeons (desde hace siglos). Smattering: I have -- (nociones) of German, there was -- (algunos) applause, praise. Seducir: (hombre y mujer) seduce; the idea appealed me. Fine: =, delgado, magnífico, excelente. Perspicacia: insight, shrewdness. Inattentive: desatento, distraído. Farcical: absurdo, ridículo. Twinge (punzada, V) → feel a -- of remorse =/= twinkle (centelleo, brillo). Fickle/skittish (cambiante, inestable, voluble, inconstante). Grow animal cells in vats (cubas, tanques). Delve (ahondar, hurgar) into... Cosy (cozy): acogedor, conveniente → -- up: tratar de quedar bien. Ec. churn (agitación). Hushed (silencioso) → in -- tones (en voz baja, en murmullo). Bullish (optimista). Stockpile: almacén, (armas) arsenal. Bankroll (fondos; mantener, financiar)er: financiero (of terrorism, ...). Unholy (impura, profana) alliance. Whoop (gritar, chillar, chillido) + goad (acosar, aguijonear) → he was --ed into whoop up (armar jolgorio). Well-heeled (con dinero) tourists. Ominously (de mal presagio) → he was -- silent (su silencio no presagiaba nada bueno). The bogeyman (cuco, terror) of Mexico. Shadowy (imprevisto, misterioso, oscuro) committee. Jasping (jadeando). Humans are wrecking (demoliendo) the ocean. Upkeep (mantenimiento). Winnow (discernir) truth from lies. People of this ilk (tipo, clase). Tilt towards (arremeter contra). China brazenly (descaradamente) interfered. The wireless technique will be shown off (se lucirá). Cohere (formar una unidad) with (ser coherente con) ←→ gibberish (incoherentes). Scam/fiddle (chanchullo). Congenial (simpático, agradable) president. Squirts (chorritos) of soda... He flipped (tiró algo, perdió la cabeza). Stickler (que insiste mucho, mira mucho los detalles). Riveting (fascinante). Endorse: (=), aprobar, promocionar. Drive an auger/ drill (taladro, barrena) through 2 feet lake ice. Be up to scratch (dar la talla, estar a la altura). Demure (recatado). Do you have any objection? (¿Tienes algo que objetar?). Commendable/praiseworthy (elogiable) ←→ indicted (acusados) outriders (escoltas + escorts) =/= outsiders: de fuera, desconocidos. Whammy (revés) + iron the garment inside out/on the inside; they suffered a major (importante) setback/serious reverse in the last elections. Lynching (linchamiento). Grown-up (pers. mayores). Earn their spurs (espuelas, estímulos,V) fighting native Americans. Drum up (despertar, conseguir) enthusiasm for the scheme (=, plan, proyecto, conspiración, Vs). Bide your time (esperar el momento preciso). At grass roots (de las bases) level. The stakeout (operación de vigilancia). A bit of a funk (miedo). Smash & grab (robo con rotura de escaparates). Be one step ahead (en situación ventajosa) on the authorities. Scrimping (escatimeo) & saving: cuidar mucho el dinero, hacer muchas Ec. Break loose (soltarse) → all hell broke loose/out (se armó la gorda). Muckraking (escándalo, trapos sucios) in Malta. Nonsensical: absurdo, disparatado. E. Piaf songs burbled (borboteaban, parloteaban) from loudspeakers. Sidestepping (eludiendo) licensing requirements. Bunch: racimo, ramo, manojo, grupo,Vs =/= blunt: (mocho, romo, desafilado,Vs) instrument; (pers.) directa, categórica, rotunda. Gota: a drop of rum, beads of sweat, they put him on a drip (el gota a gota). Brexit precludes (excluye, descarta) a change in... Scale: (magnitud, escala) of the disaster, (para pesar) balanza, escama, (montaña) escalar. Buck up (esforzarse por, apurar, levantar el ánimo a) her own party. She vaunted (se jactó de) their values of sexual equality & religious tolerance. Stomp in/out: entrar/salir pisando fuerte → the -- -- of army boots. Long-drawn-out (interminable, larguísimo). Bondage (cautiverio, esclavitud). Unwavering (inquebrantable, férreo, firme). A jolly (alegre, pasarlo bien) good time. China's deep-seated (profundamente arraigadas) bureaucratic traditions. It's outline (contorno, perfil, resumen) of social-credit scheme. Struck back (contra ataque). He did not have a criminal record/previous convictions (antecedentes penales). The spillover from the urban centres (excedentes de población de los centros urbanos). Substandards (de calidad inferior) subversions (=, trastornos, revoluciones). Hellhole (lugar horrible). Storyteller (narrador, mentiroso, cuentista). The party is broken & adrift (a la deriva). Oil patch: mancha/industria/yacimiento de petróleo. Upbeat/optimistic/optimist ←→ down--. Convocar: (elecciones, huelga) call, (manifestaciones) organize, (concurso, oposiciones) announce, (reunión, asamblea) call, convene. Coalesce: fusionar, unirse. Yore: antaño, de otros tiempos. Bask (disfrutar) in the sun, she --ed (se deleitaba) in their adulation. His office is tucked away (guardada, escondida) in a non descript (insulso, indefinido, sin nada particular) building next to London's... If they resent me (me molestan/ofenden)... + he resented her success (le molestaba que ella tuviera éxito). They begrudge (les duele, envidian) a callow (inmaduro, inexperto) colleague. He is ill-at-ease (incómodo) with writing at length (por fin, detenidamente). Assemble: montar, ensamblar; reunir, congregarse → tearful & backing off (retrocediendo) from --ed staff. They speak in mumbo-jumbo (suena a chino). Felled (derribado) by the forces of disruption (perturbación, trastorno). Agarrotar: (músculos) make stiff, (comercio, máquinas) seize up. Smutty (obscenos, indecentes) jokes. Too much slouching (arrellanarse) in front of the TV, slouched (inclinado) over the drink. Slip off: escabullirse, (zapatos) quitarse. A craving (ansia, antojo, sed) after the truth, for chocolate. The windswept (agotado por el viento) plains of Xinjiang. Loom (avecinarse) large: preponderar, dominar → the problems --ed -- in his mind. Hidebound (retrógrado, rígido) + -- industry, -- (conservador) by tradition. Keep up: (tienda, precios) mantenerse, (lluvia, ruido) continuar → -- - with sth (continuar con algo: estudios, ...); -- - with sb. (seguir en contacto con). He jotted down (anotó) & chipped in (intervino) with commendable (loable, meritorio) interest. Faint: ligero, apenas visible; desmayarse; -- of heart/--hearted (tímido); ritual chants were --ed in Iran. Pitch: campo de fútbol + field; armar, montar; tirar, arrojar + the successful pitch (punto), reach such a -- (extremo), the high - --ed (tono agudo) whir (runrún) of the Electr. car. Hilariously (increíblemente). Talking shops (tertulias, mentideros). Defuse: (bomba) desactivar, (situación) distender, (crisis, peligro) calmar. Atrocity/madness (barbaridad). Brussels has graduated (pasado) from scapegoat to the IMF's bogey (cuco, terror) enforcer (que hace respetar la ley). Strictures: críticas, restricciones. Lurking (acechando) traffic wardens (guardas, encargados). Animal droppings (excrementos), pellet (bolit/cagadita; perdigón). Ironclad/battleship (acorazado). Abide, ed: tolerar → -- by: (reglas) acatar, (compromiso) cumplir =/= abide, --ode, --ided: morar, permanecer. Rummage: hurgar, rebuscar. Rely on (contar en). Two leaders face down (hacen frente al) all comers (público en general). She had been mooted (planteado, sometido a discusión) in the hope she might garner (información: recoger; elogio: cosechar, ...) women vote. Regulators & courts are chipping away (descascaran, desconchan, socavan) at the legal immunity of internet firms. Be on off-limits (zona prohibida). American exhaustion (agotamiento) at bearing burdens. Custom/habit (costumbre). Puff up (inflar) its trade deficit. Nest-egg (ahorros). The markup (margen de beneficios) firms can charge over the production costs. The sun burps (eructa) & flings (lanza, arroja) mighty (poderosos) arcos. Dub: apodar → -- sb (a) knight (armar caballero); film: doblar. Shove: empujar → she --ed him away (la apartó de un empujón); meter → he tried to -- the blame (culpa) onto me. Shilly-shally (dudar, titubear). Tease (tomar el pelo, fastidiar, provocar) → they're –ing it to – it. Hush (silencio) - hush: super secreto. Iterations: repeticiones de acciones análogas. Barbed (mordaces,V) comments. Jerry-build (construido por chapuceros) ↔ gingerly (cautela). Extricate (sacar) sth from sth. Startling: sorprendente, asombroso, alarmante, extra → Russia has --ed (asustado, sobresaltado) European union with the annexation of Crimea. Quip (ocurrencia, salida, bromear). The ongoing (en curso) talks. Whip up (provocar, incitar) enough grassroots (bases). Resume (reanudar, reasumir, continuar) work on... Blood drenched (empapada). Dour (arisco, adusto, huraño) Mr Fillon. Prim: mojigato, santurrón, hipócrita; (jardín, casa) cuidados. Admonishment: admonición, advertencia, amonestación. He fudged (amañó, esquivó, inventó una excusa) the distinction, denouncing both IS (Islamic state) & Iran. Huddled (apiñadas) masses. The elections are shrill (estridentes, chillones, frenéticas) with accusations. A raft (montón) of relations, harrying (hostigando, acosando) the rest. Sneering: desdeñoso, despectivo, (risa) socarrona (astuta, guasona). Muse: pensar, reflexionar. Whoosh: ruido del tráfico/agua a presión/fuerte viento... Punchy: (artículo) incisivo, (campaña) con garra, (Mús.) briosa. Stilted: (conversación, manera) forzados, (lenguaje) rebuscado. Deprecation: menosprecio, reprobación. Ping: sonido metálico, (bala) silbido → the -- it emits, the bell goes -- when the meal is coocked. Rue (lamentar) → I -- the day I... The books are samey (parecidos). Slop: derramarse, volcarse → -- about/around (chapotear, deambular). Rebuke (reprimenda). Slur: difamación → cast a -- on sb; dificultad al hablar. Backwater: agua estancada, lugar retrasado. Well liked (muy querido) by... Bogus (falso/a) company: empresa fantasma. Aboveboard (limpio, legítimo) business. Shack (choza, casucha, rancho) =/= hut (choza, casucha, cabaña). Chortle: risa/carcajada (de satisfacción). Conniption: ataque de histeria/pánico/rabia. Diffident: tímido, poco seguro de sí mismo. Despondent: abatido, desanimado (+ dispirited, downhearted). Down-at heel (venidos a menos). Scurrilous: insidioso, embustero; difamatorio =/= ludicrous (redículo, absurdo) to believe the problem can be solved. Enraptured (cautivado). Smugness (suficiencia, petulancia). Slant: (planta, letra) inclinación, (tejado, suelo) pendiente,V; punto de vista, enfoque; sesgo. Flout: desobediencia, desacatar la ley. Factious: (debate, argumento) contencioso, (grupo) faccioso/ revolucionario. Flummox: desconcertar, dejar cortado. Kink: vuelta, curva, enroscar. Mar (estropear)k up: anotar, aumentar el precio, subir la nota. Hands-on (práctico/a) experience/approach. Headship (dirección) of club/college. Slumber: sueño, dormir =/= shudder: (pers.) conmover, hacer temblar, estremecimiento; (máquina) sacudida, zarandear de un lado a otro. Toss: lanzar, lanzamiento, sacudir, agitar; -- out: tirar a la basura. Shoo! (¡Fuera!), shoo (hacer entrar) the children into the house; -- the birds off/away (ahuyentar + frighten off/away, repel, ward off). Squeaky (muy; chirriante, chillón) clean. By & large (en general). A way of gauging (ancho de vía; calibre, indicador,V, calcular) how currencies stack up (se juntan/apilan/arreglan) against the $. Curdle: (leche...) cortarse, cuajarse... → bloodcurdling (espeluznante, aterrador). Bear, bore, borne (resistir, soportar) → borne by the poor. Flagrante: (mentira) blatant, (en justicia) glaring. Gross (bruto, ordinario) & crude (ordinario, rudimentario; petróleo: crudo). Hook up: abrochar, enganchar. Preclude (excluir, descartar) a nebula (nebulosa). In the wreckage (ruinas, escombros) of Arab World. Conflation (el refundir) several works/documents. Mild-mannered: afable, agradable, sociable Clamber: trepar, entrar difícilmente. Pervasive: (cultura occidental) omnipresente, (idea) dominante, (olor) penetrante. Queasiness: mareo, náuseas. It accords undue (excesivo) deference (respeto) to promoters. Dominant promoters bilking (burlando) the firms they run. Political Islam come to terms with (acepta) liberal democracies. Rebuke (reprimenda, reprender) =/= the public dressingdown (rapapolvo) of Macron. Entrust (encomendar) the direction of the company to an incompetent (inepto). Be readily (dispuesto, de buena gana) to chip in/cough up (apoquinar). Mellow: maduro, añejo, suavizar, sosegar. Drone: zángano, esclavo; zumbido; avión autodirigido. Outpouring (emanación) of solidarity. In the aftermath (período subsiguiente) of terrorism. A grim (nefasto, macabro, sombrío, huraño, insociable) familiarity with Europa. Subversion: =, trastornar, revolver, perturbar. Rub out: borrar, quitar, sacar. Harp on (insistir sobre). Scoff at (burlarse). Store: reserva, provisión; almacén, tienda,V. Genuine: =, sincero, auténtico, verdadero, propio, legítimo. Goon (matón) squad: la policía. Blithe: risueño, despreocupado =/= down-to-earth (realista, práctico). Propriety (decoro, corrección)ies: normas, convenciones. Bilious: asqueroso, nauseabundo, repugnante. Account: explicación, informe; cuenta, dar cuentas. He champions: aboga por, defiende... Shed: derramar, (piel) mudar, (vestido) quitarse, (luz) emitir, (fragancia) despedir; liberarse de; leñera, cobertizo, establo. Singlemindedness: resolución, determinación. Lean, leaned/leant → inclinación, the tower leans (está inclinada), apoyarse, the party --s (tiende) to the left; delgado, enjuto, magro. Crib: cuna (+ craddle), pesebre de Navidad (=/= manger), nacimiento; plagio (of an speech...). Wipe out: limpiar, borrar, cancelar, exterminar. A binding vote. Longstanding (antiguo, que viene de lejos) policies. Collude: complicidad en perjuicio de un tercero, apaño entre un director y los subordinados → she faced allegations (imputaciones, acusaciones) of colluding. Back - slapping (campechano). A Constitution run (hecha funcionar) by Brussels, steered (dirigida) by Germany & underwritten (garantizada, apoyada) by the USA. Grouse (gruñir, protestar, refunfuñar, murmurar) =/= a Catalan whine (aullido, queja,V). Strike down: abatir, (vida) segar; abolir, revocar, anular, destituir. NATO jets pound (machacan, aporrean, (Mil.) bombardean, palpitar) Belgrado to halt atrocities. Diplomatic treadmill (rutina, cinta de correr). Regular (habitual) client/customer. Tiresome (pesados, tediosos/molestos) partners. Commit: cometer, asignar → --ment: compromiso, obligación, responsabilidad). Give succo(u)r to the weak/ helpless (indefensos). Dishevelled: despeinado, (pelo) alborotado. Gaza strip: franja; deshacer, despojar, vaciar, estropear. Bring down: (precio, T.) bajar, (árbol, pared) tirar, (pers., animal) abatir, (avión) derribar, (gobierno) derrocar. Amid/amidst (entre, en medio de) two disappointments/letdowns (decepciones). Heist: golpe, atraco,V. Matter–of-fact (práctico, realista) → he said --ly (con toda naturalidad)... Hamstrung (atado de pies a cabeza, fracasado) by lack of money... Wattle (adobe: ladrillo secado al sol) & daub (cañas) → a wattle & daub fence. Outfit: conjunto, equipo, vestir; empresa, organización. With wanton (terco, sin sentido) falsehood (falsedad). Besmirch/sully/tarnish (ensuciar) their reputation =/= dirty/soil/ropa, suelo). Impropriety (incorrección), implausible (poco convincente). Hurtful (hiriente). Thin-skinned (susceptible). Seat: asiento, banca, (Pol.) escaño, sede. Backdrop: telón de fondo, objetivo influyendo en algo. Voucher: vale, justificante. The dictators quacked (temblaron). The Republican standard-bearer (abanderado, portaestandarte). Fairly: justamente, equitativamente, con imparcialidad; realmente, bastante + fairness (imparcialidad, hermosura). Piggybacking (ir a caballo). An electoral thumping (victoria/mayoría aplastante). Mushily (blando, sentimentaloide) patriotic show. It relinquish (cede, renuncia al) control of X to the state. Enloquecer: go crazy/mad/out of one's mind/ insane → be driven ...; I'm ... about pop music. Push around (dar empujones). Stiffen: almidonar, reforzar, entretelar; entumecer, agarrotar. America took over Brazil as the world's mightiest Ec. Manner (actitud, modo, estilo)s: modales → -- of adversaries. Récord: anotar, registrar, hacer constar. Baffed (desconcertado, frustrado, perplejo) by the words. Flashpoint (punto álgido). Make-or-break: intento desesperado, situación decisiva. He reverts (vuelve) to the ancient model →he soon --ed to type (pronto volvió a ser el de siempre). Spookily (de manera espeluznante) gifted for heroin. He tracks down (localiza, averigua)... Storm (tormenta, vociferar; tomar por asalto) into her son's swanky (pijo, fanfarrón) apartment. Secularise the state by fiat (orden decreto). Noose: soga, lazo. A mealy-mouthed (excesivamente comedida/ mirada) response. Tepid: tibio, poco entusiasta. Outrage: atrocidad, ultraje, escándalo, indignación, atentado,Vs. Reach out (tender la mano) to the president. A battered (aporreado, golpeado) enclave. Balk: obstaculizar, evitar, eludir. Lest: no sea que, por si acaso → -- he be a spy. Bedraggled: enmarañado/ enredado, desaliñado (sin orden ni aseo), despeinado. Bedevil (cargado de problemas) → three problems -- El Salvador. Endorse: aprobar, refrendar/legalizar, promocionar; (factura) endosar. Reverberate (resonancia, repercusión,V) far beyond the courtroom (sala de un tribunal). Take the stand on /against sth: adoptar una postura en/contra algo. Gloss over: pasar por alto, quitarle importancia. Pull out: the train --ed out of the station/from a side road; (página) arrancar, (suplemento/sección) separar, (mesa) alargar, (negociaciones) retirarse, (diente/enchufe) sacar. Egg on (incitar) sb to... Acquiescent (conforme) to the plan set out by... With no heed (sin considerar)..., you paid - -- to my advice. Tread (pisar) → -- softly when you go upstairs; paso: -- of marching feet; well-trodden (trillado) for... On the lookout (perspectiva, panorama; andar a la caza, puesto de observación) of a majestic job. A border fracas (altercado). Fisticuffs (tortazos, puñetazos). Angry-bargy (trifulca). Uneasy (preocupado)ness. Bhutan has shied away (rehuido) from old diplomacy. He is backtracking (retrocediendo, dando marcha atrás). Their offences (infracciones, delitos, atentados) were to storm (tormenta) into (irrumpir)... Feel jaded (harto, hastiado). Rub along: llevarse bien, ir tirando. Kowtow (doblegarse ante, rendirle pleitesía). Set off: (viaje) salir, (huelga) desencadenar, (bomba) estallar, (alarma) hacer sonar, (espectáculo) dar lugar a; hacer resaltar → the painting -- -- by the dark background. Sleaze: sordidez/suciedad/turbiedad en la profesión...; sinvergüenza. A stash (esconder) wads (montón, fajo; tapa, rellenar)... → millions stashed away (escondidos, guardados) in a Swiss bank account... Factional scheming (intriga, maquinación de facciones). Desordenar: (habitación) make untidy, mess up, (fichas, hojas) get... off order, the burglars turned the house upside down/in a terrible mess. They mixed up his index cards (fichas), card index cabinet (fichero). Excerpt: pasaje, seleccionar pasajes. Rung: (organización) peldaño, (taburete, banco) travesaño. Relish: salsa, guarnición. They tried to goad (estimular, acosar, aguijonear) her into an argument. Meddlesome: indiscreto, entrometido. All this rankles (duele, hace resentir). Strike back (contraatacar, devolver el golpe). Preventable/avoidable (evitable). The lean years of gridlock (paralización), the -- of the negotiations. Playful (juguetón, travieso). Stomach (=, barriga, tolerar) the unpalatable (desagradable). Be hard up (de algo: escaso, dinero: pelado) for ideas. Germany's loony (chiflada, disparatada) right. Not back out now (no te eches atrás ahora).

Anexos

A) Particularidades prácticas complementarias del mundo financiero, B) Grupo de palabras compuestas con up, out, aquellas con algún significado de brillar y las que contienen oo; todas ellas se prestan a confusión, C) Tablas para evitar algunas confusiones, D) Refranes, dichos y frases hechas.

A - Algunas particularidades prácticas complementarias del tan misantrópicamente manipulado universo económico y sobre todo financiero

La temática financiera es aún más complicada y útil, pero aquí sólo pretendemos divulgar los conceptos extremadamente prácticos que año tras año van apareciendo en las prestigiosas revistas como "*The economist*" y que pueden interesar a todos los técnicos, sea cual sea su especialidad:
Finca: real estate/real property (bienes inmuebles), property, land. The 2008 meltdown (debacle + fusión de un reactor). State-owned enterprises in OECD countries are worth around $ two trillions (millones de billones) minority stakes. Dollars two trillion or so in utilities & other assets hold by local governments. The real treasures are non-financial assets (building, land, subsoil ressources...) worth $ thirty five trillions. Utilities: el conjunto de servicios para los inmuebles: agua, gas, electricidad... =/= facilities: los servicios del interior: toilet --, cooking -- (equipo para cocinar) → the hotel --es are open to non-residents + credit f., overcraft f. (crédito al descubierto)... =/= have f/be very good with numbers (para los números). Unlisted market: off-board --: not dealt in the stock exchange. Over–the–counter: -- - -- market: el de valores y bonos no inscritos en bolsa + -- - -- medicine (se puede comprar sin receta) =/= under–the–counter goods: lo que se compra ilícitamente (contrabando...). Stock (capital en acciones). Share portfolio: cartera para acciones. Listed shares/securities. Equity (acciones ordinarias). Personal assets (bienes personales). Securities (valores, títulos) → government -- (bonos del estado). Fixed-

interest securities (valores de renta fija). Securitisation: building up (acumular) income streams (flujo de ingresos) -credit card, cart-loan repayments... repacking them as securities & reselling them on in tranches with varying levels of risk; transform a future income stream into a lump sum (suma global) today. Asset: ventaja, bien, partida del activo; asset<u>s</u> (bienes, activos) → dud (sin fondos, invendible) assets, personal -- (bienes personales), real -- (bienes muebles), activos, haberes, --s in hand (activos disponibles), --s & liabilities (activo & pasivo), assets-backed securities. Asset-stripping: comprar los activos de una empresa en crisis para luego venderlos y liquidar aquella. Junk: bonds that are deemed (considerados) risky & so must offer a higher interest rate than "Investment-grade" debt. Valuation: (empresa) tasación, (pers.) valoración. Give up (abandonar, renunciar a) even cursory (superficial) checks, give on (renunciar a) their borrowers credit-worthiness (solvencia). Cursory (somero, superficial) glance: a primera vista. Investors piled in (se lanzaron al ataque) blindly, snapping up (agarrando) supposedly safe tranches of bundled-up (atada) debt. The boom turned to burst & bail-outs. Tax inspector (agente tributario). Benchmark (referencia) such as the S&P 500 for American equities. Income (renta) tax. Reduction/discount (rebaja). Tax-fee area (zona franca). Bail sb. out (pagar la fianza de alguien) → the bail-out plan foresees Greece debt falling to 120% of the GDP by 2020. Layout (pago)... Share-out (repartir). Lay off (despedir en masa). Sell-off: (mercancías) liquidar, (stocks, shares) vender, privatización. Buyout (comprar todas las acciones) → management -- (las compran los gerentes), workers -- (ídem los obreros). On bail (bajo fianza). The laid off (despido) of ten workers. Write off (cancelar la deuda por considerarla impagable, declarar siniestro total) + it's too early to write off (cancelar) + desechar: -- -- sth. → -- -- as a total loss (considerar algo como totalmente perdido). Pay off: merecer la pena/dar resultado + (hipoteca) amortizar, liquidar (pagar y despedir a todos) → -- --sth., -- -- in installments (a plazos), -- -- old scores (ajuste de cuentas), (en juego) arriesgarse. On bail (bajo fianza). Payout: pago, reparto (share - out), indemnización (from insurance). Clear off: (deuda) liquidar, saldar + ¡Largarse! (-- --!). Rolling stocks (material rodante, móvil...). Estate: finca, propiedad → (housing --): urbanización; (industrial --): polígono industrial; (herencia): the -- was divided between four; (-- agent): agente inmobiliario. Capital goods (bienes de equipo). Property: propiedad, inmueble → -- insurance (seguro inmobiliario). Holding (parcela, pequeña propiedad)s: terrenos, valores en cartera → a majority /minority holding (una participación mayoritaria, minoritaria). Joint-stock (fondo social) company. S.A. (Sociedad anónima = Limited liability company). Property developer (promotor inmobiliario). Corporate taxes (impuestos sobre las sociedades). GSES (Government - sponsored enterprises): they buy American mortgages from Banks & other originators, bundle them into securities & resell them to investors with a guarantee. Turnover: movimiento de mercancías o volumen de negocios. National income (renta). Net/brut profits. Sales figure (cifra de negocios). Revenues (ingresos). Bonus (prima, incentivo). Earnings (ganancias). Trust fund (fondo fiduciario). Trust company (trust, empresa fiduciaria, de fideicomiso). Mutual funds (fondos de inversión inmobiliaria). Private equity funds (fondos invertidos en empresas privadas que no cotizan en bolsa), private equity firms. Hedge funds (fondos especulativos). Pooled funds (fondos comunes). Mutual funds (fondos de inversión mobiliaria). Secondary marked: where previously issued securities & financial instruments such as stocks, bonds, options & futures. Repo market → repurchasing agreement (pacto de recompra): contract to purchase and future repurchase of financial assets, above all treasure securities (valores y títulos) & treasure stock (bonos del tesoro).

B - Grupo de palabras compuestas con *up*, *out*, aquellas con algún significado de brillar y las que llevan "dos o"; todas ellas se prestan a confusión

Palabras compuestas con up

Add-up (calcular, sumar, hacer el cálculo). Back off (retroceder). Bone up (empollar) on (sobre). Backup (respaldar, refuerzo, hacer una copia de seguridad, poner marcha atrás). Closeup (primer plano). Cock-up (follón, lío). Higher-ups (los de arriba). Lead-up (período previo, precampaña). Letup (descanso, interrupción, pausa). Let up: (viento, tormenta) amainar, (producción, trabajo) disminuir. Locker-up (encarcelador). Markup (margen de beneficios). Pent-up: (odio, emoción) contener, (energía) acumular. Pick out (elegir, destacar, reconocer). Pick up (mejorar), pick sb up (recoger). Pick out (elegir, destacar, reconocer). Pick-up (mejora, subida) in demand, salary, prices. Pickup (de reparto) truck. Pop-ups (emergentes) schools. Puff (ráfaga, soplo, aliento) up (inflar) the Budget... Pump up (inflar, reactivar la economía). Put up (alojar) in school halls... Rack up (acumular). Run up: (total, deudas) ir acumulando, (bandera) izar, debts → -- -- against (tropezar con). Shot up: (temperatura, valor...: se disparó) by 30%. Top-notch (primera categoría). Set-up (sistema, montaje, organización). Top up (llenar, recargar baterías, and so on. Top-up: additional loans, groups of investments... Serve a top-up (un poco). Pay up-front (por adelantado). The law

Putin upholds (mantiene, defiende) in Syria... Upkeep (mantenimiento). Uplift (animación, aspiración, (economía) sostén). Upshot (resultado final). Uptick (repunte + upturn). Uptight (tenso, nervioso). Economic upturn (incremento, mejora). Whip up (incitar, provocar).

Palabras compuestas con out

Bottom out (tocar fondo). Fallout (lluvia radioactiva, secuelas). Lay out (exponer, disponer; arreglar, planear). Layout (plan, diseño, propiedad). Outcome (resultado, consecuencia). Outdo (mejorar, superar) the rest. Outsized (enorme) influence... Outfit (equipo, empresa, conjunto, vestir). Outgrow (crecer más que). Outlay (gasto) → Capital outliers (desembolsos, gastos). Outlet (desagüe, toma de electric., salida de gas o líquido, tienda). Outages (apagones). Pick out (elegir, distinguir). Sell out (apoquinar).

Palabras con algún significado de *brillar*

Aglow (radiante, brillante, resplandeciente) with happiness. Bazzle (resplandor) → --ed (deslumbrados), --y (deslumbrante, glamoroso). Beam (rayo, haz de luz, brillar). Bleamy (brillante) whales. Blaze (resplandor, llamarada, centelleo, fuego, ardor, derroche). The close-up (primer plano) glimpse (destello, vislumbre) of Plato...). Flare (llamarada, destello, bengala). Glare (deslumbrar, mirar fijamente, mirada). Glimmer (luz trémula, espejo del agua). Glitter (relumbrar, lucir, brillar, destello). Glitzy (glamoroso, deslumbrante). Gloss (brillo, lustre, glosar) → Glossy (brillante, lustroso). Glow (brillo, resplandor, brillar). The Factory glitter (destella, brilla + glint). Shimmering (brillante, resplandeciente). Twinkle (centelleo, brillo, brillar).

Palabras que contienen oo (se exceptúan los más elementales como roof, door, saloon, etc.)

Aloof (distante). Aloft (en alto, en el aire). Afoot (planear, poner en marcha). Boo-boo (meter la pata). Boorish (grosero). Be in cahoots with (conspirar, estar conchabado con, confabular, asociarse). Coo (arrullar para enamorar, adormecer un niño, divulgar cosas secretas). Co-op (cooperación). Co-opt (nombrar, invitar a formar parte). Chicken/hen coop (gallinero). Droop (ponerse mustio, flaquear). Fool (engañar). Footage (secuencia filmada). Footing (equilibrio). Hooded (encapuchado). Loony (chiflado, loco, disparatado). Loopy (chiflado, descabellado). Moot (discutible) point, sugerir. Ooze (supurar, irradiar, rezumar). Loop (cuva, meandro, serpentear; lazada). Loot (botín, saquear). Poolroom (sala de billar). Scoop (pala, cuchara, diario: exclusiva, logro financiero) up: recoger (datos, arroz...). Scoot (salir pitando). Shoo in (coser y cantar). Shoo off/away (ahuyentar). Shoot-out (tiroteo). Snoop (husmear, fisgonear; fisgón). In sooth (en verdad). Soothe (calmar, acallar). Spoof (parodia, trampa, burla, broma). Spook (fantasma, policía secreta; asustar). Stooge (títere). Stoop (agacharse, encorvarse). Whoop (gritar, chillar, chillido). Swoop: (avión) descender en picado, (policía) redada.

C - Tres tablas para evitar algunas confusiones, pues estos términos presentan un conflictivo parecido gráfico. Por complejo que parezca, todos y más han ido surgiendo de mis lecturas

1 - Algunas expresiones complementarias las encontrarán en el texto. Aquí se trata de facilitar la memorización:

Booze: bebida alcohólica, empinar el codo. **Buzz**: (insecto) zumbido, (conversación) rumor, pasar rozando, give sb a -- (telefonazo), llamar por interfono, -- off (largarse), -- --! (¡lárgate!).

Dazzle: brillo, resplandor, deslumbrar → **--ing**: resplandeciente, deslumbrante, que encandila. **Dizzy**: mareado,V, vertiginoso, atolondrado/tarambana. **Drizzle**: lloviznar.

Fizz: efervescencia, burbuja,V, silbido,V → **Fizzy** (gaseosas, efervescentes) drinks; **--le**: fracasar, silbar; -- **out**: apagarse, quedarse en nada. **Fussy**: nervioso, exigente. **Fuzzy**: (ideas) confusas; rizado, velloso, enmarañado.

Giddy: mareado, con vértigo, vertiginoso, alocado.

Hazy: brumoso, neblinoso, vago, confuso.

Seethe: (borbotear, hervir, estar furioso + fume (humear, estar furioso). **Shiver**: (frío) tiritar, (horror...) escalofrío. **Shrivel**: (planta) marchitar, (piel) arrugarse =/= **Sizzle**: chisporrotear, chispa, crepitar → **--ing**: sofocante, fulminante, crepitante, que chisporrotea. **Snazzy**: vistoso, elegante, llamativo =/= **Stifling**: agobiante, sofocante. **Stuffy** (ambiente cargado) =/= **sweltering** (calor sofocante, abrasador, bochornoso).

Wheeze: respirar con dificultad, resollar. **Whirr**: runrún, zumbido,Vs. **Wither**: (esperanzas) desvanecer, (entusiasmo) decaer, (planta, flor) marchitar, (fuerzas) mermar → **withering**: (calor) abrasador, (tono, comentario) hiriente, (mirada) fulminante. **Whizz**: pasar silBando/zumbando/como una bala, silbido, zumbido, be a -- at sth (ser un as en algo). **Wilt**: marchitarse, ponerse triste.

Varios (los más fáciles): Blizzard (ventisca, tormenta de aire). **Divvy (up)**: repartir =/= **dither**: estar nervioso,V, titubear, vacilar. **Huffy**: susceptible, enojadizo, quisquilloso, irritable. Nozzle: boquilla, pulverizador, inyector. **Puzzling**: desconcertante.

2 - **a** (más fáciles): <u>Down</u>: downgrading (decadencia). Downsides (pegas, desventajas). Downtrodden (reprimidos). Downturn (deteriorar, disminuir). Downplay (disminuir importancia a) → Play down (minimizar). Write down (anotar, apuntar, amortizar). Slow down (reducir la velocidad, ralentizar un proceso) =/= slowdown (disminución del ritmo, ralentización). Shutdown (cierre). Scale down (disminuir a escala, hacer proporcionalmente pequeño). Slim down (adelgazar, hacer régimen). Track-down (localizar, ubicar). A bring down (disminución) of 3%. Touchdown (aterrizaje). Melt down (fundir) =/= meltdown (fusión nuclear, cataclismo). Countdown (cuenta atrás). Bog (ciénaga, pantano, retrete) down: atascar. Back down (echarse atrás, retractarse). Tone down (atenuar color, reducir ruido, moderar críticas).

2 - **b** (de más <u>difícil</u> memorización): stand down (dimitir, retirarse). Settle down (sentar cabeza). Hand-down (herencia: transmitir, Jur.: imponer). Showdown (enfrentamiento). Low-down (información confidencial, poner al tanto de algo). Cla<u>mp</u>down (restricción, prohibición) → Cli<u>mb</u>-down (vuelta atrás, retroceso). Pay down (pagar al contado + cash payment). Rundown: resumen, poner al corriente, plantilla: reducción, hotel/distrito: venido a menos =/= run down (batería: descargar, servicios: ir reduciendo, e*stocks*: agotar; criticar, atropellar,

negocio: ir a pique. Winding down (disminuir poco a poco, tocar a su fin).

3 - Sue: pedir (en pleito...). Clue (indicación, pista, indicio). Hint: indirecta/insinuación/consejo (para compras...), señal/indicio.

Woe (desgracia, aflicción) → woeful (deplorable). Vow (promesa,V), foe (enemigo), hue (matiz, color) → hue & cry (griterío, clamor). Wit: inteligencia, ingenio =/= Wistful: pensativo, melancólico =/= genius. Plea (súplica).

Cue: right on cue (en el momento justo) for the photo, come in on -- (entrar en el momento preciso), cue sb in on sth (poner al corriente de algo), take one's cue (ejemplo) from sb, cue in (dar una entrada de teatro, Mús...).

D – Refranes, dichos, frases hechas (sayings/ proverbs, set phrases)

Observarán que algunos pocos están en el texto. Ha sido para no perder el hilo en las frases compuestas y largas. Veamos pues:
   There is nothing new under the sun (no hay nada nuevo bajo el sol). Look down on sb (mirar a alguien por encima del hombro). Don't try to take on too much (quien mucho abarca poco aprieta). Nothing ventured, nothing gained (quien nada arriesga, nada gana). The weakest goes to the wall (siempre se rompe la cuerda por lo más delgado). He came down on us like a ton of bricks (nos echó una bronca fenomenal). There is sth fishy going on (aquí hay gato encerrado). There's no accounting for tastes (contra gustos no hay disputas). Take sb down a peg (bajar los humos a alguien). Be too clever by half (pasarse de listo). He can't hold a candle to she (no le llega a la suela de sus zapatos). It's best to mind one's own business (cada uno a lo suyo). They're two of a kind (tal para cual). Leave sb in the lurch (sacudida, tambaleo,V): dejar tirado a alguien. Get more than you bargained for (ir por lana y salir esquilados). United we stand (la unión hace la fuerza). Get things mixed up (confundir la velocidad con el tocino). Once in a while can't hurt (una vez al año no hace daño). The cobbler/shoemaker (zapatero) should stick to his last (zapatero a tus zapatos). Birds of a feather flock together (Dios los cría y ellos se juntan). Like father, like son (de tal palo tal astilla). Look on the bright side (a mal tiempo buena cara). Better is devil you know (mejor

malo conocido que bueno por conocer). A bird in the hand is worth two in the bush (vale más pájaro en mano que cien volando). Prevention is better than cure. Better later than never. Variety is the spice of life (en las variedades está el gusto). Brain is better than brawn (fuerza muscular): vale más maña que fuerza. Get worked up about sth. (ahogarse en un vaso de agua). Life is full of surprises (la vida da muchas vueltas). He is old as the hills (es más viejo que Matusalén). You have to be cruel to be kind (quien bien te quiere te hará llorar) = spare the rod (vara, vástago) & spoil (estropear, malcriar) the child. Do good to all alike (haz bien y no mires a quién). Everything at its appointed time (no por madrugar amanece más temprano). Forewar<u>n</u>ed is forewar<u>m</u>ed (hombre prevenido vale por dos). You/he shouldn't push your/his luck (tanto va el cántaro a la fuente, que al final se rompe). He did the job any which way (hizo el trabajo a la buena de Dios). She caused a tremendous fuss/an almighty row (armó la de Dios). She is a real secretary (es una secretaria como Dios manda). Be tremendous/magnificent (estar del lado de Dios y de la ley). This is completely incomprehensible (esto no hay Dios que lo entienda). God/the Lord help us! (¡Qué Dios nos coja confesados!). The early bird catches the worm (a quien madruga Dios le ayuda). Man proposes and God disposes. I will eat my hat! (¡que venga Dios y lo vea!). God helps those who help themselves (a Dios rogando y con el mazo dando). It's an unfair world (Dios da pan a quien no tiene dientes). Always taking the opposite view (siempre llevando la contraria). We are all equal in the eyes of the Lord (el sol brilla para todos). See the mote in one's neighbour's eye and not the beam in one's own (ver una paja en el ojo ajeno y no un viga en el propio). Two heads are better than one (dos ojos ven mejor que uno). An eye for an eye and a tooth for a tooth. You need eyes in the back of your head (hay que andar con cuatro ojos). Take a dim view of sth (ver algo con malos ojos). Pull sb's ears (tirarle de las orejas a alguien). Realize sth is wrong (verle las orejas al lobo). I didn't sleep a wink (no pegué un ojo en toda la noche). Cost an arm and a leg (costar un ojo de la cara). Have a lot to be desired (dejar mucho que desear). Love your neighbour as yourself (ama a tu prójimo como a tí mismo). A whopping great lie (una mentira como una casa). The liar is sooner caught than the cripple (se coge antes a un mentiroso que a un cojo). Pin the blame on sb (cargarle el muerto a alguien). Rub sb up the wrong way (buscar las cosquillas a alguien, caer mal a alguien). Be in the pink (rosado): rebosar de salud, estar feliz. Where there is a will, there is a way (querer es poder). I'm not saying one thing or the other (no quito ni pongo). Beat (redoble, latido del corazón, compás, pegar, batir) about the bush: irse por las ramas, andarse con rodeos. He'd swallow anything (él comulga con ruedas de molino). He knows every trick in the book (se las sabe todas). Spend money like water (ser como un saco sin fondo). Stick to sb like a leech (sanguijuela): pegarse a alguien como una lapa. You reap what you sow. I don't care three hoots (bocinazos, toques de sirena...)/I couldn't care less/I don't give a damn (me importa un bledo o comino). It suits me (me sienta) like a hole in the head (tiro). Better too much than too little. Be in dip (zambullir, declive, inclinación,V...) water: estar con la soga hasta el cuello. He doesn't trust a soul (no se fía ni de sí mismo). He's not a shadow of his former self (mismo). Never say die (morir): no hay que darse nunca por vencido. Completely disregard sth (hacer tabla rasa de algo). If you live like that, you're bound to come to a bad (quien mal anda, mal acaba). A man is known by the company he keeps (dime con quién andas y te diré quién eres). One thing at a time (cada cosa a su tiempo). These things take time (las cosas de palacio van despacio) = the wheels of bureaucracy grind very slowly. One good turn deserves another (amor con amor se paga). Every man for himself (sálvese quien pueda). Be up to your elbows in sth (estar ocupadísimo haciendo algo). All have come to a naught (cero): todo ha quedado en nada. All be tarred with the same brush (todo metido en el mismo saco). Be in a sticky (pegajoso, peliagudo) wicket (terreno de juego): estar en una situación difícil/terreno resbaladizo. Be on the losing wicket (llevar las de perder). Be in/get into a rut (hacerse esclavo de una rutina + be stuck in a rut). He will simply throw in their lot with the later (unirse a su suerte). Spike sb's guns (poner trabas a los planes de alguien). Be under clouds (estar bajo sospecha/desacreditado). Dot the i's & cross the t's (dar los últimos toques). Put the squeeze on sb (apretar los tornillos a alguien). Mirar a alguien con disimulo (look at sb out of the corner of one's eye)/con recelo (look askance at sb.). Fall between two stools (nadar entre dos aguas). Wipe the slate clean (hacer borrón y cuenta nueva). That's the root of the problem (esa es la madre del cordero). Have the patience of a saint (tener más paciencia que un santo). L<u>et</u> sb off the hook (dejar escapar a alguien). G<u>et</u> sb off the hook (sacar a alguien de apuros). Running (gestión, funcionamiento) the foul (asqueroso, fétido, grosero) of the law: enfrentamiento a la justicia. Evildoers (malhechores) who had got their comeuppance (que se llevaron lo merecido). Bite (i, i, itten): morder, agarrar → we have bitten the bullet (bala): nos hemos enfrentado al toro. Be barking (ladrando) up the wrong tree: ir muy descaminado. The protests will fizzle (silbar, fracasar) out: apagarse, quedar en agua de borrajas. Know sth. to one's fingers (saberse algo al dedillo). Have a foot in both camps (tener intereses en ambos lados, nadar entre dos aguas). Penetrated every nook (rincón) & cranny (grieta) of the economy: penetró hasta el último rincón de la economía. Be/get into a fizz (efervescencia, burbujeo, silbido,Vs): estar/meterse en un problema. Not to mince (carne: picada,V) one's words: no tener pelos en la lengua. Pull oneself up by one's bootstraps (orejas): reponerse gracias a sus propias fuerzas. Bliss: dicha (suerte, placer) → ignorance is -- (ojos que no ven, corazón que no oye). He's got a screw loose (le falta un tornillo). Gravy (ganga) → clamber (trepar)/get on/about the gravy train: aprovechar la ocasión. Demand one's pound of flesh (exigir todo lo que a uno le corresponde). Be at loggerheads with sb (estar a matar con alguien). Cock a snook at sth/sb (burlarse. Be fighting for one's life (estar entre la espada y la pared). Like attracts like (Dios los cria y ellos se juntan). Be born with a silver spoon in one's mouth (haber nacido en una cuna de oro). The last nail (uña, clavo) in the coffin (ataúd): último paso hacia su destrucción. Shunt (cambiar de vía, empujón) sb about: enviar de acá para allá. The inroads (efectos) of mass tourism. It's an ill wind that blows nobody any good (no hay mal que por bien no venga) = every cloud has a silver lining (forro). They had fitted the bill (ellos han cumplido los requisitos). It runs them ragged (andrajosos): les hace sudar tinta. Blind spot (punto ciego) → computers are a -- -- with me (no son mi punto fuerte). As blind as a bat (más ciego que un topo). He's a big fish/frog in a small swimming pool (es un tuerto en el país de los ciegos). "Pull the rug (alfombrilla, tapete...) from under sb's feet". It's a hard nut to crack (es hueso difícil de roer, problema de difícil solución). Be out of one's nut (estar chiflado). Fool (tontear, engañar) about/around (hacer payasadas). Put one's foot in it (meter la pata). He's to his old antics! (¡está haciendo de las suyas!). Spanner (llave inglesa + wrench) → throw a spanner into the works (poner un palo en la rueda). Footing most of the bill (correr con los gastos). Cast a slur on sb (manchar la reputación de alguien). Put out the welcome mat (estera) (dar un recibimiento de reyes). Words are not binding (las palabras se las lleva el viento). It will all come out in the wash (todo se va a arreglar). Coax sth out of sb (sonsacar algo a alguien engatusándolo) + coax sb into/out doing sth (convencer a alguien de hacer o no hacer algo). Come to terms with sth (asumir o asimilar algo)/with sb (llegar a un acuerdo). By hook (gancho) or by crook (cayado):

por las buenas o por las malas. Know the set-up (organización, sistema): conocer el tinglado. It is all swings (oscilaciones) & roundabouts (indirectas, glorietas): lo que ganas por un lado lo pierdes por otro. Fit (adecuado, en forma; encajar, equipar...) → survival of the fittest (la ley del más fuerte). Keep going against all (tener más moral que el alcoyano). Nuts & <u>bolts</u> of a scheme (los aspectos prácticos de un proyecto). Roam (vagar) around/about (andar sin rumbo fijo). Be up in arms (en oposición feroz). Goalpost (poste) → move the -- (cambiar las reglas del juego). Give sb short shrift (despachar alguien sin rodeos), he gave that idea -- -- (mostró su disconformidad con tal idea), he got -- -- from the boss (el jefe se mostró poco compasivo con él). Cheek by Jowl (barbilla): codo a codo. Get sb off the hook (sacar a alguien las castañas del fuego). Open the floodgate (compuerta, esclusa) to sth: abrir las puertas a algo. History repeats itself (la historia se repite). He didn't pull any punches (no se andó con miramientos). Champing (mascando) at the bit (estar impaciente para hacer algo). The nub (pedazo, parte esencial) of the hard problema: el quid de la cuestión. It's a chicken & the egg situation (es aquello del huevo y la gallina). Run rings round sb. (dar mil vueltas a alguien). That is worth the wait (vale la pena esperar). He's been up & down all evening (no ha parado quieto todo el atardecer). Cut sb down to size (bajar los humos a alguien). Be off one's nut (estar chiflado). They're up to sth (están tramando algo). He does everything any old how (de cualquier manera). Put it mildly (por decirlo de alguna manera). She gets straight to the point (no se anda con rodeos). Pay off old scores (ajuste de cuentas). Come to terms with sth (asumir o asimilar algo). Put the squeeze on sb (apretar los tornillos a alguien). Be out of lunch (estar como una regadera). Strike out on their own (volar por sus propias alas). He was dogged by ill luck (le perseguía la mala suerte). Sell sb a pig in a poke (dar gato por liebre). Do sth on the fly (por la vía rápida). There are not flies on him (no tiene un pelo de tonto). A sure-footing (conoce el terreno que pisa) guide. Go with the flow (dejarse llevar por la corriente). Let bygones be bygones (olvidar el pasasdo). Make headline news (salir en primera página). The concert was a bit of a squib (fiasco, sátira) (el concierto fue decepcionante). A stitch in time saves nine (vale más prevenir que curar). Put the cart before the horse (empezar la casa por la ventana). Be on target (cible) (seguir la trayectoria prevista). Getting in (entregar, hacer entrar) on: tomar parte en algo. Cash in (cobrar) on sth: sacar provecho de algo. Pull strings/string -- pulling ("Mover palancas"). Plank (tabla, tablón, puntal) → be as thick as two short --s (ser más bruto que un arado). You really take the biscuit! (¡Eres el colmo!). Mess around (pasar el rato, hacer tonterías). Have one's feet on the ground (ser realista). Turn up trumps (salir bien) → he always -- - -- (no nos falla nunca). Supplicant fawning (adulador, servil) that licks sb's boots. Clear the logjam (atolladero): desbloquear la situación. It was arson (el incendio fue premeditado). Getting this off the ground (llegar a concretar eso). Trample (pisar, pisotear) on sb (tratar a alguien sin miramientos). Cash in on (sacar provecho de algo). Preen (arreglar con el pico) o.s. (pavonearse) on (enorgullecerse de...). Live up (darse a la gran vida) to (vivir de acuerdo con). White men ruled the roast (asado, tostado,V): llevan la batuta. Case in point (un ejemplo al respecto). Make a quick buck (dinero fácil). Work hand in glove (en estrecha colaboración) with... Save for a rainy-day (vacas flacas). Sift (tamizar) through (examen cuidadoso). Cling (pegarse, agarrarse) together: ir muy agarrados/juntos, no separarse ni un momento. Tarred with the same brush/cast in the same mold (cortados con el mismo patrón). Keep a stiff upper lip (poner a mal tiempo buena cara). Nudge (codazo, empujar suavemente) sb's memory: refrescar la memoria de alguien. Put sb through the hoop (aro): hacerle pasarlas negras. Profits pale (tenue, claro,V) into (se vuelven insignificantes). Loop (lazo, Comp.) bucle → be in the -- (en el grupo de gente informada). Clenched-fist salute (saludo con el puño cerrado). Marsh in lockstep (ir hombro a hombro (dos partidos políticos,..). Insider trading/dealing (abuso de información privilegiada) → ruinous -- -- scams (chanchullos). They got the cold-shoulders (les volvieron las espaldas). We were stood up (nos dejaron plantados). Take this on the chain (pagar el pato). They must get down to (ponerse a) do business: ponerse manos a la obra. She fell head over heels in love (se enamoró locamente) with him. Whom (a quien) God has joined together let no man put asunder (separar). Leave sb hold the bag (cargar el muerto a alguien). Partake (aceptar) in sth: ser partícipe en algo. Run with the pack (seguir la corriente). Gain the insight into sth (llegar a comprender algo). Besotted (obsesionado) → totally -- with her (perdidamente enamorado de ella). Scorch (quemar)ed -earth tactics (arrasar todo lo útil al enemigo). Take for granted (dar por sentado). He has stood up to him (le hizo frente). Take a back seat (mantenerse al margen, dejar que otros asuman la responsabilidad). Pull all one's eggs in one basket (jugárselo todo a una carta). Step in (tomar cartas en el asunto). Don't bite off more than you can shew (quien mucho abarca poco aprieta). Partir de cero (start from a scratch). In the middle of nowhere (donde Cristo perdió el gorro). Kill two birds with one stone. He was caught red handed (fue sorprendido en flagrante delito). Gargling (gárgaras) → the business went down the drain (desagüe, alcantarilla...): el negocio se fue a hacer gárgaras. Get one's hopes up/build up one's bones: hacerse ilusiones. He does everything any old how: lo hace todo de cualquier manera. Shoulders to the wheel (manos a la obra). I would manage it (me prometí conseguirlo). Put it mildly (por decirlo de alguna manera). That noise drives me up the wall (me pone negro). She gets straight to the point (no se anda con rodeos). In no times at all (en un santiamén). Get up to one's old tricks (hacer de las suyas). Make a clean sweep (hacer tabla rasa). Get one's share/take one's cut (sacar tajada). Wait & see which way the wind is blowing (por donde van los tiros). A glaring truth (una verdad como un templo). Live life to the full (vivir a tope). Have a blazing (abrasador, ardiente) row: tirarse los trastos por la cabeza. Run sb down/slag (escoria) sb off (poner verde a alguien). Make sb's life misery (amargar la vida a alguien). It'll all work out, don't worry (ya verás cómo todo se arregla). It was blowing (hacía viento) a gale: hizo un viento de mil demonios. Fall between two stools (taburetes): quedarse nadando entre dos aguas. Start with a clear bottom (hacer borrón y cuenta nueva). As God is my witness (pongo a Dios por testigo). Thinks backfired on me (me salieron los tiros por la culata). For no particular reason (sin ton ni son). Live from hand to mouth (al día). Different strokes for different folks (sobre gustos no hay nada escrito). Go off at a tangent (salirse por la tangente). Third time lucky (a la tercera va la vencida). Wait & see which way the wind is blowing (esperar y ver por donde van los tiros). Clear (airear) the air (atm.). Be on the ball (estar en todo). The root cause (la raíz de los males). Reveal the truth (tirar de la manta). There's no rose without thorn (espinas). Much & about nothing (mucho ruido y pocas nueces). This issue is suffering from overexposure (el tema perdió interés por haber sido demasiado debatido). Sweet dreams (que sueñes con los angelitos). They drew/cast lots (lo echaron a suertes).There's no accounting for taste (sobre gustos no hay disputas). Easy does it (despacio y buena letra). It's a snap (esto está tirado). Practice makes perfect (la práctica hace al maestro). Wars rose by leaps & bounds (a pasos agigantados). Bug/hassle sb (darle "la paliza a alguien"). Look before you leap (pensarlo dos veces). Stand one's ground (mantenerse en sus trece). Blot one's copybook (manchar su reputación, =). Overplaying (exagerando) his hand (pasarse, ir demasiado lejos). Pine (consumirse, languidecer) for sth/sb (suspirar por algo/alguien). Brave the storm (capear el temporal). His gaze met mine (se cruzaron nuestras miradas). Meet eyeball to eyeball with sb (enfrentarse cara a cara con alguien). Poke (pinchar, introducir) fun at sb: reírse de alguien. Be moved to tears (llorar de emoción). Taxpayers foot the bill (corren con los gastos). Flog sth to death (repetir algo hasta la saciedad). A global game of hide & seek (escondite). It's a piece of cake (eso es pan comido, coser y cantar). Get a real fright (llevarse un buen susto). That's no consolation (mal de muchos, consuelo de tontos). Political horse-trading (tira y afloja). Tip the balance/scales (inclinar la balanza a su /(mi....) favor). Through thick and thin (tanto en las duras como en las maduras). Cut the mustard (inventar una historia). Spin a yarn (inventar una historia). I'm up to the eyes in work. I'm snowed under with work (estoy hasta el tope de trabajo). A trancas y barrancas (with great difficulties/overcoming many obstacles). Third time lucky (a la tercera va la vencida). Be/get into a fizz (burbuja, efervescencia, silbido,Vs): meterse en un problema. Be in hiding (estar escondido), be on a hiding to nothing (llevar las de perder). Be down & out (no saber donde caer muerto. Have sb on a string (dominar a alguien completamente). Throw up one's hands in horror (rasgarse las vestiduras). Put one's foot in it (meter la pata). Be as tough as old boots (ser fuerte como un roble). There are worth pondering (vale la pena reflexionar). Run with the pack (seguir la corriente). Risk one's neck (jugarse el pellejo). Have the upper hand (tener la sartén por el mango). Spare nobody (no dejar títere con cabeza). Tear sb to shreds (trizas, triturar...): dejar a alguien como un trapo. Be on a losing wicket (llevar las de perder). Be under cloud (estar bajo sospecha). Stack (montón, estantería, apilar) → the cards are --ed against us (todo va contra nosotros). Have money to burn (atar perros con longanizas). Fight like cat and dog (llevarse como...). It's just a question of putting two and two together (por el hilo se saca el ovillo). It's the same person /

regime under different name (el mismo perro con distintos collares). There is honor among thieves (perro no come perros). It never rains but it pours (a perro flaco todo son pulgas). The best way to solve a problem is to attack the root cause of it (muerto el perro, se acabó la rabia). His/her bark's worse than his/her bite (perro ladrador, poco mordedor).

ÍNDICE

Publicaciones anteriores 5

Introducción 7

Metodología 11

Primera parte: el inglés más común 15

    Primera sección: vocablos variados
        y simples 19

    Segunda sección: palabras y
        pequeñas frases sencillas 28

    Primera sección: vocablos complementarios
        del capítulo anterior 79

    Segunda sección: palabras y pequeñas frases
        algo más complejas que en el capítulo I 88

Segunda parte: el inglés más técnico, incluyendo muchas explicaciones útiles redactadas directamente en inglés 177

    Primera sección: sustantivos y adjetivaciones
        variadas complejas 181

Segunda sección: las palabras y frases
de nivel superior   203

Anexos   457

    Palabras compuestas con up   463

    Palabras compuestas con out   464

    Palabras con algún significado de *brillar*   464

    Palabras que contienen oo (se exceptúan
los más elementales
como roof, door, saloon, etc.)   465

D – Refranes, dichos, frases hechas
(sayings/ proverbs, set phrases)   471

Editorial LibrosEnRed

LibrosEnRed es la Editorial Digital más completa en idioma español. Desde junio de 2000 trabajamos en la edición y venta de libros digitales e impresos bajo demanda.

Nuestra misión es facilitar a todos los autores la edición de sus obras y ofrecer a los lectores acceso rápido y económico a libros de todo tipo.

Editamos novelas, cuentos, poesías, tesis, investigaciones, manuales, monografías y toda variedad de contenidos. Brindamos la posibilidad de comercializar las obras desde Internet para millones de potenciales lectores. De este modo, intentamos fortalecer la difusión de los autores que escriben en español.

Ingrese a www.librosenred.com y conozca nuestro catálogo, compuesto por cientos de títulos clásicos y de autores contemporáneos.

www.ingramcontent.com/pod-product-compliance
Lightning Source LLC
Chambersburg PA
CBHW020117240426
43673CB00038B/514